CHRISTIAN
WORSHIP

CHRISTIAN WORSHIP

CHRISTIAN WORSHIP PUBLISHING TRUST

This selection Copyright © Christian Worship 2009

The right of Christian Worship to be identified as
the author of this work has been asserted by them in accordance with the
Copyright, Designs and Patents Act 1988.

First published in Great Britain in 2009 by
Christian Worship
PO Box 1012
Cardiff CF11 1PJ

1 3 5 7 9 10 8 6 4 2

A CIP catalogue record for this book is available
from the British Library.

ISBN: 978-0-9564195-0-7

Designed in Quadraat by Geoff Green Book Design, Cambridge
Printed in Germany by Berker Graphischer Betrieb Gmbh & Co

Every effort has been made to fulfil requirements with regard to reproducing
copyright material. The author and publisher will be glad to rectify any omissions
at the earliest opportunity.

www.christian-worship.org.uk

CONTENTS

PREFACE

O N 3 MARCH 2005, a meeting was held in Dudley, England to discuss the possibility of producing a new hymnbook to serve traditional evangelical churches in the twenty-first century. Aware of others throughout England and Wales who sensed a similar need, three Welsh ministers took the initiative of calling the meeting, and some two dozen men whelming agreement regarding its character, there was a clear mandate for action.

This was not to be just another new hymnbook. Rather, with many widely used books now falling out of print, and recent publications being of a somewhat different ethos, this book was to be moulded and shaped by five clear principles:

- The inclusion of a complete metrical Psalter
- The inclusion of many paraphrases of Psalms and other Scripture portions
- The inclusion of only traditional hymns, and not modern worship songs
- The retention of the second person singular, 'Thee', 'Thou' and 'Thine'
- The rejection of anything authored from within the Charismatic Movement

It was clear that although not popular with some, these principles were very important to many, and that such a book would meet a real need in the churches, providing a traditional hymnbook in a contemporary form.

METRICAL PSALMS

In common with many traditional books, the first 150 numbers correspond to the 150 Psalms of the Old Testament. These are metrical Psalms rather than Psalm paraphrases, and have been taken from *The Psalms of David in Metre* published in 1650. This is commonly known as The Scottish Metrical Psalter, and is without doubt the classic metrical Psalter within the English-speaking world. As has been done by others in the past, these renderings have been lightly edited. Our desire has been to remove unnecessary archaisms and unfortunate rhyming, while retaining the immediate recognition of all who are familiar with this well known and much loved Psalter. It is our deep conviction that the almost non-existence of metrical Psalms in the worship of many evangelical churches is highly regrettable, and it is our sincere hope that the inclusion of a complete metrical Psalter will go at least some way in helping to redress the balance (Eph 5:19, Col 3:16, Jas 5:13).

SCRIPTURE PARAPHRASES

As in most evangelical books, many paraphrases of Psalms and other Scripture portions are included. These are not given a section of their own, but are included among the traditional hymns under the appropriate subject headings. It is the testimony of many who have used books which place Scripture paraphrases in a separate section that these precious portions are often either forgotten or ignored, and tend to be sung very infrequently. It is hoped that marrying them to the themes of which they speak will make them more accessible, and cause them to be used more frequently to the blessing of all who sing them. These portions are identified at their head, and an index of all such is included for reference.

TRADITIONAL HYMNS

The major part of the book is comprised of some 1,041 traditional hymns. Many of these are older hymns that will be familiar to most and favourites of many. However, we have also included a significant number of newer hymns by living authors, as well as incorporating many longer-standing hymns that have fallen out of use but which are worthy of recovery. Although the majority of these traditional hymns would be immediately recognisable to many Christians, it is hoped that this collection is both familiar and fresh, and will be used of the Lord in bringing new heights and depths to our gatherings for worship.

'THEE', 'THOU' AND 'THINE'

One way in which this book goes against the tide is in its retention of the second person singular pronouns, 'Thee', 'Thou', and 'Thine'. To many this is simply archaic, but to us it is a matter of accuracy. The editors of one recent book seem to suggest that the use of these pronouns is positively unbiblical, 'Some Christians still prefer to address God in the second person singular ... They enjoy our respect and their own freedom. However, there is no biblical basis for this practice'. However, we would argue the precise opposite. They may reject the second person singular pronouns in favour of supposed increase of intelligibility, but as the Scriptures in Hebrew and Greek use the second person singular pronouns, our retention of them can only be both more accurate and more biblical.

INCLUSIONS AND EXCLUSIONS

What to include and what to exclude is always difficult. A balance is required between objective and subjective, strong doctrine and felt experience, the sovereignty of God and the responsibility of man, the darkness of sin and the light of salvation, the reality of Hell and the glory of Heaven. However, what should be done with authors whose theology is regarded as seriously errant – whether they are Romanist, Ecumenical, Unitarian, Charismatic or whatever else. Some have argued that hymns should be judged solely on the merit or otherwise of their words, while others would argue that everything must come from an unquestionably orthodox source.

Our policy is something of a middle way. We would not want to argue with C. H. Spurgeon, who in his Preface to *Our Own Hymn-Book* wrote: 'Whatever may be thought of our taste we have used it without prejudice; and a good hymn has not been rejected because of the character of its author, or the heresies of the church in whose hymnal it first occurred'. However, in the days in which we live, we are facing something Spurgeon never faced, namely the introduction of a whole new genre of material to worship, with the informal offerings of the Charismatic Movement, accompanied by its multi-instrument worldly-idiom music. Some more traditional hymns from this quarter may prove to stand the test of time, but many more will undoubtedly sweep numerous churches into oblivion in the process.

Therefore, regarding authors who have departed this world, we have made Spurgeon's practice our own, but regarding those who are still living, we have endeavoured to include only those hymns written by authors of known orthodoxy. We appreciate that there will be those on both sides of the argument who will question the rightness of our policy at this point, but we trust that they will acknowledge both that it is a tenable policy to hold, and that we have sought to implement it faithfully.

Throughout the production process we have been enormously indebted to the help, advice, and sheer hard-work of so many friends without whom this book would never have seen the light of day. We have been greatly encouraged by the generosity of the Lord's people which has enabled a vision to become a reality, and above all, we are full of praise and thanks to Almighty God who has blessed us so markedly, and whose blessing we humbly trust will rest upon this book.

In all the decisions taken, we have sought to unite rather than divide. For those of our brethren who want a book of a significantly different ethos, there are such available on the market. However, for those unhappy with other recent offerings, we have sought to produce a book that is clear about its parameters, but within which it seeks to be as broad, representative and biblically ecumenical as possible. It is our prayer that what other books have done in past generations this would do today – rallying those of like heart and mind, encouraging us to see that far more unites us than divides us, and enabling us to continue the greatest work known to man, namely worship 'in spirit and in truth'.

R. Jeremy Brooks, G. Roland Burrows, Stephen J. Ford, Dewi W. Higham,
W. Vernon Higham, David W. Kay, Neil V. Pfeiffer (Chairman), John P. Thackway
Christian Worship Publishing Trust

ACKNOWLEDGEMENTS

COPYRIGHT HOLDERS

Boorman, David, 109 Saunders Way, Sketty, Swansea, SA2 8BH
Church Mission Society, Partnership House, 157 Waterloo Road, London, SE1 8UU
Clifford, Alan Charles, 7 Woodside Park, Attleborough, Norwich, NR17 2JL
Cook, Paul Eric Graham, 55 Holly Avenue, Breaston, Derby, DE72 3BG
CopyCare, PO Box 77, Hailsham, BN27 3EF
Cordle, Caroline Jane, 7 Rectory Close, Carlton, Bedford, MK43 7JT
Dickie, Robert, 5094 Highpoint Drive, Swartz Creek, MI48473, USA
Ford, Stephen J., 4 Elm Grove Drive, Dawlish, EX7 0EU
Gibbard, Noel, 35 Caedelyn Road, Cardiff, CF14 1BH
Harrison, Eluned, 8 Stow Park Crescent, Newport, NP20 4HD
Harrison, Graham Stuart, 8 Stow Park Crescent, Newport, NP20 4HD
Higham, William Vernon, 8 Copperfield Drive, Thornhill, Cardiff, CF14 9DD
Hope Publishing Company, Carol Stream, IL60188, USA
Jones, Robert (Bobi) Maynard, Tandderwen, Heol Llanbadarn, Aberystwyth, SY23 1HB
Mynors, Sir Richard, Treago, Saint Weonards, Hereford, HR2 8QB
OMF International (UK), Station Approach, Borough Green, Svenoaks, TN15 8BG
Oxford University Press, Great Clarendon Street, Oxford, OX2 6DP
Owen, Edmund Tudor, 34 Bron-yr-ynn, Drefach, Llanelli, SA14 7AH
SIM – UK / N. Europe, Wetheringsett Manor, Wetheringsett, Stowmarket, IP14 5QX
Sykes, Hilary, 17 Palatine Grove, Littleover, Derby, DE23 7RR
World Student Christian Federation, 5 Route des Morillons, 1218 Grand-Seconnesc, Geneva, Switzerland

Although every effort has been made to trace holders of copyright, it has in some instances proved impossible to contact the present owner or to establish whether copyright does in fact exist. If for these reasons or through inadvertence any rights still surviving have not been acknowledged, then the publishers tender their apologies to those concerned and express their willingness to make any necessary corrections in subsequent reprints.

OTHER ACKNOWLEDGEMENTS

As stated in the Preface, throughout the production process the editors have been enormously indebted to the help, advice, and sheer hard-work of so many friends without whom this book would never have seen the light of day. Particular thanks go to Janet Cowie, Philip Dawe, Patricia Dunn, Esther Lim, Suzanne Norman, Ruth Pugh, Isobel Scott, Barabara Thomas and Colin Wright. The editors would also like to thank their wives, families and churches for their support and encouragement.

FOREWORD

IN INTRODUCING *Christian Worship*, I would like to give a word of explanation. There are many of us who wish to maintain a tradition that is precious to us, and well worth safeguarding. It is our hope that we will be able to maintain a warm and spiritual expression of biblical and reformed truths – what we would call experiential or experimental Calvinism or, just simply, heart religion. It is our desire to continue this great tradition of Christian worship that has been handed down to us by our forefathers. It is essential that the fundamental truths are clearly expressed in our hymns, with a warmth of Christian experience and practical application. We need our hymns to be God-centred, an inspiration in our worship and an encouragement in our lives. This is worshipping God 'in spirit and in truth'.

The hymns that we sing have a profound effect upon our attitude in the worship of God and should encourage reverence in our services. The hymns that we sing have a profound effect upon what we b lieve. What we sing, we ultimately believe and, therefore, it is essential that we keep close to the principles and truths of Scripture in the choice of material that we use. Such principles must be jealously guarded in the days in which we live. We must keep faithfully to the truths of the Bible and yet, at the same time, maintain a spiritual warmth. I believe that this will assist us in maintaining our reverence to God and the worship of God. In doing this, the name of the Lord Jesus Christ will be exalted and our hearts uplifted.

This new hymnbook has been carefully prepared by a number of men of the reformed and biblical tradition which we hold most dearly. The starting point for selecting hymns was the selection found in *Christian Hymns*, first published in 1977. A small number of subtractions and numerous additions were made for the final selection in *Christian Worship*. A number of hymns by William Gadsby and Joseph Hart are amongst the additions. There is a larger section at the beginning on the worship of the Godhead, and many more gospel hymns are included. You will note that we have a separate psalmody section. We have used the *Scottish Metrical Psalms* as a basis, with a few sensitive changes to clarify the meaning in some stanzas. However, the Psalms paraphrased by Isaac Watts and others are included in the hymn section, under their various headings. Our hope is that the inclusion of metrical Psalms will contribute to our worship and devotion.

I believe that we are all deeply concerned regarding the state of things in every sphere of life, both in this land, and throughout the world. It seems as if all that we held dear, and that seemed to be so secure, is collapsing around us. Yet, like Esther, we also are born 'for such a time as this', and must be faithful in our day.

In 1792, Thomas Charles of Bala spoke these striking words: 'I am persuaded that unless we are favoured with frequent revivals, and a strong powerful work of the Spirit of God, we shall, in a great degree, degenerate, and only have a "name to live". Religion will soon lose its vigour, the ministry will hardly retain its lustre and glory, and iniquity will, of consequence, abound.' However, we are all comforted by the fact that we have a sovereign, active God, who is working out His purposes. Let us look to Him for better times to come. Once again, may we experience a time of refreshing from the presence of the Lord. I trust that this hymnbook will have a part in maintaining the purity of the worship of God in our midst, and I warmly commend it to the Lord's people.

W. Vernon Higham

METRICAL PSALMS

1   C.M.

1 That man hath perfect blessedness
  Who walketh not astray
  In counsel of ungodly men,
  Nor stands in sinners' way,

  Nor sitteth in the scorner's chair:
2 But placeth his delight
  Upon God's law, and meditates
  On his law day and night.

3 He shall be like a tree that grows
  Near planted by a river,
  Which in his season yields his fruit,
  And his leaf fadeth never:

  And all he doth shall prosper well
4 The wicked are not so;
  But like they are unto the chaff,
  Which wind drives to and fro.

5 In judgment therefore shall not
    stand
  Such as ungodly are;
  Nor in th' assembly of the just
  Shall wicked men appear.

6 For why? the way of godly men
  Unto the Lord is known:
  Whereas the way of wicked men
  Shall quite be overthrown.

2   C.M.

1 Why rage the heathen? and vain
    things
  Why do the people mind?
2 Kings of the earth do set themselves,
  And princes are combined,

To plot against the Lord, and his
  Anointed, saying thus,
3 Let us asunder break their bands,
  And cast their cords from us.

4 He that in heaven sits shall laugh;
  The Lord shall scorn them all.
5 Then shall he speak to them in
    wrath,
  In rage he vex them shall.

6 Yet, notwithstanding, I have him
  To be my King appointed;
  And over Sion, my holy hill,
  I have him King anointed.

7 The sure decree I will declare:
  The Lord hath said to me,
  Thou art mine only Son; this day
  I have begotten thee.

8 Ask of me, and for heritage
  The heathen I'll make thine;
  And, for possession, I to thee
  Will give earth's utmost line.

9 Thou shalt, as with a weighty rod
  Of iron, break them all;
  And, as a potter's sherd, thou shalt
  Them dash in pieces small.

10 Now therefore, kings, be wise; be
    taught,
  Ye judges of the earth:
11 Serve God in fear, and see that ye
  Join trembling with your mirth.

12 Kiss ye the Son, lest in his ire
  Ye perish from the way,
  If once his wrath begin to burn:
  Blessed all that on him stay.

3 C.M.

*A Psalm of David, when he fled from
Absalom his son.*

1 O Lord, how are my foes increased?
Against me many rise.
2 Many say of my soul, For him
In God no succour lies.

3 Yet thou my shield and glory art,
The uplifter of mine head.
4 I cried, and, from his holy hill,
The Lord me answer made.

5 I laid me down and slept; I waked;
For God sustained me.
6 I will not fear though thousands ten
Set round against me be.

7 Arise, O Lord; save me, my God;
For thou with powerful stroke
Hast on the cheek-bone smote my
    foes,
The wicked's teeth hast broke.

8 Salvation doth appertain
Unto the Lord alone:
Thy blessing, Lord, for evermore
Thy people is upon.

4 C.M.

*To the chief Musician on Neginoth,
A Psalm of David.*

1 Give ear unto me when I call,
God of my righteousness:
Have mercy, hear my prayer; thou
    hast
Enlarged me in distress.

2 O ye the sons of men! how long
Will ye love vanities?
How long my glory turn to shame,
And will ye follow lies?

3 But know, that for himself the Lord
The godly man doth choose:
The Lord, when I on him do call,
To hear will not refuse.

4 Fear, and sin not; talk with your
    heart
On bed, and silent be.
5 Give offerings of righteousness,
And in the Lord trust ye.

6 O who will show us any good?
Is that which many say:
But of thy countenance the light,
Lord, lift on us alway.

7 Upon my heart, bestowed by thee,
More gladness I have found
Than they, ev'n then, when corn
    and wine
Did most with them abound.

8 I will both lay me down in peace,
and quiet sleep will take;
Because thou only me to dwell
In safety, Lord, dost make.

5 C.M.

*To the chief Musician, upon Nehiloth,
A Psalm of David.*
vv 1-7, 8-12

1 Give ear unto my words, O Lord,
My meditation weigh.
2 Hear my loud cry, my King, my God;
For I to thee will pray.

3 Lord, thou shalt early hear my voice:
I early will direct
My prayer to thee; and, looking up,
An answer will expect.

4 For thou art not a God that doth
In wickedness delight;
Neither shall evil dwell with thee,
5 Nor fools stand in thy sight.

All that ill-doers are thou hat'st;
6 Cutt'st off that liars be:
The bloody and deceitful man
Abhorred is by thee.

7 But I into thy house will come
In thine abundant grace;
And I will worship in thy fear
Toward thy holy place.

8 Because of those mine enemies,
   Lord, in thy righteousness
   Do thou me lead; do thou thy way
   Make straight before my face.

9 For in their mouth there is no truth,
   Their inward part is ill;
   Their throat's an open sepulchre,
   Their tongue doth flatter still.

10 O God, destroy them; let them be
   By their own counsel quelled:
   Them for their many sins cast out,
   For they 'gainst thee rebelled.

11 But let all joy that trust in thee,
   And still make joyful noise;
   For them thou sav'st; let all that
   love
   Thy name in thee rejoice.

12 For, Lord, unto the righteous man
   Thou wilt thy blessing yield:
   With favour thou wilt compass him
   About, as with a shield.

6 First Version   L.M.

*To the chief Musician on Neginoth upon
Sheminith, A Psalm of David.*

1 Lord, in thy wrath rebuke me not;
   Nor in thy hot rage chasten me.
2 Lord, pity me, for I am weak:
   Heal me, for my bones vexed be.
3 My soul is also vexed sore;
   But, Lord, how long stay wilt thou
   make?
4 Return, O Lord, my soul set free;
   O save me, for thy mercies' sake.

5 Because those that deceased are
   Of thee shall no remembrance have;
   And who is he that will to thee
   Give praises lying in the grave?

6 I with my groaning weary am,
   I also all the night my bed
   Have caused for to swim; and I
   With tears my couch have watered.

7 Mine eye, consumed with grief,
     grows old,
   Because of all mine enemies.
8 Hence from me, wicked workers all;
   For God hath heard my weeping
     cries.

9 God hath my supplication heard,
   My pray'r received graciously
10 Shamed and sore vexed be all my
     foes,
   Shamed and back turned suddenly.

6 Second Version   C.M.

*To the chief Musician on Neginoth upon
Sheminith, A Psalm of David.*

1 In thy great indignation,
   O Lord, rebuke me not;
   Nor on me lay thy chastening hand,
   In thy displeasure hot.

2 Lord, I am weak, therefore on me
   Have mercy, and me spare:
   Heal me, O Lord, for thou dost know
   My bones much vexed are.

3 My soul is vexed sore: but, Lord,
   How long stay wilt thou make?
4 Return, Lord, free my soul; and save
   Me, for thy mercies' sake.

5 Because of thee in death there shall
   No more remembrance be:
   Of those that in the grave do lie,
   Who shall give thanks to thee?

6 I with my groaning weary am,
   And all the night my bed
   I caused for to swim; with tears
   My couch I watered.

7 By reason of my vexing grief,
   Mine eye consumed is;
   It waxeth old, because of all
   That be mine enemies.

8 But now, depart from me all ye
   That work iniquity:
   For why? the Lord hath heard my
     voice,
   When I did mourn and cry.

9 Unto my supplication
The Lord did hearing give:
When I to him my prayer make,
The Lord will it receive.

10 Let all be shamed and troubled sore,
That enemies are to me;
Let them turn back, and suddenly
Ashamed let them be.

7   C.M.

Shiggaion of David, which he sang unto
the Lord, concerning the words of Cush
the Benjamite.
vv 1-5, 6–9, 10-17

1 O Lord my God, in thee do I
My confidence repose:
Save and deliver me from all
My persecuting foes;

2 Lest that the enemy my soul
Should, like a lion, tear,
In pieces rending it, while there
Is no deliverer.

3 O Lord my God, if it be so
That I committed this;
If it be so that in my hands
Iniquity there is:

4 If I rewarded ill to him
That was at peace with me;
(Yea, ev'n the man that without
cause
My foe was I did free;)

5 Then let the foe pursue and take
My soul, and my life thrust
Down to the earth, and let him lay
Mine honour in the dust.

6 Rise in thy wrath, Lord, raise thyself,
For my foes raging be;
And, to the judgment which thou hast
Commanded, wake for me.

7 So shall th' assembly of thy folk
About encompass thee:
Thou, therefore, for their sakes, return
Unto thy place on high.

8 The Lord he shall the people judge:
My judge, JEHOVAH, be,
After my righteousness, and mine
Integrity in me.

9 O let the wicked's malice end;
But stablish steadfastly
The righteous: for the righteous
God
The hearts and reins doth try.

10 In God, who saves th' upright in
heart,
Is my defence and stay.

11 God just men judgeth, God is wroth
With ill men ev'ry day.

12 If he do not return again,
Then he his sword will whet;
His bow he hath already bent,
And hath it ready set:

13 He also hath for him prepared
The instruments of death;
Against the persecutors he
His shafts ordained hath.

14 Behold, he with iniquity
Doth travail, as in birth;
A mischief he conceived hath,
And falsehood shall bring forth.

15 He made a pit and digged it deep,
Another there to take;
But he is fall'n into the ditch
Which he himself did make.

16 Upon his own head his mischief
Shall be returned home;
His violent dealing also down
On his own self shall come.

17 According to his righteousness
The Lord I'll magnify;
And will sing praise unto the name
Of God that is most high.

8 C.M.

To the chief Musician upon Gittith,
A Psalm of David.

1 How excellent in all the earth,
   Lord, our Lord, is thy name!
   Who hast thy glory far advanced
   Above the starry frame.

2 From infants' and from sucklings'
      mouth
   Thou didest strength ordain,
   For thy foes' cause, that so thou
      might'st
   Th' avenging foe restrain.

3 When I look up unto the heavens,
   Which thine own fingers framed,
   Unto the moon, and to the stars,
   Which were by thee ordained;

4 Then say I, What is man, that he
   Remembered is by thee?
   Or what the son of man, that thou
   So kind to him should'st be?

5 For thou a little lower hast
   Him than the angels made;
   With glory and with dignity
   Thou crowned hast his head.

6 Of thy hands' works thou madest
      him lord,
   All 'neath his feet didst lay;

7 All sheep and oxen, yea, and beasts
   That in the field do stray;

8 Fowls of the air, fish of the sea,
   All that pass through the same.

9 How excellent in all the earth,
   Lord, our Lord, is thy name!

9

To the chief Musician upon Muth-
labben, A Psalm of David.
vv 1-6, 7-10, 11-14, 15-20

1 Lord, thee I'll praise with all my
      heart,
   Thy wonders all proclaim.

2 In thee, most High, I'll greatly joy,
   And sing unto thy name.

3 When back my foes were turned,
      they fell,
   And perished at thy sight:

4 For thou maintain'dst my right and
      cause;
   On throne sat'st judging right.

5 The heathen thou rebuked hast,
   The wicked overthrown;
   Thou hast put out their names, that
      they
   May never more be known.

6 O enemy! destructions have
   An end perpetual:
   Thou cities razed; perished with
      them
   Is their memorial.

7 God shall endure for aye; he doth
   For judgment set his throne;

8 In righteousness to judge the world,
   Justice to give each one.

9 God also will a refuge be
   For those that are oppressed;
   A refuge will he be in times
   Of trouble to distressed.

10 And they that know thy name, in
      thee
   Their confidence will place:
   For thou hast not forsaken them
   That truly seek thy face.

11 O sing ye praises to the Lord,
   That dwells in Sion hill;
   And all the nations among
   His deeds record ye still.

12 When he enquireth after blood,
   He then remembereth them:
   The humble folk he not forgets
   That call upon his name.

13 Lord, pity me; behold the grief
   Which I from foes sustain;
   Ev'n thou, who from the gates of
      death
   Dost raise me up again;

14 That I, in Sion's daughters' gates,
   May all thy praise advance;
   And that I may rejoice always
   In thy deliverance.

15 The heathen are sunk in the pit
   Which they themselves prepared;
   And in the net which they have hid
   Their own feet fast are snared.

16 The Lord is by the judgment known
   Which he himself hath wrought:
   The sinners' hands do make the
      snares
   Wherewith themselves are caught.

17 They who are wicked into hell
   Each one shall turned be;
   And all the nations that forget
   To seek the Lord most high.

18 For they that needy are shall not
   Forgotten be alway;
   The expectation of the poor
   Shall not be lost for aye.

19 Arise, Lord, let not man prevail;
   Judge heathen in thy sight:
20 That they may know themselves but
      men,
   The nations, Lord, affright.

10   C.M.

vv 1–3, 4-7, 8-12, 13-18

1 What is the cause that thou, O Lord,
  Dost stand from us afar?
  And wherefore hidest thou thyself,
  When times so troublous are?

2 The wicked in his loftiness
  Doth persecute the poor:
  In these devices they have framed
  Let them be taken sure.

3 The wicked of his heart's desire
  Doth talk with boasting great;
  He blesseth him that's covetous,
  Whom yet the Lord doth hate.

4 The wicked, through his pride of
      face,
  On God he doth not call;
  And in the counsels of his heart
  The Lord is not at all.

5 His ways they always grievous are;
  Thy judgments from his sight
  Removed are: at all his foes
  He puffeth with despite.

6 Within his heart he thus hath said,
  I shall not moved be;
  And no adversity at all
  Shall ever come to me.

7 His mouth with cursing, fraud,
      deceit,
  Is filled abundantly;
  And underneath his tongue there is
  Mischief and vanity.

8 He closely sits in villages;
  He slays the innocent:
  Against the poor that pass him by
  His cruel eyes are bent.

9 He, lion-like, lurks in his den;
  He waits the poor to take;
  And when he draws him in his net,
  His prey he doth him make.

10 Himself he humbleth very low,
   He croucheth down withal,
   That so a multitude of poor
   May by his strong ones fall.

11 He thus hath said within his heart,
   The Lord hath quite forgot;
   He hides his countenance, and he
   For ever sees it not.

12 O Lord, do thou arise; O God,
   Lift up thine hand on high:
   Put not the meek afflicted ones
   Out of thy memory.

13 Why is it that the wicked man
   Thus doth the Lord despise?
   Because that God will it require
   He in his heart denies.

14 Thou hast it seen; for their mischief
And spite thou wilt repay:
The poor commits himself to thee;
Thou art the orphan's stay.

15 The arm break of the wicked man,
And of the evil one;
Do thou seek out his wickedness,
Until thou findest none.

16 The Lord is King through ages all,
Ev'n to eternity;
The heathen people from his land
Are perished utterly.

17 O Lord, of those that humble are
Thou the desire didst hear;
Thou wilt prepare their heart, and thou
To hear wilt bend thine ear;

18 To judge the fatherless, and those
That are oppressed sore;
That man, that is but of the earth,
May them oppress no more.

11 C.M.

To the chief Musician, A Psalm of David.

1 I in the Lord do put my trust:
How is it then that ye
Say to my soul, Flee, as a bird,
Unto your mountain high?

2 For, lo, the wicked bend their bow,
Their shafts on string they fit,
That those who upright are in heart
They privily may hit.

3 If the foundations be destroyed,
What hath the righteous done?
4 God in his holy temple is,
In heaven is his throne:

His eyes do see, his eye-lids try
5 Men's sons. The just he proves:
But his soul hates the wicked man,
And him that violence loves.

6 Snares, fire and brimstone, furious storms,
On sinners he shall rain:
This, as the portion of their cup,
Doth unto them pertain.

7 Because the Lord most righteous doth
In righteousness delight;
And with a pleasant countenance
Beholdeth the upright.

12 C.M.

To the chief Musician upon Sheminith, A Psalm of David.

1 Help, Lord, because the godly man
Doth daily fade away;
And from among the sons of men
The faithful do decay.

2 Unto his neighbour every one
Doth utter vanity:
They with a double heart do speak,
And lips of flattery.

3 God shall cut off all flatt'ring lips,
Tongues that speak proudly thus,
4 Our tongues prevail, our lips are ours:
Who is lord over us?

5 For poor oppressed, and for the sighs
Of needy, rise will I,
Saith God, and him in safety set
From such as him defy.

6 The words of God are words most pure;
They be like silver tried
In earthen furnace, seven times
That hath been purified.

7 Lord, thou shalt them preserve and keep
For ever from this race.
8 On each side walk the wicked, when
Vile men are high in place.

13 C.M.

To the chief Musician, A Psalm of David.

1 How long wilt thou forget me,
   Lord?
   Shall it for ever be?
   O how long shall it be that thou
   Wilt hide thy face from me?

2 How long take counsel in my soul,
   Still sad in heart, shall I?
   How long exalted over me
   Shall be mine enemy?

3 O Lord my God, consider well,
   And answer to me make:
   Mine eyes enlighten, lest the sleep
   Of death me overtake:

4 Lest that mine enemy should say,
   Against him I prevail;
   And those that trouble me rejoice,
   When I am moved and fail.

5 But I have all my confidence
   Thy mercy set upon;
   My heart within me shall rejoice
   In thy salvation.

6 I will unto the Lord my God
   Sing praises cheerfully,
   Because he hath his bounty shown
   To me abundantly.

14 C.M.

To the chief Musician, A Psalm of David.

1 That there is not a God, the fool
   Doth in his heart conclude:
   They are corrupt, their works are
   vile;
   Not one of them doth good.

2 Upon men's sons the Lord from
   heaven
   Did cast his eyes abroad,
   To see if any understood,
   And did seek after God.

3 They altogether filthy are,
   They all aside are gone;
   And there is none that doeth good,
   Yea, sure there is not one.

4 These workers of iniquity
   Do they not know at all,
   That they my people eat as bread,
   And on God do not call?

5 There feared they much; for God is
   with
   The whole race of the just.
6 You shame the counsel of the poor,
   Because God is his trust.

7 Let Israel's help from Sion come:
   When back the Lord shall bring
   His captives, Jacob shall rejoice,
   And Israel shall sing.

15 C.M.

A Psalm of David.

1 Within thy tabernacle, Lord,
   Who shall abide with thee?
   And in thy high and holy hill
   Who shall a dweller be?

2 The man that walketh uprightly,
   And worketh righteousness,
   And as he thinketh in his heart,
   So doth he truth express.

3 Who doth not slander with his
   tongue,
   Nor to his friend doth hurt;
   Nor yet against his neighbour doth
   Take up an ill report.

4 In whose eyes vile men are
   despised;
   But those that God do fear
   He honoureth; and changeth not,
   Though to his hurt he swear.

5 His coin puts not to usury,
   Nor take reward will he
   Against the guiltless. Who doth
   thus
   Shall never moved be.

16 C.M.

Michtam of David.
vv 1-5, 6-11

1 Lord, keep me; for I trust in thee.
2 To God thus was my speech,
   Thou art my Lord; and unto thee
   My goodness doth not reach:

3 To saints on earth, to the excellent,
   Where my delight is placed.
4 Their sorrows shall be multiplied
   To other gods that haste:

   Of their drink-offerings of blood
   I will no offering make;
   Yea, neither I their very names
   Up in my lips will take.

5 God is of mine inheritance
   And cup the portion;
   The lot that fallen is to me
   Thou dost maintain alone.

6 Unto me happily the lines
   In pleasant places fell;
   Yea, the inheritance I got
   In beauty doth excel.

7 I bless the Lord, because he doth
   By counsel me conduct;
   And in the seasons of the night
   My reins do me instruct.

8 Before me still the Lord I set:
   Since it is so that he
   Doth ever stand at my right hand,
   I shall not moved be.

9 Because of this my heart is glad,
   And joy shall be expressed
   Ev'n by my glory; and my flesh
   In confidence shall rest.

10 Because my soul in grave to dwell
    Shall not be left by thee;
    Nor wilt thou give thine Holy One
    Corruption to see.

11 Thou wilt me show the path of life:
    Of joys there is full store
    Before thy face; at thy right hand
    Are pleasures evermore.

17 C.M.

A Prayer of David.
vv 1-4, 5-7, 8-15

1 Lord, hear the right, attend my cry,
   Unto my prayer give heed,
   That doth not in hypocrisy
   From feigned lips proceed.

2 And from before thy presence forth
   My sentence do thou send:
   Toward these things that equal are
   Do thou thine eyes intend.

3 Thou prov'dst mine heart, thou
      visit'dst me
   By night, thou didst me try,
   Yet nothing found'st; for that my
      mouth
   Shall not sin, purposed I.

4 As for men's works, I, by the word
   That from thy lips doth flow,
   Did me preserve out of the paths
   Wherein destroyers go.

5 Hold up my goings, Lord, me
      guide
   In those thy paths divine,
   So that my footsteps may not slide
   Out of those ways of thine.

6 I called have on thee, O God,
   Because thou wilt me hear:
   That thou mayest hearken to my
      speech,
   To me incline thine ear.

7 Thy wondrous loving-kindness
      show,
   Thou that, by thy right hand,
   Sav'st them that trust in thee from
      those
   That up against them stand.

8 As the apple of the eye me keep;
   In thy wings shade me close
9 From vile oppressors, compassing
   Me round, as deadly foes.

10 In their own fat they are enclosed;
Their mouth speaks loftily.
11 Our steps they compassed; and to
ground
Down bowing set their eye.

12 He like unto a lion is
That's greedy of his prey,
Or lion young, which lurking doth
In secret places stay.

13 Arise, and disappoint my foe,
And cast him down, O Lord:
My soul save from the wicked man,
The man which is thy sword.

14 From men, which are thy hand, O
Lord,
From worldly men me save,
Which only in this present life
Their part and portion have.

Whose belly with thy treasure hid
Thou fill'st: they children have
In plenty; of their goods the rest
They to their children leave.

15 But as for me, I thine own face
In righteousness will see;
And with thy likeness, when I wake,
I satisfied shall be.

18   C.M.

vv 1-3, 4-10, 11-16, 17-19, 20-27,
28-36, 37-45, 46-50

1 Thee will I love, O Lord, my
strength.
2 My fortress is the Lord,
My rock, and he that doth to me
Deliverance afford:

My God, my strength, whom I will
trust,
A buckler unto me,
The horn of my salvation,
And my high tower, is he.

3 Upon the Lord, who worthy is
Of praises, will I cry;
And then shall I preserved be
Safe from mine enemy.

4 Floods of ill men affrighted me,
Death's pangs about me went;
5 Hell's sorrows me environed;
Death's snares did me prevent.

6 In my distress I called on God,
Cry to my God did I;
He from his temple heard my
voice,
To his ears came my cry.

7 The earth, as frighted, then did
shake,
Trembling upon it seized:
The hills' foundations moved were,
Because he was displeased.

8 Up from his nostrils came a
smoke,
And from his mouth there came
Devouring fire, and coals by it
Were turned into flame.

9 He also bowed down the heavens,
And thence he did descend;
And thickest clouds of darkness
did
Under his feet attend.

10 And he upon a cherub rode,
And thereon he did fly;
Yea, on the swift wings of the wind
His flight was from on high.

11 He darkness made his secret place:
About him, for his tent,
Dark waters were, and thickest
clouds
Of th' airy firmament.

12 And at the brightness of that light,
Which was before his eye,
His thick clouds passed away, hail-
stones
And coals of fire did fly.

13 The Lord God also in the heavens
Did thunder in his ire;
And there the Highest gave his
voice,
Hailstones and coals of fire.

14 Yea, he his arrows sent abroad,
   And them he scattered;
   His lightnings also he shot out,
   And them discomfited.

15 The waters' channels then were
      seen,
   The world's foundations vast
   At thy rebuke discovered were,
   And at thy nostrils' blast.

16 And from above the Lord sent
      down,
   And took me from below;
   From many waters he me drew,
   Which would me overflow.

17 He me rescued from my strong
      foes,
   And such as did me hate;
   Because he saw that they for me
   Too strong were, and too great.

18 They me prevented in the day
   Of my calamity;
   But even then the Lord himself
   A stay was unto me.

19 He to a place where liberty
   And room was hath me brought;
   Because he took delight in me,
   He my deliverance wrought.

20 According to my righteousness
   He did me recompense,
   He me repaid according to
   My hands' pure innocence.

21 For I God's ways kept, from my
      God
   Did not turn wickedly.
22 His judgments were before me, I
   His laws put not from me.

23 Sincere before him was my heart;
   With him upright was I;
   And watchfully I kept myself
   From mine iniquity.

24 After my righteousness the Lord
   Hath recompensed me,
   After the cleanness of my hands
   Appearing in his eye.

25 Thou gracious to the gracious art,
   To upright men upright:
26 Pure to the pure; wilt froward show
   To men of froward heart.

27 For thou wilt the afflicted save
   In grief that low do lie:
   But wilt bring down the
      countenance
   Of them whose looks are high.

28 The Lord will light my candle so,
   That it shall shine full bright:
   The Lord my God will also make
   My darkness to be light.

29 By thee through troops of men I
      break,
   And them discomfit all;
   And, by my God assisting me,
   I overleap a wall.

30 As for God, perfect is his way:
   The Lord his word is tried;
   He is a buckler to all those
   Who do in him confide.

31 Who but the Lord is God? but he
   Who is a rock and stay?
32 'Tis God that girdeth me with
      strength,
   And perfect makes my way.

33 He made my feet swift as the
      hinds,
   Set me on my high places.
34 Mine hands to war he taught, mine
      arms
   Brake bows of steel in pieces.

35 The shield of thy salvation
   Thou didst on me bestow:
   Thy right hand held me up, and
      great
   Thy kindness made me grow.

36 And in my way my steps thou hast
   Enlarged under me,
   That I go safely, and my feet
   Are kept from sliding free.

37 Mine enemies I pursued have,
And did them overtake;
Nor did I turn again till I
An end of them did make.

38 I wounded them, they could not
rise;
They at my feet did fall.

39 Thou girdedst me with strength for
war;
My foes thou brought'st down all:

40 And thou hast given to me the
necks
Of all mine enemies;
That I might them destroy and slay,
Who did against me rise.

41 They cried out, but there was none
That would or could them save;
Yea, they did cry unto the Lord,
But he no answer gave.

42 Then did I beat them small as dust
Before the wind that flies;
And I did cast them out like dirt
Upon the street that lies.

43 Thou mad'st me free from people's
strife,
And heathen's head to be:
A people whom I have not known
Shall service do to me.

44 At hearing they shall me obey,
To me they shall submit.

45 Strangers for fear shall fade away,
Who in close places sit.

46 God lives, blessed be my Rock; the
God
Of my health praised be.

47 God doth avenge me, and subdues
The people under me.

48 He saves me from mine enemies;
Yea, thou hast lifted me
Above my foes; and from the man
Of violence set me free.

49 Therefore to thee will I give thanks
The heathen folk among;
And to thy name, O Lord, I will
Sing praises in a song.

50 He great deliverance gives his king:
He mercy doth extend
To David, his anointed one,
And his seed without end.

19   C.M.

*To the chief Musician, A Psalm of
David.*
vv 1-6, 7-14

1 The heavens God's glory do
declare,
The skies his hand-works preach:
2 Day utters speech to day, and night
To night doth knowledge teach.

3 There is no speech nor tongue to
which
Their voice doth not extend:
4 Their line is gone through all the
earth,
Their words to the world's end.

In them he set the sun a tent;
5 Who, bridegroom-like, forth goes
From his house, as a strong man
doth
To run his race rejoice.

6 From heaven's end is his going
forth,
Circling to the end again;
And there is nothing from his heat
That hidden doth remain.

7 God's law is perfect, and converts
The soul in sin that lies:
God's testimony is most sure,
And makes the simple wise.

8 The statutes of the Lord are right,
And do rejoice the heart:
The Lord's command is pure, and
doth
Light to the eyes impart.

9 Unspotted is the fear of God,
And doth endure for ever:
The judgments of the Lord are true
And righteous altogether.

10 They more than gold, yea, much
        fine gold,
    To be desired are:
    Than honey, honey from the comb
    That droppeth, sweeter far.

11 Moreover, they thy servant warn
    How he his life should frame:
    A great reward provided is
    For them that keep the same.

12 Who can his errors understand?
    O cleanse thou me within
13 From secret faults. Thy servant
        keep
    From all presumptuous sin:

    And do not suffer them to have
    Dominion over me:
    Then, righteous and innocent,
    I from much sin shall be.

14 The words which from my mouth
        proceed,
    The thoughts sent from my heart,
    Accept, O Lord, for thou my strength
    And my Redeemer art.

20   C.M.

*To the chief Musician, A Psalm of
David.*
vv 1-4, 5-9

1 JEHOVAH hear thee in the day
    When trouble he doth send:
    And let the name of Jacob's God
    Thee from all ill defend.

2 O let him help send from above,
    Out of his sanctuary:
    From Sion, his own holy hill,
    Let him give strength to thee.

3 Let him remember all thy gifts,
    Accept thy sacrifice:
4 Grant thee thine heart's wish, and
        fulfil
    Thy thoughts and counsel wise.

5 In thy salvation we will joy;
    In our God's name we will
    Display our banners: and the Lord
    Thy prayers all fulfil.

6 Now know I God his king doth
        save:
    He from his holy heaven
    Will hear him, with the saving
        strength
    By his own right hand given.

7 In chariots some put confidence,
    Some horses trust upon:
    But we remember will the name
    Of our Lord God alone.

8 We rise, and upright stand, when
        they
    Are bowed down, and fall.
9 Deliver, Lord; and let the King
    Us hear, when we do call.

21   C.M.

*To the chief Musician, A Psalm of
David.*
vv 1-7, 8-13

1 The king in thy great strength, O
        Lord,
    Shall very joyful be:
    In thy salvation rejoice
    How fervently shall he!

2 Thou hast bestowed upon him
    All that his heart would have;
    And thou from him didst not with-
        hold
    Whate'er his lips did crave.

3 For thou with blessings dost him
        meet
    Of goodness manifold;
    And thou hast set upon his head
    A crown of purest gold.

4 When he desired life of thee,
    Thou life to him didst give;
    Ev'n such a length of days, that he
    For evermore should live.

5 In that salvation wrought by thee
    His glory is made great;
    Honour and comely majesty
    Thou hast upon him set.

6 Because that thou for evermore
  Most blessed hast him made;
  And thou hast with thy
        countenance
  Made him exceeding glad.

7 Because the king upon the Lord
  His confidence doth lay;
  And through the grace of the most
        High
  Shall not be moved away.

8 Thine hand shall all those men find
        out
  That enemies are to thee;
  Even thy right hand shall find out
        those
  Of thee that haters be.

9 Like fiery oven thou shalt them
        make,
  When kindled is thine ire;
  God shall them swallow in his
        wrath,
  Devour them shall the fire.

10 Their fruit from earth thou shalt
        destroy,
  Their seed men from among:
11 For they beyond their might 'gainst
        thee
  Did mischief plot and wrong.

12 Thou therefore shalt make them
        turn back,
  When thou thy shafts shalt place
  Upon thy strings, made ready all
  To fly against their face.

13 In thy great power and strength, O
        Lord,
  Be thou exalted high;
  So shall we sing with joyful hearts,
  Thy power praise shall we.

22   C.M.

To the chief Musician upon Aijeleth
Shahar, A Psalm of David.
vv 1-6, 7-12, 13-20, 21-26, 27-31

1 My God, my God, why hast thou
        me
  Forsaken? why so far
  Art thou from helping me, and
        from
  My words that roaring are?

2 All day, my God, to thee I cry,
  Yet am not heard by thee;
  And in the season of the night
  I cannot silent be.

3 But thou art holy, thou that dost
  Inhabit Israel's praise.
4 Our fathers hoped in thee, they
        hoped
  And thou didst them release.

5 When unto thee they sent their cry,
  To them deliverance came:
  Because they put their trust in thee,
  They were not put to shame.

6 But as for me, a worm I am,
  And as no man am prized:
  Reproach of men I am, and by
  The people am despised.

7 All that me see laugh me to scorn;
  Shoot out the lip do they;
  They nod and shake their heads at
        me,
  And, mocking, thus do say,

8 This man did trust in God, that he
  Would free him by his might:
  Let him deliver him, since he
  Had in him such delight.

9 But thou art he out of the womb
  That didst me safely take;
  When I was on my mother's breasts
  Thou me to hope didst make.

10 And I was cast upon thy care,
  Even from the womb till now;
  And from my mother's belly, Lord,
  My God and guide art thou.

11 Be not far off, for grief is near,
  And none to help is found.
12 Bulls many compass me, strong
    bulls
  Of Bashan me surround.

13 Their mouths they opened wide on
    me,
  Upon me gape did they,
  Like to a lion ravening
  And roaring for his prey.

14 Like water I'm poured out, my
    bones
  All out of joint do part:
  Amidst my bowels, as the wax,
  So melted is my heart.

15 My strength is like a potsherd
    dried;
  My tongue it cleaveth fast
  Unto my jaws; and to the dust
  Of death thou brought me hast.

16 For dogs have compassed me
    about:
  The wicked, that did meet
  In their assembly, me enclosed;
  They pierced my hands and feet.

17 I all my bones may tell; they do
  Upon me look and stare.
18 Upon my vesture lots they cast,
  And clothes among them share.

19 But be not far, O Lord, my
    strength;
  Haste to give help to me.
20 From sword my soul, from power
    of dogs
  My darling set thou free.

21 Out of the roaring lion's mouth
  Do thou me shield and save:
  For from the horns of unicorns
  An ear to me thou gave.

22 I will show forth thy name unto
  Those that my brethren are;
  Amidst the congregation
  Thy praise I will declare.

23 Praise ye the Lord, who do him
    fear;
  Him glorify all ye
  The seed of Jacob: fear him all
  That Israel's children be.

24 For he despised not nor abhorred
  The afflicted's misery;
  Nor from him hid his face, but
    heard
  When he to him did cry.

25 Within the congregation great
  My praise shall be of thee;
  My vows before them that him fear
  Shall be performed by me.

26 The meek shall eat, and shall be
    filled;
  They also praise shall give
  Unto the Lord that do him seek:
  Your heart shall ever live.

27 All ends of the earth remember
    shall,
  And turn the Lord unto;
  All kindreds of the nations
  To him shall homage do:

28 Because the kingdom to the Lord
  Doth appertain as his;
  Likewise among the nations
  The Governor he is.

29 Earth's fat ones eat, and worship
    shall:
  All who to dust descend
  Shall bow to him; none of them
    can
  His soul from death defend.

30 A seed shall service do to him;
  Unto the Lord it shall
  Be for a generation
  Reckoned in ages all.

31 They shall come, and they shall
    declare
  His truth and righteousness
  Unto a people yet unborn,
  And that he hath done this.

23   C.M.

A Psalm of David.

1 The Lord's my shepherd, I'll not
  want.

2 He makes me down to lie
  In pastures green: he leadeth me
  The quiet waters by.

3 My soul he doth restore again;
  And me to walk doth make
  Within the paths of righteousness,
  Even for his own name's sake.

4 Yea, though I walk in death's dark
  vale,
  Yet will I fear none ill:
  For thou art with me; and thy rod
  And staff me comfort still.

5 My table thou hast furnished
  In presence of my foes;
  My head thou dost with oil anoint,
  And my cup overflows.

6 Goodness and mercy all my life
  Shall surely follow me:
  And in God's house for evermore
  My dwelling-place shall be.

24   C.M.

vv 1-6, 7-10

1 The earth belongs unto the Lord,
  And all that it contains;
  The world that is inhabited,
  And all that there remains.

2 For the foundations thereof
  He on the seas did lay,
  And he hath it established
  Upon the floods to stay.

3 Who is the man that shall ascend
  Into the hill of God?
  Or who within his holy place
  Shall have a firm abode?

4 Whose hands are clean, whose
  heart is pure,
  And unto vanity
  Who hath not lifted up his soul,
  Nor sworn deceitfully.

5 He from the Eternal shall receive
  The blessing him upon,
  And righteousness, even from the
  God
  Of his salvation.

6 This is the generation
  That after him enquire,
  O Jacob, who do seek thy face
  With their whole heart's desire.

7 Ye gates, lift up your heads on
  high;
  Ye doors that last for aye,
  Be lifted up, that so the King
  Of glory enter may.

8 But who of glory is the King?
  The mighty Lord is this;
  Even that same Lord, that great in
  might
  And strong in battle is.

9 Ye gates, lift up your heads; ye
  doors,
  Doors that do last for aye,
  Be lifted up, that so the King
  Of glory enter may.

10 But who is he that is the King
  Of glory? who is this?
  The Lord of hosts, and none but
  he,
  The King of glory is.

25 First Version   S.M.

A Psalm of David.
vv. 1-7, 8-14, 15-22

1 To thee I lift my soul:
2 O Lord, I trust in thee:
  My God, let me not be ashamed,
  Nor foes triumph o'er me.

3 Let none that wait on thee
Be put to shame at all;
But those that without cause transgress,
Let shame upon them fall.

4 Show me thy ways, O Lord;
Thy paths, O teach thou me:
5 And do thou lead me in thy truth,
Therein my teacher be:

For thou art God that dost
To me salvation send,
And I upon thee all the day
Expecting do attend.

6 Thy tender mercies, Lord,
I pray thee to remember,
And loving-kindnesses; for they
Have been of old for ever.

7 My sins and faults of youth
Do thou, O Lord, forget:
After thy mercy think on me,
And for thy goodness great.

8 God good and upright is:
The way he'll sinners show.
9 The meek in judgment he will guide,
And make his path to know.

10 The whole paths of the Lord
Are truth and mercy sure,
To those that do his covenant keep,
And testimonies pure.

11 Now, for thine own name's sake,
O Lord, I thee entreat
To pardon mine iniquity;
For it is very great.

12 What man is he that fears
The Lord, and doth him serve?
Him shall he teach the way that he
Shall choose, and still observe.

13 His soul shall dwell at ease;
And his posterity
Shall flourish still, and of the earth
Inheritors shall be.

14 With those that fear him is
The secret of the Lord;
The knowledge of his covenant
He will to them afford.

15 Mine eyes upon the Lord
Continually are set:
For he it is that shall bring forth
My feet out of the net.

16 Turn unto me thy face,
And to me mercy show;
Because that I am desolate,
And am brought very low.

17 My heart's griefs are increased:
Me from distress relieve.
18 See mine affliction and my pain,
And all my sins forgive.

19 Consider thou my foes,
Because they many are;
And it a cruel hatred is
Which they against me bear.

20 O do thou keep my soul,
Do thou deliver me:
And let me never be ashamed,
Because I trust in thee.

21 Let uprightness and truth
Keep me, who thee attend.
22 Redemption, Lord, to Israel
From all his troubles send.

25 Second Version   C.M.

A Psalm of David.
vv 1-7, 8-14, 15-22

1 To thee I lift my soul, O Lord:
2 My God, I trust in thee:
Let me not be ashamed; let not
My foes triumph over me.

3 Yea, let thou none ashamed be
That do on thee attend:
Ashamed let them be, O Lord,
Who without cause offend.

4 Thy ways, Lord, show; teach me
thy paths:
5 Lead me in truth, teach me:
For of my safety thou art God;
All day I wait on thee.

6 Thy mercies, that most tender are,
Do thou, O Lord, remember,
And loving-kindnesses; for they
Have been of old for ever.

7 Let not the errors of my youth,
Nor sins, remembered be:
In mercy, for thy goodness' sake,
O Lord, remember me.

8 The Lord is good and gracious,
He upright is also:
He therefore sinners will instruct
In ways that they should go.

9 The meek and lowly he will guide
In judgment just alway:
To meek and poor afflicted ones
He'll clearly teach his way.

10 The whole paths of the Lord our
God
Are truth and mercy sure,
To such as keep his covenant,
And testimonies pure.

11 Now, for thine own name's sake, O
Lord,
I humbly thee entreat
To pardon mine iniquity;
For it is very great.

12 What man fears God? him shall he
teach
The way that he shall choose.

13 His soul shall dwell at ease; his
seed
The earth, as heirs, shall use.

14 The secret of the Lord is with
Such as do fear his name;
And he his holy covenant
Will manifest to them.

15 Towards the Lord my waiting eyes
Continually are set;
For he it is that shall bring forth
My feet out of the net.

16 O turn thee unto me, O God,
Have mercy me upon;
Because I solitary am,
And in affliction.

17 Enlarged the griefs are of mine
heart;
Me from distress relieve.

18 See mine affliction and my pain,
And all my sins forgive.

19 Consider thou mine enemies,
Because they many are;
And it a cruel hatred is
Which they against me bear.

20 O do thou keep my soul; O God,
Do thou deliver me:
Let me not be ashamed; for I
Do put my trust in thee.

21 O let integrity and truth
Keep me, who thee attend.

22 Redemption, Lord, to Israel
From all his troubles send.

26 C.M.

A Psalm of David.
vv 1-7, 8-12

1 Judge me, O Lord, for I have
walked
In mine integrity:
I trusted also in the Lord;
Slide therefore shall not I.

2 Examine me, and do me prove;
Try heart and reins, O God:

3 For thy love is before mine eyes,
Thy truth's paths I have trod.

4 With persons vain I have not sat,
Nor with dissemblers gone:

5 Th' assembly of ill men I hate;
To sit with such I shun.

6 Mine hands in innocence, O Lord,
I'll wash and purify;
So to thine holy altar go,
And compass it will I:

7 That I, with voice of thanksgiving,
May publish and declare,
And tell of all thy mighty works,
That great and wondrous are.

8 The habitation of thy house,
 Lord, I have loved well;
 Yea, in that place I do delight
 Where doth thine honour dwell.

9 With sinners gather not my soul,
 And such as blood would spill:
10 Whose hands mischievous plot,
  right hand
 Corrupting bribes do fill.

11 But as for me, I will walk on
 In mine integrity:
 Do thou redeem me, and, O Lord,
 Be merciful to me.

12 My foot upon an even place
 Doth stand with steadfastness:
 Within the congregations
 Th' Eternal I will bless.

27 C.M.

A Psalm of David.
vv 1-6, 7-14

1 The Lord's my light and saving
  health,
 Who shall make me dismayed?
 My life's strength is the Lord, of
  whom
 Then shall I be afraid?

2 When as mine enemies and foes,
 Most wicked persons all,
 To eat my flesh against me rose,
 They stumbled and did fall.

3 Against me though an host
  encamp,
 My heart yet fearless is:
 Though war against me rise, I will
 Be confident in this.

4 One thing I of the Lord desired,
 And will seek to obtain,
 That all days of my life I may
 Within God's house remain;

 That I the beauty of the Lord
 Behold may and admire,
 And that I in his holy place
 May rev'rently enquire.

5 For he in his pavilion shall
 Me hide in evil days;
 In secret of his tent me hide,
 And on a rock me raise.

6 And now, even at this present time,
 Mine head shall lifted be
 Above all those that are my foes,
 And round encompass me:

 Therefore unto his tabernacle
 I'll sacrifices bring
 Of joyfulness; I'll sing, yea, I
 To God will praises sing.

7 O Lord, give ear unto my voice,
 When I do cry to thee;
 Upon me also mercy have,
 And do thou answer me.

8 When thou didst say, Seek ye my
  face,
 Then unto thee reply
 Thus did my heart, Above all things
 Thy face, Lord, seek will I.

9 Far from me hide not thou thy face;
 Put not away from thee
 Thy servant in thy wrath: thou hast
 An helper been to me.

 O God of my salvation,
 Leave me not, nor forsake:
10 Though me my parents both
  should leave,
 The Lord me up will take.

11 O Lord, instruct me in thy way,
 To me a leader be
 In a plain path, because of those
 That hatred bear to me.

12 Give me not to mine enemies' will;
 For witnesses that lie
 Against me risen are, and such
 As breathe out cruelty.

13 I fainted had, unless that I
 Believed had to see
 The Lord's own goodness in the
  land
 Of them that living be.

14 Wait on the Lord, and be thou
strong,
And he shall strength afford
Unto thine heart; yea, do thou wait,
I say, upon the Lord.

28 C.M.

A Psalm of David.
vv 1-6, 7-9

1 To thee I'll cry, O Lord, my rock;
Hold not thy peace to me;
Lest like those that to pit descend
I by thy silence be.

2 The voice hear of my humble
prayers,
When unto thee I cry;
When to thine holy oracle
I lift mine hands on high.

3 With ill men draw me not away
That work iniquity;
That speak peace to their friends,
while in
Their hearts doth mischief lie.

4 Give them according to their deeds
And ills endeavoured:
And as their handiworks deserve,
To them be rendered.

5 God shall not build, but them
destroy,
Who would not understand
The Lord's own works, nor did
regard
The doing of his hand.

6 For ever blessed be the Lord,
For graciously he heard
The voice of my petitions,
And prayers did regard.

7 The Lord's my strength and shield;
my heart
Upon him did rely;
And I am helped: hence my heart
Doth joy exceedingly,

And with my song I will him
praise.

8 Their strength is God alone:
He also is the saving strength
Of his anointed one.

9 O thine own people do thou save,
Bless thine inheritance;
Them also do thou feed, and them
For evermore advance.

29 C.M.

A Psalm of David.

1 Give ye unto the Lord, ye sons
That of the mighty be,
All strength and glory to the Lord
With cheerfulness give ye.

2 Unto the Lord the glory give
That to his name is due;
And in the beauty of holiness
Unto JEHOVAH bow.

3 The Lord's voice on the waters is;
The God of majesty
Doth thunder, and on multitudes
Of waters sitteth he.

4 A powerful voice it is that comes
Out from the Lord most high;
The voice of that great Lord is full
Of glorious majesty.

5 The voice of the Eternal doth
Asunder cedars tear;
Yea, God the Lord doth cedars
break
That Lebanon doth bear.

6 He makes them like a calf to skip,
Ev'n that great Lebanon,
And, like to a young unicorn,
The mountain Sirion.

7 God's voice divides the flames of
fire;

8 The desert it doth shake:
The Lord doth make the wilderness
Of Kadesh all to quake.

9 God's voice doth make the hinds to
   calve,
   It makes the forest bare:
   And in his temple every one
   His glory doth declare.

10 The Lord sits on the floods; the
   Lord
   Sits King, and ever shall.
11 The Lord will give his people
   strength,
   And with peace bless them all.

30   C.M.

*A Psalm and Song at the dedication of
the house of David.*
vv 1-5, 6-12

1 Lord, I will thee extol, for thou
   Hast lifted me on high,
   And over me thou to rejoice
   Mad'st not mine enemy.

2 O thou who art the Lord my God,
   I in distress to thee,
   With loud cries lifted up my voice,
   And thou hast healed me.

3 O Lord, my soul thou hast brought
   up,
   And rescued from the grave;
   That I to pit should not go down,
   Alive thou didst me save.

4 O ye that are his holy ones,
   Sing praise unto the Lord;
   And give unto him thanks, when ye
   His holiness record.

5 For but a moment lasts his wrath;
   Life in his favour lies:
   Weeping may for a night endure,
   At morn doth joy arise.

6 In my prosperity I said,
   That nothing shall me move.
7 O Lord, thou hast my mountain
   made
   To stand strong by thy love:

   But when that thou, O gracious
   God,
   Didst hide thy face from me,
   Then quickly was my prosperous
   state
   Turned into misery.

8 Wherefore unto the Lord my cry
   I caused to ascend:
   My humble supplication
   I to the Lord did send.

9 What profit is there in my blood,
   When I go down to pit?
   Shall unto thee the dust give
   praise?
   Thy truth declare shall it?

10 Hear, Lord, have mercy; help me,
   Lord:
11 Thou turned hast my sadness
   To dancing; yea, my sackcloth
   loosed,
   And girded me with gladness;

12 That sing thy praise my glory may,
   And never silent be.
   O Lord my God, for evermore
   I will give thanks to thee.

31   C.M.

*To the chief Musician, A Psalm of
David.*
vv 1-6, 7-14, 15-18, 19-24

1 In thee, O Lord, I put my trust,
   Shamed let me never be;
   According to thy righteousness
   Do thou deliver me.

2 Bow down thine ear to me, with
   speed
   Send me deliverance:
   To save me, my strong rock be
   thou,
   And my house of defence.

3 Because thou art my rock, and thee
   I for my fortress take;
   Therefore do thou me lead and
   guide,
   Ev'n for thine own name's sake.

4 And since thou art my strength,
   therefore
Pull me out of the net,
Which they in subtlety for me
So privily have set.

5 Into thine hands I do commit
My spirit: thou art he,
O thou, JEHOVAH, God of truth,
That hast redeemed me.

6 Those that do lying vanities
Regard, I have abhorred:
But as for me, my confidence
Is fixed on the Lord.

7 I'll in thy mercy gladly joy:
For thou my miseries
Considered hast; thou hast my soul
Known in adversities:

8 And thou hast not enclosed me
Within the enemy's hand;
And by thee have my feet been
   made
In a large room to stand.

9 O Lord, upon me mercy have,
For trouble is on me:
Mine eye, my belly, and my soul,
With grief consumed be.

10 Because my life with grief is spent,
My years with sighs and groans:
My strength doth fail; and for my
   sin
Consumed are my bones.

11 I was a scorn to all my foes,
And to my friends a fear;
And specially reproached of those
That were my neighbours near:

When they me saw they from me
   fled.
12 Even so I am forgot,
As men are out of mind when
   dead:
I'm like a broken pot.

13 For slanders I of many heard;
Fear compassed me, while they
Against me did consult, and plot
To take my life away.

14 But as for me, O Lord, my trust
Upon thee I did lay;
And I to thee, Thou art my God,
Did confidently say.

15 My times are wholly in thine hand:
Do thou deliver me
From their hands that mine
   enemies
And persecutors be.

16 Thy countenance to shine do thou
Upon thy servant make:
Unto me give salvation,
For thy great mercies' sake.

17 Let me not be ashamed, O Lord,
For on thee called I have:
Let wicked men be shamed, let
   them
Be silent in the grave.

18 To silence put the lying lips,
That grievous things do say,
And hard reports, in pride and
   scorn,
On righteous men do lay.

19 How great's the goodness thou for
   them
That fear thee keep'st in store,
And wrought'st for them that trust
   in thee
The sons of men before!

20 In secret of thy presence thou
Shalt hide them from man's pride:
From strife of tongues thou closely
   shalt,
As in a tent, them hide.

21 All praise and thanks be to the
   Lord;
For he hath magnified
His wondrous love to me within
A city fortified.

22 For from thine eyes cut off I am,
I in my haste had said;
My voice yet heard'st thou, when to
   thee
With cries my moan I made.

23 O love the Lord, all ye his saints;
    Because the Lord doth guard
    The faithful, and he plenteously
    Proud doers doth reward.

24 Be of good courage, and he
        strength
    Unto your heart shall send,
    All ye whose hope and confidence
    Doth on the Lord depend.

32   C.M.

A Psalm of David, Maschil.
vv 1-7, 8-11

1 O blessed is the man to whom
    Is freely pardoned
    All the transgression he hath done,
    Whose sin is covered.

2 Blessed is the man to whom the
        Lord
    Imputeth not his sin,
    And in whose spirit is no guile,
    Nor fraud is found therein.

3 When as I did refrain my speech,
    And silent was my tongue,
    My bones then waxed old, because
    I roared all day long.

4 For upon me both day and night
    Thine hand did heavy lie,
    So that my moisture turned is
    To summer's drought thereby.

5 I thereupon have unto thee
    My sin acknowledged,
    And likewise mine iniquity
    I have not covered:

    I will confess unto the Lord
    My trespasses, said I;
    And of my sin thou freely didst
    Forgive the iniquity.

6 For this shall every godly one
    His prayer make to thee;
    In such a time he shall thee seek,
    As found thou mayest be.

Surely, when floods of waters great
Do swell up to the brim,
They shall not overwhelm his soul,
Nor once come near to him.

7 Thou art my hiding-place, thou
        shalt
    From trouble keep me free:
    Thou with songs of deliverance
    About shalt compass me.

8 I will instruct thee, and thee teach
    The way that thou shalt go;
    And, with mine eye upon thee set,
    I will direction show.

9 Then be not like the horse or mule,
    Which do not understand;
    Whose mouth, lest they come near
        to thee,
    A bridle must command.

10 Unto the man that wicked is
    His sorrows shall abound;
    But him that trusteth in the Lord
    Mercy shall compass round.

11 Ye righteous, in the Lord be glad,
    In him do ye rejoice:
    All ye that upright are in heart,
    For joy lift up your voice.

33   C.M.

vv 1-5, 6-11, 12-22

1 Ye righteous, in the Lord rejoice;
    It comely is and right,
    That upright men, with thankful
        voice,
    Should praise the Lord of might.

2 Praise God with harp, and unto
        him
    Sing with the psaltery;
    Upon a ten-stringed instrument
    Make ye sweet melody.

3 A new song to him sing, and play
    With loud noise skilfully;

4 For right is God's word, all his
        works
    Are done in verity.

5 To judgment and to righteousness
   A love he beareth still;
   The loving-kindness of the Lord
   The earth throughout doth fill.

6 The heavens by the word of God
   Did their beginning take;
   And by the breathing of his mouth
   He all their hosts did make.

7 The waters of the seas he brings
   Together as an heap;
   And in storehouses, as it were,
   He layeth up the deep.

8 Let earth, and all that live therein,
   With reverence fear the Lord;
   Let all the world's inhabitants
   Dread him with one accord.

9 For he did speak the word, and
      done
   It was without delay;
   Established it firmly stood,
   Whatever he did say.

10 God doth the counsel bring to
      nought
   Which heathen folk do take;
   And what the people do devise
   Of none effect doth make.

11 O but the counsel of the Lord
   Doth stand for ever sure;
   And of his heart the purposes
   From age to age endure.

12 That nation blessed is, whose God
   JEHOVAH is, and those
   A blessed people are, whom for
   His heritage he chose.

13 The Lord from heav'n sees and
      beholds
   All sons of men full well:
14 He views all from his dwelling-
      place
   That in the earth do dwell.

15 He forms their hearts alike, and all
   Their doings he observes.
16 Great hosts save not a king, much
      strength
   No mighty man preserves.

17 An horse for preservation
   Is a deceitful thing;
   And by the greatness of his
      strength
   Can no deliv'rance bring.

18 Behold on those that do him fear
   The Lord doth set his eye;
   Even those who on his mercy do
   With confidence rely.

19 From death to free their soul, in
      dearth
   Life unto them to yield.
20 Our soul doth wait upon the Lord;
   He is our help and shield.

21 Since in his holy name we trust,
   Our heart shall joyful be.
22 Lord, let thy mercy be on us,
   As we do hope in thee.

34   C.M.

*A Psalm of David, when he changed his
behaviour before Abimelech; who drove
him away, and he departed.*
vv 1-7, 8-16, 17-22

1 God will I bless all times; his
      praise
   My mouth shall still express.
2 My soul shall boast in God: the
      meek
   Shall hear with joyfulness.

3 Extol the Lord with me, let us
   Exalt his name together.
4 I sought the Lord, he heard, and
      did
   Me from all fears deliver.

5 They looked to him, and lightened
      were:
   Not shamed were their faces.
6 This poor man cried, God heard,
      and saved
   Him from all his distresses.

7 The angel of the Lord encamps,
   And round encompasseth
   All those about that do him fear,
   And them delivereth.

8 O taste and see that God is good:
  Who trusts in him is blessed.
9 Fear God his saints: none that him
    fear
  Shall be with want oppressed.

10 The lions young may hungry be,
   And they may lack their food:
   But they that truly seek the Lord
   Shall not lack any good.

11 O children, hither do ye come,
   And unto me give ear;
   I shall you teach to understand
   How ye the Lord should fear.

12 What man is he that life desires,
   To see good would live long?
13 Thy lips refrain from speaking
     guile,
   And from ill words thy tongue.

14 Depart from ill, do good, seek
     peace,
   Pursue it earnestly.
15 God's eyes are on the just; his ears
   Are open to their cry.

16 The face of God is set against
   Those that do wickedly,
   That he may quite out from the
     earth
   Cut off their memory.

17 The righteous cry unto the Lord,
   He unto them gives ear;
   And they out of their troubles all
   By him delivered are.

18 The Lord is ever nigh to them
   In heart that broken be;
   Those who in spirit contrite are
   He saveth graciously.

19 The troubles that afflict the just
   In number many be;
   But yet at length out of them all
   The Lord doth set him free.

20 He carefully his bones doth keep,
   Whatever can befall;
   That not so much as one of them
   Can broken be at all.

21 Ill shall the wicked slay; laid waste
   Shall be who hate the just.
22 The Lord redeems his servants'
     souls;
   None perish that him trust.

35   C.M.

A Psalm of David.
vv 1-10, 11-16, 17-23, 24-28

1 Plead, Lord, with those that plead;
     and fight
   With those that fight with me.
2 Of shield and buckler take thou
     hold,
   Stand up mine help to be.

3 Draw also out the spear, and do
   Against them stop the way
   That me pursue: unto my soul,
   I'm thy salvation, say.

4 Let them confounded be and
     shamed
   That for my soul have sought:
   Who plot my hurt turned back be
     they,
   And to confusion brought.

5 Let them be like unto the chaff
   That flies before the wind;
   And let the angel of the Lord
   Pursue them hard behind.

6 With darkness cover thou their
     way,
   And let it slippery prove;
   And let the angel of the Lord
   Pursue them from above.

7 For without cause have they for me
   Their net hid in a pit,
   They also have without a cause
   For my soul digged it.

8 Let ruin seize him unawares;
   His net he hid withal
   Himself let catch; and in the same
   Destruction let him fall.

9 My soul in God shall joy; and glad
In his salvation be:
10 And all my bones shall say, O Lord,
Who is like unto thee,

Which dost the poor set free from
him
That is for him too strong;
The poor and needy from the man
That spoils and does him wrong?

11 False witnesses rose; to my charge
Things I not knew they laid.
12 They, to the spoiling of my soul,
Me ill for good repaid.

13 But as for me, when they were sick,
In sackcloth sad I mourned:
My humbled soul did fast, my
prayer
Into my bosom turned.

14 Myself I did behave as he
Had been my friend or brother;
I heavily bowed down, as one
That mourneth for his mother.

15 But in my trouble they rejoiced,
Gathering themselves together;
Yea, abjects vile together did
Themselves against me gather:

I knew it not; they did me tear,
And quiet would not be.
16 With mocking hypocrites, at feasts
They gnashed their teeth at me.

17 How long, Lord, look'st thou on?
from those
Destructions they intend
Rescue my soul, from lions young
My darling do defend.

18 I will give thanks to thee, O Lord,
In the assembly great;
And where much people gathered
are
Thy praises forth will set.

19 Let not my wrongful enemies
Proudly rejoice o'er me;
Nor who me hate without a cause,
Let them wink with the eye.

20 For peace they do not speak at all;
But crafty plots prepare
Against all those within the land
That meek and quiet are.

21 With mouths set wide, they 'gainst
me said,
Ha, ha! our eye doth see.
22 Lord, thou hast seen, hold not thy
peace;
Lord, be not far from me.

23 Stir up thyself; wake, that thou
mayest
Judgment to me afford,
Ev'n to my cause, O thou that art
My only God and Lord.

24 O Lord my God, do thou me judge
After thy righteousness;
And let them not their joy 'gainst
me
Triumphantly express:

25 Nor let them say within their
hearts,
Ah, we would have it thus;
Nor suffer them to say, that he
Is swallowed up by us.

26 Shamed and confounded be they
all
That at my hurt are glad;
Let those against me that do boast
With shame and scorn be clad.

27 Let them that love my righteous
cause
Be glad, shout, and not cease
To say, The Lord be magnified,
Who loves his servant's peace.

28 Thy righteousness shall also be
Declared by my tongue;
The praises that belong to thee
Speak shall it all day long.

36 C.M.

*To the chief Musician, A Psalm of
David, the servant of the Lord.*
vv 1-4, 5-12

1 The wicked man's transgression
 Within my heart thus says,
 Undoubtedly the fear of God
 Is not before his eyes.

2 Because himself he flattereth
 In his own blinded eye,
 Until the hatefulness be found
 Of his iniquity.

3 Words from his mouth proceeding
  are,
 Fraud and iniquity:
 He to be wise, and to do good,
 Hath left off utterly.

4 He mischief, lying on his bed,
 Most cunningly doth plot:
 He sets himself in ways not good,
 Ill he abhorreth not.

5 Thy mercy, Lord, is in the heavens;
 Thy truth doth reach the clouds:
6 Thy justice is like mountains great;
 Thy judgments deep as floods:

 Lord, thou preservest man and
  beast.
7 How precious is thy grace!
 Therefore in shadow of thy wings
 Men's sons their trust shall place.

8 They with the fatness of thy house
 Shall be well satisfied;
 From rivers of thy pleasures thou
 Wilt drink to them provide.

9 Because of life the fountain pure
 Remains alone with thee;
 And in that purest light of thine
 We clearly light shall see.

10 Thy loving-kindness unto them
 Continue that thee know;
 And still on men upright in heart
 Thy righteousness bestow.

11 Let not the foot of cruel pride
 Come, and against me stand;
 And let me not removed be,
 Lord, by the wicked's hand.

12 There fallen and ruined are they
 That work iniquities:
 Cast down they are, and never shall
 Be able to arise.

37 C.M.

A Psalm of David.
vv 1-7, 8-15, 16-22, 23-33, 34-40

1 For evil-doers fret thou not
 Thyself unquietly;
 Nor do thou envy bear to those
 That work iniquity.

2 For, even like unto the grass,
 Soon be cut down shall they;
 And, like the green and tender
  herb,
 They wither shall away.

3 Set thou thy trust upon the Lord,
 And be thou doing good;
 And so thou in the land shalt
  dwell,
 And verily have food.

4 Delight thyself in God; he'll give
 Thine heart's desire to thee.
5 Thy way to God commit, him trust,
 It bring to pass shall he.

6 And, like unto the light, he shall
 Thy righteousness display;
 And he thy judgment shall bring
  forth
 Like noon-tide of the day.

7 Rest in the Lord, and patiently
 Wait for him: do not fret
 For him who, prospering in his
  way,
 Success in sin doth get.

8 Do thou from anger cease, and
  wrath
 See thou forsake also:
 Fret not thyself in any wise,
 That evil thou should'st do.

9 For those that evil doers are
Shall be cut off and fall:
But those that wait upon the Lord
The earth inherit shall.

10 For yet a little while, and then
The wicked shall not be;
His place thou shalt consider well,
But it thou shalt not see.

11 But by inheritance the earth
The meek ones shall possess:
They also shall delight themselves
In an abundant peace.

12 The wicked plots against the just,
And at him whets his teeth:
13 The Lord shall laugh at him, because
His day he coming seeth.

14 The wicked have drawn out the sword,
And bent their bow, to slay
The poor and needy, and to kill
Men of an upright way.

15 But their own sword, which they have drawn,
Shall enter their own heart:
Their bows which they have bent shall break,
And into pieces part.

16 A little that a just man hath
Is more and better far
Than is the wealth of many such
As vile and wicked are.

17 For sinners' arms shall broken be;
But God the just sustains.
18 God knows the just man's days, and still
Their heritage remains.

19 They shall not be ashamed when they
The evil time do see;
And when the days of famine are,
They satisfied shall be.

20 But wicked men, and foes of God,
As fat of lambs, decay;
They shall consume, yea, into smoke
They shall consume away.

21 The wicked borrows, but the same
Again he doth not pay;
Whereas the righteous mercy shows,
And gives his own away.

22 For such as blessed be of him
The earth inherit shall;
And they that cursed are of him
Shall be destroyed all.

23 A good man's footsteps by the Lord
Are ordered aright;
And in the way wherein he walks
He greatly doth delight.

24 Although he fall, yet shall he not
Be cast down utterly;
Because the Lord with his own hand
Upholds him mightily.

25 I have been young, and now am old,
Yet have I never seen
The just man left, nor that his seed
For bread have beggars been.

26 He's ever merciful, and lends:
His seed is blessed therefore.
27 Depart from evil, and do good,
And dwell for evermore.

28 For God loves judgment, and his saints
Leaves not in any case;
They are kept ever: but cut off
Shall be the sinner's race.

29 The just inherit shall the land,
And ever in it dwell:
30 The just man's mouth doth wisdom speak;
His tongue doth judgment tell.

31 His God's law is within his heart,
His steps slide not away.
32 The wicked man doth watch the
just,
And seeketh him to slay.

33 Yet him the Lord will not forsake,
Nor leave him in his hands:
The righteous will he not condemn,
When he in judgment stands.

34 Wait on the Lord, and keep his way,
And thee exalt shall he
Th' earth to inherit; when cut off
The wicked thou shalt see.

35 I saw the wicked great in power,
Spread like a green bay-tree:
36 He passed, yea, was not; him I
sought,
But found he could not be.

37 Mark thou the perfect, and behold
The man of uprightness;
Because that surely of this man
The latter end is peace.

38 But those men that transgressors
are
Shall be destroyed together;
The latter end of wicked men
Shall be cut off for ever.

39 But the salvation of the just
Is from the Lord above;
He in the time of their distress
Their stay and strength doth prove.

40 The Lord shall help, and them
deliver:
He shall them free and save
From wicked men; because in him
Their confidence they have.

38 C.M.

*A Psalm of David, to bring to
remembrance.*
vv 1-8, 9-15, 16-22

1 In thy great indignation,
O Lord, rebuke me not;
Nor on me lay thy chastening hand,
In thy displeasure hot.

2 For in me fast thine arrows stick,
Thine hand doth press me sore:
3 And in my flesh there is no health,
Nor soundness any more.

This grief I have, because thy wrath
Is forth against me gone;
And in my bones there is no rest,
For sin that I have done.

4 Because gone up above mine head
My great transgressions be;
And, as a weighty burden, they
Too heavy are for me.

5 My wounds do stink, and are
corrupt;
My folly makes it so.
6 I troubled am, and much bowed
down;
All day I mourning go.

7 For a disease that loathsome is
So fills my loins with pain,
That in my weak and weary flesh
No soundness doth remain.

8 So feeble and infirm am I,
And broken am so sore,
That, through disquiet of my heart,
I have been made to roar.

9 O Lord, all that I do desire
Is still before thine eye;
And of my heart the secret groans
Not hidden are from thee.

10 My heart doth pant incessantly,
My strength doth quite decay;
As for mine eyes, their wonted
light
Is from me gone away.

11 My lovers and my friends do stand
At distance from my sore;
And those do stand aloof that were
Kinsmen and kind before.

12 Yea, they that seek my life lay
snares:
Who seek to do me wrong
Speak things mischievous, and
deceits
Imagine all day long.

13 But, as one deaf, that heareth not,
I suffered all to pass;
I as a dumb man did become,
Whose mouth not opened was:

14 As one that hears not, in whose
mouth
Are no reproofs at all.
15 For, Lord, I hope in thee; my God,
Thou'lt hear me when I call.

16 For I said, Hear me, lest they
should
Rejoice o'er me with pride;
And o'er me magnify themselves,
When as my foot doth slide.

17 For I am near to halt, my grief
Is still before mine eye:
18 For I'll declare my sin, and grieve
For mine iniquity.

19 Mine enemies yet lively are,
And strong are they beside;
And they that hate me wrongfully
Are greatly multiplied.

20 And they for good that render ill,
As en'mies me withstood;
Yea, ev'n for this, because that I
Do follow what is good.

21 Forsake me not, O Lord; my God,
Far from me never be.
22 O Lord, thou my salvation art,
Haste to give help to me.

39 C.M.

*To the chief Musician, even to Jeduthun,
A Psalm of David.
vv 1-6, 7-13*

1 I said, I will look to my ways,
Lest with my tongue I sin:
In sight of wicked men my mouth
With bridle I'll keep in.

2 With silence I as dumb became,
I did myself restrain
From speaking good; but then the
more
Increased was my pain.

3 My heart within me waxed hot;
And, while I musing was,
The fire did burn; and from my
tongue
These words I did let pass:

4 Mine end, and measure of my days,
O Lord, unto me show
What is the same; that I thereby
My frailty well may know.

5 Lo, thou my days an handbreadth
mad'st;
Mine age is in thine eye
As nothing: sure each man at best
Is wholly vanity.

6 Sure each man walks in a vain
show;
They vex themselves in vain:
He heaps up wealth, and doth not
know
To whom it shall pertain.

7 And now, O Lord, what wait I for?
My hope is fixed on thee.
8 Free me from all my trespasses,
The fool's scorn make not me.

9 Dumb was I, opening not my
mouth,
Because this work was thine.
10 Thy stroke take from me; by the
blow
Of thine hand I do pine.

11 When with rebukes thou dost
correct
Man for iniquity,
Thou wastes his beauty like a
moth:
Sure each man's vanity.

12 Attend my cry, Lord, at my tears
And prayers not silent be:
I sojourn as my fathers all,
And stranger am with thee.

13 O spare thou me, that I my
strength
Recover may again,
Before from hence I do depart,
And here no more remain.

40

C.M.

To the chief Musician, A Psalm of David.
vv 1-5, 6-10, 11-17

1 I waited for the Lord my God,
And patiently did bear;
At length to me he did incline
My voice and cry to hear.

2 He took me from a fearful pit,
And from the miry clay,
And on a rock he set my feet,
Establishing my way.

3 He put a new song in my mouth,
Our God to magnify:
Many shall see it, and shall fear,
And on the Lord rely.

4 O blessed is the man whose trust
Upon the Lord relies;
Respecting not the proud, nor such
As turn aside to lies.

5 O Lord my God, full many are
The wonders thou hast done;
Thy gracious thoughts to us-ward
far
Above all thoughts are gone:

In order none can reckon them
To thee: if them declare,
And speak of them I would, they
more
Than can be numbered are.

6 No sacrifice nor offering
Didst thou at all desire;
Mine ears thou bored: sin-offering
thou
And burnt didst not require:

7 Then to the Lord these were my
words,
I come, behold and see;
Within the volume of the book
It written is of me:

8 To do thy will I take delight,
O thou my God that art;
Yea, that most holy law of thine
I have within my heart.

9 Within the congregation great
I righteousness did preach:
Lo, thou dost know, O Lord, that I
Refrained not my speech.

10 I never did within my heart
Conceal thy righteousness;
I thy salvation have declared,
And shown thy faithfulness:

Thy kindness, which most loving
is,
Concealed have not I,
Nor from the congregation great
Have hid thy verity.

11 Thy tender mercies, Lord, from me
O do thou not restrain;
Thy loving-kindness, and thy truth,
Let them me still maintain.

12 For ills past reckoning compass
me,
And mine iniquities
Such hold upon me taken have,
I cannot lift mine eyes:

They more than hairs are on mine
head,
Thence is my heart dismayed.

13 Be pleased, Lord, to rescue me;
Lord, hasten to mine aid.

14 Shamed and confounded be they
all
That seek my soul to kill;
Yea, let them backward driven be,
And shamed, that wish me ill.

15 For a reward of this their shame
Confounded let them be.
That in this manner scoffing say,
Aha, aha! to me.

16 In thee let all be glad, and joy,
Who seeking thee abide;
Who thy salvation love, say still,
The Lord be magnified.

17 I'm poor and needy, yet the Lord
Of me a care doth take:
Thou art my help and saviour,
My God, no tarrying make.

41

C.M.

To the chief Musician, A Psalm of David.
vv 1-3, 4-10, 11-13

1 Blessed is he that wisely doth
   The poor man's case consider;
   For when the time of trouble is,
   The Lord will him deliver.

2 God will him keep, yea, save alive;
   On earth he blessed shall live;
   And to his enemies' desire
   Thou wilt him not up give.

3 God will give strength when he on
        bed
   Of languishing doth mourn;
   And in his sickness sore, O Lord,
   Thou all his bed wilt turn.

4 I said, O Lord, do thou extend
   Thy mercy unto me;
   O do thou heal my soul; for why?
   I have offended thee.

5 Those that to me are enemies,
   Of me do evil say,
   When shall he die, that so his name
   May perish quite away?

6 To see me if he comes, he speaks
   Vain words: but then his heart
   Heaps mischief to it, which he tells,
   When forth he doth depart.

7 My haters jointly whispering,
   'Gainst me my hurt devise.
8 Mischief, say they, cleaves fast to
        him;
   He, lying, shall not rise.

9 Yea, ev'n mine own familiar friend,
   On whom I did rely,
   Who ate my bread, ev'n he his heel
   Against me lifted high.

10 But, Lord, be merciful to me,
   And up again me raise,
   That I may justly them requite
   According to their ways.

11 By this I know that certainly
   I favoured am by thee;
   Because my hateful enemy
   Triumphs not over me.

12 But as for me, thou me uphold'st
   In mine integrity;
   And me before thy countenance
   Thou sett'st continually.

13 The Lord, the God of Israel,
   Be blessed for ever then,
   From age to age eternally.
   Amen, yea, and amen.

42

C.M.

To the chief Musician, Maschil, for the sons of Korah.
vv 1-5, 6-11

1 Like as the hart for water-brooks
   In thirst doth pant and bray;
   So pants my longing soul, O God,
   That come to thee I may.

2 My soul for God, the living God,
   Doth thirst: when shall I near
   Unto thy countenance approach,
   And in God's sight appear?

3 My tears have unto me been meat,
   Both in the night and day,
   While unto me continually,
   Where is thy God? they say.

4 My soul is poured out in me,
   When this I think upon;
   Because that with the multitude
   I heretofore had gone:

   With them into God's house I went,
   With voice of joy and praise;
   Yea, with the multitude that kept
   The solemn holy days.

5 O why art thou cast down, my soul?
   Why in me so dismayed?
   Trust God, for I shall praise him
        yet,
   His count'nance is mine aid.

6 My God, my soul's cast down in
   me;
   Thee therefore mind I will
   From Jordan's land, the
   Hermonites,
   And ev'n from Mizar hill.

7 At noise of thy great water-spouts
   Deep unto deep doth call;
   Thy breaking waves pass over me,
   Yea, and thy billows all.

8 His loving-kindness yet the Lord
   Command will in the day,
   His song's with me by night; to
   God,
   By whom I live, I'll pray:

9 And I will say to God my rock,
   Why me forgett'st thou so?
   Why, for my foes' oppression,
   Thus mourning do I go?

10 'Tis as a sword within my bones,
   When my foes me upbraid;
   Ev'n when by them, Where is thy
   God?
   'Tis daily to me said.

11 O why art thou cast down, my soul?
   Why, thus with grief oppressed,
   Art thou disquieted in me?
   In God still hope and rest:

   For yet I know I shall him praise,
   Who graciously to me
   The health is of my countenance,
   Yea, mine own God is he.

43 C.M.

1 Judge me, O God, and plead my
   cause
   'Gainst an ungodly nation;
   From the unjust and crafty man,
   O be thou my salvation.

2 For thou the God art of my
   strength;
   Then why reject me so?
   For mine enemy's oppression,
   Why do I mourning go?

3 O send thy light forth and thy truth;
   Let them be guides to me,
   And bring me to thine holy hill,
   Ev'n where thy dwellings be.

4 Then will I to God's altar go,
   To God my chiefest joy:
   Yea, God, my God, thy name to
   praise
   My harp I will employ.

5 Why art thou then cast down, my
   soul?
   What should discourage thee?
   And why with vexing thoughts art
   thou
   Disquieted in me?

   Still trust in God; for him to praise
   Good cause I yet shall have:
   He of my countenance is health,
   My God that doth me save.

44 C.M.

*To the chief Musician for the sons of
Korah, Maschil.*
vv 1-8, 9-16, 17-26

1 O God, we with our ears have
   heard,
   Our fathers have us told,
   What works thou in their days hadst
   done,
   Ev'n in the days of old.

2 Thy hand did drive the heathen out,
   And plant them in their place;
   Thou didst afflict the nations,
   But them thou didst increase.

3 For neither got their sword the
   land,
   Nor did their arm them save;
   But thy right hand, arm,
   countenance;
   For thou them favour gave.

4 Thou art my King: for Jacob, Lord,
   Deliverances command.

5 Through thee we shall push down
   our foes,
   That do against us stand:

We, through thy name, shall tread
    down those
That risen against us have.
6 For in my bow I shall not trust,
    Nor shall my sword me save.

7 But from our foes thou hast us
    saved,
    Our haters put to shame.
8 In God we all the day do boast,
    And ever praise thy name.

9 But now we are cast off by thee,
    And us thou putt'st to shame;
    And when our armies do go forth,
    Thou goest not with the same.

10 Thou mak'st us from the enemy,
    Faint-hearted, to turn back;
    And they who hate us for
      themselves
    Our spoils away do take.

11 Like sheep for meat thou gavest us;
    'Mong heathen cast we be.
12 Thou didst for nought thy people
    sell;
    Their price enriched not thee.

13 Thou mak'st us a reproach to be
    Unto our neighbours near;
    Derision and a scorn to them
    That round about us are.

14 A by-word also thou dost us
    Among the heathen make;
    The people, in contempt and spite,
    At us their heads do shake.

15 Before me my confusion
    Continually abides;
    And of my bashful countenance
    The shame me ever hides:

16 For voice of him that doth reproach,
    And speaketh blasphemy;
    By reason of th' avenging foe,
    And cruel enemy.

17 All this is come on us, yet we
    Have not forgotten thee;
    Nor falsely in thy covenant
    Behaved ourselves have we.

18 Back from thy way our heart not
    turned;
    Our steps no straying made;
19 Though us thou brak'st in dragons'
    place,
    And cover'dst with death's shade.

20 If we God's name forgot, or
    stretched
    To a strange god our hands,
21 Shall not God search this out? for
    he
    Heart's secrets understands.

22 Yea, for thy sake we're killed all day,
    Counted as slaughter-sheep.
23 Rise, Lord, cast us not ever off;
    Awake, why dost thou sleep?

24 O wherefore hidest thou thy face?
    Forgett'st our cause distressed,
25 And our oppression? For our soul
    Is to the dust down pressed:

    Our belly also on the earth
    Fast cleaving, hold doth take.
26 Rise for our help, and us redeem,
    Ev'n for thy mercies' sake.

45 First Version   C.M.

To the chief Musician upon Shoshannim,
for the sons of Korah, Maschil, A Song
of loves.
vv 1-8, 9-17

1 My heart brings forth a goodly
    thing;
    My words that I indite
    Concern the King: my tongue's a
    pen
    Of one that swift doth write.

2 Thou fairer art than sons of men:
    Into thy lips is store
    Of grace infused; God therefore
    thee
    Hath blessed for evermore.

3 O thou that art the mighty One,
    Thy sword gird on thy thigh;
    Ev'n with thy glory excellent,
    And with thy majesty.

4 For meekness, truth, and
    righteousness,
  In state ride prosp'rously;
  And thy right hand shall thee
    instruct
  In things that fearful be.

5 Thine arrows sharply pierce the
    heart
  Of enemies of the King;
  And under thy subjection
  The people down do bring.

6 For ever and for ever is,
  O God, thy throne of might;
  The sceptre of thy kingdom is
  A sceptre that is right.

7 Thou lovest right, and hatest ill;
  For God, thy God, most high,
  Above thy fellows hath with oil
  Of joy anointed thee.

8 Of aloes, myrrh, and cassia,
  A smell thy garments had,
  Out of the ivory palaces,
  Whereby they made thee glad.

9 Among thy women honourable
  Kings' daughters were at hand:
  Upon thy right hand did the queen
  In gold of Ophir stand.

10 O daughter, hearken and regard,
  And do thine ear incline;
  Likewise forget thy father's house,
  And people that are thine.

11 Then of the King desired shall be
  Thy beauty veh'mently:
  Because he is thy Lord, do thou
  Him worship rev'rently.

12 The daughter there of Tyre shall be
  With gifts and offerings great:
  Those of the people that are rich
  Thy favour shall entreat.

13 Behold, the daughter of the King
  All glorious is within;
  And with embroideries of gold
  Her garments wrought have been.

14 She shall be brought unto the King
  In robes with needle wrought;
  Her fellow-virgins following
  Shall unto thee be brought.

15 They shall be brought with gladness
    great,
  And mirth on every side,
  Into the palace of the King,
  And there they shall abide.

16 Instead of those thy fathers dear,
  Thy children thou may'st take,
  And in all places of the earth
  Them noble princes make.

17 Thy name remembered I will make
  Through ages all to be:
  The people therefore evermore
  Shall praises give to thee.

45 Second Version   S.M.

To the chief Musician upon Shoshannim,
for the sons of Korah, Maschil, A Song
of loves.
vv 1-8, 9-17

1 My heart inditing is
  Good matter in a song:
  I speak the things that I have made,
  Which to the King belong:

  My tongue shall be as quick,
  His honour to indite,
  As is the pen of any scribe
  That useth fast to write.

2 Thou'rt fairest of all men;
  Grace in thy lips doth flow:
  And therefore blessings evermore
  On thee doth God bestow.

3 Thy sword gird on thy thigh,
  Thou that art most of might:
  Appear in dreadful majesty,
  And in thy glory bright.

4 For meekness, truth, and right,
  Ride prosp'rously in state;
  And thy right hand shall teach to
    thee
  Things terrible and great.

5   Thy shafts shall pierce their hearts
    That foes are to the King;
    Whereby into subjection
    The people thou shalt bring.

6   Thy royal seat, O Lord,
    For ever shall remain:
    The sceptre of thy kingdom doth
    All righteousness maintain.

7   Thou lov'st right, and hat'st ill;
    For God, thy God, most high,
    Above thy fellows hath with th' oil
    Of joy anointed thee.

8   Of myrrh and spices sweet
    A smell thy garments had,
    Out of the ivory palaces,
    Whereby they made thee glad.

9   And in thy glorious train
    Kings' daughters waiting stand;
    And thy fair queen, in Ophir gold,
    Doth stand at thy right hand.

10   O daughter, take good heed,
    Incline, and give good ear;
    Thou must forget thy kindred all,
    And father's house most dear.

11   Thy beauty to the King
    Shall then delightful be:
    And do thou humbly worship him,
    Because thy Lord is he.

12   The daughter then of Tyre
    There with a gift shall be,
    And all the wealthy of the land
    Shall make their suit to thee.

13   The daughter of the King
    All glorious is within;
    And with embroideries of gold
    Her garments wrought have been.

14   She cometh to the King
    In robes with needle wrought;
    The virgins that do follow her
    Shall unto thee be brought.

15   They shall be brought with joy,
    And mirth on every side,
    Into the palace of the King,
    And there they shall abide.

16   And in thy fathers' stead,
    Thy children thou mayest take,
    And in all places of the earth
    Them noble princes make.

17   I will show forth thy name
    To generations all:
    Therefore the people evermore
    To thee give praises shall.

46   C.M.

To the chief Musician, for the sons of
Korah, A Song upon Alomoth.
vv 1-7, 8-11

1   God is our refuge and our strength,
    In straits a present aid;
2   Therefore, although the earth
      remove,
    We will not be afraid:

    Though hills amidst the seas be
      cast;
3   Though waters roaring make,
    And troubled be; yea, though the
      hills,
    By swelling seas do shake.

4   A river is, whose streams rejoice
    The city of our God;
    The holy place, wherein the Lord
    Most high hath his abode.

5   God in the midst of her doth dwell;
    Nothing shall her remove:
    The Lord to her an helper will,
    And that right early, prove.

6   The heathen raged tumultuously,
    The kingdoms moved were:
    The Lord God uttered his voice,
    The earth did melt for fear.

7   The Lord of hosts upon our side
    Doth constantly remain:
    The God of Jacob's our refuge,
    Us safely to maintain.

8   Come, and behold what wondrous
      works
    Have by the Lord been wrought;
    Come, see what desolations
    He on the earth hath brought.

9 Unto the ends of all the earth
Wars into peace he turns:
The bow he breaks, the spear he
cuts,
In fire the chariot burns.

10 Be still, and know that I am God;
Among the heathen I
Will be exalted; I on earth
Will be exalted high.

11 Our God, who is the Lord of hosts,
Is still upon our side;
The God of Jacob our refuge
For ever will abide.

47 C.M.

*To the chief Musician, A Psalm for the
sons of Korah.*
vv 1-4, 5-9

1 All people, clap your hands; to God
With voice of triumph shout:
2 For dreadful is the Lord most high,
Great King the earth throughout.

3 The heathen people under us
He surely shall subdue;
And he shall make the nations
Under our feet to bow.

4 The lot of our inheritance
Choose out for us shall he,
Of Jacob, whom he loved well,
Ev'n the excellency.

5 God is with shouts gone up, the
Lord
With trumpets sounding high.
6 Sing praise to God, sing praise,
sing praise,
Praise to our King sing ye.

7 For God is King of all the earth;
With knowledge praise express.
8 God rules the nations: God sits on
His throne of holiness.

9 The princes of the people are
Assembled willingly;
Ev'n of the God of Abraham
They who the people be.

For why? the shields that do defend
The earth are only his:
They to the Lord belong; yea, he
Exalted greatly is.

48 C.M.

A Song and Psalm for the sons of Korah.
vv 1-9, 10-14

1 Great is the Lord, and greatly he
Is to be praised still,
Within the city of our God,
Upon his holy hill.

2 Mount Sion stands most beautiful,
The joy of all the land;
The city of the mighty King
On her north side doth stand.

3 The Lord within her palaces
Is for a refuge known.
4 For, lo, the kings that gathered were
Together, by have gone.

5 But when they did behold the same,
They, wond'ring, would not stay;
But, being troubled at the sight,
They thence did haste away.

6 Great terror there took hold on
them;
They were possessed with fear;
Their grief came like a woman's
pain,
When she a child doth bear.

7 Thou Tarshish ships with east wind
break'st:
8 As we have heard it told,
So, in the city of the Lord,
Our eyes did it behold;

In our God's city, which his hand
For ever stablish will.
9 We of thy loving-kindness thought,
Lord, in thy temple still.

10 O Lord, according to thy name,
Through all earth is thy praise;
And thy right hand, O Lord, is full
Of righteousness always.

11 Because thy judgments are made
known,
Let Sion mount rejoice;
Of Judah let the daughters all
Send forth a cheerful voice.

12 Walk about Sion, and go round;
The high towers thereof tell:
13 Consider ye her palaces,
And mark her bulwarks well;

That ye may tell posterity.
14 For this God doth abide
Our God for evermore; he will
Ev'n unto death us guide.

49 C.M.

*To the chief Musician, A Psalm for the
sons of Korah.*
vv 1-13, 14-20

1 Hear this, all people, and give ear,
All in the world that dwell;
2 Both low and high, both rich and
poor.
3 My mouth shall wisdom tell:

My heart shall knowledge meditate.
4 I will incline mine ear
To parables, and on the harp
My sayings dark declare.

5 Amidst those days that evil be,
Why should I, fearing, doubt?
When of my heels th' iniquity
Shall compass me about.

6 Whoe'er they be that in their wealth
Their confidence do pitch,
And boast themselves, because they
are
Become exceeding rich:

7 Yet none of these his brother can
Deliver any way;
Nor can he unto God for him
Sufficient ransom pay,

8 (Their soul's redemption precious is,
And it can never be,)
9 That still he should for ever live,
And not corruption see.

10 For why? he seeth that wise men
die,
And brutish fools also
Do perish; and their wealth, when
dead,
To others they let go.

11 Their inward thought is, that their
house
And dwelling-places shall
Stand through all ages; they their
lands
By their own names do call.

12 But yet in honour shall not man
Abide continually;
But passing hence, may be
compared
Unto the beasts that die.

13 Thus brutish folly plainly is
Their wisdom and their way;
Yet their posterity approve
What they do fondly say.

14 Like sheep they in the grave are laid,
And death shall them devour;
And in the morning upright men
Shall over them have power:

Their beauty from their dwelling
shall
Consume within the grave.
15 But from hell's hand God will me
free,
For he shall me receive.

16 Be thou not then afraid when one
Enriched thou dost see,
Nor when the glory of his house
Advanced is on high:

17 For he shall carry nothing hence
When death his days doth end;
Nor shall his glory after him
Into the grave descend.

18 Although he his own soul did bless
Whilst he on earth did live;
(And when thou to thyself dost well,
Men will thee praises give;)

19 He to his fathers' race shall go,
   They never shall see light.
20 Man honoured wanting knowledge
      is
   Like beasts that perish quite.

50 First Version   S.M.

A Psalm of Asaph.
vv 1-6, 7-15, 16-23

1 The mighty God, the Lord,
   Hath spoken, and did call
   The earth, from rising of the sun,
   To where he hath his fall.

2 From out of Sion hill,
   Which of excellency
   And beauty the perfection is,
   God shined gloriously.

3 Our God shall surely come,
   Keep silence shall not he:
   Before him fire shall waste, great
      storms
   Shall round about him be.

4 Unto the heavens clear
   He from above shall call,
   And to the earth likewise, that he
   May judge his people all.

5 Together let my saints
   Unto me gathered be,
   Those that by sacrifice have made
   A covenant with me.

6 And then the heavens shall
   His righteousness declare:
   Because the Lord himself is he
   By whom men judged are.

7 My people Israel hear,
   Speak will I from on high,
   Against thee I will testify;
   God, ev'n thine am I.

8 I for thy sacrifice
   No blame will on thee lay,
   Nor for burnt-off'rings, which to
      me
   Thou offer'dst every day.

9 I'll take no calf nor goats
   From house or fold of thine:
10 For beasts of forests, cattle all
   On thousand hills, are mine.

11 The fowls on mountains high
   Are all to me well known;
   Wild beasts which in the fields do
      lie,
   Ev'n they are all mine own.

12 Then, if I hungry were,
   I would not tell it thee;
   Because the world, and fullness all
   Thereof, belongs to me.

13 Will I eat flesh of bulls?
   Or goats' blood drink will I?
14 Thanks offer thou to God, and pay
   Thy vows to the most High.

15 And call upon me when
   In trouble thou shalt be;
   I will deliver thee, and thou
   My name shalt glorify.

16 But to the wicked man
   God saith, My laws and truth
   Should'st thou declare? how dar'st
      thou take
   My covenant in thy mouth?

17 Since thou instruction hat'st,
   Which should thy ways direct;
   And since my words behind thy
      back
   thou cast'st, and dost reject.

18 When thou a thief didst see,
   With him thou didst consent;
   And with the vile adulterers
   Partaker on thou went.

19 Thou givest thy mouth to ill,
   Thy tongue deceit doth frame;
20 Thou sitt'st, and 'gainst thy brother
      speak'st,
   Thy mother's son dost shame.

21 Because I silence kept,
   While thou these things hast
      wrought;
   That I was altogether like
   Thyself, hath been thy thought;

Yet I will thee reprove,
And set before thine eyes,
In order ranked, thy misdeeds
And thine iniquities.

22 Now, ye that God forget,
This carefully consider;
Lest I in pieces tear you all,
And none can you deliver.

23 Whoso doth offer praise
Me glorifies; and I
Will show him God's salvation,
That orders right his way.

50 Second Version   C.M.

A Psalm of Asaph.
vv 1-6, 7-15, 16-23

1 The mighty God, the Lord, hath
          spoke,
And called the earth upon,
Ev'n from the rising of the sun
Unto his going down.

2 From out of Sion, his own hill,
Where the perfection high
Of beauty is, from thence the Lord
Hath shined gloriously.

3 Our God shall come, and shall no
          more
Be silent, but speak out:
Before him fire shall waste, great
          storms
Shall compass him about.

4 He to the heavens from above,
and to the earth below,
Shall call, that he his judgments
          may
before his people show.

5 Let all my saints together be
Unto me gathered;
Those that by sacrifice with me
A covenant have made.

6 And then the heavens shall declare
His righteousness abroad:
Because the Lord himself doth
          come;
None else is judge but God.

7 Hear, O my people, and I'll speak;
O Israel by name,
Against thee I will testify;
God, ev'n thine am I.

8 I for thy sacrifices few
Reprove thee never will,
Nor for burnt-off'rings to have
          been
Before me offered still.

9 I'll take no bullock nor he-goats
From house nor folds of thine:
10 For beasts of forests, cattle all
On thousand hills, are mine.

11 The fowls are all to me well known
That mountains high do yield;
And I do challenge as mine own
The wild beasts of the field.

12 If I were hungry, I would not
To thee for need complain;
For earth, and all its fullness, doth
To me of right pertain.

13 That I to eat the flesh of bulls
Take pleasure dost thou think?
Or that I need, to quench my thirst,
The blood of goats to drink?

14 Nay, rather unto me, thy God,
Thanksgiving offer thou:
To the most High perform thy
          word,
And fully pay thy vow:

15 And in the day of trouble great
see that thou call on me;
I will deliver thee, and thou
my name shalt glorify.

16 But God unto the wicked saith,
Why should'st thou mention make
Of my commands? how dar'st thou
          in
Thy mouth my covenant take?

17 Since it is so that thou dost hate
   All good instruction;
   And since thou cast'st behind thy
      back,
   And slight'st my words each one.

18 When thou a thief didst see, then
      straight
   Thou join'dst with him in sin,
   And with the vile adulterers
   Thou hast partaker been.

19 Thy mouth to evil thou dost give,
   Thy tongue deceit doth frame.
20 Thou sitt'st, and 'gainst thy brother
      speak'st,
   Thy mother's son to shame.

21 These things thou wickedly hast
      done,
   And I have silent been:
   Thou thought'st that I was like thy-
      self,
   And did approve thy sin:

   But I will sharply thee reprove,
   And I will order right
   Thy sins and thy transgressions
   In presence of thy sight.

22 Consider this, and be afraid,
   Ye that forget the Lord,
   Lest I in pieces tear you all,
   When none can help afford.

23 Who offereth praise me glorifies:
   I will show God's salvation
   To him that ordereth aright
   His life and conversation.

51 C.M.

To the chief Musician, A Psalm of
David, when Nathan the prophet came
unto him, after he had gone in to
Bathsheba.
vv 1-8, 9-14, 15-19

1 After thy loving-kindness, Lord,
   Have mercy upon me:
   For thy compassions great, blot out
   All mine iniquity.

2 Me cleanse from sin, and throughly
      wash
   From mine iniquity:
3 For my transgressions I confess;
   My sin I ever see.

4 Against thee only have I sinned,
   In thy sight done this ill;
   That when thou speak'st thou
      may'st be just,
   And clear in judging still.

5 Behold, I in iniquity
   Was formed the womb within;
   My mother also me conceived
   In guiltiness and sin.

6 Behold, thou in the inward parts
   With truth delighted art;
   And wisdom thou shalt make me
      know
   Within the hidden part.

7 Do thou with hyssop sprinkle me,
   I shall be cleansed so;
   Yea, wash thou me, and then I shall
   Be whiter than the snow.

8 Of gladness and of joyfulness
   Make me to hear the voice;
   That so these very bones which thou
   Hast broken may rejoice.

9 All mine iniquities blot out,
   Thy face hide from my sin.
10 Create a clean heart, Lord, renew
   A right spirit me within.

11 Cast me not from thy sight, nor
      take
   Thy Holy Spirit away.
12 Restore me thy salvation's joy;
   With thy free Spirit me stay.

13 Then will I teach thy ways unto
   Those that transgressors be;
   And those that sinners are shall
      then
   Be turned unto thee.

14 O God, of my salvation God,
Me from blood-guiltiness
Set free; then shall my tongue aloud
Sing of thy righteousness.

15 My closed lips, O Lord, by thee
Let them be opened;
Then shall thy praises by my mouth
Abroad be published.

16 For sacrifice thou asketh not,
Else would I give it thee;
Nor wilt thou with burnt-offering
At all delighted be.

17 A broken spirit is to God
A pleasing sacrifice:
A broken and a contrite heart,
Lord, thou wilt not despise.

18 Show kindness, and do good, O
Lord,
To Sion, thine own hill:
The walls of thy Jerusalem
Build up of thy good will.

19 Then righteous offerings shall thee
please,
And offerings burnt, which they
With whole burnt-offerings, and
with calves,
Shall on thine altar lay.

52 C.M.

*To the chief Musician, Maschil, A Psalm
of David, when Doeg the Edomite came
and told Saul, and said unto him,
David is come to the house of Ahimelech.*

1 Why dost thou boast, O mighty
man,
Of mischief and of ill?
The goodness of Almighty God
Endureth ever still.

2 Thy tongue mischievous to defame,
Deviseth subtly,
Like to a razor sharp to cut,
Working deceitfully.

3 Ill more than good, and more than
truth
Thou lovest to speak wrong:

4 Thou lovest all-devouring words,
O thou deceitful tongue.

5 So God shall thee destroy for aye,
Remove thee, pluck thee out
Quite from thy house, out of the
land
Of life he shall thee root.

6 The righteous shall it see, and fear,
And laugh at him they shall:

7 Lo, this the man is that did not
Make God his strength at all:

But he in his abundant wealth
His confidence did place;
And he took strength unto himself
From his own wickedness.

8 But I am in the house of God
Like to an olive green:
My confidence for ever hath
Upon God's mercy been.

9 And I for ever will thee praise,
Because thou hast done this:
I on thy name will wait; for good
Before thy saints it is.

53

*To the chief Musician upon Mahalath,
Maschil, A Psalm of David.*

1 That there is not a God, the fool
Doth in his heart conclude:
They are corrupt, their works are
vile,
Not one of them doth good.

2 The Lord upon the sons of men
From heav'n did cast his eyes,
To see if any one there was
That sought God, and was wise.

3 They altogether filthy are,
They all are backward gone;
And there is none that doeth good,
No, not so much as one.

4 These workers of iniquity,
Do they not know at all,
That they my people eat as bread,
And on God do not call?

5 Ev'n there they were afraid, and
stood
With trembling, all dismayed,
Whereas there was no cause at all
Why they should be afraid:

For God his bones that thee
besieged
Hath scattered all abroad;
Thou hast confounded them, for
they
Despised are of God.

6 Let Israel's help from Sion come:
When back the Lord shall bring
His captives, Jacob shall rejoice,
And Israel shall sing.

54 C.M.

*To the chief Musician on Neginoth,
Maschil, A Psalm of David, when the
Ziphims came and said to Saul, Doth
not David hide himself with us?*

1 Save me, O God, by thy great name,
And judge me by thy strength:
2 My prayer hear, O God; give ear
Unto my words at length.

3 For they that strangers are to me
Do up against me rise;
Oppressors seek my soul, and God
Set not before their eyes.

4 The Lord my God my helper is,
Lo, therefore I am bold:
He taketh part with every one
That doth my soul uphold.

5 Unto mine enemies he shall
Mischief and ill repay:
O for thy truth's sake cut them off,
And sweep them clean away.

6 I will a sacrifice to thee
Give with free willingness;
Thy name, O Lord, because 'tis good,
With praise I will confess.

7 For he hath me delivered
From all adversities;
And his desire mine eye hath seen
Upon mine enemies.

55 C.M.

*To the chief Musician on Neginoth,
Maschil, A Psalm of David.
vv 1-8, 9-15, 16-23*

1 Lord, hear my prayer, hide not thy
self
From my entreating voice:
2 Attend and hear me; in my plaint
I mourn and make a noise.

3 Because of enemies' voice, and for
Vile men's oppression great:
On me they cast iniquity,
And they in wrath me hate.

4 Sore pained within me is my heart:
Death's terrors on me fall.
5 On me comes trembling, fear and
dread
O'erwhelming me withal.

6 O that I, like a dove, had wings,
Said I, then would I flee
Far hence, that I might find a place
Where I in rest might be.

7 Lo, then far off I wander would,
And in the desert stay;
8 From windy storm and tempest I
Would haste to escape away.

9 O Lord, on them destruction bring,
And do their tongues divide;
For in the city violence
And strife I have espied.

10 They day and night upon the walls
Do go about it round:
There mischief is, and sorrow there
In midst of it is found.

11 Abundant wickedness there is
Within her inward part;
And from her streets deceitfulness
And guile do not depart.

12 He was no foe that me reproached,
Then that endure I could;
Nor hater that did 'gainst me boast,
From him me hide I would.

13 But thou, man, who mine equal,
guide,
And mine acquaintance wast:
14 We joined sweet counsels, to God's
house
In company we past.

15 Let death upon them seize, and
down
Let them go quick to hell;
For wickedness doth much abound
Among them where they dwell.

16 I'll call on God: the Lord will save.
17 I'll pray, and make a noise
At ev'ning, morning, and at noon;
And he shall hear my voice.

18 He hath my soul delivered,
That it in peace might be
From battle that against me was;
For many were with me.

19 The Lord shall hear, and them
afflict,
Of old who hath abode:
Because they never changes have,
Therefore they fear not God.

20 'Gainst those that were at peace
with him
He hath put forth his hand:
The covenant that he had made,
By breaking he profaned.

21 More smooth than butter were his
words,
While in his heart was war;
His speeches were more soft than
oil,
And yet drawn swords they are.

22 Cast thou thy burden on the Lord,
And he shall thee sustain;
Yea, he shall cause the righteous
man
Unmoved to remain.

23 But thou, O Lord my God, those
men
In justice shalt o'erthrow,
And in destruction's dungeon dark
At last shalt lay them low:

The bloody and deceitful men
Shall not live half their days:
But upon thee with confidence
I will depend always.

56 C.M.

*To the chief Musician upon Jonath-elem-
rechokim, Michtam of David, when the
Philistines took him in Gath.*
vv 1-4, 5-13

1 Show mercy, Lord, to me, for man
Would swallow me outright;
He me oppresseth, while he doth
Against me daily fight.

2 They daily would me swallow up
That hate me spitefully;
For they be many that do fight
Against me, O most High.

3 When I'm afraid I'll trust in thee:
4 In God I'll praise his word;
I will not fear what flesh can do,
My trust is in the Lord.

5 Each day they wrest my words; their
thoughts
'Gainst me are all for ill.
6 They meet, they lurk, they mark my
steps,
Waiting my soul to kill.

7 But shall they by iniquity
Escape thy judgments so?
O God, with indignation down
Do thou the people throw.

8 My wanderings all what they have
been
Thou know'st, their number took;
Into thy bottle put my tears:
Are they not in thy book?

9 My foes shall, when I cry, turn back;
  I know God is for me.
10 In God his word I'll praise; his
  word
  In God shall praised be.

11 In God I trust; I will not fear
  What man can do to me.
12 Thy vows upon me are, O God:
  I'll render praise to thee.

13 Wilt thou not, who from death me
  saved,
  My feet from falls keep free,
  To walk before God in the light
  Of those that living be?

57 C.M.

*To the chief Musician, Al-taschith,
Michtam of David, when he fled from
Saul in the cave.
vv 1-2, 3-6, 7-11*

1 Be merciful to me, O God;
  Thy mercy unto me
  Do thou extend; because my soul
  Doth put her trust in thee:

  Yea, in the shadow of thy wings
  My refuge I will place,
  Until these sad calamities
  Do wholly overpass.

2 My cry I will cause to ascend
  Unto the Lord most high;
  To God, who doth all things for me
  Perform most perfectly.

3 From heaven he shall send down,
  and me
  From his reproach defend
  That would devour me: God his
  truth
  And mercy forth shall send.

4 My soul among fierce lions is,
  I firebrands live among,
  Men's sons, whose teeth are spears
  and darts,
  A sharp sword is their tongue.

5 Be thou exalted very high
  Above the heavens, O God;
  Let thou thy glory be advanced
  O'er all the earth abroad.

6 My soul's bowed down; for they a
  net
  Have laid, my steps to snare:
  Into the pit which they have digged
  For me, they fallen are.

7 My heart is fixed, my heart is fixed,
  O God; I'll sing and praise.
8 My glory wake; wake psaltery, harp;
  Myself I'll early raise.

9 I'll praise thee 'mong the people,
  Lord;
  'Mong nations sing will I:
10 For great to heaven thy mercy is,
  Thy truth is to the sky.

11 O Lord, exalted be thy name
  Above the heavens to stand:
  Do thou thy glory far advance
  Above both sea and land.

58 C.M.

*To the chief Musician, Al-taschith,
Michtam of David.
vv 1-5, 6-11*

1 Do ye, O congregation,
  Indeed speak righteousness?
  O ye that are the sons of men,
  Judge ye with uprightness?

2 Yea, ev'n within your very hearts
  Ye wickedness have done;
  And of your hands the violence
  Doth weigh the earth upon.

3 The wicked men estranged are,
  Ev'n from the very womb;
  They, speaking lies, do stray as soon
  As to the world they come.

4 Unto a serpent's poison like
  Their poison doth appear;
  Yea, they are like the adder deaf,
  That closely stops her ear;

5 That so she may not hear the voice
Of one that charm her would,
No, not though he most cunning were,
And charm most wisely could.

6 Their teeth, O God, within their mouth
Break thou in pieces small;
The great teeth break thou out, O Lord,
Of these young lions all.

7 Let them like waters melt away,
Which downward still do flow:
In pieces cut his arrows all,
When he shall bend his bow.

8 Like to a snail that melts away,
Let each of them be gone;
Like woman's birth untimely, that
They never see the sun.

9 He shall them take away before
Your pots the thorns can find,
Both living, and in fury great,
As with a stormy wind.

10 The righteous, when he vengeance sees,
He shall be joyful then;
The righteous one shall wash his feet
In blood of wicked men.

11 So men shall say, The righteous man
Reward shall never miss:
And verily upon the earth
A God to judge there is.

59   C.M.

*To the chief Musician, Al-taschith,
Mitcham of David; when Saul sent, and
they watched the house to kill him.*
vv 1-9, 10-17

1 My God, deliver me from those
That are mine enemies;
And do thou me defend from those
That up against me rise.

2 Do thou deliver me from them
That work iniquity;
And give me safety from the men
Of bloody cruelty.

3 For, lo, they for my soul lay wait:
The mighty do combine
Against me, Lord; not for my fault,
Nor any sin of mine.

4 They run, and, without fault in me,
Themselves do ready make:
Awake to meet me with thy help;
And do thou notice take.

5 Therefore awake, Lord God of hosts,
Thou God of Israel,
To visit heathen all: spare none
That wickedly rebel.

6 At ev'ning they go to and fro;
They make great noise and sound,
Like to a dog, and often walk
About the city round.

7 Behold, they belch out with their mouth,
And in their lips are swords:
For they do say thus, Who is he
That now doth hear our words?

8 But thou, O Lord, shalt laugh at them,
And all the heathen mock.

9 While he's in power I'll wait on thee;
For God is my high rock.

10 He of my mercy that is God
Betimes shall me prev'nt;
And on mine enemies shall let
Me see mine heart's content.

11 Them slay not, lest my folk forget;
But scatter them abroad
By thy strong power; and bring them down,
O thou our shield and God.

12 For their mouth's sin, and for the
    words
  That from their lips do fly,
  Let them be taken in their pride;
  Because they curse and lie.

13 In wrath consume them, them
    consume,
  That so they may not be:
  And that in Jacob God doth rule
  To the earth's ends let them see.

14 At ev'ning let thou them return,
  Making great noise and sound,
  Like to a dog, and often walk
  About the city round.

15 And let them wander up and down,
  In seeking food to eat;
  And let them grudge when they
    shall not
  Be satisfied with meat.

16 But of thy power I'll sing aloud;
  At morn thy mercy praise:
  For thou to me my refuge wast,
  And tower, in troublous days.

17 O God, thou art my strength, I will
  Sing praises unto thee;
  For God is my defence, a God
  Of mercy unto me.

60 C.M.

*To the chief Musician upon Shushan-
eduth, Michtam of David, to teach;
when he strove with Aram-naharaim,
and with Aram-zobah, when Joab
returned and smote of Edom, in the
valley of Salt, twelve thousand.*
vv 1-5, 6-12

1 O Lord, thou hast rejected us,
  And scattered us abroad;
  Thou justly hast displeased been;
  Return to us, O God.

2 The earth to tremble thou hast
    made;
  Therein didst breaches make:
  Do thou thereof the breaches heal,
  Because the land doth shake.

3 Unto thy people thou hard things
  Hast showed, and on them sent;
  And thou hast caused us to drink
  Wine of astonishment.

4 And yet a banner thou hast given
  To them who thee do fear;
  That it by them, because of truth,
  Displayed may appear.

5 That thy beloved people may
  Delivered be from thrall,
  Save with the power of thy right
    hand,
  And hear me when I call.

6 God in his holiness hath spoke;
  Herein I will take pleasure:
  Shechem I will divide, and forth
  Will Succoth's valley measure.

7 Gilead I claim as mine by right;
  Manasseh mine shall be;
  Ephraim is of mine head the
    strength;
  Judah gives laws for me;

8 Moab my washpot is; my shoe
  I'll over Edom throw;
  And over Palestina's land
  I will in triumph go.

9 O who is he will bring me to
  The city fortified?
  O who is he that to the land
  Of Edom will me guide?

10 O God, who hast rejected us,
  This thing wilt thou not do?
  Ev'n thou, O God, which didest not
  Forth with our armies go?

11 Help us from trouble; for the help
  Is vain which man supplies.
12 Through God we'll do great acts; he
    shall
  Tread down our enemies.

61 C.M.

To the chief Musician upon Neginoth,
A Psalm of David.
vv 1-5, 6-8

1 O God, give ear unto my cry;
   Unto my prayer attend.
2 From farthest corner of the land
   My cry to thee I'll send.

   What time my heart is
      overwhelmed,
   And in perplexity,
   Do thou me lead unto the Rock
   That higher is than I.

3 For thou hast for my refuge been
   A shelter by thy power;
   And for defence against my foes
   Thou hast been a strong tower.

4 Within thy tabernacle I
   For ever will abide;
   And under covert of thy wings
   With confidence me hide.

5 For thou the vows that I did make,
   O Lord my God, didst hear:
   Thou hast giv'n me the heritage
   Of those thy name that fear.

6 A life prolonged for many days
   Thou to the king shalt give;
   Like many generations be
   The years which he shall live.

7 He in God's presence his abode
   For evermore shall have:
   O do thou truth and mercy both
   Prepare, that may him save.

8 And so will I perpetually
   Sing praise unto thy name;
   That having made my vows, I may
   Each day perform the same.

62 C.M.

To the chief Musician, to Jeduthun,
A Psalm of David.
vv 1-4, 5-8, 9-12

1 My soul with expectation
   Depends on God indeed;
   My strength and my salvation do
   From him alone proceed.

2 He only my salvation is,
   And my strong rock is he:
   He only is my sure defence;
   Much moved I shall not be.

3 How long will ye against a man
   Plot mischief? ye shall all
   Be slain; ye as a tottering fence
   Shall be, and bowing wall.

4 They only plot to cast him down
   From his excellency:
   They joy in lies; with mouth they
      bless,
   But they curse inwardly.

5 My soul, wait thou with patience
   Upon thy God alone;
   On him dependeth all my hope
   And expectation.

6 He only my salvation is,
   And my strong rock is he;
   He only is my sure defence:
   I shall not moved be.

7 In God my glory placed is,
   And my salvation sure;
   In God the rock is of my strength,
   My refuge most secure.

8 Ye people, place your confidence
   In him continually;
   Before him pour ye out your heart:
   God is our refuge high.

9 Surely mean men are vanity,
   And great men are a lie;
   In balance laid, they wholly are
   More light than vanity.

10 Trust ye not in oppression,
In robbery be not vain;
On wealth set not your hearts, when
   as
Increased is your gain.

11 God hath it spoken once to me,
Yea, this I heard again,
That power to Almighty God
Alone doth appertain.

12 Yea, mercy also unto thee
Belongs, O Lord, alone:
For thou according to his work
Rewardest every one.

63 C.M.

A Psalm of David, when he was in the
wilderness of Judah.
vv 1-6, 7-11

1 Lord, thee my God, I'll early seek:
My soul doth thirst for thee;
My flesh longs in a dry parched
   land,
Wherein no waters be:

2 That I thy power may behold,
And brightness of thy face,
As I have seen thee heretofore
Within thy holy place.

3 Since better is thy love than life,
My lips thee praise shall give.
4 I in thy name will lift my hands,
And bless thee while I live.

5 Ev'n as with marrow and with fat
My soul shall filled be;
Then shall my mouth with joyful
   lips
Sing praises unto thee:

6 When I do thee upon my bed
Remember with delight,
And when on thee I meditate
In watches of the night.

7 In shadow of thy wings I'll joy;
For thou mine help hast been.
8 My soul thee follows hard; and me
Thy right hand doth sustain.

9 Who would destroy my soul shall
   sink
Down to earth's lowest room.
10 They by the sword shall be cut off,
And foxes' prey become.

11 Yet shall the king in God rejoice,
And each one glory shall
That swears by him: but stopped
   shall be
The mouth of liars all.

64 C.M.

To the chief Musician, A Psalm of David.

1 When I to thee my prayer make,
Lord, to my voice give ear;
My life save from the enemy,
Of whom I stand in fear.

2 Me from their secret counsel hide
Who do live wickedly;
From insurrection of those men
That work iniquity:

3 Who do their tongues with malice
   whet,
And make them cut like swords;
In whose bent bows are arrows set,
Ev'n sharp and bitter words:

4 That they may at the perfect man
In secret aim their shot;
Yea, suddenly they dare at him
To shoot, and fear it not.

5 In ill encourage they themselves,
And their snares close do lay:
Together conference they have;
Who shall them see? they say.

6 They have searched out iniquities,
A perfect search they keep:
Of each of them the inward
   thought,
And very heart, is deep.

7 God shall an arrow shoot at them,
And wound them suddenly:
8 So their own tongue shall them
   confound;
All who them see shall fly.

9 And on all men a fear shall fall,
   God's works they shall declare;
   For they shall wisely notice take
   What these his doings are.

10 In God the righteous shall rejoice,
   And trust upon his might;
   Yea, they shall greatly glory all
   In heart that are upright.

65   C.M.

To the chief Musician,
A Psalm and Song of David.
vv 1-4, 5-8, 9-13

1 Praise waits for thee in Sion, Lord:
   To thee vows paid shall be.
2 O thou that hearer art of prayer,
   All flesh shall come to thee.

3 Iniquities, I must confess,
   Prevail against me do:
   But as for our transgressions,
   Them purge away shalt thou.

4 Blessed is the man whom thou dost
      choose,
   And mak'st approach to thee,
   That he within thy courts, O Lord,
   May still a dweller be:

   We surely shall be satisfied
   With thy abundant grace,
   And with the goodness of thy
      house,
   Ev'n of thy holy place.

5 O God of our salvation,
   Thou, in thy righteousness,
   By fearful works unto our prayers
   Thine answer dost express:

   Therefore the ends of all the earth,
   And those afar that be
   Upon the sea, their confidence,
   O Lord, will place in thee.

6 Who, being girt with power, sets
      fast
   By his great strength the hills.
7 Who noise of seas, noise of their
      waves,
   And people's tumult, stills.

8 Those in the utmost parts that dwell
   Are at thy signs afraid:
   Th' outgoings of the morn and ev'n
   By thee are joyful made.

9 Earth thou dost visit, watering it;
   Thou mak'st it rich to grow
   With God's full flood; thou corn
      prepar'st,
   When thou provid'st it so.

10 Its ridges thou dost water well,
   Its furrows settlest:
   With showers thou dost her mollify,
   Her spring by thee is blessed.

11 So thou the year most liberally
   Dost with thy goodness crown;
   And all thy paths abundantly
   On us drop fatness down.

12 They drop upon the pastures wide,
   That do in deserts lie;
   The little hills on every side
   Rejoice right pleasantly.

13 With flocks the pastures clothed be,
   The vales with corn are clad;
   And now they shout and sing to
      thee,
   For thou hast made them glad.

66   C.M.

To the chief Musician, A Song or Psalm.
vv 1-4, 5-7, 8-12, 13-20

1 All lands to God in joyful sounds,
   Aloft your voices raise.
2 Sing forth the honour of his name,
   And glorious make his praise.

3 Say unto God, How terrible
In all thy works art thou!
Through thy great power thy foes to
thee
Shall be constrained to bow.

4 All on the earth shall worship thee,
They shall thy praise proclaim
In songs: they shall sing cheerfully
Unto thy holy name.

5 Come, and the works that God hath
wrought
With admiration see:
In doings to the sons of men
Most terrible is he.

6 Into dry land the sea he turned,
And they a passage had;
Ev'n marching through the flood on
foot,
There we in him were glad.

7 He ruleth ever by his power;
His eyes the nations see:
O let not the rebellious ones
Lift up themselves on high.

8 Ye people, bless our God; aloud
The voice speak of his praise:
9 Our soul in life who safe preserves,
Our foot from sliding stays.

10 For thou didst prove and try us,
Lord,
As men do silver try;
11 Brought'st us into the net, and
mad'st
Bands on our loins to lie.

12 Thou hast caused men ride o'er our
heads;
And though that we did pass
Through fire and water, yet thou
brought'st
Us to a wealthy place.

13 I'll bring burnt offerings to thy
house;
To thee my vows I'll pay,
14 Which my lips uttered, my mouth
spake,
When trouble on me lay.

15 Burnt-sacrifices of fat rams
With incense I will bring;
Of bullocks and of goats I will
Present an offering.

16 All that fear God, come, hear, I'll
tell
What he did for my soul.
17 I with my mouth unto him cried,
My tongue did him extol.

18 If in my heart I sin regard,
The Lord me will not hear:
19 But surely God me heard, and to
My prayer's voice gave ear.

20 O let the Lord, our gracious God,
For ever blessed be,
Who turned not my prayer from
him,
Nor yet his grace from me.

67 First Version S.M.

*To the chief Musician on Neginoth,
A Psalm or Song.*

1 Lord, bless and pity us,
Shine on us with thy face:
2 That the earth thy way, and nations
all
May know thy saving grace.

3 Let people praise thee, Lord;
Let people all thee praise.
4 O let the nations be glad,
In songs their voices raise:

Thou'lt justly people judge,
On earth rule nations all.
5 Let people praise thee, Lord; let
them
Praise thee, both great and small.

6 The earth her fruit shall yield,
Our God shall blessing send.
7 God shall us bless; men shall him
fear
Unto earth's utmost end.

67 Second Version   C.M.

To the chief Musician on Neginoth,
A Psalm or Song.

1 Lord, unto us be merciful,
   Do thou us also bless;
   And graciously cause shine on us
   The brightness of thy face:

2 That so thy way upon th' earth
   To all men may be known;
   Also among the nations all
   Thy saving health be shown.

3 O let the people praise thee, Lord;
   Let people all thee praise.
4 O let the nations be glad,
   And sing for joy always:

   For rightly thou shalt people judge,
   And nations rule on earth.
5 Let people praise thee, Lord; let all
   The folk praise thee with mirth.

6 Then shall the earth yield her
      increase;
   God, our God, bless us shall.
7 God shall us bless; and of the earth
   The ends shall fear him all.

68   C.M.

To the chief Musician,
A Psalm or Song of David.
vv 1-6, 7-15, 16-19, 20-23, 24-31,
32-35

1 Let God arise, and scattered
   Let all his enemies be;
   And let all those that do him hate
   Before his presence flee.

2 As smoke is driven, so drive thou
      them;
   As fire melts wax away,
   Before God's face let wicked men
   So perish and decay.

3 But let the righteous all be glad:
   Let them before God's sight
   Be very joyful; yea, let them
   Rejoice with all their might.

4 To God sing, to his name sing
      praise;
   Extol him with your voice,
   That rides on heaven, by his name
      JAH,
   Before his face rejoice.

5 Because the Lord a father is
   Unto the fatherless;
   God is the widow's judge, within
   His place of holiness.

6 God doth the solitary set
   In families: from bands
   The chained doth free; but rebels do
   Inhabit parched lands.

7 O God, what time thou didst go
      forth
   Before thy people's face;
   And when through the great
      wilderness
   Thy glorious marching was;

8 Then at God's presence shook the
      earth,
   Then drops from heaven fell;
   This Sinai shook before the Lord,
   The God of Israel.

9 O God, thou to thine heritage
   Didst send a plenteous rain,
   Whereby thou, when it weary was,
   Didst it refresh again.

10 Thy congregation then did make
   Their habitation there:
   Of thine own goodness for the
      poor,
   O God, thou didst prepare.

11 The Lord himself did give the word,
   The word abroad did spread;
   Great was the company of them
   The same who published.

12 Kings of great armies foiled were,
   And forced to flee away;
   And women, who remained at
      home,
   Did distribute the prey.

13 Though ye have lain among the
      pots,
   Like doves ye shall appear,
   Whose wings with silver, and with
      gold
   Whose feathers covered are.

14 When there th' Almighty scattered
      kings,
   Like Salmon's snow 'twas white.

15 God's hill is like to Bashan hill,
   Like Bashan hill for height.

16 Why do ye leap, ye mountains high?
   This is the hill where God
   Desires to dwell; yea, God in it
   For aye will make abode.

17 God's chariots twenty thousand are,
   Thousands of angels strong;
   God is in his most holy place,
   Mount Sinai, them among.

18 Thou hast, O Lord, most glorious,
   Ascended up on high;
   And in triumph victorious led
   Captive captivity:

   Thou hast received gifts for men,
   For such as did rebel;
   Yea, ev'n for them, that God the
      Lord
   In midst of them might dwell.

19 Blessed be the Lord, who is to us
   Of our salvation God;
   Who daily with his benefits
   Us plenteously doth load.

20 He of salvation is the God,
   Who is our God most strong;
   And unto God the Lord from death
   The issues do belong.

21 But surely God shall wound the
      head
   Of those that are his foes;
   The hairy scalp of him that still
   On in his trespass goes.

22 God said, My people I will bring
   Again from Bashan hill;
   Yea, from the sea's devouring
      depths
   Them bring again I will;

23 That in the blood of enemies
   Thy foot imbrued may be,
   And of thy dogs dipped in the same
   The tongues thou mayest see.

24 Thy goings they have seen, O God;
   The steps of majesty
   Of my God, and my mighty King,
   Within the sanctuary.

25 Before went singers, players next
   On instruments took way;
   And them among the damsels were
   That did on timbrels play.

26 Within the congregations
   Bless God with one accord:
   From Israel's fountain do ye bless
   And praise the mighty Lord.

27 With their prince, little Benjamin,
   Princes and council there
   Of Judah were, there Zebulun's
   And Napht'li's princes were.

28 Thy God commands thy strength;
      make strong
   What thou wrought'st for us, Lord.

29 For thy house at Jerusalem
   Kings shall thee gifts afford.

30 The spearmen's host, the multitude
   Of bulls, which fiercely look,
   Those calves which people have
      forth sent,
   O Lord our God, rebuke,

   Till every one submit himself,
   And silver pieces bring:
   The people that delight in war
   Disperse, O God and King.

31 Those that be princes great shall
      then
   Come out of Egypt lands;
   And Ethiopia to God
   Shall soon stretch out her hands.

32 O all ye kingdoms of the earth,
Sing praises to this King;
For he is Lord that ruleth all,
Unto him praises sing.

33 To him that rides on heavens of
heavens,
Which he of old did found;
Lo, he sends out his voice, a voice
In might that doth abound.

34 Strength unto God do ye ascribe;
For his excellency
Is over Israel, his strength
Is in the clouds most high.

35 Thou'rt from thy temple dreadful,
Lord;
Israel's own God is he,
Who gives his people strength and
power:
O let God blessed be.

69   C.M.

*To the chief Musician upon
Shoshannim, A Psalm of David.*
vv 1-6a, 6b-13, 14-21, 22-29, 30-36

1 Save me, O God, because the floods
Do so environ me,
That ev'n unto my very soul
Come in the waters be.

2 I downward in deep mire do sink,
Where standing there is none:
I am into deep waters come,
Where floods have o'er me gone.

3 I weary with my crying am,
My throat is also dried;
Mine eyes do fail, while for my God
I waiting do abide.

4 Those men that do without a cause
Bear hatred unto me,
Than are the hairs upon my head
In number more they be:

They that would me destroy, and are
Mine enemies wrongfully,
Are mighty: so what I took not,
To render forced was I.

5 Lord, thou my folly know'st, my sins
Not covered are from thee.
6 Let none that wait on thee be
shamed,
Lord God of hosts, for me.

O Lord, the God of Israel,
Let none, who search do make,
And seek thee, be at any time
Confounded for my sake.

7 For I have borne reproach for thee,
My face is hid with shame.
8 To brethren strange, to mother's
sons
An alien I became.

9 Because the zeal did eat me up,
Which to thine house I bear;
And the reproaches cast at thee,
Upon me fallen are.

10 With tears and fasting mourned my
soul,
And that was made my shame.
11 When sackcloth I did wear, to them
A proverb I became.

12 The men that in the gate do sit
Against me evil spake;
They also that vile drunkards were
Of me their song did make.

13 But, in an acceptable time,
My prayer, Lord, is to thee:
In truth of thy salvation, Lord,
And mercy great, hear me.

14 Deliver me out of the mire,
From sinking do me keep;
Free me from those that do me
hate,
And from the waters deep.

15 Let not the flood on me prevail,
Whose water overflows;
Nor deep me swallow, nor the pit
Her mouth upon me close.

16 Hear me, O Lord, because thy love
And kindness is most good;
Turn unto me, according to
Thy mercies' multitude.

17 Nor from thy servant hide thy face:
  I'm troubled, soon attend.
18 Draw near my soul, and it redeem;
  Me from my foes defend.

19 To thee is my reproach well known,
  My shame, and my disgrace:
  Those that mine adversaries be
  Are all before thy face.

20 Reproach hath broke my heart; I'm full
  Of grief: I looked for one
  To pity me, but none I found;
  Comforters found I none.

21 They also bitter gall did give
  Unto me for my meat:
  They gave me vinegar to drink,
  When as my thirst was great.

22 Before them let their table prove
  A snare; and do thou make
  Their welfare and prosperity
  A trap themselves to take.

23 Let thou their eyes so darkened be,
  That sight may them forsake;
  And let their loins be made by thee
  Continually to shake.

24 Thy fury pour thou out on them,
  And indignation;
  And let thy wrathful anger, Lord,
  Fast hold take them upon.

25 All waste and desolate let be
  Their habitation;
  And in their tabernacles all
  Inhabitants be none.

26 Because him they do persecute,
  Whom thou didst smite before;
  They talk unto the grief of those
  Whom thou hast wounded sore.

27 Add thou iniquity unto
  Their former wickedness;
  And do not let them come at all
  Into thy righteousness.

28 Out of the book of life let them
  Be 'razed and blotted quite;
  Among the righteous and the just
  Their names do thou not write.

29 But now become exceeding poor
  And sorrowful am I:
  By thy salvation, O my God,
  Let me be set on high.

30 The name of God I with a song
  Most cheerfully will praise;
  And I, in giving thanks to him,
  His name shall highly raise.

31 This to the Lord a sacrifice
  More gracious shall prove
  Than bullock, ox, or any beast
  That hath both horn and hoof.

32 When this the humble men shall see,
  It joy to them shall give:
  O all ye that do seek the Lord,
  Your hearts shall ever live.

33 For God the poor hears, and will not
  His prisoners contemn.
34 Let heaven, and earth, and seas, him praise,
  And all that move in them.

35 For God will Judah's cities build,
  And he will Sion save,
  That they may dwell therein, and it
  In sure possession have.

36 And they that are his servants' seed
  Inherit shall the same;
  So shall they have their dwelling there
  That love his blessed name.

70 First Version   S.M.

*To the chief Musician, A Psalm of
David, to bring to remembrance.*

1 Lord, haste me to deliver;
  With speed, Lord, succour me.
2 Let them that for my soul do seek
  Shamed and confounded be:

Turned back be they, and shamed,
That in my hurt delight.

3 Turned back be they, Ha, ha! that
say,
Their shaming to requite.

4 In thee let all be glad,
And joy that seek for thee:
Let them who thy salvation love
Say still, God praised be.

5 I poor and needy am;
Come, Lord, and make no stay:
My help thou and deliverer art;
O Lord, make no delay.

70 Second Version   C.M.

*To the chief Musician, A Psalm of
David, to bring to remembrance.*

1 Make haste, O God, me to preserve;
With speed, Lord, succour me.

2 Let them that for my soul do seek
Sham'd and confounded be:

Let them be turned back, and
sham'd,
That in my hurt delight.

3 Turned back be they, Ha, ha! that
say,
Their shaming to requite.

4 O Lord, in thee let all be glad,
And joy that seek for thee:
Let them who thy salvation love
Say still, God praised be.

5 But I both poor and needy am;
Come, Lord, and make no stay:
My help thou and deliverer art;
O Lord, make no delay.

71   C.M.

vv 1-5, 6-13, 14-19, 20-24

1 O Lord, my hope and confidence
Is placed in thee alone;
Then let thy servant never be
Put to confusion.

2 And let me, in thy righteousness,
From thee deliverance have;
Cause me escape, incline thine ear
Unto me, and me save.

3 Be thou my dwelling-rock, to which
I ever may resort:
Thou gav'st commandment me to
save,
Thou art my rock and fort.

4 Free me, my God, from wicked
hands,
Hands cruel and unjust:

5 For thou, O Lord God, art my hope,
And from my youth my trust.

6 Thou from the womb didst hold me
up;
Thou art the same that me
Out of my mother's bowels took;
I ever will praise thee.

7 To many I a wonder am;
Thou art my refuge strong.

8 Filled let my mouth be with thy
praise
And honour all day long.

9 O do not cast me off, when as
Old age doth overtake me;
And when my strength decayed is,
Then do not thou forsake me.

10 For those that are mine enemies
Against me speak with hate;
And they together counsel take
That for my soul lay wait.

11 They said, God leaves him; him
pursue
And take: none will him save.

12 Be thou not far from me, my God:
Thy speedy help I crave.

13 Confound, consume them, that
unto
My soul are enemies:
Clothed be they with reproach and
shame
That do my hurt devise.

14 But I with expectation
Will hope continually;
And yet with praises more and more
I will thee magnify.

15 Thy justice and salvation
My mouth abroad shall show,
Ev'n all the day; for I thereof
The numbers do not know.

16 And I will constantly go on
In strength of God the Lord;
And thine own righteousness, ev'n
thine
Alone, I will record.

17 For ev'n from my youth, O God,
By thee I have been taught;
And hitherto I have declared
The wonders thou hast wrought.

18 And now, Lord, leave me not,
when I
Old and grey-headed grow:
Till to this age thy strength and
power
To all to come I show.

19 And thy most perfect righteousness
O Lord, is very high,
Who hast so great things done: O
God,
Who is like unto thee?

20 Thou, Lord, who great adversities,
And sore, to me didst show,
Shalt quicken, and bring me again
From depths of earth below.

21 My greatness and my power thou
wilt
Increase, and far extend:
On every side against all grief
Thou wilt me comfort send.

22 Thee, ev'n thy truth, I'll also praise,
My God, with psaltery:
Thou Holy One of Israel,
With harp I'll sing to thee.

23 My lips shall much rejoice in thee,
When I thy praises sound;
My soul, which thou redeemed hast,
In joy shall much abound.

24 My tongue thy justice shall
proclaim,
Continuing all day long;
For they confounded are, and
shamed,
That seek to do me wrong.

72 C.M.

A Psalm for Solomon.
vv 1-7, 8-16, 17-19

1 O Lord, thy judgments give the
king,
His son thy righteousness.
2 With right he shall thy people
judge,
Thy poor with uprightness.

3 The lofty mountains shall bring
forth
Unto the people peace;
Likewise the little hills the same
Shall do by righteousness.

4 The people's poor ones he shall
judge,
The needy's children save;
And those shall he in pieces break
Who them oppressed have.

5 They shall thee fear, while sun and
moon
Do last, through ages all.
6 Like rain on mown grass he shall
drop,
Or showers on earth that fall.

7 The just shall flourish in his days,
And prosper in his reign:
He shall, while doth the moon
endure,
Abundant peace maintain.

8 His large and great dominion shall
From sea to sea extend:
It from the river shall reach forth
Unto earth's utmost end.

9 They in the wilderness that dwell
Bow down before him must;
And they that are his enemies
Shall lick the very dust.

10 The kings of Tarshish, and the isles,
To him shall presents bring;
And unto him shall offer gifts
Sheba's and Seba's king.

11 Yea, all the mighty kings on earth
Before him down shall fall;
And all the nations of the world
Do service to him shall.

12 For he the needy shall preserve,
When he to him doth call;
The poor also, and him that hath
No help of man at all.

13 The poor man and the indigent
In mercy he shall spare;
He shall preserve alive the souls
Of those that needy are.

14 Both from deceit and violence
Their soul he shall set free;
And in his sight right precious
And dear their blood shall be.

15 Yea, he shall live, and giv'n to him
Shall be of Sheba's gold:
For him still shall they pray, and he
Shall daily be extolled.

16 Of corn an handful in the earth
On tops of mountains high,
With prosp'rous fruit shall shake, like trees
On Lebanon that be.

The city shall be flourishing,
Her citizens abound
In number shall, like to the grass
That grows upon the ground.

17 His name for ever shall endure;
Last like the sun it shall:
Men shall be blessed in him, and blessed
All nations shall him call.

18 Now blessed be the Lord our God,
The God of Israel,
For he alone doth wondrous works,
In glory that excel.

19 And blessed be his glorious name
To all eternity:
The whole earth let his glory fill.
Amen, so let it be.

73 C.M.

A Psalm of Asaph.
vv 1-9, 10-15, 16-22, 23-28

1 Yet God is good to Israel,
To each pure-hearted one.
2 But as for me, my steps near slipped,
My feet were almost gone.

3 For I was envious, and grudged
The foolish folk to see,
When I perceived the wicked sort
Enjoy prosperity.

4 For still their strength continueth firm;
Their death of bands is free.
5 They are not toiled like other men,
Nor plagued, as others be.

6 Therefore their pride, like to a chain,
Them compasseth about;
And, as a garment, violence
Doth cover them throughout.

7 Their eyes stand out with fat; they have
More than their hearts could wish.
8 They are corrupt; their talk of wrong
Both vile and lofty is.

9 They set their mouth against the heavens
In their blasphemous talk;
And their reproaching tongue throughout
The earth at large doth walk.

10 His people oftentimes for this
Look back, and turn about;
Since waters of so full a cup
To these are poured out.

11 And thus they say, How can it be
That God these things doth know?
Or, Can there in the Highest be
Knowledge of things below?

12 Behold, these are the wicked ones,
Yet prosper at their will
In worldly things; they do increase
In wealth and riches still.

13 I verily have done in vain
My heart to purify;
To no effect in innocence
Washed my hands have I.

14 For daily, and all day throughout,
Great plagues I suffered have;
Yea, every morning I anew
Did chastisement receive.

15 If in this manner foolishly
To speak I would intend,
Thy children's generation,
behold, I should offend.

16 When I this thought to know, it was
Too hard a thing for me;
17 Till to God's sanctuary I went,
Then I their end did see.

18 Assuredly thou didst them set
A slippery place upon;
Them suddenly thou castedst down
Into destruction.

19 How in a moment suddenly
To ruin brought are they!
With fearful terrors utterly
They are consumed away.

20 Just like unto a dream, when one
From sleeping doth arise;
So thou, O Lord, when thou
awak'st,
Their image shalt despise.

21 Thus grieved was my heart in me,
And me my reins oppressed:
22 So foolish I, and ignorant,
And in thy sight a beast.

23 Nevertheless continually,
O Lord, I am with thee:
Thou dost me hold by my right
hand,
And still upholdest me.

24 Thou, with thy counsel, while I live,
Wilt me conduct and guide;
And to thy glory afterward
Receive me to abide.

25 Whom have I in the heavens high
But thee, O Lord, alone?
And in the earth whom I desire
Besides thee there is none.

26 My flesh and heart doth faint and
fail,
But God doth fail me never:
For of my heart God is the strength
And portion for ever.

27 For, lo, they that are far from thee
For ever perish shall;
Them that a whoring from thee go
Thou hast destroyed all.

28 But surely it is good for me
That I draw near to God:
In God I trust, that all thy works
I may declare abroad.

74   C.M.

Maschil of Asaph.
vv 1-9, 10-17, 18-23

1 O God, why hast thou cast us off?
Is it for evermore?
Against thy pasture-sheep why doth
Thine anger smoke so sore?

2 To thy remembrance do thou call
Thy congregation,
Which thou hast purchased of old;
Still think the same upon:

The rod of thine inheritance,
Which thou redeemed hast,
This Sion hill, wherein thou hadst
Thy dwelling in times past.

3 To these long desolations
   Thy feet lift, do not tarry;
   For all the ills thy foes have done
   Within thy sanctuary.

4 Amidst thy congregations
   Thine enemies do roar:
   Their ensigns they set up for signs
   Of triumph thee before.

5 A man was famous, and was had
   In estimation,
   According as he lifted up
   His axe thick trees upon.

6 But all at once with axes now
   And hammers they go to,
   And down the carved work thereof
   They break, and quite undo.

7 They fired have thy sanctuary,
   And have defiled the same,
   By casting down unto the ground
   The place where dwelt thy name.

8 Thus said they in their hearts, Let us
   Destroy them out of hand:
   They burnt up all the synagogues
   Of God within the land.

9 Our signs we do not now behold;
   There is not us among
   A prophet more, nor any one
   That knows the time how long.

10 How long, Lord, shall the enemy
   Thus in reproach exclaim?
   And shall the adversary thus
   Always blaspheme thy name?

11 Thy hand, ev'n thy right hand of
      might,
   Why dost thou thus draw back?
   O from thy bosom pluck it out
   For our deliverance sake.

12 For certainly God is my King,
   Ev'n from the times of old,
   Working in midst of all the earth
   Salvation manifold.

13 The sea, by thy great power, to part
   Asunder thou didst make;
   And thou the dragons' heads, O
      Lord,
   Within the waters brake.

14 The leviathan's head thou brak'st
   In pieces, and didst give
   Him to be meat unto the folk
   In wilderness that live.

15 Thou clav'st the fountain and the
      flood,
   Which did with streams abound:
   Thou driedst the mighty waters up
   Unto the very ground.

16 Thine only is the day, O Lord,
   Thine also is the night;
   And thou alone prepared hast
   The sun and shining light.

17 By thee the borders of the earth
   Were settled everywhere:
   The summer and the winter both
   By thee created were.

18 That th' enemy reproached hath,
   O keep it in record;
   And that the foolish people have
   Blasphemed thy name, O Lord.

19 Unto the multitude do not
   Thy turtle's soul deliver:
   The congregation of thy poor
   Do not forget for ever.

20 Unto thy covenant have respect;
   For earth's dark places be
   Full of the habitations
   Of horrid cruelty.

21 O let not those that be oppressed
   Return again with shame:
   Let those that poor and needy are
   Give praise unto thy name.

22 Do thou, O God, arise and plead
   The cause that is thine own:
   Remember how thou art reproached
   Still by the foolish one.

23 Do not forget the voice of those
   That are thine enemies:
   Of those the tumult ever grows
   That do against thee rise.

75 C.M.

*To the chief Musician, Al-taschith,
A Psalm or Song of Asaph.*

1 To thee, O God, do we give thanks,
   We do give thanks to thee;
   Because thy wondrous works
      declare
   Thy great name near to be.

2 I purpose, when I shall receive
   The congregation,
   That I shall judgment uprightly
   Render to every one.

3 Dissolved is the land, with all
   That in the same do dwell;
   But I the pillars thereof do
   Bear up, and stablish well.

4 I to the foolish people said,
   Do not deal foolishly;
   And unto those that wicked are,
   Lift not your horn on high.

5 Lift not your horn on high, nor
      speak
6 With stubborn neck. But know,
   That not from east, nor west, nor
      south,
   Promotion doth flow.

7 But God is judge; he puts down
      one,
   And sets another up.
8 For in the hand of God most high
   Of red wine is a cup:

   'Tis full of mixture, he pours forth,
   And makes the wicked all
   Wring out the bitter dregs thereof;
   Yea, and they drink them shall.

9 But I for ever will declare,
   I Jacob's God will praise.
10 All horns of vile men I'll cut off;
   But just men's horns will raise.

76 C.M.

*To the chief Musician on Neginoth,
A Psalm or Song of Asaph.*

1 In Judah's land God is well known,
   His name's in Israel great:
2 In Salem is his tabernacle,
   In Sion is his seat.

3 There arrows of the bow he brake,
   The shield, the sword, the war.
4 More glorious thou than hills of
      prey,
   More excellent art far.

5 Those that were stout of heart are
      spoiled,
   They slept their sleep outright;
   And none of those their hands did
      find,
   That were the men of might.

6 When thy rebuke, O Jacob's God,
   Had forth against them past,
   Their horses and their chariots both
   Were in a dead sleep cast.

7 Thou, Lord, ev'n thou art he that
      should
   Be feared; and who is he
   That may stand up before thy sight,
   If once thou angry be?

8 From heav'n thou judgment caused
      be heard;
   The earth was still with fear,
9 When God to judgment rose, to save
   All meek on earth that were.

10 Surely the very wrath of man
   Unto thy praise redounds:
   Thou to the remnant of his wrath
   Wilt set restraining bounds.

11 Vow to the Lord your God, and pay:
   All ye that near him be,
   Bring gifts and presents unto him;
   For to be feared is he.

12 He shall the spirits soon cut off
   Of those that princes are:
   Unto the kings that are on earth
   He fearful doth appear.

77   C.M.

To the chief Musician, to Jeduthun,
A Psalm of Asaph.
vv 1-6, 7-14, 15-20

1 Unto the Lord I with my voice,
I unto God did cry;
Ev'n with my voice, and unto me
His ear he did apply.

2 I in my trouble sought the Lord,
My sore by night did run,
And ceased not; my grieved soul
Did consolation shun.

3 I to remembrance God did call,
Yet trouble did remain;
And overwhelmed my spirit was,
Whilst I did sore complain.

4 Mine eyes, debarred from rest and
sleep,
Thou makest still to wake;
My trouble is so great that I
Unable am to speak.

5 The days of old to mind I called,
And oft did think upon
The times and ages that are past
Full many years agone.

6 By night my song I call to mind,
And commune with my heart;
My spirit carefully enquired
How I might ease my smart.

7 For ever will the Lord cast off,
And gracious be no more?
8 For ever is his mercy gone?
Fails his word evermore?

9 Is't true that to be gracious
The Lord forgotten hath?
And that his tender mercies he
Hath shut up in his wrath?

10 Then did I say, That surely this
Is mine infirmity:
I'll mind the years of the right hand
Of him that is most High.

11 Yea, I remember will the works
Performed by the Lord:
The wonders done of old by thee
I surely will record.

12 I also will of all thy works
My meditation make;
And of thy doings to discourse
Great pleasure I will take.

13 O God, thy way most holy is
Within thy sanctuary;
And what god is so great in power
As is our God most high?

14 Thou art the God that wonders dost
By thy right hand most strong:
Thy mighty power thou hast
declared
The nations among.

15 To thine own people with thine arm
Thou didst redemption bring;
To Jacob's sons, and to the tribes
Of Joseph that do spring.

16 The waters, Lord, perceived thee,
The waters saw thee well;
And they for fear aside did flee;
The depths on trembling fell.

17 The clouds in water forth were
poured,
Sound loudly did the sky;
And swiftly through the world
abroad
Thine arrows fierce did fly.

18 Thy thunder's voice along the
heaven
A mighty noise did make;
By lightnings lightened was the
world,
Earth trembled did and shake.

19 Thy way is in the sea, and in
The waters great thy path;
Yet are thy footsteps hid, O Lord;
None knowledge thereof hath.

20 Thy people thou didst safely lead,
Like to a flock of sheep;
By Moses' hand and Aaron's thou
Didst them conduct and keep.

78

C.M.

Maschil of Asaph.
vv 1-8, 9-18, 19-31, 32-41, 42-50,
51-54, 55-66, 67-72

1 Attend, my people, to my law;
Thereto give thou an ear;
The words that from my mouth
  proceed
Attentively do hear.

2 My mouth shall speak a parable,
And sayings dark of old;
3 The same which we have heard and
  known,
And us our fathers told.

4 We also will them not conceal
From their posterity;
Them to the generation
To come declare will we:

The praises of the Lord our God,
And his almighty strength,
The wondrous works that he hath
  done,
We will show forth at length.

5 His testimony and his law
In Israel he did place,
And charged our fathers it to show
To their succeeding race;

6 That so the race which was to come
Might well them learn and know;
And sons unborn, who should arise,
Might to their sons them show:

7 That they might set their hope in
  God,
And suffer not to fall
His mighty works out of their mind,
But keep his precepts all:

8 And might not, like their fathers, be
A stiff rebellious race;
A race not right in heart; with God
Whose spirit not fixed was.

9 The sons of Ephraim, who nor bows
Nor other arms did lack,
When as the day of battle was,
They faintly turned back.

10 They brake God's covenant, and
  refused
In his commands to go;
11 His works and wonders they forgot,
Which he to them did show.

12 Things marvellous he brought to
  pass;
Their fathers them beheld
Within the land of Egypt done,
Yea, ev'n in Zoan's field.

13 By him divided was the sea,
He caused them through to pass;
And made the waters so to stand,
As like an heap it was.

14 With cloud by day, with light of fire
All night, he did them guide.
15 In desert rocks he clave, and drink,
As from great depths, supplied.

16 He from the rock brought streams,
  like floods
Made waters to run down.
17 Yet sinning more, in desert they
Provoked the Highest One.

18 For in their heart they tempted God,
And, speaking with mistrust,
They greedily did meat require
To satisfy their lust.

19 Against the Lord himself they
  spake,
And, murmuring, said thus,
A table in the wilderness
Can God prepare for us?

20 Behold, he smote the rock, and
  thence
Came streams and waters great;
But can he give his people bread?
And send them flesh to eat?

21 The Lord did hear, and waxed
  wroth;
So kindled was a flame
'Gainst Jacob, and 'gainst Israel
Up indignation came.

22 For they believed not God, nor trust
In his salvation had;
23 Though clouds above he did
command,
And heaven's doors open made,

24 And manna rained on them, and
gave
Them corn of heaven to eat.
25 Man angels' food did eat; to them
He to the full sent meat.

26 And in the heaven he did cause
An eastern wind to blow;
And by his power he let out
The southern wind to go.

27 Then flesh as thick as dust he made
To rain down them among;
And feathered fowls, like as the
sand
Which lieth the shore along.

28 At his command amidst their camp
These showers of flesh down fell,
All round about the tabernacles
And tents where they did dwell.

29 So they did eat abundantly,
And had of meat their fill;
For he did give to them what was
Their own desire and will.

30 They from their lust had not
estranged
Their heart and their desire;
But while the meat was in their
mouths,
Which they did so require,

31 God's wrath upon them came, and
slew
The fattest of them all;
So that the choice of Israel,
O'erthrown by death, did fall.

32 Yet, notwithstanding of all this,
They sinned still the more;
And though he had great wonders
wrought,
Believed him not therefore:

33 Wherefore their days in vanity
He did consume and waste;
And by his wrath their wretched
years
Away in trouble past.

34 But when he slew them, then they
did
To seek him show desire;
Yea, they returned, and after God
Right early did enquire.

35 And that the Lord had been their
Rock,
They did remember then;
Ev'n that the high almighty God
Had their Redeemer been.

36 Yet with their mouth they flattered
him,
And spake but feignedly;
And they unto the God of truth
With their false tongues did lie.

37 For though their words were good,
their heart
With him was not sincere;
Unsteadfast and so treacherous
They in his covenant were.

38 But, full of pity, he forgave
Their sin, them did not slay;
Nor stirred up all his wrath, but oft
His anger turned away.

39 For that they were but fading flesh
To mind he did recall;
A wind that passeth soon away,
And not returns at all.

40 How often did they him provoke
Within the wilderness!
And in the desert did him grieve
With their rebelliousness!

41 Yea, turning back, they tempted
God,
And limits set upon
Him, who in midst of Israel is
The only Holy One.

42 They did not call to mind his power,
Nor yet the day when he
Delivered them out of the hand
Of their fierce enemy;

43 Nor how great signs in Egypt land
He openly had wrought;
What miracles in Zoan's field
His hand to pass had brought.

44 How lakes and rivers every where
He turned into blood;
So that nor man nor beast could drink
Of standing lake or flood.

45 He brought among them swarms of flies,
Which did them sore annoy;
And divers kinds of filthy frogs
He sent them to destroy.

46 He to the caterpillar gave
The fruits of all their soil;
Their labours he delivered up
Unto the locusts' spoil.

47 Their vines with hail, their sycamores
He with the frost did blast:
48 Their beasts to hail he gave; their flocks
Hot thunderbolts did waste.

49 Fierce burning wrath he on them cast,
And indignation strong,
Distress and trouble, angels sent
That evil were among.

50 He to his wrath made way; their soul
From death he did not save;
But over to the pestilence
The lives of them he gave.

51 In Egypt land the first-born all
He smote down everywhere;
Among the tents of Ham, ev'n these
Chief of their strength that were.

52 But his own people, like to sheep,
Thence to go forth he made;
And he, amidst the wilderness,
Them, as a flock, did lead.

53 And he them safely on did lead,
So that they did not fear;
But by the sea their enemies
Quite overwhelmed were.

54 To borders of his sanctuary
The Lord his people led,
Ev'n to the mount which his right hand
For them had purchased.

55 The nations of Canaan,
By his almighty hand,
Before their face he did expel
Out of their native land;

Which for inheritance to them
By line he did divide,
And made the tribes of Israel
Within their tents abide.

56 Yet God most high they did provoke,
And tempted ever still;
And to observe his testimonies
Did not incline their will:

57 But, like their fathers, turned back,
And dealt unfaithfully:
Aside they turned, like a bow
That shoots deceitfully.

58 For they to anger did provoke
Him with their places high;
And with their graven images
Moved him to jealousy.

59 When God heard this, he waxed wroth,
And much loathed Israel then:
60 So Shiloh's tent he left, the tent
Which he had placed with men.

61 And he his strength delivered
Into captivity;
He left his glory in the hand
Of his proud enemy.

62 His people also he gave o'er
Unto the sword's fierce rage:
So sore his wrath inflamed was
Against his heritage.

63 The fire consumed their choice
young men;
Their maids no marriage had;
64 And when their priests fell by the
sword,
Their wives no mourning made.

65 But then the Lord arose, as one
That doth from sleep awake;
And like a giant that, by wine
Refreshed, a shout doth make:

66 Upon his enemies' hinder parts
He made his stroke to fall;
And so upon them he did put
A shame perpetual.

67 Moreover, he the tabernacle
Of Joseph did refuse;
The mighty tribe of Ephraim
He would in no wise choose:

68 But he the tribe of Judah chose
To be the rest above;
And of mount Sion he made choice,
Which he so much did love.

69 And he his sanctuary built
Like to a palace high,
Like to the earth which he did
found
To perpetuity.

70 Of David, that his servant was,
He also choice did make,
And ev'n from the folds of sheep
Was pleased him to take:

71 From waiting on the ewes with
young,
He brought him forth to feed
Israel, his inheritance,
His people, Jacob's seed.

72 So after the integrity
He of his heart them fed;
And by the good skill of his hands
Them wisely governed.

79   C.M.

A Psalm of Asaph.
vv 1-7, 8-13

1 O God, the heathen entered have
Thine heritage; by them
Defiled is thy house: on heaps
They laid Jerusalem.

2 The bodies of thy servants they
Have cast forth to be meat
To ravenous fowls; thy dear saints'
flesh
They gave to beasts to eat.

3 Their blood about Jerusalem
Like water they have shed;
And there was none to bury them
When they were slain and dead.

4 Unto our neighbours a reproach
Most base become are we;
A scorn and laughing stock to them
That round about us be.

5 How long, Lord, shall thine anger
last?
Wilt thou still keep the same?
And shall thy fervent jealousy
Burn like unto a flame?

6 On heathen pour thy fury forth,
That have thee never known,
And on those kingdoms which thy
name
Have never called upon.

7 For these are they who Jacob have
Devoured cruelly;
And they his habitation
Have caused waste to lie.

8 Against us mind not former sins;
Thy tender mercies show;
Let them prev'nt us speedily,
For we're brought very low.

9 For thy name's glory help us, Lord,
Who hast our Saviour been:
Deliver us; for thy name's sake,
O purge away our sin.

10 Why say the heathen, Where's their
   God?
   Let him to them be known;
   When those who shed thy servants'
   blood
   Are in our sight o'erthrown.

11 O let the prisoner's sighs ascend
   Before thy sight on high;
   Preserve those in thy mighty power
   That are designed to die.

12 And to our neighbours' bosom
   cause
   It sev'n-fold rendered be,
   Ev'n the reproach wherewith they
   have,
   O Lord, reproached thee.

13 So we thy folk, and pasture-sheep,
   Shall give thee thanks always;
   And unto generations all
   We will show forth thy praise.

80   C.M.

To the chief musician upon Shoshannim,
Eduth, A Psalm of Asaph.
vv 1-7, 8-11, 12-16, 17-19

1 Hear, Israel's Shepherd! like a flock
  Thou that dost Joseph guide;
  Shine forth, O thou that dost
  between
  The cherubims abide.

2 In Ephraim's, and Benjamin's
  And in Manasseh's sight,
  O come for our salvation;
  Stir up thy strength and might.

3 Turn us again, O Lord our God,
  And upon us vouchsafe
  To make thy countenance to shine,
  And so we shall be safe.

4 O Lord of hosts, almighty God,
  How long shall kindled be
  Thy wrath against the prayer made
  By thine own folk to thee?

5 Thou tears of sorrow giv'st to them
  Instead of bread to eat;
  Yea, tears instead of drink thou
  giv'st
  To them in measure great.

6 Thou makest us a strife unto
  Our neighbours round about;
  Our enemies among themselves
  At us do laugh and flout.

7 Turn us again, O God of hosts,
  And upon us vouchsafe
  To make thy countenance to shine,
  And so we shall be safe.

8 A vine from Egypt brought thou
  hast,
  By thine outstretched hand;
  And thou the heathen out didst
  cast,
  To plant it in their land.

9 Before it thou a room didst make,
  Where it might grow and stand;
  Thou causedst it deep root to take,
  And it did fill the land.

10 The mountains veiled were with its
   shade,
   As with a covering;
   Like goodly cedars were the boughs
   Which out from it did spring.

11 Upon the one hand to the sea
   Her boughs she did out send;
   On th' other side unto the flood
   Her branches did extend.

12 Why hast thou then thus broken
   down,
   And torn her hedge away?
   So that all passengers do pluck,
   And make of her a prey.

13 The boar who from the forest
   comes
   Doth waste it at his pleasure;
   The wild beast of the field also
   Devours it out of measure.

14 O God of hosts, we thee beseech,
   Return now unto thine;
   Look down from heaven in love,
      behold,
   And visit this thy vine:

15 This vineyard, which thine own
      right hand
   Hath planted us among;
   And that same branch, which for
      thyself
   Thou hast made to be strong.

16 Burnt up it is with flaming fire,
   It also is cut down:
   They utterly are perished,
   When as thy face doth frown.

17 O let thy hand be still upon
   The Man of thy right hand,
   The Son of man, whom for thyself
   Thou madest strong to stand.

18 So henceforth we will not go back,
   Nor turn from thee at all:
   O do thou quicken us, and we
   Upon thy name will call.

19 Turn us again, Lord God of hosts,
   And upon us vouchsafe
   To make thy countenance to shine,
   And so we shall be safe.

81   C.M.

To the chief Musician upon Gittith,
A Psalm of Asaph.
vv 1-7, 8-16

1 Sing loud to God our strength; with
      joy
   To Jacob's God do sing.
2 Take up a psalm, the pleasant harp,
   Timbrel and psaltery bring.

3 Blow trumpets at new-moon, what
      day
   Our feast appointed is:
4 For charge to Israel, and a law
   Of Jacob's God was this.

5 To Joseph this a testimony
   He made, when Egypt land
   He travelled through, where speech
      I heard
   I did not understand.

6 His shoulder I from burdens took,
   His hands from pots did free.
7 Thou didst in trouble on me call,
   And I delivered thee:

   In secret place of thundering
   I did thee answer make;
   And at the streams of Meribah
   Of thee a proof did take.

8 O thou, my people, give an ear,
   I'll testify to thee;
   To thee, O Israel, if thou wilt
   But hearken unto me.

9 In midst of thee there shall not be
   Any strange god at all;
   Nor unto any god unknown
   Thou bowing down shalt fall.

10 I am the Lord thy God, which did
   From Egypt land thee guide;
   I'll fill thy mouth abundantly,
   Do thou it open wide.

11 But yet my people to my voice
   Would not attentive be;
   And ev'n my chosen Israel
   He would have none of me.

12 So to the lust of their own hearts
   I them delivered;
   And then in counsels of their own
   They vainly wandered.

13 O that my people had me heard,
   Israel my ways had chose!
14 Their enemies I'd soon subdued,
   My hand turned on their foes.

15 The haters of the Lord to him
   Submission should have feigned;
   But as for them, their time should
      have
   For evermore remained.

16 He should have also fed them with
The finest of the wheat;
Of honey from the rock thy fill
I should have made thee eat.

82 C.M.

A Psalm of Asaph.

1 In gods' assembly God doth stand;
He judgeth gods among.
2 How long, accepting persons vile,
Will ye give judgment wrong?

3 Defend the poor and fatherless;
To poor oppressed do right.
4 The poor and needy ones set free;
Rid them from ill men's might.

5 They know not, nor will under
stand;
In darkness they walk on:
All the foundations of the earth
Out of their course are gone.

6 I said that ye are gods, and are
Sons of the Highest all:
7 But ye shall die like men, and as
One of the princes fall.

8 O God, do thou raise up thyself,
The earth to judgment call:
For thou, as thine inheritance,
Shalt take the nations all.

83 C.M.

A Song or Psalm of Asaph.
vv 1-8, 9-18

1 Keep not, O God, we thee entreat,
O keep not silence now:
Do thou not hold thy peace, O God,
And still no more be thou.

2 For, lo, thine enemies a noise
Tumultuously have made;
And they that haters are of thee
Have lifted up the head.

3 Against thy chosen people they
Do crafty counsel take;
And they against thy hidden ones
Do consultations make.

4 Come, let us cut them off, said they,
From being a nation,
That of the name of Israel may
No more be mention.

5 For with joint heart they plot, in
league
Against thee they combine.
6 The tents of Edom, Ishm'elites,
Moab's and Hagar's line;

7 Gebal, and Ammon, Amalek,
Philistines, those of Tyre;
8 And Assur joined with them, to help
Lot's children they conspire.

9 Do to them as to Midian,
Jabin at Kison strand;
10 And Sisera, which at En-dor fell,
As dung to fat the land.

11 Like Oreb and like Zeeb make
Their noble men to fall;
Like Zeba and Zalmunna like,
Make thou their princes all;

12 Who said, For our possession
Let us God's houses take.
13 My God, them like a wheel, as chaff
Before the wind, them make.

14 As fire consumes the wood, as
flame
Doth mountains set on fire,
15 Chase and affright them with the
storm
And tempest of thine ire.

16 Their faces fill with shame, O Lord,
That they may seek thy name.
17 Let them confounded be, and vexed,
And perish in their shame:
18 That men may know that thou, to
whom
Alone doth appertain
The name Jehovah, dost most high
O'er all the earth remain.

84 C.M.

To the chief Musician upon Gittith,
A Psalm for the sons of Korah.
vv 1-7, 8-12

1 How lovely is thy dwelling-place,
O Lord of hosts, to me!
The tabernacles of thy grace
How pleasant, Lord, they be!

2 My thirsty soul longs vehemently,
Yea faints, thy courts to see:
My very heart and flesh cry out,
O living God, for thee.

3 Behold, the sparrow findeth out
An house wherein to rest;
The swallow also for herself
Hath purchased a nest;

Ev'n thine own altars, where she safe
Her young ones forth may bring,
O thou almighty Lord of hosts,
Who art my God and King.

4 Bless'd are they in thy house that dwell,
They ever give thee praise.
5 Bless'd is the man whose strength thou art,
In whose heart are thy ways:

6 Who as they pass through Baca's vale,
Therein do dig up wells;
Also the rain that falleth down
The pools with water fills.

7 So they from strength unwearied go
Still forward unto strength,
Until in Sion they appear
Before the Lord at length.

8 Lord God of hosts, my prayer hear;
O Jacob's God, give ear.
9 See God our shield, look on the face
Of thine anointed dear.

10 For in thy courts one day excels
A thousand; rather in
My God's house will I keep a door,
Than dwell in tents of sin.

11 For God the Lord's a sun and shield:
He'll grace and glory give;
And will withhold no good from them
That uprightly do live.

12 O thou that art the Lord of hosts,
That man is truly blest,
Who by assured confidence
On thee alone doth rest.

85 C.M.

To the chief Musician, A Psalm for the
sons of Korah.
vv 1-5, 6-13

1 O Lord, thou hast been favourable
To thy beloved land:
Jacob's captivity thou hast
Recalled with mighty hand.

2 Thou pardoned thy people hast
All their iniquities;
Thou all their trespasses and sins
Hast covered from thine eyes.

3 Thou took'st off all thine ire, and turn'dst
From thy wrath's furiousness.
4 Turn us, God of our health, and cause
Thy wrath 'gainst us to cease.

5 Shall thy displeasure thus endure
Against us without end?
Wilt thou to generations all
Thine anger forth extend?

6 That in thee may thy people joy,
Wilt thou not us revive?
7 Show us thy mercy, Lord, to us
Do thy salvation give.

8 I'll hear what God the Lord will speak:
To his folk he'll speak peace,
And to his saints; but let them not
Return to foolishness.

9 To them that fear him surely near
Is his salvation;

That glory in our land may have
Her habitation.

10 Truth met with mercy,
     righteousness
   And peace kissed mutually:
11 Truth springs from earth, and
     righteousness
   Looks down from heaven high.

12 Yea, what is good the Lord shall
     give;
   Our land shall yield increase:
13 Justice, to set us in his steps,
   Shall go before his face.

86   C.M.

A Prayer of David.
vv 1-7, 8-13, 14-17

1 O Lord, do thou bow down thine
     ear,
   And hear me graciously;
   Because I sore afflicted am,
   And am in poverty.

2 Because I'm holy, let my soul
   By thee preserved be:
   O thou my God, thy servant save,
   That puts his trust in thee.

3 Since unto thee I daily cry,
   Be merciful to me.
4 Rejoice thy servant's soul; for, Lord,
   I lift my soul to thee.

5 For thou art gracious, O Lord,
   And ready to forgive;
   And rich in mercy, all that call
   Upon thee to relieve.

6 Hear, Lord, my prayer; unto the
     voice
   Of my request attend;
7 In troublous times I'll call on thee;
   For thou wilt answer send.

8 Lord, there is none among the gods
   That may with thee compare;
   And like the works which thou hast
     done,
   Not any work is there.

9 All nations whom thou mad'st shall
     come
   And worship reverently
   Before thy face; and they, O Lord,
   Thy name shall glorify.

10 Because thou art exceeding great,
   And works by thee are done
   Which are to be admired; and thou
   Art God thyself alone.

11 Teach me thy way, and in thy truth,
   O Lord, then walk will I;
   Unite my heart, that I thy name
   May fear continually.

12 O Lord my God, with all my heart
   To thee I will give praise;
   And I the glory will ascribe
   Unto thy name always:

13 Because thy mercy toward me
   In greatness doth excel;
   And thou delivered hast my soul
   Out from the lowest hell.

14 O God, the proud against me rise,
   And violent men have met,
   That for my soul have sought; and
     thee
   Before them have not set.

15 But thou art full of pity, Lord,
   A God most gracious,
   Long-suffering, and in thy truth
   And mercy plenteous.

16 O turn to me thy countenance,
   And mercy on me have;
   Thy servant strengthen, and the son
   Of thine own handmaid save.

17 Show me a sign for good, that they
   Which do me hate may see,
   And be ashamed; because thou,
     Lord,
   Didst help and comfort me.

87 C.M.

A Psalm or Song for the sons of Korah.

1 Upon the hills of holiness
   He his foundation sets.
2 God, more than Jacob's dwellings
   all,
   Delights in Sion's gates.
3 Things glorious are said of thee,
   Thou city of the Lord.
4 Rahab and Babel I, to those
   That know me, will record:

   Behold ev'n Tyrus, and with it
   The land of Palestine,
   And likewise Ethiopia;
   This man was born therein.

5 And it of Sion shall be said,
   This man and that man there
   Was born; and he that is most High
   Himself shall stablish her.
6 When God the people writes, he'll
   count
   That this man born was there.
7 There be that sing and play; and all
   My well-springs in thee are.

88 C.M.

*A Song or Psalm for the sons of Korah,
to the chief Musician upon Mahalath
Leannoth, Maschil of Heman the
Ezrahite.*
vv 1-9, 10-18

1 Lord God, my Saviour, day and
   night
   Before thee cried have I.
2 Before thee let my prayer come;
   Give ear unto my cry.
3 For troubles great do fill my soul;
   My life draws nigh the grave.
4 I'm counted with those that go
   down
   To pit, and no strength have.

5 Ev'n free among the dead, like
   them
   That slain in grave do lie;
   Whom, from thy hand cut off, no
   more
   Thou hast in memory.

6 Thou hast me laid in lowest pit,
   In deeps and darksome caves.
7 Thy wrath lies hard on me, thou
   hast
   Me pressed with all thy waves.

8 Thou hast put far from me my
   friends,
   Thou mad'st them to abhor me;
   And I am so shut up, that I
   Find no evasion for me.

9 By reason of affliction
   Mine eye mourns dolefully:
   To thee, Lord, do I call, and stretch
   My hands continually.

10 Wilt thou show wonders to the
   dead?
   Shall they rise, and thee bless?
11 Shall in the grave thy love be told?
   In death thy faithfulness?

12 Shall thy great wonders in the dark,
   Or shall thy righteousness
   Be known to any in the land
   Of deep forgetfulness?

13 But, Lord, to thee I cried; my prayer
   At morn prev'nt shall thee.
14 Why, Lord, dost thou cast off my
   soul,
   And hid'st thy face from me?

15 Distressed am I, and from my youth
   I ready am to die;
   Thy terrors I have borne, and am
   Distracted fearfully.

16 The dreadful fierceness of thy wrath
   Quite over me doth go:
   Thy terrors great have cut me off,
   They did pursue me so.

17 For round about me every day,
Like water, they did roll;
And, gathering together, they
Have compassed my soul.

18 My friends thou hast put far from
me,
And him that did me love;
And those that mine acquaintance
were
To darkness didst remove.

89 C.M.

Maschil of Ethan the Ezrahite.
vv 1-4, 5-13, 14-18, 19-23, 24-28,
29-34, 35-46, 47-52

1 God's mercies I will ever sing;
And with my mouth I shall
Thy faithfulness make to be known
To generations all.

2 For mercy shall be built, said I,
For ever to endure;
Thy faithfulness, ev'n in the
heavens,
Thou wilt establish sure.

3 I with my chosen One have made
A covenant graciously;
And to my servant, whom I loved,
To David sworn have I;

4 That I thy seed establish shall
For ever to remain,
And will to generations all
Thy throne build and maintain.

5 The praises of thy wonders, Lord,
The heavens shall express;
And in the congregation
Of saints thy faithfulness.

6 For who in heaven with the Lord
May once himself compare?
Who is like God among the sons
Of those that mighty are?

7 Great fear in meeting of the saints
Is due unto the Lord;
And he of all about him should
With reverence be adored.

8 O thou that art the Lord of hosts,
What Lord in mightiness
Is like to thee? who compassed
round
Art with thy faithfulness.

9 Ev'n in the raging of the sea
Thou over it dost reign;
And when the waves thereof do
swell,
Thou stillest them again.

10 Rahab in pieces thou didst break,
Like one that slaughtered is;
And with thy mighty arm thou hast
Dispersed thine enemies.

11 The heavens are thine, thou for
thine own
The earth dost also take;
The world, and fullness of the
same,
Thy power did found and make.

12 The north and south from thee
alone
Their first beginning had;
Both Tabor mount and Hermon hill
Shall in thy name be glad.

13 Thou hast an arm that's full of
power,
Thy hand is great in might;
And thy right hand exceedingly
Exalted is in height.

14 Justice and judgment of thy throne
Are made the dwelling-place;
Mercy, accompanied with truth,
Shall go before thy face.

15 O greatly blessed the people are
The joyful sound that know;
In brightness of thy face, O Lord,
They ever on shall go.

16 They in thy name shall all the day
Rejoice exceedingly;
And in thy righteousness shall they
Exalted be on high.

17 Because the glory of their strength
Doth only stand in thee;
And in thy favour shall our horn
And power exalted be.

18 For God is our defence; and he
To us doth safety bring:
The Holy One of Israel
Is our almighty King.

19 In vision to thy Holy One
Thou saidst, I help upon
A strong one laid; out of the folk
I raised a chosen one;

20 Ev'n David, I have found him out
A servant unto me;
And with my holy oil my King
Anointed him to be.

21 With whom my hand shall
stablished be;
Mine arm shall make him strong.
22 On him the foe shall not exact,
Nor son of mischief wrong.

23 I will beat down before his face
All his malicious foes;
I will them greatly plague who do
With hatred him oppose.

24 My mercy and my faithfulness
With him yet still shall be;
And in my name his horn and
power
Men shall exalted see.

25 His hand and power shall reach
afar;
I'll set it in the sea;
And his right hand established
Shall in the rivers be.

26 Thou art my Father, he shall cry,
Thou art my God alone;
And he shall say, Thou art the Rock
Of my salvation.

27 I'll make him my first-born, more
high
Than kings of any land.
28 My love I'll ever keep for him,
My covenant fast shall stand.

29 His seed I by my power will make
For ever to endure;
And, as the days of heaven, his
throne
Shall stable be, and sure.

30 But if his children shall forsake
My laws, and go astray,
And in my judgments shall not
walk,
But wander from my way:

31 If they my laws break, and do not
Keep my commandments all;
32 I'll visit then their faults with rods,
Under my stripes they'll fall.

33 Yet I'll not take my love from him,
Nor false my promise make.
34 My covenant I'll not break, nor
change
What with my mouth I spake.

35 Once by my holiness I sware,
To David I'll not lie;
36 His seed and throne shall, as the
sun,
Before me last for aye.

37 It, like the moon, shall ever be
Established steadfastly;
And like to that which in the *heaven*
Doth witness faithfully.

38 But thou, displeased, hast cast off,
Thou didst abhor and loathe;
With him that thine anointed is
Thou hast been very wroth.

39 Thou hast thy servant's covenant
Made void, and quite cast by;
Thou hast profaned his crown,
while it
Cast on the ground doth lie.

40 Thou all his hedges hast broke
down,
His strong holds down hast torn.
41 He to all passers-by a spoil,
To neighbours is a scorn.

42 Thou hast set up his foes' right
   hand;
   Madest all his enemies glad:
43 Turned his sword's edge, and him
   to stand
   In battle hast not made.

44 His glory thou hast made to cease,
   His throne to ground down cast;
45 Shortened his days of youth, and
   him
   With shame thou covered hast.

46 How long, Lord, wilt thou hide
   thyself?
   For ever, in thine ire?
   And shall thine indignation
   Burn like unto a fire?

47 Remember, Lord, how short a time
   I shall on earth remain:
   O wherefore is it so that thou
   Has made all men in vain?

48 What man is he that liveth here,
   And death shall never see?
   Or from the power of the grave
   What man his soul shall free?

49 Thy former loving-kindnesses,
   O Lord, where be they now?
   Those which in truth and
   faithfulness
   To David sworn hast thou?

50 Mind, Lord, thy servant's sad
   reproach;
   How I in bosom bear
   The scornings of the people all,
   Who strong and mighty are.

51 Wherewith thy raging enemies
   Reproached, O Lord, think on;
   Wherewith they have reproached
   the steps
   Of thine anointed one.

52 All blessing to the Lord our God
   Let be ascribed then:
   For evermore so let it be.
   Amen, yea, and amen.

90 C.M.

A Prayer of Moses the man of God.
vv 1-7, 8-12, 13-17

1 Lord, thou hast been our dwelling-
   place
   In generations all.
2 Before thou ever hadst brought
   forth
   The mountains great or small;

   Ere ever thou hadst formed the
   earth,
   And all the world abroad;
   Ev'n thou from everlasting art
   To everlasting God.

3 Thou dost unto destruction
   Man that is mortal turn;
   And unto them thou sayest, Again,
   Ye sons of men, return.

4· Because a thousand years appear
   No more before thy sight
   Than yesterday, when it is past,
   Or than a watch by night.

5 As with an overflowing flood
   Thou carry'st them away:
   They like a sleep are, like the grass
   That grows at morn are they.

6 At morn it flourishes and grows,
   Cut down at ev'n doth fade.
7 For by thine anger we're consumed,
   Thy wrath makes us afraid.

8 Our sins thou and iniquities
   Dost in thy presence place,
   And sett'st our secret faults before
   The brightness of thy face.

9 For in thine anger all our days
   Do pass on to an end;
   And as a tale that hath been told,
   So we our years do spend.

10 Threescore and ten years do sum up
   Our days and years, we see;
   Or, if, by reason of more strength,
   In some fourscore they be:

Yet doth the strength of such old men
But grief and labour prove;
For it is soon cut off, and we
Fly hence, and soon remove.

11 Who knows the power of thy wrath?
According to thy fear
12 So is thy wrath: Lord, teach thou us
Our end in mind to bear;

And so to count our days, that we
Our hearts may still apply
To learn thy wisdom and thy truth,
That we may live thereby.

13 Turn yet again to us, O Lord,
How long thus shall it be?
Let it repent thee now for those
That servants are to thee.

14 O with thy tender mercies, Lord,
Us early satisfy;
So we rejoice shall all our days,
And still be glad in thee.

15 According as the days have been,
Wherein we grief have had,
And years wherein we ill have seen,
So do thou make us glad.

16 O let thy work and power appear
Thy servants' face before;
And show unto their children dear
Thy glory evermore:

17 And let the beauty of the Lord
Our God be us upon:
And our hands' works establish
thou,
Establish them each one.

91   C.M.

vv 1-4, 5-13, 14-16

1 He that doth in the secret place
Of the most High reside,
Under the shade of him that is
The Almighty shall abide.

2 I of the Lord my God will say,
He is my refuge still,
He is my fortress, and my God,
And in him trust I will.

3 Assuredly he shall thee save,
And give deliverance
From subtle fowler's snare, and
from
The noisome pestilence.

4 His feathers shall thee hide; thy
trust
Under his wings shall be:
His faithfulness shall be a shield
And buckler unto thee.

5 Thou shalt not need to be afraid
For terrors of the night;
Nor for the arrow that doth fly
By day, while it is light;

6 Nor for the pestilence, that walks
In darkness secretly;
Nor for destruction, that doth
waste
At noon-day openly.

7 A thousand at thy side shall fall,
On thy right hand shall lie
Ten thousand dead; yet unto thee
It shall not once come nigh.

8 Only thou with thine eyes shalt
look,
And a beholder be;
And thou therein the just reward
Of wicked men shalt see.

9 Because the Lord, who constantly
My refuge is alone,
Ev'n the most High, is made by
thee
Thy habitation;

10 No plague shall near thy dwelling
come;
No ill shall thee befall:
11 For thee to keep in all thy ways
His angels charge he shall.

12 They in their hands shall bear thee
up,
Still waiting thee upon;
Lest thou at any time should'st
dash
Thy foot against a stone.

13 Upon the adder thou shalt tread,
   And on the lion strong;
   Thy feet on dragons trample shall,
   And on the lions young.

14 Because on me he set his love,
   I'll save and set him free;
   Because my great name he hath
      known,
   I will him set on high.

15 He'll call on me, I'll answer him;
   I will be with him still
   In trouble, to deliver him,
   And honour him I will.

16 With length of days unto his mind
   I will him satisfy;
   I also my salvation
   Will cause his eyes to see.

92 C.M.

A Psalm or Song for the Sabbath day.
vv 1-4, 5-11, 12-15

1 To render thanks unto the Lord
   It is a comely thing,
   And to thy name, O thou most
      High,
   Due praise aloud to sing.

2 Thy loving-kindness to show forth
   When shines the morning light;
   And to declare thy faithfulness
   With pleasure ev'ry night.

3 On a ten-stringed instrument,
   Upon the psaltery,
   And on the harp with solemn
      sound,
   And grave sweet melody.

4 For thou, Lord, by thy mighty works
   Hast made my heart right glad;
   And I will triumph in the works
   Which by thine hands were made.

5 How great, Lord, are thy works!
      each thought
   Of thine a deep it is:
6 A brutish man it knoweth not;
   Fools understand not this.

7 When ev'n like unto the grass
   Springs up the wicked race,
   And workers of iniquity
   Do flourish all apace;

   It is that they for ever may
   Destroyed be and slain;
8 But thou, O Lord, art the most
      High,
   For ever to remain.

9 For, lo, thine enemies, O Lord,
   Thine enemies perish shall;
   The workers of iniquity
   Shall be dispersed all.

10 But thou shalt, like unto the horn
   Of th' unicorn, exalt
   My horn on high: thou with fresh
      oil
   Anoint me also shalt.

11 Mine eyes shall also my desire
   See on mine enemies;
   Mine ears shall of the wicked hear
   That do against me rise.

12 But like the palm-tree flourishing
   Shall be the righteous one;
   He shall like to the cedar grow
   That is in Lebanon.

13 Those that within the house of God
   Are planted by his grace,
   They shall grow up, and flourish all
   In our God's holy place.

14 And in old age, when others fade,
   They fruit still forth shall bring;
   They shall be fat, and full of sap,
   And aye be flourishing;

15 To show that upright is the Lord:
   He is a rock to me;
   And he from all unrighteousness
   Is altogether free.

93 C.M.

1 The Lord doth reign, and clothed is
    he
  With majesty most bright;
  His works do show him clothed to
    be,
  And girt about with might.

  The world is also stablished,
  That it cannot depart.
2 Thy throne is fixed of old, and thou
  From everlasting art.

3 The floods, O Lord, have lifted up,
  They lifted up their voice;
  The floods have lifted up their
    waves,
  And made a mighty noise.

4 But yet the Lord, that is on high,
  Is more of might by far
  Than noise of many waters is,
  Or great sea-billows are.

5 Thy testimonies ev'ry one
  In faithfulness excel;
  And holiness for ever, Lord,
  Thine house becometh well.

94 C.M.

vv 1-8, 9-13, 14-19, 20-23

1 O Lord God, unto whom alone
  All vengeance doth belong;
  O mighty God, who vengeance
    own'st,
  Shine forth, avenging wrong.

2 Lift up thyself, thou of the earth
  The sovereign Judge that art;
  And unto those that are so proud
  A due reward impart.

3 How long, O mighty God, shall
    they
  Who vile and wicked be,
  How long shall they who wicked
    are
  Thus triumph haughtily?

4 How long shall things most hard
    by them
  Be uttered and told?
  And all that work iniquity
  To boast themselves be bold?

5 Thy folk they break in pieces, Lord,
  Thine heritage oppress:
6 The widow they and stranger slay,
  And kill the fatherless.

7 Yet say they, God it shall not see,
  Nor God of Jacob know.
8 Ye brutish people! understand;
  Fools! when wise will ye grow?

9 The Lord did plant the ear of man,
  And hear then shall not he?
  He only formed the eye, and then
  Shall he not clearly see?

10 He that the nations doth correct,
  Shall he not chastise you?
  He knowledge unto man doth
    teach,
  And shall himself not know?

11 Man's thoughts to be but vanity
  The Lord doth well discern.
12 Blessed is the man thou
    chastenest, Lord,
  And mak'st thy law to learn:

13 That thou mayest give him rest
    from days
  Of sad adversity,
  Until the pit be digged for those
  That work iniquity.

14 For sure the Lord will not cast off
  Those that his people be,
  Neither his own inheritance
  Quit and forsake will he:

15 But judgment unto righteousness
  Shall yet return again;
  And all shall follow after it
  That are right-hearted men.

16 Who will rise up for me against
Those that do wickedly?
Who will stand up for me 'gainst
those
That work iniquity?

17 Unless the Lord had been my help
When I was sore oppressed,
Almost my soul had in the house
Of silence been at rest.

18 When I had uttered this word,
(My foot doth slip away,)
Thy mercy held me up, O Lord,
Thy goodness did me stay.

19 Amidst the multitude of thoughts
Which in my heart do fight,
My soul, lest it be overcharged,
Thy comforts do delight.

20 Shall of iniquity the throne
Have fellowship with thee,
Which mischief, cunningly
contrived,
Doth by a law decree?

21 Against the righteous souls they
join,
They guiltless blood condemn.
22 But of my refuge God's the rock,
And my defence from them.

23 On them their own iniquity
The Lord shall bring and lay,
And cut them off in their own sin;
Our Lord God shall them slay.

95 C.M.

1 O come, let us sing to the Lord:
Come, let us every one
A joyful noise make to the Rock
Of our salvation.

2 Let us before his presence come
With praise and thankful voice;
Let us sing psalms to him with
grace,
And make a joyful noise.

3 For God, a great God, and great
King,
Above all gods he is.
4 Depths of the earth are in his hand,
The strength of hills is his.

5 To him the spacious sea belongs,
For he the same did make;
The dry land also from his hands
Its form at first did take.

6 O come, and let us worship him,
Let us bow down withal,
And on our knees before the Lord
Our Maker let us fall.

7 For he's our God, the people we
Of his own pasture are,
And of his hand the sheep; to-day,
If ye his voice will hear,

8 Then harden not your hearts, as in
The provocation,
As in the desert, on the day
Of the temptation:

9 When me your fathers tempt'd and
prov'd,
And did my working see;
10 Ev'n for the space of forty years
This race hath grieved me.

I said, This people errs in heart,
My ways they do not know:
11 To whom I sware in wrath, that to
My rest they should not go.

96 C.M.

vv 1-7, 8-13

1 O sing a new song to the Lord:
Sing all the earth to God.
2 To God sing, bless his name, show
still
His saving health abroad.

3 Among the heathen nations
His glory do declare;
And unto all the people show
His works that wondrous are

4 For great's the Lord, and greatly he
   Is to be magnified;
   Yea, worthy to be feared is he
   Above all gods beside.

5 For all the gods are idols dumb,
   Which blinded nations fear;
   But our God is the Lord, by whom
   The heavens created were.

6 Great honour is before his face,
   And majesty divine;
   Strength is within his holy place,
   And there doth beauty shine.

7 Do ye ascribe unto the Lord,
   Of people every tribe,
   Glory do ye unto the Lord,
   And mighty power ascribe.

8 Give ye the glory to the Lord
   That to his name is due;
   Come ye into his courts, and bring
   An offering with you.

9 In beauty of his holiness,
   O do the Lord adore;
   Likewise let all the earth
      throughout
   Tremble his face before.

10 Among the heathen say, God
      reigns;
   The world shall stedfastly
   Be fixed from moving; he shall
      judge
   The people righteously.

11 Let heavens be glad before the
      Lord,
   And let the earth rejoice;
   Let seas, and all that is therein,
   Cry out, and make a noise.

12 Let fields rejoice, and every thing
   That springeth of the earth:
   Then woods and every tree shall
      sing
   With gladness and with mirth

13 Before the Lord; because he comes,
   To judge the earth comes he:
   He'll judge the world with
      righteousness,
   The people faithfully.

97 C.M.

vv 1-7, 8-12

1 God reigneth, let the earth be glad,
   And isles rejoice each one.
2 Dark clouds him compass; and in
      right
   With judgment dwells his throne.

3 Fire goes before him, and his foes
   It burns up round about:
4 His lightnings lighten did the
      world;
   Earth saw, and shook throughout.

5 Hills at the presence of the Lord,
   Like wax, did melt away;
   Ev'n at the presence of the Lord
   Of all the earth, I say.

6 The heavens declare his
      righteousness,
   All men his glory see.
7 All who serve graven images,
   Confounded let them be.

   Who do of idols boast themselves,
   Let shame upon them fall:
   Ye that are called gods, see that
   Ye do him worship all.

8 Sion did hear, and joyful was,
   Glad Judah's daughters were;
   They much rejoiced, O Lord,
      because
   Thy judgments did appear.

9 For thou, O Lord, art high above
   All things on earth that are;
   Above all other gods thou art
   Exalted very far.

10 Hate ill, all ye that love the Lord:
   His saints' souls keepeth he;
   And from the hands of wicked men
   He sets them safe and free.

11 For all those that be righteous
Sown is a joyful light,
And gladness sown is for all those
That are in heart upright.

12 Ye righteous, in the Lord rejoice;
Express your thankfulness,
When ye into your memory
Do call his holiness.

98 C.M.

1 O sing a new song to the Lord,
For wonders he hath done:
His right hand and his holy arm
Him victory hath won.

2 The Lord God his salvation
Hath caused to be known;
His justice in the heathen's sight
He openly hath shown.

3 He mindful of his grace and truth
To Israel's house hath been;
And the salvation of our God
All ends of the earth have seen.

4 Let all the earth unto the Lord
Send forth a joyful noise;
Lift up your voice aloud to him,
Sing praises, and rejoice.

5 With harp, with harp, and voice of
psalms,
Unto Jehovah sing:
6 With trumpets, cornets, gladly
sound
Before the Lord the King.

7 Let seas and all their fullness roar;
The world, and dwellers there;
8 Let floods clap hands, and let the
hills
Together joy declare

9 Before the Lord; because he comes,
To judge the earth comes he:
He'll judge the world with
righteousness,
His folk with equity.

99 C.M.

vv 1-5, 6-9

1 Th' eternal Lord doth reign as king,
Let all the people quake;
He sits between the cherubims,
Let th' earth be moved and shake.

2 The Lord in Sion great and high
Above all people is;
3 Thy great and dreadful name (for it
Is holy) let them bless.

4 The king's strength also judgment
loves;
Thou settlest equity:
Just judgment thou dost execute
In Jacob righteously.

5 The Lord our God exalt on high,
And reverently do ye
Before his footstool worship him:
The Holy One is he.

6 Moses and Aaron 'mong his
priests,
Samuel, with them that call
Upon his name: these called on
God,
And he them answered all.

7 Within the pillar of the cloud
He unto them did speak:
The testimonies he them taught,
And laws, they did not break.

8 Thou answeredst them, O Lord our
God;
Thou wast a God that gave
Pardon to them, though on their
deeds
Thou wouldest vengeance have.

9 Do ye exalt the Lord our God,
And at his holy hill
Do ye him worship: for the Lord
Our God is holy still.

100 First Version

L.M.

A Psalm of praise.

1 All people that on earth do dwell,
Sing to the Lord with cheerful
voice.

2 Gladly him serve, his praise forth
tell,
Come ye before him and rejoice.

3 Know that the Lord is God indeed;
Without our aid he did us make:
We are his flock, he doth us feed,
And for his sheep he doth us take.

4 O enter then his gates with praise,
Approach with joy his courts unto:
Praise, laud, and bless his name
always,
For it is seemly so to do.

5 For why? the Lord our God is good,
His mercy is for ever sure;
His truth at all times firmly stood,
And shall from age to age endure.

100 Second Version

C.M.

A Psalm of praise.

1 O all ye lands, unto the Lord
Make ye a joyful noise.

2 Serve God with gladness, him
before
Come with a singing voice.

3 Know ye the Lord that he is God;
Not we, but he us made:
We are his people, and the sheep
Within his pasture fed.

4 Enter his gates and courts with
praise,
To thank him go ye thither:
To him express your thankfulness,
And bless his name together.

5 Because the Lord our God is good,
His mercy faileth never;
And to all generations
His truth endureth ever.

101

C.M.

A Psalm of David.

1 I mercy will and judgment sing,
Lord, I will sing to thee.

2 With wisdom in a perfect way
Shall my behaviour be.

O when, in kindness unto me,
Wilt thou be pleased to come?
I with a perfect heart will walk
Within my house at home.

3 I will endure no wicked thing
Before mine eyes to be:
I hate their work that turn aside,
It shall not cleave to me.

4 A stubborn and a froward heart
Depart quite from me shall;
A person giv'n to wickedness
I will not know at all.

5 I'll cut him off that slandereth
His neighbour privily:
The haughty heart I will not bear,
Nor him that looketh high.

6 Upon the faithful of the land
Mine eyes shall be, that they
May dwell with me: he shall me
serve
That walks in perfect way.

7 Who of deceit a worker is
In my house shall not dwell;
And in my presence shall he not
Remain that lies doth tell.

8 Yea, all the wicked of the land
Early destroy will I;
All from God's city to cut off
That work iniquity.

102 First Version C.M.

A Prayer of the afflicted, when he is
overwhelmed, and poureth out his
complaint before the Lord.
vv 1-12, 13-22, 23-28

1 O Lord, unto my prayer give ear,
My cry let come to thee;
2 And in the day of my distress
Hide not thy face from me.

Give ear to me; what time I call,
To answer me make haste:
3 For, as an hearth, my bones are
    burnt,
My days, like smoke, do waste.

4 My heart within me smitten is,
And it is withered
Like very grass; so that I do
Forget to eat my bread.

5 By reason of my groaning voice
My bones cleave to my skin.
6 Like pelican in wilderness
Forsaken I have been:

I like an owl in desert am,
That nightly there doth moan;
7 I watch, and like a sparrow am
On the house-top alone.

8 My bitter enemies all day
Reproaches cast on me;
And, being mad at me, with rage
Against me sworn they be.

9 For why? I ashes eaten have
Like bread, in sorrows deep;
My drink I also mingled have
With tears that I did weep.

10 Thy wrath and indignation
Did cause this grief and pain;
For thou hast lifted me on high,
And cast me down again.

11 My days are like unto a shade,
Which doth declining pass;
And I am dried and withered,
Ev'n like unto the grass.

12 But thou, Lord, everlasting art,
And thy remembrance shall
Continually endure, and be
To generations all.

13 Thou shalt arise, and mercy have
Upon thy Sion yet;
The time to favour her is come,
The time that thou hast set.

14 For in her rubbish and her stones
Thy servants pleasure take;
Yea, they the very dust thereof
Do favour for her sake.

15 So shall the heathen people fear
The Lord's most holy name;
And all the kings on earth shall
    dread
Thy glory and thy fame.

16 When Sion by the mighty Lord
Built up again shall be,
In glory then and majesty
To men appear shall he.

17 The prayer of the destitute
He surely will regard;
Their prayer will he not despise,
By him it shall be heard.

18 For generations yet to come
This shall be on record:
So shall the people that shall be
Created praise the Lord.

19 He from his sanctuary's height
Hath downward cast his eye;
And from his glorious throne in
    heaven
The Lord the earth did spy;

20 That of the mournful prisoner
The groanings he might hear,
To set them free that unto death
By men appointed are:

21 That they in Sion may declare
The Lord's most holy name,
And publish in Jerusalem
The praises of the same;

22 When as the people gather shall
In troops with one accord,
When kingdoms shall assembled
be
To serve the highest Lord.

23 My wonted strength and force he
hath
Abated in the way,
And he my days hath shortened:
24 Thus therefore did I say,

My God, in mid-time of my days
Take thou me not away:
From age to age eternally
Thy years endure and stay.

25 The firm foundation of the earth
Of old time thou hast laid;
The heavens also are the work
Which thine own hands have
made.

26 Thou shalt for evermore endure,
But they shall perish all;
Yea, every one of them wax old,
Like to a garment, shall:

Thou, as a vesture, shalt them
change,
And they shall changed be:
27 But thou the same art, and thy
years
Are to eternity.

28 The children of thy servants shall
Continually endure;
And in thy sight, O Lord, their seed
Shall be established sure.

102 Second Version   L.M.

*A Prayer of the afflicted, when he is
overwhelmed, and poureth out his
complaint before the Lord.*
vv 1-12, 13-22, 23-28

1 Lord, hear my prayer, and let my
cry
Have speedy access unto thee;
2 In day of my calamity
O hide not thou thy face from me.

Hear when I call to thee; that day
An answer speedily return:
3 My days, like smoke, consume
away,
And, as an hearth, my bones do
burn.

4 My heart is wounded very sore,
And withered, like grass doth fade:
I am forgetful grown therefore
To take and eat my daily bread.

5 By reason of my smart within,
And voice of my most grievous
groans,
My flesh consumed is, my skin,
All parched, doth cleave unto my
bones.

6 The pelican of wilderness,
The owl in desert, I do match;
7 And, sparrow-like, companionless,
Upon the house's top, I watch.

8 I all day long am made a scorn,
Reproached by my malicious foes:
The madmen are against me
sworn,
The men against me that arose.

9 For I have ashes eaten up,
To me as if they had been bread;
And with my drink I in my cup
Of bitter tears a mixture made.

10 Because thy wrath was not
appeased,
And dreadful indignation:
Therefore it was that thou me
raised,
And thou again didst cast me
down.

11 My days are like a shade alway,
Which doth declining swiftly pass;
And I am withered away,
Much like unto the fading grass.

12 But thou, O Lord, shalt still
endure,
From change and all mutation free,
And to all generations sure
Shall thy remembrance ever be.

13 Thou shalt arise, and mercy yet
Thou to mount Sion shalt extend:
Her time for favour which was set,
Behold, is now come to an end.

14 Thy saints take pleasure in her
stones,
Her very dust to them is dear.
15 All heathen lands and kingly
thrones
On earth thy glorious name shall
fear.

16 God in his glory shall appear,
When Sion he builds and repairs.
17 He shall regard and lend his ear
Unto the needy's humble prayers:

Th' afflicted's prayer he will not
scorn.
18 All times this shall be on record:
And generations yet unborn
Shall praise and magnify the Lord.

19 He from his holy place looked
down,
The earth he viewed from heaven
on high;
20 To hear the prisoner's mourning
groan,
And free them that are doomed to
die;

21 That Sion, and Jerusalem too,
His name and praise may well
record,
22 When people and the kingdoms do
Assemble all to praise the Lord.

23 My strength he weakened in the
way,
My days of life he shortened.
24 My God, O take me not away
In mid-time of my days, I said:

Thy years throughout all ages last.
25 Of old thou hast established
The earth's foundation firm and
fast:
Thy mighty hands the heavens have
made.

26 They perish shall, as garments do,
But thou shalt evermore endure;
As vestures, thou shalt change
them so;
And they shall all be changed sure:

27 But from all changes thou art free;
Thy endless years do last for aye.
28 Thy servants, and their seed who
be,
Established shall before thee stay.

103 C.M.

A Psalm of David.
vv 1-7, 8-12, 13- 18, 19-22

1 O thou my soul, bless God the
Lord;
And all that in me is
Be stirred up his holy name
To magnify and bless.

2 Bless, O my soul, the Lord thy God,
And not forgetful be
Of all his gracious benefits
He hath bestowed on thee.

3 All thine iniquities who doth
Most graciously forgive:
Who thy diseases all and pains
Doth heal, and thee relieve.

4 Who doth redeem thy life, that
thou
To death mayest not go down;
Who thee with loving-kindness
doth
And tender mercies crown:

5 Who with abundance of good
things
Doth satisfy thy mouth;
So that, ev'n as the eagle's age,
Renewed is thy youth.

6 God righteous judgment executes
For all oppressed ones.
7 His ways to Moses, he his acts
Made known to Israel's sons.

8 The Lord our God is merciful,
And he is gracious,
Long-suffering, and slow to wrath,
In mercy plenteous.

9 He will not chide continually,
Nor keep his anger still.
10 With us he dealt not as we sinned,
Nor did requite our ill.

11 For as the heaven in its height
The earth surmounteth far;
So great to those that do him fear
His tender mercies are:

12 As far as east is distant from
The west, so far hath he
From us removed, in his love,
All our iniquity.

13 Such pity as a father hath
Unto his children dear;
Like pity shows the Lord to such
As worship him in fear.

14 For he remembers we are dust,
And he our frame well knows.
15 Frail man, his days are like the
grass,
As flower in field he grows:

16 For over it the wind doth pass,
And it away is gone;
And of the place where once it was
It shall no more be known.

17 But unto them that do him fear
God's mercy never ends;
And to their children's children
still
His righteousness extends:

18 To such as keep his covenant,
And mindful are alway
Of his most just commandments
all,
That they may them obey.

19 The Lord prepared hath his throne
In heavens firm to stand;
And everything that being hath
His kingdom doth command.

20 O ye his angels, that excel
In strength, bless ye the Lord;
Ye who obey what he commands,
And hearken to his word.

21 O bless and magnify the Lord,
Ye glorious hosts of his;
Ye ministers, that do fulfil
Whate'er his pleasure is.

22 O bless the Lord, all ye his works,
Wherewith the world is stored
In his dominions everywhere.
My soul, bless thou the Lord.

104   C.M.

vv 1-9, 10-18, 19-24, 25-30, 31-35

1 Bless God, my soul. O Lord my
God,
Thou art exceeding great;
With honour and with majesty
Thou clothed art in state.

2 With light, as with a robe, thyself
Thou coverest about;
And, like unto a curtain, thou
The heavens stretchest out.

3 Who of his chambers doth the
beams
Within the waters lay;
Who doth the clouds his chariot
make,
On wings of wind make way.

4 Who flaming fire his ministers,
His angels spir'ts, doth make:
5 Who earth's foundations did lay,
That it should never shake.

6 Thou didst it cover with the deep,
As with a garment spread:
The waters stood above the hills,
When thou the word but said.

7 But at the voice of thy rebuke
They fled, and would not stay;
They at thy thunder's dreadful
voice
Did haste them fast away.

8 They by the mountains do ascend,
And by the valley-ground
Descend, unto that very place
Which thou for them didst found.

9 Thou hast a bound unto them set,
That they may not pass over,
That they do not return again
The face of earth to cover.

10 He to the valleys sends the springs,
Which run among the hills:

11 They to all beasts of field give
drink,
Wild asses drink their fills.

12 By them the fowls of heaven shall
have
Their habitation,
Which do among the branches
sing
With delectation.

13 He from his chambers watereth
The hills, when they are dried:
With fruit and increase of thy
works
The earth is satisfied.

14 For cattle he makes grass to grow,
He makes the herb to spring
For use of man, that food to him
He from the earth may bring;

15 And wine, that to the heart of man
Doth cheerfulness impart,
Oil that his face makes shine, and
bread
That strengtheneth his heart.

16 The trees of God are full of sap;
The cedars that do stand
In Lebanon, which planted were
By his almighty hand.

17 Birds of the air upon their boughs
Do choose their nests to make;
As for the stork, the fir-tree she
Doth for her dwelling take.

18 The lofty mountains for wild goats
A place of refuge be;
The conies also to the rocks
Do for their safety flee.

19 He sets the moon in heav'n, there
by
The seasons to discern:
From him the sun his certain time
Of going down doth learn.

20 Thou darkness mak'st, 'tis night,
then beasts
Of forests creep abroad.

21 The lions young roar for their prey,
And seek their meat from God.

22 The sun doth rise, and home they
flock,
Down in their dens they lie.

23 Man goes to work, his labour he
Doth to the ev'ning ply.

24 How manifold, Lord, are thy
works!
In wisdom wonderful
Thou every one of them hast made;
Earth of thy wealth is full:

25 So is this great and spacious sea,
Wherein things creeping are,
Which numbered cannot be; and
beasts
Both great and small are there.

26 There ships go; there thou mak'st
to play
Leviathan the great.

27 These all wait on thee, that thou
mayest
In due time give them meat.

28 That which thou givest unto them
They gather for their food;
Thine hand thou openest liberally,
They filled are with good.

29 Thou hid'st thy face; they troubled
are,
Their breath thou tak'st away;
Then do they die, and to their dust
Return again do they.

30 Thy quick'ning spirit thou sendest
forth,
Then they created be;
And then the earth's decayed face
Renewed is by thee.

31 The glory of the mighty Lord
Continue shall for ever:
The Lord Jehovah shall rejoice
In all his works together.

32 Earth, as affrighted, trembleth all,
If he on it but look;
And if the mountains he but touch,
They presently do smoke.

33 I will sing to the Lord most high,
So long as I shall live;
And while I being have I shall
To my God praises give.

34 Of him my meditation shall
Sweet thoughts to me afford;
And as for me, I will rejoice
In God, my only Lord.

35 From earth let sinners be consumed,
Let bad men no more be.
O thou my soul, bless thou the
Lord.
Praise to the Lord give ye.

105   C.M.

vv 1-7, 8-15, 16-22, 23-37, 38-45

1 Give thanks to God, call on his
name;
To men his deeds make known.
2 Sing ye to him, sing psalms;
proclaim
His wondrous works each one.

3 See that ye in his holy name
To glory do accord;
And let the heart of every one
Rejoice that seeks the Lord.

4 The Lord Almighty, and his
strength,
With steadfast hearts seek ye:
His blessed and his gracious face
Seek ye continually.

5 Think on the works that he hath
done,
Which admiration breed;
His wonders, and the judgments
all
Which from his mouth proceed;

6 O ye that are of Abraham's race,
His servant well approv'n;
And ye that Jacob's children are,
Whom he chose for his own.

7 Because he, and he only, is
The mighty Lord our God;
And his most righteous judgments
are
In all the earth abroad.

8 His cov'nant he remembered hath,
That it may ever stand:
To thousand generations
The word he did command.

9 Which covenant he firmly made
With faithful Abraham,
And unto Isaac, by his oath,
He did renew the same:

10 And unto Jacob, for a law,
He made it firm and sure,
A covenant to Israel,
Which ever should endure.

11 He said, I will give Canaan's land
For heritage to you;
12 While they were strangers there,
and few,
In number very few:

13 While yet they went from land to
land
Without a sure abode;
And while through sundry
kingdoms they
Did wander far abroad;

14 Yet, notwithstanding suffered he
No man to do them wrong:
Yea, for their sakes, he did reprove
Kings, who were great and strong.

15 Thus did he say, Touch ye not those
   That mine anointed be,
   Nor do the prophets any harm
   That do pertain to me.

16 He called for famine on the land,
   He brake the staff of bread:
17 But yet he sent a man before,
   By whom they should be fed;

   Ev'n Joseph, whom unnat'rally
   Sell for a slave did they;
18 Whose feet with fetters they did
   hurt,
   And he in irons lay;

19 Until the time that his word came
   To give him liberty;
   The word and purpose of the Lord
   Did him in prison try.

20 Then sent the king, and did
   command
   That he enlarged should be:
   He that the people's ruler was
   Did send to set him free.

21 A lord to rule his family
   He raised him, as most fit;
   To him of all that he possessed
   He did the charge commit:

22 That he might at his pleasure bind
   The princes of the land;
   And he might teach his senators
   Wisdom to understand.

23 The people then of Israel
   Down into Egypt came;
   And Jacob also sojourned
   Within the land of Ham.

24 And he did greatly by his power
   Increase his people there;
   And stronger than their enemies
   They by his blessing were.

25 Their heart he turned to envy
   His folk maliciously,
   With those that his own servants
   were
   To deal in subtlety.

26 His servant Moses he did send,
   Aaron his chosen one.
27 By these his signs and wonders
   great
   In Ham's land were made known.

28 Darkness he sent, and made it dark;
   His word they did obey.
29 He turned their waters into blood,
   And he their fish did slay.

30 The land in plenty brought forth
   frogs
   In chambers of their kings.
31 His word all sorts of flies and lice
   In all their borders brings.

32 He hail for rain, and flaming fire
   Into their land he sent:
33 And he their vines and fig-trees
   smote:
   Trees of their coasts he rent.

34 He spake, and caterpillars came,
   Locusts did much abound;
35 Which in their land all herbs
   consumed,
   And all fruits of their ground.

36 He smote all first-born in their
   land,
   Chief of their strength each one.
37 With gold and silver brought them
   forth,
   Weak in their tribes were none.

38 Egypt was glad when forth they
   went,
   Their fear on them did light.
39 He spread a cloud for covering,
   And fire to shine by night.

40 They asked, and he brought quails:
   with bread
   Of heaven he filled them.
41 He opened rocks, floods gushed,
   and ran
   In deserts like a stream.

42 For on his holy promise he,
   And servant Abraham, thought.
43 With joy his people, his elect
   With gladness, forth he brought.

44 And unto them the pleasant lands
He of the heathen gave;
That of the people's labour they
Inheritance might have.

45 That they his statutes might
observe
According to his word;
And that they might his laws obey.
Give praise unto the Lord.

106 C.M.

vv 1-5, 6-8, 9-15, 16-18, 19-27,
28-31, 32-42, 43-48

1 Give praise and thanks unto the
Lord,
For bountiful is he;
His tender mercy doth endure
Unto eternity.

2 God's mighty works who can
express?
Or show forth all his praise?

3 Blessed are they that judgment
keep,
And justly do always.

4 Remember me, Lord, with that love
Which thou to thine dost bear;
With thy salvation, O my God,
To visit me draw near:

5 That I thy chosen's good may see,
And in their joy rejoice;
And may with thine inheritance
Triumph with cheerful voice.

6 We with our fathers sinned have,
And of iniquity
Too long we have the workers
been;
We have done wickedly.

7 The wonders great, which thou, O
Lord,
Didst work in Egypt land,
Our fathers, though they saw, yet
them
They did not understand:

And they thy mercies' multitude
Kept not in memory;
But at the sea, ev'n the Red sea,
Provoked him grievously.

8 Nevertheless he saved them,
Ev'n for his own name's sake;
That so he might to be well known
His mighty power make.

9 When he the Red sea did rebuke,
Then dried up it was:
Through depths, as through the
wilderness,
He safely made them pass.

10 From hands of those that hated
them
He did his people save;
And from the enemy's cruel hand
To them redemption gave.

11 The waters overwhelmed their
foes;
Not one was left alive.

12 Then they believed his word, and
praise
No him in songs did give.

13 But soon did they his mighty works
Forget unthankfully,
And on his counsel and his will
Did not wait patiently;

14 They lusted in the wilderness,
In desert God did tempt.

15 He gave them what they sought,
but to
Their soul he leanness sent.

16 And against Moses in the camp
Their envy did appear;
At Aaron they, the saint of God,
Envious also were.

17 Therefore the earth did open wide,
And Dathan did devour,
And all Abiram's company
Did cover in that hour.

18 Likewise among their company
A fire was kindled then;
And so the hot consuming flame
Burnt up these wicked men.

19 Upon the hill of Horeb they
An idol-calf did frame,
A molten image they did make,
And worshipped the same.

20 And thus their glory, and their
God,
Most vainly changed they
Into the likeness of an ox
That eateth grass or hay.

21 They did forget the mighty God,
That had their saviour been,
By whom such great things
brought to pass
They had in Egypt seen.

22 In Ham's land he did wondrous
works,
Things terrible did he,
When he his mighty hand and arm
Stretched out at the Red sea.

23 Then said he, He would them
destroy,
Had not, his wrath to stay,
His chosen Moses stood in breach,
That them he should not slay.

24 Yea, they despised the pleasant
land,
Believed not his word:

25 But in their tents they murmured,
Not hearkening to the Lord.

26 Therefore in desert them to slay
He lifted up his hand:

27 'Mong nations to o'erthrow their
seed,
And scatter in each land.

28 They unto Baal-peor did
Themselves associate;
The sacrifices of the dead
They did profanely eat.

29 Thus, by their vile inventions,
They did provoke his ire;
And then upon them suddenly
The plague brake in as fire.

30 Then Phinehas rose, and justice
did,
And so the plague did cease;

31 That to all ages counted was
To him for righteousness.

32 And at the waters, where they
strove,
They did him angry make,
In such sort, that it fared ill
With Moses for their sake:

33 Because they there his spirit meek
Provoked bitterly,
So that he uttered with his lips
Words unadvisedly.

34 Nor, as the Lord commanded
them,
Did they the nations slay:

35 But with the heathen mingled
were,
And learned of them their way.

36 And they their idols served, which
did
A snare unto them turn.

37 Their sons and daughters they to
devils
In sacrifice did burn.

38 In their own children's guiltless
blood
Their hands they did imbrue,
Whom to Canaan's idols they
For sacrifices slew:

So was the land defiled with blood.

39 They stained with their own way,
And with their own inventions
A whoring they did stray.

40 Against his people kindled was
The wrath of God therefore,
Insomuch that he did his own
Inheritance abhor.

41 He gave them to the heathen's
hand;
Their foes did them command.

42 Their enemies them oppressed,
they were
Made subject to their hand.

43 He many times delivered them;
But with their counsel so
They him provoked, that for their
  sin
They were brought very low.

44 Yet their affliction he beheld,
When he did hear their cry:
45 And he for them his covenant
Did call to memory;

After his mercies' multitude
46 He did repent: And made
Them to be pitied of all those
Who did them captive lead.

47 O Lord our God, us save, and
  gather
The heathen from among,
That we thy holy name may praise
In a triumphant song.

48 Bless'd be JEHOVAH, Israel's God,
To all eternity:
Let all the people say, Amen.
Praise to the Lord give ye.

107 C.M.

vv 1-9, 10-16, 17-22, 23-32, 33-38,
39-43

1 Praise God, for he is good: for still
His mercies lasting be.
2 Let God's redeemed say so, whom
  he
From the en'my's hand did free;

3 And gathered them out of the
  lands,
From north, south, east, and west.
4 They strayed in desert's pathless
  way,
No city found to rest.

5 For thirst and hunger in them
  faints
6 Their soul. When straits them press,
They cry unto the Lord, and he
Them frees from their distress.

7 Them also in a way to walk
That right is he did guide,
That they might to a city go,
Wherein they might abide.

8 O that men to the Lord would give
Praise for his goodness then,
And for his works of wonder done
Unto the sons of men!

9 For he the soul that longing is
Doth fully satisfy;
With goodness he the hungry soul
Doth fill abundantly.

10 Such as shut up in darkness deep,
And in death's shade abide,
Whom strongly hath affliction
  bound,
And irons fast have tied:

11 Because against the words of God
They wrought rebelliously,
And they the counsel did contemn
Of him that is most High:

12 Their heart he did bring down with
  grief,
They fell, no help could have.
13 In trouble then they cried to God,
He them from straits did save.

14 He out of darkness did them bring,
And from death's shade them take;
These bands, wherewith they had
  been bound,
Asunder quite he brake.

15 O that men to the Lord would give
Praise for his goodness then,
And for his works of wonder done
Unto the sons of men!

16 Because the mighty gates of brass
In pieces he did tear,
By him in sunder also cut
The bars of iron were.

17 Fools, for their sin, and their
  offence,
Do sore affliction bear;
18 All kind of meat their soul abhors;
They to death's gates draw near.

19 In grief they cry to God; he saves
   Them from their miseries.
20 He sends his word, them heals, and them
   From their destructions frees.

21 O that men to the Lord would give
   Praise for his goodness then,
   And for his works of wonder done
   Unto the sons of men!

22 And let them sacrifice to him
   Offerings of thankfulness;
   And let them show abroad his works
   In songs of joyfulness.

23 Who go to sea in ships, and in
   Great waters trading be,
24 Within the deep these men God's works
   And his great wonders see.

25 For he commands, and forth in haste
   The stormy tempest flies,
   Which makes the sea with rolling waves
   Aloft to swell and rise.

26 They mount to heaven, then to the depths
   They do go down again;
   Their soul doth faint and melt away
   With trouble and with pain.

27 They reel and stagger like one drunk,
   at their wit's end they be:
28 Then they to God in trouble cry,
   Who them from straits doth free.

29 The storm is changed into a calm
   At his command and will;
   So that the waves, which raged before,
   Now quiet are and still.

30 Then are they glad, because at rest
   And quiet now they be:
   So to the haven he them brings,
   Which they desired to see.

31 O that men to the Lord would give
   Praise for his goodness then,
   And for his works of wonder done
   Unto the sons of men!

32 Among the people gathered
   Let them exalt his name;
   Among assembled elders spread
   His most renowned fame.

33 He to dry land turns water-springs,
   And floods to wilderness;
34 For sins of those that dwell therein,
   Fat land to barrenness.

35 The burnt and parched wilderness
   To water-pools he brings;
   The ground that was dried up before
   He turns to water-springs:

36 And there, for dwelling, he a place
   Doth to the hungry give,
   That they a city may prepare
   Commodiously to live.

37 There sow they fields, and vineyards plant,
   To yield fruits of increase.
38 His blessing makes them multiply,
   Lets not their beasts decrease.

39 Again they are diminished,
   And very low brought down,
   Through sorrow and affliction,
   And great oppression.

40 He upon princes pours contempt,
   And causeth them to stray,
   And wander in a wilderness,
   Wherein there is no way.

41 Yet setteth he the poor on high
   From all his miseries,
   And he, much like unto a flock,
   Doth make him families.

42 They that are righteous shall rejoice,
   When they the same shall see;
   And, as ashamed, stop her mouth
   Shall all iniquity.

43 Whoso is wise, and will these
     things
   Observe, and them record,
   Ev'n they shall understand the love
   And kindness of the Lord.

108   C.M.

A Song or Psalm of David.
vv 1-6, 7-13

1 My heart is fixed, Lord; I will sing,
   And with my glory praise.
2 Awake up psaltery and harp;
   Myself I'll early raise.

3 I'll praise thee 'mong the people,
     Lord;
   'Mong nations sing will I:
4 For above heav'n thy mercy's great,
   Thy truth doth reach the sky.

5 Be thou above the heavens, Lord,
   Exalted gloriously;
   Thy glory all the earth above
   Be lifted up on high.

6 That those who thy beloved are
   Delivered may be,
   O do thou save with thy right hand,
   And answer give to me.

7 God in his holiness hath said,
   Herein I will take pleasure;
   Shechem I will divide, and forth
   Will Succoth's valley measure.

8 Gilead I claim as mine by right;
   Manasseh mine shall be;
   Ephraim is of my head the
     strength;
   Judah gives laws for me;

9 Moab's my washing-pot; my shoe
   I'll over Edom throw;
   Over the land of Palestine
   I will in triumph go.

10 O who is he will bring me to
   The city fortified?
   O who is he that to the land
   Of Edom will me guide?

11 O God, thou who hadst cast us off,
   This thing wilt thou not do?
   And wilt not thou, ev'n thou, O
     God,
   Forth with our armies go?

12 Do thou from trouble give us help,
   For helpless is man's aid.
13 Through God we shall do valiantly;
   Our foes he shall down tread.

109   C.M.

To the chief Musician, A Psalm of
David.
vv 1-5, 6-11, 12-20, 21-27, 28-31

1 O thou the God of all my praise,
   Do thou not hold thy peace;
2 For mouths of wicked men to
     speak
   Against me do not cease:

   The mouths of vile deceitful men
   Against me opened be;
   And with a false and lying tongue
   They have accused me.

3 They did beset me round about
   With words of hateful spite:
   And though to them no cause I
     gave,
   Against me they did fight.

4 They for my love became my foes,
   But I me set to pray.
5 Evil for good, hatred for love,
   To me they did repay.

6 Set thou the wicked over him;
   And upon his right hand
   Against him in the judgment give,
   Ev'n Satan, leave to stand.

7 And when by thee he shall be
     judged,
   Let him condemned be;
   And let his prayer be turned to sin,
   When he shall call on thee.

8 Few be his days, and in his room
   His charge another take.
9 His children let be fatherless,
   His wife a widow make.

10 His children let be vagabonds,
And beg continually;
And from their places desolate
Seek bread for their supply.

11 Let covetous extortioners
Catch all he hath away:
Of all for which he laboured hath
Let strangers make a prey.

12 Let there be none to pity him,
Let there be none at all
That on his children fatherless
Will let his mercy fall.

13 Let his posterity from earth
Cut off for ever be,
And in a later age their name
Be blotted out by thee.

14 Let God his father's wickedness
Still to remembrance call;
And never let his mother's sin
Be blotted out at all.

15 But let them all before the Lord
Appear continually,
That he may wholly from the earth
Cut off their memory.

16 Because he mercy minded not,
But persecuted still
The poor and needy, that he might
The broken-hearted kill.

17 As he in cursing pleasure took,
So let it to him fall;
As he delighted not to bless,
So bless him not at all.

18 As cursing he like clothes put on,
Into his bowels so,
Like water, and into his bones,
Like oil, down let it go.

19 Like to the garment let it be
Which doth himself array,
And for a girdle, wherewith he
Is girt about alway.

20 From God let this be their reward
That en'mies are to me,
And their reward that speak against
My soul maliciously.

21 But do thou, for thine own name's
sake,
O God the Lord, for me:
Since good and sweet thy mercy is,
From trouble set me free.

22 For I am poor and indigent,
Afflicted sore am I,
My heart within me also is
Wounded exceedingly.

23 I pass like a declining shade,
Am like the locust tossed:
24 My knees through fasting
weakened are,
My flesh hath fatness lost.

25 I also am a vile reproach
Unto them made to be;
And they that did upon me look
Did shake their heads at me.

26 O do thou help and succour me,
Who art my God and Lord:
And, for thy tender mercy's sake,
Safety to me afford:

27 That thereby they may know that
this
Is thy almighty hand;
And that thou, Lord, hast done the
same,
They may well understand.

28 Although they curse with spite, yet,
Lord,
Bless thou with loving voice:
Let them ashamed be when they
rise;
Thy servant let rejoice.

29 Let thou mine adversaries all
With shame be clothed over;
And let their own confusion
Them, as a mantle, cover.

30 But as for me, I with my mouth
Will greatly praise the Lord;
And I among the multitude
His praises will record.

31 For he shall stand at his right hand
   Who is in poverty,
   To save him from all those that
      would
   Condemn his soul to die.

110 C.M.

A Psalm of David.

1 The Lord did say unto my Lord,
   Sit thou at my right hand,
   Until I make thy foes a stool,
   Whereon thy feet may stand.

2 The Lord shall out of Sion send
   The rod of thy great power:
   In midst of all thine enemies
   Be thou the governor.

3 A willing people in thy day
   Of power shall come to thee,
   In holy beauties from morn's
      womb;
   Thy youth like dew shall be.

4 The Lord himself hath made an
      oath,
   And will repent him never,
   Of th' order of Melchisedec
   Thou art a priest for ever.

5 The glorious and mighty Lord,
   That sits at thy right hand,
   Shall, in his day of wrath, strike
      through
   Kings that do him withstand.

6 He shall among the heathen judge,
   He shall with bodies dead
   The places fill: o'er many lands
   He wound shall every head.

7 The brook that runneth in the way
   With drink shall him supply;
   And, for this cause, in triumph he
   Shall lift his head on high.

111 C.M.

1 Praise ye the Lord: with my whole
      heart
   I will God's praise declare,
   Where the assemblies of the just
   And congregations are.

2 The whole works of the Lord our
      God
   Are great above all measure,
   Sought out they are of every one
   That doth therein take pleasure.

3 His work most honourable is,
   Most glorious and pure,
   And his untainted righteousness
   For ever doth endure.

4 His works most wonderful he hath
   Made to be thought upon:
   The Lord is gracious, and he is
   Full of compassion.

5 He giveth meat unto all those
   That truly do him fear;
   And evermore his covenant
   He in his mind will bear.

6 He did the power of his works
   Unto his people show,
   When he the heathen's heritage
   Upon them did bestow.

7 His handiworks are truth and right;
   All his commands are sure:
8 And, done in truth and uprightness,
   They evermore endure.

9 He sent redemption to his folk;
   His covenant for aye
   He did command: holy his name
   And reverend alway.

10 Wisdom's beginning is God's fear:
   Good understanding they
   Have all that his commands fulfil:
   His praise endures for aye.

112 C.M.

vv 1-4, 5-10

1 Praise ye the Lord. The man is
    blessed
  That fears the Lord aright,
  He who in his commandments all
  Doth greatly take delight.

2 His seed and offspring powerful
  Shall be the earth upon:
  Of upright men blessed shall be
  The generation.

3 Riches and wealth shall ever be
  Within his house in store;
  And his unspotted righteousness
  Endures for evermore.

4 Unto the upright light doth rise,
  Though he in darkness be:
  Compassionate, and merciful,
  And righteous, is he.

5 A good man doth his favour show,
  And doth to others lend:
  He with discretion his affairs
  Will guide unto the end.

6 Surely there is not any thing
  That ever shall him move:
  The righteous man's memorial
  Shall everlasting prove.

7 When he shall evil tidings hear,
  He shall not be afraid:
  His heart is fixed, his confidence
  Upon the Lord is stayed.

8 His heart is firmly stablished,
  Afraid he shall not be,
  Until upon his enemies
  He his desire shall see.

9 He hath dispersed, giv'n to the
    poor;
  His righteousness shall be
  To ages all; with honour shall
  His horn be raised high.

10 The wicked shall it see, and fret,
   His teeth gnash, melt away:
   What wicked men do most desire
   Shall utterly decay.

113 C.M.

1 Praise God: ye servants of the Lord,
  O praise, the Lord's name praise.
2 Yea, blessed be the name of God
  From this time forth always.

3 From rising sun to where it sets,
  God's name is to be praised.
4 Above all nations God is high,
  His glory highly raised.

5 Unto the Lord our God that dwells
  On high, who can compare?
6 Himself that humbleth things to see
  In heav'n and earth that are.

7 He from the dust doth raise the
    poor,
  That very low doth lie;
  And from the dunghill lifts the man
  Oppressed with poverty;

8 That he may highly him advance,
  And with the princes set;
  With those that of his people are
  The chief, ev'n princes great.

9 The barren woman house to keep
  He maketh, and to be
  Of sons a mother full of joy.
  Praise to the Lord give ye.

114 C.M.

1 When Israel out of Egypt went,
  And did his dwelling change,
  When Jacob's house went out from
    those
  That were of language strange,

2 He Judah did his sanctuary,
  His kingdom Israel make:
3 The sea it saw, and quickly fled,
  Jordan was driven back.

4 Like rams the mountains, and like
    lambs
  The hills skipped to and fro.
5 O sea, why fledd'st thou? Jordan,
    back
  Why wast thou driven so?

6 Ye mountains great, wherefore was
 it
 That ye did skip like rams?
 And wherefore was it, little hills,
 That ye did leap like lambs?

7 O at the presence of the Lord,
 Earth, tremble thou for fear,
 While as the presence of the God
 Of Jacob doth appear:

8 Who from the hard and stony rock
 Did standing water bring;
 And by his power did turn the flint
 Into a water-spring.

115 C.M.

vv 1-11, 12-18

1 Not unto us, Lord, not to us,
 But do thou glory take
 Unto thy name, ev'n for thy truth,
 And for thy mercy's sake.

2 O wherefore should the heathen
 say,
 Where is their God now gone?

3 But our God in the heavens is,
 What pleased him he hath done.

4 Their idols silver are and gold,
 Work of men's hands they be.

5 Mouths have they, but they do not
 speak;
 And eyes, but do not see;

6 Ears have they, but they do not hear;
 Noses, but savour not;

7 Hands, feet, but handle not, nor
 walk;
 Nor speak they through their
 throat.

8 Like them their makers are, and all
 On them their trust that build.

9 O Israel, trust thou in the Lord,
 He is their help and shield.

10 O Aaron's house, trust in the Lord,
 Their help and shield is he.

11 Ye that fear God, trust in the Lord,
 Their help and shield he'll be.

12 The Lord of us hath mindful been,
 And he will bless us still:
 He will the house of Israel bless,
 Bless Aaron's house he will.

13 Both small and great, that fear the
 Lord,
 He will them surely bless.

14 The Lord will you, you and your
 seed,
 Yet more and more increase.

15 O blessed are ye of the Lord,
 Who made the earth and heaven.

16 The heaven, ev'n heavens, are
 God's, but he
 Earth to men's sons hath given.

17 The dead, nor who to silence go,
 God's praise do not record.

18 But henceforth we for ever will
 Bless God. Praise ye the Lord.

116 C.M.

vv 1-8, 9-19

1 I love the Lord, because my voice
 And prayers he did hear.

2 I, while I live, will call on him,
 Who bowed to me his ear.

3 Of death the cords and sorrows did
 About me compass round;
 The pains of hell took hold on me,
 I grief and trouble found.

4 Upon the name of God the Lord
 Then did I call, and say,
 Deliver thou my soul, O Lord,
 I do thee humbly pray.

5 God merciful and righteous is,
 Yea, gracious is our Lord.

6 God saves the meek: I was brought
 low,
 He did me help afford.

7 O thou my soul, do thou return
 Unto thy quiet rest;
 For largely, lo, the Lord to thee
 His bounty hath expressed.

8 For my distressed soul from death
Delivered was by thee:
Thou didst my mourning eyes from
tears,
My feet from falling, free.

9 I in the land of those that live
Will walk the Lord before.

10 I did believe, therefore I spake:
I was afflicted sore.

11 I said, when I was in my haste,
That all men liars be.

12 What shall I render to the Lord
For all his gifts to me?

13 I'll of salvation take the cup,
On God's name will I call:

14 I'll pay my vows now to the Lord
Before his people all.

15 Dear in God's sight is his saints'
death.

16 Thy servant, Lord, am I;
Thy servant sure, thine handmaid's
son:
My bands thou didst untie.

17 Thank-off'rings I to thee will give,
And on God's name will call.

18 I'll pay my vows now to the Lord
Before his people all;

19 Within the courts of God's own
house,
Within the midst of thee,
O city of Jerusalem.
Praise to the Lord give ye.

117 C.M.

1 O give ye praise unto the Lord,
All nations that be;
Likewise, ye people all, accord
His name to magnify.

2 For great to us-ward ever are
His loving-kindnesses:
His truth endures for evermore.
The Lord O do ye bless.

118 C.M.

vv 1-9, 10-14, 15-18, 19-29

1 O praise the Lord, for he is good;
His mercy lasteth ever.

2 Let those of Israel now say,
His mercy faileth never.

3 Now let the house of Aaron say,
His mercy lasteth ever.

4 Let those that fear the Lord now say,
His mercy faileth never.

5 I in distress called on the Lord;
The Lord did answer me:
He in a large place did me set,
From trouble made me free.

6 The mighty Lord is on my side,
I will not be afraid;
For anything that man can do
I shall not be dismayed.

7 The Lord doth take my part with
them
That help to succour me:
Therefore on those that do me hate
I my desire shall see.

8 Better it is to trust in God
Than trust in man's defence;

9 Better to trust in God than make
Princes our confidence.

10 The nations, joining all in one,
Did compass me about:
But in the Lord's most holy name
I shall them all root out.

11 They compassed me about; I say,
They compassed me about:
But in the Lord's most holy name
I shall them all root out.

12 Like bees they compassed me
about;
Like unto thorns that flame
They quenched are: for them shall I
Destroy in God's own name.

13 Thou sore hast thrust, that I might
    fall,
    But my Lord helped me.
14 God my salvation is become,
    My strength and song is he.

15 In dwellings of the righteous
    Is heard the melody
    Of joy and health: the Lord's right
    hand
    Doth ever valiantly.

16 The right hand of the mighty Lord
    Exalted is on high;
    The right hand of the mighty Lord
    Doth ever valiantly.

17 I shall not die, but live, and shall
    The works of God discover.
18 The Lord hath me chastised sore,
    But not to death given over.

19 O set ye open unto me
    The gates of righteousness;
    Then will I enter into them,
    And I the Lord will bless.

20 This is the gate of God, by it
    The just shall enter in.
21 Thee will I praise, for thou me
    heard'st
    And hast my safety been.

22 That stone is made head corner-
    stone,
    Which builders did despise:
23 This is the doing of the Lord,
    And wondrous in our eyes.

24 This is the day God made, in it
    We'll joy triumphantly.
25 Save now, I pray thee, Lord; I pray,
    Send now prosperity.

26 Blessed is he in God's great name
    That cometh us to save:
    We, from the house which to the
    Lord
    Pertains, you blessed have.

27 God is the Lord, who unto us
    Hath made light to arise:
    Bind ye unto the altar's horns
    With cords the sacrifice.

28 Thou art my God, I'll thee exalt;
    My God, I will thee praise.
29 Give thanks to God, for he is good:
    His mercy lasts always.

119   C.M.

Aleph – First Part

1   Blessed are they that undefiled,
    And straight are in the way;
    Who in the Lord's most holy law
    Do walk, and do not stray.

2   Blessed are they who to observe
    His statutes are inclined;
    And who do seek the living God
    With their whole heart and mind.

3   Such in his ways do walk, and they
    Do no iniquity.
4   Thou hast commanded us to keep
    Thy precepts carefully.

5   O that thy statutes to observe
    Thou would'st my ways direct!
6   Then shall I not be shamed, when I
    Thy precepts all respect.

7   Then with integrity of heart
    Thee will I praise and bless,
    When I the judgments all have
    learned
    Of thy pure righteousness.

8   That I will keep thy statutes all
    Firmly resolved have I:
    O do not then, most gracious
    God,
    Forsake me utterly.

Beth – Second Part

9   By what means shall a young man
    learn
    His way to purify?
    If he according to thy word
    Thereto attentive be.

10 Unfeignedly thee have I sought
    With all my soul and heart:
    O let me not from the right path
    Of thy commands depart.

11 Thy word I in my heart have hid,
   That I offend not thee.
12 O Lord, thou ever blessed art,
   Thy statutes teach thou me.
13 The judgments of thy mouth each
   one
   My lips declared have:
14 More joy thy testimonies' way
   Than riches all me gave.
15 I will thy holy precepts make
   My meditation;
   And carefully I'll have respect
   Unto thy ways each one.
16 Upon thy statutes my delight
   Shall constantly be set:
   And, by thy grace, I never will
   Thy holy word forget.

Gimel – Third Part

17 With me thy servant, in thy grace,
   Deal bountifully, Lord;
   That by thy favour I may live,
   And duly keep thy word.
18 Open mine eyes, that of thy law
   The wonders I may see.
19 I am a stranger on this earth,
   Hide not thy laws from me.
20 My soul within me breaks, and
   doth
   Much fainting still endure,
   Through longing that it hath all
   times
   Unto thy judgments pure.
21 Thou hast rebuked the cursed
   proud,
   Who from thy precepts swerve.
22 Reproach and shame remove from
   me,
   For I thy laws observe.
23 Against me princes spake with
   spite,
   While they in council sat:
   But I thy servant did upon
   Thy statutes meditate.

24 My comfort, and my heart's delight,
   Thy testimonies be;
   And they, in all my doubts and
   fears,
   Are counsellors to me.

Daleth – Fourth Part

25 My soul to dust cleaves: quicken me,
   According to thy word.
26 My ways I showed, and me thou
   heard'st:
   Teach me thy statutes, Lord.
27 The way of thy commandments
   just
   Make me aright to know;
   So all thy works that wondrous are
   I shall to others show.
28 My soul doth melt, and drop away,
   For heaviness and grief:
   To me, according to thy word,
   Give strength, and send relief.
29 From me the wicked way of lies
   Let far removed be;
   And graciously thy holy law
   Do thou grant unto me.
30 I chosen have the perfect way
   Of truth and verity:
   Thy judgments that most
   righteous are
   Before me laid have I.
31 I to thy testimonies cleave;
   Shame do not on me cast.
32 I'll run thy precepts' way, when
   thou
   My heart enlarged hast.

He – Fifth Part

33 Teach me, O Lord, the perfect way
   Of thy precepts divine,
   And to observe it to the end
   I shall my heart incline.
34 Give understanding unto me,
   So keep thy law shall I;
   Yea, ev'n with my whole heart I
   shall
   Observe it carefully.

35 In thy law's path make me to go;
    For I delight therein.
36 My heart unto thy testimonies,
    And not to greed, incline.

37 Turn thou away my sight and eyes
    From viewing vanity;
    And in thy good and holy way
    Be pleased to quicken me.

38 Confirm to me thy gracious word,
    Which I did gladly hear,
    Ev'n to thy servant, Lord, who is
    Devoted to thy fear.

39 Turn thou away my feared
      reproach;
    For good thy judgments be.
40 Lo, for thy precepts I have longed;
    In thy truth quicken me.

Vau - Sixth Part

41 Let thy sweet mercies also come
    And visit me, O Lord;
    Ev'n thy benign salvation,
    According to thy word.

42 So shall I have wherewith I may
    Give him an answer just,
    Who spitefully reproacheth me;
    For in thy word I trust.

43 The word of truth out of my
      mouth
    Take thou not utterly;
    For on thy judgments righteous
    My hope doth still rely.

44 So shall I keep for evermore
    Thy law continually.
45 And, since that I thy precepts
      seek,
    I'll walk at liberty.

46 I'll speak thy word to kings, and I
    With shame shall not be moved;
47 And will delight myself always
    In thy laws, which I loved.

48 To thy commandments, which I
      loved,
    My hands lift up I will;
    And I will also meditate
    Upon thy statutes still.

Zain - Seventh Part

49 Remember, Lord, thy gracious
      word
    Thou to thy servant spake,
    Which, for a ground of my sure
      hope,
    Thou causedst me to take.

50 This word of thine my comfort is
    In mine affliction:
    For in my straits I am revived
    By this thy word alone.

51 The men whose hearts with pride
      are filled
    Did greatly me deride;
    Yet from thy straight
      commandments all
    I have not turned aside.

52 Thy judgments righteous, O Lord,
    Which thou of old forth gave,
    I did remember, and myself
    By them sweet comfort have.

53 Horror took hold on me, because
    Ill men thy law forsake.
54 I in my house of pilgrimage
    Thy laws my songs do make.

55 Thy name by night, Lord, I did
      mind,
    And I have kept thy law.
56 And this I had, because thy word
    I kept, and stood in awe.

Cheth - Eight Part

57 Thou my sure portion art alone,
    Which I did choose, O Lord:
    I have resolved, and said, that I
    Would keep thy holy word.

58 With my whole heart I did entreat
    Thy face and favour free:
    According to thy gracious word
    Be merciful to me.

59 I thought upon my former ways,
    And did my life well try;
    And to thy testimonies pure
    My feet then turned I.

60 I did not stay, nor linger long,
As those that slothful are;
But hastily thy laws to keep
Myself I did prepare.

61 Bands of the wicked me beset,
Thy law I did not slight.

62 I'll rise at midnight thee to praise,
Ev'n for thy judgments right.

63 I am companion to all those
Who fear, and thee obey.

64 O Lord, thy mercy fills the earth:
Teach me thy laws, I pray.

Teth - Ninth Part

65 Well hast thou with thy servant
dealt,
As thou didst promise give.

66 Good judgment me, and
knowledge teach,
For I thy word believe.

67 Ere I afflicted was I strayed;
But now I keep thy word.

68 Good art thou, and thou doest
good:
Teach me thy statutes, Lord.

69 The men whose hearts are full of
pride
Against me forged a lie;
Yet thy commandments to observe
With my whole heart will I.

70 Their hearts, through worldly ease
and wealth,
As fat as grease they be:
But in thy holy law I take
Delight continually.

71 It hath been very good for me
That I afflicted was,
That I might well instructed be,
And learn thy holy laws.

72 The word that cometh from thy
mouth
Is better unto me
Than many thousands and great
sums
Of gold and silver be.

Jod - Tenth Part

73 Thou mad'st and fashion'dst me:
thy laws
To know give wisdom, Lord.

74 So who thee fear shall joy to see
Me trusting in thy word.

75 That very right thy judgments are
I know, and do confess;
And that thou hast afflicted me
In truth and faithfulness.

76 O let thy kindness merciful,
I pray thee, comfort me,
As to thy servant faithfully
Was promised by thee.

77 And let thy tender mercies come
To me, that I may live;
Because thy holy laws to me
Sweet delectation give.

78 Lord, let the proud ashamed be;
For they, without a cause,
With me perversely dealt: but I
Will muse upon thy laws.

79 Let such as fear thee, and have
known
Thy statutes, turn to me.

80 My heart let in thy laws be sound,
That shamed I never be.

Caph - Eleventh Part

81 My soul for thy salvation faints;
Yet I thy word believe.

82 Mine eyes fail for thy word: I say,
When wilt thou comfort give?

83 For like a bottle I'm become,
That in the smoke is set:
But still thy righteous statutes,
Lord,
I never do forget.

84 How many are thy servant's days?
When wilt thou execute
Just judgment on these wicked
men
That do me persecute?

85   The proud have digged pits for
     me,
     Which is against thy laws.
86   Thy words all faithful are: help
     me,
     Pursued without a cause.

87   They so consumed me, that on
     earth
     My life they scarce did leave:
     Thy precepts yet forsook I not,
     But close to them did cleave.

88   After thy loving-kindness, Lord,
     Me quicken, and preserve:
     The testimony of thy mouth
     So shall I still observe.

Lamed – Twelfth Part

89   Thy word for ever is, O Lord,
     In heaven settled fast;
90   Unto all generations
     Thy faithfulness doth last:

     The earth thou hast established,
     And it abides by thee.
91   This day they stand as thou
     ordain'dst;
     For all thy servants be.

92   Unless in thy most perfect law
     My soul delights had found,
     I should have perished, when as
     My troubles did abound.

93   Thy precepts I will ne'er forget;
     They quickening to me brought.
94   Lord, I am thine; O save thou me:
     Thy precepts I have sought.

95   For me the wicked have laid wait,
     Me seeking to destroy:
     But I thy testimonies true
     Consider will with joy.

96   An end of all perfection
     Here have I seen, O God:
     But as for thy commandment just,
     It is exceeding broad.

Mem – Thirteenth Part

97   O how love I thy law! it is
     My study all the day:
98   It makes me wiser than my foes;
     For it doth with me stay.

99   Than all my teachers now I have
     More understanding far;
     Because my meditation
     Thy testimonies are.

100 In understanding I excel
     Ev'n those that aged be;
     Because thy precepts to observe
     I have sought earnestly.

101 My feet from each bad way I
     stayed,
     That I may keep thy word.
102 I from thy judgments have not
     swerved;
     For thou hast taught me, Lord.

103 How sweet unto my taste, O Lord,
     Are all thy words of truth!
     Yea, I do find them sweeter far
     Than honey to my mouth.

104 I through thy precepts, that are
     pure,
     Do understanding get;
     I therefore every way that's false
     With all my heart do hate.

Nun – Fourteenth Part

105 Thy word is to my feet a lamp,
     And to my path a light.
106 Sworn have I, and I will perform,
     To keep thy judgments right.

107 I am with sore affliction
     Ev'n overwhelmed, O Lord:
     In mercy raise and quicken me,
     According to thy word.

108 The free-will offerings of my
     mouth
     Accept, I thee beseech:
     And unto me thy servant, Lord,
     Thy judgments clearly teach.

109 Though still my soul be in my
    hand,
    Thy laws I'll not forget.
110 I erred not from them, though for
    me
    The wicked snares did set.

111 I of thy testimonies have
    Above all things made choice,
    To be my heritage for aye;
    For they my heart rejoice.

112 I carefully inclined have
    My heart still to attend;
    That I thy statutes may perform
    Alway unto the end.

Samech - Fifteenth Part

113 I hate the thoughts of vanity,
    But love thy law do I.
114 My shield and hiding-place thou
    art:
    I on thy word rely.

115 All ye that evil-doers are
    From me depart away;
    For the commandments of my
    God
    I purpose to obey.

116 According to thy faithful word
    Uphold and stablish me,
    That I may live, and of my hope
    Ashamed never be.

117 Hold thou me up, so shall I be
    In peace and safety still;
    And to thy statutes have respect
    Continually I will.

118 Thou tread'st down all that love
    to stray;
    False their deceit doth prove.
119 Vile men, like dross, away thou
    putt'st;
    Therefore thy law I love.

120 For fear of thee my very flesh
    Doth tremble, all dismayed;
    And of thy righteous judgments,
    Lord,
    My soul is much afraid.

Ain - Sixteenth Part

121 To all men I have judgment done,
    Performing justice right;
    Then let me not be left unto
    My fierce oppressors' might.

122 For good unto thy servant, Lord,
    Thy servant's surety be:
    From the oppression of the proud
    Do thou deliver me.

123 Mine eyes do fail with looking
    long
    For thy salvation,
    He word of thy pure righteousness
    While I do wait upon.

124 In mercy with thy servant deal,
    Thy laws me teach and show.
125 I am thy servant, wisdom give,
    That I thy laws may know.

126 'Tis time thou work, Lord; for
    they have
    Made void thy law divine.
127 Therefore thy precepts more I
    love
    Than gold, yea, gold most fine.

128 Concerning all things thy
    commands
    All right I judge therefore;
    And every false and wicked way
    I perfectly abhor.

Pe - Seventeenth Part

129 Thy statutes, Lord, are wonderful,
    My soul them keeps with care.
130 The entrance of thy words gives
    light,
    Makes wise who simple are.

131 My mouth I have wide opened,
    And panted earnestly,
    While after thy commandments all
    I longed exceedingly.

132 Look on me, Lord, and merciful
    Do thou unto me prove,
    As thou art wont to do to those
    Thy name who truly love.

133 O let my footsteps in thy word
Aright still ordered be:
Let no iniquity obtain
Dominion over me.

134 From man's oppression save thou
me;
So keep thy laws I will.

135 Thy face make on thy servant
shine;
Teach me thy statutes still.

136 Rivers of waters from mine eyes
Did run down, when I saw
How wicked men run on in sin,
And do not keep thy law.

Tzaddi – Eighteenth Part

137 O Lord, thou art most righteous;
Thy judgments are upright.

138 Thy testimonies thou command'st
Most faithful are and right.

139 My zeal hath ev'n consumed me,
Because mine enemies
Thy holy words forgotten have,
And do thy laws despise.

140 Thy word's most pure, therefore
on it
Thy servant's love is set.

141 Small, and despised I am, yet I
Thy precepts not forget.

142 Thy righteousness is
righteousness
Which ever doth endure:
Thy holy law, Lord, also is
The very truth most pure.

143 Trouble and anguish have me
found,
And taken hold on me:
Yet in my trouble my delight
Thy just commandments be.

144 Eternal righteousness is in
Thy testimonies all:
Lord, to me understanding give,
And ever live I shall.

Koph – Nineteenth Part

145 With my whole heart I cried, Lord,
hear;
I will thy word obey.

146 I cried to thee; save me, and I
Will keep thy laws alway.

147 I of the morning did prev'nt
The dawning, and did cry:
For all mine expectation
Did on thy word rely.

148 Mine eyes did wakefully prev'nt
The watches of the night,
That in thy word with careful
mind
Then meditate I might.

149 After thy loving-kindness hear
My voice, that calls on thee:
According to thy judgment, Lord,
Revive and quicken me.

150 Who follow mischief they draw
nigh;
They from thy law are far:

151 But thou art near, Lord; most firm
truth
All thy commandments are.

152 As for thy testimonies all,
Of old this have I tried,
That thou hast surely founded
them
For ever to abide.

Resh – Twentieth Part

153 Consider mine affliction,
In safety do me set:
Deliver me, O Lord, for I
Thy law do not forget.

154 After thy word revive thou me:
Save me, and plead my cause.

155 Salvation is from sinners far;
For they seek not thy laws.

156 O Lord, both great and manifold
Thy tender mercies be:
According to thy judgments just,
Revive and quicken me.

157 My persecutors many are,
And foes that do combine;
Yet from thy testimonies pure
My heart doth not decline.

158 I saw transgressors, and was
grieved;
For they keep not thy word.

159 See how I love thy law! as thou
Art kind, me quicken, Lord.

160 From the beginning all thy word
Hath been most true and sure:
Thy righteous judgments every
one
For evermore endure.

Schin - Twenty-First Part

161 Princes have persecuted me,
Although no cause they saw:
But still of thy most holy word
My heart doth stand in awe.

162 I at thy word rejoice, as one
Of spoil that finds great store.

163 Thy law I love; but lying all
I hate and do abhor.

164 Sev'n times a-day it is my care
To give due praise to thee;
Because of all thy judgments,
Lord,
Which righteous ever be.

165 Great peace have they who love thy
law;
Offence they shall have none.

166 I hoped for thy salvation, Lord,
And thy commands have done.

167 My soul thy testimonies pure
Observed carefully;
On them my heart is set, and them
I love exceedingly.

168 Thy testimonies and thy laws
I kept with special care;
For all my works and ways each
one
Before thee open are.

Tau - Twenty-Second Part

169 O let my earnest prayer and cry
Come near before thee, Lord:
Give understanding unto me,
According to thy word.

170 Let my request before thee come:
After thy word me free.

171 My lips shall utter praise, when
thou
Hast taught thy laws to me.

172 My tongue of thy most blessed
word
Shall speak, and it confess;
Because that thy commandments
all
Are perfect righteousness.

173 Let thy strong hand make help to
me:
Thy precepts are my choice.

174 I longed for thy salvation, Lord,
And in thy law rejoice.

175 O let my soul live, and it shall
Give praises unto thee;
And let thy judgments gracious
Be helpful unto me.

176 I, like a lost sheep, went astray;
Thy servant seek, and find:
For thy commands I suffered not
To slip out of my mind.

120   C.M.

A Song of degrees.

1 In my distress to God I cried,
And he gave ear to me.

2 From lying lips, and guileful
tongue,
O Lord, my soul set free.

3 What shall be giv'n thee? or what
shall
Be done to thee, false tongue?

4 Ev'n burning coals of juniper,
Sharp arrows of the strong.

5 Woe's me that I in Mesech am
A sojourner so long;
That I in tabernacles dwell
To Kedar that belong.

6 My soul with him that hateth peace
Hath long a dweller been.
7 I am for peace; but when I speak,
For battle they are keen.

121   C.M.

A Song of degrees.

1 I to the hills will lift mine eyes,
From whence doth come mine aid.
2 My safety cometh from the Lord,
Who heaven and earth hath made.

3 Thy foot he'll not let slide, nor will
He slumber that thee keeps.
4 Behold, he that keeps Israel,
He slumbers not, nor sleeps.

5 The Lord thee keeps, the Lord thy shade
On thy right hand doth stay:
6 The moon by night thee shall not smite,
Nor yet the sun by day.

7 The Lord shall keep thy soul; he shall
Preserve thee from all ill.
8 Henceforth thy going out and in
God keep for ever will.

122   C.M.

A Song of degrees of David.

1 I joyed when to the house of God,
Go up, they said to me.
2 Jerusalem, within thy gates
Our feet shall standing be.

3 Jerusalem a city, is
Compactly built together:
4 Unto that place the tribes go up,
The tribes of God go thither:

To Israel's testimony, there
To God's name thanks to pay.
5 For thrones of judgment, ev'n the thrones
Of David's house, there stay.

6 Pray that Jerusalem may have
Peace and felicity:
Let them that love thee and thy peace
Have still prosperity.

7 Therefore I wish that peace may still
Within thy walls remain,
And ever may thy palaces
Prosperity retain.

8 Now, for my friends' and brethren's sakes,
Peace be in thee, I'll say.
9 And for the house of God our Lord,
I'll seek thy good alway.

123   C.M.

A Song of degrees.

1 O thou that dwellest in the heavens,
I lift mine eyes to thee.
2 Behold, as servants' eyes do look
Their masters' hand to see,

As handmaid's eyes her mistress' hand;
So do our eyes attend
Upon the Lord our God, until
To us he mercy send.

3 O Lord, be gracious to us,
Unto us gracious be;
Because replenished with contempt
Exceedingly are we.

4 Our soul is filled with scorn of those
That at their ease abide,
And with the insolent contempt
Of those that swell in pride.

124 First Version C.M.

A Song of degrees of David.

1 Had not the Lord been on our side,
  May Israel now say;
2 Had not the Lord been on our side,
  When men rose us to slay;

3 They had us swallowed quick, when
    as
  Their wrath 'gainst us did flame:
4 Waters had covered us, our soul
  Had sunk beneath the stream.

5 Then had the waters, swelling high,
  Over our soul made way.
6 Bless'd be the Lord, who to their
    teeth
  Us gave not for a prey.

7 Our soul's escaped, as a bird
  Out of the fowler's snare;
  The snare asunder broken is,
  And we escaped are.

8 Our sure and all-sufficient help
  Is in Jehovah's name;
  His name who did the heaven create,
  And who the earth did frame.

124 Second Version 10. 10. 10. 10. 10.

A Song of degrees of David.

1 Now Israel may say, and that truly,
  If that the Lord had not our cause
    maintained;
2 If that the Lord had not our right
    sustained,
  When cruel men against us furiously
  Rose up in wrath, to make of us
    their prey;

3 Then certainly they had devoured us
    all,
  And swallowed quick, for ought
    that we could deem;
  Such was their rage, as we might
    well esteem.
4 And as fierce floods before them all
    things drown,
  So had they brought our soul to
    death quite down.

5 The raging streams, with their
    proud swelling waves,
  Had then our soul o'erwhelmed in
    the deep.
6 But blessed be God, who doth us
    safely keep,
  And hath not given us for a living
    prey
  Unto their teeth, and bloody cruelty.

7 Ev'n as a bird out of the fowler's
    snare
  Escapes away, so is our soul set
    free:
  Broke are their nets, and thus
    escaped we.
8 Therefore our help is in the Lord's
    great name,
  Who heaven and earth by his great
    power did frame.

125 C.M.

A Song of degrees.

1 They in the Lord that firmly trust
  Shall be like Sion hill,
  Which at no time can be removed,
  But standeth ever still.

2 As round about Jerusalem
  The mountains stand alway,
  The Lord his folk doth compass so,
  From henceforth and for aye.

3 For ill men's rod upon the lot
  Of just men shall not lie;
  Lest righteous men stretch forth
    their hands
  Unto iniquity.

4 Do thou to all those that be good
  Thy goodness, Lord, impart;
  And do thou good to those that are
  Upright within their heart.

5 But as for such as turn aside
  After their crooked way,
  God shall lead forth with wicked
    men:
  On Israel peace shall stay.

126 C.M.

A Song of degrees.

1 When Sion's bondage God turned
   back,
   As men that dreamed were we.
2 Then filled with laughter was our
   mouth,
   Our tongue with melody:

   They 'mong the heathen said, The
   Lord
   Great things for them hath
   wrought.
3 The Lord hath done great things for
   us,
   Whence joy to us is brought.

4 As streams of water in the south,
   Our bondage, Lord, recall.
5 Who sow in tears, a reaping time
   Of joy enjoy they shall.

6 That man who, bearing precious
   seed,
   In going forth doth mourn,
   He doubtless, bringing back his
   sheaves,
   Rejoicing shall return.

127 C.M.

A Song of degrees for Solomon.

1 Except the Lord do build the house,
   The builders lose their pain:
   Except the Lord the city keep,
   The watchmen watch in vain.

2 'Tis vain for you to rise betimes,
   Or late from rest to keep,
   To feed on sorrows' bread; so gives
   He his beloved sleep.

3 Lo, children are God's heritage,
   The womb's fruit his reward.
4 The sons of youth as arrows are,
   For strong men's hands prepared.

5 O happy is the man that hath
   His quiver filled with those;
   They unashamed in the gate
   Shall speak unto their foes.

128 C.M.

A Song of degrees.

1 Bless'd is each one that fears the
   Lord,
   And walketh in his ways;
2 For of thy labour thou shalt eat,
   And happy be always.

3 Thy wife shall as a fruitful vine
   By thy house' sides be found:
   Thy children like to olive-plants
   About thy table round.

4 Behold, the man that fears the Lord,
   Thus blessed shall he be.
5 The Lord shall out of Sion give
   His blessing unto thee:

   Thou shalt Jerusalem's good behold
   Whilst thou on earth dost dwell.
6 Thou shalt thy children's children
   see,
   And peace on Israel.

129 C.M.

A Song of degrees.

1 Oft did they vex me from my youth,
   May Israel now declare;
2 Oft did they vex me from my youth,
   Yet not victorious were.

3 The ploughers ploughed upon my
   back;
   They long their furrows drew.
4 The righteous Lord did cut the
   cords
   Of the ungodly crew.

5 Let Sion's haters all be turned
   Back with confusion.
6 As grass on houses' tops be they,
   Which fades ere it be grown:

7 Whereof enough to fill his hand
   The mower cannot find;
   Nor can the man his bosom fill,
   Whose work is sheaves to bind.

8 Neither say they who do go by,
God's blessing on you rest:
We in the name of God the Lord
Do wish you to be blessed.

130 C.M.

A Song of degrees.

1 Lord, from the depths to thee I cried.
2 My voice, Lord, do thou hear:
Unto my supplication's voice
Give an attentive ear.

3 Lord, who shall stand, if thou, O
Lord,
Should'st mark iniquity?
4 But yet with thee forgiveness is,
That feared thou mayest be.

5 I wait for God, my soul doth wait,
My hope is in his word.
6 More than they that for morning
watch,
My soul waits for the Lord;

I say, more than they that do watch
The morning light to see.
7 Let Israel hope in the Lord,
For with him mercies be;

And plenteous redemption
Is ever found with him.
8 And from all his iniquities
He Israel shall redeem.

131 C.M.

A Song of degrees of David.

1 My heart not haughty is, O Lord,
Mine eyes not lofty be;
Nor do I deal in matters great,
Or things too high for me.

2 I surely have myself behaved
With spirit still and mild,
As child of mother weaned: my soul
Is like a weaned child.

3 Upon the Lord let all the hope
Of Israel rely,
Ev'n from the time that present is
Unto eternity.

132 C.M.

A Song of degrees.
vv 1-9, 10-18

1 David, and his afflictions all,
Lord, do thou think upon;
2 How unto God he sware, and vowed
To Jacob's mighty One.

3 I will not come within my house,
Nor rest in bed at all;
4 Nor shall mine eyes take any sleep,
Nor eyelids slumber shall;

5 Till for the Lord a place I find,
Where he may make abode;
A place of habitation
For Jacob's mighty God.

6 Lo, at the place of Ephratah
Of it we understood;
And we did find it in the fields,
And city of the wood.

7 We'll go into his tabernacles,
And at his footstool bow.
8 Arise, O Lord, into thy rest,
Th' ark of thy strength, and thou.

9 O let thy priests be clothed, Lord,
With truth and righteousness;
And let all those that are thy saints
Shout loud for joyfulness.

10 For thine own servant David's sake,
Do not deny thy grace;
Nor of thine own anointed one
Turn thou away the face.

11 The Lord in truth to David sware,
He will not turn from it,
I of thy body's fruit will make
Upon thy throne to sit.

12 My covenant if thy sons will keep,
And laws to them made known,
Their children then shall also sit
For ever on thy throne.

13 For God of Sion hath made choice;
There he desires to dwell.
14 This is my rest, here still I'll stay;
For I do like it well.

15 Her food I'll greatly bless; her poor
   With bread will satisfy.
16 Her priests I'll clothe with health;
   her saints
   Shall shout forth joyfully.

17 And there will I make David's horn
   To bud forth pleasantly:
   For him that mine anointed is
   A lamp ordained have I.

18 As with a garment I will clothe
   With shame his en'mies all:
   But yet the crown that he doth wear
   Upon him flourish shall.

133 C.M.

A Song of degrees of David.

1 Behold, how good a thing it is,
   And how becoming well,
   Together such as brethren are
   In unity to dwell!

2 Like precious ointment on the head,
   That down the beard did flow,
   Ev'n Aaron's beard, and to the
   skirts,
   Did of his garments go.

3 As Hermon's dew, the dew that
   doth
   On Sion hills descend:
   For there the blessing God
   commands,
   Life that shall never end.

134 C.M.

A Song of degrees.

1 Behold, bless ye the Lord, all ye
   That his attendants are,
   Ev'n you that in God's temple be,
   And praise him nightly there.

2 Your hands within God's holy place
   Lift up, and praise his name.
3 From Sion hill the Lord thee bless,
   That heaven and earth did frame.

135 C.M.

vv 1-5, 6-12, 13-21

1 Praise ye the Lord, the Lord's name
   praise;
   His servants, praise ye God.
2 Who stand in God's house, in the
   courts
   Of our God make abode.

3 Praise ye the Lord, for he is good;
   Unto him praises sing:
   Sing praises to his name, because
   It is a pleasant thing.

4 For Jacob to himself the Lord
   Did choose of his good pleasure,
   And he hath chosen Israel
   For his peculiar treasure.

5 Because I know assuredly
   The Lord is very great,
   And that our Lord above all gods
   In glory hath his seat.

6 What things soever pleased the
   Lord,
   That in the heaven did he,
   And in the earth, the seas, and all
   The places deep that be.

7 He from the ends of earth doth
   make
   The vapours to ascend;
   With rain he lightnings makes, and
   wind
   Doth from his treasures send.

8 Egypt's first-born, from man to
   beast
9 Who smote. Strange tokens he
   On Pharaoh and his servants sent,
   Egypt, in midst of thee.

10 He smote great nations, slew great
   kings:
11 Sihon of Heshbon king,
   And Og of Bashan, and to nought
   Did Canaan's kingdoms bring:

12 And for a wealthy heritage
  Their pleasant land he gave,
  An heritage which Israel,
  His chosen folk, should have.

13 Thy name, O Lord, shall still
    endure,
  And thy memorial
  With honour shall continued be
  To generations all.

14 For why? the righteous God will
    judge
  His people righteously;
  Concerning those that do him
    serve,
  Himself repent will he.

15 The idols of the nations
  Of silver are and gold,
  And by the hands of men is made
  Their fashion and mould.

16 Mouths have they, but they do not
    speak;
  Eyes, but they do not see;
17 Ears have they, but hear not; and in
  Their mouths no breathing be.

18 Their makers are like them; so are
  All that on them rely.
19 O Israel's house, bless God; bless
    God,
  O Aaron's family.

20 O bless the Lord, of Levi's house
  Ye who his servants are;
  And bless the holy name of God,
  All ye the Lord that fear.

21 And blessed be the Lord our God
  From Sion's holy hill,
  Who dwelleth at Jerusalem.
  The Lord O praise ye still.

136 First Version   8 7. 8 7

vv 1-6, 7-12, 13-22, 23-26

1 Give thanks to God, for good is he:
  For mercy hath he ever.
2 Thanks to the God of gods give ye:
  For his grace faileth never.

3 Thanks give the Lord of lords unto:
  For mercy hath he ever.
4 Who only wonders great can do:
  For his grace faileth never.

5 Who by his wisdom made heavens
    high:
  For mercy hath he ever.
6 Who stretched the earth above the
    sea:
  For his grace faileth never.

7 To him that made the great lights
    shine:
  For mercy hath he ever.
8 The sun to rule till day decline:
  For his grace faileth never.

9 The moon and stars to rule by night:
  For mercy hath he ever.
10 Who Egypt's first-born killed out
    right:
  For his grace faileth never.

11 And Israel brought from Egypt
    land:
  For mercy hath he ever.
12 With stretched-out arm, and with
    strong hand:
  For his grace faileth never.

13 By whom the Red sea parted was:
  For mercy hath he ever.
14 And through its midst made Israel
    pass:
  For his grace faileth never.

15 But Pharaoh and his host did
    drown:
  For mercy hath he ever.
16 Who through the desert led his own:
  For his grace faileth never.

17 To him great kings who overthrew:
  For he hath mercy ever.
18 Yea, famous kings in battle slew:
  For his grace faileth never.

19 Ev'n Sihon king of Amorites:
  For he hath mercy ever.
20 And Og the king of Bashanites:
  For his grace faileth never.

21 Their land in heritage to have:
For mercy hath he ever.
22 His servant Israel right he gave:
For his grace faileth never.

23 In our low state who on us thought:
For he hath mercy ever.
24 And from our foes our freedom
wrought:
For his grace faileth never.

25 Who doth all flesh with food
relieve:
For he hath mercy ever.
26 Thanks to the God of heaven give:
For his grace faileth never.

136 Second Version   6 6. 6 6. 8 8

vv 1-6, 7-12, 13-22, 23-26

1 Praise God, for he is kind:
His mercy lasts for aye.
2 Give thanks with heart and mind
To God of gods alway:
For certainly
His mercies dure
Most firm and sure
Eternally.

3 The Lord of lords praise ye,
Whose mercies still endure.
4 Great wonders only he
Doth work by his great power
For certainly
His mercies dure
Most firm and sure
Eternally.

5 Which God omnipotent,
By might and wisdom high,
The heaven and firmament
Did frame, as we may see:
For certainly
His mercies dure
Most firm and sure
Eternally.

6 To him who did outstretch
This earth so great and wide,
Above the waters' reach
Making it to abide:

For certainly
His mercies dure
Most firm and sure
Eternally.

7 Great lights he made to be;
For his grace lasteth aye:
8 Such as the sun we see,
To rule the lightsome day:
For certainly
His mercies dure
Most firm and sure
Eternally.

9 Also the moon so clear,
Which shineth in our sight;
The stars that do appear,
To rule the darksome night:
For certainly
His mercies dure
Most firm and sure
Eternally.

10 To him that Egypt smote,
Who did his message scorn;
And in his anger hot
Did kill all their first-born:
For certainly
His mercies dure
Most firm and sure
Eternally.

11 Thence Israel out he brought;
For his grace lasteth ever.
12 With a strong hand he wrought,
And stretched-out arm deliver:
For certainly
His mercies dure
Most firm and sure
Eternally.

13 The sea he cut in two;
For his grace lasteth still.
14 And through its midst to go
Made his own Israel:
For certainly
His mercies dure
Most firm and sure
Eternally.

15 But overwhelmed and lost
Was proud king Pharaoh,
With all his mighty host,
And chariots there also:
For certainly
His mercies dure
Most firm and sure
Eternally.

16 To him who powerfully
His chosen people led,
Ev'n through the desert dry,
And in that place them fed:
For certainly
His mercies dure
Most firm and sure
Eternally.

17 To him great kings who smote;
For his grace hath no bound.

18 Who slew, and spared not
Kings famous and renowned:
For certainly
His mercies dure
Most firm and sure
Eternally.

19 Sihon the Amorites' king;
For his grace lasteth ever:

20 Og also, who did reign
The land of Bashan over:
For certainly
His mercies dure
Most firm and sure
Eternally.

21 Their land by lot he gave;
For his grace faileth never,

22 That Israel might it have
In heritage for ever:
For certainly
His mercies dure
Most firm and sure
Eternally.

23 Who hath remembered
Us in our low estate;

24 And us delivered
From foes which did us hate:
For certainly
His mercies dure
Most firm and sure
Eternally.

25 Who to all flesh gives food;
For his grace faileth never.

26 Give thanks to God most good,
The God of heaven, for ever:
For certainly
His mercies dure
Most firm and sure
Eternally.

137 C.M.

1 By Babel's streams we sat and wept,
When Sion we thought on.

2 In midst thereof we hanged our harps
The willow-trees upon.

3 For there a song required they,
Who did us captive bring:
Our spoilers called for mirth, and
said,
A song of Sion sing.

4 O how the Lord's song shall we sing
Within a foreign land?

5 If thee, Jerusalem, I forget,
Skill part from my right hand.

6 My tongue to my mouth's roof let
cleave,
If I do thee forget,
Jerusalem, and thee above
My chief joy do not set.

7 Remember Edom's children, Lord,
Who in Jerusalem's day,
Ev'n unto its foundation,
Raze, raze it quite, did say.

8 O daughter thou of Babylon,
Near to destruction;
Bless'd shall he be that thee rewards,
As thou to us hast done.

9 Yea, happy surely shall he be
Thy tender little ones
Who shall lay hold upon, and them
Shall dash against the stones.

138 C.M.

A Psalm of David.
vv 1-5, 6-8

1 Thee will I praise with all my heart,
I will sing praise to thee
2 Before the gods: And worship will
Toward thy sanctuary.

I'll praise thy name, ev'n for thy
truth,
And kindness of thy love;
For thou thy word hast magnified
All thy great name above.

3 Thou didst me answer in the day
When I to thee did cry;
And thou my fainting soul with
strength
Didst strengthen inwardly.

4 All kings upon the earth that are
Shall give thee praise, O Lord,
When as they from thy mouth shall
hear
Thy true and faithful word.

5 Yea, in the righteous ways of God
With gladness they shall sing:
For great's the glory of the Lord;
Who doth for ever reign.

6 Though God be high, yet he
respects
All those that lowly be;
Whereas the proud and lofty ones
Afar off knoweth he.

7 Though I in midst of trouble walk,
I life from thee shall have:
'Gainst my foes' wrath thou'lt
stretch thine hand;
Thy right hand shall me save.

8 Surely that which concerneth me
The Lord will perfect make:
Lord, still thy mercy lasts; do not
Thine own hands' works forsake.

139 C.M.

To the chief Musician, A Psalm of
David.
vv 1-12, 13-18, 19-24

1 O Lord, thou hast me searched and
known.
2 Thou knowest my sitting down,
And rising up; yea, all my thoughts
Afar to thee are known.

3 My footsteps, and my lying down,
Thou compassest always;
Thou also most entirely art
Acquaint with all my ways.

4 For in my tongue, before I speak,
Not any word can be,
But altogether, lo, O Lord,
It is well known to thee.

5 Behind, before, thou hast beset,
And laid on me thine hand.
6 Such knowledge is too strange for
me,
Too high to understand.

7 Where from thy Spirit shall I go?
Or from thy presence fly?
8 Ascend I heaven, lo, thou art there;
There, if in hell I lie.

9 Take I the morning wings, and dwell
In utmost parts of sea;
10 Ev'n there, Lord, shall thy hand me
lead,
Thy right hand hold shall me.

11 If I do say that darkness shall
Me cover from thy sight,
Then surely shall the very night
About me be as light.

12 Yea, darkness hideth not from thee,
But night doth shine as day:
To thee the darkness and the light
Are both alike alway.

13 For thou possessed hast my reins,
And thou hast covered me,
When I within my mother's womb
Enclosed was by thee.

14 Thee will I praise; for fearfully
And strangely made I am;
Thy works are marvellous, right
well
My soul doth know the same.

15 My substance was not hid from
thee,
When as in secret I
Was made; and in earth's lowest
parts
Was wrought most curiously.

16 Thine eyes my substance did
behold,
Yet being unperfect;
And in the volume of thy book
My members all were writ;

Which after in continuance
Were fashioned every one,
When as they yet all shapeless were,
And of them there was none.

17 How precious also are thy thoughts,
O gracious God, to me!
And in their sum how passing great
And numberless they be!

18 If I should count them, than the
sand
They more in number be:
What time soever I awake,
I ever am with thee.

19 Thou, Lord, wilt sure the wicked
slay:
Hence from me bloody men.
20 Thy foes against thee loudly speak,
And take thy name in vain.

21 Do not I hate all those, O Lord,
That hatred bear to thee?
With those that up against thee rise
Can I but grieved be?

22 With perfect hatred them I hate,
My foes I them do hold.
23 Search me, O God, and know my
heart,
Try me, my thoughts unfold:

24 And see if any wicked way
There be at all in me;
And in thine everlasting way
To me a leader be.

140 C.M.

*To the chief Musician, A Psalm of
David.*
vv 1-7, 8-13

1 Lord, from the ill and froward man
Give me deliverance,
And do thou safe preserve me from
The man of violence:

2 Who in their heart things
mischievous
Are meditating ever;
And they for war assembled are
Continually together.

3 Much like unto a serpent's tongue
Their tongues they sharp do make;
And underneath their lips there lies
The poison of a snake.

4 Lord, keep me from the wicked's
hands,
From violent men me save;
Who utterly to overthrow
My goings purposed have.

5 The proud for me a snare have hid,
And cords; yea, they a net
Have by the way-side for me spread;
They gins for me have set.

6 I said unto the Lord, Thou art
My God: unto the cry
Of all my supplications,
Lord, do thine ear apply.

7 O God the Lord, who art the
strength
Of my salvation:
A covering in the day of war
My head thou hast put on.

8 Unto the wicked man, O Lord,
His wishes do not grant;
Nor further thou his ill device,
Lest they themselves should vaunt.

9 As for the head and chief of those
  About that compass me,
  Ev'n by the mischief of their lips
  Let thou them covered be.

10 Let burning coals upon them fall,
   Them throw in fiery flame,
   And in deep pits, that they no more
   May rise out of the same.

11 Let not an evil speaker be
   On earth established:
   Mischief shall hunt the violent man,
   Till he be ruined.

12 I know God will the afflicted's
   cause
   Maintain, and poor men's right.
13 Surely the just shall praise thy
   name;
   The just dwell in thy sight.

141   C.M.

A Psalm of David.
vv 1-5, 6-10

1 O Lord, I unto thee do cry,
  Do thou make haste to me,
  And give an ear unto my voice,
  When I cry unto thee.

2 As incense let my prayer be
  Directed in thine eyes;
  And the uplifting of my hands
  As th' ev'ning sacrifice.

3 Set, Lord, a watch before my
  mouth,
  Keep of my lips the door.
4 My heart incline thou not unto
  The ills I should abhor,

  To practise wicked works with men
  That work iniquity;
  And of their dainties let me not
  With them partaker be.

5 Let him that righteous is me smite,
  It shall a kindness be;
  Let him reprove, I shall it count
  A precious oil to me:

Such smiting shall not break my
  head;
For yet the time shall fall,
When I in their calamities
To God pray for them shall.

6 When as their judges down shall be
  In stony places cast,
  Then shall they hear my words; for
  they
  Shall sweet be to their taste.

7 About the grave's devouring mouth
  Our bones are scattered round,
  As wood which men do cut and
  cleave
  Lies scattered on the ground.

8 But unto thee, O God the Lord,
  Mine eyes uplifted be:
  My soul do not leave destitute;
  My trust is set on thee.

9 Lord, keep me safely from the
  snares
  Which they for me prepare;
  And from the subtle gins of them
  That wicked workers are.

10 Let workers of iniquity
   Into their own nets fall,
   Whilst I do, by thine help, escape
   The danger of them all.

142   C.M.

Maschil of David; A Prayer when he
was in the cave.

1 I with my voice cried to the Lord,
  With it made my request:
2 Poured out to him my plaint, to him
  My trouble I expressed.

3 When overwhelmed my spirit is,
  Then well thou knew'st my way;
  Where I did walk a snare for me
  They privily did lay.

4 I looked on my right hand, and
viewed,
But none to know me were;
All refuge failed me, no man
Did for my soul take care.

5 I cried to thee; I said, Thou art
My refuge, Lord, alone;
And in the land of those that live
Thou art my portion.

6 Because I am brought very low,
Attend unto my cry:
Me from my persecutors save,
Who stronger are than I.

7 From prison bring my soul, that I
Thy name may glorify:
The just shall compass me, when
thou
With me deal'st bounteously.

143 First version   C.M.

A Psalm of David.
vv 1-5, 6-12

1 Lord, hear my prayer, attend my
suits;
And in thy faithfulness
Give thou an answer unto me,
And in thy righteousness.

2 Thy servant also bring thou not
In judgment to be tried:
Because no living man can be
In thy sight justified.

3 For th' enemy pursued my soul,
My life to ground down tread:
In darkness he hath made me dwell,
As who have long been dead.

4 My spirit thus is overwhelmed
In me perplexedly;
Within me is my very heart
Amazed wondrously.

5 I call to mind the days of old,
I think upon thy deeds;
On all the works I meditate
Which from thy hand proceeds.

6 My hands to thee I stretch; my soul
Thirsts, as dry land, for thee.

7 Haste, Lord, to hear, my spirit fails:
Hide not thy face from me;

Lest like to them I do become
That go down to the dust.

8 At morn let me thy kindness hear;
For in thee do I trust.

Teach me the way that I should
walk:
I lift my soul to thee.

9 Lord, free me from my foes; I flee
To thee to cover me.

10 Because thou art my God, to do
Thy will do me instruct:
Thy Sp'rit is good, me to the land
Of uprightness conduct.

11 Revive and quicken me, O Lord,
Ev'n for thine own name's sake;
And do thou, for thy righteousness,
My soul from trouble take.

12 And of thy mercy slay my foes;
Let all destroyed be
That do afflict my soul: for I
A servant am to thee.

143 Second Version   6 6. 6 6. D

A Psalm of David.
vv 1-5, 6-12

1 Oh, hear my prayer, Lord,
And unto my desire
To bow thine ear accord,
I humbly thee require;
And, in thy faithfulness,
Unto me answer make,
And, in thy righteousness,
Upon me pity take.

2 In judgment enter not
With me thy servant poor;
For why, this well I wot,
No sinner can endure
The sight of thee, O God:
If thou his deeds shalt try,
He dare make none abode
Himself to justify.

3 Behold, the cruel foe
Me persecutes with spite,
My soul to overthrow:
Yea, he my life down quite
Unto the ground hath smote,
And made me dwell full low
In darkness, as forgot,
Or men dead long ago.

4 Therefore my spirit vexed,
O'erwhelmed is me within;
My heart right sore perplexed
And desolate hath been.

5 Yet I do call to mind
What ancient days record,
Thy works of every kind
I think upon, O Lord.

6 Lo, I do stretch my hands
To thee, my help alone;
For thou well understands
All my complaint and moan:
My thirsting soul desires,
And longeth after thee,
As thirsty ground requires
With rain refreshed to be.

7 Lord, let my prayer prevail,
To answer it make speed;
For, lo, my sp'rit doth fail:
Hide not thy face in need;
Lest I be like to those
That do in darkness sit,
Or him that downward goes
Into the dreadful pit.

8 Because I trust in thee,
O Lord, cause me to hear
Thy loving-kindness free,
When morning doth appear:
Cause me to know the way
Wherein my path should be;
For why, my soul on high
I do lift up to thee.

9 From my fierce enemy
In safety do me guide,
Because I flee to thee,
Lord, that thou mayest me hide.

10 My God alone art thou,
Teach me thy righteousness:
Thy Spirit's good, lead me to
The land of uprightness.

11 O Lord, for thy name's sake,
Be pleased to quicken me;
And, for thy truth, forth take
My soul from misery.

12 And of thy grace destroy
My foes, and put to shame
All who my soul annoy;
For I thy servant am.

144 C.M.

A Psalm of David.
vv 1-10, 11-15

1 O blessed ever be the Lord,
Who is my strength and might,
Who doth instruct my hands to war,
My fingers teach to fight.

2 My goodness, fortress, my high
tower,
Deliverer, and shield,
In whom I trust: who under me
My people makes to yield.

3 Lord, what is man, that thou of him
Dost so much knowledge take?
Or son of man, that thou of him
So great account dost make?

4 Man is like vanity; his days,
As shadows, pass away.

5 Lord, bow thy heav'ns, come down,
touch thou
The hills, and smoke shall they.

6 Cast forth thy lightning, scatter
them;
Thine arrows shoot, them rout.

7 Thine hand send from above, me
save;
From great depths draw me out;

And from the hand of children
strange,

8 Whose mouth speaks vanity;
And their right hand is a right hand
That works deceitfully.

9 A new song I to thee will sing,
Lord, on a psaltery;
I on a ten-stringed instrument
Will praises sing to thee.

10 Ev'n he it is that unto kings
Salvation doth send;
Who his own servant David doth
From hurtful sword defend.

11 O free me from strange children's
hand,
Whose mouth speaks vanity;
And their right hand a right hand is
That works deceitfully.

12 That, as the plants, our sons may be
In youth grown up that are;
Our daughters like to corner-
stones,
Carved like a palace fair.

13 That to afford all kind of store
Our garners may be filled;
That our sheep thousands, in our
streets
Ten thousands they may yield.

14 That strong our oxen be for work,
That no in-breaking be,
Nor going out; and that our streets
May from complaints be free.

15 Those people blessed are who be
In such a case as this;
Yea, blessed all those people are,
Whose God Jehovah is.

145 First Version   C.M.

David's Psalm of praise.
vv 1-7, 8-16, 17-21

1 I'll thee extol, my God, O King;
I'll bless thy name always.

2 Thee will I bless each day, and will
Thy name for ever praise.

3 Great is the Lord, much to be
praised;
His greatness search exceeds.

4 Race unto race shall praise thy
works,
And show thy mighty deeds.

5 I of thy glorious majesty
The honour will record;
I'll speak of all thy mighty works,
Which wondrous are, O Lord.

6 Men of thine acts the might shall
show,
Thine acts that dreadful are;
And I, thy glory to advance,
Thy greatness will declare.

7 The memory of thy goodness great
They largely shall express;
With songs of praise they shall extol
Thy perfect righteousness.

8 The Lord is very gracious,
In him compassions flow;
In mercy he is very great,
And is to anger slow.

9 The Lord Jehovah unto all
His goodness doth declare;
And over all his other works
His tender mercies are.

10 Thee all thy works shall praise, O
Lord,
And thee thy saints shall bless;

11 They shall thy kingdom's glory
show,
Thy power by speech express:

12 To make the sons of men to know
His acts done mightily,
And of his kingdom's excellent
And glorious majesty.

13 Thy kingdom shall for ever stand,
Thy reign through ages all.

14 God raiseth all that are bowed
down,
Upholdeth all that fall.

15 The eyes of all things wait on thee,
The giver of all good;
And thou, in time convenient,
Bestow'st on them their food:

16 Thine hand thou openest liberally,
And of thy bounty gives
Enough to satisfy the need
Of every thing that lives.

17 The Lord is just in all his ways,
Holy in his works all.
18 God's near to all that call on him,
In truth that on him call.

19 He will accomplish the desire
Of those that do him fear:
He also will deliver them,
And he their cry will hear.

20 The Lord preserves all who him
love,
That nought can them annoy:
But he all those that wicked are
Will utterly destroy.

21 My mouth the praises of the Lord
To publish cease shall never:
Let all flesh bless his holy name
For ever and for ever.

145 Second Version L.M.

David's Psalm of praise.
vv 1-7, 8-16, 17-21

1 O Lord, thou art my God and King;
Thee will I magnify and praise:
I will thee bless, and gladly sing
Unto thy holy name always.

2 Each day I rise I will thee bless,
And praise thy name time without
end.
3 Much to be praised, and great God
is;
His greatness none can
comprehend.

4 Race shall thy works praise unto
race,
The mighty acts show done by thee.
5 I will speak of the glorious grace,
And honour of thy majesty;

Thy wondrous works I will record.
6 By men the might shall be extolled
Of all thy dreadful acts, O Lord:
And I thy greatness will unfold.

7 They utter shall abundantly
The memory of thy goodness great;
And shall sing praises cheerfully,
Whilst they thy righteousness
relate.

8 The Lord our God is gracious,
Compassionate is he also;
In mercy he is plenteous,
But unto wrath and anger slow.

9 Good unto all men is the Lord:
O'er all his works his mercy is.
10 Thy works all praise to thee afford:
Thy saints, O Lord, thy name shall
bless.

11 The glory of thy kingdom show
Shall they, and of thy power tell:
12 That so men's sons his deeds may
know,
His kingdom's grace that doth
excel.

13 Thy kingdom hath none end at all,
It doth through ages all remain.
14 The Lord upholdeth all that fall,
The cast-down raiseth up again.

15 The eyes of all things, Lord, attend,
And on thee wait that here do live,
And thou, in season due, dost send
Sufficient food them to relieve.

16 Yea, thou thine hand dost open
wide,
And every thing dost satisfy
That lives, and doth on earth abide,
Of thy great liberality.

17 The Lord is just in his ways all,
And holy in his works each one.
18 He's near to all that on him call,
Who call in truth on him alone.

19 God will the just desire fulfil
Of such as do him fear and dread:
Their cry regard, and hear he will,
And save them in the time of need.

20 The Lord preserves all, more and
  less,
  That bear to him a loving heart:
  But workers all of wickedness
  Destroy will he, and clean subvert.

21 Therefore my mouth and lips I'll
  frame
  To speak the praises of the Lord:
  To magnify his holy name
  For ever let all flesh accord.

146 C.M.

1 Praise God. The Lord praise, O my
  soul.
2 I'll praise God while I live;
  While I have being to my God
  In songs I'll praises give.

3 Trust not in princes, nor man's son,
  In whom there is no stay:
4 His breath departs, to earth he turns;
  That day his thoughts decay.

5 O happy is that man and blessed,
  Whom Jacob's God doth aid;
  Whose hope upon the Lord doth
  rest,
  And on his God is stayed:

6 Who made the earth and heavens
  high,
  Who made the swelling deep,
  And all that is within the same;
  Who truth doth ever keep:

7 Who righteous judgment executes
  For those oppressed that be,
  Who to the hungry giveth food;
  God sets the captives free.

8 The Lord doth give the blind their
  sight,
  The bowed down doth raise:
  The Lord doth dearly love all those
  That walk in upright ways.

9 The stranger's shield, the widow's
  stay,
  The orphan's help, is he:
  But yet by him the wicked's way
  Turned upside down shall be.

10 The Lord shall reign for evermore:
  Thy God, O Sion, he
  Reigns to all generations.
  Praise to the Lord give ye.

147 C.M.

vv 1-5, 6-11, 12-20

1 Praise ye the Lord; for it is good
  Praise to our God to sing:
  For it is pleasant, and to praise
  It is a comely thing.

2 God doth build up Jerusalem;
  And he it is alone
  That the dispersed of Israel
  Doth gather into one.

3 Those that are broken in their heart,
  And grieved in their minds,
  He healeth, and their painful
  wounds
  He tenderly up-binds.

4 He counts the number of the stars;
  He names them every one.
5 Great is our Lord, and of great
  power;
  His wisdom search can none.

6 The Lord lifts up the meek; and
  casts
  The wicked to the ground.
7 Sing to the Lord, and give him
  thanks;
  On harp his praises sound;

8 Who covereth the heaven with
  clouds,
  Who for the earth below
  Prepareth rain, who maketh grass
  Upon the mountains grow.

9 He gives the beast his food, he
feeds
The ravens young that cry.
10 His pleasure not in horses'
strength,
Nor in man's legs, doth lie.

11 But in all those that do him fear
The Lord doth pleasure take;
In those that to his mercy do
By hope themselves betake.

12 The Lord praise, O Jerusalem;
Sion, thy God confess:
13 For thy gates' bars he maketh
strong;
Thy sons in thee doth bless.

14 He in thy borders maketh peace;
With fine wheat filleth thee.
15 He sends forth his command on
earth,
His word runs speedily.

16 Hoar-frost, like ashes, scattereth he;
Like wool he snow doth give:
17 Like morsels casteth forth his ice;
Who in its cold can live?

18 He sendeth forth his mighty word,
And melteth them again;
His wind he makes to blow, and
then
The waters flow amain.

19 The doctrine of his holy word
To Jacob he doth show;
His statutes and his judgments he
Gives Israel to know.

20 To any nation never he
Such favour did afford;
For they his judgments have not
known.
O do ye praise the Lord.

148 First Version
C.M.

1 Praise God. From heavens praise
the Lord,
In heights praise to him be.
2 All ye his angels, praise ye him;
His hosts all, praise him ye.

3 O praise ye him, both sun and
moon,
Praise him, all stars of light.
4 Ye heavens of heavens him praise,
and floods
Above the heavens' height.

5 Let all the creatures praise the name
Of our almighty Lord:
For he commanded, and they were
Created by his word.

6 He also, for all times to come,
Hath them established sure;
He hath appointed them a law,
Which ever shall endure.

7 Praise ye Jehovah from the earth,
Dragons, and every deep:
8 Fire, hail, snow, vapour, stormy
wind,
His word that fully keep.

9 All hills and mountains, fruitful
trees,
And all ye cedars high:
10 Beasts, and all cattle, creeping
things,
And all ye birds that fly.

11 Kings of the earth, all nations,
Princes, earth's judges all:
12 Both young men, yea, and maidens
too,
Old men, and children small.

13 Let them God's name praise; for his
name
Alone is excellent:
His glory reacheth far above
The earth and firmament.

14 His people's horn, the praise of all
His saints, exalteth he;
Israel's seed, a people near
To him. The Lord praise ye.

148 Second Version 6 6. 6 6. 8 8

1 The Lord of heaven confess,
On high his glory raise.
2 Him let all angels bless,
Him all his armies praise.
3 Him glorify
Sun, moon, and stars;
4 Ye higher spheres,
And cloudy sky.

5 From God your beings are,
Him therefore famous make;
You all created were,
When he the word but spake.
6 And from that place,
Where fixed you be
By his decree,
You cannot pass.

7 Praise God from earth below,
Ye dragons, and ye deeps:
8 Fire, hail, clouds, wind, and snow.
Whom in command he keeps.
9 Praise ye his name,
Hills great and small,
Trees low and tall;
10 Beasts wild and tame;

All things that creep or fly.
11 Ye kings, ye common throng,
All princes mean or high;
12 Both men and virgins young,
Ev'n young and old,
13 Exalt his name;
For much his fame
Should be extolled.

O let God's name be praised
Above both earth and sky;
14 For he his saints hath raised,
And set their horn on high;
Ev'n those that be
Of Israel's race,
Near to his grace.
The Lord praise ye.

149 C.M.

1 Praise ye the Lord: unto him sing
A new song, and his praise
In the assembly of his saints
In sweet psalms do ye raise.

2 Let Isr'el in his Maker joy,
And to him praises sing:
Let all that Sion's children are
Be joyful in their King.

3 O let them unto his great name
Give praises in the dance;
Let them with timbrel and with harp
In songs his praise advance.

4 For God doth pleasure take in those
That his own people be;
And he with his salvation
The meek will beautify.

5 And in his glory excellent
Let all his saints rejoice:
Let them to him upon their beds
Aloud lift up their voice.

6 Let in their mouth aloft be raised
The high praise of the Lord,
And let them have in their right
hand
A sharp two-edged sword;

7 To execute the vengeance due
Upon the heathen all,
And make deserved punishment
Upon the people fall.

8 And ev'n with chains, as prisoners,
bind
Their kings that them command;
Yea, and with iron fetters strong,
The nobles of their land.

9 On them the judgment to perform
Found written in his word:
This honour is to all his saints.
O do ye praise the Lord.

150 C.M.

1 Praise ye the Lord. God's praise
   within
   His sanctuary raise;
   And to him in the firmament
   Of his power give ye praise.

2 Because of all his mighty acts,
   With praise him magnify:
   O praise him, as he doth excel
   In glorious majesty.

3 Praise him with trumpet's sound;
   his praise
   With psaltery advance:

4 With timbrel, harp, stringed
   instruments,
   And organs, in the dance.

5 Praise him on cymbals loud; him
   praise
   On cymbals sounding high.

6 Let each thing breathing praise the
   Lord.
   Praise to the Lord give ye.

THE WORSHIP OF GOD

151
85.85.843

'Thou hast created all things, and for thy pleasure they are and were created'
Revelation 4 v 11

1 Angel voices, ever singing
Round Thy throne of light,
Angel harps, for ever ringing,
Rest not day nor night;
Thousands only live to bless Thee,
And confess Thee
Lord of might.

2 Thou who art beyond the farthest
Mortal eye can scan,
Can it be that Thou regardest
Songs of sinful man?
Can we know that Thou art near us
And wilt hear us?
Yes, we can.

3 In Thy house, great God, we offer
Of Thine own to Thee,
And for Thine acceptance proffer,
All unworthily,
Hearts, and minds, and hands, and voices
In our choicest
Psalmody.

4 Honour, glory, might, and merit
Thine shall ever be,
Father, Son, and Holy Spirit,
Blessed Trinity.
Of the best that Thou hast given
Earth and heaven
Render Thee.

Francis Pott (1832–1909)

152
L.M.

Based on Psalm 100

1 Before Jehovah's awesome throne,
Ye nations, bow with sacred joy;
Know that the Lord is God alone,
He can create, and He destroy.

2 His sovereign power, without our aid,
Made us of clay, and formed us men;
And when like wandering sheep we strayed,
He brought us to His fold again.

3 We are His people, we His care,
Our souls and all our mortal frame;
What lasting honours shall we rear,
Almighty Maker, to Thy name?

4 We'll crowd Thy gates with thankful songs,
High as the heavens our voices raise;
And earth, with her ten thousand tongues,
Shall fill Thy courts with sounding praise.

5 Wide as the world is Thy command,
Vast as eternity Thy love;
Firm as a rock Thy truth shall stand,
When rolling years shall cease to move.

Isaac Watts (1674–1748)
Alt. John Wesley (1703–91)

153
L.M. (with Hallelujahs)

Based on Psalm 117

1 From all that dwell below the skies
Let the Creator's praise arise:
Hallelujah!
Let the Redeemer's name be sung,
Through every land, by every tongue.
Hallelujah!

2 Eternal are Thy mercies, Lord;
Eternal truth attends Thy Word:
Hallelujah!
Thy praise shall sound from shore to
shore,
Till suns shall rise and set no more.
Hallelujah!

Isaac Watts (1674–1748)

154
L.M.

Based on Psalm 136

1 Give to our God immortal praise;
Mercy and truth are all His ways;
Wonders of grace to God belong,
Repeat His mercies in your song.

2 Give to the Lord of lords renown,
The King of kings with glory crown:
His mercies ever shall endure,
When lords and kings are known no
more.

3 He built the earth, He spread the sky,
And fixed the starry lights on high:
Wonders of grace to God belong,
Repeat His mercies in your song.

4 He fills the sun with morning light,
He bids the moon direct the night:
His mercies ever shall endure,
When suns and moons shall shine
no more.

5 He sent His Son with power to save
From guilt and darkness and the
grave:
Wonders of grace to God belong,
Repeat His mercies in your song.

6 Through this vain world He guides
our feet,
And leads us to His heavenly seat:
His mercies ever shall endure,
When this vain world shall be no
more.

Isaac Watts (1674–1748)

155
87.87

Based on Psalm 145 vv 1-10

1 God, my King, Thy might
confessing,
Ever will I bless Thy name;
Day by day Thy throne addressing,
Still will I Thy praise proclaim.

2 Honour great our God befitteth,
Who His majesty can reach?
Age to age His works transmitteth,
Age to age His power shall teach.

3 They shall talk of all Thy glory,
On Thy might and greatness dwell,
Speak of Thy dread acts the story,
And Thy deeds of wonder tell.

4 Nor shall fail from memory's
treasure
Works by love and mercy wrought;
Works of love surpassing measure,
Works of mercy passing thought.

5 Full of kindness and compassion,
Slow to anger, vast in love,
God is good to all creation;
All His works His goodness prove.

6 All Thy works, O Lord, shall bless
Thee;
Thee shall all Thy saints adore:
King supreme shall they confess
Thee,
And proclaim Thy sovereign power.

Richard Mant (1776–1848)

156

C.M.

'His understanding is infinite'
Psalm 147 v 5

1 Great God! how infinite art Thou!
What worthless worms are we;
Let the whole race of creatures bow,
And pay their praise to Thee.

2 Thy throne eternal ages stood,
Ere seas or stars were made:
Thou art the ever-living God.
Were all the nations dead.

3 Nature and time quite naked lie
To Thine immense survey,
From the formation of the sky
To the great burning day.

4 Eternity, with all its years,
Stands present in Thy view;
To Thee there's nothing old
     appears;
Great God! there's nothing new.

5 Our lives through various scenes are
     drawn
And vexed with trifling cares,
While Thine eternal thought moves
     on
Thine undisturbed affairs.

6 Great God! how infinite art Thou!
What worthless worms are we;
Let the whole race of creatures bow,
And pay their praise to Thee.

Isaac Watts (1674–1748)

157

8 7. 8 7. D

Based on Psalm 146

1 Hallelujah, praise Jehovah,
O my soul, Jehovah praise;
I will sing the glorious praises
Of my God through all my days.
Put no confidence in princes,
Nor for help on man depend;
He shall die, to dust returning,
And his purposes shall end.

2 Happy is the man that chooses
Israel's God to be his aid;
He is blest whose hope of blessing
On the Lord his God is stayed.
Heaven and earth the Lord created,
Seas and all that they contain;
He delivers from oppression,
Righteousness He will maintain.

3 Food He daily gives the hungry,
Sets the mourning prisoner free,
Raises those bowed down with
     anguish,
Makes the sightless eyes to see.
Well Jehovah loves the righteous,
And the stranger He befriends,
Helps the fatherless and the widow,
Judgment on the wicked sends.

4 Hallelujah, praise Jehovah,
O my soul, Jehovah praise;
I will sing the glorious praises
Of my God through all my days.
Over all God reigns forever,
Through all ages He is King;
Unto Him, thy God, O Zion,
Joyful hallelujahs sing.

The Psalter 1912

158

8 7. 8 7. D

'Grace, mercy, and peace, from God our
Father and Jesus Christ our Lord'
1 Timothy 1 v 2

1 Holy Father full of mercy,
O most high and mighty God.
There is none on earth beside Thee,
Thou alone the living God.
From Thy throne-room look upon us,
Fill our hearts with saving grace,
Send Thy Spirit to embrace us,
Grant us light to see Thy face.

2 Holy Father and Creator,
Sovereign God who rules on high,
Thou alone our soul's protector,
Bend Thine ear to hear our cry.
For we need Thy grace and mercy
To resist indwelling sin.
We Thy children cry for pity,
Grant us strength to fight and win.

3   Holy Father, King Immortal,
    God of love and God of grace.
    Thou alone who art eternal,
    Descend now upon this place.
    Fill our hearts with Thy sweet
        presence,
    Shed abroad Thy holy love,
    May the perfume of Thy fragrance,
    Come upon us from above.

© The Author   *Robert Dickie (b.1950)*

159   D.C.M.

*'How precious also are thy thoughts unto
me, O God!' Psalm 139 v 17*

1   How shall I sing that majesty
    Which angels do admire?
    Let dust in dust and silence lie;
    Sing, sing, ye heavenly choir.
    Thousands of thousands stand
        around
    Thy throne, O God most high;
    Ten thousand times ten thousand
        sound
    Thy praise; but who am I?

2   Thy brightness unto them appears,
    Whilst I Thy footsteps trace;
    A sound of God comes to my ears,
    But they behold Thy face.
    They sing because Thou art their
        sun;
    Lord, send a beam on me;
    For where heaven is but once begun
    There hallelujahs be.

3   Enlighten with faith's light my heart,
    Inflame it with love's fire;
    Then shall I sing and bear a part
    With that celestial choir.
    I shall, I fear, be dark and cold,
    With all my fire and light;
    Yet when Thou dost accept their
        gold,
    Lord, treasure up my mite.

4   How great a being, Lord, is Thine,
    Which doth all beings keep!
    Thy knowledge is the only line
    To sound so vast a deep.
    Thou art a sea without a shore,
    A sun without a sphere;
    Thy time is now and evermore,
    Thy place is everywhere.

                    John Mason (c.1646–94)

160   8 8. 88. 88

*'While I live will I praise the LORD'
Psalm 146 v 2*

1   I'll praise my Maker while I've
        breath,
    And when my voice is lost in death,
    Praise shall employ my nobler
        powers;
    My days of praise shall ne'er be past,
    While life, and thought, and being
        last,
    Or immortality endures.

2   Happy the man whose hopes rely
    On Israel's God! He made the sky,
    And earth, and seas, with all their
        train:
    His truth for ever stands secure;
    He saves the oppressed, He feeds the
        poor,
    And none shall find His promise
        vain.

3   The Lord gives eyesight to the blind;
    The Lord supports the fainting
        mind;
    He sends the labouring conscience
        peace;
    He helps the stranger in distress,
    The widow and the fatherless,
    And grants the prisoner sweet
        release.

4 I'll praise Him while He lends me
     breath,
   And when my voice is lost in death,
   Praise shall employ my nobler powers;
   My days of praise shall ne'er be past,
   While life, and thought, and being
     last,
   Or immortality endures.

                    Isaac Watts (1674–1748)

161   C.M.

'Lord, teach us to pray' Luke 11 v 1

1 In Thy great name, O Lord, we come
   To worship at Thy feet!
   O pour Thy Holy Spirit down
   On all that now shall meet!

2 Teach us to pray, and praise, and hear,
   And understand Thy Word;
   To feel Thy blissful presence near,
   And trust our living Lord.

3 This house with grace and glory fill,
   This congregation bless:
   Thy great salvation now reveal,
   Thy glorious righteousness.

                    Joseph Hoskins (1745–88)

162   88.88.88

'Holy, holy, holy is the LORD of hosts'
Isaiah 6 v 3

1 Infinite God, to Thee we raise
   Our hearts in solemn songs of
     praise;
   By all Thy works on earth adored,
   We worship Thee, the common
     Lord;
   The everlasting Father own,
   And bow our souls before Thy
     throne.

2 Thee all the choir of angels sings,
   The Lord of hosts, the King of kings;
   Cherubs proclaim Thy praise aloud,
   And seraphs shout the Triune God;
   And, Holy, holy, holy! cry,
   Thy glory fills both earth and sky!

3 God of the patriarchal race,
   The ancient seers record Thy praise,
   The goodly apostolic band
   In highest joy and glory stand;
   And all the saints and prophets join
   To extol Thy majesty divine.

4 Head of the martyrs' noble host,
   Of Thee they justly make their boast;
   The church, to earth's remotest
     bounds,
   Her heavenly Founder's praise
     resounds;
   And strives, with those around the
     throne,
   To hymn the mystic Three in One.

5 Father of endless majesty,
   All might and love they render Thee;
   Thy true and only Son adore,
   The same in dignity and power;
   And God the Holy Ghost declare,
   The saints' eternal Comforter.

                        Ambrose (c.339–97)
                  Tr. Charles Wesley (1707–88)

163   88. 88. 88

'Your heart shall rejoice, and your joy no
man taketh from you' John 16 v 22

1 Messiah, joy of every heart,
   Thou, Thou the King of glory art!
   The Father's everlasting Son!
   Thee it delights thy church to own;
   For all our hopes on Thee depend,
   Whose glorious mercies never end.

2 Bent to redeem a sinful race,
   Thou, Lord, with unexampled grace,
   Into our lower world didst come,
   And stoop to a poor virgin's womb;
   Whom all the heavens cannot
     contain,
   Our God appeared a child of man!

3 When thou hadst rendered up Thy
     breath,
   And dying drawn the sting of death,
   Thou didst from earth triumphant
     rise,

And open the portals of the skies,
That all who trust in Thee alone
Might follow, and partake Thy
    throne.

4 Seated at God's right hand again,
Thou dost in all His glory reign;
Thou dost, thy Father's image, shine
In all the attributes divine;
And Thou with judgment clad shalt
    come
To seal our everlasting doom.

5 Wherefore we now for mercy pray;
O Saviour, take our sins away!
Before Thou as our Judge appear,
In dreadful majesty severe,
Appear our advocate with God,
And save the purchase of Thy blood!

6 Hallow, and make Thy servants
    meet,
And with Thy saints in glory seat;
Sustain and bless us by Thy sway,
And keep to that tremendous day,
When all Thy church shall chant
    above
The new eternal song of love.

Charles Wesley (1707–88)

164   8 8. 8 8. 8 8

'*Looking for that blessed hope, and the
glorious appearing of the great God*'
Titus 2 *v* 13

1 Saviour, we now rejoice in hope,
That Thou at last wilt take us up;
With daily triumph we proclaim,
And bless and magnify Thy name;
And wait Thy greatness to adore
When time and death shall be no
    more.

2 Till then with us vouchsafe to stay,
And keep us pure from sin today;
Thy great confirming grace bestow,
And guard us all our days below;
And ever mightily defend,
And save Thy servants to the end.

3 Still let us, Lord, by Thee be blest,
Who in Thy guardian mercy rest:
Extend Thy mercy's arms to me,
The weakest soul that trusts in Thee;
And never let me lose Thy love,
Till I, even I, am crowned above.

Charles Wesley (1707–88)

165   10 4. 6 6. 6 6. 10 4

'*My God, my King*' Psalm 68 *v* 24

1 Let all the world in every corner sing
My God and King.
The heavens are not too high,
His praise may thither fly:
The earth is not too low,
His praises there may grow.
Let all the world in every corner sing
My God and King.

2 Let all the world in every corner sing
My God and King.
The Church with psalms must shout,
No door can keep them out:
But above all, the heart
Must bear the longest part.
Let all the world in every corner sing
My God and King.

George Herbert (1593–1632)

166   7 7. 7 7

'*His mercy endureth for ever*'
Psalm 136 *v* 1

1 Let us with a gladsome mind
Praise the Lord for He is kind;
For His mercies shall endure,
Ever faithful, ever sure.

2 That by He all-commanding might,
Filled the new-made world with
    light;
For His mercies shall endure,
Ever faithful, ever sure.

3 All things living He doth feed,
His full hand supplies their need;
For His mercies shall endure,
Ever faithful, ever sure.

4 He His chosen race did bless
In the wasteful wilderness;
For His mercies shall endure,
Ever faithful, ever sure.

5 He hath with a piteous eye,
Looked upon our misery:
For His mercies shall endure,
Ever faithful, ever sure.

6 Let us with a gladsome mind
Praise the Lord for He is kind;
For His mercies shall endure,
Ever faithful, ever sure.

John Milton (1608–74) Altd

167
88.88.88

Based on Genesis 28 vv 16-17

1 Lo! God is here! Let us adore,
And own how dreadful is this place!
Let us within us feel His power
And silent bow before His face;
Who know His power, His grace
who prove,
Serve Him with awe, with reverence
love.

2 Lo! God is here! Him day and night
The united choirs of angels sing;
To Him, enthroned above all height,
Heaven's host their noblest praises
bring;
Disdain not, Lord, our meaner song,
Who praise Thee with a stammering
tongue.

3 Being of beings! May our praise
Thy courts with grateful fragrance
fill;
Still may we stand before Thy face,
Still hear and do Thy sovereign will;
To Thee may all our thoughts arise,
Ceaseless, accepted sacrifice.

Gerhard Tersteegen (1697–1769)
Tr. John Wesley (1703–91)

168
C.M.

Based on Psalm 145

1 Long as I live I'll bless Thy name,
My King, my God of love;
My work and joy shall be the same
In the bright world above.

2 Great is the Lord, His power
unknown,
And let His praise be great:
I'll sing the honours of Thy throne,
Thy works of grace repeat.

3 Thy grace shall dwell upon my
tongue,
And while my lips rejoice,
The men that hear my sacred song
Shall join their cheerful voice.

4 Fathers to sons shall teach Thy
name,
And children learn Thy ways;
Ages to come Thy truth proclaim,
And nations sound Thy praise.

5 Thy glorious deeds of ancient date
Shall through the world be known;
Thine arm of power, Thy heavenly
state,
With public splendour shown.

6 The world is managed by Thy hands,
Thy saints are ruled by love;
And Thine eternal kingdom stands,
Though rocks and hills remove.

Isaac Watts (1674–1748)

169
C.M.

'For the LORD is a great God, and a great
King above all gods' Psalm 95 v 3

1 My God, how wonderful Thou art,
Thy majesty how bright!
How beautiful Thy mercy-seat,
In depths of burning light!

2 How dread are Thine eternal years,
O everlasting Lord,
By prostrate spirits day and night
Incessantly adored?

3 How wonderful, how beautiful,
  The sight of Thee must be,
  Thine endless wisdom, boundless
      power,
  And awesome purity!

4 O how I fear Thee, living God,
  With deepest, tenderest fears,
  And worship Thee with trembling
      hope
  And penitential tears!

5 Yet I may love Thee, too, O Lord,
  Almighty as Thou art;
  For Thou hast stooped to ask of me
  The love of my poor heart.

6 No earthly father loves like Thee;
  No mother, e'er so mild,
  Bears and forbears as Thou hast done
  With me, Thy sinful child.

7 Father of Jesus, love's reward,
  What rapture will it be
  Prostrate before Thy throne to lie,
  And ever gaze on Thee!

Frederick William Faber (1814–63)

170 S.M.

Based on Psalm 103 vv 1-7

1 O bless the Lord, my soul;
  Let all within me join,
  And aid my tongue to bless His name
  Whose favours are divine.

2 O bless the Lord, my soul,
  Nor let His mercies lie
  Forgotten in unthankfulness,
  And without praises die.

3 'Tis He forgives thy sins,
  'Tis He relieves thy pain,
  'Tis He that heals thy sicknesses,
  And makes thee young again.

4 He crowns thy life with love,
  When ransomed from the grave;
  He that redeemed my soul from hell
  Hath sovereign power to save.

5 He fills the poor with good,
  He gives the sufferers rest;
  The Lord hath judgements for the
      proud,
  And justice for the oppressed.

6 His wondrous works and ways
  He made by Moses known;
  But sent the world His truth and
      grace
  By His belovèd Son.

Isaac Watts (1674–1748)

171 D.L.M.

'Faith ... the gift of God' Ephesians 2 v 8

1 O glorious Majesty on high,
  Eternal splendour is Thy dress,
  Where seraphim for ever fly,
  With songs of sweetest holiness.
  Beyond the confines of our mind,
  In realms outreaching human sight,
  In perfect blessedness we find,
  By faith, Thy glorious image bright.

2 The joy of truth shines in Thy face,
  Of sovereign grace and mercy's
      smile;
  And in the bosom of Thy grace
  Election cradled without guile.
  Thy perfect will becomes our joy
  When we have seen Thy heart of
      love;
  Our eager lips we now employ
  To sing the praise of God above.

3 Thy perfect plan for all Thine own
  Is born in every chosen heart;
  Forbid it then that we should roam,
  Or ever seek from Thee to part.
  To Thee predestined to conform,
  And bear Thine image in our lives,
  With glorious gown and shining
      crown,
  And all this from Thy grace derives!

4 Who brings this grace unto the
    dead,
With quickening life and serious
    call?
It is the Saviour who has led
A host of souls since Adam's fall.
With costly merit, pardon pure,
He has redeemed His chosen flock;
The faith He gives will now endure,
And stand for ever on this Rock.

© The Author   *William Vernon Higham (b.1926)*

172   L.M.

'Who is like thee, glorious in holiness,
fearful in praises, doing wonders?'
Exodus 15 v 11

1 O God, Thou bottomless abyss!
Thee to perfection who can know?
O height immense! What words suffice
Thy countless attributes to show?

2 Unfathomable depths Thou art;
O plunge me in Thy mercy's sea!
Void of true wisdom is my heart;
With love embrace and cover me!

3 While Thee, all infinite, I set
By faith before my ravished eye,
My weakness bends beneath the
    weight;
O'erpowered I sink, I faint, I die!

4 Eternity Thy fountain was,
Which, like Thee, no beginning
    knew;
Thou wast ere time began his race,
Ere glowed with stars the ethereal
    blue.

5 Greatness unspeakable is Thine,
Greatness, whose undiminished ray,
When short-lived worlds are lost,
    shall shine
When earth and heaven are fled away.

6 All creatures praise the eternal
    Name;
Ye hosts that to His court belong,
Cherubic choirs, seraphic flames,
Awake the everlasting song!

7 Thrice holy! Thine the kingdom is,
The power of omnipotence is Thine;
And when created nature dies,
Thy never-ceasing glories shine.

Ernst Lange (1650–1727)
Tr. John Wesley (1703–91)

173   10 10. 11 11

'And they sang praises with gladness'
2 Chronicles 29 v 30

1 O heavenly King, look down from
    above;
Assist us to sing Thy mercy and love:
So sweetly o'erflowing, so plenteous
    the store,
Thou still art bestowing and giving
    us more.

2 O God of our life, we hallow Thy
    name;
Our business and strife is Thee to
    proclaim.
Accept our thanksgiving for creating
    grace;
The living, the living shall show
    forth Thy praise.

3 Our Father and Lord, almighty art
    Thou;
Preserved by Thy word, we worship
    Thee now;
The bountiful donor of all we enjoy,
Our tongues, to Thine honour, and
    lives we employ.

4 But O above all, Thy kindness we
    praise,
From sin and from thrall which
    saves the lost race;
Thy Son Thou hast given the world
    to redeem,
And bring us to heaven whose trust
    is in Him.

5 Wherefore of Thy love we sing and
    rejoice,
  With angels above we lift up our
    voice:
  Thy love each believer shall gladly
    adore,
  For ever and ever, when time is no
    more.

Charles Wesley (1707–88)

174   5 5. 5 5. 6 5. 6 5

*'Let everything that hath breath praise
the LORD. Praise ye the LORD'
Psalm 150 v 6*

1 O praise ye the Lord!
  Praise Him in the height;
  Rejoice in His word,
  Ye angels of light;
  Ye heavens, adore Him
  By whom ye were made,
  And worship before Him,
  In brightness arrayed.

2 O praise ye the Lord!
  Praise Him upon earth,
  In tuneful accord,
  Ye sons of new birth;
  Praise Him who hath brought you
  His grace from above,
  Praise Him who hath taught you
  To sing of His love.

3 O praise ye the Lord!
  Thanksgiving and song
  To Him be outpoured
  All ages along:
  For love in creation,
  For heaven restored,
  For grace of salvation
  O praise ye the Lord!

Henry Williams Baker (1821–77)

175   12 10. 12 10

*'Worship the LORD in the beauty of
holiness' Psalm 29 v 2*

1 O worship the Lord in the beauty of
    holiness;
  Bow down before Him, His glory
    proclaim;
  With gold of obedience and incense
    of lowliness,
  Kneel and adore Him, the Lord is
    His name.

2 Low at His feet lay thy burden of
    carefulness;
  High on His heart He will bear it for
    thee,
  Comfort thy sorrows, and answer
    thy prayerfulness,
  Guiding thy steps as may best for
    thee be.

3 Fear not to enter His courts in the
    slenderness
  Of the poor wealth thou wouldst
    reckon as thine;
  Truth in its beauty and love in its
    tenderness,
  These are the offerings to lay on His
    shrine.

4 These, though we bring them in
    trembling and fearfulness,
  He will accept for the name that is
    dear;
  Mornings of joy give for evenings of
    tearfulness,
  Trust for our trembling, and hope
    for our fear.

5 O worship the Lord in the beauty of
    holiness;
  Bow down before Him, His glory
    proclaim;
  With gold of obedience and incense
    of lowliness,
  Kneel and adore Him, the Lord is
    His name.

John Samuel Bewley Monsell (1811–75)

176 L.M.

'Praise waiteth for thee. O God, in Zion'
Psalm 65 v 1

1 Praise, Lord, for Thee in Zion waits;
 Prayer shall besiege Thy temple
  gates;
 All flesh shall to Thy throne repair;
 And find, through Christ, salvation
  there.

2 Our spirits faint, our sins prevail;
 Leave not our trembling hearts to
  fail:
 O Thou that hearest prayer, descend,
 And still be found the sinner's
  friend.

3 How blest Thy saints! How safely led!
 How surely kept! How richly fed!
 Saviour of all in earth and sea,
 How happy they who rest in Thee!

4 Thy hand sets fast the mighty hills,
 Thy voice the troubled ocean stills;
 Evening and morning hymn Thy
  praise,
 And earth Thy bounty wide displays.

5 The year is with Thy goodness
  crowned;
 Thy clouds drop wealth the world
  around;
 Through Thee the deserts laugh and
  sing,
 And nature smiles, and owns her King.

6 Lord, on our souls Thy Spirit pour;
 The moral waste within restore;
 O let Thy love our spring-time be,
 And make us all bear fruit to Thee.

Henry Francis Lyte (1793–1847)

177 87.87.47

Based on Psalm 103

1 Praise, my soul, the King of heaven,
 To his feet thy tribute bring;
 Ransomed, healed, restored,
  forgiven,
 Who like thee His praise should
  sing?
 Praise Him! Praise Him!
 Praise the everlasting King.

2 Praise Him for His grace and favour
 To our fathers in distress;
 Praise Him still the same for ever,
 Slow to chide and swift to bless:
 Praise Him! Praise Him!
 Glorious in His faithfulness.

3 Father-like, He tends and spares us,
 Well our feeble frame He knows;
 In His hands He gently bears us,
 Rescues us from all our foes:
 Praise Him! Praise Him!
 Widely as His mercy flows.

4 Frail as summer's flower we
  flourish;
 Blows the wind, and it is gone;
 But while mortals rise and perish
 God endures unchanging on.
 Praise Him! Praise Him!
 Praise the high eternal one.

5 Angels, help us to adore Him;
 Ye behold Him face to face;
 Sun and moon, bow down before
  Him,
 Dwellers all in time and space.
 Praise Him! Praise Him!
 Praise with us the God of grace.

Henry Francis Lyte (1793 –1847)

178   7 7. 7 7. (with Hallelujahs)

'Let everything that hath breath praise the LORD' Psalm 150 v 6

1 Praise the Lord, His glories show,
Hallelujah!
Saints within His courts below,
Angels round His throne above,
All that see and share His love.

2 Earth to heaven, and heaven to earth,
Tell His wonders, sing His worth;
Age to age and shore to shore,
Praise Him, praise Him evermore!

3 Praise the Lord, His mercies trace;
Praise His providence and grace,
All that He for man hath done,
All He sends us through His Son.

4 Join each voice and sing each heart,
In His worship bear your part;
All that breathe, your Lord adore,
Praise Him, praise Him evermore.

Henry Francis Lyte (1793–1847)

179   6 6. 8 4. D

'Praise him according to his excellent greatness' Psalm 150 v 2

1 Praise to the living God!
All praisèd be His name,
Who was, and is, and is to be,
Ever the same!
The one eternal God
Ere aught that now appears:
The First, the Last, beyond all
thought
His timeless years!

2 Formless, all lovely forms
Declare His loveliness;
Holy, no holiness of earth
Can His express.
Lo, He is Lord of all!
Creation speaks His praise,
And everywhere, above, below,
His will obeys.

3 His Spirit floweth free,
High surging where it will:
In prophet's word He spake of old,
He speaketh still.
Established is His law,
And changeless it shall stand,
Written upon the human heart,
On sea, on land.

4 Eternal life hath He
Implanted in the soul;
His love shall be our strength and
stay,
While ages roll.
Praise to the living God!
All praisèd be His name,
Who was, and is, and is to be,
Ever the same.

Jewish Doxology (Medieval)
Tr. Max Landsberg (1845–1928)
and Newton Mann (1836–1926)

180   14 14. 4 7 8

'Let everything that hath breath praise the LORD' Psalm 150 v 6

1 Praise to the Lord, the Almighty, the
King of creation;
O my soul, praise Him, for He is thy
health and salvation;
All ye who hear,
Brothers and sisters, draw near,
Praise Him in glad adoration.

2 Praise to the Lord, who doth prosper
thy work and defend thee;
Surely His goodness and mercy here
daily attend thee;
Ponder anew
What the Almighty can do,
Who with His love doth befriend thee.

3 Praise to the Lord, who when
tempests their warfare are waging,
Who, when the elements madly
around thee are raging,
Biddeth them cease,
Turneth their fury to peace,
Whirlwinds and waters assuaging.

4 Praise to the Lord, who, when
   darkness and sin are abounding,
   Who, when the godless do triumph,
   all virtue confounding,
   Sheddeth His light,
   Chaseth the horrors of night,
   Saints with His mercy surrounding.

5 Praise to the Lord! O let all that is in
   me adore Him!
   All that hath life and breath, come
   now with praises before Him!
   Let the Amen
   Sound from His people again:
   Gladly for aye we adore Him.

Joachim Neander (1650–80)
Tr. Catherine Winkworth (1827–78) and others

181 87.87.D

'And one cried unto another, and said,
Holy, holy, holy' Isaiah 6 v 3

1 Round the Lord in glory seated,
   Cherubim and seraphim
   Filled His temple, and repeated
   Each to each the alternate hymn:

   Lord, Thy glory fills the heaven,
   Earth is with Thy fullness stored;
   Unto Thee be glory given,
   Holy, holy, holy Lord!

2 Heaven is still with glory ringing,
   Earth takes up the angels' cry,
   Holy, holy, holy singing,
   Lord of hosts, the Lord most high:

3 With His seraph-train before Him,
   With His holy church below,
   Thus unite we to adore Him,
   Bid we thus our anthem flow:

Richard Mant (1776–1848) Altd

182 77.77

'Blessed be thy glorious name'
Nehemiah 9 v 5

1 Songs of praise the angels sang,
   Heaven with hallelujahs rang,
   When creation was begun,
   When God spake and it was done.

2 Songs of praise awoke the morn,
   When the Prince of Peace was born;
   Songs of praise arose, when He
   Captive led captivity.

3 Heaven and earth must pass away,
   Songs of praise shall crown that day;
   God will make new heavens, new
   earth,
   Songs of praise shall hail their birth.

4 And shall man alone be dumb,
   Till that glorious kingdom come?
   No! the church delights to raise
   Psalms, and hymns, and songs of
   praise.

5 Saints below, with heart and voice,
   Still in songs of praise rejoice,
   Learning here, by faith and love,
   Songs of praise to sing above.

6 Borne upon their latest breath,
   Songs of praise shall conquer death;
   Then, amidst eternal joy,
   Songs of praise their powers employ.

James Montgomery (1771–1854)

183 S.M.

'Stand up and bless the LORD your God'
Nehemiah 9 v 5

1 Stand up, and bless the Lord,
   Ye people of His choice:
   Stand up, and bless the Lord your
   God
   With heart and soul and voice.

2 Though high above all praise,
   Above all blessings high,
   Who would not fear His holy name,
   And laud and magnify?

3 O for the living flame
From His own altar brought,
To touch our lips, our minds inspire,
And wing to heaven our thought!

4 God is our strength and song,
And His salvation ours;
Then be His love in Christ
proclaimed
With all our ransomed powers.

5 Stand up, and bless the Lord,
The Lord your God adore;
Stand up, and bless His glorious
name
Henceforth for evermore.

James Montgomery (1771–1854)

184   D.C.M.

Based on Nehemiah 9

1 Stand up and bless the Lord your
God
Both now and for always,
And blessed be Thy glorious name
Above all other praise.
Thou, even Thou, art Lord alone,
Who all things Thou didst form;
The hosts of heaven do give Thee
praise,
Who keeps us from all harm.

2 Full many are Thy wonders Lord,
And mercies daily shown;
But sinful hearts are slow to thank
And sooner sigh and groan.
But God is plenteous to forgive,
And full of love and grace,
Is slow to anger, and most kind
If we but seek His face.

3 A fiery, cloudy pillar, Thou
The way to us will show,
And by Thy light, if we but look,
The right way we will go.
Thy Spirit also sheds us light,
To teach and show us good,
And satisfies our mouth each day
With water and with food.

4 We nothing lack through all our
days,
All comes from Thy great hand,
If we but follow all Thy Word,
Obey each great command.
Our God is gracious, merciful,
Great things for us hath done;
Now therefore, praise to God be
given,
The great and mighty one!

© The Author   *Caroline Jane Cordle (b.1978)*

185   9 8. 9 8. D

Based on Psalm 118

1 Unto the Lord come, raise together
Glad songs of praise from earth
below;
To Him whose mercy lasts for ever
True thankfulness now let us show:
When, in distress, my cry ascended,
He answered me and set me free;
I will not fear, by Him defended:
What can man do now unto me?

2 Better it is on Him relying
Than confidence in man to place;
My enemies around defying,
Undaunted in His name I'll face:
My strength, my song and my
salvation,
All has the Lord become to me!
Praise, then, with joyful
acclamation,
His hand that brings the victory.

3 Thee will I praise – Thou hast
protected
When Thou didst hear my helpless
cry;
The stone by builders once rejected
Now in its place is set on high.
Save, Lord, we plead, Thou great
defender,
Send to us now prosperity;
With grateful hearts we then will
render
Our sacrifice of praise to Thee.

© The Author   *Graham Stuart Harrison (b.1935)*

186   6 6. 6 6. 4 4. 4 4

'Sing unto the LORD, bless his name'
Psalm 96 v 2

1 Ye holy angels bright,
  Who wait at God's right hand,
  Or through the realms of light
  Fly at your Lord's command,
    Assist our song,
    Or else the theme
    Too high doth seem
    For mortal tongue.

2 Ye blessèd souls at rest,
  Who ran this earthly race,
  And now, from sin released,
  Behold the Saviour's face,
    God's praises sound,
    As in His sight
    With sweet delight
    Ye do abound.

3 Ye saints, who toil below,
  Adore your heavenly King,
  And onward as ye go,
  Some joyful anthem sing;
    Take what He gives
    And praise Him still
    Through good and ill,
    Who ever lives.

4 My soul, bear thou thy part,
  Triumph in God above,
  And with a well-tuned heart
  Sing thou the songs of love.
    Let all thy days
    Till life shall end,
    Whate'er He send,
    Be filled with praise.

        Richard Baxter (1615–91) Altd

187   C.M.

'God is love' 1 John 4 v 16

1 Come, ye that know and fear the
    Lord,
  And raise your thoughts above;
  Let every heart and voice accord
  To sing that God is love.

2 This precious truth His Word
    declares
  And all His mercies prove;
  Jesus, the gift of gifts, appears
  To show that God is love.

3 Behold His patience bearing long
  With those who from Him rove,
  Till mighty grace their hearts subdue,
  To teach them God is love.

4 The work begun is carried on
  By power from heaven above;
  And every step, from first to last,
  Declares that God is love.

5 O, may we all while here below
  This best of blessings prove,
  Till warmer hearts, in brighter
    worlds,
  Proclaim that God is love.

        George Burder (1752–1832)

188   8 6. 8 8 6

'The King of kings, and Lord of lords ...
dwelling in light which no man can
approach unto' 1 Timothy 5 vv 15,16

1 Eternal Light! Eternal Light!
  How pure the soul must be,
  When, placed within Thy searching
    sight,
  It shrinks not, but with calm delight
  Can live and look on Thee.

2 The spirits that surround Thy throne
  May bear the burning bliss;
  But that is surely theirs alone,
  Since they have never, never known
  A fallen world like this.

3 O how shall I, whose native sphere
  Is dark, whose mind is dim,
  Before the Ineffable appear,
  And on my naked spirit bear
  The uncreated beam?

4 There is a way for man to rise
  To that sublime abode:
  An offering and a sacrifice,
  A Holy Spirit's energies,
  An advocate with God.

5 These, these prepare us for the sight
Of holiness above;
The sons of ignorance and night
Can dwell in the eternal light,
Through the eternal love.

Thomas Binney (1798–1874)

189   L.M.

'For there are three that bear record in heaven' 1 John 5 v 7

1 Father of heaven, whose love
    profound
A ransom for our souls hath found,
Before Thy throne we sinners bend;
To us Thy pardoning love extend.

2 Almighty Son, Incarnate Word,
Our Prophet, Priest, Redeemer, Lord,
Before Thy throne we sinners bend;
To us Thy saving grace extend.

3 Eternal Spirit, by whose breath
The soul is raised from sin and death,
Before Thy throne we sinners bend;
To us Thy quickening power extend.

4 Thrice holy: Father, Spirit, Son;
Mysterious Godhead, Three in One,
Before Thy throne we sinners bend;
Grace, pardon, life to us extend.

Edward Cooper (1770–1833)

190   L.M.

Based on Psalm 36 vv 5-9

1 High in the heavens, eternal God,
Thy goodness in full glory shines;
Thy truth shall break through every
    cloud
That veils and darkens Thy designs.

2 For ever firm Thy justice stands,
As mountains their foundations keep;
Wise are the wonders of Thy hands;
Thy judgments are a mighty deep.

3 Thy providence is kind and large,
Both man and beast Thy bounty
    share:

The whole creation is Thy charge,
But saints are Thy peculiar care.

4 My God, how excellent Thy grace,
Whence all our hope and comfort
    springs!
The sons of Adam in distress
Fly to the shadow of Thy wings.

5 From the provisions of Thy house
We shall be fed with sweet repast;
There mercy like a river flows,
And brings salvation to our taste.

6 Life, like a fountain rich and free,
Springs from the presence of the
    Lord;
And in Thy light our souls shall see
The glories promised in Thy Word.

Isaac Watts (1674–1748)

191   7 7. 7 7. D

'And God saw every thing that he had made, and, behold, it was very good' Genesis 1 v 31

1 Holy, holy, holy Lord,
God of hosts, when heaven and earth
Out of darkness, at Thy word,
Issued into glorious birth,
All Thy works before Thee stood,
And Thine eye beheld them good;
While they sang with sweet accord,
Holy, holy, holy Lord!

2 Holy, holy, holy! Thee,
One Jehovah evermore,
Father, Son and Spirit, we,
Dust and ashes, would adore:
Lightly by the world esteemed,
From that world by Thee redeemed,
Sing we here with glad accord,
Holy, holy, holy Lord!

3 Holy, holy, holy! all
  Heaven's triumphant choirs shall
    sing,
  When the ransomed nations fall
  At the footstool of their King:
  Then shall saints and seraphim,
  Harps and voices, swell one hymn,
  Blending in sublime accord,
  Holy, holy, holy Lord!

James Montgomery (1771–1854)

192   11 11. 11 11

'The Lord is my portion, saith my soul'
Lamentations 3 v 24

1 Immortal, invisible, God only wise,
  In light inaccessible hid from our
    eyes,
  Most blessed, most glorious, the
    Ancient of Days,
  Almighty, victorious, Thy great name
    we praise.

2 Unresting, unhasting, and silent as
    light,
  Nor wanting, nor wasting, Thou
    rulest in might;
  Thy justice like mountains high
    soaring above,
  Thy clouds which are fountains of
    goodness and love.

3 To all life Thou givest, to both great
    and small;
  In all life thou livest, the true life of
    all;
  We blossom and flourish as leaves
    on the tree,
  And wither and perish – but nought
    changeth Thee.

4 Great Father of glory, pure Father of
    light,
  Thine angels adore Thee, all veiling
    their sight;
  All laud we would render; O help us
    to see
  'Tis only the splendour of light
    hideth thee.

5 Immortal, invisible, God only wise,
  In light inaccessible hid from our
    eyes,
  Most blessed, most glorious, the
    Ancient of Days,
  Almighty, victorious, Thy great name
    we praise.

Walter Chalmers Smith (1824–1908)

193   8 7. 8 7

'Stand up and bless the LORD your God
for ever' Nehemiah 9 v 5

1 Praise to Thee, Thou great Creator!
  Praise be Thine from every tongue:
  Join my soul, with every creature,
  Join the universal song.

2 Father! Source of all compassion!
  Pure unbounded grace is Thine;
  Hail the God of our salvation!
  Praise Him for His love divine.

3 For ten thousand blessings given,
  For the hope of future joy,
  Sound his praise through earth and
    heaven,
  Sound Jehovah's praise on high.

4 Joyfully on earth adore Him,
  Till in heaven our song we raise;
  There, enraptured, fall before Him,
  Lost in wonder, love and praise.

John Fawcett (1739–1817)

194   10 10. 10 10

Based on Luke 1 vv 46-55

1 Tell out, my soul, the greatness of
    the Lord!
  Unnumbered blessings, give my
    spirit voice;
  Tender to me the promise of His
    Word;
  In God my Saviour shall my heart
    rejoice.

2 Tell out, my soul, the greatness of
    His name!
  Make known His might, the deeds
    His arm has done;
  His mercy sure, from age to age the
    same;
  His holy name, the Lord, the Mighty
    One.

3 Tell out, my soul, the greatness of
    His might!
  Powers and dominions lay their
    glory by.
  Proud hearts and stubborn wills are
    put to flight,
  The hungry fed, the humble lifted
    high.

4 Tell out, my soul, the glories of His
    Word!
  Firm is His promise, and His mercy
    sure.
  Tell out, my soul, the greatness of
    the Lord
  To children's children and for
    evermore!

© The Author,   Timothy Dudley-Smith (b.1926)
Administered by OUP

195   L.M.

'The Lord God omnipotent reigneth'
Revelation 19 v 6

1 The Lord is King; lift up thy voice,
  O earth, and all ye heavens rejoice!
  From world to world the joy shall
    ring:
  'The Lord Omnipotent is King!'

2 The Lord is King! who then shall
    dare
  Resist His will, distrust His care,
  Or murmur at His wise decrees,
  Or doubt His royal promises?

3 The Lord is King! child of the dust,
  The Judge of all the earth is just:
  Holy and true are all His ways;
  Let every creature speak His praise.

4 He reigns! ye saints, exalt your
    strains:
  Your God is King, your Father reigns;
  And He is at the Father's side,
  The Man of Love, the Crucified.

5 Come, make your wants, your
    burdens known:
  He will present them at the throne;
  And angel bands are waiting there,
  His messages of love to bear.

6 One Lord, one empire, all secures:
  He reigns – and life and death are
    yours;
  Through earth and heaven one song
    shall ring,
  'The Lord Omnipotent is King!'

                    Josiah Conder (1789–1855)

196   8 8 8. D

'They that sow in tears shall reap in joy'
Psalm 126 v 5

1 Thee will I praise with all my heart,
  And tell mankind how good Thou art,
  How marvellous Thy works of grace;
  Thy name I will in songs record,
  And joy and glory in my Lord,
  Extolled above all thanks and praise.

2 The Lord will save His people here;
  In times of need their help is near
  To all by sin and hell oppressed;
  And they that know Thy name will
    trust
  In Thee, who, to Thy promise just,
  Hast never left a soul distressed.

3 The Lord is by His judgements known;
  He helps His poor afflicted one,
  His sorrows all He bears in mind;
  The mourner shall not always weep,
  Who sows in tears in joy shall reap,
  With grief who seeks with joy shall
    find.

4 A helpless soul that looks to Thee
Is sure at last Thy face to see,
And all Thy goodness to partake;
The sinner who for Thee doth grieve,
And longs, and labours to believe,
Thou never, never wilt forsake.

Charles Wesley (1707–88)

197 C.M.

'The LORD, the LORD God, merciful and
gracious' Exodus 34 v 6

1 Thy ceaseless, unexhausted love,
Unmerited and free,
Delights our evil to remove,
And help our misery.

2 Thou waitest to be gracious still;
Thou dost with sinners bear,
That, saved, we may Thy goodness
feel,
And all Thy grace declare.

3 Thy goodness and Thy truth to me,
To every soul, abound,
A vast, unfathomable sea,
Where all our thoughts are drowned.

4 Its streams the whole creation reach,
So plenteous is the store,
Enough for all, enough for each,
Enough for evermore.

5 Faithful, O Lord, Thy mercies are,
A rock that cannot move:
A thousand promises declare
Thy constancy of love.

6 Throughout the universe it reigns,
Unalterably sure;
And while the truth of God remains,
The goodness must endure.

Charles Wesley (1707–88)

198 11 11. 11 11

'I will sing of the mercies of the Lord'
Psalm 89 v 1

1 Thy mercy, my God, is the theme of
my song,
The joy of my heart, and the boast of
my tongue;
Thy free grace alone, from the first
to the last,
Hath won my affections, and bound
my soul fast.

2 Thy mercy is more than a match for
my heart,
Which wonders to feel its own
hardness depart;
Dissolved by Thy goodness I fall to
the ground,
And weep to the praise of the mercy
I found.

3 The door of Thy mercy stands open
all day
To the poor and the needy who
knock by the way;
No sinner shall ever be empty sent
back,
Who comes seeking mercy for
Jesus's sake.

4 Thy mercy in Jesus exempts me from
hell;
Its glories I'll sing and its wonders
I'll tell;
'Twas Jesus, my friend, when He
hung on the tree,
Who opened the channel of mercy
for me.

5 Great Father of mercies, Thy
goodness I own,
And the covenant love of Thy
crucified Son;
All praise to the Spirit, whose
whisper divine
Seals mercy, and pardon, and
righteousness mine.

John Stocker (Gospel Magazine 1776)

199

668.668.33.66

'A name which is above every name'
Philippians 2 v 9

1 Wondrous King, all-glorious,
Sovereign Lord victorious,
O receive our praise with favour!
From Thee welled God's kindness,
Though we in our blindness
Strayed from Thee, our blessèd
   Saviour.
Strengthen Thou,
Help us now,
Let our tongues be singing,
Thee our praises bringing.

2 Heavens, spread the story
Of our Maker's glory,
All the pomp of earth obscuring.
Sun, thy rays be sending,
Thy bright beams expecting,
Light to all the earth assuring.
Moon and star,
Praise afar
Him who glorious made you;
The vast heavens aid you.

3 O my soul, rejoicing,
Sing, thy praises voicing,
Sing, with hymns of faith adore Him!
All who here have being,
Shout, your voices freeing;
Bow down in the dust before Him.
His is God
Sabaoth;
Praise the Lord who loves us
From our sins and saves us.

4 Hallelujahs render
To the Lord most tender,
Ye who know and love the Saviour.
Hallelujahs sing ye,
Ye redeemed, O bring ye
Hearts that yield Him glad behaviour.
Blest are ye
Endlessly;
Sinless there for ever,
Ye shall laud Him ever.

Joachim Neander (1650–80)
Tr. William J. Schaefer (b.1891)

200

Irregular

'Worthy is the Lamb that was slain'
Revelation 5 v 12

1 All glory and praise
To the Lamb that was slain,
Who has borne all our sins
And has cleansed every stain.

Hallelujah! Thine the glory,
Hallelujah! we sing;
Hallelujah! Thine the glory,
Our praise now we bring.

2 We praise Thee, O God,
For Thy Spirit of light,
Who has shown us our Saviour
And scattered our night.

3 All glory and praise
To the God of all grace,
Who has bought us, and sought us,
And shown us His face.

William P. Mackay (1839–85)

201

C.M.

'Thy faithfulness shalt thou establish in
the very heavens' Psalm 89 v 2

1 Begin, my soul, some heavenly
   theme;
Awake, my voice, and sing
The mighty works, or mightier
   name,
Of our eternal King.

2 Tell of His wondrous faithfulness,
And sound His power abroad;
Sing the sweet promise of His grace,
And the performing God.

3 Proclaim salvation from the Lord,
For wretched, dying men:
His hand hath writ the sacred word
With an immortal pen.

4 Engraved as in eternal brass,
The mighty promise shines;
Nor can the powers of darkness
   'rase
Those everlasting lines.

5 His every word of grace is strong
  As that which built the skies;
  The voice that rolls the stars along
  Speaks all the promises.

6 Now shall my fainting heart rejoice
  To know my heaven secure;
  I trust the all-creating voice,
  And faith desires no more.

Isaac Watts (1674–1748) Altd

202   6 6 4. 6 6. 6 4

'Let God arise, let his enemies be scattered'
Psalm 68 v 1

1 Come, Thou Almighty King,
  Help us Thy name to sing,
  Help us to praise:
  Father all-glorious,
  O'er all victorious,
  Come and reign over us,
  Ancient of Days!

2 Come, Thou Incarnate Word,
  Gird on Thy mighty sword,
  Our prayers attend;
  Come, and Thy people bless,
  And give Thy Word success;
  Spirit of holiness,
  On us descend!

3 Come, Holy Comforter,
  Thy sacred witness bear
  In this glad hour:
  Thou, who almighty art,
  Now rule in every heart,
  And ne'er from us depart,
  Spirit of power!

4 To the great One in Three,
  Eternal praises be,
  Hence evermore:
  His sovereign majesty
  May we in glory see,
  And to eternity
  Love and adore!

Anonymous (c.1757)

203   L.M.

'The LORD commanded the blessing'
Psalm 133 v 3

1 Command Thy blessing from above,
  O God! on all assembled here;
  Behold us with a Father's love,
  While we look up with filial fear.

2 Command Thy blessing, Jesus, Lord!
  May we Thy true disciples be;
  Speak to each heart the mighty
    word,
  Say to the weakest, 'Follow me!'

3 Command Thy blessing in this hour,
  Spirit of truth! And fill this place
  With humbling and exalting power,
  With quickening and confirming
    grace.

4 O Thou, our Maker, Saviour, Guide,
  One true, eternal God confessed,
  May nought in life or death divide
  The saints in Thy communion blest!

5 With Thee and these for ever bound,
  May all, who here in prayer unite,
  With harps and songs Thy throne
    surround,
  Rest in Thy love, and reign in light.

James Montgomery (1771–1854) Altd

204   D.S.M.

*'For in him we live, and move, and have
our being' Acts 17 v 28*

1 Father, in whom we live,
  In whom we are, and move,
  The glory, power, and praise receive
  Of Thy creating love.
  Let all the angel throng
  Give thanks to God on high;
  While earth repeats the joyful song,
  And echoes to the sky.

2 Incarnate Deity,
Let all the ransomed race
Render in thanks their lives to Thee,
For Thy redeeming grace.
The grace to sinners showed
Ye heavenly choirs proclaim,
And cry: Salvation to our God,
Salvation to the Lamb!

3 Spirit of holiness,
Let all Thy saints adore
Thy sacred energy, and bless
Thine heart-renewing power.
Not angel tongues can tell
Thy love's ecstatic height,
The glorious joy unspeakable,
The beatific sight.

4 Eternal, triune Lord!
Let all the hosts above,
Let all the sons of men, record
And dwell upon Thy love.
When heaven and earth are fled
Before Thy glorious face,
Sing all the saints Thy love hath made,
Thine everlasting praise.

Charles Wesley (1707–88)

205   8 7. 8 7. 4 7

'Give unto the LORD the glory due unto his name' 1 Chronicles 16 v 29

1 Glory be to God the Father,
Glory be to God the Son,
Glory be to God the Spirit,
Great Jehovah, Three in One:
Glory, glory,
While eternal ages run!

2 Glory be to Him who loved us,
Washed us from each spot and stain;
Glory be to Him whom bought us,
Made us kings with Him to reign:
Glory, glory,
To the Lamb that once was slain!

3 Glory to the King of angels,
Glory to the church's King,
Glory to the King of nations,
Heaven and earth your praises bring:
Glory, glory,
To the King of glory bring!

4 'Glory, blessing, praise eternal!'
Thus the choir of angels sings;
'Honour, riches, power, dominion!'
Thus its praise creation brings.
Glory, glory,
Glory to the King of kings!

Horatius Bonar (1808–89)

206   L.M.

*'Bless the Lord O my soul: and all that is within me, bless his holy name'
Psalm 103 v 1*

1 God is a name my soul adores,
The almighty Three, the eternal One;
Nature and grace, with all their powers,
Confess the infinite Unknown.

2 Thy voice produced the sea and spheres,
Bade the waves roar, the planets shine;
But nothing like Thyself appears
Through all these spacious works of Thine.

3 Still restless nature dies and grows,
From change to change the creatures run:
Thy being no succession knows,
And all Thy vast designs are one.

4 A glance of Thine runs through the globe,
Rules the bright worlds, and moves their frame;
Of light Thou form'st Thy dazzling robe,
Thy ministers are living flame.

5 How shall polluted mortals dare
To sing Thy glory or Thy grace?
Beneath Thy feet we lie afar,
And see but shadows of Thy face.

6 Who can behold the blazing light?
Who can approach consuming
flame?
None but Thy wisdom knows Thy
might,
None but Thy word can speak Thy
name.

Isaac Watts (1674–1748)

207   6 6 8. 6 6 8. 3 3. 6 6

'The LORD is in his holy temple'
Psalm 11 v 4

1 God is in His temple,
The Almighty Father,
Round His footstool let us gather;
Him with adoration
Serve, the Lord most holy,
Who hath mercy on the lowly.
Let us raise
Hymns of praise,
For His great salvation:
God is in His temple!

2 Christ comes to His temple:
We, His word receiving,
Are made happy in believing.
Lo! From sin delivered,
He hath turned our sadness,
Our deep gloom, to light and
gladness.
Let us raise
Hymns of praise,
For our bonds are severed:
Christ comes to His temple!

3 Come and claim Thy temple,
Gracious Holy Spirit!
In our hearts Thy home inherit:
Make in us Thy dwelling,
Thy high work fulfilling,
Into ours Thy will instilling;
Till we raise
Hymns of praise,
Beyond mortal telling,
In the eternal temple.

William Tidd Matson (1833–99)

208   C.M.

'Holy, holy, holy, Lord God Almighty'
Revelation 4 v 8

1 Hail! holy, holy, holy Lord!
Whom One in Three we know;
By all Thy heavenly host adored,
By all Thy church below.

2 One undivided Trinity
With triumph we proclaim;
Thy universe is full of Thee,
And speaks Thy glorious name.

3 Thee, Holy Father, we confess,
Thee, Holy Son, adore,
Thee, Spirit of trust and holiness,
We worship evermore.

4 Three Persons equally divine
We magnify and love;
And saints in earth and heaven shall
join,
To sing Thy praise above.

5 Hail! holy, holy, holy Lord,
Our heavenly song shall be,
Supreme, essential One, adored
In co-eternal Three.

Charles Wesley (1707–88)

209   11 12. 12 10

'Which was, and is, and is to come'
Revelation 4 v 8

1 Holy, holy, holy, Lord God Almighty!
Early in the morning our song shall
rise to Thee;
Holy, holy, holy! merciful and
mighty,
God in Three Persons, blessed
Trinity!

2 Holy, holy, holy! all the saints adore
Thee,
Casting down their golden crowns
around the glassy sea;
Cherubim and seraphim falling
down before Thee,
Who wert, and art, and evermore
shalt be.

3 Holy, holy, holy! though the
   darkness hide Thee,
   Though the eye of sinful man Thy
   glory may not see,
   Only Thou art holy, there is none
   beside Thee
   Perfect in power, in love, and purity.

4 Holy, holy, holy, Lord God Almighty!
   All Thy works shall praise Thy name,
   in earth and sky and sea;
   Holy, holy, holy! merciful and mighty,
   God in Three Persons, blessèd
   Trinity!

Reginald Heber (1783–1826)

210   L.M.

'Thy face, LORD, will I seek' Psalm 27 v 8

1 Lord Jesus Christ, be present now,
   Our hearts in true devotion bow;
   Thy Spirit send with grace divine,
   And let Thy truth within us shine.

2 Unseal our lips to sing Thy praise;
   Our souls to Thee in worship raise;
   Make strong our faith, increase our
   light,
   That we may know Thy name aright:

3 Until we join the hosts that cry
   'Holy art Thou, O Lord most high!'
   And in the light of that blest place
   For e'er behold Thee face to face.

4 Glory to God the Father, Son,
   And Holy Spirit, Three in One!
   To Thee, O blessèd Trinity,
   Be praise throughout eternity!

Anonymous (1651)
Tr. Catherine Winkworth (1827–78)

211   6 7. 6 7. 6 6. 6 6

*'O clap your hands, all ye people; shout
unto God with the voice of triumph'
Psalm 47 v 1*

1 Now thank we all our God,
   With hearts, and hands, and voices;
   Who wondrous things hath done,
   In whom His world rejoices;
   Who, from our mothers' arms,
   Hath blessed us on our way
   With countless gifts of love,
   And still is ours today.

2 O may this bounteous God
   Through all our life be near us,
   With ever-joyful hearts
   And blessèd peace to cheer us,
   And keep us in His grace,
   And guide us when perplexed,
   And free us from all ills
   In this world and the next.

3 All praise and thanks to God
   The Father now be given,
   The Son, and Him who reigns
   With them in highest heaven:
   The one eternal God,
   Whom earth and heaven adore;
   For thus it was, is now,
   And shall be evermore.

Martin Rinkart (1586–1649)
Tr. Catherine Winkworth (1827–78)

212   11 10. 11 10

'Praise ye the LORD' Psalm 148 v 1

1 Praise ye Jehovah! praise the Lord
   most holy,
   Who cheers the contrite, girds with
   strength the weak;
   Praise Him who will with glory
   crown the lowly,
   And with salvation beautify the
   meek.

2 Praise ye the Lord, for all His
    lovingkindness,
  And all the tender mercies He hath
    shown;
  Praise Him who pardons all our sin
    and blindness,
  And calls us sons, and takes us for
    His own.

3 Praise ye Jehovah, source of all our
    blessing!
  Before His gifts earth's richest
    boons wax dim;
  Resting in Him, His peace and joy
    possessing,
  All things are ours, for we have all in
    Him.

4 Praise ye the Father, God the Lord,
    who gave us,
  With full and perfect love, His only
    Son;
  Praise ye the Son who died Himself
    to save us;
  Praise ye the Spirit, praise the Three
    in One!

Margaret Cockburn-Campbell (1808–41)

213   6 6. 8 4. D

*'I have taken upon me to speak unto the
Lord, which am but dust and ashes'
Genesis 18 v 27*

1 The God of Abraham praise,
  Who reigns enthroned above,
  Ancient of everlasting days,
  And God of love.
  Jehovah! Great I AM!
  By earth and heaven confessed;
  I bow and bless the sacred name
  For ever blessed.

2 The God of Abraham praise,
  At whose supreme command
  From earth I rise, and seek the joys
  At His right hand.
  I all on earth forsake –
  Its wisdom, fame, and power –
  And Him my only portion make,
  My shield and tower.

3 The God of Abraham praise,
  Whose all-sufficient grace
  Shall guide me all my happy days
  In all my ways.
  He is my faithful Friend,
  He is my gracious God;
  And He shall save me to the end
  Through Jesus' blood.

4 He by Himself hath sworn,
  I on His oath depend,
  I shall, on eagles' wings upborne,
  To heaven ascend;
  I shall behold His face,
  I shall His power adore,
  And sing the wonders of His grace
  For evermore.

5 There dwells the Lord our King,
  The Lord our Righteousness,
  Triumphant o'er the world and sin,
  The Prince of Peace;
  On Zion's sacred height
  His kingdom He maintains,
  And glorious with His saints in light
  For ever reigns.

6 The whole triumphant host
  Give thanks to God on high
  Hail, Father, Son, and Holy Ghost!
  They ever cry.
  Hail, Abraham's God, and mine!
  I join the heavenly lays;
  All might and majesty are Thine,
  And endless praise.

Thomas Olivers (1725–99)

214   6 6. 6 6. 8 8

*'Ye have not chosen me but I have chosen
you' John 15 v 16*

1 To Him that chose us first,
  Before the world began;
  To Him that bore the curse
  To save rebellious man;
  To Him that formed our hearts
    anew,
  Is endless praise and glory due.

2 The Father's love shall run
  Through our immortal songs;
  We bring to God the Son
  Hosannas on our tongues;
  Our lips address the Spirit's name,
  With equal praise and zeal the same.

3 Let every saint above,
  And angel round the throne,
  For ever bless and love
  The sacred Three in One;
  Thus heaven shall raise His honours
     high,
  When earth and time grow old and
     die.

Isaac Watts (1674–1748)

215   6 6. 6 6. 8 8

'Salvation is of the Lord' Jonah 2 v 9

1 We give immortal praise
  To God the Father's love,
  For all our comforts here,
  And better hopes above;
  He sent His own eternal Son,
  To die for sins that man had done.

2 To God the Son belongs
  Immortal glory too,
  Who bought us with His blood
  From everlasting woe:
  And now He lives, and now He
     reigns,
  And sees the fruit of all His pains.

3 To God the Spirit's name
  Immortal worship give,
  Whose new-creating power
  Makes the dead sinner live;
  His work completes the great design,
  And fills the soul with joy divine.

4 Almighty God, to Thee
  Be endless honours done,
  The undivided Three,
  And the mysterious One:
  Where reason fails, with all her
     powers,
  There faith prevails, and love adores.

Issac Watts (1674–1748)

216   L.M.

'Holy, holy, holy' Isaiah 6 v 3

1 We praise, we worship Thee, O God;
  Thy sovereign power we sound
     abroad;
  All nations bow before Thy throne,
  And Thee the eternal Father own.

2 Loud hallelujahs to Thy name
  Angels and seraphim proclaim;
  The heavens and all the powers on
     high
  With rapture consistantly do cry.

3 'O holy, holy, holy Lord,
  Thou God of hosts, by all adored,
  Earth and the heavens are full of
     Thee,
  Thy light, Thy power, Thy majesty.'

4 Apostles join the glorious throng,
  And swell the loud immortal song;
  Prophets enraptured hear the sound,
  And spread the hallelujahs round.

5 Victorious martyrs join their praise
  And shout the omnipotence of grace,
  While all Thy church through all the
     earth
  Acknowledge and extol Thy worth.

6 Glory to Thee, O God most high!
  Father, we praise Thy majesty:
  The Son, the Spirit we adore;
  One Godhead, blest for evermore.

Gell's Collection 1815

217   6 6. 6 6. 8 8

'God is love' 1 John 4 v 8

1 What was it, O our God,
  Led Thee to give Thy Son,
  To yield Thy Well-beloved
  For us by sin undone?
  'Twas love unbounded led Thee thus
  To give Thy Well-beloved for us.

2 What led the Son of God
   To leave His throne on high,
   To shed His precious blood,
   To suffer and to die?
   'Twas love, unbounded love to us,
   Led Him to die and suffer thus.

3 What moved Thee to impart
   Thy Spirit from above,
   That He might fill our heart
   With heavenly peace and love?
   'Twas love, unbounded love to us,
   Moved Thee to give Thy Spirit thus.

4 What love to Thee we owe,
   Our God, for all Thy grace!
   Our hearts may well o'erflow
   In everlasting praise:
   Help us, O Lord, to praise Thee thus
   For all Thy boundless love to us.

                    Ann Gilbert (1782–1866)

218   C.M.

'And very early in the morning the first
day of the week, they came unto the
sepulchre at the rising of the sun'
Mark 16 v 2

1 Blest morning, whose first dawning
      rays
   Beheld the Son of God
   Arise triumphant from the grave,
   And leave His dark abode!

2 Wrapt in the silence of the tomb
   The great Redeemer lay,
   Till the revolving skies had brought
   The third, the appointed day.

3 Hell and the grave combined their
      force
   To hold our Lord, in vain;
   Sudden the Conqueror arose,
   And burst their feeble chain.

4 To Thy great name, Almighty Lord,
   We sacred honours pay,
   And loud hosannas shall proclaim
   The triumphs of the day.

5 Salvation and immortal praise
   To our victorious King!
   Let heaven and earth, and rocks and
      seas,
   With glad hosannas ring!

                    Isaac Watts (1674–1748)

219   8 8. 8 8. 8 8.

'This is the day which the LORD hath
made' Psalm 118 v 24

1 Come, let us with our Lord arise,
   Our Lord, who made both earth and
      skies;
   Who died to save the world He made,
   And rose triumphant from the dead;
   He rose, the Prince of life and peace,
   And stamped the day for ever His.

2 This is the day the Lord hath made,
   That all may see His love displayed,
   May feel His resurrection's power,
   And rise again to fall no more,
   In perfect righteousness renewed,
   And filled with all the life of God.

3 Then let us render Him His own,
   With solemn prayer approach the
      throne,
   With meekness hear the gospel
      word,
   With thanks His dying love record;
   Our joyful hearts and voices raise,
   And fill the courts with songs of
      praise.

4 Honour and praise to Jesus pay
   Throughout His consecrated day;
   Be all in Jesu's praise employed,
   Nor leave a single moment void;
   With utmost care the time improve,
   And only breathe His praise and
      love.

                    Charles Wesley (1707–88)

220

L.M.

'The sabbath of rest' Exodus 31 v 15

1 How welcome to the saints, when
      pressed
   With six days' noise, and care, and
      toil,
   Is the returning day of rest,
   Which hides them from the world
      awhile!

2 Now from the throng withdrawn
      away,
   They seem to breathe a different air;
   Composed and softened by the day,
   All things another aspect wear.

3 How happy if their lot is cast
   Where statedly the gospel sounds!
   The Word is honey to their taste,
   Renews their strength, and heals
      their wounds.

4 With joy they hasten to the place
   Where they their Saviour oft have
      met;
   And while they feast upon His grace,
   Their burdens and their griefs forget.

5 This favoured lot, my friends, is ours;
   May we the priv'lege highly prize,
   And find these consecrated hours
   Sweet earnests of immortal joys!

                    John Newton (1725–1807)

221

C.M.

*'O LORD, I beseech thee, send now
prosperity'* Psalm 118 v 25

1 Now, gracious God, Thine arm
      reveal,
   And make Thy glory known,
   Now let us all Thy presence feel,
   And soften hearts of stone.

2 Help us to venture near Thy throne,
   And plead a Saviour's name,
   For all that we can call our own
   Is vanity and shame.

3 From all the guilt of former sin
   May mercy set us free;
   And let the week we now begin
   Begin and end with Thee.

4 Send down Thy Spirit from above,
   That saints may love Thee more;
   And sinners now may learn to love,
   Who never loved before.

                    John Newton (1725–1807)

222

7 6. 7 6. D

'I was in the Spirit on the Lord's day'
Revelation 1 v 10

1 O day of rest and gladness,
   O day of joy and light,
   O balm of care and sadness,
   Most beautiful, most bright!
   On thee the high and lowly,
   Through ages joined in tune,
   Sing: Holy, holy, holy,
   To the great God Triune.

2 On thee, at the creation,
   The light first had its birth;
   On thee, for our salvation,
   Christ rose from depths of earth;
   On thee, our Lord victorious
   The Spirit sent from heaven:
   And thus on Thee most glorious
   A triple light was given.

3 Today on weary nations
   The heavenly manna falls;
   To holy convocations
   The silver trumpet calls,
   Where gospel light is glowing
   With pure and radiant beams,
   And living water flowing
   With soul-refreshing streams.

4 New graces ever gaining
   From this our day of rest,
   We reach the rest remaining
   To spirits of the blest.
   To Holy Ghost be praises,
   To Father and to Son;
   The church her voice upraises
   To Thee, blest Three in One.

              Christopher Wordsworth (1807–85)

223
C.M.

'Let my beloved come into his garden,
and eat his pleasant fruits'
Song of Solomon 4 v 16

1 Once more we come before our God;
   Once more His blessing ask;
   O may not duty seem a load,
   Nor worship prove a task.

2 Father, Thy quickening Spirit send
   From heaven, in Jesus' name,
   To make our waiting minds attend,
   And put our souls in frame.

3 May we receive the word we hear,
   Each in an honest heart;
   Hoard up the precious treasure
      there,
   And never with it part.

4 To seek thee all our hearts dispose;
   To each thy blessings suit;
   And let the seed thy servant sows
   Produce a copious fruit.

5 Bid the refreshing north wind wake;
   Say to the south wind, Blow;
   Let every plant the power partake,
   And all the garden grow.

6 Revive the parched with heavenly
      showers;
   The cold with warmth divine;
   And as the benefit is ours,
   Be all the glory Thine.

Joseph Hart (1712–1768)

224
87.87.887

'For thine is the kingdom, and the power,
and the glory' Matthew 6 v 13

1 Our Father God, Thy name we
      praise,
   To Thee our hymns addressing,
   And joyfully our voices raise
   Thy faithfulness confessing;
   Assembled by Thy grace, O Lord,
   We seek fresh guidance from Thy
      Word;
   Now grant anew Thy blessing.

2 Touch, Lord, the lips that speak for
      Thee;
   Set words of truth before us,
   That we may grow in constancy,
   The light of wisdom o'er us.
   Give us this day our daily bread;
   May hungry souls again be fed;
   May heavenly food restore us.

3 As with our brethren here we meet,
   Thy grace alone can feed us.
   As here we gather at Thy feet
   We pray that Thou wilt heed us.
   The power is Thine, O Lord divine,
   The kingdom and the rule are Thine.
   May Jesus Christ still lead us!

Anabaptist Ausbund 16th Century
© Copyright Control   *Tr. E. A. Payne (1902–1980)*

225
L.M.

Based on Psalm 92

1 Sweet is the work, my God, my King,
   To praise Thy name, give thanks and
      sing;
   To show Thy love by morning light,
   And talk of all Thy truth at night.

2 Sweet is the day of sacred rest,
   No mortal cares disturb my breast;
   O may my heart in tune be found,
   Like David's harp of solemn sound!

3 My heart shall triumph in the Lord,
   And bless His works and bless His
      Word;
   Thy works of grace, how bright they
      shine,
   How deep Thy counsels, how divine!

4 And I shall share a glorious part
   When grace has well refined my
      heart;
   And fresh supplies of joy are shed,
   Like holy oil, to cheer my head.

5 Sin, my worst enemy before,
   Shall vex my eyes and ears no more;
   My inward foes shall all be slain,
   Nor Satan break my peace again.

6 Then shall I see, and hear, and know
All I desired or wished below;
And every power find sweet employ
In that eternal world of joy.

Isaac Watts (1674–1748)

226 L.M.

'The Lord's day' Revelation 1 v 10

1 This day, at Thy creating Word
First o'er the earth the light was
    poured:
O Lord, this day upon us shine
And fill our souls with light divine.

2 This day the Lord for sinners slain
In might victorious rose again:
O Jesus, may we raisèd be
From death of sin to life in Thee!

3 This day the Holy Spirit came
With fiery tongues of cloven flame:
O Spirit, fill our hearts this day
With grace to hear and grace to pray.

4 O Day of light and life and grace!
From earthly toil sweet resting place,
Thy hallowed hours, blest gift of
    love,
Give we again to God above.

5 All praise to God the Father be,
All praise, eternal Son, to Thee,
Whom with the Spirit, we adore
For ever and for evermore.

William Walsham How (1823–97)

227 S.M.

*'And God said, Let there be light: and
there was light' Genesis 1 v 3*

1 This is the day of light:
Let there be light today;
O Day-spring, rise upon our night,
And chase its gloom away.

2 This is the day of rest:
Our failing strength renew;
On weary brain and troubled breast
Shed Thou Thy freshening dew.

3 This is the day of peace:
Thy peace our spirits fill;
Bid Thou the blasts of discord cease,
The waves of strife be still.

4 This is the day of prayer:
Let earth to heaven draw near;
Lift up our hearts to seek thee there,
Come down to meet us here.

5 This is the first of days:
Send forth Thy quickening breath,
And wake dead souls to love and
    praise,
O Vanquisher of death!

John Ellerton (1826–93)

228 C.M.

Based on Psalm 118 vv 24-26

1 This is the day the Lord hath made;
He calls the hours His own;
Let heaven rejoice, let earth be glad,
And praise surround the throne.

2 Today He rose and left the dead,
And Satan's empire fell;
Today the saints His triumphs
    spread,
And all His wonders tell.

3 Hosanna to the anointed King,
To David's holy Son;
Help us, O Lord; descend and bring
Salvation from Thy throne.

4 Blest be the Lord, who comes to
    men
With messages of grace;
Who comes in God His Father's
    name,
To save our sinful race.

5 Hosanna in the highest strains
The Church on earth can raise;
The highest heav'ns, in which He
    reigns,
Shall give Him nobler praise.

Isaac Watts (1674–1748)

229 88. 88. 88

'My word ... shall not return unto me
void' Isaiah 55 v 11

1 Thy presence, gracious God, afford:
Prepare us to receive Thy word;
Now let Thy voice engage our ear,
And faith be mixed with what we
hear.
Thus, Lord, Thy waiting servants bless,
And crown Thy gospel with success.

2 Distracting thoughts and cares
remove,
And fix our hearts and hopes above;
With food divine may we be fed,
And satisfied with living bread.

3 To us the sacred word apply
With sovereign power and energy:
And may we, in Thy faith and fear,
Reduce to practice what we hear.

4 Father, in us Thy Son reveal,
Teach us to know and do Thy will:
Thy saving power and love display,
And guide us to the realms of day.

John Fawcett (1740–1817)

230 L.M.

'From the rising of the sun unto the going
down of the same the LORD's name is to
be praised' Psalm 113 v3

1 All praise to Thee, who safe hast
kept,
And hast refreshed me while I slept!
Grant, Lord, when I from death shall
wake,
I may of endless light partake.

2 Lord, I my vows to Thee renew;
Disperse my sins as morning dew;
Guard my first springs of thought
and will,
And with Thyself my spirit fill.

3 Direct, control, suggest, this day,
All I design, or do, or say,
That all my powers, with all their
might,
In Thy sole glory may unite.

4 Praise God, from whom all blessings
flow;
Praise Him, all creatures here below;
Praise Him above, ye heavenly host;
Praise Father, Son, and Holy Ghost.

Thomas Ken (1637–1710)

231 LM

'My voice shalt thou hear in the
morning, O LORD' Psalm 5 v 3

1 Awake, my soul, and with the sun
Thy daily stage of duty run,
Shake off dull sloth, and joyful rise
To pay thy morning sacrifice.

2 Thy precious time mis-spent
redeem,
Each present day thy last esteem;
Improve thy talent with due care;
For the great day thyself prepare.

3 Let all thy converse be sincere;
Thy conscience as the noonday clear;
Think how all-seeing God thy ways
And all thy secret thoughts surveys.

4 By influence of light divine
Let thy own light in good works shine;
Reflect all heaven's propitious ways
In ardent love and cheerful praise.

5 Wake, and lift up thyself, my heart,
And with the angels bear thy part,
Who all night long unwearied sing
High praise to the eternal King.

6 Praise God, from whom all blessings
flow;
Praise Him, all creatures here below;
Praise Him above, ye heavenly host;
Praise Father, Son, and Holy Ghost.

Thomas Ken (1637–1710)

232   S.M.

'O sing unto the LORD a new song'
Psalm 96 v 1

1 Begin the day with God:
He is the rising Sun,
His is the radiance of thy dawn,
His the fresh day begun.

2 Sing a new song at morn;
Join the glad woods and hills;
Join the fresh winds and seas and
    plains;
Join the bright flowers and rills.

3 Awake, cold lips, and sing;
Arise, dull heart, and pray;
Lift up, O man, thy heart and eyes;
Brush slothfulness away.

4 Cast every weight aside;
Do battle with each sin;
Fight with the faithless world
    without,
The faithless heart within.

5 Look up beyond these clouds,
Thither thy pathway lies;
Mount up, away, and linger not,
Thy goal is yonder skies!

Horatius Bonar (1808–89)

233   C.M.

'Whatsoever ye do, do all to the glory of
God' 1 Corinthians 10 v 31

1 My Father, for another night
Of quiet sleep and rest,
For all the joy of morning light
Thy holy name be blest.

2 Now with the new-born day I give
Myself anew to Thee,
That as Thou willest I may live,
And what Thou willest be.

3 Whate'er I do, things great or small,
Whate'er I speak or frame,
Thy glory may I seek in all,
Do all in Jesu's name.

4 My Father, for His sake, I pray,
Thy child accept and bless;
And lead me by Thy grace today
In paths of righteousness.

Henry Williams Baker (1821–77)

234   L.M.

'He that followeth me shall not walk in
darkness, but shall have the light of life'
John 8 v 12

1 O Jesus, Lord of heavenly grace,
Thou brightness of Thy Father's
    face,
Thou fountain of eternal light,
Whose beams disperse the shades of
    night;

2 Come, holy Sun of heavenly love,
Shower down Thy radiance from
    above,
And to our inmost hearts convey
The Holy Spirit's cloudless ray.

3 And we the Father's help will claim,
And sing the Father's glorious
    name;
His powerful succour we implore,
That we may stand, to fall no more.

4 May He our actions deign to bless,
And loose the bonds of wickedness,
From sudden falls our feet defend,
And guide us safely to the end.

5 May faith, deep-rooted in the soul,
Subdue our flesh, our minds control;
May guile depart, and discord cease,
And all within be joy and peace.

6 O hallowed be the approaching day;
Let meekness be our morning ray,
And faithful love our noonday light,
And hope our sunset, calm and
    bright.

7 O Christ, with each returning morn
Thine image to our hearts is borne;
O may we ever clearly see
Our Saviour and our God in Thee.

Ambrose (c.339–97)
Tr. John Chandler (1806–76)

235 666.D

'Daily shall he be praised' Psalm 72 *v* 15

1 When morning gilds the skies
My heart awaking cries,
May Jesus Christ be praised!
Alike at work and prayer,
To Jesus I repair:
May Jesus Christ be praised!

2 To Thee my God above,
I cry with glowing love,
May Jesus Christ be praised!
The fairest graces spring
In hearts that ever sing,
May Jesus Christ be praised!

3 Does sadness fill my mind?
A solace here I find,
May Jesus Christ be praised!
Or fades my earthly bliss?
My comfort still is this,
May Jesus Christ be praised!

4 When evil thoughts molest,
With this I shield my breast,
May Jesus Christ be praised!
The powers of darkness fear
When this sweet chant they hear,
May Jesus Christ be praised!

5 Be this, while life is mine,
My canticle divine,
May Jesus Christ be praised!
Sing this eternal song
Through all the ages long,
May Jesus Christ be praised!

German 19th Century
Tr. Edward Caswell (1814–78)

GOD THE FATHER

236
77.77.77

1 All things praise Thee; Lord most
high:
Heaven and earth and sea and sky,
All were for Thy glory made,
That Thy greatness thus displayed
Should all worship bring to Thee;
All things praise Thee: Lord, may we.

2 All things praise Thee; night to night
Sings in silent hymns of light;
All things praise Thee; day to day
Chants Thy power, in burning ray;
Time and space are praising Thee,
All things praise Thee: Lord, may we.

3 All things praise Thee; high and low,
Rain and dew and seven – hued bow,
Crimson sunset, fleecy cloud,
Running stream and tempest loud;
Summer, winter, all to Thee
Glory render: Lord, may we.

4 All things praise Thee; gracious Lord,
Great Creator, powerful Word,
Omnipresent Spirit, now
At Thy feet we humbly bow,
Lift our hearts in praise to Thee:
All things praise Thee; Lord, may we.

5 All things praise Thee; shall not they,
Who Thy wondrous cross survey,
Greatest of all wonders shown;
God's own Son for sin to atone.
Let the Church in triumph sing,
We will praise Thee, Christ our King.

George William Conder (1821–74)

237
87.87.D

Based on Psalm 91

1 Call Jehovah thy salvation,
Rest beneath the Almighty's shade,
In His secret habitation
Dwell, and never be dismayed:
There no tumult shall alarm thee,
Thou shalt dread no hidden snare:
Guile nor violence can harm thee,
In eternal safeguard there.

2 From the sword at noon-day
wasting,
From the noisome pestilence,
In the depth of midnight blasting,
God shall be thy sure defence.
He shall charge His angel legions
Watch and ward o'er thee to keep,
Though thou walk through hostile
regions,
Though in deserts wild thou sleep.

3 Since with pure and firm affection,
Thou on God hast set thy love,
With the wings of His protection
He will shield thee from above.
Thou shalt call on Him in trouble,
He will hearken, He will save,
Here for grief reward thee double,
Crown with life beyond the grave.

James Montgomery (1771–1854)

238 S.M.

'Commit thy way unto the LORD'
Psalm 37 v 5

1 Commit thou all thy griefs
And ways into His hands,
To His sure truth and tender care,
Who heaven and earth commands.

2 Who points the clouds their course,
Whom winds and seas obey,
He shall direct thy wandering feet,
He shall prepare thy way.

3 Thou on the Lord rely,
So safe shalt thou go on;
Fix on His work thy steadfast eye,
So shall thy work be done.

4 No profit canst thou gain
By self-consuming care:
To Him commend thy cause; His ear
Attends the softest prayer.

5 He everywhere hath sway,
And all things serve His might;
His every act pure blessing is,
His path unsullied light.

6 When He makes bare His arm,
Who shall His work withstand?
When He His people's cause
defends,
Who, who shall stay His hand?

7 Put thou thy trust in God,
In duty's path go on;
Walk in His strength with faith and
hope,
So shall thy work be done.

Paul Gerhardt (1607–76)
Tr. John Wesley (1703–91)

239 C.M.

'How excellent is thy name in all the
earth!' Psalm 8 v 1

1 I sing the almighty power of God,
That made the mountains rise,
That spread the flowing seas abroad,
And built the lofty skies.

2 I sing the wisdom that ordained
The sun to rule the day;
The moon shines full at His
command,
And all the stars obey.

3 I sing the goodness of the Lord,
That filled the earth with food;
He formed the creatures with His
word,
And then pronounced them good.

4 There's not a plant or flower below
But makes His glories known;
And clouds arise, and tempests
blow,
By order from His throne.

5 Creatures, as numerous as they be,
Are subject to His care;
There's not a place where we can
flee
But God is present there.

6 In heaven He shines with beams of
love,
With wrath in hell beneath:
'Tis on His earth I stand or move,
And 'tis His air I breathe.

7 His hand is my perpetual guard,
He guides me with His eye;
Why should I then forget the Lord,
Who is for ever nigh?

Isaac Watts (1674–1748)

240 L.M.

'In him was life: and the life was the
light of men' John 1 v 4

1 Lord of all being, throned afar,
Thy glory flames from sun and star;
Centre and soul of every sphere,
Yet to each loving heart how near.

2 Sun of our life, Thy quickening ray
Sheds on our path the glow of day;
Star of our hope, Thy softened light
Cheers the long watches of the
night.

3 Our midnight is Thy smile
    withdrawn;
  Our noontide is Thy gracious dawn;
  Our rainbow arch, Thy mercy's sign;
  All, save the clouds of sin, are Thine.

4 Lord of all life, below, above,
  Whose light is truth, whose warmth
    is love,
  Before Thy ever-blazing throne
  We ask no lustre of our own.

5 Grant us Thy truth to make us free,
  And kindling hearts that burn for
    Thee,
  Till all Thy living altars claim
  One holy light, one heavenly flame.

Oliver Wendell Holmes (1809–94)

241   5 5. 5 5. 6 5. 6 5

Based on Psalm 104

1 O worship the King,
  All-glorious above;
  O gratefully sing
  His power and His love:
  Our Shield and Defender,
  The Ancient of Days,
  Pavilioned in splendour
  And girded with praise.

2 O tell of His might,
  O sing of His grace,
  Whose robe is the light,
  Whose canopy space;
  His chariots of wrath
  The deep thunder-clouds form,
  And dark is His path
  On the wings of the storm.

3 The earth, with its store
  Of wonders untold,
  Almighty, Thy power
  Hath founded of old;
  Hath stablished it fast
  By a changeless decree,
  And round it hath cast,
  Like a mantle, the sea.

4 Thy bountiful care
  What tongue can recite?
  It breathes in the air,
  It shines in the light;
  It streams from the hills,
  It descends to the plain,
  And sweetly distils
  In the dew and the rain.

5 Frail children of dust,
  And feeble as frail,
  In Thee do we trust,
  Nor find Thee to fail;
  Thy mercies how tender,
  How firm to the end,
  Our Maker, Defender,
  Redeemer and Friend!

6 O measureless might!
  Ineffable love!
  While angels delight
  To hymn Thee above,
  Thy humbler creation,
  Though feeble their lays,
  With true adoration
  Shall lisp to Thy praise.

Robert Grant (1779–1838)

242   8 7. 8 7. D

Based on Psalm 148

1 Praise the Lord! Ye heavens, adore Him;
  Praise Him, angels in the height;
  Sun and moon, rejoice before Him;
  Praise Him, all ye stars and light.
  Praise the Lord! For He hath spoken;
  Worlds His mighty voice obeyed;
  Laws, that never shall be broken,
  For their guidance He hath made.

2 Praise the Lord! For He is glorious;
  Never shall His promise fail;
  God hath made His saints
    victorious;
  Sin and death shall not prevail.
  Praise the God of our salvation!
  Hosts on high His power proclaim;
  Heaven and earth, and all creation,
  Laud and magnify His name.

Anonymous
Foundling Hospital Collection (c.1802)

243 L.M.

Based on Psalm 147

1 Praise ye the Lord; 'tis good to raise
Our hearts and voices in His praise:
His nature and His works invite
To make His duty our delight.

2 He formed the stars, those heavenly
flames,
He counts their numbers, calls their
names;
His wisdom's vast, and knows no
bounds,
A deep where all our thoughts are
drowned.

3 Sing to the Lord, exalt Him high,
Who spreads His clouds along the
sky;
There He prepares the fruitful rain,
Nor lets the drops descend in vain.

4 He makes the grass on hills adorn,
And clothes the smiling fields with
corn;
The beasts with food His hands
supply,
And the young ravens when they cry.

5 What is the creature's skill or force,
The sprightly man, the warlike
horse,
The nimble wit, the active limb?
All are too mean delights for Him.

6 But saints are lovely in His sight;
He views His children with delight;
He sees their hope, He knows their
fear,
And looks, and loves His image
there.

Isaac Watts (1674–1748)

244 L.M.

'The heavens declare the glory of God'
Psalm 19 v 1

1 The spacious firmament on high,
With all the blue ethereal sky,
And spangled heavens, a shining
frame,
Their great Original proclaim.

2 The unwearied sun, from day to day
Does his Creator's power display;
And publishes to every land
The work of an almighty hand.

3 Soon as the evening shades prevail,
The moon takes up the wondrous
tale,
And nightly to the listening earth
Repeats the story of her birth.

4 While all the stars that round her
burn,
And all the planets in their turn,
Confirm the tidings as they roll,
And spread the truth from pole to
pole.

5 What though in solemn silence all
Move round this dark terrestrial ball?
What though no real voice nor
sound
Amidst their radiant orbs be found.

6 In reason's ear they all rejoice,
And utter forth a glorious voice;
For ever singing, as they shine,
The hand that made us is divine.

Joseph Addison (1672–1719)

245 6 6. 7 7. 7 7

'For in him we live, and move, and have
our being' Acts 17 v 28

1 Far off we need not rove
To find the God of love;
In His providential care,
Ever intimately near,
All His various works declare,
God, the bounteous God is here.

2 We live, and move, and are,
  Through His preserving care;
  He doth still in life maintain
  Every soul that moves and lives;
  Gives us back our breath again
  Being every moment gives.

3 Who live O God in Thee,
  Entirely Thine should be:
  Thine we are, a heaven-born race,
  Only to Thy glory move,
  Thee with all our powers we praise,
  Thee with all our being love.

Charles Wesley (1707–88)

246   L.M.

Based on Psalm 46

1 God is the refuge of His saints,
  When storms of sharp distress
    invade;
  Ere we can offer our complaints,
  Behold Him present with His aid.

2 Let mountains from their seats be
    hurled
  Down to the deep, and buried there:
  Convulsions shake the solid world;
  Our faith shall never yield to fear.

3 Loud may the troubled ocean roar,
  In sacred peace our souls abide;
  While every nation, every shore,
  Trembles, and dreads the swelling
    tide.

4 There is a stream whose gentle flow
  Makes glad the city of our God,
  Life, love, and joy, still gliding
    through,
  And watering our divine abode.

5 This sacred stream, Thy holy Word,
  Thus all our raging fear controls;
  Sweet peace Thy promises afford,
  And give new strength to fainting
    souls.

6 Zion enjoys her Monarch's love,
  Secure against the threatening hour;
  Nor can her firm foundations move,
  Built on His truth, armed with His
    power.

Isaac Watts (1674–1748)

247   C.M.

*'How unsearchable are his judgments,
and his ways past finding out!'*
Romans 11 v 33

1 God moves in a mysterious way
  His wonders to perform;
  He plants His footsteps in the sea,
  And rides upon the storm.

2 Deep in unfathomable mines
  Of never-failing skill
  He treasures up His bright designs,
  And works His sovereign will.

3 Ye fearful saints, fresh courage take;
  The clouds ye so much dread
  Are big with mercy, and shall break
  In blessings on your head.

4 Judge not the Lord by feeble sense,
  But trust Him for His grace;
  Behind a frowning providence
  He hides a smiling face.

5 His purposes will ripen fast,
  Unfolding every hour;
  The bud may have a bitter taste,
  But sweet will be the flower.

6 Blind unbelief is sure to err,
  And scan His work in vain;
  God is His own interpreter,
  And He will make it plain.

William Cowper (1731–1800)

248   C.M.

*'The LORD God ... abundant in goodness
and truth'* Exodus 34 v 6

1 God shall alone the refuge be
  And comfort of my mind:
  Too wise to be mistaken, He,
  Too good to be unkind.

2 In all His holy, sovereign will,
He is, I daily find,
Too wise to be mistaken still,
Too good to be unkind.

3 When I the tempter's rage endure,
'Tis God supports my mind;
Too wise to be mistaken, sure!
Too good to be unkind.

4 Though I cannot His goings see,
Nor all His footsteps find;
Too wise to be mistaken, He,
Too good to be unkind.

5 Hereafter He will make me know
And I shall surely find,
He was too wise to err, and O
Too good to be unkind!

Samuel Medley (1738–99)

249 Irregular

'Great is thy faithfulness'
Lamentations 3 v 23

1 'Great is Thy faithfulness', O God
my Father,
There is no shadow of turning with
Thee,
Thou changest not, Thy compas-
sions they fail not;
As Thou hast been Thou for ever wilt
be.

*'Great is Thy faithfulness! Great is
Thy faithfulness!'
Morning by morning new mercies I see!
All I have needed Thy hand hath
provided –
'Great is Thy faithfulness', Lord unto me!*

2 Summer and winter, and springtime
and harvest,
Sun, moon and stars in their courses
above,
Join with all nature in manifold
witness
To Thy great faithfulness, mercy and
love.

3 Pardon for sin and a peace that
endureth,
Thy own dear presence to cheer and
to guide,
Strength for today and bright hope
for tomorrow,
Blessings all mine, with ten
thousand beside!

©1923 Renewed 1951 *Thomas O. Chisholm (1866–1960)*
Hope Publishing Company

250 6 4. 6 4. 6 6. 6 4

'A time for every purpose under heaven'
Ecclesiastes 3 v 1

1 Great providence of heaven –
What wonders shine
In its profound display
Of God's design:
It guards the dust of earth,
Commands the hosts above,
Fulfils the mighty plan
Of His great love.

2 The kingdoms of this world
Lie in its hand;
See how they rise and fall
At its command!
Through sorrow and distress,
Tempestuous storms that rage,
God's kingdom yet endures
From age to age.

3 Its darkness dense is but
A radiant light;
Its oft-perplexing ways
Are ordered right.
Soon all its winding paths
Will end, and then the tale
Of wonder shall be told
Beyond the veil.

David Charles (1762–1834)
Tr. Edmund Tudor Owen (b.1935)

251   C.M.

Based on Isaiah 40 vv 28-31

1 Hast thou not known, hast thou not
   heard,
   That firm remains on high
   The everlasting throne of Him
   Who formed the earth and sky?

2 Art thou afraid His power shall fail
   When comes thy evil day?
   And can an all-creating arm
   Grow weary or decay?

3 Supreme in wisdom as in power
   The Rock of Ages stands;
   Though Him thou canst not see, nor
   trace
   The working of His hands.

4 He gives the conquest to the weak,
   Supports the fainting heart;
   And courage in the evil hour
   His heavenly aids impart.

5 Mere human power shall fast decay,
   And youthful vigour cease;
   But they who wait upon the Lord
   In strength shall still increase.

6 The saints shall mount on eagles'
   wings,
   And taste the promised bliss,
   Till their unwearied feet arrive
   Where perfect pleasure is.

Isaac Watts (1674–1748)

252   C.M.

*'I am with thee, and will keep thee in all
places whither thou goest' Genesis 28 v 15*

1 How are Thy servants blest, O Lord!
   How sure is their defence!
   Eternal wisdom is their guide,
   Their help omnipotence.

2 From all my griefs and fears, O Lord,
   Thy mercy sets me free,
   Whilst in the confidence of prayer
   My heart takes hold on Thee.

3 In midst of dangers, fears and death,
   Thy goodness I'll adore,
   And praise Thee for Thy mercies
   past,
   And humbly hope for more.

4 My life, while Thou preserv'st my
   life,
   Thy sacrifice shall be;
   And O may death, when death shall
   come,
   Unite my soul to Thee!

Joseph Addison (1672–1719)

253   S.M.

*'His commandments are not grievous'
1 John 5 v 3*

1 How gentle God's commands,
   How kind His precepts are!
   Come, cast your burdens on the
   Lord,
   And trust His constant care.

2 While providence supports,
   Let saints securely dwell;
   That hand which bears all nature up
   Shall guide His children well.

3 Why should this anxious load
   Press down your weary mind?
   Haste to your Heavenly Father's
   throne,
   And sweet refreshment find.

4 His goodness stands approved,
   Down to the present day;
   I'll drop my burden at His feet,
   And bear a song away.

Philip Doddridge (1702–51)

254

10 10. 10 10. 10 10

'Hide not thy face far from me'
Psalm 27 v 9

1 Lord, if one moment Thou Thy face
      shouldst hide,
   Or cloud Thy glory, or Thy smile deny,
   Then would all nature veil her
      mournful eyes,
   And vent her grief in universal cries:
   Then certain death, with all its
      dismal train,
   Would o'er the nations spread its
      tragic reign.

2 See all creation, in such splendour
      born,
   Now, with her hosts to native dust
      return;
   But when again Thy glory is dis-
      played,
   She shall revive and lift her radiant
      head;
   New rising forms Thine order shall
      obey,
   And life rekindle at Thy stirring ray.

3 United thanks replenished nature
      pays,
   And heaven and earth resound their
      Maker's praise!
   When time shall in eternity be lost,
   And aging nature languish into dust;
   For ever young, new marvels shall
      remain,
   Vast as Thy being, endless as Thy
      reign.

4 When, at Thy word, my soul
      excursive flies
   Through earth and air into Thy regal
      skies,
   From world to world, new wonders
      shall I find,
   As all the Godhead dawns upon my
      mind!
   To Thee, my soul shall endless
      praises pay:
   Joined with the angels in eternal day.

Thomas Blacklock (1721–91)

255

L.M.

'O God of hosts: look down from heaven'
Psalm 80 v 14

1 Lord, my weak thought in vain
      would climb
   To search the starry vault profound,
   In vain would wing her flight sublime
   To find creation's utmost bound.

2 But weaker yet that thought must
      prove
   To search Thy great eternal plan,
   Thy sovereign counsels, born of love
   Long ages ere the world began.

3 When my dim reason would demand
   Why that, or this, Thou dost ordain,
   By some vast deep I seem to stand,
   Whose secrets I must ask in vain.

4 When doubts disturb my troubled
      breast,
   And all is dark as night to me,
   Here, as on solid rock, I rest –
   That so it seemeth good to Thee.

5 Be this my joy, that evermore
   Thou rulest all things at Thy will;
   Thy sovereign wisdom I adore,
   And calmly, sweetly, trust in Thee.

Ray Palmer (1808–1887)

256

8 4. 8 4. 8 4

'We glory in tribulations also' Romans 5 v 3

1 My God, I thank Thee, who hast
      made
   The earth so bright,
   So full of splendour and of joy,
   Beauty and light;
   So many glorious things are here,
   Noble and right.

2 I thank Thee, too, that Thou hast
      made
   Joy to abound,
   So many gentle thoughts and deeds
   Circling us round,
   That in the darkest spot of earth
   Some love is found.

3 I thank Thee more, that all our joy
Is touched with pain,
That shadows fall on brightest
hours,
That thorns remain;
So that earth's bliss may be our
guide,
And not our chain.

4 For Thou, who knowest, Lord, how
soon
Our weak heart clings,
Hast given us joys, tender and true,
Yet all with wings,
So that we see, gleaming on high,
Diviner things.

5 I thank Thee, Lord, that Thou hast
kept
The best in store:
We have enough, but not too much
To long for more –
A yearning for a deeper peace
Not known before.

6 I thank Thee, Lord, that here our
souls,
Though amply blest,
Can never find, although they seek,
A perfect rest,
Nor ever shall, until they lean
On Jesus' breast.

Adelaide Anne Procter (1825–64)

257 C.M.

'I said, Thou art my God' Psalm 31 v 14

1 My God, my Father, blissful name!
O may I call Thee mine!
May I with sweet assurance claim
A portion so divine!

2 This only can my fears control,
And bid my sorrows fly;
What harm can ever reach my soul
Beneath my Father's eye?

3 Whate'er Thy providence denies
I calmly would resign,
For Thou art just and good and wise;
O bend my will to Thine!

4 Whate'er Thy sacred will ordains,
O give me strength to bear;
And let me know my Father reigns,
And trust His tender care.

5 If pain and sickness rend this frame,
And life almost depart,
Is not Thy mercy still the same
To cheer my drooping heart?

6 Of cares and sorrows me surround,
Their power why should I fear?
My inward peace they cannot
wound,
If Thou, my God, art near.

Anne Steele (1717–78)

258 D.C.M

Based on Psalm 23

1 My Shepherd will supply my need,
Jehovah is His name;
In pastures fresh He makes me feed
Beside the living stream.
He brings my wandering spirit back
When I forsake His ways;
And leads me for His mercy's sake
In paths of truth and grace.

2 When I walk through the shades of
death,
Thy presence is my stay;
A word of Thy supporting breath
Drives all my fears away.
Thy hand in sight of all my foes
Doth still my table spread;
My cup with blessings over flows,
Thine oil anoints my head.

3 The sure provisions of my God
Attend me all my days:
O may Thy house be mine abode,
And all my work be praise!
There would I find a settled rest,
While others go and come;
No more a stranger or a guest,
But like a child at home.

Isaac Watts (1674–1748)

259 L.M.

'*My voice shalt Thou hear in the morning, O LORD*' Psalm 5 v 3

1 New every morning is the love
Our wakening and uprising prove;
Through sleep and darkness safely
brought,
Restored to life and power and
thought.

2 New mercies, each returning day,
Hover around us while we pray;
New perils past, new sins forgiven,
New thoughts of God, new hopes of
heaven.

3 If on our daily course our mind
Be set to hallow all we find,
New treasures still, of countless
price,
God will provide for sacrifice.

4 Old friends, old scenes, will lovelier
be,
As more of heaven in each we see:
Some softening gleam of love and
prayer
Shall dawn on every cross and care.

5 The trivial round, the common task,
Will furnish all we ought to ask;
Room to deny ourselves; a road
To bring us, daily, nearer God.

6 Only, O Lord, in Thy dear love
Fit us for perfect rest above;
And help us, this and every day,
To live more nearly as we pray.

John Keble (1792–1866)

260 C.M.

Based on Psalm 90

1 Our God, our help in ages past,
Our hope for years to come,
Our shelter from the stormy blast,
And our eternal home;

2 Beneath the shadow of Thy throne
Thy saints have dwelt secure;
Sufficient is Thine arm alone,
And our defence is sure.

3 Before the hills in order stood,
Or earth received her frame,
From everlasting Thou art God,
To endless years the same.

4 A thousand ages in Thy sight
Are like an evening gone,
Short as the watch that ends the
night
Before the rising sun.

5 Time, like an ever-rolling stream,
Bears all its sons away;
They fly forgotten, as a dream
Dies at the opening day.

6 Our God, our help in ages past,
Our hope for years to come,
Be Thou our guard while troubles
last,
And our eternal home.

Isaac Watts (1674–1748)

261 7 7.7 7

'*A time to every purpose under the heaven*'
Ecclesiastes 3 v 1

1 Sovereign Ruler of the skies!
Ever gracious, ever wise!
All my times are in Thy hand,
All events at Thy command.

2 His decree, who formed the earth,
Fixed my first and second birth;
Parents, native place, and time,
All appointed were by Him.

3 He that formed me in the womb,
He shall guide me to the tomb;
All my times shall ever be
Ordered by His wise decree.

4 Times of sickness, times of health;
Times of penury and wealth;
Times of trial and of grief;
Times of triumph and relief.

5 Times the tempter's power to prove;
Times to taste a Saviour's love –
All shall come, and last, and end
As shall please my heavenly Friend.

6 Plagues and deaths around me fly;
Till He bids I cannot die;
Not a single shaft can hit
Till the God of love sees fit.

John Ryland (1753–1825)

262   6 6. 6 6. 8 8

Based on Psalm 84

1 The Lord Jehovah reigns;
His throne is built on high,
The garments He assumes
Are light and majesty:
His glories shine with beams so
bright,
No mortal eye can bear the sight.

2 The thunders of His hand
Keep the wide world in awe;
His wrath and justice stand
To guard His holy law;
And where His love resolves to bless,
His truth confirms and seals the
grace.

3 Through all His mighty works
Amazing wisdom shines,
Confounds the powers of hell,
And breaks their dark designs;
Strong is His arm, and shall fulfil
His great decrees and sovereign will.

4 And will this mighty King
Of glory condescend?
And will He write His name
My Father and my Friend?
I love His name, I love His Word,
Join all my powers to praise the
Lord.

Isaac Watts (1674–1748)

263   C.M.

Based on Psalm 34

1 Through all the changing scenes of
life,
In trouble and in joy,
The praises of my God shall still
My heart and tongue employ.

2 Of His deliverance I will boast,
Till all that are distressed
From my example comfort take,
And charm their griefs to rest.

3 O magnify the Lord with me,
With me exalt His name;
When in distress to Him I called,
He to my rescue came.

4 The hosts of God encamp around
The dwellings of the just;
Deliverance He affords to all
Who on His succour trust.

5 O make but trial of His love,
Experience will decide
How blessed are they, and only they,
Who in His truth confide.

6 Fear Him, ye saints, and you will then
Have nothing else to fear;
Make you His service your delight,
Your wants shall be His care.

Nahum Tate (1652–1715)
and Nicholas Brady (1659–1726)

264   C.M.

'I will sing of the mercies of the LORD for
ever' Psalm 89 v 1

1 When all Thy mercies, O my God,
My rising soul surveys,
Transported with the view, I'm lost
In wonder, love and praise.

2 Unnumbered comforts on my soul
Thy tender care bestowed,
Before my infant heart conceived
From whom those comforts flowed.

3 When worn with sickness, oft hast
  Thou
  With health renewed my face;
  And, when in sins and sorrows
  sunk,
  Revived my soul with grace.

4 Ten thousand thousand precious
  gifts
  My daily thanks employ;
  Nor is the last a cheerful heart
  That tastes those gifts with joy.

5 Through every season of my life
  Thy goodness I'll pursue
  And after death in distant worlds,
  The glorious theme renew.

6 Through all eternity to Thee
  A joyful song I'll raise;
  But O! eternity's too short
  To utter all Thy praise!

Joseph Addison (1672–1719)

265   C.M.

'Why art thou cast down, O my soul?'
Psalm 42 v 11

1 When storms of life engulf my way,
  And sorrows crowd my breast,
  One thought prevails, and is my
  stay –
  Thy providence is best.

2 Unmoveable, Thy providence
  Remains secure and still,
  Provides the grace for my defence
  In face of every ill.

3 Why does my soul within me fear?
  Why does my heart grow cold?
  When in Thy sight I am most dear;
  Such love should make me bold.

4 Thy mercies past have never failed,
  Nor has Thy goodness waned;
  Thy faithful kindness has prevailed,
  Thy will has always reigned.

5 Thy person and Thy work remain
  In perfect harmony;
  Unswerving in Thy purpose plain,
  Thy providence to me.

6 Come all my foes to crush my heart,
  Come Satan's host to kill;
  Then come my Lord to take my part
  My cup with joy to fill.

7 In every place I'll praise Thy name,
  And never doubt Thy care;
  Thy providence remains the same,
  For Thou art always there.

© The Author   *William Vernon Higham (b.1926)*

266   87.87.337

'My help cometh from the LORD'
Psalm 121 v 2

1 All my hope on God is founded;
  He doth still my trust renew,
  Me through change and chance He
  guideth,
  Only good and only true.
  God unknown,
  He alone
  Calls my heart to be His own.

2 Pride of man and earthly glory,
  Sword and crown betray his trust;
  What with care and toil he buildeth,
  Tower and temple, fall to dust.
  But God's power,
  Hour by hour,
  Is my temple and my tower.

3 God's great goodness aye endureth,
  Deep His wisdom, passing thought:
  Splendour, light, and life attend Him,
  Beauty springeth out of nought.
  Evermore
  From His store
  New-born worlds rise and adore.

4 Daily doth the Almighty Giver
  Bounteous gifts on us bestow;
  His desire our soul delighteth,
  Pleasure leads us where we go.
  Love doth stand
  At His hand;

Joy doth wait on His command.

5 Still from man to God eternal
Sacrifice of praise be done,
High above all praises praising
For the gift of Christ His Son.
Christ doth call
One and all:
Ye who follow shall not fall.

Robert Seymour Bridges (1844–1930)
From Joachim Neander (1650–80)

267   L.M.

'The LORD hath laid on him the iniquity
of us all' Isaiah 53 v 6

1 God of salvation, we adore
Thy saving love, Thy saving power,
And to our utmost stretch of thought
Hail the redemption Thou hast
wrought.

2 We love the stroke that breaks our
chain,
The sword by which our sins are
slain;
And while abased in dust we bow,
We sing the grace that lays us low.

3 Perish each thought of human pride,
Let God alone be magnified;
His glory let the heavens resound,
Shouted from earth's remotest
bound.

4 Saints who His full salvation know,
Saints who but taste it here below,
Join with the angelic choir to raise
Transporting songs of deathless
praise.

Philip Doddridge (1702–51)

268   88.88.88

'Who is a God like unto thee?'
Micah 7 v 18

1 Great God of wonders! all Thy ways
Are matchless, godlike, and divine;
But the fair glories of Thy grace,
More godlike and unrivalled shine.

Who is a pardoning God like Thee?
Or who has grace so rich and free?

2 Such dire offences to forgive,
Such guilty, daring worms to spare:
This is Thy grand prerogative,
And in the honour none shall share.

3 Angels and men, resign your claim
To pity, mercy, love, and grace:
These glories crown Jehovah's name
With an incomparable blaze.

4 In wonder lost, with trembling joy,
We take the pardon of our God,
Pardon for sins of deepest dye,
A pardon sealed with Jesus' blood.

5 O may this strange, this matchless
grace,
This godlike miracle of love,
Fill the wide earth with grateful
praise
And all the angelic choirs above.

Samuel Davies (1723–61)

269   L.M.

'His wonderful works' Psalm 111 v 4

1 How wondrous are the works of God,
Displayed through all the world
abroad!
Immensely great, immensely small!
Yet one strange work exceeds them
all.

2 He formed the sun, fair fount of
light,
The moon and stars to rule the
night;
But night and stars, and moon and
sun
Are little works compared with one.

3 The highest heavens are short of this;
'Tis deeper than the vast abyss:
'Tis more than thought can e'er
    conceive,
Or hope expect, or faith believe.

4 Almighty God sighed human breath!
The Lord of life experienced death!
How it was done we can't discuss,
But this we know, 'twas done for us.

5 Blest with this faith, then, let us
    raise
Our heart in love, our voice in praise;
We now believe, but soon shall know
The greatest glories God can show.

Joseph Hart (1712–68)

270 S.M.

Based on Psalm 103 vv 8-18

1 My soul, repeat His praise
Whose mercies are so great,
Whose anger is so slow to rise,
So ready to abate.

2 High as the heavens are raised
Above the ground we tread,
So far the riches of His grace
Our highest thoughts exceed.

3 His power subdues our sins;
And His forgiving love,
Far as the east is from the west,
Doth all our guilt remove.

4 The pity of the Lord
To those that fear His name
Is such as tender parents feel;
He knows our feeble frame.

5 Our days are as the grass,
Or like the morning flower;
If one sharp blast sweep o'er the
    field,
It withers in an hour.

6 But Thy compassions, Lord,
To endless years endure;
And children's children ever find
Thy words of promise sure.

Isaac Watts (1674–1748)

271 L.M.

'Having made peace through the blood of his cross' Colossians 1 v 20

1 Nature with open volume stands
To spread her Maker's praise abroad,
And every labour of His hands
Shows something worthy of a God.

2 But in the grace that rescued man
His brightest form of glory shines;
Here on the cross 'tis fairest drawn
In precious blood and crimson lines.

3 Here His whole name appears
    complete;
Nor wit can guess, nor reason prove,
Which of the letters best is writ,
The power, the wisdom, or the love.

4 Here I behold His inmost heart,
Where grace and vengeance
    strangely join,
Piercing His Son with sharpest
    smart,
To make the purchased pleasures
    mine.

5 O the sweet wonders of that cross
Where God the Saviour loved and
    died!
Her noblest life my spirit draws
From His dear wounds and bleeding
    side.

6 I would for ever speak His name
In sounds to mortal ears unknown;
With angels join to praise the Lamb,
And worship at His Father's throne.

Isaac Watts (1674–1748)

272 L.M.

'And to know the love of Christ, which passeth knowledge' Ephesians 3 v 19

1 O Lord, enlarge our scanty thought,
To know the wonders Thou hast
    wrought;
Unloose our stammering tongues to
    tell
Thy love immense, unsearchable.

2 What are our works but sin and
     death,
  Till Thou Thy quickening Spirit
     breathe;
  Thou giv'st the power Thy grace to
     move:
  O wondrous grace! O boundless
     love!

3 How can it be, Thou heavenly King,
  That Thou shouldst us to glory
     bring;
  Make slaves the partners of Thy
     throne,
  Decked with a never-fading crown?

4 Our hearts then melt, our eyes
     o'erflow,
  Our words are lost, nor will we
     know,
  Nor will we think of aught beside,
  My Lord, my Love, is crucified!

5 First-born of many brethren Thou;
  To Thee, lo! all our souls we bow;
  To Thee our hearts and hands we
     give:
  Thine may we die, Thine may we
     live!

Nicolaus Ludwig von Zinzendorf (1700–60) v 1
Johann Nitschmann (1712–83) vv 2-4
Anna Nitschmann (1715–60) v 5
Tr. John Wesley (1703–91)

273   L.M.

'Hereby perceive we the love of God'
1 John 3 v 16

1 O love of God, how strong and true;
  Eternal, and yet ever new;
  Uncomprehended and unbought,
  Beyond all knowledge and all
     thought!

2 O love of God, how deep and great,
  Far deeper than man's deepest hate;
  Self-fed, self-kindled like the light,
  Changeless, eternal, infinite!

3 O heavenly love, how precious still,
  In days of weariness and ill,
  In nights of pain and helplessness,
  To heal, to comfort, and to bless!

4 O wide-embracing, wondrous love,
  We read thee in the sky above;
  We read thee in the earth below,
  In seas that swell and streams that
     flow.

5 We read thee best in Him who came
  To bear for us the cross of shame,
  Sent by the Father from on high,
  Our life to live, our death to die.

6 We read thy power to bless and save,
  E'en in the darkness of the grave;
  Still more in resurrection light
  We read the fulness of thy might.

7 O love of God, our shield and stay
  Through all the perils of our way;
  Eternal love, in thee we rest,
  For ever safe, for ever blest.

Horatius Bonar (1808–89)

274   87.87.47

'The glory of the LORD shall be revealed'
Isaiah 40 v 5

1 O what matchless condescension
  The eternal God displays,
  Claiming our supreme attention
  To His boundless works and ways;
  His own glory
  He reveals in gospel days.

2 In the person of the Saviour
  All His majesty is seen,
  Love and justice shine for ever;
  And without a veil between,
  We approach Him,
  And rejoice in His dear name.

3 Would we view His highest glory,
  Here it shines in Jesus' face;
  Sing and tell the pleasing story,
  O ye sinners saved by grace;
  And with pleasure,
  Bid the guilty Him embrace.

4 In His highest work, redemption,
See His glory in a blaze;
Nor can angels ever mention
Aught that more of God displays.
Grace and justice
Here unite in endless days.

5 True, 'tis sweet and solemn
pleasure,
God to view in Christ the Lord;
Here He smiles, and smiles forever;
May my soul His name record,
Praise and bless Him,
And His wonders spread abroad.

William Gadsby (1773–1844)

275　　　　　8 7. 8 7. 8 8 7

'Sing unto God, sing praise to his name'
Psalm 68 v 4

1 Sing praise to God who reigns
above,
The God of all creation,
The God of wonders, power and
love,
The God of our salvation.
With healing balm my soul He fills,
The God who every sorrow stills –
To God all praise and glory!

2 What God's almighty power hath
made
His gracious mercy keepeth;
By morning dawn or evening shade
His watchful eye ne'er sleepeth;
Within the kingdom of His might,
Lo, all is just and all is right –
To God all praise and glory!

3 I cried to Him in time of need:
Lord God, O hear my calling!
For death He gave me life indeed
And kept my feet from falling.
For this my thanks shall endless be;
O thank Him, thank our God, with
me –
To God all praise and glory!

4 The Lord forsaketh not His flock,
His chosen generation;
He is their refuge and their rock,
Their peace and their salvation.
As with a mother's tender hand
He leads His own, his chosen band –
To God all praise and glory!

5 Then come before His presence now
And banish fear and sadness;
To your Redeemer pay your vow
And sing with joy and gladness:
Though great distress my soul
befell,
The Lord, my God, did all things
well –
To God all praise and glory!

Johann Jakob Schutz (1640–90)
Tr. Frances Elizabeth Cox (1812–97)

276　　　　11 11. 11 11 (with refrain)

'Give unto the Lord the glory'
Psalm 29 v 2

1 To God be the glory! Great things He
hath done!
So loved He the world that He gave
us His Son;
Who yielded His life an atonement
for sin,
And opened the life-gate that all may
go in.

Praise the Lord! Praise the Lord! Let the
earth hear His voice!
Praise the Lord! Praise the Lord! Let the
people rejoice!
O come to the Father through Jesus the
Son:
And give Him the glory! Great things He
hath done!

2 O perfect redemption, the purchase
of blood!
To every believer the promise of
God;
The vilest offender who truly
believes,
That moment from Jesus a pardon
receives.

3 Great things He hath taught us,
  great things He hath done,
And great our rejoicing through
  Jesus the Son;
But purer and higher and greater
  will be
Our wonder, our transport, when
  Jesus we see!

Frances Jane Crosby (1820–1915)

277 S.M.

'To the only wise God our Saviour, be
glory' Jude v 25

1 To God, the only wise,
  Our Saviour and our King,
  Let all the saints below the skies
  Their humble praises bring.

2 'Tis His almighty love,
  His counsel, and His care,
  Preserve us safe from sin and death,
  And every hurtful snare.

3 He will present our souls,
  Unblemished and complete,
  Before the glory of His face,
  With joys divinely great.

4 Then all the chosen seed
  Shall meet around the throne,
  Shall bless the conduct of His grace,
  And make His wonders known.

5 To our redeemer God
  Wisdom and power belongs,
  Immortal crowns of majesty
  And everlasting songs.

Isaac Watts (1674–1748)

278 7 6. 7 6. D

'The glory of the LORD shall be revealed'
Isaiah 11 v 5

1 'Twas God that made the ocean,
  And laid its sandy bed;
  He gave the stars their motion,
  And built the mountain's head;
  He made the rolling thunder,
  The lightning's flashing flame;
  His works are full of wonder,
  All-glorious is His name.

2 And must it not surprise us
  That one so high and great,
  Should see and not despise us,
  Poor sinners, at His feet?
  Yet day by day He gives us
  Our raiment and our food;
  In sickness He relieves us,
  And is in all things good.

3 But things that are far greater
  His mighty hand hath done,
  And sent us blessings sweeter
  Through Christ, His only Son,
  Who, when He saw us dying
  In sin and sorrow's night,
  On wings of mercy flying
  Came down with life and light.

4 He gives His Word to teach us
  Our danger and our wants,
  And kindly doth beseech us
  To take the life He grants.
  His Holy Spirit frees us
  From Satan's deadly powers,
  Leads us by faith to Jesus,
  And makes His glory ours.

George Burden Bubier (1823–69)

GOD THE SON

279

8 8. 8 8. D

'A name which is above every name'
Philippians 2 v 9

1 A beautiful name I have heard,
With sound of salvation to me;
God's only begotten and Word,
This Jesus of blest Calvary.
Eternal, yet born into time,
Unchanging, for ever the same,
A Saviour in person sublime
Has taken our sin and our shame.

2 The burdens of life press me hard,
And weariness weighs like the hills;
Then Satan with wiles to retard
Surrounds my poor soul with all ills.
I then look to Jesus my Lord,
And find anew grace for the day;
New mercies fresh manna afford,
Which drive all my terrors away.

3 His person I'll never exhaust,
Unchanging yet ever anew:
Without Him I'm weak and I'm lost,
But with Him my strength does
renew.
The mountains of hard unbelief
I'll move with the power of His
name;
Although all I am is but brief,
My Saviour is ever the same.

4 Whenever I look on Thy face,
New beauties I'll ever behold:
I'll ever discover new grace,
The half cannot ever be told.

A Saviour so constant and true,
Immortal, eternal and pure;
Thy mercy is fresh as the dew
Reviving with grace to endure.

© The Author   William Vernon Higham (b.1926)

280

C.M.

'A friend loveth at all times'
Proverbs 17 v 17

1 A friend there is – your voices join,
Ye saints, to praise His name!
Whose truth and kindness are
divine,
Whose love's a constant flame.

2 When most we need His helping
hand,
This friend is always near;
With heaven and earth at His
command
He waits to answer prayer.

3 His love no end or measure knows,
No change can turn its course:
Immutably the same it flows
From one eternal source.

4 When frowns appear to veil His face,
And clouds surround His throne,
He hides the purpose of His grace,
To make it better known.

5 And if our dearest comforts fall
Before His sovereign will,
He never takes away our all;
Himself He gives us still.

6 Our sorrows in the scale He weighs,
   And measures out our pains;
   The wildest storm His word obeys;
   His word its rage restrains.

Joseph Swain (1761–1796)

281   10 10. 11 11

'Of his fullness have all we received'
John 1 v 16

1 A fulness resides in Jesus our Head,
   And ever abides to answer our need:
   The Father's good pleasure has laid
      up in store
   A plentiful treasure, to give to the
      poor.

2 Whate'er be our wants, we need not
      to fear,
   Our numerous complaints His
      mercy will hear:
   His fulness shall yield us abundant
      supplies;
   His power shall shield us when
      dangers arise.

3 The fountain o'erflows our woes to
      redress,
   Still more He bestows and grace
      upon grace;
   His gifts in abundance we daily
      receive,
   Rich treasures in plenty for all that
      believe.

4 Whatever distress awaits us below,
   Such plentiful grace will Jesus
      bestow,
   And still shall support us, and
      silence our fear,
   For nothing can hurt us while Jesus
      is near.

5 When troubles attend, or danger, or
      strife,
   His love will defend and guard us
      through life;
   And when we are fainting, and ready
      to die,
   Whatever is wanting His hand will
      supply.

John Fawcett (1739–1817)

282   7 6. 7 6. D

'Out of the mouths of babes and
sucklings' Psalm 8 v 2

1 All glory, laud, and honour
   To Thee, Redeemer, King,
   To whom the lips of children
   Made sweet hosannas ring!
   Thou art the King of Israel,
   Thou David's royal Son,
   Who in the Lord's name comest,
   The King and blessèd One.

2 The company of angels
   Are praising Thee on high,
   And mortal men and all things
   Created make reply.
   The people of the Hebrews
   With palms before Thee went;
   Our praise and prayer and anthems
   Before Thee we present.

3 To Thee before Thy passion
   They sang their hymns of praise;
   To Thee now high exalted
   Our melody we raise.
   Thou didst accept their praises;
   Accept the prayers we bring,
   Who in all good delightest,
   Thou good and gracious King.

Theodulph of Orleans (c.750–821)
Tr. John Mason Neale (1818–66)

283
C.M.

'KING OF KINGS, AND LORD OF
LORDS' *Revelation 19 v 16*

1 All hail the power of Jesus' name!
Let angels prostrate fall;
Bring forth the royal diadem
To crown Him Lord of all.

2 Crown Him, ye martyrs of our God,
Who from His altar call;
Extol the stem of Jesse's rod,
And crown Him Lord of all.

3 Ye seed of Israel's chosen race,
Ye ransomed from the fall,
Hail Him who saves you by His
    grace,
And crown Him Lord of all.

4 Ye Gentile sinners, ne'er forget
The wormwood and the gall;
Go spread your trophies at His feet,
And crown Him Lord of all.

5 Let every kindred, every tribe,
On this terrestrial ball,
To Him all majesty ascribe,
And crown Him Lord of all.

6 O that with yonder sacred throng
We at His feet may fall,
Join in the everlasting song,
And crown Him Lord of all!

Edward Perronet (1726–92)
and John Rippon (1751–1836)

284
7 7.7 7

'THE LORD OUR RIGHTEOUSNESS'
Jeremiah 23 v 6

1 Brethren, let us join to bless
Christ, the Lord our Righteousness;
Let our praise to Him be given,
High at God's right hand in heaven.

2 Son of God, to Thee we bow,
Thou art Lord, and only Thou;
Thou the blessèd Virgin's Seed,
Glory of Thy church, and Head.

3 Thee the angels ceaseless sing,
Thee we praise, our Priest and King;
Worthy is Thy name of praise,
Full of glory, full of grace.

4 Thou hast the glad tidings brought
Of salvation by Thee wrought;
Wrought to set Thy people free,
Wrought to bring our souls to Thee.

5 May we follow and adore
Thee, our Saviour, more and more;
Guide and bless us with Thy love,
Till we join Thy saints above.

John Cennick (1718-55)

285
C.M.

'Worthy is the Lamb that was slain'
Revelation 5 v 12

1 Come, let us join our cheerful songs
With angels round the throne;
Ten thousand thousand are their
    tongues,
But all their joys are one.

2 'Worthy the Lamb that died', they
    cry,
'To be exalted thus!'
'Worthy the Lamb', our lips reply,
'For He was slain for us!'

3 Jesus is worthy to receive
Honour and power divine;
And blessings, more than we can
    give,
Be, Lord, for ever Thine.

4 Let all that dwell above the sky,
And air, and earth, and seas,
Conspire to lift Thy glories high,
And speak Thine endless praise.

5 The whole creation join in one,
To bless the sacred name
Of Him that sits upon the throne,
And to adore the Lamb.

Isaac Watts (1674–1748)

286   C.M.

'He hath put a new song in my mouth,
even praise unto our God' Psalm 40 v 3

1 Come, ye that love the Saviour's
        name,
   And joy to make it known;
   The Sovereign of your heart proclaim,
   And bow before His throne.

2 Behold your King, your Saviour
        crowned
   With glories all divine;
   And tell the wondering nations
        round
   How bright those glories shine.

3 Infinite power and boundless grace
   In Him unite their rays:
   You that have e'er beheld His face,
   Can you forbear His praise?

4 When in His earthly courts we view
   The glories of our King,
   We long to love as angels do,
   And wish like them to sing.

5 And shall we long and wish in vain?
   Lord, teach our songs to rise!
   Thy love can animate the strain,
   And bid it reach the skies.

6 O, happy season! glorious day!
   When heaven and earth shall raise
   With all their power, the raptured lay
   To celebrate Thy praise.

Anne Steele (1717–78)

287   S.M.D.

'On his head were many crowns'
Revelation 19 v 12

1 Crown Him with many crowns,
   The Lamb upon His throne;
   Hark! how the heavenly anthem
        drowns
   All music but its own.
   Awake, my soul, and sing
   Of Him who died for thee,
   And hail Him as thy chosen King
   Through all eternity.

2 Crown Him the Son of God,
   Before the worlds began:
   And ye, who tread where He hath
        trod,
   Crown Him the Son of man:
   Who every grief hath known
   That wrings the human breast,
   And takes and bears them for His
        own,
   That all in Him may rest.

3 Crown Him the Lord of love!
   Behold His hands and side,
   Rich wounds, yet visible above,
   In beauty glorified:
   No angel in the sky
   Can fully bear that sight,
   But downward bends his burning eye
   At mysteries so bright.

4 Crown Him the Lord of life,
   Who triumphed o'er the grave,
   And rose victorious in the strife
   For those He came to save:
   His glories now we sing
   Who died, and rose on high;
   Who died eternal life to bring,
   And lives that death may die.

5 Crown Him the Lord of peace,
   Whose power a sceptre sways
   From pole to pole, that wars may
        cease,
   And all be prayer and praise:
   His reign shall know no end,
   And round His pierced feet
   Fair flowers of paradise extend
   Their fragrance ever sweet.

6 Crown Him the Lord of years,
   The Potentate of time,
   Creator of the rolling spheres,
   Ineffably sublime!
   All hail, Redeemer, hail!
   For Thou hast died for me:
   Thy praise shall never, never fail
   Throughout eternity.

Matthew Bridges (1800–94)
and Godfrey Thring (1823–1903)

288

664.666.4

'Worthy is the Lamb' Revelation 5 v 12

1 Glory to God on high!
Let earth to heaven reply,
'Praise ye His name!'
Angles His love adore,
Who all our sorrows bore;
And saints cry evermore,
'Worthy the Lamb!'

2 All they around the throne
Cheerfully join in one,
Praising His name;
We, who have felt His blood
Sealing our peace with God,
Sound His dear name abroad,
'Worthy the Lamb!'

3 Join, all ye ransomed race,
Our Lord and God to bless:
Praise ye His name:
In Him we will rejoice,
Making a cheerful noise,
Shouting with heart and voice,
'Worthy the Lamb!'

4 Though we must change our place,
Yet we shall never cease
Praising His name!
To Him we'll tribute bring,
Hail Him our gracious King,
And withouth ceasing sing,
'Worthy the Lamb!'

James Allen (1734–1804) Altd

289

10 10. 10 10 (with refrain)

'The glorious gospel of the blessed God'
1 Timothy 1 v 11

1 Great is the gospel of our glorious
God,
Where mercy met the anger of God's
rod;
A penalty was paid and pardon
bought,
And sinners lost at last to Him were
brought:

O let the praises of my heart by Thine,
For Christ has died that I may call Him
mine,
That I may sing with those who dwell
above,
Adoring, praising Jesus, King of love.

2 Great is the mystery of godliness,
Great is the work of God's own
holiness;
It moves my soul, and causes me to
long
For greater joys than to the earth
belong:

3 The Spirit vindicated Christ our
Lord,
And angels sang with joy and sweet
accord;
The nations heard, a dark world
flamed with light –
When Jesus rose in glory and in
might:

© The Author   William Vernon Higham (b.1926)

290

87.87.D

'Worthy is the Lamb that was slain'
Revelation 5 v 12

1 Hail, Thou once despisèd Jesus!
Hail, Thou Galilean King!
Thou didst suffer to release us;
Thou didst free salvation bring.
Hail, Thou agonizing Saviour,
Bearer of our sin and shame!
By Thy merits we find favour;
Life is given through Thy name.

2 Paschal Lamb, by God appointed,
All our sins on Thee were laid;
By almighty love anointed,
Thou hast full atonement made:
All Thy people are forgiven
Through the virtue of Thy blood;
Opened is the gate of heaven;
Peace is made 'twixt man and God.

3 Jesus, hail! enthroned in glory,
There for ever to abide;
All the heavenly hosts adore Thee,
Seated at Thy Father's side:
There for sinners Thou art pleading,
There Thou dost our place prepare,
Ever for us interceding,
Till in glory we appear.

4 Worship, honour, power, and
   blessing,
Thou art worthy to receive;
Loudest praises without ceasing,
Meet it is for us to give.
Help, ye bright, angelic spirits!
Bring your sweetest, noblest lays;
Help to sing our Saviour's merits,
Help to chant Immanuel's praise!

John Bakewell (1721–1819)

291   C.M.

'Thou shalt call his name JESUS'
Matthew 1 v 21

1 How sweet the name of Jesus sounds
In a believer's ear!
It soothes his sorrows, heals his
   wounds,
And drives away his fear.

2 It makes the wounded spirit whole,
And calms the troubled breast;
'Tis manna to the hungry soul,
And to the weary rest.

3 Dear name! the rock on which I
   build,
My shield and hiding-place,
My never-failing treasury filled
With boundless stores of grace.

4 Jesus! my Shepherd, Brother, Friend,
My Prophet, Priest and King,
My Lord, my Life, my Way, my End,
Accept the praise I bring.

5 Weak is the effort of my heart,
And cold my warmest thought;
But when I see Thee as Thou art,
I'll praise Thee as I ought.

6 Till then I would Thy love proclaim
With every fleeting breath;
And may the music of Thy name
Refresh my soul in death!

John Newton (1725–1807)

292   10 10. 10 10

'I know that my redeemer liveth'
Job 19 v 25

1 I greet Thee who my sure Redeemer
art,
My only trust and Saviour of my heart,
Who pain didst undergo for my poor
sake:
I pray Thee from our hearts all cares
to take.

2 Thou art the King of mercy and of
grace,
Reigning omnipotent in every place:
So come, O King, and our whole
being sway;
Shine on us with the light of Thy
pure day.

3 Thou art the Life, by which alone we
live,
And all our substance and our
strength receive;
O comfort us in death's approaching
hour,
Strong-hearted then to face it by Thy
power.

4 Thou hast the true and perfect
gentleness,
No harshness hast Thou, and no
bitterness;
O grant to us the grace we find in Thee,
That we may dwell in perfect unity.

5 Our hope is in no other save in Thee;
Our faith is built upon Thy promise
free;
Come, give us peace, make us so
strong and sure,
That we may conquerors be, and ills
endure.

Strasbourg Psalter (1545)
Tr. Elizabeth Lee Smith (1817-98) Altd

293   87.87.D

'O LORD, my strength, and my redeemer'
Psalm 19 v 14

1   I will sing of my Redeemer,
    And His wondrous love to me;
    On the cruel cross He suffered,
    From the curse to set me free.

    Sing, O sing, of my Redeemer!
    With His blood He purchased me,
    On the cross He sealed my pardon,
    Paid the debt and made me free.

2   I will tell the wondrous story,
    How my lost estate to save,
    In His boundless love and mercy,
    He the ransom freely gave.

3   I will praise my dear Redeemer,
    His triumphant power I'll tell,
    How the victory He giveth
    Over sin and death and hell.

4   I will sing of my Redeemer,
    And His heavenly love to me;
    He from death to life hath brought
       me,
    Son of God, with Him to be.

                      Philipp Paul Bliss (1838–76)

294   C.M.

'Ye are complete in him' Colossians 2 v 10

1   I've found the pearl of greatest price,
    My heart doth sing for joy;
    And sing I must, for Christ is mine,
    Christ shall my song employ.

2   Christ is my Prophet, Priest, and
       King:
    My Prophet full of light,
    My great High Priest before the
       throne,
    My King of heavenly might.

3   For He indeed is Lord of lords,
    And He the King of kings;
    He is the Sun of Righteousness,
    With healing in His wings.

4   Christ is my peace; He died for me,
    For me He gave His blood;
    And, as my wondrous sacrifice,
    Offered Himself to God.

5   Christ Jesus is my All-in-all,
    My comfort and my love;
    My life below; and He shall be
    My glory-crown above.

                          John Mason (c.1646–94)

295   88.88.88

'What is thy beloved more than another
beloved?' Song of Solomon 5 v 9

1   If gazing strangers want to know
    What makes me sing of Jesus so;
    I love His name, 'tis very dear,
    And would His loveliness declare:
    A single smile from Jesus given
    Will lift a drooping soul to heaven.

2   His eyes are full of melting love,
    More soft and sparkling than the
       dove;
    And sweet instruction He conveys,
    To warm my heart and guide my
       ways:
    A single smile from Jesus given
    Will lift a drooping soul to heaven.

3   No sinful taint His bosom knows,
    But with amazing kindness glows;
    He wrought a righteousness divine,
    And gives me faith to call it mine:
    A single smile from Jesus given
    Will lift a drooping soul to heaven.

4   His mercies, like Himself, endure,
    And like His love are ever sure;
    And when our eyes His worth can
       view,
    Our hearts will love and trust Him
       too.
    A single smile from Jesus given
    Will lift a drooping soul to heaven.

                         John Berridge (1716–93)

296
10 10. 10 10

'The Lord is my helper, and I will not
fear what man shall do unto me'
Hebrews 13 v 6

1 Immortal honours rest on Jesus'
　head,
　My God, my portion, and my living
　Bread;
　In Him I live, upon Him cast my
　care;
　He saves from death, destruction
　and despair.

2 He is my refuge in each deep
　distress,
　The Lord my strength and glorious
　righteousness.
　Through floods and flames He leads
　me safely on,
　And daily makes His sovereign
　goodness known.

3 My every need He richly will supply,
　Nor will His mercy ever let me die;
　In Him there dwells a treasure all
　divine,
　And matchless grace has made that
　treasure mine.

4 O that my soul could love and praise
　Him more,
　His beauties trace, His majesty
　adore,
　Live near His heart, upon His bosom
　lean,
　Obey His voice and all His will
　esteem.

William Gadsby (1773–1844)

297
10 10. 10 10. 4

'The love of Christ, which passeth
knowledge' Ephesians 3 v 19

1 It passeth knowledge, that dear love
　of Thine,
　My Saviour, Jesus, yet this soul of
　mine
　Would of Thy love, in all its breadth
　and length,

Its height and depth, its everlasting
　strength,
Know more and more.

2 It passeth telling, that dear love of
　Thine,
　My Saviour, Jesus, yet these lips of
　mine
　Would fain proclaim to sinners, far
　and near,
　A love which can remove all guilty
　fear,
　And love beget.

3 It passeth praises, that dear love of
　Thine,
　My Saviour, Jesus, yet this heart of
　mine
　Would sing that love, so full, so rich,
　so free,
　Which brings a rebel sinner, such as
　me,
　Nigh unto God.

4 But though I cannot sing, or tell, or
　know
　The fulness of Thy love while here
　below,
　My empty vessel I may freely bring:
　O Thou who art of love the living
　spring,
　My vessel fill.

5 O fill me, Jesus, Saviour, with Thy
　love!
　Lead, lead me to the living fount
　above;
　Thither may I, in simple faith, draw
　nigh,
　And never to another fountain fly,
　But unto Thee.

6 And when my Jesus face to face I see,
　When at His lofty throne I bow the
　knee,
　Then of His love, in all its breadth
　and length,
　Its height and depth, its everlasting
　strength,
　My soul shall sing!

Mary Shekleton (1827–83)

298 C.M.

'Blessed are they that mourn: for they shall be comforted' Matthew 5 v 4

1 Jesus, the glories of Thy face
My songs of praise record:
I sing the overflowing grace
Of my belovèd Lord.

2 Thou art the Father's chief delight:
Thy beauty angels view:
Thou art all fair in Zion's sight,
And my Belovèd too.

3 Of Thee the ancient prophets wrote:
Of Thee let Israel sing;
And heaven's vast choir, in every
note,
Praise my belovèd King.

4 Thy precious name shall joy impart
To all that are Thine own:
In life and death, O may my heart
Be my Belovèd's throne.

Joseph Irons (1785–1852)

299 C.M.

'A name which is above every other name' Philippians 2 v 9

1 Jesus! the name high over all,
In hell, or earth, or sky;
Angels and men before it fall,
And devils fear and fly.

2 Jesus! the name to sinners dear,
The name to sinners given;
It scatters all their guilty fear,
It turns their hell to heaven.

3 Jesus! the prisoner's fetters breaks,
And bruises Satan's head;
Power into strengthless souls it
speaks,
And life into the dead.

4 O that the world might taste and see
The riches of His grace!
The arms of love that compass me
Would all mankind embrace.

5 His only righteousness I show,
His saving truth proclaim;
'Tis all my business here below
To cry, 'Behold the Lamb!'

6 Happy, if with my latest breath
I may but gasp His name;
Preach Him to all, and cry in death,
'Behold, behold the Lamb!'

Charles Wesley (1707–88)

300 L.M.

'A friend of publicans and sinners!' Luke 7 v 34

1 Jesus, the sinner's Friend, to Thee,
Lost and undone, for aid I flee,
Weary of earth, myself, and sin;
Open Thine arms, and take me in!

2 Pity, and heal my sin-sick soul;
'Tis Thou alone canst make me
whole;
Fall'n, till in me Thine image shine,
And cursed I am, till Thou art mine.

3 At last I own it cannot be
That I should fit myself for Thee:
Here then to Thee I all resign;
Thine is the work, and only Thine.

4 What shall I say Thy grace to move?
Lord, I am sin, but Thou art love:
I give up every plea beside –
Lord, I am lost, but Thou hast died!

Charles Wesley (1707–88)

301 S.M.

'He hath made us accepted in the beloved' Ephesians 1 v 6

1 Jesus! the sinner's Friend,
We hide ourselves in Thee!
God looks upon Thy sprinkled blood;
It is our only plea.

2 He hears Thy precious name;
We plead Thy name alone;
The Father must accept and bless
His well-beloved Son.

3 He sees Thy spotless robe;
  It covers all our sin;
  The golden gates have welcomed
    Thee,
  And we may enter in.

4 Thou hast fulfilled the law,
  And we are justified;
  Ours is the blessing, Thine the
    curse:
  We live, for Thou hast died.

5 Jesus! The sinner's Friend,
  We cannot speak Thy praise:
  No mortal voice can sing the song
  That ransomed hearts would raise.

6 But when before the throne,
  Upon the glassy sea,
  Clothed in our blood-washed robes
    of white,
  We stand complete in Thee.

7 Jesus! we'll give Thee then
  Such praises as are meet,
  And cast ten thousand golden
    crowns,
  Adoring, at Thy feet!

Catherine Pennefather (d.1893)

302   C.M.

'Unto you therefore which believe he is
precious' 1 Peter 2 v 7

1 Jesus, the very thought of Thee
  With sweetness fills my breast;
  But sweeter far Thy face to see,
  And in Thy presence rest.

2 Nor voice can sing, nor heart can
    frame,
  Nor can the memory find
  A sweeter sound than Thy blest
    name,
  O Saviour of mankind!

3 O hope of every contrite heart,
  O joy of all the meek,
  To those who fall how kind Thou art!
  How good to those who seek!

4 But what to those who find? Ah! this
  Nor tongue nor pen can show:
  The love of Jesus, what it is
  None but His loved ones know.

5 Jesus, our only joy be Thou,
  As Thou our prize wilt be;
  Jesus, be Thou our glory now,
  And through eternity.

Bernard of Clairvaux (1091–1153)
Tr. Edward Caswall (1814–78)

303   C.M.

'Blessed are they that have not seen and
yet have believed' John 20 v 29

1 Jesus, these eyes have never seen
  That radiant form of Thine;
  The veil of sense hangs dark
    between
  Thy blessèd face and mine.

2 I see Thee not, I hear Thee not,
  Yet art Thou oft with me;
  And earth hath ne'er so dear a spot,
  As where I meet with Thee.

3 Like some bright dream that comes
    unsought,
  When slumbers o'er me roll,
  Thine image ever fills my thought,
  And charms my ravished soul.

4 Yet, though I have not seen, and still
  Must rest in faith alone,
  I love Thee, dearest Lord, and will,
  Unseen, but not unknown.

5 When death these mortal eyes shall
    seal,
  And still this throbbing heart,
  The rending veil shall Thee reveal
  All glorious as Thou art.

Ray Palmer (1808–87)

304

L.M.

'They shall enter into the king's palace'
Psalm 45 v 15

1 Jesus, Thou everlasting King,
Accept the tribute which we bring;
Accept the well-deserved renown,
And wear our praises as Thy crown.

2 Let every act of worship be
Like our espousals, Lord, to Thee;
Like the dear hour when from above
We first received Thy pledge of love.

3 The gladness of that happy day –
Our hearts would wish it long to
stay;
Nor let our faith forsake its hold,
Nor comfort sink, nor love grow
cold.

4 Each following minute as it flies,
Increase Thy praise, improve our
joys,
Till we are raised to sing Thy name
At the great supper of the Lamb.

5 O that the months would roll away
And bring that coronation day!
The King of grace shall fill the
throne,
His Father's glory all His own.

Isaac Watts (1674–1748)

305

L.M.

'For he satisfieth the longing soul'
Psalm 107 v 9

1 Jesus, Thou joy of loving hearts,
Thou fount of life, Thou light of
men,
From the best bliss that earth
imparts,
We turn unfilled to Thee again.

2 Thy truth unchanged hath ever
stood;
Thou savest those that on Thee call;
To them that seek Thee Thou art
good,
To them that find Thee, all in all.

3 We taste Thee, O Thou living Bread,
And long to feast upon Thee still;
We drink of Thee, the fountain-
head,
And thirst our souls from Thee to
fill.

4 Our restless spirits yearn for Thee
Where'er our changeful lot is cast;
Glad, when Thy gracious smile we
see;
Blest, when our faith can hold Thee
fast.

5 O Jesus, ever with us stay;
Make all our moments calm and
bright;
Chase the dark night of sin away;
Shed o'er our souls Thy holy light.

Latin c.11th Century
Tr. Ray Palmer (1808–87)

306

6 6. 6 6. 8 8

*'He that glorieth, let him glory in the
Lord' 2 Corinthians 10 v 17*

1 Join all the glorious names
Of wisdom, love, and power,
That ever mortals knew,
That angels ever bore;
All are too mean to speak His worth,
Too mean to set my Saviour forth.

2 Great Prophet of my God,
My tongue would bless Thy name:
By Thee the joyful news
Of our salvation came;
The joyful news of sins forgiven,
Of hell subdued, and peace with
heaven.

3 Jesus, my great High Priest,
Offered His blood and died;
My guilty conscience seeks
No sacrifice beside;
His powerful blood did once atone,
And now it pleads before the throne.

4 My Saviour and my Lord,
  My Conqueror and my King,
  Thy sceptre and Thy sword,
  Thy reigning grace I sing;
  Thine is the power: behold, I sit
  In willing bonds beneath Thy feet.

5 Now let my soul arise,
  And tread the tempter down:
  My Captain leads me forth
  To conquest and a crown:
  A feeble saint shall win the day,
  Though death and hell obstruct the
    way.

6 Should all the hosts of death,
  And powers of hell unknown,
  Put their most dreadful forms
  Of rage and malice on,
  I shall be safe, for Christ displays
  Superior power and guardian grace.

Isaac Watts (1674–1748)

307   L.M.

'Him hath God exalted' Acts 5 v 31

1 Join, all who love the Saviour's
    name,
  To sing His everlasting fame;
  Great God! prepare each heart and
    voice
  In Him for ever to rejoice.

2 Of Him what wondrous things are
    told!
  In Him what glories I behold!
  For Him I gladly all things leave;
  To Him, my soul, for ever cleave.

3 In Him my treasure's all contained;
  By Him my feeble soul's sustained;
  From Him I all things now receive;
  Through Him my soul shall ever live.

4 With Him I daily love to walk;
  Of Him my soul delights to talk;
  On Him I cast my every care;
  Like Him one day I shall appear.

5 Bless Him, my soul, from day to day,
  Trust Him to bring thee on thy way;
  Give Him thy poor, weak, sinful
    heart;
  With Him, O never, never part.

6 Take Him for strength and
    righteousness;
  Make Him thy refuge in distress;
  Love Him above all earthly joy,
  And Him in everything employ.

7 Praise Him in cheerful, grateful
    songs;
  To Him your highest praise belongs;
  'Tis He who does your heaven
    prepare,
  And Him you'll sing for ever there.

Samuel Medley (1738–99)

308   66.88.88

'The Lord and Saviour Jesus Christ'
2 Peter 2 v 20

1 Let earth and heaven agree,
  Angels and men be joined,
  To celebrate with me
  The Saviour of mankind;
  To adore the all-atoning Lamb,
  And bless the sound of Jesu's name.

2 Jesus, transporting sound!
  The joy of earth and heaven;
  No other help is found,
  No other name is give,
  By which we can salvation have;
  But Christ eternal born to save.

3 Jesus, harmonious name!
  That charms the hosts above;
  They ever more proclaim
  And wonder at His love;
  'Tis all their happiness to gaze,
  'Tis heaven to see our Jesu's face.

4 His name the sinners hears,
  And is from sin set free;
  'Tis music in his ears,
  'Tis life and victory;
  New songs do now his lips employ,
  And dances his glad heart for joy.

5 O unexampled love!
O free abounding grace!
How swiftly didst Thou move
To save a fallen race:
What shall we do to make it known
What Thou for sinners lost hath
done?

Charles Wesley (1707–88)

309 6 6. 6 6. 8 8

Based on Philippians 2 vv 1-11

1 Let joyful tongues unite
And sing with fervent voice,
To praise our Saviour's might
And His triumphant grace!
Rejoice with awe,
For through His love
We'll dwell above,
For evermore!

2 He left His courts on high,
His Father's peace to bring,
That through His blood brought
nigh,
We'd to His mercy sing;
Our guilty souls,
Though bound for hell,
To Zion's hill
Are brought, with praise!

3 Behold the cruel cross
On which the Saviour died;
His suffering ends our loss,
God's law is satisfied;
His mercy's just,
So at His throne
His love we own,
We can Him trust.

4 We'll sing eternally
And bless that sacred name;
With joy we bend the knee
To Him who took our shame;
We worship bring!
O may our days
Be full of praise,
Immortal King!

© The Author   *Alan Charles Clifford (b.1941)*

310 11 6. 11 6

'I am the light of the world' John 9 v 5

1 Light of the world, for ever, ever
shining,
There is no change in Thee;
True Light of life, all joy and health
enshrining,
Thou canst not fade nor flee.

2 Thou hast arisen, but declinest
never;
Today shines as the past;
All that Thou wast Thou art, and
shalt be ever,
Brightness from first to last.

3 Night visits not Thy sky, nor storm,
nor sadness;
Day fills up all its blue,
Unfailing beauty and unfaltering
gladness,
And love for ever new!

4 Light of the world! undimming and
unsetting,
O shine each mist away;
Banish the fear, the falsehood and
the fretting;
Be our unchanging Day.

Horatius Bonar (1808–89)

311 8 7. 8 7. 4 7

*'They shall abundantly utter the memory
of thy great goodness' Psalm 145 v 7*

1 Lord, enthroned in heavenly splendour,
First begotten from the dead,
Thou alone, our strong Defender,
Liftest up Thy people's head.
Hallelujah,
Jesus, true and living Bread!

2 Price of life, for us Thou livest,
By Thy body souls are healed;
Price of peace, Thy peace Thou
givest,
By Thy blood is pardon sealed.
Hallelujah,
Word of God, in flesh revealed!

3 Paschal Lamb, Thine offering
  finished
  Once for all when Thou wast slain,
  In its fullness undiminished
  Shall forevermore remain.
  Hallelujah,
  Cleansing souls from every stain!

4 Life imparting heavenly Manna,
  Smitten Rock with streaming side,
  Heaven and earth with loud hosanna
  Worship Thee, the Lamb who died.
  Hallelujah,
  Risen, ascended, glorified!

George Hugh Bourne (1840–1925)

312   8 7. 8 7. 3 3 7

'A name which is above every other name'
Philippians 2 v 9

1 Mighty Christ from time eternal,
  Mighty, He man's nature takes,
  Mighty, when on Calv'ry dying,
  Mighty, death itself He breaks.
  See His might,
  Infinite,
  King of heaven and earth by right!

2 Mighty was He in heaven's purpose,
  Mighty, in the pledge to save,
  Mighty, from His birth to Calv'ry,
  Mighty, bursting from the grave.
  Still will He
  Mighty be
  When things hidden now we see.

3 Great my Jesus in His person,
  Great as God and man is He,
  Great His comeliness and beauty,
  White and ruddy, fair to see.
  Great that sight,
  Sovereign might,
  Throned secure on heaven's height!

Titus Lewis (1773 – 1811) vv 1-3
Anonymous v 2
© The Author   *Tr. Graham Stuart Harrison (b.1935)*

313   8 7. 8 7. D

'The brightness of his glory … upholding
all things' Hebrews 1 v 3

1 Mighty God, while angels bless
    Thee,
  May a mortal lisp Thy name?
  Lord of men, as well as angels,
  Thou art every creature's theme.
  Lord of every land and nation,
  Ancient of eternal days,
  Sounded through the wide creation
  Be Thy just and lawful praise.

2 For the grandeur of Thy nature,
  Grand beyond a seraph's thought;
  For created works of power,
  Works with skill and kindness
    wrought;
  For Thy providence, that governs
  Through Thine empire's wide
    domain,
  Wings an angel, guides a sparrow;
  Blessed be Thy gentle reign.

3 But Thy rich, Thy free redemption,
  Dark through brightness all along –
  Thought is poor, and poor
    expression –
  Who dare sing that awesome song?
  Brightness of the Father's glory,
  Shall Thy praise unuttered lie?
  Fly my tongue, such guilty silence!
  Sing the Lord who came to die.

4 From the highest throne in glory,
  To the cross of deepest woe,
  All to ransom guilty captives:
  Flow, my praise, for ever flow!
  Go, return, immortal Saviour!
  Leave Thy footstool, take Thy
    throne;
  Thence return, and reign for ever,
  Be the kingdom all Thine own!

Robert Robinson (1735–90)

314
L.M.

'He is before all things, and by him all things consist' Colossians 1 v 17

1 My song shall bless the Lord of all,
My praise shall climb to His abode;
Thee, Saviour, by that name I call,
The great Supreme, the mighty God.

2 Without beginning or decline,
Object of faith and not of sense;
Eternal ages saw Him shine,
He shines eternal ages hence.

3 As much when in the manger laid
Almighty Ruler of the sky,
As when the six days' work He made
Filled all the morning stars with joy.

4 Of all the crowns Jehovah wears,
Salvation is His dearest claim;
That gracious sound, well pleased,
      He hears,
And owns Emmanuel for His name.

5 A cheerful confidence I feel,
My well-placed hopes with joy I see;
My bosom glows with heavenly zeal,
To worship Him who died for me.

6 As man, He pities my complaint,
His power and truth are all divine;
He will not fail, He cannot faint;
Salvation's sure, and must be mine.

William Cowper (1731–1800)

315
7 7.7 7

'He hath by inheritance obtained a more excellent name' Hebrews 1 v 4

1 Name of Jesus! highest name!
Name that earth and heaven adore!
From the heart of God it came,
Leads me to God's heart once more.

2 Name of Jesus! living tide!
Days of drought for me are past;
How much more than satisfied
Are the thirsty lips at last.

3 Name of Jesus! dearest name!
Bread of heaven, and balm of love:
Oil of gladness, surest claim
To the treasures stored above.

4 Jesus gives forgiveness free
Jesus cleanses all my stains;
Jesus gives His life to me,
Jesus always He remains.

5 Only Jesus! fairest name!
Life, and rest, and peace, and bliss.
Jesus, evermore the same,
He is mine, and I am His.

Gerhard Tersteegen (1697– 1769)
Tr. Emma Frances Bevan (1827–1909)

316
L.M.

'The glory of God in the face of Jesus Christ' 2 Corinthians 4 v 6

1 Now to the Lord a noble song!
Awake, my soul! awake, my tongue!
Hosanna to the eternal name,
And all His boundless love proclaim.

2 See where it shines in Jesus' face,
The brightest image of His grace;
God, in the Person of His Son,
Has all His mightiest works
      outdone.

3 The spacious earth and spreading
      flood
Proclaim the wise and powerful
      God;
And Thy rich glories from afar
Sparkle in every rolling star.

4 But in His looks a glory stands,
The noblest labour of Thy hands;
The pleasing lustre of His eyes
Outshines the wonders of the skies.

5 Grace! 'tis a sweet, a charming
      theme;
My thoughts rejoice at Jesus' name:
Ye angels, dwell upon the sound!
Ye heavens, reflect it to the ground!

6 O may I live to reach the place
   Where He unveils His lovely face;
   There all His beauties to behold,
   And sing His name to harps of gold!

Isaac Watts (1674–1748)

317   C.M.

'His name shall be called Wonderful'
Isaiah 9 v 6

1 O Jesus, King most wonderful,
   Thou Conqueror renowned,
   Thou sweetness most ineffable,
   In whom all joys are found!

2 When once Thou visitest the heart,
   Then truth begins to shine;
   Then earthly vanities depart,
   Then kindles love divine.

3 O Jesus, light of all below,
   Thou fount of life and fire,
   Surpassing all the joys we know,
   And all we can desire:

4 May every heart confess Thy name,
   And ever Thee adore;
   And, seeking Thee, itself inflame
   To seek Thee more and more.

5 Thee may our tongues for ever bless,
   Thee may we love alone,
   And ever in our lives express
   The image of Thine own.

6 Grant us, while here on earth we stay,
   Thy love to feel and know;
   And when from hence we pass away,
   To us Thy glory show.

Latin c.11th Century
Tr. Edward Caswall (1814–78)

318   8 7. 8 7. D

'The love of Christ, which passeth
knowledge' Ephesians 3 v 19

1 O the deep, deep love of Jesus!
   Vast, unmeasured, boundless, free,
   Rolling as a mighty ocean
   In its fullness over me.

Underneath me, all around me,
   Is the current of Thy love;
   Leading onward, leading homeward,
   To my glorious rest above.

2 O the deep, deep love of Jesus!
   Spread His praise from shore to
     shore,
   How He loveth, ever loveth,
   Changeth never, nevermore;
   How He watches o'er His loved
     ones,
   Died to call them all His own;
   How for them He intercedeth,
   Watcheth o'er them from the throne.

3 O the deep, deep love of Jesus!
   Love of every love the best;
   'Tis an ocean vast of blessing,
   'Tis a haven sweet of rest.
   O the deep, deep love of Jesus!
   'Tis a heaven of heavens to me;
   And it lifts me up to glory,
   For it lifts me up to Thee.

Samuel Trevor Francis (1834–1925)

319   L.M.

'Greater love hath no man' John 15 v 13

1 O Thou, my soul, forget no more
   The Friend who all thy misery bore;
   Let every idol be forgot,
   But, O my soul, forget Him not.

2 Jesus for thee a body takes,
   Thy guilt assumes, thy fetters breaks,
   Discharging all thy dreadful debt:
   And canst thou e'er such love forget?

3 Renounce thy works and ways with
     grief,
   And fly to this most sure relief;
   Nor Him forget who left His throne,
   And for thy life gave up His own.

4 Infinite truth and mercy shine
   In Him, and He Himself is thine;
   And canst thou, then, with sin beset,
   Such charms, such matchless
     charms, forget?

5 Ah no! till life itself depart,
His name shall cheer and warm my
heart;
And lisping this, from earth I'll rise,
And join the chorus of the skies.

6 Ah no! when all things else expire,
And perish in the general fire,
This name all others shall survive,
And through eternity shall live.

Krishna Pal (1764–1822)
Tr. Joshua Marshman (1768–1837)

320   7 6. 7 6. D

'For in him dwelleth all the fullness of the
Godhead bodily' Colossians 2 v 9

1 Oh for a faith's perception
Which heavenly host adores.
To understand redemption,
This rich mysterious store.
Two natures in one person,
Inseparable lie.
This pure and blessed union
Distinct in harmony.

2 Our souls gaze on His glory,
This wondrous Son divine.
Entrust our lives entirely
And tell Him we are Thine.
His manhood sympathises
With our frail burdened frame.
Yet He is God that rises
Supreme o'er hell and shame.

Ann Griffiths (1776–1805)
© The Translator   *Tr. William Vernon Higham (b.1926)*

321   11 10. 11 10 (with refrain)

'The day of Jesus Christ'
Philippians 1 v 6

1 One day when heaven was filled with
His praises,
One day when sin was sick as could
be,
Jesus came forth to be born of a
virgin –
Dwelt amongst men, my example is
He!

Living, He loved me; dying, He saved me;
Buried, He carried my sins far away!
Rising, He justified freely for ever;
One day He's coming – O glorious day!

2 One day they led Him up Calvary's
mountain,
One day they nailed Him to die on
the tree;
Suffering anguish, despised and
rejected;
Bearing our sins, my Redeemer is
He!

3 One day they left Him alone in the
garden,
One day He rested, from suffering
free;
Angels came down o'er His tomb to
keep vigil;
Hope of the hopeless, my Saviour is
He!

4 One day the grave could conceal
Him no longer,
One day the stone rolled away from
the door;
He had arisen, o'er death He had
conquered;
Now is ascended, my Lord evermore!

5 One day the trumpet will sound for
His coming,
One day the skies with His glory will
shine;
Wonderful day, His beloved ones
bringing;
Glorious Saviour, this Jesus is mine!

J. Wilbur Chapman (1859–1918)

322   8 7. 8 7. 7 7

'A friend that sticketh closer than a
brother' Proverbs 18 v 24

1 One there is above all others,
Well deserves the name of Friend;
His is love beyond a brother's,
Costly, free and knows no end:
They who once His kindness prove,
Find it everlasting love.

2 Which of all our friends, to save us,
  Could, or would, have shed his blood?
  But the Saviour died to have us
  Reconciled in Him to God:
  This was boundless love indeed;
  Jesus is a Friend in need.

3 When He lived on earth abased
  Friend of sinners was His name;
  Now above all glory raised,
  He rejoices in the same;
  Still He calls them brethren, friends,
  And to all their wants attends.

4 Could we bear from one another
  What He daily bears from us?
  Yet this glorious Friend and Brother
  Loves us though we treat Him thus;
  Though for good we render ill,
  He accounts us brethren still.

5 O for grace our hearts to soften!
  Teach us, Lord, at length to love:
  We, alas! forget too often
  What a Friend we have above;
  But, when home our souls are
    brought,
  We shall love Thee as we ought.

John Newton (1725–1807)

323   Irregular

'Jesus Christ, to whom be praise'
1 Peter 4 v 11

1 Praise Him, praise Him! Jesus, our
    blessed Redeemer;
  Sing, O earth, His wonderful love
    proclaim!
  Hail Him, hail Him! highest
    archangels in glory,
  Strength and honour give to His holy
    name.
  Like a shepherd, Jesus will guard His
    children,
  In His arms He carries them all day
    long;
  O ye saints that dwell in the
    mountains of Zion,
  Praise him, praise Him! ever in joyful
    song.

2 Praise Him, praise Him! Jesus, our
    blessed Redeemer;
  For our sins He suffered and bled
    and died.
  He, our Rock, our hope of eternal
    salvation,
  Hail Him, hail Him! Jesus the
    crucified.
  Loving Saviour, meekly enduring
    sorrow,
  Crowned with thorns that cruelly
    pierced His brow;
  Once for us rejected, despised, and
    forsaken,
  Prince of glory, ever triumphant
    now.

3 Praise Him, praise him! Jesus, our
    blessed Redeemer;
  Heavenly portals loud with hosannas
    ring!
  Jesus, Saviour, reigneth for ever and
    ever,
  Crown Him, crown Him! Prophet
    and Priest and King!
  Death is vanquished, tell it with joy,
    ye faithful!
  Where is now thy victory, boasting
    grave?
  Jesus lives, no longer thy portals are
    cheerless;
  Jesus lives, the mighty and strong to
    save.

Frances Jane Crosby (1820–1915)

324   888.5

*'Let us offer the sacrifice of praise
continually' Hebrews 13 v 15*

1 Praise the Saviour, ye who know
    Him!
  Who can tell how much we owe
    Him?
  Gladly let us render to Him
  All we have and are.

2 Jesus is the name that charms us,
   He for conflict fits and arms us;
   Nothing moves, and nothing harms
       us,
   When we trust in Him.

3 Trust in Him, ye saints, for ever;
   He is faithful, changing never;
   Neither force nor guile can sever
   Those He loves from Him.

4 Keep us, Lord, O keep us cleaving
   To Thyself, and still believing,
   Till the hour of our receiving
   Promised joys in heaven.

5 Then we shall be where we would
       be,
   Then we shall be what we should be,
   That which is not now, nor could be,
   Then shall be our own.

Thomas Kelly (1769–1855)

325   87.87.47

'My soul thirsteth for God' Psalm 42 v 2

1 Precious Jesus! Friend of sinners;
   We, as such, to Thee draw near;
   Let Thy spirit now dwell in us,
   And with love our souls inspire;
   Fill, O fill us
   With that love which casts out fear.

2 Matchless Saviour; let us view Thee
   As the Lord our Righteousness;
   Cause each soul to cleave unto Thee,
   Come, and with Thy presence bless.
   Dear Immanuel,
   Feast us with Thy sovereign grace.

3 Open now Thy precious treasure;
   Let the blessings freely flow;
   Give to each a gracious measure
   Of Thy glory here below;
   Loving Bridegroom,
   'Tis Thyself we want to know.

4 Come, and claim us as Thy portion,
   And let us lay claim to Thee;
   Leave us not to empty notion,
   But from bondage set us free;
   King of glory!
   We would live and reign with Thee.

William Gadsby (1773–1884)

326   C.M.

'His dear Son' Colossians 1 v 13

1 Son of His love – the image of
   The great Invisible!
   First-born of all created things –
   His glories who can tell?

2 Son of His love – pre-eminent,
   The Church's risen Head;
   Before all things, and bond of all,
   The first-born from the dead.

3 It pleased the Father that in Him
   Should all the fulness dwell:
   It pleased Him by the blood-stained
       cross
   All enmity to quell.

4 Son of His love – the sweetest name
   Of all that Jesus bears:
   For in the love that crowns the Head
   The meanest member shares.

5 Son of His love – and this dear Son
   Declares His passion too:
   E'en as the Father hath loved Me,
   I also have loved you.

6 O love of loves! O joy of joys!
   What happy souls are we!
   God loves us as He loves His Son,
   And Jesus loves as He!

Thomas Spurgeon (1856–1917)

327   C.M.

'The name of Jesus' Philippians 2 v 10

1 There is a name I love to hear,
   I love to sing its worth;
   It sounds like music in mine ear,
   The sweetest name on earth.

2 It tells me of a Saviour's love,
Who died to set me free;
It tells me of His precious blood,
The sinner's perfect plea.

3 It tells of One whose loving heart
Can feel my deepest woe,
Who in each sorrow bears
A part that none can bear below.

4 Jesus, the name I love so well,
The name I love to hear:
No saint on earth its worth can tell,
No heart conceive how dear.

5 This name shall shed its fragrance
    still
Along life's thorny road,
Shall sweetly smooth the rugged hill
That leads me up to God.

6 And there with all the blood-bought
    throng,
From sin and sorrow free,
I'll sing the new eternal song
Of Jesus' love for me.

Frederick Whitfield (1829–1904)

328   8 6. 8 6. 8 8

*'At the name of Jesus every knee should
bow' Philippians 2 v 10*

1 Thou art the everlasting Word,
The Father's only Son;
God manifestly seen and heard,
And heaven's beloved One.

*Worthy, O Lamb of God, art Thou
That every knee to thee should bow!*

2 In Thee, most perfectly expressed,
The Father's glories shine:
Of the full Deity possessed,
Eternally divine:

3 True image of the Infinite,
Whose essence is concealed;
Brightness of uncreated light;
The heart of God revealed:

4 But the high mysteries of Thy name
An angel's grasp transcend:
The Father only – glorious claim! –
The Son can comprehend:

5 Throughout the universe of bliss
The centre Thou, and sun,
The eternal theme of praise is this,
To heaven's belovèd One.

Josiah Conder (1789–1855)

329   C.M.

*'I am the way, the truth, and the life'
John 14 v 6*

1 Thou art the Way; to Thee alone
From sin and death we flee:
And he who would the Father seek
Must seek Him, Lord, by Thee.

2 Thou art the Truth; Thy Word alone
True wisdom can impart;
Thou only canst inform the mind,
And purify the heart.

3 Thou art the Life; the rending tomb
Proclaims Thy conquering arm;
And those who put their trust in
    Thee
Nor death nor hell shall harm.

4 Thou art the Way, the Truth, the Life;
Grant us that Way to know,
That Truth to keep, that Life to win,
Whose joys eternal flow.

George Washington Doane (1799–1859)

330   8 4. 8 4. 8 8 8. 4

'Worthy is the Lamb' Revelation 5 v 12

1 'Tis the church triumphant singing,
Worthy the Lamb!
Heaven throughout with praises
    ringing,
Worthy the Lamb!
Thrones and powers before Him
    bending,
Odours sweet with voice ascending
Swell the chorus never ending,
Worthy the Lamb!

2 Every kindred, tongue and nation—
Worthy the Lamb!
Join to sing the great salvation;
Worthy the Lamb!
Loud as mighty thunders roaring,
Floods of mighty waters pouring,
Prostrate at His feet adoring,
Worthy the Lamb!

3 Harps and songs for ever sounding
Worthy the Lamb!
Mighty grace o'er sin abounding;
Worthy the Lamb!
By His blood He dearly bought us;
Wandering from the fold He sought
us;
And to glory safely brought us:
Worthy the Lamb!

4 Sing with blest anticipation,
Worthy the Lamb!
Through the vale of tribulation,
Worthy the Lamb!
Sweetest notes, all notes excelling,
On the theme for ever dwelling,
Still untold, though ever telling,
Worthy the Lamb!

John Kent (1766–1843)

331 C.M.

'Greater love hath no man than this'
John 15 v 13

1 To our Redeemer's glorious name,
Awake the sacred song;
O may His love – immortal flame –
Tune every heart and tongue.

2 His love, what mortal thought can
reach
What mortal tongue display?
Imagination's utmost stretch
In wonder dies away.

3 Let wonder still with love unite,
And gratitude and joy;
Jesus be our supreme delight,
His praise our blest employ.

4 Jesus who left His throne on high,
Left the bright realms of bliss,
And came to earth to bleed and die!
Was ever love like this?

5 O may the sweet, the blissful theme
Fill every heart and tongue;
Till strangers love Thy charming
name,
And join the sacred song.

Anne Steele (1716–1778)

332 87.87.87

'Thou shalt call his name JESUS'
Matthew 1 v 21

1 To the name of our salvation,
Laud and honour let us pay,
Which for many a generation
Hid in God's foreknowledge lay,
But with holy exultation
We may sing aloud today.

2 Jesus is the name we treasure,
Name beyond what words can tell;
Name of gladness, name of
pleasure,
Ear and heart delighting well;
Name of sweetness, passing
measure,
Saving us from sin and hell.

3 Jesus is the name exalted
Over every other name;
In this name, whene'er assaulted,
We can put our foes to shame;
Strength to them who else had
halted,
Eyes to blind, and feet to lame.

4 Therefore we, in love adoring,
This most blessed name revere:
Holy Jesus, Thee imploring
So to write it in us here,
That, hereafter heavenward soaring,
We may sing with angels there.

Anonymous 15th Century
Tr. John Mason Neale (1818–66)

333

D.C.M.

'The Word was made flesh, and dwelt among us' John 1 v 14

1 We know, by faith we surely know,
The Son of God is come,
Is manifested here below,
And makes our hearts His home:
To us He hath, in gracious love,
An understanding given,
To recognise Him from above,
The Lord of earth and heaven.

2 The self-existing God supreme,
Our Saviour we adore,
Fountain of life eternal, Him
We worship evermore:
Out of His plenitude receive
Ineffable delight,
And shall through endless ages live
Triumphant in His sight.

Charles Wesley (1707–88)

334

11 11. 11 11

'We thank thee, and praise thy glorious name' 1 Chronicles 29 v 13

1 We praise Thee, we bless Thee, our
Father and Friend,
O let our devotions before Thee
ascend;
In youth and in childhood, together
we come,
To pray that Thy will in our hearts
may be done.

2 We thank Thee for blessings
received every day,
For which Thou hast taught us
unceasing to pray;
But O, for the treasures Thy Word
hath in store,
Thy name, O our Father, we bless
and adore.

3 Protect us – defend us from sin and
from harm,
And gather, dear Shepherd, the
lambs with Thy arms.
O nourish and strengthen our souls
now in youth
With mercy and wisdom and
goodness and truth.

Frances Jane Crosby (1820–1915)

335

C.M.

'A name written, KING OF KINGS, AND LORD OF LORDS' Revelation 19 v 16

1 When oceans vast their depths reveal
And moons have ceased to wane,
The Lamb who died and rose again,
On Zion's hill shall reign.

2 His glorious name must long
endure
When suns have ceased to shine,
And through eternity the saints
Will sing His praise divine.

3 As countless as the drops of dew,
Or sand upon the shore,
Are blessings which the ransomed
have
In Him for evermore.

4 Let every other name recede,
His name alone extol;
In Him reserved, there is the grace
To satisfy my soul.

Morgan Rhys (1716–79)
Tr. Edward Mason Powell (1852–1928)

336

11 12 (with refrain)

'Unto him that loved us, and washed us from our sins' Revelation 1 v 5

1 With harps and with vials there
stand a great throng
In the presence of Jesus, and sing
this new song:

*Unto Him who hath loved us and
washed us from sin,
Unto Him be the glory forever, Amen.*

2 All these once were sinners, defiled
  in His sight,
  Now arrayed in pure garments in
  praise they unite:

3 He maketh the rebel a priest and a
  king,
  He hath bought us, and taught us
  this new song to sing:

4 How helpless and hopeless we
  sinners had been
  If He never had loved us till cleansed
  from our sin!

5 Aloud in His praises our voices shall
  ring,
  So that others, believing, this new
  song shall sing:

Arthur Tappan Pierson (1837–1911)

337   5 5. 5 5. 6 5. 6 5

'God ... working salvation'
Psalm 74 v 12

1 Ye servants of God,
  Your Master proclaim,
  And publish abroad
  His wonderful name:
  The name all-victorious
  Of Jesus extol;
  His kingdom is glorious,
  And rules over all.

2 God ruleth on high,
  Almighty to save;
  And still He is nigh,
  His presence we have;
  The great congregation
  His triumph shall sing,
  Ascribing salvation
  To Jesus, our King.

3 'Salvation to God,
  Who sits on the throne!'
  Let all cry aloud,
  And honour the Son:
  The praises of Jesus
  The angels proclaim,
  Fall down on their faces
  And worship the Lamb.

4 Then let us adore
  And give Him His right,
  All glory and power,
  All wisdom and might;
  All honour and blessing,
  With angels above,
  And thanks never-ceasing
  And infinite love.

Charles Wesley (1707–88)

338   8. 3 3. 6. D

'She brought forth her first-born son ...
and laid Him in a manger' *Luke 2 v 7*

1 All my heart this night rejoices,
  As I hear,
  Far and near,
  Sweetest angel voices:
  'Christ is born!' Their choirs are
  singing,
  Till the air,
  Everywhere,
  Now with joy is ringing.

2 Hark! a voice from yonder manger,
  Soft and sweet,
  Doth entreat:
  'Flee from woe and danger;
  Brethren, come: from all that grieves
  you
  You are freed;
  All you need
  I will surely give you.'

3 Come, then, let us hasten yonder;
  Here let all,
  Great and small,
  Kneel in awe and wonder;
  Love Him who with love is yearning;
  Hail the star
  That from far
  Bright with hope is burning.

4 Ye who pine in weary sadness,
  Weep no more,
  For the door
  Now is found of gladness;
  Cling to Him, for He will guide you
  Where no cross,
  Pain or loss
  Can again betide you.

5 Blessed Saviour, let me find Thee;
  Keep Thou me
  Close to Thee;
  Cast me not behind Thee;
  Life of life, my heart Thou stillest,
  Calm I rest
  On Thy breast,
  All this void Thou fillest.

6 Thee, dear Lord, with heed I'll
    cherish,
  Live to Thee,
  And with Thee
  Dying, shall not perish,
  But shall dwell with Thee for ever
  Far on high,
  In the joy
  That can alter never.

                    Paul Gerhardt (1607–76)
          Tr. Catherine Winkworth (1827–78)

339   L.M.

'He became poor' 2 Corinthians 8 v 9

1 All praise to Thee, Eternal Lord,
  Clothed in a garb of flesh and blood;
  Choosing a manger for Thy throne,
  While worlds on worlds are Thine
    alone.

2 Once did the skies before Thee bow;
  A virgin's arms contain Thee now;
  Angels who did in Thee rejoice
  Now listen for Thine infant voice.

3 A little Child, Thou art our Guest,
  That weary ones in Thee may rest;
  Forlorn and lowly is Thy birth,
  That we may rise to heaven from
    earth.

4 Thou comest in the darksome night
  To make us children of the light,
  To make us, in the realms divine,
  Like Thine own angels round Thee
    shine.

5 All this for us Thy love hath done;
  By this to Thee our love is won:
  For this we tune our cheerful lays,
  And shout our thanks in ceaseless
    praise.

                  Tr. from Martin Luther (1483–1546)

340   8 7. 8 7 (with refrain)

'Born King of the Jews' Matthew 2 v 2

1 Angels from the realms of glory,
  Wing your flight o'er all the earth;
  Ye who sang creation's story,
  Now proclaim Messiah's birth;

  Come and worship,
  Worship Christ the new-born King.

2 Shepherds, in the field abiding,
  Watching o'er your flocks by night,
  God with man is now residing;
  Yonder shines the infant light;

3 Sages, leave your contemplations;
  Brighter visions beam afar;
  Seek the great Desire of nations;
  Ye have seen His natal star;

4 Saints, before the altar bending,
  Watching long in hope and fear,
  Suddenly the Lord, descending,
  In His temple shall appear;

5 Sinners, wrung with true repentance,
  Doomed for guilt to endless pains,
  Justice now revokes the sentence,
  Mercy calls you – break your chains;

                    James Montgomery (1771–1854)

341   8 7. 8 7. D

'His righteousness remaineth for ever'
2 Corinthians 9 v 9

1 Angels gaze amazed in wonder,
  Glorious sight to faith displayed.
  See our Maker and Sustainer
  Perfect in His work arrayed.
  In a manger gently rocking,
  With no place to lay His head.
  Yet with heavenly host adoring
  Worship Him in humble bed.

2 Let us praise with loud thanksgiving
Praise Him with our latest breath
Now my soul with joy is singing
With such words outlive our death.
In our nature was afflicted
With the weakness of mankind.
He was fully man, yet sinless,
Yet in Him the Godhead find.

3 Hear Mount Sinai loudly thunder
And the trumpet sound the call.
Safe are we in love and wonder
In our Saviour cannot fall.
In the righteousness of Jesus
Faith is born and fear is dead.
In His sacrifice made for us
We have nothing more to dread.

Ann Griffiths (1776–1805)
© The Translator   Tr. *William Vernon Higham (b.1926)*

342   7 7.7 7.7 7

*'When they saw the star, they rejoiced
with exceeding great joy' Matthew 2 v 10*

1 As with gladness men of old
Did the guiding star behold,
As with joy they hailed its light,
Leading onward, beaming bright –
So, most gracious Lord, may we
Evermore be led to Thee.

2 As with joyful steps they sped,
Saviour, to Thy lowly bed,
There to bend the knee before
Thee, whom heaven and earth
    adore –
So may we with willing feet
Ever seek Thy mercy-seat.

3 As they offered gifts most rare
At Thy cradle rude and bare –
So may we with holy joy,
Pure, and free from sin's alloy,
All our costliest treasures bring,
Christ, to Thee, our heavenly King.

4 Holy Jesus, every day
Keep us in the narrow way;
And, when earthly things are past,
Bring our ransomed souls at last
Where they need no star to guide,
Where no clouds Thy glory hide.

5 In the heavenly country bright
Need they no created light;
Thou its light, its joy, its crown,
Thou its sun which goes not down;
There for ever may we sing
Hallelujahs to our King.

William Chatterton Dix (1837–98)

343   C.M.

*'The Word was made flesh, and dwelt
among us' John 1 v 14*

1 Behold, the great Creator makes
Himself a house of clay:
A robe of human flesh He takes
Which He will wear for aye.

2 Hark, hark, the wise eternal Word
Like a weak infant cries!
In form of servant is the Lord,
And God in cradle lies.

3 This wonder struck the world
    amazed,
It shook the starry frame;
Squadrons of spirits stood and
    gazed,
Then down in troops they came.

4 Glad shepherds ran to view the
    sight;
A choir of angels sings,
And eastern sages with delight
Adore this King of kings.

5 Join then, all hearts that are not
    stone,
And all our voices prove,
To celebrate this holy One,
The God of peace and love.

Thomas Pestel (c.1584–c.1659)

344
11 10. 11 10

'We have seen his star in the east'
Matthew 2 v 2

1 Brightest and best of the sons of the
   morning,
   Dawn on our darkness, and lend us
   thine aid;
   Stars of the east, the horizon adorning,
   Guide where our infant Redeemer is
   laid.

2 Cold on His cradle the dew-drops
   are shining;
   Low lies His head with the beasts of
   the stall;
   Angels adore Him in slumber
   reclining,
   Maker, and Monarch, and Saviour of
   all.

3 Say, shall we yield Him, in costly
   devotion,
   Odours of Edom, and offerings
   divine,
   Gems of the mountains and pearls
   of the ocean,
   Myrrh from the forest or gold from
   the mine?

4 Vainly we offer each ample oblation,
   Vainly with gifts would His favour
   secure;
   Richer by far is the heart's
   adoration,
   Dearer to God are the prayers of the
   poor.

5 Brightest and best of the sons of the
   morning,
   Dawn on our darkness, and lend us
   thine aid;
   Star of the east, the horizon
   adorning,
   Guide where our infant Redeemer is
   laid.

Reginald Heber (1783–1826)

345
5 5. 5 3. D

'Behold, a virgin shall conceive, and bear
a son' Isaiah 7 v 14

1 Child in the manger,
   Infant of Mary;
   Outcast and stranger,
   Lord of all!
   Child who inherits
   All our transgressions,
   All our demerits
   On Him fall.

2 Once the most holy
   Child of salvation,
   Gently and lowly
   Livèd below;
   Now as our glorious
   Mighty Redeemer,
   See Him victorious
   O'er each foe.

3 Prophets foretold Him,
   Infant of wonder;
   Angels behold Him
   On His throne;
   Worthy our Saviour
   Of all their praises;
   Happy for ever
   Are His own.

Mary Macdonald (1789–1872)
Tr. Lachlan Macbean (1853–1931)

346
10 10. 10 10. 10 10

'For unto you is born this day ... a
Saviour, which is Christ the Lord'
Luke 2 v 11

1 Christians, awake! Salute the happy
   morn,
   Whereon the Saviour of the world
   was born;
   Rise to adore the mystery of love
   Which hosts of angels chanted from
   above:
   With them the joyful tidings first
   begun
   Of God Incarnate, and the Virgin's
   Son.

2 Then to the watchful shepherds it
was told,
Who heard the angelic herald's
voice, 'Behold,
I bring good tidings of a Saviour's
birth
To you and all the nations upon earth;
This day hath God fulfilled His
promised word,
This day is born a Saviour, Christ the
Lord.'

3 He spake; and straightway the
celestial choir
In hymns of joy unknown before
conspire;
The praises of redeeming love they
sang,
And heaven's whole orb with
hallelujahs rang;
God's highest glory was their
anthem still,
'Peace upon earth, and unto men
goodwill.'

4 O may we keep and ponder in our
mind
God's wondrous love in saving lost
mankind;
Trace we the Babe who hath
retrieved our loss
From His poor manger to His bitter
cross;
Tread in His steps, assisted by His
grace,
Till man's first heavenly state again
takes place.

5 Then may we hope, the angelic
thrones among,
To sing, redeemed, a glad triumphal
song:
He that was born upon this joyful
day
Around us all His glory shall display;
Saved by His love, incessant we shall
sing
Eternal praise to heaven's Almighty
King.

John Byrom (1692–1763)

347 C.M.

'Let us now go even unto Bethlehem'
Luke 2 v 15

1 Come, ye redeemed of the Lord,
Your grateful tribute bring;
And celebrate with one accord
The birthday of our King.

2 Let us with humble hearts repair,
Faith will point out the road,
To little Bethlehem and there
Adore our infant God.

3 The crowded inn, like sinners'
hearts,
O ignorance extreme!
For other guests, of various sorts,
Had room; but none for Him.

4 But see what different thoughts arise
In our and angels' breasts;
To hail His birth they left the skies,
We lodged Him with the beasts!

5 Yet let believers cease their fears
Nor envy heavenly powers;
If sinless innocence be theirs,
Redemption all is ours.

Joseph Hart (1712–68)

348 87.87.87

'When the fullness of the time was come'
Galatians 4 v 4

1 Earth was waiting, spent and
restless,
With a mingled hope and fear;
And the faithful few were sighing,
Surely, Lord, the day is near;
The Desire of all the nations,
It is time He should appear.

2 In the sacred courts of Zion,
Where the Lord had His abode,
There the money-changers
trafficked,
And the sheep and oxen trod;
And the world, because of wisdom,
Knew not either Lord or God.

3 Then the Spirit of the Highest
On a virgin meek came down,
And He burdened her with blessing,
And He pained her with renown;
For she bare the Lord's Anointed,
For His cross and for His crown.

4 Earth for Him had groaned and
travailed
Since the ages first began;
For in Him was hid the secret
That through all the ages ran –
Son of Mary, Son of David,
Son of God, and Son of man.

Walter Chalmers Smith (1824–1908)

349   L.M.

'God was manifest in the flesh'
1 Timothy 3 v 16

1 Ere the blue heavens were stretched
abroad,
From everlasting was the Word;
With God He was; the Word was
God;
And must divinely be adored.

2 By his own power were all things
made;
By him supported all things stand;
He is the whole creation's Head,
And angels fly at His command.

3 Ere sin was born, or Satan fell,
He led the host of morning stars;
Thy generation who can tell,
Or count the number of thy years?

4 But lo! He leaves those heavenly
forms;
The Word descends and dwells in
clay,
That he may hold converse with
worms,
Dressed in such feeble flesh as they.

5 Mortals with joy behold His face
The eternal Father's only Son;
How full of truth! How full of grace!
When through his eyes the Godhead
shone.

6 Bless'd angels leave their high
abode,
To learn new mysteries here, and tell
The loves of our descending God,
The glories of Immanuel.

Isaac Watts (1674–1748)

350   L.M.

*'For unto you is born this day in the City
of David a Saviour, which is Christ the
Lord' Luke 2 v 11*

1 From heaven above to earth I come,
To bear good news to every home;
Glad tidings of great joy I bring,
Whereof I now will say and sing:

2 To you this night is born a Child,
Of Mary, chosen virgin mild;
This little Child, of lowly birth,
Shall be the joy of all the earth.

3 These are the tokens ye shall mark:
The swaddling clothes and manger
dark;
There ye shall find the Infant laid
By whom the heavens and earth were
made.

4 'Tis Christ our God, who far on high
Hath heard your sad and bitter cry;
Himself will your salvation be;
Himself from sin will make you free.

5 Welcome to earth, Thou noble guest,
Through whom the sinful world is
blest!
Thou com'st to share my misery:
What thanks shall I return to Thee?

6 Ah, dearest Jesus, holy Child,
Make Thee a bed, soft, undefiled,
Within my heart, that it may be
A quiet chamber kept for Thee.

7 My heart for very joy doth leap;
My lips no more can silence keep;
I too must raise with joyful tongue
That sweetest ancient cradle song –

8 'Glory to God in highest heaven,
   Who unto man His Son hath given!'
   While angels sing with holy mirth
   A glad new year to all the earth.

Martin Luther (1483–1546)
Tr. Catherine Winkworth (1827–78)

351   7 6. 7 6. 7 7. 7 6

'Christ that died ... maketh intercession
for us' Romans 8 v 34

1 Glory be to God on high,
   And peace on earth descend:
   God comes down, He bows the sky,
   And shows Himself our Friend:
   God the invisible appears:
   God, the blest, the great I AM,
   Sojourns in this vale of tears,
   And Jesus is His name.

2 Him the angels all adored,
   Their Maker and their King;
   Tidings of their humbled Lord
   They now to mortals bring.
   Emptied of His majesty,
   Of His dazzling glories shorn,
   Being's source begins to be
   And God Himself is born!

3 See the eternal Son of God
   A mortal Son of man;
   Dwelling in an earthly clod,
   Whom heaven cannot contain.
   Stand amazed, ye heavens, at this!
   See the Lord of earth and skies;
   Humbled to the dust He is,
   And in a manger lies.

4 We, the sons of men, rejoice,
   The Prince of Peace proclaim;
   With heaven's host lift up our voice,
   And shout Immanuel's name:
   Knees and hearts to Him we bow;
   Of our flesh and of our bone,
   Jesus is our Brother now,
   And God is all our own.

Charles Wesley (1707–88)

352   C.M.

'Unto him be glory' Ephesians 3 v 21

1 Glory to God! The angels said,
   Good tidings, lo! I bring;
   In David's city is a babe –
   Your Lord and Saviour – King.

2 Glory to God, and peace on earth,
   Goodwill to man is shown;
   Let heavenly joy at Jesus' birth
   Be through the nations known.

3 Glory to God! Let man reply,
   For Christ the Lord is come;
   Behold Him in a manger lie –
   A stable is His home.

4 Glory to God! For love so mild;
   How wonderful the plan,
   That Jesus once became a child,
   To save rebellious man!

5 Glory to God! Let all the earth
   Join in the heavenly song,
   And praise Him for the Saviour's
        birth,
   In every land and tongue.

Silver Street Collection 1821

353   C.M.

'The Lord hath anointed me to preach
good tidings' Isaiah 61 v 1

1 Hark, the glad sound! the Saviour
        comes,
   The Saviour promised long;
   Let every heart prepare a throne,
   And every voice a song.

2 He comes the prisoners to release,
   In Satan's bondage held;
   The gates of brass before Him burst,
   The iron fetters yield.

3 He comes, from thickest films of
        vice
   To clear the mental ray,
   And on the eyeballs of the blind
   To pour celestial day.

4 He comes the broken heart to bind,
The bleeding soul to cure,
And with the treasures of His grace
To enrich the humble poor.

5 Our glad hosannas, Prince of Peace,
Thy welcome shall proclaim,
And heaven's eternal arches ring
With Thy belovèd name.

Philip Doddridge (1702–51)

354   7 7. 7 7. D (with refrain)

*'For unto you is born … a Saviour, which
is Christ the Lord' Luke 2 v 11*

1 Hark! the herald angels sing
Glory to the new-born King,
Peace on earth, and mercy mild,
God and sinners reconciled.
Joyful, all ye nations, rise,
Join the triumph of the skies;
With the angelic host proclaim,
'Christ is born in Bethlehem.'

*Hark! the herald angels sing
Glory to the new-born King.*

2 Christ, by highest heaven adored,
Christ, the everlasting Lord,
Late in time behold Him come,
Offspring of a virgin's womb.
Veiled in flesh the Godhead see!
Hail the incarnate Deity!
Pleased as Man with men to dwell,
Jesus, our Immanuel.

3 Hail, the heaven-born Prince of
Peace!
Hail, the Sun of Righteousness!
Light and life to all He brings,
Risen with healing in His wings.
Mild He lays His glory by,
Born that man no more may die,
Born to raise the sons of earth,
Born to give them second birth.

4 Come, Desire of nations, come,
Fix in us Thy humble home;
Rise, the woman's conquering Seed,
Bruise in us the serpent's head.

Now display Thy saving power,
Ruined nature now restore;
Now in mystic union join
Thine to ours, and ours to Thine!

Charles Wesley (1707–88)

355   D.C.M.

*'And suddenly there was with the angel a
multitude of the heavenly host praising
God' Luke 2 v 13*

1 It came upon the midnight clear,
That glorious song of old,
From angels bending near the earth
To touch their harps of gold:
'Peace on the earth, goodwill to
men,
From heaven's all-gracious King!'
The world in solemn stillness lay
To hear the angels sing.

2 Still through the cloven skies they
come,
With peaceful wings unfurled,
And still their heavenly music floats
O'er all the weary world;
Above its sad and lowly plains
They bend on hovering wing,
And ever o'er its Babel sounds
The blessèd angels sing.

3 Yet with the woes of sin and strife
The world has suffered long;
Beneath the angels' strain have
rolled
Two thousand years of wrong;
And man, at war with man, hears
not
The love-song which they bring:
O hush the noise, ye men of strife,
And hear the angels sing.

4 And ye, beneath life's crushing load
Whose forms are bending low,
Who toil along the climbing way
With painful steps and slow,
Look up! for glad and golden hours
Come swiftly on the wing;
O rest beside the weary road,
And hear the angels sing.

5 For lo! the days are hastening on,
By prophet bards foretold,
When with the ever-circling years
Comes round the age of gold;
When peace shall over all the earth
Its ancient splendours fling,
And the whole world send back the
   song
Which now the angels sing.

Edmund Hamilton Sears (1810–76)

356   C.M.

'Rejoice greatly, O daughter of Zion'
Zechariah 9 v 9

1 Joy to the world! The Lord is come!
Let earth receive her King;
Let every heart prepare Him room,
And heaven and nature sing.

2 Joy to the earth! The Saviour reigns!
Let men their songs employ;
While fields and floods, rocks, hills
   and plains,
Repeat the sounding joy.

3 No more let sins and sorrows grow,
Nor thorns infest the ground;
He comes to make His blessings
   flow
Far as the curse is found.

4 He rules the earth with truth and
   grace,
And makes the nations prove
The glories of His righteousness,
The wonders of His love.

Isaac Watts (1674–1748)

357   6 6. 6 6. 8 8

'He humbled himself' Philippians 2 v 8

1 Let earth and heaven combine,
Angels and men agree,
To praise in songs divine,
The incarnate Deity,
Our God contracted to a span,
Incomprehensibly made man.

2 He laid His glory by,
He wrapped Him in our clay;
Unmarked by human eye,
The latent Godhead lay;
Infant of days He here became,
And bore the mild Immanuel's
   name.

3 Unsearchable the love
That hath the Saviour bought;
The grace is far above
Or man or angel's thought;
Suffice for us that God, we know,
Our God, is manifest below.

4 He deigns in flesh to appear,
Widest extremes to join;
To bring our vileness near,
And make us all divine:
And we the life of God shall know,
For God is manifest below.

5 Made perfect by His love,
And sanctified by grace,
We shall from earth remove,
And see His glorious face:
Then shall His love be fully showed,
And man shall then be lost in God.

Charles Wesley (1707–88)

358   Irregular

'Let us now go even unto Bethlehem'
Luke 2 v 15

1 O come, all ye faithful,
Joyful and triumphant,
O come ye, O come ye to Bethlehem;
Come and behold Him
Born the King of angels:

O come, let us adore Him,
O come, let us adore Him,
O come, let us adore Him, Christ the Lord!

2 God of God,
Light of Light,
Lo, He abhors not the Virgin's
   womb;
Very God,
Begotten, not created:

3 Sing, choirs of angels,
  Sing in exultation,
  Sing, all ye citizens of heaven above;
  'Glory to God
  In the highest!'

4 Yea, Lord, we greet Thee,
  Born this happy morning,
  Jesus, to Thee be glory given;
  Word of the Father,
  Now in flesh appearing:

Latin 17th Century
Tr. Frederick Oakeley (1802-80) Altd

359   Irregular

'Emmanuel ... God with us'
Matthew 1 v 23

1 O little town of Bethlehem,
  How still we see thee lie!
  Above thy deep and dreamless sleep
  The silent stars go by:
  Yet in thy dark street shineth
  The everlasting Light;
  The hopes and fears of all the years
  Are met in thee tonight.

2 O morning stars, together
  Proclaim the holy birth,
  And praises sing to God the King,
  And peace to men on earth;
  For Christ is born of Mary;
  And, gathered all above,
  While mortals sleep, the angels keep
  Their watch of wondering love.

3 How silently, how silently,
  The wondrous gift is given!
  So God imparts to human hearts
  The blessings of His heaven.
  No ear may hear His coming;
  But in this world of sin,
  Where meek souls will receive Him, still
  The dear Christ enters in.

4 O holy Child of Bethlehem,
  Descend to us, we pray;
  Cast out our sin, and enter in;
  Be born in us today.
  We hear the Christmas angels
  The great glad tidings tell;
  O come to us, abide with us,
  Our Lord Immanuel.

Phillips Brooks (1835–93)

360   87.87.77

'[Christ Jesus] was made in the likeness of
men' Philippians 2 v 7

1 Once in royal David's city
  Stood a lowly cattle-shed,
  Where a mother laid her Baby
  In a manger for His bed.
  Mary was that mother mild,
  Jesus Christ her little Child.

2 He came down to earth from heaven
  Who is God and Lord of all,
  And His shelter was a stable,
  And His cradle was a stall.
  With the poor, and mean, and lowly
  Lived on earth our Saviour holy.

3 And through all His wondrous
      childhood
  He would honour and obey,
  Love, and watch the lowly mother
  In whose gentle arms He lay.
  Christian children all must be
  Mild, obedient, good as He.

4 For He is our childhood's pattern:
  Day by day like us He grew;
  He was little, weak, and helpless;
  Tears and smiles like us He knew;
  And He feeleth for our sadness,
  And He shareth in our gladness.

5 And our eyes at last shall see Him,
  Through His own redeeming love;
  For that Child so dear and gentle
  Is our Lord in heaven above;
  And He leads His children on
  To the place where He is gone.

6 Not in that poor lowly stable,
  With the oxen standing by,
  We shall see Him, but in heaven,
  Set at God's right hand on high;
  When like stars His children
    crowned
  All in white shall wait around.

Cecil Frances Alexander (1818–95)

361   7 7. 7 7 (with refrain)

'Unto you is born ... a Saviour'
Luke 2 v 11

1 See, amid the winter's snow,
  Born for us on earth below,
  See, the Lamb of God appears,
  Promised from eternal years.

  Hail, thou ever-blessed morn!
  Hail, redemption's happy dawn!
  Sing through all Jerusalem:
  Christ is born in Bethlehem!

2 Lo, within a manger lies
  He who built the starry skies,
  He who, throned in height sublime,
  Sits amid the cherubim.

3 Say, ye holy shepherds, say,
  What your joyful news today;
  Wherefore have ye left your sheep
  On the lonely mountain steep?

4 As we watched at dead of night,
  Lo, we saw a wondrous light:
  Angels, singing peace on earth,
  Told us of the Saviour's birth.

5 Sacred Infant, all divine,
  What a tender love was Thine,
  Thus to come from highest bliss
  Down to such a world as this!

6 Teach, O teach us, holy Child,
  By Thy face so meek and mild,
  Teach us to resemble Thee
  In Thy sweet humility.

Edward Caswall (1814–78)

362   8 7. 8 7. D

'Ye shall find the babe ... lying in a
manger' Luke 2 v 12

1 See He lies there in the manger
  Who once made the earth and sky.
  Down from heaven He's come, a
    stranger;
  Newly born, yet born to die.
  Hands almighty, now lie helpless
  Round His mother's finger curled;
  Lips so gracious, now yet
    speechless,
  Soon will speak to all the world.

2 Shepherds hasten to adore Him,
  Wise men offer gifts so rare.
  See the lowly maiden rocks Him
  Gently, with a mother's care.
  Made a man for man's salvation,
  Yet eternal God is He;
  Born to save from every nation,
  From their chains to set men free.

3 Now they worship and adore Him
  As they hear the Baby's cries;
  But the crowds will mock and scorn
    Him
  As He helpless hangs and dies.
  Christ incarnate, come to save us,
  Rid our hearts of wretched pride;
  Reign alone as Sovereign o'er us –
  Thou art worthy! Thou hast died!

4 Well might angels sing in wonder
  As they herald forth His birth;
  Even they can scarcely ponder
  Why God's Son came down to earth.
  See Him now, enthroned in glory,
  Earth awaiting His return.
  While our hearts recount his story
  May these hearts within us burn.

Graham Stuart Harrison (b.1935)

363　　Irregular

'And they came with haste, and found Mary, and Joseph, and the babe lying in a manger' Luke 2 v 16

1 Silent night! holy night!
All is calm, all is bright
Round yon virgin mother and Child,
Holy Infant so tender and mild,
Sleep in heavenly peace!

2 Silent night! holy night!
Shepherds quake at the sight!
Glories stream from heaven afar,
Heavenly hosts sing hallelujah;
Christ the Saviour is born!

3 Silent night! holy night!
Son of God, love's pure light
Radiant beams from Thy holy face,
With the dawn of redeeming grace,
Jesus, Lord, at Thy birth.

Joseph Mohr (1792–1848)
Tr. Anonymous

364　　77.77.77

'For unto us a child is born, unto us a son is given' Isaiah 9 v 6

1 Sing, O sing, this blessed morn!
Unto us a Child is born,
Unto us a Son is given,
God Himself comes down from heaven;

Sing, O sing this blessed morn,
Jesus Christ today is born!

2 God of God and Light of light
Comes with mercies infinite,
Joining in a wondrous plan
Heaven to earth, and God to man.

3 God with us, Emmanuel,
Deigns for ever now to dwell;
He on Adam's fallen race
Sheds the fulness of His grace.

4 God comes down that man may rise,
Lifted by Him to the skies,
Christ is Son of man that we
Sons of God in Him may be.

5 O renew us, Lord, we pray,
With Thy Spirit day by day,
That we ever one may be,
With the Father and with Thee.

Christopher Wordsworth (1807–85)

365　　C.M.

'The people that walked in darkness have seen a great light' Isaiah 9 v 2

1 The race that long in darkness pined
Have seen a glorious Light;
The people dwell in day, who dwelt
In death's surrounding night.

2 To hail Thy rise, Thou better Sun,
The gathering nations come,
Joyous as when the reapers bear
The harvest-treasures home.

3 To us a Child of hope is born,
To us a Son is given;
Him shall the tribes of earth obey,
Him all the hosts of heaven.

4 His name shall be the Prince of Peace,
For evermore adored,
The Wonderful, the Counsellor,
The great and mighty Lord.

5 His power increasing still shall spread,
His reign no end shall know:
Justice shall guard His throne above,
And peace abound below.

John Morison (1749–98)

366　　Irregular

'Though he was rich, yet for your sakes he became poor' 2 Corinthians 8 v 9

1 Thou didst leave Thy throne
And Thy kingly crown,
When Thou camest to earth for me;
But in Bethlehem's home
Was there found no room
For Thy holy nativity:
O come to my heart, Lord Jesus!
There is room in my heart for Thee.

2 Heaven's arches rang
When the angel's sang,
Proclaiming Thy royal degree;
But of lowly birth
Cam'st Thou, Lord, on earth,
And in great humility:
O come to my heart, Lord Jesus!
There is room in my heart for Thee.

3 The foxes found rest,
And the birds their nest,
In the shade of the cedar tree;
But Thy couch was the sod,
O Thou Son of God,
In the deserts of Galilee:
O come to my heart, Lord Jesus!
There is room in my heart for Thee.

4 Thou camest, O Lord,
With the living word,
That should set Thy people free;
But, with mocking scorn,
And with crown of thorn,
They bore Thee to Calvary:
O come to my heart, Lord Jesus!
Thy cross is my only plea.

5 When heaven's arches ring,
And her choirs shall sing,
At Thy coming to victory,
Let Thy voice call me home,
Saying, 'Yet there is room,
There is room at My side for Thee!'
And my heart shall rejoice, Lord
Jesus,
When Thou comest and callest for
me.

Emily Elizabeth Steele Elliott (1836–97)

367   9 8. 9 8. 9 8

'Though he was rich, yet for your sakes
he became poor' 2 Corinthians 8 v 9

1 Thou who wast rich beyond all
splendour,
All for love's sake becamest poor;
Thrones for a manger didst
surrender,
Sapphire-paved courts for stable
floor.

Thou who wast rich beyond all
splendour,
All for love's sake becamest poor.

2 Thou who art God beyond all
praising,
All for love's sake becamest Man;
Stooping so low, but sinners raising
Heavenwards by Thine eternal plan.
Thou who art God beyond all
praising,
All for love's sake becamest Man.

3 Thou who art love beyond all telling,
Saviour and King, we worship Thee.
Immanuel, within us dwelling,
Make us what Thou wouldst have us
be.
Thou who art love beyond all telling,
Saviour and King, we worship Thee.

© OMF International (UK)   Frank Houghton (1894–1972)

368   L.M.

'Now the birth of Jesus Christ was on this
wise' Matthew 1 v 18

1 To us a Child of royal birth,
Heir of the promises, is given;
The Invisible appears on earth,
The Son of man, the God of heaven.

2 A Saviour born, in love supreme
He comes our fallen souls to raise;
He comes His people to redeem
With all His plenitude of grace.

3 The Christ, by raptured seers
foretold,
Filled with the eternal Spirit's power,
Prophet, and Priest, and King
behold,
And Lord of all the worlds adore.

4 The Lord of hosts, the God most
High,
Who quits His throne on earth to
live,
With joy we welcome from the sky,
With faith into our hearts receive.

Charles Wesley (1707–88)

369 C.M.

'Good tidings of great joy' Luke 2 v 10

1 While shepherds watched their
    flocks by night,
All seated on the ground,
The angel of the Lord came down,
And glory shone around.

2 'Fear not!' said he, for mighty dread
Had seized their troubled mind;
'Glad tidings of great joy I bring
To you and all mankind.

3 'To you, in David's town, this day
Is born of David's line
A Saviour, who is Christ the Lord;
And this shall be the sign:

4 'The heavenly Babe you there shall
    find
To human view displayed,
All meanly wrapped in swathing
    bands,
And in a manger laid.'

5 Thus spake the seraph, and
    forthwith
Appeared a shining throng
Of angels praising God, and thus
addressed their joyful song:

6 'All glory be to God on high,
And to the earth be peace:
Good will henceforth from heaven to
    men
Begin and never cease.'

Nahum Tate (1652–1715)

370 C.M.

'The word was made flesh, and dwelt among us' John 1 v 14

1 From heaven's eternal throne there
    came
A word of strong decree:
Light up the world with grace and
    truth
And set the captives free!

2 Forth from the courts of heavenly
    bliss
Down to this world of shame,
The Son of God with light and life
In glad obedience came.

3 The Word made flesh in human
    form
Entered the world He made;
The darkness fled and glory shone
Around where He was laid.

4 While circling years in time revealed
The plan of God in grace,
The Son of man unfurled the truth
Prophets had learned to trace.

5 Borne to a cross by cruel hands
Of men in darkness held,
Judgment and death eclipsed the
    Son,
Whilst lies deceived the world.

6 Out from a tomb of dark despair
The Prince of light arose;
The truth prevails and grace
    abounds,
In all the world it flows.

7 Now fix your gaze, O sons of light,
On heaven's exalted King!
The Lamb of God will soon return
And full salvation bring.

© The Author   *Paul Eric Graham Cook (b.1932)*

371 L.M.

'Come unto me, all ye that labour and are heavy laden' Matthew 11 v 28

1 How sweetly flowed the gospel's
    sound
From lips of gentleness and grace;
When listening thousands gathered
    round
And joy and reverence filled the
    place.

2 From heaven He came, of heaven He
   spoke,
To heaven He led His followers' way;
Dark clouds of gloomy night He
   broke,
Unveiling an immortal day.

3 'Come, wanderers, to my Father's
   home;
Come, all ye weary ones, and rest.'
Yes! gracious Saviour, we will come,
Obey Thee, love Thee, and be blest.

               John Bowring (1792–1872)

372   L.M.

'I have given you an example'
John 13 v 15

1 My dear Redeemer and my Lord,
I read my duty in Thy Word;
But in Thy life the law appears
Drawn out in living characters.

2 Such was Thy truth, and such Thy
   zeal,
Such deference to Thy Father's will,
Such love, and meekness so divine,
I would transcribe and make them
   mine.

3 Cold mountains and the midnight
   air
Witnessed the fervour of Thy prayer;
The desert Thy temptations knew,
Thy conflict, and Thy victory too.

4 Be Thou my pattern: make me bear
More of Thy gracious image here;
Then God the Judge shall own my
   name
Amongst the followers of the Lamb.

               Isaac Watts (1674–1748)

373   L.M.

*'They shall call his name Emmanuel,
which being interpreted is, God with us'*
Matthew 1 v 23

1 Thou Son of God and Son of Man,
Beloved, adored Immanuel;
Who didst, before all time began,
In glory with Thy Father dwell:

2 We sing Thy love, who didst in time
For us humanity assume;
To answer for the sinner's crime,
To suffer in the sinner's room.

3 The ransomed church Thy glory
   sings;
The hosts of heaven Thy will obey;
And, Lord of lords and King of
   kings,
We celebrate Thy blessèd sway.

4 A servant's form Thou didst sustain;
And with delight the law obey;
And then endure amazing pain,
Whilst all our sorrows on Thee lay.

5 Blest Saviour! We are wholly Thine;
So freely loved, so dearly bought,
Our souls to Thee we would resign,
To Thee would subject every
   thought.

               John Ryland (1753–1825)

374   8 8. 8 8. 8 8

'For we walk by faith, not by sight'
2 Corinthians 5 v 7

1 We saw Thee not when Thou didst
   come
To this poor world of sin and death,
Nor e'er beheld Thy cottage-home,
In that despisèd Nazareth;
But we believe Thy footsteps trod
Its streets and plains, Thou Son of
   God.

2 We did not see Thee lifted high
  Amid that wild and savage crew,
  Nor heard Thy meek, imploring cry,
  'Forgive, they know not what they
    do!'
  Yet we believe the deed was done,
  That shook the earth and veiled the
    sun.

3 We stood not by the empty tomb
  Where late Thy sacred body lay;
  Nor sat within that upper room,
  Nor met Thee on the open way:
  But we believe that angels said,
  'Why seek the living with the dead?'

4 We did not mark the chosen few,
  When Thou didst through the clouds
    ascend,
  First lift to Heaven their wondering
    view,
  Then to the earth all prostrate bend;
  But we believe that mortal eyes
  Beheld that journey to the skies.

5 And now that Thou dost reign on
    high,
  And thence Thy waiting people
    bless,
  No ray of glory from the sky
  Doth shine upon our wilderness;
  But we believe Thy faithful Word,
  And trust in our redeeming Lord.

> John Hampden Gurney (1802–62)
> Based on Anne Richter (1792–1857)

375   C.M.

'We shall be like him' 1 John 3 v 2

1 What grace, O Lord, and beauty
    shone
  Around Thy steps below!
  What patient love was seen in all
  Thy life and death of woe!

2 For, ever on Thy burdened heart
  A weight of sorrow hung,
  Yet no ungentle, murmuring word
  Escaped Thy silent tongue.

3 Thy foes might hate, despise, revile,
  Thy friends unfaithful prove:
  Unwearied in forgiveness still,
  Thy heart could only love.

4 O give us hearts to love like Thee,
  Like Thee, O Lord, to grieve
  Far more for others' sins than all
  The wrongs that we receive.

5 One with Thyself, may every eye
  In us, Thy brethren, see
  The gentleness and grace that spring
  From union, Lord, with Thee.

> Edward Denny (1796–1889)

376   7 7 (with refrain)

'He humbled himself' Philippians 2 v 8

1 Who is He in yonder stall,
  At Whose feet the shepherds fall?

'Tis the Lord! O wondrous story!
'Tis the Lord! the King of glory!
At His feet we humbly fall;
Crown Him! crown Him, Lord of all!

2 Who is He to Whom they bring
  All the sick and sorrowing?

3 Who is He in deep distress,
  Fasting in the wilderness?

4 Who is He that stands and weeps
  At the grave where Lazarus sleeps?

5 Lo! at midnight, who is He
  Prays in dark Gethsemane?

6 Who is He on yonder tree
  Dies in grief and agony?

7 Who is He that from the grave
  Comes to succour, help and save?

8 Who is He that from His throne
  Rules through all the world alone?

> Benjamin Russell Hanby (1833–67)

377   87.87.D

'He was in the world ... and the world knew him not' John 1 v 10

1 Who is this, so weak and helpless,
Child of lowly Hebrew maid,
Rudely in a stable sheltered,
Coldly in a manger laid?
'Tis the Lord of all creation,
Who this wondrous path hath trod;
He is God from everlasting,
And to everlasting God.

2 Who is this, a Man of sorrows,
Walking sadly life's hard way,
Homeless, weary, sighing, weeping
Over sin and Satan's sway?
'Tis our God, our glorious Saviour,
Who above the starry sky
Now for us a place prepareth,
Where no tear can dim the eye.

3 Who is this? Behold Him shedding
Drops of blood upon the ground!
Who is this, despised, rejected,
Mocked, insulted, beaten, bound?
'Tis our God, who gifts and graces
On His church now poureth down;
Who shall smite in righteous
    judgment
All His foes beneath His throne.

4 Who is this that hangeth dying,
While the rude world scoffs and
    scorns;
Numbered with the malefactors,
Torn with nails, and crowned with
    thorns?
'Tis the God Who ever liveth,
'Mid the shining ones on high,
In the glorious golden city,
Reigning everlastingly.

William Walsham How (1823–97)

378   87.87.47

'And when he was come into Jerusalem, all the city was moved, saying, Who is this?' Matthew 21 v 10

1 Who is this, with joy approaching
Happy men who see His face?
'Tis the Saviour, healing, speaking,
Full of truth and full of grace.
Son of David,
Grant me sight, and Thine embrace.

2 Who is this, with men acclaiming,
Born the Son of David's line,
Hallelujahs, palm leaves waving?
'Tis the Christ, the Son divine.
Loud hosannas!
Come, O Lord, for Thee we pine.

3 Who is this, on cross so lonely,
Hanging there for men to see?
'Tis the Lord of all the glory,
Bearing penalty for me.
O forgive me!
Plead my cause eternally.

4 Who is this, in glory standing,
Victor over death and shame,
Risen glorious, ever pleading?
'Tis a sweet and wondrous name!
Blessed Jesus!
Praise the Lord who took my blame!

© The Author   William Vernon Higham (b.1926)

379   C.M.

'An high priest, who is set on the right hand of the throne' Hebrews 8 v 1

1 A Man there is, a real Man,
With wounds still gaping wide,
From which rich streams of blood
    once ran,
In hands, and feet, and side.

2 'Tis no wild fancy of our brains,
No metaphor we speak;
The same dear Man in heaven now
    reigns,
That suffered for our sake.

3 This wondrous Man of whom we
  tell,
  Is true Almighty God;
  He bought our souls from death and
  hell;
  The price, His own heart's blood.

4 That human heart He still retains,
  Though throned in highest bliss;
  And feels each tempted member's
  pains;
  For our affliction's His.

5 Come, then, repenting sinner, come;
  Approach with humble faith;
  Owe what thou wilt, the total sum
  Is cancelled by His death!

6 His blood can cleanse the blackest
  soul,
  And wash our guilt away;
  He will present us sound and whole
  In that tremendous day.

Joseph Hart (1712-68)

380   C.M.

'Who loved me, and gave himself for me'
Galatians 2 v 20

1 Alas! and did my Saviour bleed
  And did my Sovereign die?
  Would He devote that sacred head
  For such a worm as I?

2 Was it for crimes that I had done.
  He groaned upon the tree?
  Amazing pity! Grace unknown!
  And love beyond degree!

3 Well might the sun in darkness hide,
  And shut His glories in,
  When God, the mighty Maker, died
  For man, the creature's sin.

4 Thus might I hide my blushing face
  While His dear cross appears;
  Dissolve my heart in thankfulness,
  And melt my eyes to tears.

5 But drops of grief can ne'er repay
  The debt of love I owe:
  Here, Lord, I give myself away;
  'Tis all that I can do.

Isaac Watts (1674–1748)

381   5 5 11. D

'Is it nothing to you, all ye that pass by?'
Lamentations 1 v 12

1 All ye that pass by,
  To Jesus draw nigh;
  To you is it nothing that Jesus
  should die?
  Your ransom and peace,
  Your surety He is,
  Come, see if there ever was sorrow
  like His.

2 He dies to atone,
  For sins not His own;
  Your debt He hath paid, and your
  work He hath done.
  Ye all may receive
  The peace He did leave,
  Who made intercession, 'My Father,
  forgive!'

3 For you and for me
  He prayed on the tree:
  The prayer is accepted, the sinner is
  free.
  That sinner am I
  Who on Jesus rely,
  And come for the pardon God
  cannot deny.

4 His death is my plea;
  My Advocate see,
  And hear the blood speak that hath
  answered for me;
  He purchased the grace
  Which now I embrace;
  O Father, Thou know'st He hath
  died in my place.

Charles Wesley (1707–78)

382   C.M.

'Redemption through his blood'
Ephesians 1 v 7

1 And did the Holy and the Just,
  The Sovereign of the skies,
  Stoop down to wretchedness and dust,
  That guilty worms might rise.

2 Yes; the Redeemer left His throne,
  His radiant throne on high –
  Surprising mercy! love unknown! –
  To suffer, bleed and die.

3 He took the dying traitor's place,
  And suffered in his stead:
  For man – O miracle of grace! –
  For man the Saviour bled!

4 Dear Lord, what heavenly wonders
    dwell
  In Thy atoning blood!
  By this are sinners snatched from hell,
  And rebels brought to God.

5 Jesus, my soul adoring bends
  To love so full, so free;
  And may I hope that love extends
  Its sacred power to me?

6 What glad return can I impart
  For favours so divine?
  O take my all, this worthless heart,
  And make it only Thine.

Anne Steele (1717–78)

383   S.M.

'For Christ also hath once suffered for
sins, the just for the unjust, that he
might bring us to God' 1 Peter 3 v 18

1 And was it for my sin
  That Jesus suffered so,
  When moved by His all-powerful
    love
  He came to earth below?

2 Thy holy law fulfilled,
  Atonement now is made,
  And our great debt, too great for us,
  He now has fully paid.

3 He suffered pain and death,
  When on the hill brought low;
  His blood will wash the guilty clean,
  As pure and white as snow.

4 For in His death our death
  Died with Him on the tree,
  And a great number by His blood
  Will go to heaven made free.

5 When Jesus bowed His head
  And, dying, took our place,
  The veil was rent, a way was found
  To that pure home of grace.

6 He conquered blackest hell;
  He trod the serpent down;
  A host from fetters He'll set free
  By grace to be God's own.

John Elias (1774–1841)
© The Translator   *Tr. Noel Gibbard (b.1932)*

384   S.M.

'My voice shalt thou hear in the
morning, O LORD' Psalm 5 v 3

1 Awake, my soul, and rise
  Amazed, and yonder see
  How hangs the mighty Saviour God
  Upon a cursèd tree!

2 How gloriously fulfilled
  Is that most ancient plan,
  Contrived in the eternal mind
  Before the world began.

3 Here depths of wisdom shine,
  Which angels cannot trace;
  The highest rank of cherubim
  Still lost in wonder gaze.

4 Here free salvation reigns,
  And carries all before;
  And this shall for the guilty race
  Be refuge evermore.

5 Now hell in all her strength,
  Her rage, and boasted sway,
  Can never snatch a wandering sheep
  From Jesus' arms away.

William Williams (1717–91)

385 S.M.

'And they crucified him'
Matthew 27 v 35

1 Behold the amazing sight!
The Saviour lifted high;
The Son of God, His soul's delight,
Expires in agony.

2 For whom, for whom, my heart,
Were all these sorrows borne?
Why did He feel that piercing smart,
And wear that crown of thorn?

3 For us in love He bled,
For us in anguish died;
'Twas love that bowed His sacred
head,
And pierced His precious side.

4 We see, and we adore,
We trust that dying love;
We feel its strong attractive power
To lift our souls above.

5 Behold the amazing sight!
Nor trace His griefs alone,
But from the cross pursue the flight
To His triumphant throne.

Philip Doddridge (1702–51)

386 L.M.

'A living sacrifice, which is your
reasonable service' Romans 12 v 1

1 Extended on a cursed tree,
Besmeared with dust, and sweat,
and blood,
See there, the King of glory see!
Sinks and expires the Son of God.

2 Who, who, my Saviour, this hath
done?
Who could Thy sacred body wound?
No guilt Thy spotless heart hath
known,
No guile hath in Thy lips been
found.

3 I, I alone, have done the deed!
'Tis I Thy sacred flesh have torn;
My sins have caused Thee, Lord, to
bleed,
Pointed the nail, and fixed the thorn.

4 The burden, for me to sustain
Too great, on Thee, my Lord, was
laid;
To heal me, Thou hast born my pain;
To bless me, Thou a curse wast
made.

5 My Saviour, how shall I proclaim?
How pay the mighty debt I owe?
Let all I have and all I am,
Ceaseless to all Thy glory show.

6 Too much to Thee I cannot give;
Too much I cannot do for Thee;
Let all Thy love, and all Thy grief,
Graven on my heart for ever be!

7 The meek, the still, the lowly mind,
O may I learn from Thee, my God,
And love, with softest pity joined,
For those that trample on Thy blood!

8 Still let Thy tears, Thy groans, Thy
sighs,
O'erflow my eyes, and heave my
breast,
Till loose from flesh and earth I rise,
And ever in Thy bosom rest.

Paul Gerhardt (1607–76)
Tr. John Wesley (1703–91)

387 Irregular

'Behold the Lamb of God!' John 1 v 36

1 Give me a sight, O Saviour,
Of Thy wondrous love to me,
Of the love that brought Thee down
to earth,
To die on Calvary.

O make me understand it,
Help me to take it in,
What it meant to Thee, the Holy One,
To bear away my sin.

2 Was it the nails, O Saviour,
  That bound Thee to the tree?
  Nay, 'twas Thine everlasting love,
  Thy love for me, for me.

3 O wonder of all wonders,
  That through Thy death for me
  My open sins, my secret sins,
  Can all forgiven be!

4 Then melt my heart, O Saviour,
  Bend me, yes, break me down,
  Until I own Thee Conqueror,
  And Lord and Sovereign crown.

Katharine Agnes May Kelly (1869–1942)
© HarperCollins Religious, Administered by CopyCare

388   65.65

'The precious blood of Christ'
1 Peter 1 v 19

1 Glory be to Jesus,
  Who, in bitter pains,
  Poured for me the life-blood
  From His sacred veins.

2 Grace and life eternal
  In that blood I find;
  Blest be His compassion,
  Infinitely kind!

3 Blest through endless ages
  Be the precious stream,
  Which from endless torments
  Did the world redeem.

4 Abel's blood for vengeance
  Pleaded to the skies;
  But the blood of Jesus
  For our pardon cries.

5 Oft as it is sprinkled
  On our guilty hearts,
  Satan, in confusion
  Terror-struck departs.

6 Oft as earth exulting
  Wafts its praise on high,
  Angel-hosts rejoicing
  Make their glad reply.

7 Lift ye then your voices;
  Swell the mighty flood;
  Louder still and louder
  Praise the Lamb of God.

Italian c.1815
Tr. Edward Caswall (1814–78)

389   87.87.47

'To him be glory both now and forever'
2 Peter 3 v 18

1 Glory, glory everlasting
  Be to Him who bore the cross!
  Who redeemed our souls, by tasting
  Death, the death deserved by us:
  Spread His glory,
  Who redeemed His people thus.

2 His is love, 'tis love unbounded,
  Without measure, without end;
  Human thought is here confounded,
  'Tis too vast to comprehend:
  Praise the Saviour!
  Magnify the sinner's Friend.

3 While we hear the wondrous story
  Of the Saviour's cross and shame,
  Sing we 'Everlasting glory
  Be to God, and to the Lamb!'
  Saints and angels,
  Give ye glory to His name!

Thomas Kelly (1769–1855)

390   77.77.77

'Let this mind be in you, which was also
in Christ Jesus' Philippians 2 v 5

1 Go to dark Gethsemane,
  Ye that feel the tempter's power;
  Your Redeemer's conflict see;
  Watch with Him one bitter hour;
  Turn not from His griefs away;
  Learn of Jesus Christ to pray.

2 Follow to the judgment-hall;
  View the Lord of life arraigned.
  O the wormwood and the gall!
  O the pangs His soul sustained!
  Shun not suffering, shame, or loss:
  Learn of Him to bear the cross.

3 Calvary's mournful mountain climb;
There, adoring at His feet,
Mark that miracle of time,
God's own sacrifice complete.
'It is finished!' – hear Him cry:
Learn of Jesus Christ to die.

4 Early hasten to the tomb
Where they laid His breathless clay:
All is solitude and gloom;
Who hath taken Him away?
Christ is risen! He meets our eyes:
Saviour, teach us so to rise.

James Montgomery (1771–1854)

391
87.87.D

*'We have a great high priest, that is
passed into the heavens'
Hebrews 4 v 14*

1 Great High Priest, we view Thee
      stooping
With our names upon Thy breast,
In the garden groaning, drooping,
To the ground with horrors pressed;
Holy angels stood confounded,
To behold their Maker thus;
And can we remain unmoved,
When we know 'twas all for us?

2 On the cross Thy body broken
Cancels every penal tie;
Tempted souls produce this token,
All demands to satisfy.
All is finished, do not doubt it,
But believe your dying Lord;
Never reason more about it,
Only trust His sacred Word.

3 Lord, we fain would trust Thee
      solely;
'Twas for us Thy blood was spilt;
Bruisèd Bridegroom, take us wholly,
Take, and make us what Thou wilt.
Thou hast borne the bitter sentence
Passed on man's accursed race;
True belief and true repentance
Are Thy gifts, Thou God of grace.

Joseph Hart (1712–68)

392
87.87.47

'It is finished' John 19 v 30

1 Hark! the voice of love and mercy
Sounds aloud from Calvary;
See, it rends the rocks asunder,
Shakes the earth and veils the sky:
'It is finished!'
Hear the dying Saviour cry.

2 'It is finished!' What assurance
Do the wondrous words afford!
Heavenly blessings without measure
Flow to us from Christ the Lord:
'It is finished!'
Saints the dying words record.

3 Finished all the types and shadows
Of the ceremonial law,
Finished all that God had promised;
Death and hell no more shall awe.
'It is finished!'
Saints, from hence your comfort
      draw.

4 Saints and angels shout His praises,
His great finished work proclaim;
All on earth and all in heaven
Join to bless Immanuel's name:
Hallelujah!
Endless glory to the Lamb!

Jonathan Evans (1749–1809)

393
D.L.M.

*'O grave, I will be thy destruction'
Hosea 13 v 14*

1 He dies! the Friend of sinners dies!
Lo! Salem's daughters weep around;
A solemn darkness veils the skies,
A sudden trembling shakes the
      ground.
Come, saints, and drop a tear or two
For Him who groaned beneath your
      load:
He shed a thousand drops for you,
A thousand drops of richer blood.

2 Here's love and grief beyond degree:
The Lord of Glory dies for men!
But lo! what sudden joys we see,
Jesus, the dead, revives again!
The rising God forsakes the tomb;
The tomb in vain forbids His rise;
Cherubic legions guard Him home,
And shout Him welcome to the
    skies.

3 Break off your fears, ye saints, and
    tell
How high your great Deliv'rer
    reigns;
Sing how He spoiled the hosts of hell,
And led the monster death in chains!
Say, 'Live forever, wondrous King!
Born to redeem, and strong to save;'
Then ask the monster, 'Where's thy
    sting?'
And, 'Where's thy vict'ry, boasting
    grave?'

Charles Wesley (1707–1788)

394   8 7. 8 7. D

'Unto him that loved us, and washed us
from our sins in his own blood'
Revelation 1 v 5

1 Here is love, vast as the ocean,
Lovingkindness as the flood,
When the Prince of life, our ransom,
Shed for us His precious blood.
Who His love will not remember?
Who can cease to sing His praise?
He can never be forgotten
Throughout heaven's eternal days.

2 On the Mount of Crucifixion
Fountains opened deep and wide;
Through the floodgates of God's
    mercy
Flowed a vast and gracious tide.
Grace and love, like mighty rivers,
Poured incessant from above,
And heaven's peace and perfect justice
Kissed a guilty world in love.

William Rees (1802–83)
Tr. William Edwards (1848–1929)

395   8 8. 8 8

'No man taketh it from me, but I lay it
down of myself' John 10 v 18

1 How willing was Jesus to die,
That we, fellow-sinners, might live!
The life they could not take away,
How ready was Jesus to give!

2 They pierced both His hands and
    His feet –
His hands and His feet He resigned;
The pangs of His body were great,
But greater the pangs of His mind.

3 That wrath would have kindled a hell
Of never-abating despair
In millions of creatures, which fell
On Jesus, and spent itself there.

4 'Twas justice that burst in a blaze
Of vengeance on Jesus our Head;
Divinity's indwelling rays
Sustained Him till nature was dead.

5 Divinity back to His frame
The life He had yielded restored;
And Jesus entombed was the same
With Jesus in glory adored.

6 No nearer we venture than this,
To gaze on a deep so profound;
But tread, whilst we taste of the
    bliss,
With reverence the hallowed ground.

Joseph Swain (1761–96)

396   Irregular

'And being in an agony he prayed more
earnestly' Luke 22 v 44

1 I stand amazed in the presence
Of Jesus the Nazarene,
And wonder how He could love me,
A sinner, condemned, unclean.

How marvellous! how wonderful!
And my song shall ever be
How marvellous! how wonderful
Is my Saviour's love to me!

2 For me it was in the garden
  He prayed – 'Not My will, but
      Thine';
  He had no tears for His own griefs,
  But sweat drops of blood for mine.

3 In pity angels beheld Him,
  And came from the world of light
  To comfort Him in the sorrows
  He bore for my soul that night.

4 He took my sins and my sorrows,
  He made them His very own;
  He bore the burden to Calvary,
  And suffered and died alone.

5 When with the ransomed in glory
  His face I at last shall see,
  'Twill be my joy through the ages
  To sing of His love for me.

Charles Homer Gabriel (1856–1932)

397   8 7 8.7 8 7

'It is finished' John 19 v 30

1 'It is finished!' sinners hear it,
  'Tis the dying Victor's cry;
  'It is finished!' angels bear it –
  Bear the joyful truth on high:
  'It is finished!'
  Tell it through the earth and sky

2 Justice, from her awesome station,
  Bars the sinner's peace no more;
  Justice views with approbation
  What the Saviour did and bore;
  Grace and mercy
  Now display their boundless store.

3 'It is finished!' all is over;
  He the cup of wrath has drained;
  Such the truth these words discover,
  Thus our victory was obtained:
  'Tis a victory
  None but Jesus could have gained!

Thomas Kelly (1769–1855)

398   6 4. 6 4. 6 6. 6 4

'There they crucified him' Luke 23 v 33

1 Jesus was slain for me,
  At Calvary;
  Crownèd with thorns was he
  At Calvary.
  There He in anguish died,
  There from His opened side
  Poured forth the crimson tide,
  At Calvary.

2 Pardoned is all my sin,
  At Calvary;
  Cleansed is my heart within,
  At Calvary.
  Now robes of praise I wear,
  Gone are my grief and care,
  Christ bore my burdens there,
  At Calvary.

3 Wondrous His love for me,
  At Calvary;
  Glorious His victory,
  At Calvary.
  Vanquished are death and hell,
  O, let His praises swell,
  Ever my tongue shall tell
  At Calvary.

George Perfect

399   C.M. (with refrain)

'A place called Gethsemane'
Matthew 26 v 36

1 King of my life, I crown Thee now,
  Thine shall the glory be;
  Lest I forget Thy thorn-crowned brow,
  Lead me to Calvary.

  Lest I forget Gethsemane,
  Lest I forget Thine agony,
  Lest I forget Thy love for me,
  Lead me to Calvary.

2 Show me the tomb where Thou wast
      laid
  Tenderly mourned and wept:
  Angels in robes of light arrayed
  Guarded Thee whilst Thou slept.

3 Let me, like Mary, hear the voice
That called her by her name,
And bade her mourning heart rejoice
And her dear Master claim.

4 May I be willing, Lord, to bear
Daily my cross for Thee;
Even Thy cup of grief to share –
Thou hast borne all for me.

5 Fill me, O Lord, with Thy desire
For all who know not Thee;
Then touch my lips with holy fire,
To speak of Calvary.

© 1921, Renewed 1949   *Jenny Evelyn Hussey (1874–1958)*
Hope Publishing Company

400   7 7 7 . 8

'A man of sorrows' Isaiah 53 v 3

1 Man of sorrows! What a name
For the Son of God, who came
Ruined sinners to reclaim!
Hallelujah! what a Saviour!

2 Bearing shame and scoffing rude,
In my place condemned He stood;
Sealed my pardon with His blood:
Hallelujah! what a Saviour!

3 Guilty, vile, and helpless, we;
Spotless Lamb of God was He:
Full atonement! – can it be?
Hallelujah! what a Saviour!

4 Lifted up was He to die,
'It is finished!' was His cry;
Now in heaven exalted high:
Hallelujah! what a Saviour!

5 When He comes, our glorious King,
All His ransomed home to bring,
Then anew this song we'll sing:
Hallelujah! what a Saviour!

Philip Paul Bliss (1838–76)

401   6 6 . 6 6 . 4 4 . 4 4

*'Having loved his own ... he loved them
unto the end' John 13 v 1*

1 My song is love unknown,
My Saviour's love to me,
Love to the loveless shown,
That they might lovely be.
O who am I,
That for my sake
My Lord should take
Frail flesh, and die?

2 He came from His blest throne,
Salvation to bestow:
But men made strange, and none
The longed-for Christ would know.
But O, my Friend!
My Friend indeed,
Who at my need
His life did spend!

3 Sometimes they strew His way,
And His sweet praises sing;
Resounding all the day
Hosannas to their King.
Then 'Crucify!'
Is all their breath,
And for His death
They thirst and cry.

4 They rise and needs will have
My dear Lord made away;
A murderer they save,
The Prince of life they slay,
Yet cheerful He
To suffering goes,
That He His foes
From thence might free.

5 In life, no house, no home
My Lord on earth might have;
In death, no friendly tomb
But what a stranger gave.
What may I say?
Heaven was His home:
But mine the tomb,
Wherein He lay.

6 Here might I stay and sing,
No story so divine;
Never was love, dear King,
Never was grief like Thine!
This is my Friend,
In whose sweet praise
I all my days
Could gladly spend.

Samuel Crossman (1624–83)

402   7 7.7 7

'They that are Christ's have crucified the flesh' Galatians 5 v 24

1 Never further than Thy cross,
Never higher than Thy feet;
Here earth's precious things seem
dross,
Here earth's bitter things grow
sweet.

2 Gazing thus our sin we see,
Learn Thy love while gazing thus;
Sin which laid the cross on Thee,
Love which bore the cross for us.

3 Here we learn to serve and give,
And, rejoicing, self deny;
Here we gather love to live,
Here we gather faith to die.

4 Symbols of our liberty
And our service here unite;
Captives, by Thy cross set free,
Soldiers of Thy cross, we fight.

5 Pressing onwards as we can,
Still to this our hearts must tend;
Where our earliest hopes began,
There our last aspirings end.

6 Till amid the hosts of light
We, in Thee redeemed, complete,
Through Thy cross made pure and
white,
Cast our crowns before Thy feet.

Elizabeth Charles (1828–96)

403   8 8.8 8.8 8

'The Son of God, who loved me, and gave himself for me' Galatians 2 v 20

1 O Love Divine! what hast Thou
done?
The immortal God hath died for me!
The Father's co-eternal Son
Bore all my sins upon the tree;
The immortal God for me hath died!
My Lord, my Love is crucified.

2 Behold Him, ye that pass Him by,
The bleeding Prince of life and
peace!
Come, sinners, see your Maker die,
And say, was ever grief like His?
Come, feel with me His blood
applied:
My Lord, my Love is crucified:

3 Is crucified for me and you,
To bring us rebels back to God:
Believe, believe the record true,
Ye now are bought with Jesus' blood,
Pardon for sin flows from His side:
My Lord, my Love is crucified.

4 Then let us sit beneath His cross,
And gladly catch the healing stream,
All things for Him account but loss,
And give up all our hearts to Him;
Of nothing think or speak beside:
My Lord, my Love is crucified.

Charles Wesley (1707–88)

404   S.M.

'It is finished' John 19 v 30

1 O perfect life of love!
All, all is finished now,
All that He left His throne above
To do for us below.

2 No work is left undone
Of all the Father willed;
His toil and sorrows, one by one,
The scriptures have fulfilled.

3 No pain that we can share
But He has felt its smart;
All forms of human grief and care
Have pierced that tender heart.

4 And on His thorn-crowned head,
And on His sinless soul,
Our sins in all their guilt were laid,
That He might make us whole.

5 In perfect love He dies:
For me He dies, for me!
O all-atoning Sacrifice,
I cling by faith to Thee.

6 In every time of need,
Before the judgement throne,
Thy work, O Lamb of God, I'll plead,
Thy merits, not my own.

7 Yet work, O Lord, in me
As Thou for me hast wrought;
And let my love the answer be
To grace Thy love has brought.

Henry Williams Baker (1821–77)

405

7 6. 7 6. D

'He was wounded for our transgressions'
Isaiah 53 v 5

1 O sacred head! sore wounded,
With grief and shame bowed down,
How scornfully surrounded
With thorns, Thine only crown!
How pale art Thou with anguish,
With sore abuse and scorn!
How does that visage languish
Which once was bright as morn!

2 Thy grief and bitter passion
Were all for sinners' gain:
Mine, mine was the transgression,
But Thine the deadly pain:
Lo! here I fall, my Saviour;
'Tis I deserve Thy place;
Look on me with Thy favour,
Vouchsafe to me Thy grace.

3 What language shall I borrow
To thank Thee, dearest Friend,
For this Thy dying sorrow,
Thy pity without end?
O make me Thine for ever;
And should I fainting be,
Lord, let me never, never
Outlive me love to thee!

4 Be near me when I'm dying;
O show Thy cross to me;
Thy death, my hope supplying,
From death shall set me free.
These eyes, new faith receiving,
From Jesus shall not move;
For he who dies believing
Dies safely through Thy love.

Paul Gerhardt (1607-76)
From Salve Caput Cruentatum

Attributed to Bernard of Clairvaux (1091–1153)
Tr. James Waddell Alexander (1804–59) Altd

406

8 10. 10 4

'God commendeth his love towards us, in
that, while we were yet sinners, Christ
died for us' Romans 5 v 8

1 O Son of man, O Son of God,
Eternal grace Thy painful path had
    planned,
A heavy cross and agony of shame –
The way ordained.

2 O death of Christ, O blood divine,
O perfect life He lived, all for our
    gain,
Fulfilling all the law's demands, and
    more,
He did attain.

3 O bitter cup, O costly task,
To meet the wrath of God's own
    holiness!
The Saviour stood, and in my stead
    He died,
My soul to bless.

4 O love of God, O wondrous grace,
That such an angry death of anguish
sore
Should pay my penalty and make me
whole –
O boundless store!

5 O wondrous flood of grace and love,
Both mingled in the blood as He
implored:
Can this be so, all this for me, my
Lord?
Thou art adored.

6 Peace through the blood of Christ
alone,
Peace with my God and peace within
my soul,
Peace in that day when He will come
at last,
My All in all.

© The Author   William Vernon Higham (b.1926)

407   L.M.

'Hosanna in the highest' Matthew 21 v 9

1 Ride on! ride on in majesty!
Hark! all the tribes 'Hosanna' cry;
O Saviour meek, pursue Thy road
With palms and scattered garments
strowed.

2 Ride on, ride on in majesty!
In lowly pomp ride on to die;
O Christ, Thy triumphs now begin
O'er captive death and conquered
sin.

3 Ride on, ride on in majesty!
The angel armies of the sky
Look down with sad and wondering
eyes
To see the approaching sacrifice.

4 Ride on, ride on in majesty!
Thy last and fiercest strife is nigh:
The Father on His sapphire throne
Awaits His own anointed Son.

5 Ride on! ride on in majesty!
In lowly pomp ride on to die;
Bow Thy meek head to mortal pain,
Then take, O God, Thy power, and
reign.

Henry Hart Milman (1791–1868)

408   8.7.8.7.D

'This man offered one sacrifice for sins for
ever' Hebrews 10 v 12

1 Stricken, smitten, and afflicted,
See Him dying on the tree!
'Tis the Christ by man rejected;
Yes, my soul, 'tis He, 'tis He!
'Tis the long expected Prophet,
David's Son, yet David's Lord;
By His Son God now has spoken:
'Tis the true and faithful Word.

2 Tell me, ye who hear Him groaning,
Was there ever grief like His?
Friends through fear His cause
disowning,
Foes insulting His distress;
Many hands were raised to wound
Him,
None would interpose to save;
But the deepest stroke that pierced
Him
Was the stroke that justice gave.

3 Ye who think of sin but lightly
Nor suppose the evil great
Here may view its nature rightly,
Here its guilt may estimate.
Mark the sacrifice appointed,
See who bears the awful load;
'Tis the Word, the Lord's Anointed,
Son of man and Son of God.

4 Here we have a firm foundation,
Here the refuge of the lost;
Christ's the Rock of our salvation,
His the name of which we boast.
Lamb of God, for sinners wounded,
Sacrifice to cancel guilt!
None shall ever be confounded
Who on Him their hope have built.

Thomas Kelly (1769–1854)

409
C.M.

*'The chastisement of our peace was upon
him' Isaiah 53 v 5*

1 The enormous load of human guilt
Was on my Saviour laid;
With woes as with a garment He
For sinners was arrayed.

2 And in the fearful pangs of death
He wept, He prayed for me;
Loved and embraced my guilty soul
When nailèd to the tree.

3 O love amazing! love beyond
The reach of human tongue;
Love which shall be the subject of
An everlasting song.

4 Eternity, though infinite,
Is short enough to trace
The virtues of His healing wounds,
The wonders of His grace.

5 Ye men, rejoice in Jesu's blood,
Ye angels, join your lays;
In one harmonious endless choir
Sing His eternal praise.

William Williams (1717–91)

410
C.M.

*'A fountain opened ... for sin and for
uncleanness' Zechariah 13 v 1*

1 There is a fountain filled with blood
Drawn from Immanuel's veins;
And sinners, plunged beneath that
flood,
Lose all their guilty stains.

2 The dying thief rejoiced to see
That fountain in his day;
And there may I, though vile as he,
Wash all my sins away.

3 Dear dying Lamb, Thy precious
blood
Shall never lose its power,
Till all the ransomed church of God
Be saved, to sin no more.

4 E'er since, by faith, I saw the stream
Thy flowing wounds supply,
Redeeming love has been my theme,
And shall be till I die.

5 Then in a nobler, sweeter song
I'll sing Thy power to save,
When this poor lisping, stammering
tongue
Lies silent in the grave.

William Cowper (1731–1800)

411
L.M.

*'God forbid that I should glory, save in
the cross of our Lord Jesus Christ'
Galatians 6 v 14*

1 We sing the praise of Him Who died,
Of Him Who died upon the cross;
The sinner's hope let men deride,
For this we count the world but loss.

2 Inscribed upon the cross we see
In shining letters, 'God is love';
He bears our sins upon the tree;
He brings us mercy from above.

3 The cross! it takes our guilt away;
It holds the fainting spirit up;
It cheers with hope the gloomy day,
And sweetens every bitter cup.

4 It makes the coward spirit brave,
And nerves the feeble arm for fight;
It takes the terror from the grave,
And gilds the bed of death with
light.

5 The balm of life, the cure of woe,
The measure and the pledge of love,
The sinner's refuge here below,
The angels' theme in heaven above.

Thomas Kelly (1769–1855)

412   L.M.

*'I count all things but loss for the
excellency of the knowledge of Christ Jesus
my Lord' Philippians 3 v 8*

1 When I survey the wondrous cross,
   On which the Prince of glory died,
   My richest gain I count but loss,
   And pour contempt on all my pride.

2 Forbid it, Lord, that I should boast
   Save in the death of Christ my God:
   All the vain things that charm me
      most,
   I sacrifice them to His blood.

3 See from His head, His hands, His
      feet,
   Sorrow and love flow mingled down;
   Did e'er such love and sorrow meet,
   Or thorns compose so rich a crown?

4 His dying crimson, like a robe,
   Spreads o'er His body on the tree:
   Then I am dead to all the globe,
   And all the globe is dead to me.

5 Were the whole realm of nature
      mine,
   That were an offering far too small;
   Love so amazing, so divine,
   Demands my soul, my life, my all.

Isaac Watts (1674–1748)

413   8 7. 8 7. D (with refrain)

*'He is risen from the dead'
Matthew 28 v 7*

1 Christ is risen! Hallelujah!
   Risen our victorious Head!
   Sing His praises! Hallelujah!
   Christ is risen from the dead.
   Gratefully our hearts adore Him
   As His light once more appears,
   Bowing down in joy before Him,
   Rising up from grief and tears.

   *Christ is risen! Hallelujah!
   Risen our victorious Head!
   Sing His praises! Hallelujah!
   Christ is risen from the dead.*

2 Christ is risen! All the sadness
   Of His earthly life is o'er;
   Through the open gates of gladness
   He returns to life once more;
   Death and hell before Him bending ,
   He doth rise, the Victor now,
   Angels on His steps attending,
   Glory round His wounded brow.

3 Christ is risen! Henceforth never
   Death or hell shall us enthral;
   We are Christ's, in Him for ever
   We have triumphed over all;
   All the doubting and dejection
   Of our trembling hearts have ceased;
   'Tis the day of resurrection,
   Let us rise and keep the feast.

John Samuel Bewley Monsell (1811–75)

414   7 7. 7 7 (with Hallelujahs)

*'The firstfruits of them that slept'
1 Corinthians 15 v 20*

1 Christ, the Lord, is risen today,
   Hallelujah!
   Sons of men and angels say:
   Raise your joys and triumphs high;
   Sing, ye heavens, and earth reply.

2 Love's redeeming work is done;
   Fought the fight, the battle won.
   Lo! our Sun's eclipse is o'er;
   Lo! He sets in blood no more.

3 Vain the stone, the watch, the seal!
   Christ hath burst the gates of hell;
   Death in vain forbids Him rise;
   Christ hath opened paradise.

4 Lives again our glorious King!
   'Where, O death, is now thy sting?'
   Once He died our souls to save;
   'Where's thy victory, boasting
      grave?'

5 Soar we now where Christ hath led,
   Following our exalted Head;
   Made like Him, like Him we rise;
   Ours the cross, the grave, the skies.

6 King of glory! Soul of bliss!
Everlasting life is this,
Thee to know, Thy power to prove,
Thus to sing, and thus to love.

Charles Wesley (1707–88)

415 87.87.47

'Come, see the place where the Lord lay'
Matthew 28 v 6

1 Come, ye saints, look here and
    wonder,
See the place where Jesus lay;
He has burst His bands asunder,
He has borne our sins away.
Joyful tidings!
Yes, the Lord is risen today.

2 Jesus triumphs! O sing praises!
By His death He overcame:
Thus the Lord His glory raises;
Thus He fills His foes with shame.
O sing praises!
Praises to the Victor's name.

3 Jesus triumphs! Countless legions
Come from heaven to meet their
    King;
Soon in yonder blessed regions
They shall join His praise to sing.
Songs eternal
Shall through heaven's high arches
    ring.

Thomas Kelly (1769–1855)

416 87.87.D

'Now is Christ risen from the dead'
1 Corinthians 15 v 20

1 Hallelujah! Hallelujah!
Hearts to heaven and voices raise;
Sing to God a hymn of gladness,
Sing to God a hymn of praise;
He who on the cross a victim
For the world's salvation bled,
Jesus Christ, the King of glory,
Now is risen from the dead.

2 Christ is risen, Christ the first-fruits
Of the holy harvest field,
Which will all its full abundance
At His second coming yield;
Then the golden ears of harvest
Will their heads before Him wave,
Ripened by His glorious sunshine
From the furrows of the grave.

3 Christ is risen, we are risen:
Shed upon us heavenly grace,
Rain and dew and gleams of glory
From the brightness of Thy face;
That we, with our hearts in heaven,
Here on earth may fruitful be,
And by angel hands be gathered,
And be ever, Lord, with Thee.

4 Hallelujah! Hallelujah!
Glory be to God on high;
Hallelujah to the Saviour
Who has gained the victory;
Hallelujah to the Spirit,
Fount of love and sanctity;
Hallelujah! Hallelujah!
To the Triune Majesty!

Christopher Wordsworth (1807–85)

417 L.M.

'I know that my redeemer liveth'
Job 19 v 25

1 I know that my Redeemer lives:
What joy the blest assurance gives!
He lives, He lives, who once was
    dead;
He lives, my everlasting Head.

2 He lives, triumphant from the grave;
He lives, eternally to save;
He lives, all glorious in the sky;
He lives, exalted there on high.

3 He lives to bless me with His love,
And still He pleads for me above;
He lives to raise me from the grave,
And me eternally to save.

4 He lives, my kind, wise, constant
  Friend,
Who still will keep me to the end;
He lives, and while He lives I'll sing,
Jesus, my Prophet, Priest, and King.

5 He lives my mansion to prepare;
And He will bring me safely there;
He lives, all glory to His name!
Jesus, unchangeably the same!

Samuel Medley (1738–99)

418   7 8. 7 8. 4

'Because I live, ye shall live also'
John 14 v 19

1 Jesus lives! thy terrors now
Can, O death, no more appal us;
Jesus lives! by this we know
Thou, O grave, canst not enthral us.
Hallelujah!

2 Jesus lives! henceforth is death
But the gate of life immortal;
This shall calm our trembling
  breath,
When we pass its gloomy portal.

3 Jesus lives! for us He died;
Then, alone to Jesus living,
Pure in heart may we abide,
Glory to our Saviour giving.

4 Jesus lives! our hearts know well
Nought from us His love shall sever;
Life, nor death, nor powers of hell
Tear us from His keeping ever.

5 Jesus lives! to Him the throne
Over all the world is given;
May we go where He is gone,
Rest and reign with Him in heaven.

Christian Furchtegott Gellert (1715–69)
Tr. Frances Elizabeth Cox (1812–97)

419   Irregular

'Why seek ye the living among the dead?
He is not here, but is risen'
Luke 24 vv 5–6

1 Low in the grave He lay,
Jesus, my Saviour!
Waiting the coming day,
Jesus, my Lord!

Up from the grave He arose,
With a mighty triumph o'er His foes;
He arose a Victor from the dark domain,
And He lives for ever with His saints to
  reign:
He arose! He arose!
Hallelujah! Christ arose!

2 Vainly they watch His bed,
Jesus, my Saviour!
Vainly they seal the dead,
Jesus, my Lord!

3 Death cannot keep his prey,
Jesus, my Saviour!
He tore the bars away,
Jesus, my Lord!

Robert Lowry (1826–99)

420   8 7. 8 7. 8 7

'By him therefore let us offer the sacrifice
of praise to God continually'
Hebrews 13 v 15

1 Praise the Saviour, now and ever,
Praise Him, all beneath the skies;
Prostrate lying, suffering, dying,
On the cross a sacrifice;
Victory gaining, life obtaining,
Now in glory He doth rise.

2 Man's work faileth, Christ availeth,
He is all our righteousness;
He, our Saviour, has for ever
Set us free from dire distress.
Through His merit we inherit
Life and peace and happiness.

3 Sin's bonds severed, we're delivered;
   Christ has bruised the serpent's
      head.
   Death no longer is the stronger;
   Hell itself is captive led.
   Christ has risen from death's prison;
   O'er the tomb He light has shed.

4 For His favour, praise for ever
   Unto God the Father sing.
   Praise the Saviour, praise Him ever,
   Son of God, our Lord and King.
   Praise the Spirit; through Christ's
      merit
   He doth our salvation bring.

Venantius Fortunatus (c.530–609)

© Copyright Control   *Tr. Augustus Nelson*

421   6 6. 8 4. D

'He is not here: for he is risen'
Matthew 28 v 6

1 See Christ the Victor raised
   In resurrection life,
   The mighty arm of God displayed,
   Who ends the strife.
   He is the Lord of all,
   Whose arm is shortened not;
   See devils' flight, and Satan's fall,
   And hell their lot.

2 The sting of death is sin,
   The power of law declares;
   But Jesus Christ the Son doth win,
   Our guilt He bears.
   Behold, ye sinners, now,
   And look to Christ alone;
   Behold the blood upon His brow –
   He did atone.

3 Immortal is my dress,
   Corruption fled away,
   Now robed in Him, yes, nothing less,
   In bright array.
   O death, where is thy sting?
   O grave, thy victory?
   The living Christ on mercy's wing
   Grants peace to me.

© The Author   *William Vernon Higham (b.1926)*

422   7 6. 7 6. D

'He rose again' 1 Corinthians 15 v 4

1 The day of resurrection!
   Earth, tell it out abroad;
   The passover of gladness,
   The passover of God!
   From death to life eternal,
   From earth unto the sky,
   Our Christ hath brought us over
   With hymns of victory.

2 Our hearts be pure from evil,
   That we may see aright
   The Lord in rays eternal
   Of resurrection light,
   And, listening to His accents,
   May hear, so calm and plain,
   His own 'All hail!' and hearing,
   May raise the victor-strain.

3 Now let the heavens be joyful;
   Let earth her song begin;
   The round world keep high triumph,
   And all that is therein;
   Let all things seen and unseen,
   Their notes of gladness blend:
   For Christ the Lord hath risen,
   Our joy that hath no end.

John of Damascus, 8th Century
Tr. John Mason Neale (1818–66)

423   6 6. 6 6. 8 8

'Thou hast led captivity captive'
Psalm 68 v 18

1 The happy morn is come;
   Triumphant o'er the grave,
   The Saviour leaves the tomb,
   Omnipotent to save:

   Captivity is captive led,
   For Jesus liveth, who was dead.

2 Who now accuseth them
   For whom their Surety died?
   Or who shall those condemn
   Whom God hath justified?

3 Christ hath the ransom paid;
The glorious work is done;
On Him our help is laid,
By Him our victory won:

4 Hail, Thou triumphant Lord!
The Resurrection Thou;
Hail, Thou incarnate Word!
Before Thy throne we bow:

Thomas Haweis (1733–1820)

424   S.M.

*'The Lord is risen indeed, and hath
appeared' Luke 24 v 34*

1 The Lord is risen indeed,
And are the tidings true?
Yes, they beheld the Saviour bleed,
And saw Him living too.

2 The Lord is risen indeed,
Then justice asks no more;
Mercy and truth are now agreed,
Who stood opposed before.

3 The Lord is risen indeed,
Then is His work performed:
The captive surety now is freed,
And death, our foe, disarmed.

4 The Lord is risen indeed,
Then hell has lost its prey;
With Him is risen the ransomed
seed,
To reign in endless day.

5 The Lord is risen indeed,
He lives to die no more;
He lives the sinner's cause to plead,
Whose curse and shame He bore.

6 Then take your golden lyres,
And strike each cheerful chord,
Join all the bright celestial choirs,
To sing our risen Lord.

Thomas Kelly (1769–1854)

425   8 8 8. 4

*'Death is swallowed up in victory'
1 Corinthians 15 v 54*

1 The strife is o'er, the battle done;
The victory of life is won;
The song of triumph has begun:
Hallelujah !

2 The powers of death have done their
worst,
But Christ their legions hath
dispersed;
Let shouts of holy joy outburst:

3 The three sad days have quickly
sped;
He rises glorious from the dead;
All glory to our risen Head:

4 He broke the bonds of death and hell;
The bars from heaven's high portals
fell;
Let hymns of praise His triumph tell:

5 Lord, by the stripes which wounded
Thee,
From death's dread sting Thy
servants free,
That we may live and sing to Thee:

*Latin c.12th Century
Tr. Francis Pott (1832–1909)*

426   10 11. 11 11 (with refrain)

*'Thanks be to God, which giveth us the
victory through our Lord Jesus Christ'
1 Corinthians 15 v 7*

1 Thine be the glory, risen, conquering
Son,
Endless is the victory Thou o'er
death hast won;
Angels in bright raiment rolled the
stone away,
Kept the folded grave-clothes, where
Thy body lay.

*Thine be the glory, risen, conquering Son,
Endless is the victory Thou o'er death hast
won!*

2 Lo! Jesus meets us, risen from the
  tomb;
Lovingly He greets us, scatters fear
  and gloom;
Let the church with gladness hymns
  of triumph sing,
For her Lord now liveth, death hath
  lost its sting.

3 No more we doubt Thee, glorious
  Prince of life;
Life is nought without Thee, aid us
  in our strife;
Make us more than conquerors,
  through Thy deathless love;
Bring us safe through Jordan to Thy
  home above.

©WSCF   *Edmond Louis Budry (1854–1932)*
Tr. Richard Birch Hoyle (1875–1939)

427   C.M.

'He is risen' Mark 16 v 6

1 Ye humble souls that seek the Lord,
Chase all your fears away;
And bow with rapture down to see
The place where Jesus lay.

2 Thus low the Lord of life was
  brought,
Such wonders love can do;
Thus cold in death that bosom lay,
Which throbbed and bled for you.

3 But raise your eyes, and tune your
  songs;
The Saviour lives again:
Not all the bolts and bars of death
The Conqueror could detain.

4 High o'er the angelic bands He rears
His once dishonoured head;
And through unnumbered years He
  reigns,
Who dwelt among the dead.

5 With joy like His shall every saint
His vacant tomb survey;
Then rise with His ascending Lord
To realms of endless day.

Philip Doddridge (1702–51)

428   6 6. 6 6. 4 4. 4 4

'Knowing that Christ being raised from
the dead dieth no more' Romans 6 v 9

1 Yes, the Redeemer rose,
The Saviour left the dead,
And o'er our hellish foes
High raised His conquering head;
In wild dismay
The guards around
Fell to the ground
And sunk away.

2 Lo! The angelic bands
In full assembly meet,
To wait His high commands
And worship at His feet;
Joyful they come,
And wing their way
From realms of day
To Jesus' tomb.

3 Then back to heaven they fly,
And the glad tidings bear;
Hark! As they soar on high,
What music fills the air!
Their anthems say,
'Jesus, who bled,
Hath left the dead,
He rose today.'

4 Ye mortals, catch the sound
Redeemed by Him from hell,
And send the echo round
The globe on which you dwell;
Transported cry,
'Jesus, who bled,
Hath left the dead,
No more to die.'

5 All hail, triumphant Lord,
Who sav'st us with Thy blood!
Wide be Thy name adored,
Thou risen, reigning God!
With Thee we rise,
With Thee we reign,
And empires gain
Beyond the skies.

Philip Doddridge (1702–51)

429 C.M.

'Father, I will that they also ... be with me' John 17 v 24

1 Awake, sweet gratitude, and sing
   The ascended Saviour's love:
   Sing how He lives to carry on
   His people's cause above.

2 With cries and tears He offered up
   His humble suit below;
   But with authority He asks,
   Enthroned in glory now.

3 For all that come to God by Him,
   Salvation He demands;
   Points to their names upon His
      breast,
   And spreads His wounded hands.

4 His sweet atoning sacrifice
   Gives sanction to His claim:
   Father, I will that all My saints
   Be with Me where I am.

5 Eternal life, at His request,
   To every saint is given:
   Safety on earth, and after death
   The plenitude of heaven.

6 Founded on right, Thy prayer avails,
   The Father smiles on Thee;
   And now Thou in Thy kingdom art,
   Dear Lord, remember me.

Augustus M. Toplady (1740–78)

430 77.77

Based on Psalm 47

1 Clap your hands, ye people all,
   Praise the God on whom ye call;
   Lift your voice and shout His praise,
   Triumph in His sovereign grace!

2 Glorious is the Lord most high,
   Terrible in majesty;
   He His sovereign sway maintains,
   King o'er all the earth He reigns.

3 Jesus is gone up on high,
   Takes His seat above the sky:
   Shout the angel-choirs aloud,
   Echoing to the trump of God.

4 Sons of earth, the triumph join:
   Praise Him with the host divine;
   Emulate the heavenly powers;
   Their victorious Lord is ours.

5 Shout the God enthroned above,
   Trumpet forth His conquering love;
   Praises to our Jesus sing,
   Praises to our glorious King!

6 Power is all to Jesus given,
   Power o'er hell, and earth, and
      heaven;
   Power He now to us imparts:
   Praise Him with believing hearts.

7 Wonderful in saving power,
   Him let all our hearts adore;
   Earth and heaven repeat the cry –
   'Glory be to God most high!'

Charles Wesley (1707–88)

431 8 7. 8 7. 7 7. 7 7

'While he blessed them, he was parted from them, and carried up into heaven' Luke 24 v 51

1 Conquering Prince and Lord of
      glory,
   Majesty enthroned in light;
   All the heavens are bowed before
      Thee,
   Far beyond them spreads Thy might;
   Shall not I fall at Thy feet,
   And my heart with rapture beat,
   Now Thy glory is displayed,
   Thine ere yet the worlds were made?

2 As I watch Thee far ascending
   To the right hand of the throne,
   See the host before Thee bending,
   Praising Thee in sweetest tone;
   Shall not I too at Thy feet
   Here the angels' strain repeat,
   And rejoice that heaven doth ring
   With the triumph of my King?

3 Power and Spirit are o'erflowing,
  On me also be they poured;
  Every hindrance overthrowing,
  Make Thy foes Thy footstool, Lord!
  Yea, let earth's remotest end
  To Thy righteous sceptre bend,
  Make Thy way before Thee plain,
  O'er all hearts and spirits reign.

4 Lo! Thy presence now is filling
  All Thy church in every place;
  Fill my heart too; make me willing
  In this season of Thy grace;
  Come, Thou King of glory, come,
  Deign to make my heart Thy home,
  There abide and rule alone,
  As upon Thy heavenly throne!

Gerhard Tersteegen (1697–1769)
Tr. Catherine Winkworth (1827–78)

432   C.M.

'The Word was made flesh, and dwelt
amongst us' John 1 v 14

1 It is my sweetest comfort, Lord,
  And will for ever be,
  To muse upon the gracious truth
  Of Thy humanity.

2 O joy! there sitteth in our flesh,
  Upon a throne of light,
  One of a human mother born,
  In perfect Godhead bright!

3 Though earth's foundations should
    be moved,
  Down to their lowest deep;
  Though all the trembling universe
  Into destruction sweep;

4 For ever God, for ever Man,
  My Jesus shall endure;
  And fixed on Him, my hope remains
  Eternally secure.

Edward Caswall (1814–78)

433   8 7. 8 7. 4 7

'We see Jesus ... crowned with glory'
Hebrews 2 v 9

1 Look, ye saints! the sight is glorious:
  See the Man of sorrows now;
  From the fight returned victorious,
  Every knee to Him shall bow;
  Crown Him, crown Him,
  Crowns become the Victor's brow.

2 Crown the Saviour! angels, crown
    Him;
  Rich the trophies Jesus brings;
  In the seat of power enthrone Him,
  While the vault of heaven rings;
  Crown Him, crown Him,
  Crown the Saviour King of kings.

3 Sinners in derision crowned Him,
  Mocking thus the Saviour's claim;
  Saints and angels crowd around
    Him,
  Own His title, praise His name;
  Crown Him, crown Him,
  Spread abroad the Victor's fame.

4 Hark, those bursts of acclamation!
  Hark, those loud triumphant chords!
  Jesus takes the highest station;
  O what joy the sight affords!
  Crown Him, crown Him,
  King of kings and Lord of lords!

Thomas Kelly (1769–1855)

434   C.M.

Based on Psalm 47

1 O for a shout of sacred joy
  To God, the sovereign King:
  Let every land their tongues employ,
  And hymns of triumph sing.

2 Jesus our God ascends on high;
  His heavenly guards around
  Attend Him rising through the sky,
  With trumpet's joyful sound.

3 While angels shout and praise their
    King,
  Let mortals learn their strains;
  Let all the earth His honours sing;
  O'er all the earth He reigns.

4 Rehearse His praise with awe
    profound.
  Let knowledge lead the song;
  Nor mock Him with a solemn sound
  Upon a thoughtless tongue.

5 In Israel stood His ancient throne;
  He loved that chosen race;
  But now He calls the world His own,
  And heathens taste His grace.

Isaac Watts (1674–1748)

435   L.M.

Based on Psalm 24 vv 7-10

1 Our Lord is risen from the dead!
  Our Jesus is gone up on high!
  The powers of hell are captive led,
  Dragged to the portals of the sky.

2 There His triumphal chariot waits,
  And angels chant the solemn lay:
  Lift up your heads, ye heavenly gates;
  Ye everlasting doors, give way.

3 Loose all your bars of massy light,
  And wide unfold the ethereal scene:
  He claims these mansions as His
    right;
  Receive the King of glory in!

4 Who is this King of glory? who?
  The Lord that all our foes o'ercame,
  The world, sin, death, and hell
    o'erthrew;
  And Jesus is the Conqueror's name.

5 Lo! His triumphal chariot waits,
  And angels chant the solemn lay:
  Lift up your heads, ye heavenly gates;
  Ye everlasting doors, give way!

6 Who is this King of glory? who?
  The Lord, of glorious power
    possessed;
  The King of saints, and angels too,
  God over all, for ever blessed!

Charles Wesley (1707–88)

436   Irregular

*'We will be glad and rejoice in his
salvation' Isaiah 25 v 9*

1 Rejoice and be glad! the Redeemer
    hath come:
  Go, look on His cradle, His cross,
    and His tomb.

  *Sound His praises, tell the story of Him
    who was slain;
  Sound His praises, tell with gladness He
    liveth again.*

2 Rejoice and be glad! it is sunshine at
    last;
  The clouds have departed, the
    shadows are past.

3 Rejoice and be glad! for the blood
    hath been shed;
  Redemption is finished, the price
    hath been paid.

4 Rejoice and be glad! now the pardon
    is free;
  The Just for the unjust hath died on
    the tree.

5 Rejoice and be glad! for the Lamb
    that was slain
  O'er death is triumphant, and liveth
    again.

6 Rejoice and be glad! for our King is
    on high;
  He pleadeth for us on His throne in
    the sky.

7 Rejoice and be glad! for He cometh
    again;
  He cometh in glory, the Lamb that
    was slain.

Horatius Bonar (1808–89)

437
66.66.88

*'I shall give thee ... the uttermost parts of
the earth for thy possession'* Psalm 2 v 8

1 Rejoice, the Saviour reigns
Among the sons of men;
He breaks the prisoners' chains,
And makes them free again:
Let hell oppose God's only Son,
In spite of foes His cause goes on.

2 The baffled prince of hell
In vain new projects tries,
Truth's empire to repel
By cruelty and lies:
The infernal gates shall rage in vain,
Conquest awaits the Lamb once
  slain.

3 He died, but soon arose
Triumphant o'er the grave;
And now Himself He shows
Omnipotent to save:
Let rebels kiss the victor's feet,
Eternal bliss His subjects meet.

4 All power is in His hand,
His people to defend;
To His most high command
Shall millions more attend:
All heaven with smiles approves His
  cause;
And distant isles receive His laws.

John Ryland (1753–1825)

438
87.87.D

*'And it came to pass ... he was parted
from them, and carried up into heaven'*
Luke 24 v 51

1 See, the Conqueror mounts in
    triumph,
See the King in royal state
Riding on the clouds His chariot
To His heavenly palace gate;
Hark! The choirs of angel voices
Joyful hallelujahs sing,
And the portals high are lifted
To receive their heavenly King.

2 Who is this that comes in glory,
With the trump of jubilee?
Lord of battles, God of armies,
He has gained the victory;
He who on the cross did suffer,
He who from the grave arose,
He has vanquished sin and Satan,
He by death has spoiled His foes.

3 He has raised our human nature
In the clouds to God's right hand;
There we sit in heavenly places,
There with Him in glory stand:
Jesus reigns, adored by angels;
Man with God is on the throne;
Mighty Lord, in Thine ascension
We by faith behold our own.

4 Glory be to God the Father;
Glory be to God the Son,
Dying, risen, ascending for us,
Who the heavenly realm has won;
Glory to the Holy Spirit;
To One God in Persons Three
Glory both in earth and heaven,
Glory, endless glory, be!

Christopher Wordsworth (1807–85)

439
C.M.

'I go to prepare a place for you'
John 14 v 2

1 The golden gates are lifted up,
The doors are opened wide;
The King of glory is gone in
Unto His Father's side.

2 Thou art gone up before us, Lord,
To make for us a place,
That we may be where now Thou art,
And look upon God's face.

3 And ever on our earthly path
A gleam of glory lies;
A light still breaks behind the cloud
That veiled Thee from our eyes.

4 Lift up our hearts, lift up our minds;
Let Thy dear grace be given,
That, while we wander here below,
Our treasure be in heaven;

5 That where Thou art at God's right
hand,
Our hope, our love, may be.
Dwell Thou in us, that we may dwell
For evermore in Thee.

Cecil Frances Alexander (1818–95)

440   C.M.

*'If we suffer, we shall also reign with
him' 2 Timothy 2 v 12*

1 The head that once was crowned
with thorns
Is crowned with glory now;
A royal diadem adorns
The mighty Victor's brow.

2 The highest place that heaven
affords
Is His by sovereign right,
The King of kings, and Lord of
lords,
And heaven's eternal light.

3 The joy of all who dwell above,
The joy of all below,
To whom He manifests His love,
And grants His name to know.

4 To them the cross, with all its
shame,
With all its grace, is given:
Their name an everlasting name,
Their joy the joy of heaven.

5 They suffer with their Lord below,
They reign with Him above;
Their profit and their joy to know
The mystery of His love.

6 The cross He bore is life and health,
Though shame and death to Him;
His people's hope, His people's
wealth,
Their everlasting theme.

Thomas Kelly (1769–1855)

441   8 8 7. D

*'He that ... ascended up far above all
heavens, that he might fill all things'
Ephesians 4 v 10*

1 The Lord ascendeth up on high,
The Lord hath triumphed gloriously,
In power and might excelling;
The grave and hell are captive led,
Lo! He returns, our glorious Head,
To His eternal dwelling.

2 The heavens with joy receive their
Lord,
By saints, by angel hosts adorned;
O day of exultation!
O earth, adore thy glorious King!
His rising, His ascension sing
With grateful adoration!

3 Our great High Priest hath gone
before,
Now on His church His grace to
pour,
And still His love He giveth:
O may our hearts to Him ascend;
May all within us upward tend
To Him who ever liveth!

Arthur Tozer Russell (1806–74)

442   6 6. 8 4. D

*'And when he had spoken these things,
while they beheld, he was taken up; and
a cloud received Him out of their sight'
Acts 1 v 9*

1 The Saviour now ascends
Before the Father's throne;
He pleads for us and now defends
Who are His own.
He gave us noble birth,
An act of grace in time,
He called us His, and prayed on
earth,
'For they are Thine'.

2 Because He went on high,
On God's right hand to stand,
The Holy Spirit brings Him nigh
To every land.
Sweet messenger of grace,
Companion in our ways,
This wondrous name we'll not
    disgrace
In all our days.

3 A constant presence now,
Our Advocate and Friend;
Before our Saviour all will bow,
And to Him bend.
A comfort to each heart
With knowledge that He cares;
In life or death He'll not depart:
His kingdom shares.

© The Author   *William Vernon Higham (b.1926)*

443   D.S.M.

'This same Jesus ... shall so come'
Acts 1 v 11

1 Thou art gone up on high
Triumphant o'er the grave,
And captive led captivity,
Thy ransomed ones to save.
Thou art gone up on high!
O help us to ascend,
And there with Thee continually
In heart and spirit blend.

2 Thou art gone up on high
To mansions in the skies;
And round Thy throne unceasingly
The songs of praise arise:
But we are lingering here
With sin and care oppressed;
O let the Comforter be near
To lead us to our rest.

3 Thou art gone up on high;
But Thou didst first come down,
Through earth's most bitter agony
To pass unto Thy crown:
And girt with griefs and fears
Our onward course must be;
But only let that path of tears
Lead us at last to Thee.

4 Thou art gone up on high;
But Thou shalt come again
With all the bright ones of the sky
Attendant on Thy train.
O by Thy saving power
So make us live and die,
That we may stand in that dread
    hour
At Thy right hand on high.

Emma Toke (1812–78)

444   C.M.

'While they beheld, he was taken up'
Acts 1 v 9

1 Triumphant, Christ ascends on high,
The glorious work complete;
Sin, death and hell now vanquished
    lie
Beneath His aweful feet.

2 There, with eternal glory crowned,
The Lord, the Conqueror, reigns,
His praise the heavenly choirs
    resound,
In their immortal strains.

3 Amid the splendours of His throne
Unchanging love appears;
The names He purchased for His
    own
Still on His heart He bears.

4 O the rich depths of love divine!
Of bliss, a boundless store:
Dear Saviour, let me call Thee mine,
I cannot wish for more.

5 On Thee alone my hope relies,
Beneath Thy cross I fall,
My Lord, my Life, my Sacrifice,
My Saviour, and my All.

Anne Steele (1717–78)

445

66.66.88

'Christ being come an high priest'
Hebrews 9 v 11

1 A good High Priest is come,
Supplying Aaron's place,
And taking up his room,
Dispensing life and grace,
The law by Aaron's priesthood came,
But grace and truth by Jesus' name.

2 He once temptations knew,
Of every sort and kind,
That He might succour show
To every tempted mind:
In every point the Lamb was tried
Like us, and then for us He died.

3 He died: but lives again,
And by the throne He stands,
There shows how He was slain,
Opening His pierced hands:
Our Priest abides and pleads the cause
Of us who have transgressed His
laws.

4 I other priests disclaim,
And laws and offerings too;
None but the bleeding Lamb
The mighty work can do:
He shall have all the praise; for He
Has loved, and lived, and died for me.

John Cennick (1718–55)

446

L.M.

'Seeing he ever liveth to make intercession'
Hebrews 7 v 25

1 Before the throne of God above
I have a strong, a perfect plea,
A great High Priest, whose name is
Love,
Who ever lives and pleads for me.

2 My name is graven on His hands,
My name is written on His heart;
I know that while in heaven He
stands,
No tongue can bid me thence
depart.

3 When Satan tempts me to despair,
And tells me of the guilt within,
Upward I look, and see Him there
Who made an end of all my sin.

4 Because the sinless Saviour died,
My sinful soul is counted free;
For God the Just is satisfied
To look on Him, and pardon me.

5 Behold Him there! The risen Lamb,
My perfect, spotless righteousness,
The great unchangeable I AM,
The King of glory and of grace!

6 One with Himself, I cannot die,
My soul is purchased by His blood;
My life is hid with Christ on high,
With Christ, my Saviour and my God.

Charitie Lees De Chenez (1841–1923)

447

66.66.88

'It is finished' John 19 v 30

1 Done is the work that saves,
Once and for ever done;
Finished the righteousness
That clothes the unrighteous one.
The love that blesses us below
Is flowing freely to us now.

2 The sacrifice is o'er,
The veil is rent in twain,
The mercy-seat is red
With blood of Victim slain;
Why stand ye then without, in fear?
The blood divine invites us near.

3 The gate is open wide;
The new and living way
Is clear and free and bright
With love and peace and day.
Into the holiest now we come,
Our present and our endless home.

4 Upon the mercy-seat
The High Priest sits within;
The blood is in His hand
Which makes and keeps us clean.
With boldness let us now draw near;
That blood has banished every fear.

5 Then to the Lamb once slain
Be glory, praise and power,
Who died and lives again,
Who liveth evermore,
Who loved and washed us in His blood,
Who makes us kings and priests to God.

Horatius Bonar (1809–89)

448
88.88.88

*'This man, because he continueth ever,
hath an unchangeable priesthood'
Hebrews 7 v 24*

1 Entered the holy place above,
Covered with meritorious scars,
The tokens of His dying love
Our great High-priest in glory bears;
He pleads His passion on the tree,
He shows Himself to God for me.

2 Before the throne my Saviour stands,
My Friend and Advocate appears;
My name is graven on His hands,
And Him the Father always hears;
While low at Jesu's cross I bow,
He hears the blood of sprinkling now.

3 This instant now I may receive
The answer of His powerful prayer;
This instant now by Him I live,
His prevalence with God declare;
And soon my spirit, in His hands,
Shall stand where my Forerunner stands.

Charles Wesley (1707–88)

449
C.M.

*'He ... hath an unchangeable priesthood'
Hebrews 7 v 24*

1 Jesus, in Thee our eyes behold
A thousand glories more
Than the rich gems and polished gold
The sons of Aaron wore.

2 They first their own burnt-offerings brought,
To purge themselves from sin:
Thy life was pure, without a spot,
And all Thy nature clean.

3 Fresh blood, as constant as the day,
Was on their altar spilt:
But Thy one offering takes away
For ever all our guilt.

4 Their priesthood ran through several hands,
For mortal was their race:
Thy never-changing office stands
Eternal as Thy days.

5 Once, in the circuit of a year,
With blood, but not their own,
Did they within the veil appear,
Before the golden throne.

6 But Christ, by His own powerful blood,
Ascends above the skies;
And in the presence of our God
Shows His own sacrifice.

7 Jesus, the King of glory, reigns
On Zion's heavenly hill,
Looks like a Lamb that has been slain,
And wears His priesthood still.

8 He ever lives to intercede
Before His Father's face:
Give Him, my soul, thy cause to plead,
Nor doubt the Father's grace.

Isaac Watts (1674–1748)

450   66.66.88

*'A great high priest, that is passed into
the heavens' Hebrews 4 v 14*

1 The atoning work is done;
  The Victim's blood is shed;
  And Jesus now is gone,
  His people's cause to plead.
  He stands in heaven, their great
    High Priest,
  And bears their names upon His
    breast.

2 He sprinkles with His blood
  The mercy-seat above;
  Else justice had withstood
  The purposes of love;
  But justice now objects no more,
  And mercy yields her boundless
    store.

3 No temple made with hands
  His place of service is;
  In heaven itself He stands –
  A heavenly Priesthood His!
  In Him the shadows of the law
  Are all fulfilled, and now withdraw.

4 And though awhile He be
  Hid from the eyes of men,
  His people look to see
  Their great High Priest again;
  In brightest glory He will come,
  And take His waiting people home.

                          Thomas Kelly (1769–1855)

451   88.88.D

*'By his own blood he entered in once into
the holy place' Hebrews 9 v 12*

1 The Saviour to glory is gone;
  His sufferings and sorrows are past;
  His work is completed and done,
  And shall to eternity last.
  For ever He lives to bestow
  The blessings He purchased so dear;
  Our bosoms with gratitude glow,
  Whilst to Him, by faith, we draw
    near.

2 Expecting from Him to receive
  All fullness of glory and grace,
  Rejoicing in hope, we believe,
  His promises thankful embrace.
  Our King shall protect us from
    harms,
  Our Advocate make our plea good;
  Our Shepherd will bear in His arms
  The sheep which He bought with
    His blood.

3 Our Prophet will point out the way
  Which leads to the mansions above;
  Our Priest all our ransom shall pay,
  Our Friend of unchangeable love.
  But whilst to the Lamb on His
    throne
  Our hearts and our voices we raise,
  His glory exalted we own
  Above all our blessings and praise.

                          Thomas Haweis (1733–1820)

452   C.M.

*'The veil of the temple was rent in twain'
Matthew 27 v 51*

1 The veil is rent: lo! Jesus stands
  Before the throne of grace;
  And clouds of incense from His
    hands
  Fill all that glorious place.

2 His precious blood is sprinkled
    there,
  Before and on the throne;
  And His own wounds in heaven
    declare
  His work on earth is done.

3 'Tis finished!' on the cross, He said,
  In agonies and blood;
  'Tis finished!' now He lives to plead
  Before the face of God.

4 'Tis finished!' here our souls can
    rest,
  His work can never fail;
  By Him, our Sacrifice and Priest,
  We enter through the veil.

5 Within the holiest of all,
Cleansed by His precious blood,
Before Thy throne Thy children fall,
And worship Thee, our God.

James George Deck (1802–84)

453 L.M.

'We have a great high priest'
Hebrews 4 v 14

1 Where high the heavenly temple
stands,
The house of God not made with
hands,
A great High Priest our nature
wears,
The Saviour of mankind appears.

2 He who for men their surety stood,
And poured on earth His precious
blood,
Pursues in heaven His mighty plan,
The Saviour and the Friend of man.

3 Though now ascended up on high,
He bends on earth a brother's eye;
Partaker of the human name,
He knows the frailty of our frame.

4 Our fellow-sufferer yet retains
A fellow-feeling of our pains,
And still remembers in the skies
His tears, His agonies, and cries.

5 In every pang that rends the heart,
The Man of sorrows had a part;
He sympathizes with our grief,
And to the sufferer sends relief.

6 With boldness, therefore, at the
throne,
Let us make all our sorrows known;
And ask the aids of heavenly power
To help us in the evil hour.

Michael Bruce (1746–67) Altd

454 L.M.

'He ever liveth to make intercession for us'
Hebrews 7 v 25

1 Wherewith, O God, shall I draw
near,
And bow myself before Thy face?
How in Thy purer eyes appear?
What shall I bring to gain Thy grace?

2 Whoe'er to Thee themselves approve
Must take the path Thyself has
showed,
Justice pursue, and mercy love,
And humbly walk by faith with God.

3 But though my life henceforth be
Thine,
Present for past can ne'er atone;
Though I to Thee the whole resign,
I only give Thee back Thine own.

4 What have I then wherein to trust?
I nothing have, I nothing am;
Excluded is my every boast,
My glory swallowed up in shame.

5 Guilty I stand before Thy face,
On me I feel Thy wrath abide;
'Tis just – the sentence should take
place;
'Tis just – but O, Thy Son hath died!

6 Jesus, the Lamb of God, hath bled;
He bore our sins upon the tree;
Beneath our curse He bowed His
head;
'Tis finished! He hath died for me!

7 See where before the throne He
stands,
And pours the all-prevailing prayer,
Points to His side, and lifts His
hands,
And shows that I am graven here.

8 He ever lives for me to pray;
He prays that I with Him may reign:
Amen to what my Lord doth say!
Jesus, Thou canst not pray in vain.

Charles Wesley (1707-88)

455   C.M.

*'But was in all points tempted like as we
are, yet without sin' Hebrews 4 v 15*

1 With joy we meditate the grace
Of our High Priest above;
His heart is made of tenderness,
And overflows with love.

2 Touched with a sympathy within,
He knows our feeble frame;
He knows what sore temptations
mean,
For He has felt the same.

3 But spotless, innocent, and pure,
The great Redeemer stood,
While Satan's fiery darts He bore,
And did resist to blood.

4 He in the days of feeble flesh
Poured out His cries and tears;
And, though exalted, feels afresh
What every member bears.

5 He'll never quench the smoking flax,
But raise it to a flame;
The bruisèd reed He never breaks,
Nor scorns the meanest name.

6 Then let our humble faith address
His mercy and His power:
We shall obtain delivering grace
In the distressing hour.

Isaac Watts (1674–1748)

456   6 5. 6 5. D

*'All kings shall fall down before him'
Psalm 72 v 11*

1 At the name of Jesus
Every knee shall bow,
Every tongue confess Him
King of glory now.
'Tis the Father's pleasure
We should call Him Lord,
Who from the beginning
Was the mighty Word.

2 Humbled for a season,
To receive a name
From the lips of sinners
Unto whom He came,
Faithfully He bore it
Spotless to the last,
Brought it back victorious
When from death He passed.

3 Name Him, brothers, name Him,
With love strong as death,
But with awe and wonder,
And with bated breath;
He is God the Saviour,
He is Christ the Lord,
Ever to be worshipped,
Trusted, and adored.

4 In your hearts enthrone Him;
There let Him subdue
All that is not holy,
All that is not true;
Crown Him as your Captain
In temptation's hour;
Let His will enfold you
In its light and power.

5 Brothers, this Lord Jesus
Shall return again
With His Father's glory,
With His angel train;
For all wreaths of empire
Meet upon His brow,
And our hearts confess Him
King of glory now.

Caroline Maria Noel (1817–77)

457   8 7. 8 7

*'When he had by himself purged our sins,
sat down on the right hand of the
Majesty on high' Hebrews 1 v 3*

1 Christ, above all glory seated!
King triumphant, strong to save!
Dying, Thou hast death defeated;
Buried, Thou hast spoiled the grave.

2 Thou art gone where now is given
What no mortal might could gain,
On the eternal throne of heaven,
In Thy Father's power to reign.

3 There Thy kingdoms all adore Thee,
   Heaven above and earth below;
   While the depths of hell before Thee,
   Trembling and defeated, bow.

4 We, O Lord, with hearts adoring,
   Follow Thee above the sky;
   Hear our prayers, Thy grace
      imploring;
   Lift our souls to Thee on high.

5 So when Thou again in glory
   On the clouds of heaven shalt shine,
   We Thy flock may stand before Thee,
   Owned for evermore as Thine.

6 Hail, all hail! In Thee confiding,
   Jesus, Thee shall all adore,
   In Thy Father's might abiding
   With one Spirit evermore!

Latin c. 5th Century
Tr. James Russell Woodford (1820–85)

458   87.87

'The desire of all nations shall come'
Haggai 2 v 7

1 Come, Thou long-expected Jesus,
   Born to set Thy people free;
   From our fears and sins release us,
   Let us find our rest in Thee.

2 Israel's strength and consolation,
   Hope of all the earth Thou art;
   Dear desire of every nation,
   Joy of every loving heart.

3 Born Thy people to deliver,
   Born a child, and yet a king;
   Born to reign in us for ever,
   Now Thy gracious kingdom bring.

4 By Thine own eternal Spirit
   Rule in all our hearts alone;
   By Thine all-sufficient merit
   Raise us to Thy glorious throne.

Charles Wesley (1707–88)

459   77.77

'All power is given unto me in heaven
and in earth' Matthew 28 v 18

1 Earth, rejoice, our Lord is King!
   Sons of men, His praises sing;
   Sing ye in triumphant strains,
   Jesus the Messiah reigns!

2 Power is all to Jesus given,
   Lord of hell, and earth, and heaven,
   Every knee to Him shall bow;
   Satan, hear, and tremble now!

3 Angels and archangels join,
   All triumphantly combine,
   All in Jesu's praise agree,
   Carrying on His victory.

4 Though the sons of night
      blaspheme,
   More there are with us than them;
   God with us, we cannot fear;
   Fear, ye fiends, for Christ is here!

5 Lo! to faith's enlightened sight,
   All the mountain flames with light;
   Hell is nigh, but God is nigher,
   Circling us with hosts of fire.

6 Christ the Saviour is come down,
   Points us to the victor's crown,
   Bids us take our seats above,
   More than conquerors in His love.

Charles Wesley (1707–88)

460   66.66.88

'He ascended up on high' Ephesians 4 v 8

1 God is gone up on high,
   With a triumphant noise;
   The clarions of the sky
   Proclaim the angelic joys!

   Join all on earth, rejoice and sing,
   Glory ascribe to glory's King.

2 God in the flesh below,
   For us He reigns above:
   Let all the nations know
   Our Jesu's conquering love!

3 All power to our great Lord
  Is by the Father given;
  By angel hosts adored,
  He reigns supreme in heaven:

4 High on His holy seat
  He bears the righteous sway;
  His foes beneath His feet
  Shall sink and die away:

5 His foes and ours are one,
  Satan, the world, and sin;
  But He shall tread them down,
  And bring His kingdom in:

6 Till all the earth, renewed
  In righteousness divine,
  With all the hosts of God
  In one great chorus join:

Charles Wesley (1707–88)

461   77.77.D

'He shall reign for ever and ever'
Revelation 11 v 15

1 Hark! the song of jubilee,
  Loud as mighty thunders' roar:
  Or the fulness of the sea,
  When it breaks upon the shore.
  Hallelujah! for the Lord
  God Omnipotent shall reign:
  Hallelujah! let the word
  Echo round the earth and main.

2 Hallelujah! Hark! The sound,
  From the depths unto the skies,
  Wakes above, beneath, around,
  All creation's harmonies;
  See Jehovah's banner furled:
  Sheathed His sword; He speaks –
     'tis done:
  And the kingdoms of this world
  Are the kingdoms of His Son.

3 He shall reign from pole to pole
  With illimitable sway:
  He shall reign, when, like a scroll,
  Yonder heavens have passed away;
  Then the end – beneath His rod
  Man's last enemy shall fall;
  Hallelujah! Christ in God,
  God in Christ, is All in all.

James Montgomery (1771–1854)

462   L.M.

'The Lord God omnipotent reigneth'
Revelation 19 v 6

1 Jesus, immortal King, go on;
  The glorious day will soon be won;
  Thine enemies prepare to flee,
  And leave the conquered world to
     Thee.

2 Gird on Thy sword, victorious Chief!
  The captive sinner's soul relief;
  Cast the usurper from his throne,
  And make the universe Thine own.

3 Then shall contending nations rest,
  For love shall reign in every breast;
  Weapons, for war designed, shall
     cease,
  Or then be implements of peace.

4 Thy footsteps, Lord, with joy we
     trace,
  And mark the conquests of Thy
     grace;
  Finish the work Thou hast begun,
  And let Thy will on earth be done.

5 Hark! how the hosts triumphant
     sing,
  'The Lord Omnipotent is King!'
  Let all the saints rejoice at this,
  The kingdoms of the world are His!

Thomas Kelly (1769–1855)

463 L.M.

'He shall have dominion also from sea to sea' Psalm 72 v 8

1 Jesus shall reign where'er the sun
Doth his successive journeys run;
His kingdom stretch from shore to
shore,
Till moons shall wax and wane no
more.

2 For Him shall endless prayer be
made,
And praises throng to crown His head;
His name, like sweet perfume, shall
rise
With every morning sacrifice.

3 People and realms of every tongue
Dwell on His love with sweetest
song;
And infant voices shall proclaim
Their early blessings on His name.

4 Blessings abound where'er He
reigns:
The prisoner leaps to lose his
chains;
The weary find eternal rest,
And all the sons of want are blest.

5 Where He displays His healing
power,
Death and the curse are known no
more;
In Him the tribes of Adam boast
More blessings than their father lost.

6 Let every creature rise and bring
Peculiar honours to our King;
Angels descend with songs again,
And earth repeat the loud Amen.

Isaac Watts (1674–1748)

464 87.87.D

'This same Jesus' Acts 1 v 11

1 Lamb of God, Thou now art seated
High upon Thy Father's throne,
All Thy gracious work completed,
All Thy mighty victory won;
Every knee in heaven is bending
To the Lamb for sinners slain;
Every voice and harp is swelling –
Worthy is the Lamb to reign!

2 Lord, in all Thy power and glory,
Still Thy thoughts and eyes are here;
Watching o'er Thy ransomed people,
To Thy gracious heart so dear;
Thou for them art interceding –
Everlasting is Thy love –
And a blessed rest preparing
In our Father's house above.

3 Lamb of God, Thou soon in glory
Wilt to this sad earth return;
All thy foes shall quake before Thee,
All that now despise Thee, mourn:
Then Thy saints shall rise to meet
Thee,
With Thee in Thy kingdom reign;
Thine the praise and Thine the glory,
Lamb of God for sinners slain.

James George Deck (1802–84)

465 66.66.88

'Let the children of Zion be joyful in their King' Psalm 149 v 2

1 Rejoice, the Lord is King!
Your Lord and King adore;
Mortals, give thanks and sing
And triumph evermore:

*Life up your heart, lift up your voice;
Rejoice, again I say, Rejoice.*

2 Jesus the Saviour reigns,
The God of truth and love:
When He had purged our stains,
He took His seat above:

3 His kingdom cannot fail;
He rules o'er earth and heaven;
The keys of death and hell
Are to our Jesus given:

4 He sits at God's right hand
Till all His foes submit,
And bow to His command,
And fall beneath His feet:

5 He all His foes shall quell,
Shall all our sins destroy,
And every bosom swell
With pure seraphic joy:

6 Rejoice in glorious hope;
Jesus the Judge shall come,
And take His servants up
To their eternal home:

We soon shall hear the archangel's voice;
The trump of God shall sound, Rejoice!

Charles Wesley (1707–88)

466   8 7. 8 7. D

'But ye are come unto mount Sion, and
unto the city of the living God'
Hebrews 12 v 22

1 Shake the earth, O mighty Saviour!
Let Thy voice like trumpet sound,
Full of strength and purest grandeur,
Stirring all the lost now found.
Sinners trembling, saints rejoicing,
As He calls His heavenly throng;
Hear new voices now proclaiming
Hallelujah gospel song!

2 We are come to this assembly
Of our Judge and of the Lamb,
Triune splendour dressed in mercy;
None of His shall come to harm.
See the firstfruits, Christ-begotten;
Read their names upon His palm;
They shall never be forgotten –
This shall be their happy psalm.

3 See the Saviour's exultation,
Son of God and Son of man!
Now we see the consummation
And fulfilment of His plan.
Listen to the acclamation,
Ringing loud the heavens to hear,
Thanking God for our salvation
And for Jesus Christ so dear.

© The Author   William Vernon Higham (b.1926)

467   L.M.

'They shall bring all your brethren …
out of all nations' Isaiah 66 v 20

1 Shout, for the blessèd Jesus reigns;
Through distant lands His triumphs
spread;
And sinners, freed from endless
pains,
Own Him their Saviour and their
Head.

2 He calls His chosen from afar,
They all at Zion's gates arrive;
Those who were dead in sin before
By sovereign grace are made alive.

3 Gentiles and Jews His laws obey;
Nations remote their offerings bring
And unconstrained their homage
pay
To their exalted God and King.

4 O may His holy church increase,
His word and Spirit still prevail,
While angels celebrate His praise,
And saints His growing glories hail.

5 Loud hallelujahs to the Lamb,
From all below, and all above!
In lofty songs exalt His name,
In songs as lasting as His love.

Benjamin Beddome (1717–95)

468   C.M.

'Behold, the bridegroom cometh'
Matthew 25 v 6

1 The Lord will come, and not be slow;
   His footsteps cannot err;
   Before Him righteousness shall go,
   His royal harbinger.

2 Mercy and truth that long were
      missed,
   Now joyfully are met;
   Sweet peace and righteousness have
      kissed,
   And hand in hand are set.

3 Truth from the earth, like to a
      flower,
   Shall bud and blossom then;
   And justice, from her heavenly
      bower,
   Look down on mortal men.

4 Rise, Lord, judge Thou the earth in
      might,
   This longing earth redress;
   For Thou art He who shall by right
   The nations all possess.

5 The nations all whom Thou hast
      made
   Shall come, and all shall frame
   To bow them low before Thee, Lord,
   And glorify Thy name.

6 For great Thou art, and wonders
      great
   By Thy strong hand are done:
   Thou in Thine everlasting seat
   Remainest God alone.

                   John Milton (1608–74)

469   87.87.47

'Thou King of saints' Revelation 15 v 3

1 'Tis to Thee we owe allegiance,
   God our Saviour and our King;
   May we render true obedience,
   Every day our tribute bring;
   And with rapture
   Of Thy love and glory sing.

2 May we bow to Thy dominion,
   Yielding to Thy righteous sway;
   Careless of the world's opinion,
   May we all Thy will obey;
   Saviour, lead us,
   Lead us in the perfect way.

3 Thine is greatness never wasting,
   High Thou art, with glory crowned;
   Thine a kingdom everlasting,
   Grace and truth Thy throne
      surround;
   While all others
   Vanish, and no more are found.

4 Happy they whom Thou dost govern!
   Great their peace, their honour
      great;
   Thee beholding, Thee their
      Sovereign,
   Thee enthroned in royal state.
   Happy people!
   Who before Thee ever wait!

                   Thomas Kelly (1769–1855)

470   87.87.47

'Maranatha' 1 Corinthians 16 v 22

1 Christ is coming! let creation
   From her groans and travails cease;
   Let the glorious proclamation
   Hope restore and faith increase:
   Christ is coming!
   Come, Thou blessèd Prince of Peace.

2 Earth can now but tell the story
   Of Thy bitter cross and pain:
   She shall yet behold Thy glory,
   When Thou comest back to reign.
   Christ is coming!
   Let each heart repeat the strain!

3 Long Thine exiles have been pining,
   Far from rest and home and Thee;
   But in heavenly vestures shining
   They their loving Lord shall see.
   Christ is coming!
   Haste the joyous jubilee.

4 With that blessèd hope before us,
  Let our joyful songs be sung;
  Let the mighty advent chorus
  Onward roll from tongue to tongue.
  Christ is coming!
  Come, Lord Jesus, quickly come!

John Ross Macduff (1818–95)

471   S.M.

'Return, O LORD, how long?'
Psalm 90 v 13

1 Come, Lord, and tarry not;
  Bring the long-looked for day;
  O why these years of waiting here,
  These ages of delay?

2 Come, for Thy saints still wait;
  Daily ascends their sigh;
  The Spirit and the bride say, Come;
  Wilt Thou not hear the cry?

3 Come in Thy glorious might,
  Come with the iron rod;
  Scattering Thy foes before Thy face,
  Most mighty Son of God.

4 Come, and make all things new;
  Build up this ruined earth;
  Restore our faded paradise,
  Creation's second birth.

5 Come, and begin Thy reign
  Of everlasting peace;
  Come, take the kingdom to Thyself,
  Great King of Righteousness!

Horatious Bonar (1808–89)

472   87.87.47

'The judgment of the great day' Jude v 6

1 Day of judgment! day of wonders!
  Hark! the trumpet's aweful sound,
  Louder than a thousand thunders,
  Shakes the vast creation round:
  How the summons
  Will the sinner's heart confound!

2 See the Judge, our nature wearing,
  Clothed in majesty divine:
  Ye who long for His appearing
  Then shall say, This God is mine!
  Gracious Saviour,
  Own me in that day for Thine.

3 At His call the dead awaken,
  Rise to life from earth and sea;
  All the powers of nature, shaken
  By His look, prepare to flee;
  Careless sinner,
  What will then become of thee?

4 But to those who have confessèd,
  Loved and served the Lord below,
  He will say, Come near, ye blessèd,
  See the kingdom I bestow;
  You for ever
  Shall my love and glory know.

John Newton (1725–1807)

473   8 8 8. 4

'This same Jesus ... shall so come in like
manner as ye have seen him go into
heaven' Acts 1 v 11

1 From far we see the glorious day,
  When He who bore our sins away
  Will all His majesty display.
  Hallelujah!

2 A Man of sorrows once below,
  His visage marred by grief and woe,
  His steps were watched by many a
      foe.

3 He groaned beneath sin's awful
      load,
  For in the sinner's place He stood,
  And died to bring us nigh to God.

4 But now He reigns, with glory
      crowned,
  While angel hosts His throne
      surround,
  And aye His lofty praise resound.

5 And soon the glorious day will
   come,
When He shall take His people
   home,
And seat them with Him on the
   throne.

6 Lord, may Thy love, Thy cross still
   be
Our theme, as witnesses for Thee,
Till we Thy glorious face shall see!

7 Come, Lord, come quickly from
   above,
That we may see Thee, and may
   prove
The depths of everlasting love!

Anonymous

474   8 7. 8 7. 8 8 7

*'I saw the dead, small and great, stand
before God' Revelation 20 v 12*

1 Great God, what do I see and hear!
The end of things created:
The Judge of mankind doth appear
On clouds of glory seated;
The trumpet sounds, the graves
   restore
The dead which they contained
   before:
Prepare, my soul, to meet Him!

2 The dead in Christ shall first arise
At the last trumpet's sounding,
Caught up to meet Him in the skies,
With joy their Lord surrounding.
No gloomy fears their souls dismay,
His presence sheds eternal day
On those prepared to meet Him.

3 The ungodly, filled with guilty fears,
Behold His wrath prevailing;
For they shall rise and find their
   tears
And sighs are unavailing:
The day of grace is past and gone;
Trembling they stand before His
   throne,
All unprepared to meet Him.

4 Great Judge, to Thee our prayers we
   pour,
In deep abasement bending;
O shield us through that last dread
   hour,
Thy wondrous love extending.
May we in this our trial day,
With faithful hearts Thy Word obey,
And thus prepare to meet Thee.

*v 1 Anonymous 1802
vv 2 & 3 William Bengo Collyer (1782–1854)
and Thomas Cotterill (1779–1823)
v 4 Anonymous*

475   8 7. 8 7. D

*'... until the day dawn, and the day star
arise in your hearts' 2 Peter 1 v 18*

1 I am waiting for the dawning
Of the bright and blessèd day,
When the darksome night of sorrow
Shall have vanished far away;
When for ever with the Saviour,
Far beyond this vale of tears,
I shall swell the song of worship
Through the everlasting years.

2 I am looking at the brightness,
(See it shineth from afar)
Of the clear and joyous beaming
Of the Bright and Morning Star.
Through the dark grey mist of
   morning
Do I see its glorious light;
Then away with every shadow
Of this sad and weary night.

3 I am waiting for the coming
Of the Lord who died for me;
O His words have thrilled my spirit:
I will come again for thee.
I can almost hear His footfall
On the threshold of the door,
And my heart, my heart is longing
To be with Him evermore.

Samuel Trevor Frances (1834–1925)

476
87.87.D

'Lead me, O LORD' Psalm 5 v 8

1 Lead, Lord Jesus, my frail spirit
To the Rock so strong and high,
Standing sure midst surging tempest,
Safe when pounding waves are nigh:
In the Rock of Ages hiding,
Come there flood of fiery blaze,
When the whole creation crumbles,
Rock of Ages, Thee I'll praise.

2 When earth's rocks are cleft asunder
By the terror of that day,
When, as cruel storms beat on them,
Strong men cringe in fear away,
That sure Rock will still be standing,
Midst the waters, midst the blaze;
There on heaven's eternal ocean,
Rock of Ages Thee I'll praise.

S. J. Griffith (1850–93)
© The Translator   *Tr. Graham Stuart Harrison (b.1935)*

477
87.87.47

*'Behold he cometh with clouds; and every
eye shall see him' Revelation 1 v 7*

1 Lo! He comes with clouds
descending,
Once for favoured sinners slain;
Thousand thousand saints
attending,
Swell the triumph of His train:
Hallelujah!
God appears on earth to reign.

2 Every eye shall now behold Him
Robed in dreadful majesty;
Those who set at naught and sold
Him,
Pierced and nailed Him to the tree,
Deeply wailing,
Shall the true Messiah see.

3 Every island, sea, and mountain,
Heav'n and earth, shall flee away;
All who hate Him must, confounded,
Hear the trump proclaim the day:
Come to judgment!
Come to judgment! Come away!

4 Now redemption, long expected,
See in solemn pomp appear;
All His saints, by man rejected,
Now shall meet Him in the air:
Hallelujah!
See the day of God appear!

5 Yea, Amen! let all adore Thee,
High on Thine eternal throne!
Saviour, take the power and glory,
Claim the kingdom for Thine own;
O come quickly!
Hallelujah! Come, Lord, come!

*John Cennick (1718–55)
and Charles Wesley (1707–88)*

478
87.87.D

'This man receiveth sinners' Luke 15 v 2

1 Lord, in love Thou didst receive us,
Ere creation, as Thine own;
And that love will never leave us,
But will raise us to Thy throne.
Thou wilt come and we shall meet
Thee;
Then the saints whom Thou wilt raise
Will with those remaining greet Thee,
Joining in the song of praise.

2 Then shall we, Thine image bearing,
Know Thee, Lord, as we are known,
With our blood-washed robes
declaring
What for us Thy death has done.
Thus we all, our joys expressing,
Shall for ever praise Thy name:
Glory, power, dominion, blessing,
Be to God and to the Lamb.

*Anonymous
From James Kelly's Collections 1849*

479
L.M.

*'For the Son of man shall come'
Matthew 16 v 27*

1 Now to the Lord that makes us know
The wonders of His dying love,
Be humble honours paid below,
And strains of nobler praise above.

2 'Twas He that cleansed our foulest
   sins,
   And washed us in His richest blood;
   'Tis He that makes us priests and
   kings,
   And brings us rebels near to God.

3 To Jesus, our atoning Priest,
   To Jesus, our superior King,
   Be everlasting power confessed,
   And every tongue His glory sing.

4 Behold! on flying clouds He comes,
   And all the earth's nations then shall
   see
   The glorious face of Him from whom
   Both heaven and earth away shall
   flee.

5 The unbelieving world shall wail,
   While we rejoice to see the day;
   Come, Lord, nor let Thy promise
   fail,
   Nor let Thy chariots long delay!

Isaac Watts (1674–1748)

480   7 7. 7 7. D

'A great multitude, which no man could
number' Revelation 7 v 9

1 See the ransomed millions stand,
   Palms of conquest in their hand;
   This before the throne their strain:
   'Hell is vanquished, death is slain;
   Blessing, honour, glory, might,
   Are the Conqueror's native right;
   Thrones and powers before Him fall,
   Lamb of God, and Lord of all.'

2 Hasten, Lord, the promised hour!
   Come in glory and in power!
   Still Thy foes are unsubdued;
   Nature sighs to be renewed;
   Time has nearly reached its sum;
   All things, with Thy bride, say 'Come!'
   Jesus, whom all worlds adore,
   Come and reign for evermore!

Josiah Conder (1789–1855)

481   7 6. 8 6. D

'The glory which shall be revealed in us'
Romans 8 v 18

1 Ten thousand times ten thousand,
   In sparkling raiment bright,
   The armies of the ransomed saints
   Throng up the steeps of light;
   'Tis finished, all is finished,
   Their flight with death and sin;
   Fling open wide the golden gates,
   And let the victors in.

2 What rush of hallelujahs
   Fills all the earth and sky!
   What ringing of a thousand harps
   Bespeaks the triumph nigh!
   O day for which creation
   And all its tribes were made!
   O joy, for all its former woes
   A thousand-fold repaid!

3 O then what raptured greetings
   On Canaan's happy shore,
   What knitting severed friendships
   up
   Where partings are no more!
   Then eyes with joy shall sparkle
   That brimmed with tears of late;
   Orphans no longer fatherless,
   Nor widows desolate.

4 Bring near Thy great salvation,
   Thou Lamb for sinners slain;
   Fill up the roll of Thine elect,
   Then take Thy power and reign;
   Appear, Desire of nations,
   Thine exiles long for home;
   Show in the heavens Thy promised
   sign;
   Thou Prince and Saviour, come.

Henry Alford (1810–71)

482   87.887.77.77

'Surely I come quickly'
Revelation 22 v 20

1 Thou art coming, O my Saviour,
Thou art coming, O my King,
In Thy beauty all-resplendent,
In Thy glory all-transcendent;
Well may we rejoice and sing.
Coming! In the opening east
Herald brightness slowly swells;
Coming! O my glorious Priest,
Hear we not Thy golden bells?

2 Thou art coming, Thou art coming;
We shall meet Thee on Thy way,
We shall see Thee, we shall know
        Thee,
We shall bless Thee, we shall show
        Thee
All our hearts could never say.
What an anthem that will be,
Ringing out our love to Thee,
Pouring out our rapture sweet,
At Thine own all-glorious feet!

3 O the joy to see Thee reigning,
Thee, my own belovèd Lord!
Every tongue Thy name confessing,
Worship, honour, glory, blessing,
Brought to Thee with glad accord –
Thee, my Master and my Friend,
Vindicated and enthroned,
Unto earth's remotest end
Glorified, adored, and owned!

Frances Ridley Havergal (1836–79)

483   D.S.M.

'For we must all appear before the judg-
ment seat of Christ' 2 Corinthians 5 v 10

1 Thou Judge of quick and dead,
Before whose bar severe,
With holy joy, or guilty dread,
We all shall soon appear;
Our cautioned souls prepare
For that tremendous day,
And fill us now with watchful care,
And stir us up to pray –

2 To pray, and wait the hour,
That awesome hour unknown,
When, robed in majesty and power,
Thou shalt from heaven come down,
The immortal Son of Man,
To judge the human race,
With all Thy Father's dazzling train,
With all Thy glorious grace.

3 O may we thus be found
Obedient to His Word,
Attentive to the trumpet's sound,
And looking for our Lord!
O may we thus ensure
A lot among the blest;
And watch a moment to secure
An everlasting rest!

Charles Wesley (1707–88)

484   66.66.88

'Young man, I say unto thee, Arise'
Luke 7 v 14

1 Ye slumbering souls, arise!
With all the dead awake;
Unto salvation wise,
Oil in your vessels take;
Upstarting at the midnight cry,
'Behold the heavenly Bridegroom
        nigh.'

2 He comes, He comes, to call
The nations to His bar,
And take to glory all
Who meet for glory are:
Make ready for your free reward,
Go forth with joy to meet your Lord.

3 Go, meet Him in the sky,
Your everlasting Friend;
Your Head to glorify,
With all His saints ascend;
Ye pure in heart, obtain the grace
To see, without a veil, His face!

4 Ye that have here received
The unction from above,
And in His Spirit lived,
And thirsted for His love,
Jesus shall claim you for his bride:
Rejoice with all the sanctified.

5 Rejoice in glorious hope
   Of that great day unknown,
   When you shall be caught up
   To stand before His throne;
   Called to partake the marriage feast,
   And lean on our Immanuel's breast.

6 The everlasting doors
   Shall soon the saints receive,
   Above yon angel powers
   In glorious joy to live;
   Far from a world of grief and sin,
   With God eternally shut in.

Charles Wesley (1707–88)

GOD THE HOLY SPIRIT

485
5 5. 5 11

'Oh how great is thy goodness'
Psalm 31 v 19

1 Away with our fears,
Our troubles and tears:
The Spirit is come,
The witness of Jesus returned to His
home.

2 The pledge of our Lord
To His heaven restored
Is sent from the sky,
And tells us our Head is exalted on
high.

3 Our Advocate there
By His blood and His prayer
The gift hath obtained,
For us He hath prayed, and the
Comforter gained.

4 Our glorified Head
His Spirit hath shed,
With His people to stay,
And never again will He take Him
away.

5 Our heavenly Guide
With us shall abide,
His comforts impart,
And set up His kingdom of love in
the heart.

6 The heart that believes
His kingdom receives,
His power and His peace,
His life, and His joy's everlasting
increase.

7 Then let us rejoice
In heart and in voice,
Our Leader pursue,
And shout as we travel the
wilderness through:

8 With the Spirit remove
To Zion above,
Triumphant arise,
And walk with our God, till we fly to
the skies.

Charles Wesley (1707–88)

486
6 6 11. D

'The love of God is shed abroad in our
hearts by the Holy Ghost' Romans 5 v 5

1 Come down, O Love divine,
Seek Thou this soul of mine,
And visit it with Thine own ardour
glowing;
O Comforter, draw near,
Within my heart appear,
And kindle it, Thy holy flame
bestowing.

2 O let it freely burn,
Till earthly passions turn
To dust and ashes, in its heat
consuming;
And let Thy glorious light
Shine ever on my sight,
And clothe me round, the while my
path illuming.

3 Let holy charity
Mine outward vesture be,
And lowliness become mine inner
clothing;
True lowliness of heart,
Which takes the humbler part,
And o'er its own shortcomings
weeps with loathing.

4 And so the yearning strong,
With which the soul will long,
Shall far outpass the power of
human telling;
For none can guess its grace,
Till he become the place
Wherein the Holy Spirit makes His
dwelling.

Bianco da Siena (c.1350–1434)
Tr. Richard Frederick Littledale (1833–90)

487 L.M.

'Led by the Spirit of God' Romans 8 v 14

1 Come, gracious Spirit, heavenly
Dove,
With light and comfort from above,
Be Thou our guardian, Thou our
guide,
O'er every thought and step preside.

2 The light of truth to us display,
And make us know and choose Thy
way;
Plant holy fear in every heart,
That we from God may ne'er depart.

3 Lead us to Christ, the living Way,
Nor let us from His pastures stray;
Lead us to holiness, the road
That we must take to dwell with God.

4 Lead us to heaven, that we may share
Fulness of joy for ever there;
Lead us to God, our final rest,
To be with Him for ever blest.

Simon Browne (1680–1732)

488 88.88.88

'They were all filled with the Holy Ghost'
Acts 2 v 4

1 Come, Holy Ghost, all-quickening
fire,
Come, and in me delight to rest;
Drawn by the lure of strong desire,
O come and consecrate my breast;
The temple of my soul prepare,
And fix Thy sacred presence there.

2 Eager for Thee I ask and pant;
So strong, the principle divine
Carries me out, with sweet
constraint,
Till all my hallowed soul is Thine;
Plunged in the Godhead's deepest
sea,
And lost in Thine immensity.

3 My peace, my life, my comfort Thou,
My treasure and my all Thou art;
True witness of my sonship, now
Engraving pardon on my heart,
Seal of my sins in Christ forgiven,
Earnest of love, and pledge of
heaven.

4 Come then, my God, mark out Thine
heir,
Of heaven a larger earnest give;
With clearer light Thy witness bear,
More sensibly within me live;
Let all my powers Thine entrance
feel,
And deeper stamp Thyself the seal.

Charles Wesley (1707–88)

489 C.M.

'Holy men of God spake as they were
moved by the Holy Ghost' 2 Peter 1 v 21

1 Come, Holy Ghost, our hearts
inspire,
Let us Thine influence prove,
Source of the old prophetic fire,
Fountain of light and love.

2 Come, Holy Ghost, for moved by
   Thee
The prophets wrote and spoke;
Unlock the truth, Thyself the key,
Unseal the sacred Book.

3 Expand Thy wings, celestial Dove,
Brood o'er our nature's night;
On our disordered spirits move,
And let there now be light.

4 God, through Himself, we then shall
   know,
If Thou within us shine,
And sound, with all Thy saints
   below,
The depths of love divine.

Charles Wesley (1707–88)

490   S.M.

'He shall give you another Comforter'
John 14 v 16

1 Come, Holy Spirit, come,
Let Thy bright beams arise;
Dispel the sorrow from our minds,
The darkness from our eyes.

2 Cheer our desponding hearts,
Thou heavenly Paraclete;
Give us to lie with humble hope
At our Redeemer's feet.

3 Revive our drooping faith,
Our doubts and fears remove,
And kindle in our breasts the flame
Of never-dying love.

4 Convince us of our sin,
Then lead to Jesus' blood;
And to our wondering view reveal
The secret love of God.

5 'Tis Thine to cleanse the heart,
To sanctify the soul,
To pour fresh life in every part,
And new create the whole.

6 Dwell, therefore, in our hearts;
Our minds from bondage free:
Then shall we know, and praise, and
   love,
The Father, Son, and Thee.

Joseph Hart (1712–68) Altd

491   L.M.

'The fruit of the Spirit' Galatians 5 v 22

1 Come, Holy Spirit, God and Lord!
Be all Thy graces now outpoured
On the believer's mind and soul,
To strengthen, save, and make us
   whole.

2 Thou strong Defence, Thou holy
   Light,
Teach us to know our God aright,
And call Him Father from the heart;
The Word of life and truth impart;

3 That we may love no stranger's
   creed,
Nor follow other teacher's lead,
But Jesus for our Master own,
And put our trust in Him alone.

4 From every error keep us free;
Let none but Christ our Master be,
That we in living faith abide,
In Him with all our might confide.

Martin Luther (1483–1546)
Tr. Catherine Winkworth (1827–78)

492   11 10. 11 10

*'And they were all filled with the Holy
Ghost' Acts 2 v 4*

1 Come, Holy Spirit, like a dove
   descending,
Rest Thou upon us while we meet to
   pray;
Show us the Saviour, His great love
   revealing;
Lead us to Him, the Life, the Truth,
   the Way.

2 Come, Holy Spirit, every cloud
   dispelling;
   Fill us with gladness, through the
     Master's name:
   Bring to our memory words that He
     hath spoken;
   Then shall our tongues His
     wondrous grace proclaim.

3 Come, Holy Spirit, sent from God
   the Father,
   Thou Friend and Teacher, Comforter
   and Guide;
   Our thoughts directing, keep us
     close to Jesus,
   And in our hearts for evermore
     abide.

Robert Bruce

493   7 7.7 5

'Made partakers of the Holy Ghost'
Hebrews 6 v 4

1 Come to our poor nature's night
   With Thy blessèd inward light,
   Holy Ghost the Infinite,
   Comforter divine.

2 We are sinful – cleanse us, Lord;
   Sick and faint – Thy strength afford;
   Lost, until by Thee restored,
   Comforter divine.

3 Like the dew Thy peace distil;
   Guide, subdue our wayward will,
   Things of Christ unfolding still,
   Comforter divine.

4 Gentle, awesome, holy Guest,
   Make Thy temple in each breast;
   There Thy presence be confessed,
   Comforter divine.

5 With us, for us, intercede,
   And with voiceless groanings plead
   Our unutterable need,
   Comforter divine.

6 Search for us the depths of God;
   Upwards by the starry road
   Bear us to Thy high abode,
   Comforter divine.

George Rawson (1807–89)

494   L.M.

'The comfort of the Holy Ghost'
Acts 9 v 31

1 Dear Lord, and shall Thy Spirit rest
   In such a wretched heart as mine?
   Unworthy dwelling! glorious Guest!
   Favour astonishing, divine!

2 When sin prevails, and gloomy fear,
   And hope almost expires in night,
   Lord, can Thy Spirit then be here,
   Great Spring of comfort, life and
     light?

3 Sure the blest Comforter is nigh;
   'Tis He sustains my fainting heart;
   Else would my hopes for ever die,
   And every cheering ray depart.

4 When some kind promise glads my
     soul,
   Do I not find His healing voice,
   The tempest of my fears control,
   And bid my drooping powers
     rejoice?

5 Whene'er to call the Saviour mine,
   With ardent wish my heart aspires,
   Can it be less than power divine,
   Which animates these strong
     desires?

6 What less than Thy almighty word,
   Can raise my heart from earth and
     dust,
   And bid me cleave to Thee, my Lord,
   My Life, my Treasure and my Trust?

Anne Steele (1717–78)

495 L.M.

*'God hath revealed them unto us by his
Spirit' 1 Corinthians 2 v 10*

1 Descend from heaven, immortal
  Dove!
  Stoop down and take us on Thy
    wings,
  And mount and bear us far above
  The reach of these inferior things;

2 Beyond, beyond this lower sky,
  Up where eternal ages roll,
  Where solid pleasures never die,
  And fruits immortal feast the soul.

3 O for a sight, a pleasing sight,
  Of our Almighty Father's throne!
  There sits our Saviour crowned with
    light,
  Clothed in a body like our own.

4 Adoring saints around Him stand,
  And thrones and powers before Him
    fall;
  The God shines gracious through
    the Man,
  And sheds sweet glories on them all.

5 O what amazing joys they feel,
  While to their golden harps they
    sing,
  Do His commands with heavenly
    zeal,
  And spread the triumphs of their
    King!

6 When shall the day, dear Lord,
    appear,
  That I shall mount to dwell above,
  And stand and bow amongst them
    there,
  And see Thy face, and sing thy love.

Isaac Watts (1674–1748)

496 C.M.

*'If I depart, I will send him unto you'
John 16 v 7*

1 Enthroned on high, Almighty Lord,
  The Holy Ghost sent down;
  Fulfil in us Thy faithful word,
  And all Thy mercies crown.

2 Though on our heads no tongues of
    fire
  Their wondrous powers impart,
  Grant, Saviour, what we more
    desire,
  Thy Spirit in our heart.

3 Spirit of life and light and love,
  Thy heavenly influence give;
  Quicken our souls, born from above,
  In Christ that we may live.

4 To our benighted souls reveal
  The glories of His grace;
  And bring us where no clouds
    conceal
  The brightness of His face.

5 His love within us shed abroad,
  Life's ever-springing well:
  Till God in us, and we in God,
  In love eternal dwell.

Thomas Haweis (1733–1820)

497 8 8 8. D

*'I will send unto you ... the Spirit of
truth' John 15 v 26*

1 Father of everlasting grace,
  Thy goodness and Thy truth we
    praise,
  Thy goodness and Thy truth we
    prove;
  Thou hast, in honour of Thy Son,
  The gift unspeakable sent down,
  The Spirit of life, and power, and
    love.

2 Send us the Spirit of Thy Son,
   To make the depths of Godhead
      known,
   To make us share the life divine;
   Send Him the sprinked blood to
      apply,
   Send Him our souls to sanctify,
   And show and seal us ever Thine.

3 So shall we pray, and never cease,
   So shall we thankfully confess
   Thy wisdom, truth, and power, and
      love;
   With joy unspeakable adore,
   And bless and praise Thee evermore,
   And serve Thee as Thy hosts above.

4 Till, added to that heavenly choir,
   We raise our songs of triumph
      higher,
   And praise Thee in a bolder strain,
   Out-soar the first-born seraph's
      flight,
   And sing, with all our friends in
      light,
   Thy everlasting love to man.

Charles Wesley (1707–88)

498   77.77

*'Who also hath given unto us the earnest
of the Spirit' 2 Corinthians 5 v 5*

1 Gracious Spirit, Dove divine,
   Let Thy light within me shine;
   All my guilty fears remove,
   Fill me full of heaven and love.

2 Speak Thy pardoning grace to me,
   Set the burdened sinner free;
   Lead me to the Lamb of God,
   Wash me in His precious blood.

3 Life and peace to me impart,
   Seal salvation on my heart;
   Breathe Thyself into my breast,
   Earnest of immortal rest.

4 Let me never from Thee stray,
   Keep me in the narrow way;
   Fill my soul with joy divine,
   Keep me, Lord, for ever Thine.

John Stocker 1777

499   87.87

*'For he dwelleth with you, and shall be
in you' John 14 v 17*

1 Holy Ghost, dispel our sadness,
   Pierce the clouds of sinful night:
   Come, Thou source of sweetest
      gladness,
   Breathe Thy life, and spread Thy
      light.

2 From the height which knows no
      measure,
   As a gracious shower descend;
   Bringing down the richest treasure
   Man can wish or God can send.

3 Author of the new creation,
   Come, with unction and with power;
   Make our hearts Thy habitation,
   On our souls Thy graces shower.

4 Come, Thou best of all donations
   God can give, or we implore;
   Having Thy sweet consolations
   We need wish for nothing more.

Paul Gerhardt (1607–76)
Tr. John Christian Jacobi (1670–1750)
Alt. Augustus Montague Toplady (1740–78)

500   77.77

*'Strengthened with might by his Spirit in
the inner man' Ephesians 3 v 16*

1 Holy Spirit, truth divine,
   Dawn upon this soul of mine;
   Word of God, and inward light,
   Wake my spirit, clear my sight.

2 Holy Spirit, love divine,
   Glow within this heart of mine;
   Kindle every high desire;
   Perish self in Thy pure fire.

3 Holy Spirit, power divine,
Fill and nerve this will of mine;
By Thee may I strongly live,
Bravely bear, and nobly strive.

4 Holy Spirit, right divine,
King within my conscience reign;
Be my Lord, and I shall be
Firmly bound, for ever free.

5 Holy Spirit, peace divine,
Still this restless heart of mine;
Speak to calm this tossing sea,
Stayed in Thy tranquillity.

6 Holy Spirit, joy divine,
Gladden Thou this heart of mine;
In the desert ways I'll sing:
Spring, O Well, for ever spring!

Samuel Longfellow (1819–92)

501   L.M.

*'He shall give you another Comforter,
that he may abide with you for ever'*
John 14 v 16

1 Jesus, we on the word depend
Spoken by Thee while present here:
The Father in My name shall send
The Holy Ghost, the Comforter.

2 That promise made to Adam's race,
Now, Lord, in us, even us, fulfil;
And give the Spirit of Thy grace,
To teach us all Thy perfect will.

3 That heavenly Teacher of mankind,
That Guide infallible impart,
To bring Thy sayings to our mind,
And write them on our faithful
    heart.

4 He only can the words apply
Through which we endless life
    possess;
And deal to each his legacy,
His Lord's unutterable peace.

5 That peace of God, that peace of
    Thine,
O might He now to us bring in,
And fill our souls with power divine,
And make an end of fear and sin.

6 The length and breadth of love
    reveal,
The height and depth of Deity;
And all the sons of glory seal,
And change, and make us all like
    Thee.

Charles Wesley (1707–88)

502   S.M.

'Wait for the promise of the Father'
Acts 1 v 4

1 Lord God the Holy Ghost,
In this accepted hour,
As on the day of Pentecost,
Descend in all thy power.

2 We meet with one accord
In our appointed place,
And wait the promise of our Lord,
The Spirit of all grace.

3 Like mighty rushing wind
Upon the waves beneath,
Move with one impulse every mind,
One soul, one feeling, breathe.

4 The young, the old inspire
With wisdom from above;
And give us hearts and tongues of
    fire,
To pray and praise and love.

5 Spirit of light, explore,
And chase our gloom away,
With luster shining more and more
Unto the perfect day.

6 Spirit of truth, be Thou
In life and death our Guide;
O Spirit of adoption, now
May we be sanctified.

James Montgomery (1771–1854)

503 C.M.

*'Awake, O north wind; and come, thou
south; blow upon my garden'*
Song of Solomon 4 v 16

1 O Holy Ghost, Thy people bless
Who long to feel Thy might,
And fain would grow in holiness,
As children of the light.

2 To Thee we bring, who art the Lord,
Ourselves to be Thy throne;
Let every thought and deed and word
Thy pure dominion own.

3 Life-giving Spirit, o'er us move,
As on the formless deep;
Give life and order, light and love,
Where now is death or sleep.

4 Great Gift of our ascended King,
His saving truth reveal;
Our tongues inspire His praise to
sing,
Our hearts His love to feel.

5 O Holy Ghost, of sevenfold might,
All graces come from Thee;
Grant us to know and serve aright
One God in Persons Three.

Henry Williams Baker (1821–77)

504 L.M.

*'When he, the Spirit of truth is come, he
will guide you into all truth' John 16 v 13*

1 O Holy Spirit, come,
And Jesus' love declare:
O tell us of our heavenly home,
And guide us safely there.

2 Our unbelief remove
By Thine almighty breath:
O work the wondrous work of love,
The mighty work of faith.

3 Come with resistless power,
Come with almighty grace,
Come with the long-expected shower,
And fall upon this place.

Oswald Allen (1816–78)

505 L.M.

'I will pour out my spirit upon all flesh'
Joel 2 v 28

1 O Spirt of the living God,
In all Thy plenitude of grace,
Where'er the foot of man hath trod,
Descend on our apostate race.

2 Give tongues of fire and hearts of
love
To preach the reconciling word;
Give power and unction from above,
Whene'er the joyful sound is heard.

3 Be darkness, at Thy coming, light;
Confusion, order in Thy path;
Souls without strength inspire with
might;
Bid mercy triumph over wrath.

4 O Spirit of the Lord, prepare
All the round earth her God to meet;
Breathe Thou abroad like morning
air,
Till hearts of stone begin to beat.

5 Baptise the nations; far and nigh
The triumphs of the cross record;
The name of Jesus glorify
Till every kindred call Him Lord.

6 God from eternity hath willed
All flesh shall His salvation see;
So be the Father's love fulfilled,
The Saviour's sufferings crowned
through Thee.

James Montgomery (1771–1854)

506 8 6. 8 4

*'I will pray the Father, and he shall give
you another Comforter' John 14 v 16*

1 Our blest Redeemer, ere He breathed
His tender last farewell,
A Guide, a Comforter, bequeathed
With us to dwell.

2 He came in semblance of a dove,
  With sheltering wings outspread,
  The holy balm of peace and love
  On earth to shed.

3 He came in tongues of living flame,
  To teach, convince, subdue;
  All-powerful as the wind He came,
  As viewless too.

4 He came sweet influence to impart,
  A gracious, willing Guest,
  While He can find one humble heart
  Wherein to rest.

5 And His that gentle voice we hear,
  Soft as the breath of even,
  That checks each fault, that calms
      each fear,
  And speaks of heaven.

6 And every virtue we possess,
  And every conquest won,
  And every thought of holiness,
  Are His alone.

7 Spirit of purity and grace,
  Our weakness, pitying, see:
  O make our hearts Thy dwelling-place,
  And worthier Thee.

Henriette Auber (1773–1862)

507   C.M.

*'I will pray the Father, and he shall give
you another Comforter' John 14 v 16*

1 Spirit divine, attend our prayers,
  And make our hearts Thy home;
  Descend with all Thy gracious
      powers,
  O come, great Spirit, come!

2 Come as the light, to us reveal
  Our emptiness and woe;
  And lead us in those paths of life
  Where all the righteous go.

3 Come as the fire, and purge our
      hearts
  Like sacrificial flame;
  Let our whole soul an offering be
  To our Redeemer's name.

4 Come as the dew, and sweetly bless
  This consecrated hour;
  May barrenness rejoice to own
  Thy fertilizing power.

5 Come as the dove, and spread Thy
      wings,
  The wings of peaceful love;
  And let Thy church on earth become
  Blest as the church above.

6 Come as the wind, with rushing
      sound
  And Pentecostal grace;
  That all of woman born may see
  The glory of Thy face.

7 Spirit divine, attend our prayers;
  Make a lost world Thy home;
  Descend with all Thy gracious
      powers,
  O come, great Spirit, come!

Andrew Reed (1787–1862)

508   D.S.M.

'The Spirit of truth' John 16 v 13

1 Spirit of faith, come down,
  Reveal the things of God;
  And make to us the Godhead
      known,
  And witness with the blood.
  'Tis Thine the blood to apply,
  And give us eyes to see
  Who did for guilty sinners die
  Hath surely died for me.

2 No man can truly say
  That Jesus is the Lord,
  Unless Thou take the veil away,
  And breathe the living word;
  Then, only then, we feel
  Our interest in His blood,
  And cry, with joy unspeakable:
  Thou art my Lord, my God!

3 O that the world might know
   The all-atoning Lamb!
   Spirit of faith, descend, and show
   The virtue of His name;
   The grace which all may find,
   The saving power impart;
   And testify to all mankind,
   And speak in every heart.

4 Inspire the living faith,
   Which whosoe'er receives,
   The witness in himself he hath,
   And consciously believes;
   The faith that conquers all,
   And doth the mountain move,
   And saves whoe'er on Jesus call,
   And perfects them in love.

   Charles Wesley (1707–88)

509　　10 10. 10 10

'Grace to help in time of need'
Hebrews 4 v 16

1 Spirit of God, descend upon my
   heart;
   Wean it from earth, through all its
   pulses move;
   Stoop to my weakness, mighty as
   Thou art,
   And make me love Thee as I ought to
   love.

2 Hast Thou not bid me love Thee,
   God and King –
   All, all Thine own, soul, heart and
   strength and mind?
   I see Thy cross – there teach my
   heart to cling:
   O let me seek Thee, and O let me
   find!

3 Teach me to feel that Thou art
   always nigh;
   Teach me the struggles of the soul to
   bear,
   To check the rising doubt, the rebel
   sigh;
   Teach me the patience of
   unanswered prayer.

4 Teach me to love Thee as Thine
   angels love,
   One holy passion filling all my
   frame –
   The baptism of the heaven-descended
   Dove,
   My heart an altar, and Thy love the
   flame.

   George Croly (1780–1860)

510　　L.M.

'I will put my spirit within you'
Ezekiel 36 v 27

1 Spirit of God, that moved of old
   Upon the waters' darkened face,
   Come, when our faithless hearts are
   cold,
   And stir them with an inward grace.

2 Thou who art power and peace
   combined,
   All highest strength, all purest love,
   The rushing of the mighty wind,
   The brooding of the gentle dove,

3 Come, give us still Thy powerful aid,
   And urge us on, and make us Thine;
   Nor leave the hearts that once were
   made
   Fit temples for Thy grace divine;

4 Nor let us quench Thy sevenfold
   light;
   But still with softest breathings stir
   Our wayward souls, and lead us
   right,
   O Holy Ghost, the Comforter.

   Cecil Frances Alexander (1818–95)

511
C.M.

'Ye are sealed with that holy Spirit of promise' Ephesians 1 v 13

1 Why should the children of a King
Go mourning all their days?
Great Comforter, descend and bring
Some tokens of Thy grace.

2 Dost Thou not dwell in all the saints,
And seal the heirs of heaven?
When wilt Thou banish my
complaints,
And show my sins forgiven?

3 Assure my conscience of her part
In the Redeemer's blood,
And bear Thy witness with my heart
That I am born of God.

4 Thou art the earnest of His love,
The pledge of joys to come,
And Thy soft wings, celestial Dove,
Will safe convey me home.

Isaac Watts (1674–1748)

THE WORD OF GOD

512 C.M.

'The seed is the word of God' Luke 8 v 11

1 Almighty God, Thy Word is cast
Like seed into the ground;
Now let the dew of heaven descend,
And righteous fruits abound.

2 Let not the foe of Christ and man
This holy seed remove,
But give it root in every heart
To bring forth fruits of love.

3 Let not the world's deceitful cares
The rising plant destroy,
But let it yield an hundredfold
The fruits of peace and joy.

4 Oft as the precious seed is sown,
Thy quickening grace bestow,
That all whose souls the truth
    receive
Its saving power may know.

John Cawood (1775–1852)

513 6 4. 6 4. D

'Jesus said unto them, I am the bread of life' John 6 v 35

1 Break Thou the Bread of Life,
Dear Lord, to me,
As Thou didst break the bread
Beside the sea.
Beyond the sacred page
I seek Thee, Lord;
My spirit longs for Thee,
O living Word!

2 Thou art the Bread of Life,
O Lord, to me,
Thy holy Word the truth
That saveth me.
Give me to eat and live
With Thee above,
Teach me to love Thy truth,
For Thou art love.

3 O send Thy Spirit, Lord,
Now unto me,
That He may touch my eyes,
And make me see.
Show me the truth concealed
Within Thy Word,
That in Thy Book revealed
I see Thee, Lord.

4 Bless thou the Bread of Life
To me, to me,
As thou didst bless the loaves
By Galilee;
Then shall all bondage cease,
All fetters fall;
And I shall find my peace,
My All in all.

Mary Artemisia Lathbury (1841–1913)
v 2 Alexander Groves (1842–1909)

514 C.M.

'The law of thy mouth is better unto me than thousands of gold and silver' Psalm 119 v 72

1 Father of mercies, in Thy Word
What endless glory shines!
For ever be Thy name adored
For these celestial lines.

2 Here may the blind and hungry
   come,
   And light and food receive;
   Here shall the lowliest guest have
   room,
   And taste and see and live.

3 Here springs of consolation rise
   To cheer the fainting mind,
   And thirsting souls receive supplies,
   And sweet refreshment find.

4 Here the Redeemer's welcome voice
   Spreads heavenly peace around;
   And life and everlasting joys
   Attend the blissful sound.

5 O may these heavenly pages be
   My ever dear delight;
   And still new beauties may I see,
   And still increasing light!

6 Divine Instructor, gracious Lord,
   Be Thou for ever near;
   Teach me to love Thy sacred Word,
   And view my Saviour there.

Anne Steele (1717–78)

515   8 7. 8 7. D

'And God said' Genesis 1 v 3

1 God hath spoken by His prophets,
   Spoken His unchanging Word;
   Each from age to age proclaiming
   God the One, the righteous Lord!
   Mid the world's despair and turmoil
   One firm anchor holding fast,
   God is on His throne eternal,
   He alone the first and last.

2 God hath spoken by Christ Jesus,
   Christ, the everlasting Son,
   Brightness of the Father's glory,
   With the Father ever one;
   Spoken by the Word Incarnate,
   God of God ere time began,
   Light of Light, to earth descending
   Man, revealing God to man.

3 God yet speaketh by His Spirit
   Speaking to the hearts of men,
   In the age-long Word declaring
   God's own message, now as then.
   Through the rise and fall of nations
   One sure faith yet standeth fast:
   God abides, His Word unchanging,
   God alone the first and last.

© 1953, Renewed 1981   *George Wallace Briggs (1875–1959)*
Hope Publishing Company

516   C.M.

'Thy word is a lamp unto my feet'
Psalm 119 v 105

1 How precious is the Book divine,
   By inspiration given!
   Bright as a lamp its doctrines shine,
   To guide our souls to heaven.

2 Its light, descending from above,
   Our gloomy world to cheer,
   Displays a Saviour's boundless love,
   And brings His glories near.

3 It shows to man his wandering ways,
   And where his feet have trod;
   And brings to view the matchless
   grace
   Of a forgiving God.

4 When once it penetrates the mind
   It conquers every sin;
   The enlightened soul begins to find
   The path of peace divine.

5 It sweetly cheers our drooping hearts,
   In this dark vale of tears;
   Life, light, and joy it still imparts,
   And quells our rising fears.

6 O'er all the strait and narrow way
   Its radiant beams are cast;
   A light whose ever-cheering ray
   Grows brightest at the last.

7 This lamp through all the tedious
   night
   Of life shall guide our way,
   Till we behold the clearer light
   Of an eternal day.

John Fawcett (1739–1817)

517

88.88.88

'All Scripture is given by inspiration of God, and is profitable' 2 Timothy 3 v 16

1 Inspirer of the ancient seers,
  Who wrote from Thee the sacred
      page,
  The same through all succeeding
      years,
  To us, in our degenerate age,
  The Spirit of Thy Word impart,
  And breathe the life into our heart.

2 While now Thine oracles we read,
  With earnest prayer and strong
      desire,
  O let Thy Spirit from Thee proceed,
  Our souls to awaken and inspire,
  Our weakness help, our darkness
      chase,
  And guide us by the light of grace!

3 Whene'er in error's paths we rove,
  The living God through sin forsake,
  Our conscience by Thy Word
      reprove,
  Convince and bring the wanderers
      back,
  Deep wounded by Thy Spirit's
      sword,
  And then by Gilead's balm restored.

4 The sacred lessons of Thy grace,
  Transmitted through Thy Word,
      repeat,
  And train us up in all Thy ways
  To make us in Thy will complete;
  Fulfil Thy love's redeeming plan,
  And bring us to a perfect man.

5 Furnished out of Thy treasury,
  O may we always ready stand
  To help the souls redeemed by Thee,
  In what their various states demand;
  To teach, convince, correct, reprove,
  And build them up in holiest love!

Charles Wesley (1707–88)

518

C.M.

Thy word is a lamp unto my feet'
Psalm 119 v 105

1 Lamp of our feet, whereby we trace
  Our path when wont to stray;
  Stream from the fount of heavenly
      grace,
  Brook by the traveller's way;

2 Bread of our souls, whereon we feed;
  True manna from on high;
  Our guide and chart, wherein we
      read
  Of realms beyond the sky;

3 Pillar of fire, through watches dark,
  And radiant cloud by day;
  When waves would whelm our
      tossing bark,
  Our anchor and our stay;

4 Word of the ever-living God,
  Will of His glorious Son –
  Without Thee how could earth be trod,
  Or heaven itself be won?

5 Lord, grant us all aright to learn
  The wisdom it imparts,
  And to its heavenly teaching turn
  With simple, childlike hearts.

Bernard Barton (1784–1849) Altd

519

66.66

'The word of the Lord which liveth and abideth for ever' 1 Peter 1 v 23

1 Lord, Thy Word abideth,
  And our footsteps guideth;
  Who its truth believeth
  Light and joy receiveth.

2 When our foes are near us,
  Then Thy Word doth cheer us,
  Word of consolation,
  Meassage of salvation.

3 When the storms are o'er us,
  And dark clouds before us,
  Then its light directeth,
  And our way protecteth.

4 Who can tell the pleasure,
Who recount the treasure,
By Thy Word imparted,
To the simple-hearted?

5 Word of mercy, giving
Succour to the living;
Word of life, supplying
Comfort to the dying!

6 O that we, discerning
Its most holy learning,
Lord, may love and fear Thee,
Evermore be near Thee!

Henry Williams Baker (1821–77)

520   L.M.

'God hath revealed them unto us by his
Spirit' 1 Corinthians 2 v 10

1 O God, who didst Thy will unfold
In wondrous ways to saints of old,
By dream, by oracle, or seer,
Wilt Thou not still Thy people hear?

2 What though no answering voice is
heard?
Thine oracles, the written Word,
Counsel and guidance still impart,
Responsive to the upright heart.

3 What though no more by dreams is
shown
That future things to God are
known?
Enough the promises reveal:
Wisdom and love the rest conceal.

4 Faith asks no signal from the skies
To show that prayers accepted rise;
Our Priest is in the holy place,
And answers from the throne of grace.

5 No need of prophets to inquire:
The Sun is risen, the stars retire.
The Comforter is come, and sheds
His holy unction on our heads.

6 Lord, with this grace our hearts
inspire;
Answer our sacrifice with fire,
And by Thy mighty acts declare
Thou art the God who hearest
prayer.

Josiah Conder (1789–1855)

521   7 6. 7 6. D

'Thy word is a lamp unto my feet'
Psalm 119 v 105

1 O Word of God incarnate,
O Wisdom from on high,
O Truth unchanged, unchanging,
O Light of our dark sky,
We praise Thee for the radiance
That from the hallowed page,
A lantern to our footsteps,
Shines on from age to age.

2 The church from her dear Master
Received the gift divine,
And still that light she lifteth,
O'er all the earth to shine.
It is the golden casket
Where gems of truth are stored;
It is the heaven-drawn picture
Of Christ, the living Word.

3 It floateth like a banner
Before God's host unfurled;
It shineth like a beacon
Above the darkling world;
It is the chart and compass
That, o'er life's surging sea,
'Mid mists and rocks and
quicksands
Still guides, O Christ, to Thee.

4 O make Thy church, dear Saviour,
A lamp of burnished gold,
To bear before the nations
Thy true light, as of old.
O teach Thy wandering pilgrims
By this their path to trace,
Till, clouds and darkness ended,
They see Thee face to face.

William Walsham How (1823–97)

522 L.M.

Based on Psalm 19

1 The heavens declare Thy glory, Lord,
   In every star Thy wisdom shines;
   But when our eyes behold Thy Word,
   We read Thy name in fairer lines.

2 The rolling sun, the changing light,
   And night and day, Thy power
      confess;
   But the blest volume Thou hast writ
   Reveals Thy justice and Thy grace.

3 Sun, moon, and stars convey Thy
      praise
   Round the whole earth, and never
      stand:
   So when Thy truth began its race,
   It touched and glanced on every
      land.

4 Nor shall Thy spreading gospel rest
   Till through the world Thy truth has
      run;
   Till Christ has all the nations blest,
   That see the light, or feel the sun.

5 Great Sun of righteousness, arise,
   Bless the dark world with heavenly
      light:
   Thy gospel makes the simple wise;
   Thy laws are pure, Thy judgements
      right.

6 Thy noblest wonders here we view,
   In souls renewed, and sins forgiven:
   Lord, cleanse my sins, my soul
      renew,
   And make Thy Word my guide to
      heaven.

Isaac Watts (1674–1748)

523 C.M.

'The entrance of thy words giveth light'
Psalm 119 v 130

1 The Spirit breathes upon the Word,
   And brings the truth to sight;
   Precepts and promises afford
   A sanctifying light.

2 A glory gilds the sacred page,
   Majestic, like the sun;
   It gives a light to every age;
   It gives, but borrows none.

3 The hand that gave it still supplies
   The gracious light and heat;
   Its truths upon the nations rise;
   They rise, but never set.

4 Let everlasting thanks be Thine,
   For such a bright display,
   As makes a world of darkness shine
   With beams of heavenly day.

5 My soul rejoices to pursue
   The steps of Him I love,
   Till glory breaks upon my view,
   In brighter worlds above.

William Cowper (1731–1800)

524 8 8. 8 8. 8 8.

'His delight is in the law of the LORD'
Psalm 1 v 2

1 When quiet in my house I sit,
   Thy Book be my companion still,
   My joy Thy sayings to repeat,
   Talk o'er the records of Thy will,
   And search the oracles divine,
   Till every heartfelt word be mine.

2 O may the gracious words divine
   Subject of all my converse be!
   So will the Lord His follower join,
   And walk and talk Himself with me;
   So shall my heart His presence
      prove,
   And burn with everlasting love.

3 Oft as I lay me down to rest,
  O may the reconciling word
  Sweetly compose my weary breast!
  While, on the bosom of my Lord,
  I sink in blissful dreams away,
  And visions of eternal day.

4 Rising to sing my Saviour's praise,
  Thee may I publish all day long;
  And let Thy precious word of grace
  Flow from my heart, and fill my
    tongue;
  Fill all my life with purest love,
  And join me to the Church above.

Charles Wesley (1707–88)

525 C.M.

'He hath made with me an everlasting covenant' 2 Samuel 23 v 5

1 Come, saints, and sing in sweet
    accord,
  With solemn pleasure tell
  The cov'nant made with David's
    Lord,
  In all things ordered well.

2 This cov'nant stood ere time began,
  That God with man might dwell;
  Eternal wisdom drew the plan,
  In all things ordered well.

3 This cov'nant, O believer, stands,
  Thy rising fears to quell;
  Sealed by the Surety's bleeding
    hands,
  In all things ordered well.

4 'Twas made with Jesus, for His
    bride,
  Before the sinner fell;
  'Twas signed, and sealed, and
    ratified,
  In all things ordered well.

5 In glory, soon, with Christ their King
  His saints shall surely dwell,
  And this blest cov'nant ever sing,
  In all things ordered well.

John Kent (1766–1843)

526 10 10. 10 10

'The faithful God, which keepeth covenant and mercy with them that love him' Deuteronomy 7 v 9

1 Far before time, beyond creation's
    dawn,
  Before the sun and moon and stars
    were born,
  Salvation's way for sinners lost,
    undone
  Was counselled forth by God the
    Three in One.

2 A store of grace unlimited was laid
  In Jesus Christ before the seas were
    made;
  And precious cov'nant mercies did
    abound
  In floods of blessing all the world
    around.

3 The trumpet sounds the note of glad
    release
  On Calvary, by God's atoning grace:
  Glad hymns of praise in every
    tongue shall be
  For Jesu's blood and death that set
    us free.

Peter Jones (1775–1845)
© The Translator   Tr. Edmund Tudor Owen (b.1935)

527   87.87

'Whose goings forth have been from of old' Micah 5 v 2

1 Far beyond all comprehension
  Is Jehovah's covenant love:
  Who can fathom its dimension
  Or its unknown limits prove?

2 Ere the earth upon its basis
  By creating power was built.
  His designs were wise and gracious
  For removing human guilt.

3 He displayed His grand intention
  On the mount of Calvary.
  When He died for our redemption,
  Lifted high upon the tree.

4 O, how sweet to view the flowing
  Of His soul-redeeming blood!
  With divine assurance, knowing
  That it made my peace with God.

5 Freely Thou wilt bring to heaven
  All Thy chosen, ransomed race.
  Who to Thee, their Head, were given
  In the covenant of grace.

Richard Lee c.1794

528   87.87.47

'According as he hath chosen us in him before the foundation of the world' Ephesians 1 v 4

1 Father, 'twas Thy love that knew us
  Earth's foundation long before;
  That same love to Jesus drew us
  By its sweet constraining power,
  And will keep us
  Safely now, and evermore.

2 Pause, my soul, adore and wonder!
  Ask, O why such love to me?
  Grace hath put me in the number
  Of the Saviour's family;
  Hallelujah!
  Thanks, eternal thanks, to Thee!

3 Since that love had no beginning,
  And shall never, never cease;
  Keep, O keep me, Lord, from sinning,
  Guide me in the way of peace!
  Make me walk in
  All the paths of holiness.

4 God of love, our souls adore Thee!
  We would still Thy grace proclaim,
  Till we cast our crowns before Thee,
  And in glory praise Thy name:
  Hallelujah
  Be to God and to the Lamb!

vv 1 & 4 James George Deck (1802–84)
vv 2 & 3 Anonymous

529   L.M.

'To testify the gospel of the grace of God' Acts 20 v 24

1 God, in the gospel of His Son,
  Makes His eternal counsels known;
  Where love in all its glory shines,
  And truth is drawn in fairest lines.

2 Here sinners of a humble frame
  May taste His grace, and learn His name;
  May read, in characters of blood,
  The wisdom, power, and grace of God.

3 The prisoner here may break his chains;
  The weary rest from all his pains;
  The captive feel his bondage cease;
  The mourner find the way of peace.

4 Here faith reveals to mortal eyes
  A brighter world beyond the skies;
  Here shines the light which guides our way
  From earth to realms of endless day.

5 O grant us grace, Almighty Lord,
  To read and mark Thy holy Word;
  Its truths with meekness to receive,
  And by its holy precepts live.

Benjamin Beddome (1717–95)
and Thomas Cotterill (1779–1823)

530 11 10. 11 10

'An everlasting covenant'
2 Samuel 23 v 5

1 God of the covenant, Triune
   Jehovah,
   Marvels of mercy adoring we see;
   Seeker of souls, in the counsels
   eternal
   Binding Thy lost ones for ever to
   Thee.

2 Not now by words bringing death to
   transgressors,
   Grace unto life the new covenant
   brings,
   Jesus our Surety, our Kinsman-
   Redeemer,
   Round us the robe of His
   righteousness flings.

3 Blessings on blessings through ages
   unending,
   Covenant fulness in glorious flood;
   Ours is a hope which no mortal can
   measure,
   Brought in by Jesus and sealed in
   His blood.

4 God of the covenant – changeless,
   eternal,
   Father, Son, Spirit in blessing agree;
   Thine be the glory, our weakness
   confessing,
   Triune Jehovah, we rest upon Thee.

© Copyright Control   *Jessie F. Webb (1866–1964)*

531 L.M.

'According to his mercy he saved us'
Titus 3 v 5

1 Now to the power of God supreme
   Be everlasting honours given;
   He saves from hell – we bless His
   name;
   He calls our wandering feet to
   heaven.

2 Not for our duties or deserts,
   But of His own abounding grace
   He works salvation in our hearts,
   And forms a people for His praise.

3 'Twas His own purpose that begun
   To rescue rebels doomed to die;
   He gave us grace in Christ His Son
   Before He spread the starry sky.

4 Jesus the Lord appears at last,
   And makes His Father's counsels
   known;
   Declares the great transactions past,
   And brings immortal blessings
   down.

5 He dies – and in that dreadful night
   Did all the powers of hell destroy;
   Rising, He brought our heaven to
   light,
   And took possession of the joy.

Isaac Watts (1674–1748)

532 L.M.

'That he might be just, and the justifier
of him which believeth in Jesus'
Romans 3 v 26

1 O Love, beyond conception great,
   That formed the vast stupendous
   plan,
   Where all divine perfections meet,
   To reconcile rebellious man.

2 There wisdom shines in fullest blaze
   And justice all her rights maintains;
   Astonished angels stoop to gaze,
   While mercy o'er the guilty reigns.

3 Yes, mercy reigns, and justice too;
   In Christ, they both harmonious
   meet;
   He paid to justice all its due,
   And now he fills the mercy-seat.

4 Such are the wonders of our God,
   And the amazing depths of grace,
   To save from wrath's vindictive rod,
   The chosen sons of Adam's race.

William Tucker (1731–1814)

533   87.87.47

*'Where sin abounded, grace did much
more abound' Romans 5 v 20*

1 Sovereign grace o'er sin abounding,
   Ransomed souls, the tidings swell;
   'Tis a deep that knows no sounding;
   Who its breadth or length can tell?
   On its glories
   Let my soul for ever dwell.

2 What from Christ that soul shall
          sever,
   Bound by everlasting bands?
   Once in Him, in Him for ever,
   Thus the eternal cov'nant stands:
   None shall pluck thee
   From the strength of Israel's hands.

3 Heirs of God, joint-heirs with Jesus,
   Long ere time its race begun;
   To His name eternal praises;
   O what wonders He hath done!
   One with Jesus,
   By eternal union one.

4 On such love, my soul, still ponder,
   Love so great, so rich and free;
   Say, while lost in holy wonder,
   'Why, O Lord, such love to me?'
   Hallelujah!
   Grace shall reign eternally.

                    John Kent (1766–1843)

534   C.M.

*'For by grace are ye saved'
Ephesians 2 v 8*

1 Amazing grace! how sweet the
          sound,
   That saved a wretch like me!
   I once was lost, but now am found;
   Was blind but now I see.

2 'Twas grace that taught my heart to
          fear,
   And grace my fears relieved;
   How precious did that grace appear
   The hour I first believed!

3 Through many dangers, toils and
          snares
   I have already come;
   'Tis grace has brought me safe thus
          far,
   And grace will lead me home.

4 The Lord has promised good to me,
   His Word my hope secures;
   He will my shield and portion be
   As long as life endures.

5 Yes, when this flesh and heart shall fail,
   And mortal life shall cease,
   I shall possess within the veil
   A life of joy and peace.

6 When I've been there a thousand
          years,
   Bright shining as the sun,
   I've no less days to sing God's praise
   Than when I first begun.

                    John Newton (1725–1807)

535   C.M.

*'Let the inhabitants of the rock sing'
Isaiah 42 v 11*

1 Arise, my soul, my joyful powers,
   And triumph in my God;
   Awake, my voice, and loud proclaim
   His glorious grace abroad.

2 He raised me from the depths of sin,
   The gates of gaping hell,
   And fixed my standing more secure
   Than 'twas before I fell.

3 The arms of everlasting love
   Beneath my soul He placed;
   And on the Rock of Ages set
   My slippery footsteps fast.

4 The city of my blest abode
   Is walled around with grace;
   Salvation for a bulwark stands
   To shield the sacred place.

5 Satan may vent His sharpest spite,
   And all his legions roar:
   Almighty mercy guards my life,
   And bounds his raging power.

6 Arise, my soul, awake, my voice,
And tunes of pleasure sing;
Loud hallelujahs shall address
My Saviour and my King.

Isaac Watts (1674-1748)

536 C.M.

'*Called, and chosen, and faithful*'
Revelation 17 v 14

1 Chosen of God ere time begun,
His sovereignty we prove;
With Christ our Head accounted one
In bonds of covenant love!

2 Chosen as sons and heirs of God,
Our names are there in heaven;
Chosen to life through Jesus' blood,
Our sins are all forgiven.

3 Chosen as witnesses, we speak
Of all our God has done;
Chosen to holiness, we seek
Our all in Christ alone.

4 Chosen to run the heavenly race,
The glorious prize to gain;
Chosen to persevere through grace,
We shall the crown obtain.

5 Thus chosen, we shall surely meet
On Zion's heights above;
And stand before the Lord complete,
Unblameable in love.

David Denham (1791–1848)

537 S.M.

'*By grace ye are saved*' Ephesians 2 v 5

1 Grace, 'tis a charming sound,
Harmonious to the ear;
Heaven with the echo shall resound,
And all the earth shall hear.

2 Grace first contrived a way
To save rebellious man;
And all the steps that grace display,
Which drew the wondrous plan.

3 Grace first inscribed my name
In God's eternal book;
'Twas grace that gave me to the
Lamb,
Who all my sorrows took.

4 Grace turned my wandering feet
To tread the heavenly road;
And new supplies each hour I meet,
While pressing on to God.

5 Grace taught my soul to pray,
And made my eyes o'erflow;
'Tis grace that kept me to this day,
And will not let me go.

6 Grace all the work shall crown,
Through everlasting days;
It lays in heaven the topmost stone,
And well deserves the praise.

vv 1,2,4 & 6, Philip Doddridge (1702–51)
vv 3 & 5, Augustus Montague Toplady (1740–78)

538 S.M.

'*Christ Jesus … wisdom, and righteousness, and sanctification, and redemption*'
1 Corinthians 1 v 30

1 How heavy is the night
That hangs upon our eyes,
Till Christ, with His reviving light,
Over our souls arise!

2 Our guilty spirits dread
To meet the wrath of heaven;
But in His righteousness arrayed,
We see our sins forgiven.

3 Unholy and impure
Are all our thoughts and ways:
His hands infected nature cure
With sanctifying grace.

4 The powers of hell agree
To hold our souls in vain;
He sets the sons of bondage free,
And breaks the accursed chain.

5 Lord, we adore Thy ways
  To bring us near to God,
  Thy sovereign power, Thy healing
     grace,
  And Thine atoning blood.

Isaac Watts (1674–1748)

539   D.C.M.

'Called ... unto holiness'
1 Thessalonians 4 v 7

1 How vast the benefits divine
  Which we in Christ possess!
  We are redeemed from sin and
     shame,
  And called to holiness.
  'Tis not for works that we have
     done,
  These all to Him we owe;
  But He of His electing love
  Salvation doth bestow.

2 To Thee, O Lord, alone is due
  All glory and renown;
  Aught to ourselves we dare not take,
  Or rob Thee of Thy crown.
  Thou wast Thyself our surety
  In God's redemption plan;
  In Thee His grace was given us,
  Long ere the world began.

3 Safe in the arms of sovereign love
  We ever shall remain;
  Nor shall the rage of earth or hell
  Make Thy sure counsel vain.
  Not one of all the chosen race
  But shall to heaven attain;
  Here they will share abounding
     grace,
  And there with Jesus reign.

Augustus Montague Toplady (1740–78)
Alt. Dewey Westra 1931

540   10 10. 10 6

'We love him, because he first loved us.'
1 John 4 v 19

1 I sought the Lord, and afterward I
     knew,
  He moved my soul to seek Him seek-
     ing me;
  It was not that I found, O Saviour
     true;
  For I was found by Thee.

2 Thou didst reach forth Thy hand and
     mine enfold;
  I walked, and sank not, on the
     storm-vexed sea;
  'Twas not so much that I on Thee
     took hold,
  As Thou, dear Lord, on me.

3 I find, I walk, I love, but O, the
     whole
  Of love is but my answer, Lord, to
     Thee!
  For long beforehand Thou didst
     bless my soul;
  And ever hast loved me.

The Pilgrim Hymnal 1904

541   8 8. 8 8. 8 8

'If any man ... open the door, I will come
in to him' Revelation 3 v 20

1 Lift up your heads, ye mighty gates,
  Behold, the King of glory waits!
  The King of kings is drawing near,
  The Saviour of the world is here;
  Life and salvation doth He bring,
  Wherefore rejoice and gladly sing.

2 The Lord is just, a helper tried,
  Mercy is ever at His side;
  His kingly crown is holiness;
  His sceptre, pity in distress;
  The end of all our woe He brings,
  Wherefore the earth is glad and
     sings.

3 O blest the land, the city blest,
  Where Christ the ruler is confessed!
  O happy hearts and happy homes,
  To whom this King in triumph
    comes!
  The cloudless Sun of joy He is,
  Who bringeth pure delight and bliss.

4 Fling wide the portals of your heart,
  Make it a temple set apart
  From earthly use, for heaven's
    employ,
  Adorned with prayer, and love, and
    joy;
  So shall your Sovereign enter in,
  And new and nobler life begin.

5 Redeemer, come, we open wide,
  Our hearts to Thee; here, Lord abide!
  Thine inner presence let us feel,
  Thy grace and love in us reveal,
  Thy Holy Spirit guide us on,
  Until the glorious goal is won!

Georg Weissel (1590–1635)
Tr. Catherine Winkworth (1827–78)

542   6 4. 6 4. 6 7. 6 4

'The grace of God that bringeth salvation'
Titus 2 v 11

1 O how the grace of God
  Amazes me!
  It loosed me from my bonds
  And set me free!
  What made it happen so?
  'Twas His will, this much I know
  Set me, as now I show,
  At liberty.

2 My God has chosen me,
  Though one of nought,
  To sit beside my King
  In heaven's court.
  Hear what my Lord has done;
  O the love that made Him run
  To meet His erring son!
  This has God wrought.

3 Not for my righteousness,
  For I have none,
  But for His mercy's sake,
  Jesus, God's Son,
  Suffered on Calvary's tree –
  Crucified with thieves was He –
  Great was His grace to me,
  His wayward one!

4 And when I think of how,
  At Calvary,
  He bore sin's penalty
  Instead of me,
  Amazed, I wonder why
  He, the sinless One, should die
  For one so vile as I:
  My Saviour He!

5 Now all my heart's desire
  Is to abide
  In Him, my Saviour dear,
  In Him to hide.
  My shield and buckler He,
  Cov'ring and protecting me:
  From Satan's darts I'll be
  Safe at His side.

6 Lord Jesus, hear my prayer,
  Thy grace impart;
  When evil thoughts arise
  Through Satan's art,
  Oh, drive them all away
  And do Thou, from day to day,
  Keep me beneath Thy sway,
  King of my heart.

7 Come now the whole of me,
  Eyes, ears and voice,
  Join me, Creation all,
  With joyful noise:
  Praise Him who broke the chain
  Holding me in sin's domain,
  And set me free again!
  Sing and rejoice!

E. T. Sibomana (1910–1975)
© Church Mission Society   *Tr. R. Guillebaud (1915–2002)*

543   L.M.

*'This mystery ... Christ in you, the hope
of glory' Colossians 1 v 27*

1 Of all the works of God we see,
None greater than the mystery;
How guilty man by sin defiled
To God through Christ was
reconciled.

2 Shall seraphs try the same to prove?
'Tis buried in eternal love:
'Tis lost in this unfathomed sea,
And swallowed up, great God in
thee.

3 Here the divine perfections meet
Mercy and truth each other greet;
Justice and peace in Christ we see;
United in sweet harmony.

4 Great was the mystery of that grace
That chose, from Adam's fallen race,
Ten thousand, thousand sons to
praise
Its glories through eternal days.

5 By man came death, sin, hell and
shame;
By man the resurrection came;
He bruised the subtle serpent's
head,
And captive all his legions led.

6 Great was the mystery, truly great,
That hell's designs should hell
defeat;
But here eternal wisdom shined,
For Satan wrought what God
designed.

7 Great was the mystery of that love,
When Jesus left His throne above,
Yielded His life and precious blood,
To bring rebellious man to God.

8 May I Lord of Thy wondrous grace,
By this blest mystery have a place;
Amongst those Thou hast redeemed
to praise
Thy mercy through eternal days.

John Kent (1766–1843)

544   C.M.

*'In due time Christ died for the ungodly'
Romans 5 v 6*

1 Plunged in a gulf of deep despair
We wretched sinners lay,
Without one cheerful beam of hope,
Or spark of glimmering day.

2 With pitying eyes, the Prince of
grace
Beheld our helpless grief;
He saw, and, O amazing love!
He flew to our relief.

3 Down from the shining seats above,
With joyful haste He fled;
Entered the grave in mortal flesh,
And dwelt among the dead.

4 O! for this love, let rocks and hills
Their lasting silence break,
And all harmonious human tongues
The Saviour's praises speak!

5 Angels, assist our mighty joys,
Strike all your harps of gold!
But when you raise your highest
notes,
His love can ne'er be told.

Isaac Watts (1674–1748)

545   S.M.

*'A people prepared for the Lord'
Luke 1 v 17*

1 Prepare me, gracious God,
To stand before Thy face!
Thy Spirit must the work perform,
For it is all of grace.

2 In Christ's obedience clothe,
And wash me in His blood:
So shall I lift my head with joy
Among the sons of God.

3 Do Thou my sins subdue;
Thy sovereign love make known;
The spirit of my mind renew,
And save me in Thy Son.

4 Let me attest Thy power;
  Let me Thy goodness prove,
  Till my full soul can hold no more
  Of everlasting love.

Robert Elliott 1763

546   8 7. 8 7. 4 7

'According as he hath chosen us in him
before the foundation of the world'
Ephesians 1 v 4

1 Sons we are, through God's election,
  Who in Jesus Christ believe;
  By eternal destination,
  Saving grace we here receive;
  Our Redeemer
  Does both grace and glory give.

2 Every soul of man, by sinning,
  Merits everlasting pain;
  But Thy love, without beginning,
  Formed and fixed salvation's plan.
  Countless millions
  Shall in life through Jesus reign.

3 Pause, my soul! Adore and wonder!
  Ask, 'O why such love to me?'
  Grace has put me in the number
  Of the Saviour's family;
  Hallelujah!
  Thanks, Eternal Love, to Thee!

4 These are springs of consolation,
  To converted sons of grace;
  Finished, free, and full salvation
  Shining in the Saviour's face!
  Free grace only
  Suits the wretched sinner's case.

5 When in that blest habitation,
  Which my God for me ordained;
  When in glory's full possession,
  I with saints and angels stand;
  Free grace only
  Shall resound through Canaan's
  land!

Gospel Magazine 1777

547   10 10. 10 10 (with refrain)

'The voice of him that crieth in the
wilderness, Prepare ye the way of the
LORD' Isaiah 40 v 3

1 The highway of the Lord hast thou
  not known?
  Prepared by grace for men to find a
  way;
  A path declared, His gospel made
  renown:
  The Prince of glory takes our sin
  away.

  The valleys give their voices now to raise,
  And mountains melt before Thy powerful
  name;
  Good tidings come and Zion fills with
  praise
  For God has come His gospel to proclaim.

2 The glory of the Lord is now
  revealed,
  A voice has cried and all the earth
  hast heard
  The message of the God in Christ
  who healed
  The sorrow and the sin against His
  Word.

3 He fainteth not nor faileth in His
  love,
  Yet youths shall fall in all their
  vanity;
  But those who call and wait for Him
  above,
  Like eagles rise and see His Calvary.

4 This is the God to whom all nations
  bend,
  For time and space are nestled in His
  hand.
  He is the Lord, and will the heavens
  rend
  And blessing pour upon a thirsty
  land.

5 O comfort, comfort let there ever be
  For He is God and ever reigns
      supreme;
  Our sorrows banished by His love's
      decree,
  O love of God, in Christ who doth
      redeem.

© The Author   William Vernon Higham (b.1926)

548   L.M.

'They shall come with weeping'
Jeremiah 31 v 9

1 There is a season known to God
  When all his sheep, redeemed by
      blood,
  Shall leave the hateful ways of sin,
  Turn to the fold, and enter in.

2 At peace with hell, with God at war,
  In sin's dark maze they wander far,
  Indulge their lust, and still go on
  As far from God as sheep can run.

3 But see how heaven's indulgent care
  Attends their wanderings here and
      there;
  Still hard at heel where'er they stray,
  With pricking thorns to hedge their
      way.

4 When wisdom calls, they stop their
      ear,
  And headlong urge the mad career;
  Judgments nor mercies ne'er can
      sway
  Their roving feet to wisdom's way.

5 Glory to God, they ne'er shall rove
  Beyond the limits of his love;
  Fenced with Jehovah's shalls and
      wills,
  Firm as the everlasting hills.

6 The appointed time rolls on apace,
  Not to propose but call by grace;
  To change the heart, renew the will,
  And turn the feet to Zion's hill.

John Kent (1766–1843)

549   7 6. 7 6. D

'Ye have not chosen me, but I have chosen
you' John 15 v 16

1 'Tis not that I did choose Thee,
  For, Lord, that could not be;
  This heart would still refuse Thee
  Hadst Thou not chosen me.
  Thou from the sin that stained me
  Hast cleansed and set me free;
  Of old Thou hast ordained me,
  That I should live to Thee.

2 'Twas sovereign mercy called me,
  And taught my opening mind;
  The world had else enthralled me,
  To heavenly glories blind.
  My heart owns none above Thee;
  For Thy rich grace I thirst;
  This knowing, if I love Thee,
  Thou must have loved me first.

Josiah Conder (1789–1855)

550   D.C.M.

'Who shall lay anything to the charge of
God's elect' Romans 8 v 33

1 We stand before the Judge of time,
  His throne a place of fear;
  And gaze upon the King sublime,
  With trembling hearts draw near.
  But none can charge the elect of
      Christ
  With lies and wickedness,
  There richly robed, surpassing price,
  Imputed righteousness.

2 Secure the bonds of blessedness
  On Calvary wrought with love;
  No famine, sword or nakedness,
  Can make our faith remove.
  For who can separate the saint
  When links are forged by Him,
  Who chose His path without
      complaint,
  And bore the weight of sin?

3 No space beyond, no scheme or plan,
  No circumstance can change;
  For present past and future span
  Are in His sovereign range.
  His grace persuades and tells my
      heart,
  That conqueror I shall be;
  From sin and death and judgement's
      dart,
  Secure eternally.

4 The love of Christ is vast and deep,
  No measurement can tell;
  His sacrifice our death-like sleep
  Will evermore dispel.
  If we are killed or we are torn
  With persecution's hate,
  We never, never are forlorn –
  We are regenerate.

5 Predestined from the depths divine,
  Deep in the will of God;
  Displayed in time, of David's line,
  This earth a Saviour trod.
  He bled and died for sin and shame,
  And rose to justify;
  His majesty is all our fame,
  Our Christ we glorify.

© The Author   *William Vernon Higham (b.1926)*

551   C.M.

*'O the depth of the riches both of the
wisdom and knowledge of God!'
Romans 11 v 33*

1 What shall I do, my God to love,
  My loving God to praise?
  The length, and breadth, and height
      to prove,
  And depth of sovereign grace?

2 My trespass was grown up to heaven;
  But far above the skies
  In Christ abundantly forgiven,
  I see thy mercies rise.

3 The depth of all-redeeming love
  What angel tongue can tell?
  O may I to the utmost prove
  The gift unspeakable!

4 Deeper than hell, it plucked me
      thence;
  Deeper than inbred sin,
  Jesu's great love the heart doth
      cleanse
  When Jesus enters in.

5 Come quickly, gracious Lord, and
      take
  Possession of Thine own;
  My longing heart vouchsafe to make
  Thine everlasting throne!

6 Assert Thy claim, maintain Thy
      right,
  Come quickly from above;
  And sink me to perfection's height,
  The depth of humble love.

Charles Wesley (1707–88)

552   66.66.88

Based on Psalm 18

1 Whom should we love like Thee,
  Our God, our Guide, our King,
  The Tower to which we flee,
  The Rock to which we cling?
  O for a thousand tongues to show
  The mercies which to Thee we owe!

2 The storm upon us fell,
  The floods around us rose;
  The depths of death and hell
  Seemed on our souls to close;
  To God we cried in strong despair;
  He heard, and came to help our
      prayer.

3 He came, the King of kings,
  He bowed the stable sky;
  And on the tempest's wings
  Rode glorious down from high;
  The earth before her Maker shook
  The mountains quaked at His rebuke.

4 Above the storm He stood,
  And awed it to repose;
  He drew us from the flood,
  And scattered all our foes.
  He set us in a spacious place,
  And there upholds us by His grace.

5 Whom should we love like Thee,
Our God, our Guide, our King,
The Tower to which we flee,
The Rock to which we cling?
O for a thousand tongues to show
The mercies which to thee we owe!

Henry Francis Lyte (1793–1847)

553   L.M.

'For he hath made him to be sin for us'
2 Corinthians 5 v 21

1 Behold a scene of matchless grace,
'Tis Jesus in the sinner's place;
Heaven's brightest glory sunk in
shame
That rebels might adore His name.

2 Tremendous clouds of wrath and
dread,
In vengeance burst upon His head;
Ten thousand horrors seize His soul,
And vengeful mountains on Him
roll.

3 He sighed; He groaned; He sweat;
He cried;
Through awful floods He passed and
died;
All penal wrath to Zion due,
Infinite justice on Him threw.

4 He rose in triumph from the dead;
Justice declared the debt was paid;
Then Christ with kingly grandeur
flew,
And took His throne in glory too.

5 Come saints with solemn pleasure
trace
The boundless treasures of His
grace;
He bore almighty wrath for you,
That you might all His glory view.

William Gadsby (1773–1844)

554   C.M.

'He humbled himself, and became
obedient unto death, even the death of the
cross' Philippians 2 v 8

1 Behold the Saviour of mankind
Nailed to the shameful tree!
How vast the love that Him inclined
To bleed and die for thee!

2 Hark, how He groans! while nature
shakes,
And earth's strong pillars bend;
The temple's veil in sunder breaks,
The solid marbles rend.

3 'Tis done! the precious ransom's
paid;
Receive my soul! He cries:
See where He bows His sacred head!
He bows His head, and dies!

4 But soon He'll break death's envious
chain,
And in full glory shine:
O Lamb of God, was ever pain,
Was ever love, like Thine?

Samuel Wesley (1662–1735)

555   C.M.

'The glory of the LORD shall be revealed'
Isaiah 40 v 5

1 Father, how wide Thy glory shines!
How high Thy wonders rise!
Known through the earth by
thousand signs
By thousands through the skies.

2 Those mighty orbs proclaim Thy
power,
Their motion speaks Thy skill;
And on the wings of every hour
We read Thy patience still.

3 But when we view Thy strange
design
To save rebellious worms,
Where vengeance and compassion
join
In their divinest forms.

4 Here the whole Deity is known;
   Nor dares a creature guess
   Which of the glories brightest
      shone –
   The justice or the grace.

5 Now the full glories of the Lamb
   Adorn the heavenly plains;
   The saints above sing Jesus' name
   And praise in choicest strains.

6 O, may I bear some glorious part
   In that immortal song!
   Wonder and joy shall tune my heart,
   And love command my tongue.

Isaac Watts (1674–1748)

556   D.C.M.

'For with thee is the fountain of life'
Psalm 36 v 9

1 Fountain of never-ceasing grace,
   Thy saints' exhaustless theme,
   Great object of immortal praise,
   Essentially supreme;
   We bless Thee for the glorious fruits
   Thine incarnation gives;
   Thy righteousness which grace
      imputes,
   And faith alone receives.

2 Whom heaven's angelic host adores,
   Was slaughtered for our sin;
   The guilt, O Lord, was wholly ours,
   The punishment was Thine;
   Our God in flesh, to set us free,
   Was manifested here;
   And meekly bore our sins, that we
   His righteousness might wear.

3 In Him we have a righteousness,
   By God Himself approved,
   Our rock, our sure foundation this,
   Which never can be moved.
   Our ransom by His death He paid,
   For all His people given,
   The law He perfectly obeyed,
   That they might enter heaven.

4 As all, when Adam sinned alone,
   In His transgression died,
   So by the righteousness of One
   Are sinners justified;
   We to Thy merit, precious Lord,
   With humblest joy submit,
   Again to paradise restored,
   In Thee alone complete.

Augustus Montague Toplady (1740–78)

557   8 8 6. D

'Fear not, for I have redeemed thee'
Isaiah 63 v 1

1 From whence this fear and
      unbelief?
   Hath not the Father put to grief
   His spotless Son for me?
   And will the righteous Judge of men
   Condemn me for that debt of sin
   Which, Lord, was laid on Thee?

2 Complete atonement Thou hast
      made,
   And to the utmost Thou hast paid
   Whate'er Thy people owed;
   How then can wrath on me take
      place,
   If sheltered in Thy righteousness,
   And sprinkled with Thy blood?

3 If Thou hast my discharge procured,
   And freely in my room endured
   The whole of wrath divine;
   Payment God cannot twice demand,
   First at my bleeding Surety's hand,
   And then again at mine.

4 Turn then, my soul, into thy rest!
   The merits of thy great High Priest
   Have bought thy liberty;
   Trust in His efficacious blood,
   Nor fear thy banishment from God,
   Since Jesus died for thee.

Augustus Montague Toplady (1740–78)

558
C.M.

'No man cometh unto the Father, but by me' John 14 v 6

1 Great God! from Thee there's
   nought concealed,
  Thou seest my inward frame;
  To Thee I always stand revealed
   Exactly as I am!

2 Since I can hardly, therefore, bear
   What in myself I see;
  How vile and stained must I appear,
   Most holy God, to Thee!

3 But since my Saviour stands
   between,
  In garments dyed in blood,
  'Tis He, instead of me is seen,
   When I approach to God.

4 Thus, though a sinner, I am safe;
  He pleads, before the throne,
  His life and death in my behalf,
   And calls my sins His own.

5 What wondrous love, what
   mysteries,
  In this appointment shine!
  My breaches of the law are His,
   And His obedience mine.

John Newton (1725–1807)

559
8 7. 8 7. D

'The precious blood of Christ'
1 Peter 1 v 19

1 Here behold a place of mercy,
  In His blood, acceptance find.
  Here a haven for the guilty,
  Heals my wounds, Physician kind.
  Near the Godhead blessed shelter,
  Where the sinner finds a nest.
  Heaven's pure justice now in wonder
  Granting me eternal rest.

2 God in glory planned salvation
  Rescues us by pow'r divine.
  There in Eden God's salvation
  He pronounce of woman's line.
  Now he justifies the godless,
  Bringing life unto the dead.
  Justice smiles on sinners helpless,
  Now at peace with God their head.

Ann Griffiths (1776–1805)
© The Author   *Tr. William Vernon Higham (b.1926)*

560
8 8 6. D

'He was wounded for our transgressions,
he was bruised for our iniquities'
Isaiah 53 v 5

1 In Eden – sad indeed that day –
  My countless blessings fled away,
   My crown fell in disgrace.
  But on victorious Calvary
  That crown was won again for me –
   My life shall all be praise.

2 Faith, see the place, and see the tree
  Where heaven's Prince, instead of
   me,
   Was nailed to bear my shame.
  Bruised was the dragon by the Son,
  Though two had wounds, there
   conquered One –
   And Jesus was His name.

William Williams (1717–91)
© The Translator   *Tr. Robert (Bobi) Maynard Jones (b.1929)*

561
L.M.

'THE LORD OUR RIGHTEOUSNESS'
Jeremiah 23 v 6

1 Jesus, Thy blood and righteousness
  My beauty are, my glorious dress:
  Midst flaming worlds, in these
   arrayed,
  With joy shall I lift up my head.

2 Bold shall I stand in that great day,
  For who aught to my charge shall lay?
  Fully absolved through Thee I am,
  From sin and fear, from guilt and
   shame.

3 The holy, meek, unspotted Lamb,
Who from the Father's bosom came,
Who died for me, even me, to atone,
Now for my Lord and God I own.

4 This spotless robe the same appears
When ruined nature sinks in years;
No age can change its glorious hue,
The robe of Christ is ever new.

5 When from the dust of death I rise
To claim my mansion in the skies,
E'en then shall this be all my plea,
Jesus hath lived, hath died for me.

6 O let the dead now hear Thy voice!
Now bid Thy banished ones rejoice!
Their beauty this, their glorious
    dress,
Jesus, the Lord our Righteousness.

Nicolaus Ludwig von Zinzendorf (1700–60)
Tr. John Wesley (1703–91)

562   L.M.

*'What things were gain to me, those I
counted loss for Christ' Philippians 3 v 7*

1 No more, my God, I boast no more
Of all the duties I have done;
I quit the hopes I held before,
To trust the merits of Thy Son.

2 Now for the love I bear His name,
What was my gain I count my loss;
My former pride I call my shame,
And nail my glory to His cross.

3 Yes, and I must and will esteem
All things but loss for Jesus' sake:
O may my soul be found in Him,
And of His righteousness partake!

4 The best obedience of my hands
Dares not appear before Thy throne:
But faith can answer Thy demands
By pleading what my Lord has done.

Isaac Watts (1674–1748)

563   S.M.

*'For it is not possible that the blood of
bulls and of goats should take away sins'
Hebrews 10 v 4*

1 Not all the blood of beasts,
On Jewish altars slain,
Could give the guilty conscience
    peace
Or wash away the stain.

2 But Christ, the heavenly Lamb,
Takes all our sins away;
A sacrifice of nobler name,
And richer blood than they.

3 My faith would lay her hand
On that dear head of Thine,
While like a penitent I stand,
And there confess my sin.

4 My soul looks back to see
The burden Thou didst bear
When hanging on the cursèd tree,
And knows her guilt was there.

5 Believing, we rejoice
To see the curse remove;
We bless the Lamb with cheerful
    voice,
And sing His wondrous love.

Isaac Watts (1674–1748)

564   S.M.

*'Not by works of righteousness which we
have done' Titus 3 v 5*

1 Not what these hands have done
Can save this guilty soul;
Not what this toiling flesh has borne
Can make my spirit whole.

2 Not what I feel or do
Can give me peace with God;
Not all my prayers, and sighs, and
    tears
Can bear my awful load.

3 Thy work alone, O Christ,
Can ease this weight of sin;
Thy blood alone, O Lamb of God,
Can give me peace within.

4 Thy love to me, O God,
Not mine, O Lord, to Thee,
Can rid me of this dark unrest,
And set my spirit free.

5 Thy grace alone, O God,
To me can pardon speak;
Thy power alone, O Son of God,
Can this sore bondage break.

6 I bless the Christ of God,
I rest in love divine,
And with unfaltering lip and heart,
I call this Saviour mine.

Horatius Bonar (1808–89)

565   5 5 11. D

*'Where sin abounded, grace did much
more abound' Romans 5 v 20*

1 O God of all grace,
Thy goodness we praise;
Thy Son Thou hast given to die in
    our place.
He came from above
Our curse to remove;
He hath loved, He hath loved us,
    because He would love.

2 Love moved Him to die,
And on this we rely;
He hath loved, He hath loved us: we
    cannot tell why;
But this we can tell,
He hath loved us so well
As to lay down His life to redeem us
    from hell.

3 He hath ransomed our race;
O how shall we praise
Or worthily sing Thy unspeakable
    grace?
Nothing else will we know
In our journey below,
But singing Thy grace to Thy
    paradise go.

4 Nay, and when we remove
To Thy presence above,
Our heaven shall be still to sing of
    Thy love.
We all shall commend
The love of our Friend,
For ever beginning what never shall
    end.

Charles Wesley (1707–88)

566   7 6. 7 6. D

*'For God so loved the world, that he gave
his only begotten Son' John 3 v 16*

1 O Lord, how shall I meet Thee,
How welcome Thee aright?
Thy people long to greet Thee,
My hope, my heart's delight!
O kindle, Lord most holy,
Thy lamp within my breast,
To do, in spirit lowly,
All that may please Thee best.

2 Love caused Thine incarnation,
Love brought Thee down to me;
Thy thirst for my salvation
Procured my liberty.
O love beyond all telling,
That led Thee to embrace,
In love all love excelling,
Our lost and fallen race!

3 Rejoice, then, ye sad-hearted,
Who sit in deepest gloom,
Who mourn o'er joys departed,
And tremble at your doom.
Despair not, He is near you,
Yea, standing at the door,
Who best can help and cheer you,
And bids you weep no more.

4 Sin's debt, that fearful burden,
Let not your souls distress;
Your guilt the Lord will pardon,
And cover by His grace.
He comes, for men procuring
The peace of sin forgiven,
For all God's sons securing
Their heritage in heaven.

Paul Gerhardt (1607–76)
Composite translation

567

65.65

'And I, if I be lifted up from the earth, will draw all men unto me' John 12 v 32

1 O my Saviour, lifted
From the earth for me,
Draw me, in Thy mercy,
Nearer unto Thee.

2 Lift my earth-bound longings,
Fix them, Lord, above;
Draw me with the magnet
Of Thy mighty love.

3 And I come, Lord Jesus;
Dare I turn away?
No! Thy love hath conquered,
And I come today.

4 Bringing all my burdens,
Sorrow, sin, and care;
At Thy feet I lay them,
And I leave them there.

William Walsham How (1823–97)

568

77.77.77

'Lead me to the rock that is higher than I' Psalm 61 v 2

1 Rock of Ages, cleft for me,
Let me hide myself in Thee;
Let the water and the blood,
From Thy riven side which flowed,
Be of sin the double cure,
Cleanse me from its guilt and power.

2 Not the labours of my hands
Can fulfil Thy law's demands;
Could my zeal no respite know,
Could my tears for ever flow,
All for sin could not atone:
Thou must save, and Thou alone.

3 Nothing in my hand I bring,
Simply to Thy cross I cling;
Naked, come to Thee for dress;
Helpless, look to Thee for grace;
Foul, I to the fountain fly;
Wash me, Saviour, or I die.

4 While I draw this fleeting breath,
When my eyelids close in death,
When I soar through tracts
    unknown,
See Thee on Thy judgment throne;
Rock of Ages, cleft for me,
Let me hide myself in Thee.

Augustus Montague Toplady (1740–78)

569

86.886

'Wash me, and I shall be whiter than snow' Psalm 51 v 7

1 The blood of Christ, Thy spotless
    Lamb,
O God, is all my plea:
Nought else could for my sin atone,
I have no merit of my own
Which I can bring to Thee.

2 No sacrifice save His who bore
My load upon the tree;
No other plea which lips could
    frame,
No other blood, no other name,
Accepted is for me.

3 Since Christ has entered by His
    blood
The holiest on high;
By that same hallowed blood-stained
    track
Thou welcomest the wanderer back,
And biddest me draw nigh.

4 O wondrous cross! O precious
    blood!
O death by which I live!
The sinless One, for me made sin,
Doth now His wondrous heart
    within
Eternal refuge give!

5 By that blest cross, that cleansing
    blood,
I know His power to save;
The merits of His work confessed,
I stand in Him completely blest,
A conqueror o'er the grave.

William Samuel Warren Pond (d.1919)

570   73.73.77.73.73

*'The blood of Jesus Christ his Son
cleanseth us from all sin' 1 John 1 v 7*

1 There is a path of pardon
  In His blood;
  There is a sure salvation
  In His blood.
  The law's full consummation,
  A Father's approbation –
  Hear Zion's acclamation!
  In His blood –
  Atonement and redemption
  In His blood!

2 O come, ye sons of Adam,
  And rejoice!
  Now trust the God of Abraham
  And rejoice!
  O hasten, happy sinner,
  To life in Christ for ever,
  To bonds that nought can sever:
  O rejoice!
  In full and glad surrender
  Come, rejoice!

William Williams (1801–76)
© The Translator   *Tr. William Vernon Higham (b.1926)*

571   66.66.88

*'Not by works ... but according to his
mercy he saved us' Titus 3 v 5*

1 Thy works, not mine, O Christ,
  Speak gladness to this heart;
  They tell me all is done,
  They bid my fear depart.
  To whom save Thee, who canst
    alone
  For sin atone, Lord, shall I flee?

2 Thy wounds, not mine, O Christ,
  Can heal my bruisèd soul;
  Thy stripes, not mine, contain
  The balm that makes me whole.
  To whom save Thee, who canst
    alone
  For sin atone, Lord, shall I flee?

3 Thy cross, not mine, O Christ,
  Has borne the awful load
  Of sins that none could bear
  But the incarnate God.
  To whom save Thee, who canst
    alone
  For sin atone, Lord, shall I flee?

4 Thy death, not mine, O Christ,
  Has paid the ransom due;
  Ten thousand deaths like mine
  Would have been all too few.
  To whom save Thee, who canst
    alone
  For sin atone, Lord, shall I flee?

5 Thy righteousness, O Christ,
  Alone can cover me;
  No righteousness avails
  Save that which is of Thee:
  To whom save Thee, who canst
    alone
  For sin atone, Lord, shall I flee?

Horatius Bonar (1808–89)

572   D.L.M.

*'He said, It is finished: and he bowed his
head, and gave up the ghost' John 19 v 30*

1 'Tis finished! The Messiah dies,
  Cut off for sins, but not His own;
  Accomplished is the sacrifice,
  The great redeeming work is done.
  'Tis finished! All the debt is paid;
  Justice divine is satisfied;
  The grand and full atonement made;
  God for a guilty world hath died.

2 The veil is rent in Christ alone;
  The living way to heaven is seen;
  The middle wall is broken down,
  And all mankind may enter in.
  The types and figures are fulfilled;
  Exacted is the legal pain;
  The precious promises are sealed;
  The spotless Lamb of God is slain.

3 The reign of sin and death is o'er,
   And all may live from sin set free;
   Satan hath lost his mortal power;
   'Tis swallowed up in victory.
   Saved from the legal curse I am,
   My Saviour hangs on yonder tree:
   See there the meek, expiring Lamb!
   'Tis finished! He expires for me.

4 Accepted in the Well-beloved,
   And clothed in righteousness divine,
   I see the bar to heaven removed,
   And all Thy merits, Lord, are mine.
   Death, hell, and sin are now
        subdued;
   All grace is now to sinners given;
   And lo, I plead the atoning blood,
   And in Thy right I claim Thy heaven.

Charles Wesley (1707–88)

573 C.M.

*'For by grace are ye saved through faith
... not of works' Ephesians 2 vv 8, 9*

1 'Tis not by works of righteousness
   Which our own hands have done,
   But we are saved by sovereign grace,
   Abounding through the Son.

2 'Tis from the mercy of our God
   That all our hopes begin;
   'Tis by the water and the blood
   Our souls are washed from sin.

3 'Tis through the purchase of His
        death
   Who hung upon the tree,
   The Spirit is sent down to breathe
   On such dry bones as we.

4 Raised from the dead, we live anew;
   And, justified by grace,
   We shall appear in glory too,
   And see our Father's face.

Isaac Watts (1674–1748)

THE GOSPEL ...
ITS PROCLAMATION

—

574 S.M.

'For God shall bring every work into judgment' Ecclesiastes 12 v 14

1 And will the judge descend?
And must the dead arise?
And not a single soul escape
His all-discerning eyes?

2 How will my heart endure
The terrors of that day,
When earth and heaven before His
face
Astonished shrink away?

3 But ere the trumpet shake
The mansions of the dead,
Hark! from the gospel's cheering
sound,
What joyful tidings spread!

4 Ye sinners, seek His grace,
Whose wrath ye cannot bear;
Fly to the shelter of His cross,
And find salvation there!

5 So shall the curse remove
By which the Saviour bled,
And the last aweful day shall pour
His blessings on your head.

Philip Doddridge (1702–51)

575 8 5. 8 3

'Come unto me, all ye that labour and are heavy laden, and I will give you rest' Matthew 11 v 28

1 Art thou weary, art thou languid,
Art thou sore distressed?
'Come to Me', saith One, 'and
coming,
Be at rest!'

2 Hath He marks to lead me to Him,
If He be my Guide?
In His feet and hands are wound-
prints,
And His side.

3 Hath He diadem as Monarch
That His brow adorns?
Yea, a crown in very surety,
But of thorns!

4 If I find Him, if I follow,
What His payment here?
Many a sorrow, many a labour,
Many a tear.

5 If I still hold closely to Him,
What hath He at last?
Sorrow vanquished, labour ended,
Jordan past.

6 If I ask Him to receive me,
Will He say me nay?
Not till earth and not till heaven
Pass away.

7 Finding, following, keeping,
   struggling,
Is He sure to bless?
Saints, apostles, prophets, martyrs,
Answer: Yes!

John Mason Neale (1818–66)
Based on Stephen the Sabaite (725–94)

576 C.M.

'*Come unto me ... and I will give you*
rest' *Matthew 11 v 28*

1 Come, every soul by sin oppressed,
   There's mercy with the Lord;
   And He will surely give you rest,
   By trusting in His word.

2 For Jesus shed His precious blood
   Rich blessings to bestow;
   Plunge now into the crimson flood
   That washes white as snow.

3 Yes, Jesus is the Truth, the Way
   That leads you into rest;
   Believe in Him without delay,
   And you are fully blest.

4 Come then and join this holy band
   And on to glory go,
   To dwell in that celestial land
   Where joys immortal flow.

John H. Stockton (1813–1877)

577 10 4. 10 7. 4 10

'*For his great love wherewith he loved us*'
Ephesians 2 v 4

1 Come, let us sing of a wonderful
   love,
   Tender and true;
   Out of the heart of the Father above,
   Streaming to me and to you:
   Wonderful love
   Dwells in the heart of the Father
   above.

2 Jesus, the Saviour, this gospel to tell
   Joyfully came;
   Came with the helpless and hopeless
   to dwell,
   Sharing their sorrow and shame;
   Seeking the lost,
   Saving, redeeming at measureless
   cost.

3 Jesus is seeking the wanderers yet;
   Why do they roam?
   Love only waits to forgive and forget;
   Home! weary wanderer, home!
   Wonderful love
   Dwells in the heart of the Father
   above.

4 Come to my heart, O Thou
   wonderful love!
   Come and abide,
   Lifting my life till it rises above
   Envy and falsehood and pride,
   Seeking to be
   Lowly and humble, a learner of
   Thee.

Robert Walmsley (1831–1905)

578 6 6. 6 6. D

'*Come unto me ... and I will give you*
rest' *Matthew 11 v 28*

1 Come to the Saviour now!
   He gently calleth thee;
   In true repentance bow,
   Before Him bend the knee.
   He waiteth to bestow
   Salvation, peace and love,
   True joy on earth below,
   A home in heaven above.
   Come, come, come!

2 Come to the Saviour now!
   He suffered all for thee,
   And in His merits thou
   Hast an unfailing plea.
   No vain excuses frame,
   For feelings do not stay;
   None who to Jesus came
   Were ever sent away.
   Come, come, come!

3 Come to the Saviour now,
Ye who have wandered far;
Renew your solemn vow,
For His by right you are.
Come like poor wandering sheep
Returning to His fold;
His arm will safely keep,
His love will ne'er grow cold.
Come, come, come!

4 Come to the Saviour, all,
Whate'er your burdens be;
Hear now His loving call –
'Cast all your care on Me.'
Come, and for every grief,
In Jesus you will find
A sure and safe relief,
A loving Friend and kind.
Come, come, come!

John Murch Wigner (1844–1911)

579   7 6. 7 6. D

*'Him that cometh to me I will in no wise
cast out' John 6 v 37*

1 'Come unto Me, ye weary,
And I will give you rest.'
O blessed voice of Jesus,
Which comes to hearts oppressed!
It tells of benediction,
Of pardon, grace and peace,
Of joy that hath no ending,
Of love that cannot cease.

2 'Come unto Me, ye wanderers,
And I will give you light.'
O loving voice of Jesus,
Which comes to cheer the night!
Our hearts were filled with sadness,
And we had lost our way;
But morning brings us gladness,
And songs the break of day.

3 'Come unto Me, ye fainting,
And I will give you life.'
O cheering voice of Jesus,
Which comes to aid our strife!
The foe is stern and eager,
The fight is fierce and long;
But Thou hast made us mighty,
And stronger than the strong.

4 'And whosoever cometh
I will not cast him out.'
O welcome voice of Jesus,
Which drives away our doubt,
Which calls us, very sinners,
Unworthy though we be
Of love so free and boundless,
To come, dear Lord, to Thee!

William Chatterton Dix (1837–98)

580   8 7. 8 7. 4 7

*'The gospel of the grace of God'
Acts 20 v 24*

1 Come, ye sinners, poor and
wretched,
Weak and wounded, sick and sore;
Jesus ready stands to save you,
Full of pity joined with power;
He is able,
He is willing; doubt no more!

2 Come, ye needy, come and welcome;
God's free bounty glorify!
True belief and true repentance,
Every grace that brings us nigh,
Without money,
Come to Jesus Christ and buy!

3 Let not conscience make you linger,
Nor of fitness fondly dream;
All the fitness He requireth,
Is to feel your need of Him:
This He gives you;
'Tis the Spirit's rising beam!

4 Come, ye weary, heavy-laden,
Bruised and broken by the fall;
If you tarry till you're better,
You will never come at all:
Not the righteous –
Sinners Jesus came to call!

5 View Him prostrate in the garden;
On the ground your Maker lies;
Then on Calvary's tree behold Him,
Hear Him cry, before He dies,
'It is finished!'
Sinner, will not this suffice?

6 Lo! the incarnate God, ascended,
Pleads the merit of His blood;
Venture on Him, venture wholly,
Let no other trust intrude;
None but Jesus
Can do helpless sinners good.

Joseph Hart (1712–68)

581   8 7. 8 7. 4 7

*'Come unto me ... take my yoke upon
you' Matthew 11 vv 28, 29*

1 Come, ye souls by sin afflicted,
Bowed with fruitless sorrow down,
By the broken law convicted,
Through the cross behold the
    crown;
Look to Jesus;
Mercy flows through Him alone.

2 Blessèd are the eyes that see Him,
Blest the ears that hear His voice;
Blessèd are the souls that trust Him,
And in Him alone rejoice;
His commandments
Then become their happy choice.

3 Sweet as home to pilgrims weary,
Light to newly opened eyes,
Flowing springs in deserts dreary,
Is the rest the cross supplies;
All who taste it
Shall to bliss immortal rise.

4 Take His easy yoke and wear it;
Love will make obedience sweet;
Christ will give you strength to bear
    it,
While His wisdom guides your feet
Safe to glory,
Where His ransomed captives meet.

Joseph Swain (1761–96)

582   7 7. 7 7. 7 7. 7 7

*'Ye shall find rest for your souls'
Jeremiah 6 v 16*

1 Does the gospel word proclaim
Rest for those who weary be?
Then, my soul, put in thy claim;
Sure that promise speaks to thee.
Marks of grace I cannot show;
All polluted is my breast;
Yet I weary am, I know,
And the weary long for rest.

2 Burdened with a load of sin;
Harassed with tormenting doubt;
Hourly conflicts from within;
Hourly crosses from without;
All my little strength is gone;
Sink I must without supply;
Sure upon the earth there's none
Can more weary be than I.

3 In the ark the weary dove
Found a welcome resting-place;
Thus my spirit longs to prove
Rest in Christ, the Ark of grace.
Tempest-tossed I long have been
And the flood increases fast;
Open, Lord, and take me in
Till the storm be overpast.

John Newton (1725–1807)

583   L.M.

*'The great trumpet shall be blown'
Isaiah 27 v 13*

1 Hark! how the gospel trumpet
    sounds!
Christ and free grace therein
    abounds;
Free grace to such as sinners be;
And if free grace, why not for me?

2 The Saviour died, and by His blood
Brought rebel sinners near to God;
He died to set the captives free;
And why, my soul, why not for thee?

3 The blood of Christ, how sweet it
   sounds,
To cleanse and heal the sinner's
   wounds!
The streams thereof are rich and
   free;
And why, my soul, why not for thee?

4 Thus Jesus came the poor to bless,
To clothe them with His
   righteousness;
The robe is spotless, full and free;
And why, my soul, why not for thee?

5 Eternal life by Christ is given
And ruined rebels raised to heaven;
Then sing of grace so rich and free
And say, my soul, why not for thee?

Charles Cole (1733–1813)

584   11 9. 11 9 (with refrain)

*'And have washed their robes, and made
them white in the blood of the Lamb'*
Revelation 7 v 14

1. Have you been to Jesus for the
   cleansing power?
Are you washed in the blood of the
   Lamb?
Are you fully trusting in His grace
   this hour?
Are you washed in the blood of the
   Lamb?

Are you washed in the blood,
In the soul-cleansing blood of the Lamb?
Are your garments spotless? Are they white
as snow?
Are you washed in the blood of the Lamb?

2 Are you walking daily by the
   Saviour's side?
Are you washed in the blood of the
   Lamb?
Do you rest each moment in the
   Crucified?
Are you washed in the blood of the
   Lamb?

3 When the Bridegroom cometh, will
   your robes be white,
Pure and white in the blood of the
   Lamb?
Will your soul be ready for the
   mansions bright,
And be washed in the blood of the
   Lamb?

4 Lay aside the garments that are
   stained by sin,
And be washed in the blood of the
   Lamb;
There's a fountain flowing for the
   soul unclean,
O be washed in the blood of the Lamb!

Elisha A. Hoffman (1839–1929)

585   8 7. 8 7. D

*'Whom shall I send, and who will go for
us? Then said I, Here am I; send me'*
Isaiah 6 v 8

1 Have you heard the voice of Jesus
Softly pleading with your heart?
Have you felt His presence glorious,
As He calls your soul apart,
With a love so true and loyal,
Love divine that ever flows
From a Saviour, righteous, royal,
And a cross that mercy shows?

2 Have you heard the voice of mercy
Granting peace and pardon pure?
Have you felt the balm of Calvary
Binding all your wounds secure?
Was there ever such salvation,
Was there ever care like this?
See the Saviour's grief and passion,
Grace and mercy's gentle kiss.

3 Have you heard the Saviour calling
All to leave and follow Him?
Have you felt His Person drawing
With compulsion lives to win?
Hearken to His invitation,
To the music of God's grace;
Let the peace of God's salvation
Fill your soul, and love embrace.

© The Author   *William Vernon Higham (b.1926)*

586   87.87.47

'The love of Christ' 2 Corinthians 5 v 14

1 High beyond imagination
  Is the love of God to man;
  Far too deep for human reason;
  Fathom that it never can;
  Love eternal
  Richly dwells in Christ the Lamb.

2 Love like Jesus' none can measure,
  Nor can its dimensions know;
  'Tis a boundless, endless river,
  And its waters freely flow.
  O ye thirsty,
  Come and taste its streams below.

3 Jesus loved, and loves for ever;
  Zion on His heart does dwell;
  He will never, never, never
  Leave His church a prey to hell.
  All is settled,
  And my soul approves it well.

William Gadsby (1773–1844)

587   66.66.88

'If thou be the Son of God, come down from the cross' Matthew 27 v 40

1 Himself He could not save,
  He on the cross must die,
  Or mercy cannot come
  To ruined sinners nigh.
  Yes, Christ, the Son of God, must bleed,
  That sinners might from sin be freed.

2 Himself He could not save,
  For justice must be done;
  And sin's full weight must fall
  Upon a sinless One;
  For nothing less can God accept
  In payment for the fearful debt.

3 Himself He could not save,
  For He the surety stood
  For all who now rely
  Upon His precious blood;
  He bore the penalty of guilt
  When on the cross His blood was spilt.

4 Himself He could not save,
  Yet now a Saviour He:
  Come, sinner, to Him come,
  He waits to welcome thee.
  Believe in Him, and thou shalt prove
  His saving power, His deathless love.

Albert Midlane (1825–1909)

588   87.87

'Repent, and be baptised every one of you' Acts 2 v 38

1 Humble souls, who seek salvation
  Through the Lamb's redeeming blood,
  Hear the voice of revelation,
  Tread the path that Jesus trod.

2 Flee to Him, your only Saviour,
  In His mighty name confide;
  In the whole of your behaviour
  Own Him as your sovereign Guide.

3 Hear the blest Redeemer call you,
  Listen to His heavenly voice:
  Dread no ills that can befall you,
  While you make His ways your choice.

4 Jesus says, Let each believer
  Be baptized in My name;
  He Himself in Jordan's river
  Was immersed beneath the stream.

5 Plainly here His footsteps tracing,
  Follow Him without delay,
  Gladly His command embracing,
  Lo! your Captain leads the way.

6 View the rite with understanding,
  Jesus' grave before you lies;
  Be interred at His commanding,
  After His example rise.

John Fawcett (1740–1817)

589   8 7. 8 7. 8 7. 8 7

'My soul doth magnify the Lord'
Luke 1 v 46

1 Jesus is our God and Saviour,
  Guide and Counsellor and Friend,
  Bearing all our misbehaviour,
  Kind and loving to the end.
  Trust Him; He will not deceive us,
  Though we hardly of Him deem;
  He will never, never leave us;
  Nor will let us quite leave Him.

2 Nothing but Thy blood, O Jesus,
  Can relieve us from our smart;
  Nothing else from guilt release us;
  Nothing else can melt the heart.
  Law and terrors do but harden,
  All the while they work alone:
  But a sense of blood-bought pardon
  Soon dissolves a heart of stone.

3 Jesus, all our consolations
  Flow from Thee, the Sovereign
      good,
  Love and faith and hope and
      patience,
  All are purchased by Thy blood.
  From Thy fulness we receive them;
  We have nothing of our own;
  Freely Thou delight'st to give them
  To the needy, who have none.

                    John Newton (1725–1807)

590   6 6. 8 6. 10 12

'For it is not possible that the blood of
bulls and goats should take away sins'
Hebrews 10 v 4

1 No blood, no altar now:
  The sacrifice is o'er;
  No flame, no smoke ascends on
      high,
  The lamb is slain no more.
  But richer blood has flowed from
      nobler veins,
  To purge the soul from guilt and
      cleanse the reddest stains.

2 We thank Thee for the blood,
  The blood of Christ, Thy Son:
  The blood by which our peace is
      made,
  The victory is won;
  Great victory o'er hell and sin and
      woe,
  That needs no second fight and
      leaves no second foe.

3 We thank Thee for the grace,
  Descending from above,
  That overflows our widest guilt –
  The eternal Father's love,
  Love of the Father's everlasting Son
  Love of the Holy Ghost – Jehovah,
      Three in One.

                    Horatius Bonar (1808–89)

591   L.M.

'The voice of the LORD' Psalm 29 v 4

1 Now may the gospel's conquering
      power
  Be felt by all assembled here;
  So shall this prove a joyful hour,
  And God's own arm of strength
      appear.

2 Lord! Let Thy mighty voice be heard;
  Speak in the Word, and speak with
      power;
  So shall Thy glorious name be feared
  By those who never feared before.

3 O pity those who sleep in sin,
  Preserve them from the sinner's
      doom:
  Show them the Ark, and take them
      in,
  And save them from the wrath to
      come.

4 So shall Thy people joyful be,
  And angels shall more loudly sing,
  And both ascribe the praise to Thee,
  To Thee, the everlasting King!

                    Thomas Kelly (1769–1855)

592 C.M.

'The glorious gospel of the blessed God'
1 Timothy 1 v 11

1 O for a thousand tongues to sing
My great Redeemer's praise,
The glories of my God and King,
The triumphs of His grace!

2 My gracious Master and my God,
Assist me to proclaim,
To spread through all the earth
abroad
The honours of Thy name.

3 Jesus! the name that charms our
fears.
That bids our sorrows cease;
'Tis music in the sinner's ears,
'Tis life, and health, and peace.

4 He breaks the power of cancelled
sin,
He sets the prisoner free;
His blood can make the foulest
clean,
His blood availed for me.

5 He speaks, and, listening to His
voice,
New life the dead receive,
The mournful, broken hearts rejoice,
The humble poor believe.

6 Hear Him, ye deaf; His praise, ye
dumb,
Your loosened tongues employ;
Ye blind, behold your Saviour come,
And leap, ye lame, for joy.

7 Look unto Him, ye nations, own
Your God, ye fallen race;
Look, and be saved through faith
alone,
Be justified by grace.

Charles Wesley (1707–88)

593 L.M.

'And Enoch walked with God'
Genesis 5 vv 22 & 24

1 O walk with Jesus, wouldst thou
know
How deep, how wide His love can
flow!
They only fail His love to prove
Who in the ways of sinners rove.

2 Walk thou with Him; that way is
light,
All other pathways end in night:
Walk thou with Him; that way is
rest;
All other pathways are unblest.

3 O walk with Jesus! to thy view
He will make all things sweet and
new;
Will bring new fragrance from each
flower,
And hallow every passing hour.

4 Jesus, a great desire have we
To walk life's troubled path with
Thee:
Come to us now, in converse stay;
And O walk with us day by day!

Edwin Paxton Hood (1820–85)

594 Irregular

'Come unto me' Matthew 11 v 28

1 O what a Saviour that He died for
me!
From condemnation He hath made
me free;
'He that believeth on the Son', saith
He,
'Hath everlasting life.'

'Verily, verily,' I say unto you,
'Verily, verily,' message ever new;
'He that believeth on the Son,' tis true,
'Hath everlasting life.'

2 All my iniquities on Him were laid,
  All my indebtedness by Him was
    paid;
  All who believe on Him, the Lord
    hath said,
  'Have everlasting life.'

3 Though poor and needy I can trust
    my Lord,
  Though weak and sinful I believe
    His Word;
  O glad message! every child of God
  'Hath everlasting life'.

4 Though all unworthy, yet I will not
    doubt,
  For him that cometh He will not cast
    out.
  He that believeth, O the good news
    shout,
  'Hath everlasting life.'

James McGranahan (1840–1907)

595   87.87.47

'Prepare to meet thy God' Amos 4 v 12

1 Pause, my soul! and ask the
    question,
  Art thou ready to meet God?
  Am I made a real christian,
  Washed in the Redeemer's blood?
  Have I union
  With the church's living Head?

2 Am I quickened by His Spirit;
  Live a life of faith and prayer?
  Trusting wholly to His merit;
  Casting on Him all my care?
  Daily longing
  In His likeness to appear?

3 If my hope on Christ is stayed,
  Let Him come when He thinks best;
  O my soul! Be not dismayed,
  Lean upon His loving breast;
  He will cheer thee
  With the smilings of His face.

4 But, if still a total stranger
  To His precious name and blood,
  Thou art on the brink of danger;
  Canst thou face a holy God?
  Think and tremble,
  Death is now upon the road.

William Gadsby (1773–1844)

596   77.77.77

'This man receiveth sinners' Luke 15 v 2

1 Sinners Jesus will receive:
  Tell this word of grace to all
  Who the heavenly pathway leave,
  All who linger, all who fall;
  This can bring them back again:
  Christ receiveth sinful men.

2 Shepherds seek their wandering
    sheep
  O'er the mountains bleak and cold;
  Jesus such a watch doth keep
  O'er the lost ones of His fold,
  Seeking them o'er moor and fen:
  Christ receiveth sinful men.

3 Sick and sorrowful and blind,
  I with all my sins draw nigh;
  O my Saviour, Thou canst find
  Help for sinners such as I;
  Speak that word of love again:
  Christ receiveth sinful men.

4 Christ receiveth sinful men,
  Even me with all my sin;
  Openeth to me heaven again;
  With Him I may enter in.
  Death hath no more sting nor pain:
  Christ receiveth sinful men.

Erdmann Neumeister (1671–1756)
Tr. Emma Frances Bevan (1827–1909)

597 7 6. 7 6. D (with refrain)

'He being not a forgetful hearer'
James 1 v 25

1 Tell me the old, old story
Of unseen things above,
Of Jesus and His glory,
Of Jesus and His love:
Tell me the story simply,
As to a little child,
For I am weak and weary,
And helpless and defiled.

Tell me the old, old story,
Tell me the old, old story,
Tell me the old, old story,
Of Jesus and His love.

2 Tell me the story slowly,
That I may take it in –
That wonderful redemption,
God's remedy for sin.
Tell me the story often,
For I forget so soon;
The early dew of morning
Has passed away at noon.

3 Tell me the story softly,
With earnest tones and grave:
Remember, I'm the sinner
Whom Jesus came to save.
Tell me that story always,
If you would really be,
In any time of trouble,
A comforter to me.

4 Tell me the same old story
When you have cause to fear
That this world's empty glory
Is costing me too dear.
Yes, and when that world's glory
Is dawning on my soul,
Tell me the old, old story –
Christ Jesus makes thee whole.

Arabella Catherine Hankey (1834–1911)

598 7 6. 7 6. D

'And this gospel of the kingdom shall be
preached in all the world for a witness
unto all nations' Matthew 24 v 14

1 The gospel is most precious,
A sacred holy ground,
And it shall be victorious,
For all those heaven-bound.
It comes with every blessing,
To capture God's elect,
And fills their hearts with praising,
No flaws can one detect.

2 The gospel is the glory
Of God's own precious Son,
For it's about the story
Of how our hearts were won.
We were all lost in darkness,
Until we heard the Word,
And though we were not righteous,
Christ died to be our Lord.

3 The gospel is the promise
Of God to Abraham.
'Thy seed shall be most num'rous
Drawn out from every land.
A great and mighty nation
Will be thy holy Son's,
From every place and station,
To Jesus they shall come.'

4 The gospel of the Kingdom
Shall spread through all the world,
And like a mighty banner,
Its glory is unfurled.
The Rock cut from the mountain
Became the Cornerstone,
And like a living fountain,
He gives life to His own.

5 The gospel is the highway
That leads to life above,
It is the sacred pathway
That brings us to God's love.
There is no other message
That tells us where to hide,
There is no other passage,
That leads to Jesus' side.

6 The gospel of the Saviour
Fills all our hearts with praise.
It is a sweet, sweet savour
Perfuming all our days.
It drives away our sadness
And brings us joy and peace,
It fills our souls with gladness
That shall not ever cease.

© The Author   Robert Dickie (b.1950)

599   L.M.

*'The law of the LORD is perfect,
converting the soul' Psalm 19 v 7*

1 The law of God is good and wise,
And sets His will before our eyes;
Shows us the way of righteousness
And dooms to death when we
    transgress.

2 Its light of holiness imparts
The knowledge of our sinful hearts,
That we may see our lost estate
And seek deliverance ere too late.

3 To those who help in Christ have
    found,
And would in works of love abound,
It shows what deeds are His delight
And should be done as good and
    right.

4 When men the offered help disdain,
And wilfully in sin remain,
Its terror in their ear resounds
And keeps their wickedness in
    bounds.

5 The law is good, but since the fall,
Its holiness condemns us all;
It dooms us for our sins to die
And has no power to justify.

6 To Jesus we for refuge flee
Who from the curse has set us free,
And humbly worship at His throne,
Saved by His grace, through faith
    alone.

Mathias Loy (1828–1915)

600   C.M.

*'And whosoever will, let him take the
water of life freely' Revelation 22 v 17*

1 The Saviour calls, let every ear
Attend the heavenly sound;
Ye doubting souls, dismiss your fear,
Hope smiles reviving round.

2 For every thirsty, longing heart,
Here streams of bounty flow;
And life and health and bliss impart,
To banish mortal woe.

3 Ye sinners, come, 'tis mercy's voice;
The gracious call obey;
Mercy invites to heavenly joys,
And can you yet delay?

4 Dear Saviour, draw reluctant hearts,
To Thee let sinners fly,
And take the bliss Thy love imparts,
And drink and never die.

Anne Steele (1717–78)

601   7 6. 7 6. D

'Where art thou?' Genesis 3 v 9

1 The voice of God eternal
Was heard in Eden far,
'Mid silence that was fearful,
For sin had come to mar.
Where art thou, child created,
Where hidest thou from Me?
For sin has man defeated,
God's face he could not see.

2 A separation woeful
From God and hope and life,
Despair and death so painful,
A way of grief and strife.
The serpent so beguiling
Enticed mankind to fall,
The whole creation writhing,
From Satan's tempting call.

3 The Saviour to the victory
From heaven to earth came down;
He came to show God's mercy
And move the Father's frown.
Upon His blessèd shoulders
Our Saviour took our shame,
And paid the price for sinners;
Who can forget His name?

4 Where art thou, O poor sinner,
In death and sin's dark night?
O listen to the wonder
Of words of truth and light.
O turn thy gaze to Calvary
Where Jesus calls thee back;
From hiding come for mercy,
In Christ thou wilt not lack.

5 O wondrous restoration,
An act of grace sublime!
The news of man's salvation
Was planned by love divine.
What peace and joy is given
To those who hear His voice
To come and be forgiven,
And in His grace rejoice.

© The Author   William Vernon Higham (b.1926)

602   Irregular

'Look unto me, and be ye saved, all the
ends of the earth' Isaiah 45 v 22

1 There is life for a look at the
    Crucified One,
There is life at this moment for thee;
Then look, sinner, look unto Him
    and be saved,
Unto Him who was nailed to the tree.

Look! look! look and live!
There is life for a look at the Crucified One,
There is life at this moment for thee.

2 It is not thy tears of repentance or
    prayers,
But the blood that atones for the
    soul;
On Him, then, who shed it, thou
    mayest at once
Thy weight of iniquities roll.

3 His anguish of soul on the cross
    hast thou seen?
His cry of distress hast thou heard?
Then why, if the terrors of wrath He
    endured,
Should pardon to thee be deferred?

4 Then doubt not thy welcome,
    since God has declared
There remaineth no more to be
    done;
That once in the end of the world He
    appeared,
And completed the work He begun.

5 But take with rejoicing from Jesus at
    once
The life everlasting He gives;
And know with assurance thou never
    canst die,
Since Jesus, thy righteousness, lives.

Amelia Matilda Hull (1825–82)

603   Irregular

'Rejoice with me: for I have found my
sheep which was lost' Luke 15 v 6

1 There were ninety and nine that
    safely lay
In the shelter of the fold,
But one was out on the hills away,
Far off from the gates of gold,
Away on the mountains wild and
    bare,
Away from the tender Shepherd's
    care,
Away from the tender Shepherd's
    care.

2 Lord, Thou hast here Thy ninety and
    nine;
Are they not enough for Thee?
But the Shepherd made answer: This
    of Mine
Has wandered away from Me;
And although the road be rough and
    steep,
I go to the desert to find My sheep,
I go to the desert to find My sheep.

3 But none of the ransomed ever knew
  How deep were the waters crossed;
  Nor how dark was the night that the
    Lord passed through
  Ere He found His sheep that was
    lost.
  Out in the desert He heard its cry,
  Sick and helpless, and ready to die,
  Sick and helpless, and ready to die.

4 Lord, whence are those blood-drops
    all the way
  That mark out the mountain's track?
  They were shed for one who had
    gone astray
  Ere the Shepherd could bring him
    back.
  Lord, whence are Thy hands so rent
    and torn?
  They are pierced tonight by many a
    thorn,
  They are pierced tonight by many a
    thorn.

5 But all through the mountains,
    thunder-riven,
  And up from the rocky steep,
  There arose a cry to the gate of heaven,
  Rejoice! I have found My sheep!
  And the angels echoed around the
    throne.
  Rejoice, for the Lord brings back His
    own!
  Rejoice, for the Lord brings back His
    own!

Elizabeth Cecilia Clephane (1830–69)

604   7 6. 7 6. D

'Today if ye will hear his voice'
Psalm 95 v 7

1 Today Thy mercy calls us
  To wash away our sin,
  However great our trespass,
  Whatever we have been;
  However long from mercy
  Our hearts have turned away,
  Thy blood, O Christ, can cleanse us
  And make us white today.

2 Today Thy gate is open,
  And all who enter in
  Shall find a Father's welcome,
  And pardon for their sin;
  The past shall be forgotten,
  A present joy be given,
  A future grace be promised,
  A glorious crown in heaven.

3 O all-embracing mercy!
  O ever-open door!
  What should we do without Thee
  When heart and eye run o'er?
  When all things seem against us,
  To drive us to despair,
  We know one gate is open,
  One ear will hear our prayer.

Oswald Allen (1816–78)

605   7 7.7 7.7 7

'Come unto me, all ye that labour and
are heavy laden, and I will give you rest'
Matthew 11 v 28

1 Weary souls, that wander wide
  From the central point of bliss,
  Turn to Jesus crucified,
  Fly to those dear wounds of His;
  Sink into the purple flood;
  Rise into the life of God!

2 Find in Christ the way of peace,
  Peace unspeakable, unknown;
  By His pain He gives you ease,
  Life by His expiring groan;
  Rise, exalted by His fall,
  Find in Christ your All in all.

3 Believe the record true:
  God to you His Son hath given!
  Ye may now be happy too,
  Find on earth the life of heaven,
  Live the life of heaven above,
  All the life of glorious love.

Charles Wesley (1707–88)

606

7 7. 7 7

'Come; for all things are now ready'
Luke 14 v 17

1 Welcome, welcome! sinner, hear!
Hang not back through shame or
    fear:
Doubt not, nor distrust the call;
Mercy is proclaimed to all.

2 Welcome, weeping penitent!
Grace has made thy heart relent:
Welcome, long estrangèd child!
God in Christ is reconciled.

3 Welcome to the cleansing fount
Springing from the sacred mount:
Welcome to the feast divine,
Bread of life and living wine.

4 All ye weary and distressed,
Welcome to relief and rest!
All is ready, hear the call,
There is ample room for all!

5 None can come that shall not find
Mercy called whom grace inclined!
Nor shall any willing heart
Hear the bitter word, Depart!

6 O! The virtue of that price.
That redeeming sacrifice!
Come, ye bought, but not with gold,
Welcome to the sacred fold.

Josiah Conder (1789–1855)

607

C.M.

'The gospel of peace' Romans 10 v 15

1 What a divine harmonious sound
The gospel trumpet gives;
No music can with it compare;
The soul that knows it lives.

2 Ten thousand blessings it contains,
Divinely rich and free,
For helpless, wretched, ruined man,
Though vile and base as we.

3 It speaks of pardon full and free,
Through Christ, the lamb once slain;
Whose blood can cleanse the foulest
    soul,
And take away all stain.

4 The vilest sinner out of hell,
Who lives to feel his need,
Is welcome to a throne of grace,
The Saviour's blood to plead.

5 The Lord delights to hear them cry,
And knock at mercy's door;
'Tis grace that makes them feel their
    need,
And pray to Him for more.

6 Nor will He send them empty back,
Nor fright them from the door;
The Father has in Jesus stored
All blessings for the poor.

William Gadsby (1773–1844)

608

8 8. 8 8. D

'What think ye of Christ?'
Matthew 22 v 42

1 What think ye of Christ? Is the test
To try both your state and your
    scheme,
You cannot be right in the rest,
Unless you think rightly of Him.
As Jesus appears in your view,
As He is belovèd or not;
So God is desposèd to you,
And mercy or wrath is your lot.

2 Some take Him a creature to be,
A man, or an angel at most;
Sure these have not feelings like me,
Nor know themselves wretched and
    lost:
So guilty, so helpless am I,
I dare not confide in His blood,
Nor on His protection rely,
Unless I was sure He is God.

3 If asked what of Jesus I think,
  Though still my best thoughts are
     but poor,
  I say He's my Meat and my Drink,
  My Life, and my Strength, and my
     Store;
  My Shepherd, my Husband, my
     Friend,
  My Saviour from sin and from thrall;
  My Hope from beginning to end,
  My Portion, my Lord, and my All.

John Newton (1726–1807)

609   Irregular

*'An anchor of the soul, both sure and
steadfast' Hebrews 6 v 19*

1 Will your anchor hold in the storms
     of life,
  When the clouds unfold their wings
     of strife?
  When the strong tides lift, and the
     cables strain,
  Will your anchor drift, or firm
     remain?

  *We have an anchor that keeps the soul
  Steadfast and sure while the billows roll,
  Fastened to the Rock which cannot move,
  Grounded firm and deep in the Saviour's
     love.*

2 Will your anchor hold in the straits
     of fear,
  When the breakers roar and the reef
     is near?
  While the surges rave, and the wild
     winds blow,
  Shall the angry waves then your bark
     o'erflow?

3 Will you anchor hold in the floods of
     death,
  When the waters cold chill our latest
     breath?
  On the rising tide it can never fail,
  While your anchor holds within the
     veil.

4 Will your eyes behold through the
     morning light
  The city of gold and the harbour
     bright?
  Will you anchor safe by the heavenly
     shore,
  When life's storms are past for
     evermore?

Priscilla Jane Owens (1829–1907)

610   Irregular

*'Made nigh by the blood of Christ'
Ephesians 2 v 13*

1 Would you be free from your burden
     of sin?
  There's power in the blood, power in
     the blood;
  Would you o'er evil a victory win?
  There's wonderful power in the
     blood.

  *There is power, power, wonder-working
     power
  In the blood of the Lamb;
  There is power, power, wonder-working
     power
  In the precious blood of the Lamb.*

2 Would you be free from your passion
     and pride?
  There's power in the blood, power in
     the blood;
  Come for a cleansing to Calvary's
     tide,
  There's wonderful power in the
     blood.

3 Would you be whiter, much whiter
    than snow?
  There's power in the blood, power in
    the blood;
  Sin-stains are lost in its life-giving
    flow,
  There's wonderful power in the
    blood.

4 Would you do service for Jesus your
    King?
  There's power in the blood, power in
    the blood;
  Would you live daily His praises to
    sing?
  There's wonderful power in the
    blood.

L. E. Jones

611   C.M.

'Fear not ... he will come and save you'
Isaiah 35 v 4

1 Ye trembling souls, dismiss your
    fears,
  Be mercy all your theme;
  Mercy, which like a river flows
  In one perpetual stream.

2 Fear not the powers of earth and
    hell;
  God will those powers restrain;
  His arm shall all their rage repel,
  And make their efforts vain.

3 Fear not the want of outward good,
  God for His own provides;
  Grants them supplies of daily food,
  And all they need besides.

4 Fear not that He will e'er forsake
  Or leave His work undone;
  He's faithful to His promises,
  And faithful to His Son.

5 Fear not the terrors of the grave,
  Or death's tremendous sting;
  He will from endless wrath preserve,
  To endless glory bring.

Benjamin Beddome (1717–1795)

THE GOSPEL ...
ITS BEGINNINGS AND RECEPTION

———

612

C.M.

'For by grace are ye saved'
Ephesians 2 v 8

1 All that I was, my sin, my guilt,
My death, was all my own;
All that I am I owe to Thee,
My gracious God, alone.

2 The evil of my former state
Was mine, and only mine;
The good in which I now rejoice
Is Thine, and only Thine.

3 The darkness of my former state,
The bondage – all was mine;
The light of life in which I walk,
The liberty is Thine.

4 Thy grace first made me feel my sin,
And taught me to believe;
Then, in believing, peace I found,
And now in Christ I live.

5 All that I am while here on earth,
All that I hope to be,
When Jesus comes and glory dawns,
I owe it, Lord, to Thee.

Horatius Bonar (1808–89)

613

88.88.88

'In whom we have redemption through
his blood, the forgiveness of sins'
Ephesians 1 v 7

1 And can it be that I should gain
An interest in the Saviour's blood?
Died He for me, who caused His
pain?

For me, who Him to death pursued?
Amazing love! How can it be
That Thou, my God, shouldst die for
me?

2 'Tis mystery all! The Immortal dies!
Who can explore His strange
design?
In vain the first-born seraph tries
To sound the depths of love divine!
'Tis mercy all! Let earth adore,
Let angel minds inquire no more.

3 He left His Father's throne above –
So free, so infinite His grace –
Emptied Himself of all but love,
And bled for Adam's helpless race:
'Tis mercy all, immense and free;
For, O my God, it found out me!

4 Long my imprisoned spirit lay
Fast bound in sin and nature's night;
Thine eye diffused a quickening ray,
I woke, the dungeon flamed with
light;
My chains fell off, my heart was free,
I rose, went forth, and followed
Thee.

5 No condemnation now I dread;
Jesus, and all in Him, is mine!
Alive in Him, my living Head,
And clothed in righteousness divine,
Bold I approach the eternal throne,
And claim the crown, through Christ
my own.

Charles Wesley (1707–78)

614 C.M.

'Is not my word like as a fire saith the LORD' Jeremiah 23 v 29

1 Come, O Thou all-victorious Lord,
Thy power to us make known;
Strike with the hammer of Thy
Word,
And break these hearts of stone.

2 O that we all might now begin
Our foolishness to mourn,
And turn at once from every sin,
And to our Saviour turn!

3 Give us ourselves and Thee to know,
In this our gracious day;
Repentance unto life bestow,
And take our sins away.

4 Conclude us first in unbelief,
And freely then release;
Fill every soul with sacred grief,
And then with sacred peace.

5 Impoverish, Lord, and then relieve,
And then enrich the poor;
The knowledge of our sickness give,
The knowledge of our cure.

6 That blessèd sense of guilt impart,
And then remove the load;
Trouble, and wash the troubled
heart
In the atoning blood.

7 Our desperate state through sin
declare,
And speak our sins forgiven;
In perfect holiness prepare,
And take us up to heaven.

Charles Wesley (1707–88)

615 10 10. 10 10

'Rise; he calleth thee' Mark 10 v 49

1 God calleth yet: at last shall I not
heed?
How long shall I refuse the grace I
need?
While pleasure fades, and time's
swift moments fly,
Still shall my soul in mortal peril lie?

2 God calleth yet: at length shall I not
turn?
Dare I once more His faithful
pleading spurn?
Though I have known full well what
I should be,
My will rebelled: yet now He
beckoneth me.

3 God calleth yet: alas, this stubborn
heart!
I feared His yoke, shrank from the
nobler part;
God and my soul how oft have I
betrayed!
He draws me still: rise, heart, be not
afraid.

4 Yield to Him now, once and for ever
yield;
Make God thy portion, and His
grace thy shield.
What though the world its pleasures
still display?
God calleth yet: O heart, do thou
obey!

Gerhard Tersteegen (1697–1769)
© Copyright Control *Tr. Howell Elvet Lewis (1860–1953)*

616 C.M.

'A fountain opened ... for sin and for uncleanness' Zechariah 13 v 1

1 How sad our state by nature is!
Our sin how deep it stains!
And Satan binds our captive minds
Fast in his slavish chains.

2 But there's a voice of sovereign grace
Sounds from the sacred Word –
Ho! ye despairing sinners, come,
And trust upon the Lord.

3 My soul obeys the almighty call,
And runs to this relief;
I would believe Thy promise, Lord;
O help my unbelief!

4 To the dear fountain of Thy blood,
Incarnate God, I fly;
Here let me wash my guilty soul
From crimes of deepest dye.

5 A guilty, weak and helpless wretch,
On Thy kind arms I fall;
Be Thou my strength and
  righteousness,
My Jesus and my all.

Isaac Watts (1674–1748)

617
8 7. 8 7. D

*'Harden not your heart, as in the
provocation' Psalm 95 v 8*

1 Hush, my soul, what voice is
  pleading?
Thou canst feel its silent power;
Who is this that speaks so gently
In this solemn evening hour?
'Stay, poor sinner; life is fleeting,
And thy soul is dark within;
Wilt thou wait till outer darkness
Close in gloom thy life of sin?'

2 Hark! it is a voice of sweetness,
Tenderly it speaks, and true!
Dark and sad, yet strangely yearning,
For a peace I never knew.
Half inclined to stay and listen,
Half inclined to go away;
Still I linger, for it whispers,
'Harden not thy heart today'.

3 What is this that steals beside me?
Can it be that at my side,
In His own mysterious presence,
Stands the wondrous Crucified?
'Why poor sinner, wilt thou linger?
I am waiting to forgive;
See the meaning of these wound
  prints;
I have died that thou mayest live!'

4 Hush, my soul! It is thy Saviour!
And He seeks His lost one now;
He is waiting, flee not from Him,
Venture near, before Him bow;
Tell Thy sins; He will forgive thee;
And He will not love thee less;
For the human heart of Jesus
Overflows with tenderness.

John E. Lester (c.1845–c.1900)

618
S.M. (with refrain)

*'Him that cometh to me I will in no wise
cast out' John 6 v 37*

1 I hear Thy welcome voice
That calls me, Lord, to Thee,
For cleansing in Thy precious blood
That flowed on Calvary.

*I am coming, Lord,
Coming now to Thee:
Wash me, cleanse me, in the blood
That flowed on Calvary.*

2 Though coming weak and vile,
Thou dost my strength assure;
Thou dost my vileness fully cleanse,
Till spotless all and pure.

3 'Tis Jesus calls me on
To perfect faith and love,
To perfect hope and peace and trust,
For earth and heaven above.

4 'Tis Jesus who confirms
The blessed work within,
By adding grace to welcomed grace,
Where reigned the power of sin.

5 All hail, atoning blood!
All hail, redeeming grace!
All hail, the gift of Christ our Lord,
Our strength and righteousness!

Lewis Hartsough (1828–1919)

619   L.M.

'Jesus saith unto him, I am the way'
John 14 v 6

1 Jesus, my All, to heaven is gone,
He whom I fix my hopes upon:
His track I see, and I'll pursue
The narrow way till Him I view.

2 The way the holy prophets went,
The road that leads from
        banishment,
The King's highway of holiness,
I'll go, for all His paths are peace.

3 This is the way I long have sought,
And mourned because I found it not;
My grief and burden long have been,
Because I could not cease from sin.

4 The more I strove against its power,
I sinned and stumbled but the more;
Till late I heard my Saviour say,
'Come hither, soul, I am the way!'

5 Lo! glad I come; and Thou, blest
        Lamb,
Shalt take me to Thee as I am!
Nothing but sin have I to give;
Nothing but love shall I receive.

6 Now will I tell to sinners round
What a dear Saviour I have found!
I'll point to Thy redeeming blood,
And say, 'Behold the way to God!'

John Cennick (1718–55)

620   C.M.

'Lord, help me' Matthew 15 v 25

1 Jesus! Redeemer, Saviour, Lord,
The weary sinner's Friend,
Come to my help, pronounce the
        word,
And bid my troubles end.

2 Deliverance to my soul proclaim,
And life, and liberty;
Shed forth the virtue of Thy name,
And Jesus prove to me!

3 Faith to be healed Thou know'st I
        have,
For Thou that faith hast given;
Thou canst, Thou wilt the sinner
        save,
And make me meet for heaven.

4 Thou canst o'ercome this heart of
        mine,
Thou wilt victorious prove;
For everlasting strength is Thine,
And everlasting love.

5 Thy powerful Spirit shall subdue
Unconquerable sin,
Cleanse this foul heart, and make it
        new,
And write Thy law within.

6 Bound down with twice ten
        thousand ties,
Yet let me hear Thy call,
My soul in confidence shall rise,
Shall rise and break through all.

Charles Wesley (1707–88)

621   L.M.

*'But God ... hath quickened us together
with Christ' Ephesians 2 vv 4,5*

1 Lord, I was blind: I could not see
In Thy marred visage any grace;
But now the beauty of Thy face
In radiant vision dawns on me.

2 Lord, I was deaf: I could not hear
The thrilling music of Thy voice;
But now I hear Thee and rejoice,
And all Thine uttered words are
        dear.

3 Lord, I was dumb: I could not speak
The grace and glory of Thy name;
But now, as touched with living
        flame,
My lips Thine eager praises wake.

4 Lord, I was dead: I could not stir
My lifeless soul to come to Thee;
But now, since Thou hast quickened
me,
I rise from sin's dark sepulchre.

5 Lord, Thou hast made the blind to
see,
The deaf to hear, the dumb to speak,
The dead to live; and lo, I break
The chains of my captivity.

William Tidd Matson (1833–99)

622
C.M.

*'My people shall be satisfied with my
goodness' Jeremiah 31 v 14*

1 O Christ, in Thee my soul hath
found,
And found in Thee alone,
The peace, the joy I sought so long,
The bliss till now unknown.

*Now none but Christ can satisfy,
None other name for me!
There's love and life and lasting joy,
Lord Jesus found in Thee.*

2 I sighed for rest and happiness,
I yearned for them, not Thee;
But, while I passed my Saviour by,
His love laid hold on me.

3 I tried the broken cisterns, Lord,
But, ah, the waters failed!
Even as I stooped to drink they fled,
And mocked me as I wailed.

4 The pleasures lost I sadly mourned,
But never wept for Thee,
Till grace the sightless eyes received
Thy loveliness to see.

Anonymous

623
L.M.

*'My heart is fixed, O God, my heart is
fixed: I will sing and give praise'
Psalm 57 v 7*

1 O happy day, that fixed my choice
On Thee my Saviour and my God!
Well may this glowing heart rejoice,
And tell its raptures all abroad.

2 O happy bond, that seals my vows
To Him who merits all my love!
Let cheerful anthems fill this house
While to that sacred place I move.

3 'Tis done! the great transaction's
done!
I am my Lord's and He is mine;
He drew me, and I followed on,
Charmed to confess the voice divine.

4 Now rest, my long-divided heart;
Fixed on this blissful centre, rest;
With ashes who would grudge to
part,
When called on angels' food to
feast?

5 High heaven, that heard the solemn
vow,
That vow renewed shall daily hear,
Till in life's latest hour I bow,
And bless in death a bond so dear.

Philip Doddridge (1702–51)

624
87.887

*'For to me to live is Christ'
Philippians 1 v 21*

1 O the bitter shame and sorrow,
That a time could ever be,
When I let the Saviour's pity
Plead in vain, and proudly answered,
'All of self, and none of Thee!'

2 Yet He found me; I beheld Him
Bleeding on the accursèd tree,
Heard Him pray, 'Forgive them,
Father!'
And my wistful heart said faintly,
'Some of self, and some of Thee!'

3 Day by day, His tender mercy,
Healing, helping, full and free,
Sweet and strong, and, ah! so
    patient,
Brought me lower, while I whispered,
'Less of self, and more of Thee!'

4 Higher than the highest heavens,
Deeper than the deepest sea,
Lord, Thy love at last hath
    conquered;
Grant me now my supplication –
'None of self, and all of Thee!'

Theodore Monod (1836–1921)

625   8 8 6. D

*'They shall look on him whom they
pierced' John 19 v 37*

1 O Thou who hast redeemed of old,
And bidd'st me of Thy strength take
    hold,
And be at peace with Thee,
Help me Thy benefits to own,
And hear me tell what Thou hast
    done,
O dying Lamb, for me.

2 Vouchsafe the eye of faith to see
The Man transfixed on Calvary,
To know Thee who Thou art –
The one eternal God and true;
And let the sight affect, subdue,
And break my stubborn heart.

3 Lover of souls, to rescue mine,
Reveal the charity divine
That suffered in my stead;
That made Thy soul a sacrifice,
And quenched in death those
    gracious eyes,
And bowed that sacred head.

4 The veil of unbelief remove;
And by Thy manifested love,
And by Thy sprinkled blood,
Destroy the love of sin in me,
And get Thyself the victory,
And bring me back to God.

Charles Wesley (1707–88)

626   C.M.

*'If any man thirst, let him come unto me,
and drink' John 7 v 37*

1 O what amazing words of grace
Are in the gospel found,
Suited to every sinner's case
Who knows the joyful sound.

2 Poor, sinful, thirsty, fainting souls
Are freely welcome here;
Salvation, like a river, rolls
Abundant, free and clear.

3 Come, then, with all your wants and
    wounds,
Your every burden bring:
Here love, unchanging love,
    abounds,
A deep, celestial spring.

4 Millions of sinners, vile as you,
Have here found life and peace!
Come then and prove its virtues too,
And drink, adore and bless.

Samuel Medley (1738–99)

627   8 7. 8 7. D

*'But godliness with contentment is great
gain' 1 Timothy 6 v 6*

1 Oh to search the wondrous wisdom
Of the one and living Lord,
To degrees that slay rebellion
With a sharp convicting sword.
Firm in faith believing fully
In God's purest holiness,
That will judge all men as guilty,
Standing there with none to bless.

2 See the glorious God and mighty
Yet a God of perfect love.
Fear enfolds me in the mem'ry,
Wounds my soul, I cannot move.
Yet within the place of mercy
There His peace will comfort me.
There upon His throne regarding
Peace in Christ, I need not flee.

3 God my Father and my Haven,
Strong and high for all to gaze.
Now a pathway free to heaven,
Now gives strength in flood and
 blaze.
In Him dwells my full contentment,
For His sake all foes I'll face.
Without Him there's no fulfilment
Only death and hell's disgrace.

Ann Griffiths (1776–1805)
© The Translator   *Tr. William Vernon Higham (b.1926)*

628
7 8. 7 8 (with refrain)

'Without shedding of blood is no
remission' Hebrews 9 v 22

1 What can wash away my stain?
Nothing but the blood of Jesus.
What can make me whole again?
Nothing but the blood of Jesus.

*Oh, precious is the flow
That makes me white as snow;
No other fount I know,
Nothing but the blood of Jesus.*

2 For my cleansing this I see –
Nothing but the blood of Jesus;
For my pardon this my plea –
Nothing but the blood of Jesus.

3 Nothing can for sin atone,
Nothing but the blood of Jesus;
Nought of good that I have done,
Nothing but the blood of Jesus.

4 This is all my hope and peace –
Nothing but the blood of Jesus;
He is all my righteousness –
Nothing but the blood of Jesus.

5 Now by this I overcome:
Nothing but the blood of Jesus;
Now by this I'll reach my home:
Nothing but the blood of Jesus!

Robert Lowry (1826–1899)

629
8 8. 8 8. 8 8.

'Father, forgive them; for they know not
what they do' Luke 23 v 34

1 Would Jesus have the sinner die?
Why hangs He then on yonder tree?
What means that strange expiring
 cry?
Sinners, He prays for you and me:
'Forgive them, Father, O forgive!
They know not that by Me they live'.

2 Thou loving, all atoning Lamb,
Thee, by Thy painful agony,
Thy sweat of blood, Thy grief and
 shame,
Thy cross and passion on the tree,
Thy precious death and life – I pray:
Take all, take all my sins away!

3 Oh let Thy love my heart, constrain
Thy love for guilty sinner's free,
That every hungry soul of man
May taste the grace that found out
 me;
That all may come and with me
 prove
Thy sovereign everlasting love.

Charles Wesley (1707–1788)

630
8 8 6. D

'It is appointed unto men once to die'
Hebrews 9 v 27

1 And am I only born to die?
And must I suddenly comply
With nature's stern decree?
What after death for me remains?
Celestial joys, or hellish pains,
To all eternity?

2 How then ought I on earth to live,
While God prolongs the kind
 reprieve
And props the house of clay?
My sole concern, my single care,
To watch, and tremble, and prepare
Against the fatal day.

3 No room for mirth or trifling here,
For worldly hope, or worldly fear,
If life so soon is gone:
If now the Judge is at the door,
And all mankind must stand before
The inexorable throne!

4 No matter which my thoughts
employ,
A moment's misery, or joy;
But O! when both shall end,
Where shall I find my destined
place?
Shall I my everlasting days
With fiends, or angels spend?

5 Nothing is worth a thought beneath
But how I may escape the death
That never, never dies;
How make mine own election sure,
And, when I fail on earth, secure
A mansion in the skies.

6 Jesus, vouchsafe a pitying ray,
Be Thou my guide, be Thou my way
To glorious happiness;
Ah, write the pardon on my heart,
And whensoe'er I hence depart,
Let me depart in peace.

Charles Wesley (1707–88)

631 S.M.

'How should man be just with God?'
Job 9 v 2

1 Answer for me, my Lord;
On Thee my cause I lay;
I dare not stand and plead myself;
Answer for me, I pray!

2 Condemned beneath the law,
I hear its awful word:
The soul that sinneth it shall die;
Answer for me, my Lord!

3 Without the spotless Lamb,
Without the blood outpoured,
There is no pardon for my soul;
Answer for me, my Lord!

4 Answer for me till life
Hath loosed her silver chord;
And as I sink in death's embrace,
Answer for me, my Lord!

5 No righteousness of mine
A shelter can afford;
But when I stand before the throne,
Answer for me, my Lord!

C.W.C.

632 66.66.88

'For by one offering he hath perfected for
ever them that are sanctified'
Hebrews 10 v 14

1 Arise, my soul, arise,
Shake off Thy guilty fears;
The bleeding Sacrifice
In my behalf appears:
Before the throne my Surety stands,
My name is written on His hands.

2 He ever lives above,
For me to intercede,
His all-redeeming love,
His precious blood, to plead;
His blood atoned for this our race,
And sprinkles now the throne of grace.

3 Five bleeding wounds He bears,
Received on Calvary;
They pour effectual prayers,
They strongly speak for me:
Forgive him, O forgive! they cry,
Nor let the ransomed sinner die!

4 The Father hears Him pray,
His dear Anointed One;
He cannot turn away
The presence of His Son:
His Spirit answers to the blood,
And tells me I am born of God.

5 My God is reconciled,
His pardoning voice I hear;
He owns me for His child,
I can no longer fear;
With confidence I now draw nigh,
And Father, Abba, Father! cry.

Charles Wesley (1707–88)

633

76.86.86.86

'A refuge from the storm, a shadow from the heat' Isaiah 25 v 4

1 Beneath the cross of Jesus
I fain would take my stand,
The shadow of a mighty rock
Within a weary land;
A home within the wilderness,
A rest upon the way,
From the burning of the noontide heat,
And the burden of the day.

2 O safe and happy shelter!
O refuge tried and sweet!
O trysting-place where heaven's love
And heaven's justice meet!
As to the holy patriarch
That wondrous dream was given,
So seems my Saviour's cross to me
A ladder up to heaven.

3 There lies beneath its shadow,
But on the farther side,
The darkness of an awful grave
That gapes both deep and wide:
And there between us stands the
cross,
Two arms outstretched to save,
Like a watchman set to guard the way
From that eternal grave.

4 Upon that cross of Jesus,
Mine eye at times can see
The very dying form of One
Who suffered there for me;
And from my stricken heart, with
tears,
Two wonders I confess –
The wonders of His glorious love,
And my own worthlessness.

5 I take, O cross, thy shadow,
For my abiding-place;
I ask no other sunshine than
The sunshine of His face;
Content to let the world go by,
To know no gain nor loss –
My sinful self my only shame,
My glory all – the cross.

Elizabeth Cecilia Clephane (1830–69)

634

6 10. 10 6

'If God be for us, who can be against us?'
Romans 8 v 31

1 Blessèd be God, our God!
Who gave for us His well-beloved
Son,
The gift of gifts, all other gifts in
one –
Blessèd be God, our God!

2 What will He not bestow?
Who freely gave this mighty gift
unbought,
Unmerited, unheeded, and
unsought –
What will He not bestow?

3 He sparèd not His Son!
'Tis this that silences each rising
fear;
'Tis this that bids the hard thought
disappear –
He sparèd not His Son!

4 Who shall condemn us now?
Since Christ hath died, and risen,
and gone above,
For us to plead at the right hand of
Love,
Who shall condemn us now?

5 'Tis God that justifies!
Who shall recall the pardon or the
grace,
Or who the broken chain of guilt
replace?
'Tis God that justifies!

6 The victory is ours!
For us in might came forth the
Mighty One;
For us He fought the fight, the
triumph won –
The victory is ours!

Horatius Bonar (1808–89)

635   98.98.88

'For by grace are ye saved through faith'
Ephesians 2 v 8

1 By grace I'm saved, grace free and
        boundless;
   My soul, believe and doubt it not.
   Why stagger at this word of
        promise?
   Hath scripture ever falsehood
        taught?
   No! then this word must true
        remain:
   By grace thou, too, shalt heaven
        obtain.

2 By grace! None dare lay claim to
        merit;
   Our works and conduct have no
        worth.
   God in His love sent our Redeemer,
   Christ Jesus, to this sinful earth;
   His death did for our sins atone
   And we are saved by grace alone.

3 By grace! O, mark this word of
        promise
   When thou art by thy sins
        oppressed,
   When Satan plagues thy troubled
        conscience
   And when thy heart is seeking rest.
   What reason cannot comprehend
   God by His grace to thee doth send.

4 By grace! This ground of faith is
        certain;
   So long as God is true, it stands.
   What saints have penned by
        inspiration,
   What in His Word our God
        commands,
   What our whole faith must rest
        upon,
   Is grace alone, grace in His Son.

                    Christian L. Scheidt (1709–61)

636   77.77.77

*'The dayspring from on high hath visited
us'* Luke 1 v 78

1 Christ, whose glory fills the skies,
   Christ, the true, the only Light.
   Sun of Righteousness, arise,
   Triumph o'er the shades of night;
   Day-spring from on high, be near;
   Day-star, in my heart appear.

2 Dark and cheerless is the morn
   Unaccompanied by Thee;
   Joyless is the day's return,
   Till Thy mercy's beams I see,
   Till they inward light impart,
   Glad my eyes, and warm my heart.

3 Visit then this soul of mine;
   Pierce the gloom of sin and grief;
   Fill me, Radiancy divine;
   Scatter all my unbelief;
   More and more Thyself display,
   Shining to the perfect day.

                    Charles Wesley (1707–88)

637   L.M.

*'To know the love of Christ, which
passeth knowledge'* Ephesians 3 v 19

1 Eternal depth of love divine,
   In Jesus, God with us, displayed;
   How bright Thy beaming glories
        shine!
   How wide Thy healing streams are
        spread!

2 With whom dost Thou delight to
        dwell?
   Sinners, a vile and thankless race:
   O God, what tongue aright can tell
   How vast Thy love, how great Thy
        grace!

3 The dictates of Thy sovereign will
   With joy our grateful hearts receive:
   All Thy delight in us fulfil;
   Lo! all we are to Thee we give.

4 To Thy sure love, Thy tender care,
Our flesh, soul, spirit, we resign:
O fix Thy sacred presence there,
And seal the abode for ever Thine!

5 O King of Glory, Thy rich grace
Our feeble thought surpasses far;
Yea, even our sins, though
numberless,
Less numerous than Thy mercies
are.

6 Still, Lord, Thy saving health display,
And arm our souls with heavenly
zeal;
So fearless shall we urge our way,
Through all the powers of earth and
hell.

Nicolaus Ludwig von Zinzendorf (1700–60)
Tr. John Wesley (1703–91)

638   C.M.

'The Son of God, who loved me, and gave himself for me' Galatians 2 v 20

1 For ever here my rest shall be,
Close to Thy bleeding side;
This all my hope, and all my plea,
For me the Saviour died!

2 My dying Saviour, and my God,
Fountain for guilt and sin,
Sprinkle me ever with Thy blood,
And cleanse, and keep me clean.

3 Wash me, and make me thus Thine
own,
Wash me, and mine Thou art,
Wash me, but not my feet alone,
My hands, my head, my heart.

4 The atonement of Thy blood apply,
Till faith to sight improve,
Till faith in full fruition die,
And all my soul be love.

Charles Wesley (1707–88)

639   10 10. 10 10

'The first man Adam was made a living soul' 1 Corinthians 15 v 45

1 God made me for Himself, to serve
Him here,
With love's pure service and in filial
fear;
To show His praise, for Him to
labour now;
Then see His glory, where the angels
bow.

2 All needful grace was mine through
His dear Son,
Whose life and death my full
salvation won;
The grace that would have
strengthened me, and taught;
Grace that would crown me when
my work was wrought.

3 And I, poor sinner, cast it all away;
Lives for the toil or pleasure of each
day;
As if no Christ had shed His
precious blood,
As if I owed no homage to my God.

4 O Holy Spirit, with Thy fire divine,
Melt into tears this thankless heart
of mine;
Teach me to love what once I seemed
to hate,
And live to God before it be too late.

Henry Williams Baker (1821–77)

640   C.M.

'The power of the Lord was present to heal them' Luke 5 v 17

1 Heal us, Immanuel; hear our prayer;
We wait to feel Thy touch:
Deep-wounded souls to Thee repair,
And, Saviour, we are such.

2 Our faith is feeble, we confess;
We faintly trust Thy word:
But wilt Thou pity us the less?
Be that far from Thee, Lord!

3 Remember him who once applied
  With trembling for relief;
  'Lord, I believe!' with tears he cried,
  'O help my unbelief!'

4 She, too, who touched Thee in the
    press,
  And healing virtue stole,
  Was answered: 'Daughter, go in
    peace;
  Thy faith hath made thee whole.'

5 Like her, with hopes and fears we
    come,
  To touch Thee, if we may:
  O send us not despairing home,
  Send none unhealed away.

                    William Cowper (1731–1800)

641   8 7. 8 7. D

*'Let us therefore come boldly unto the
throne of grace' Hebrews 4 v 16*

1 Here I stand in sin by nature,
  Of the living I am chief.
  Grace alone secures my future,
  God in sorrow sees my grief.
  Jesus stands in law's fulfilment,
  To transgressors mercy gives.
  God and man in glad contentment
  In this peace my soul now lives.

2 Boldly now my soul approaching,
  Golden sceptre in God's hand
  Reaching forth, to hear my pleading
  Then His gracious sweet command.
  Here I stand in sin beseeching.
  Yes, I'll fall before His feet.
  Oh for pardon and for cleansing
  In His blood, His grace to greet.

                           Ann Griffiths (1776–1805)
© The Translator   *Tr. William Vernon Higham (b.1926)*

642   8 5. 8 3

*'In thee, O LORD, do I put my trust'
Psalm 71 v 1*

1 I am trusting Thee, Lord Jesus,
  Trusting only Thee,
  Trusting Thee for full salvation,
  Great and free.

2 I am trusting Thee for pardon,
  At Thy feet I bow;
  For Thy grace and tender mercy,
  Trusting now.

3 I am trusting Thee for cleansing
  In the crimson flood;
  Trusting Thee to make me holy
  By Thy blood.

4 I am trusting Thee to guide me:
  Thou alone shalt lead,
  Every day and hour supplying
  All my need.

5 I am trusting Thee for power;
  Thine can never fail;
  Words which Thou Thyself shalt give
    me
  Must prevail.

6 I am trusting Thee, Lord Jesus;
  Never let me fall;
  I am trusting Thee for ever,
  And for all.

                   Frances Ridley Havergal (1836–79)

643   6 6. 6 6. 8 8

*'And great multitudes came ... and cast
them down at Jesus' feet; and he healed
them' Matthew 15 v 30*

1 I bring my sins to Thee,
  The sins I cannot count,
  That all may cleans'd be
  In Thy once-opened fount:
  I bring them, Saviour, all to Thee;
  The burden is too great for me.

2 My heart to Thee I bring,
The heart I cannot read,
A faithless, wandering thing,
An evil heart indeed:
I bring it, Saviour, now to Thee,
That fixed and faithful it may be.

3 My life I bring to Thee,
I would not be my own;
O Saviour, let me be
Thine ever, Thine alone!
My heart, my life, my all, I bring
To Thee, my Saviour and my King.

Frances Ridley Havergal (1836 –79)

644   D.C.M.

'Rest in the LORD' Psalm 37 v 7

1 I heard the voice of Jesus say,
'Come unto Me and rest;
Lay down, thou weary one, lay down
Thy head upon My breast!'
I came to Jesus as I was,
Weary, and worn, and sad;
I found in Him a resting-place,
And He has made me glad.

2 I heard the voice of Jesus say,
'Behold, I freely give
The living water – thirsty one,
Stoop down, and drink, and live!'
I came to Jesus, and I drank
Of that life-giving stream;
My thirst was quenched, my soul
revived,
And now I live in Him.

3 I heard the voice of Jesus say,
'I am this dark world's Light;
Look unto Me, thy morn shall rise,
And all thy day be bright!'
I looked to Jesus, and I found
In Him my Star, my Sun;
And in that light of life I'll walk
Till travelling days are done.

Horatius Bonar (1808–89)

645   10 10 (with refrain)

'Bow down thine ear, O LORD, hear me:
for I am poor and needy' Psalm 86 v 1

1 I need Thee every hour, most
gracious Lord;
No tender voice like Thine can peace
afford.

I need Thee, O I need Thee! every hour I
need Thee;
O bless me now, my Saviour! I come to
Thee.

2 I need Thee every hour; stay Thou
near by;
Temptations lose their power when
Thou art nigh.

3 I need Thee every hour, in joy or
pain;
Come quickly and abide, or life is
vain.

4 I need Thee every hour; teach me
Thy will,
And Thy rich promises in me fulfil.

5 I need Thee every hour, most Holy
One;
O make me Thine indeed, Thou
blessed Son!

Annie Sherwood Hawks (1835–1918)

646   7 6. 7 6. D

'Unto you therefore which believe he is
precious' 1 Peter 2 v 7

1 I need Thee, precious Jesus!
For I am full of sin;
My soul is dark and guilty,
My heart is dead within:
I need the cleansing fountain,
Where I can always flee,
The blood of Christ most precious,
The sinner's perfect plea.

2 I need Thee, precious Jesus!
For I am very poor;
A stranger and a pilgrim,
I have no earthly store:
I need the love of Jesus
To cheer me on my way,
To guide my doubting footsteps,
To be my strength and stay.

3 I need Thee, precious Jesus!
I need a friend like Thee;
A friend to soothe and comfort,
A friend to care for me:
I need the heart of Jesus
To feel each anxious care,
To tell my every trouble
And all my sorrows share.

4 I need Thee, precious Jesus!
And hope to see Thee soon,
Encircled with the rainbow,
And seated on Thy throne;
There with Thy blood-bought
children
My joy shall ever be,
To sing Thy praise, Lord Jesus,
To gaze, my Lord, on Thee.

Frederick Whitfield (1829–1904)

647   C.M.

'He looked on me' Luke 1 v 25

1 In evil long I took delight,
Unawed by shame or fear,
Till a new object struck my sight,
And stopped my wild career.

2 I saw One hanging on a tree,
In agonies and blood,
Who fixed His loving eyes on me,
As near His cross I stood.

3 Sure never till my latest breath
Can I forget that look;
It seemed to charge me with His
death,
Though not a word He spoke.

4 My conscience felt and owned the
guilt,
And plunged me in despair;
I saw my sins His blood had spilt,
And helped to nail Him there.

5 A second look He gave, which said,
'I freely all forgive;
This blood is for thy ransom paid;
I die that thou may'st live.'

John Newton (1725–1807)

648   7 6.7 6

'O LORD, truly I am thy servant'
Psalm 116 v 16

1 In full and glad surrender
I give myself to Thee,
Thine utterly and only
And evermore to be.

2 O Son of God, who lov'st me,
I will be Thine alone;
And all I have and am, Lord,
Shall henceforth be Thine own.

3 Reign over me, Lord Jesus;
O make my heart Thy throne!
It shall be Thine, dear Saviour,
It shall be Thine alone.

4 O come and reign, Lord Jesus;
Rule over everything!
And keep me always loyal
And true to Thee, my King.

Frances Ridley Havergal (1836–79)

649   7 7.7 7. D

'To lay hold upon the hope set before us'
Hebrews 6 v 18

1 Jesu, Lover of my soul,
Let me to Thy bosom fly,
While the nearer waters roll,
While the tempest still is high:
Hide me, O my Saviour, hide,
Till the storm of life be past;
Safe into the haven guide;
O receive my soul at last!

2 Other refuge have I none;
Hangs my helpless soul on Thee;
Leave, ah! leave me not alone,
Still support and comfort me:
All my trust on Thee is stayed,
All my help from Thee I bring;
Cover my defenceless head
With the shadow of Thy wing.

3 Thou, O Christ, art all I want;
More than all in Thee I find;
Raise the fallen, cheer the faint,
Heal the sick, and lead the blind:
Just and holy is Thy name,
I am all unrighteousness;
False and full of sin I am,
Thou art full of truth and grace.

4 Plenteous grace with Thee is found,
Grace to cover all my sin;
Let the healing streams abound,
Make and keep me pure within:
Thou of life the fountain art,
Freely let me take of Thee;
Spring Thou up within my heart,
Rise to all eternity.

Charles Wesley (1707–88)

650
6 5. 6 5. D

'Behold, God is my salvation'
Isaiah 12 v 2

1 Jesus, I will trust Thee,
Trust Thee with my soul;
Guilty, lost, and helpless,
Thou canst make me whole:
There is none in heaven
Or on earth like Thee:
Thou hast died for sinners –
Therefore, Lord for me.

2 Jesus, I must trust Thee,
Pondering Thy ways,
Full of love and mercy
All Thine earthly days:
Sinners gathered round Thee,
Lepers sought Thy face;
None too vile or loathsome
For a Saviour's grace.

3 Jesus, I can trust Thee,
Trust Thy written Word,
Though Thy voice of pity
I have never heard:
When Thy Spirit teacheth,
To my taste how sweet!
Only may I hearken,
Sitting at Thy feet.

4 Jesus, I do trust Thee,
Trust without a doubt;
Whosoever cometh
Thou wilt not cast out:
Faithful is Thy promise,
Precious is Thy blood:
These my soul's salvation,
Thou my Saviour God!

Mary Jane Walker (1816–78)

651
L.M.

'Neither is there salvation in any other'
Acts 4 v 12

1 Jesus, the spring of joys divine,
Whence all my hopes and comforts
flow
Jesus, no other name but thine,
Can save me from eternal woe.

2 In vain would boasting reason find
The way to happiness and God;
Her weak directions leave the mind
Bewildered in a dubious road.

3 No other name will heaven approve;
Thou art the true, the living way,
Ordain'd by everlasting love,
To the bright realms of endless day.

4 Here let my constant feet abide,
Nor from the heavenly path depart;
O let thy Spirit, gracious guide,
Direct my steps, and cheer my heart.

5 Safe lead me through this world of
night,
And bring me to the blissful plains,
The regions of unclouded light,
Where perfect joy for ever reigns.

Anne Steele (1716–1778)

652
L.M.

'For the Son of man is come to seek and to save that which was lost' Luke 19 v 10

1 Jesus, Thy far-extended fame
My drooping soul exults to hear;
Thy name, Thy all-restoring name,
Is music in a sinner's ear.

2 Sinners of old Thou didst receive
With comfortable words and kind,
Their sorrows cheer, their wants relieve,
Heal the diseased, and cure the blind.

3 And art Thou not the Saviour still,
In every place and age the same?
Hast Thou forgot Thy gracious skill,
Or lost the virtue of Thy name?

4 Faith in Thy changeless name I have;
The good, the kind physician, Thou
Art able now our souls to save,
Art willing to restore them now.

5 Wouldst Thou the body's health restore,
And not regard the sin-sick soul?
The sin-sick soul Thou lov'st much more,
And surely Thou shalt make it whole.

6 All my disease, my every sin,
To Thee, O Jesus, I confess;
In pardon, Lord, my cure begin,
And perfect it in holiness.

Charles Wesley (1707–88)

653
8 8 8. 6

'And he arose, and came to his father' Luke 15 v 20

1 Just as I am, without one plea
But that Thy blood was shed for me,
And that Thou bidd'st me come to Thee,
O Lamb of God, I come.

2 Just as I am, and waiting not
To rid my soul of one dark blot,
To Thee, whose blood can cleanse each spot,
O Lamb of God, I come.

3 Just as I am, though tossed about
With many a conflict, many a doubt,
Fightings and fears within, without,
O Lamb of God, I come.

4 Just as I am, poor, wretched, blind:
Sight, riches, healing of the mind,
Yea, all I need, in Thee to find,
O Lamb of God, I come.

5 Just as I am, Thou wilt receive,
Wilt welcome, pardon, cleanse, relieve;
Because Thy promise I believe,
O Lamb of God, I come.

6 Just as I am – Thy love unknown
Has broken every barrier down –
Now to be Thine, yea, Thine alone,
O Lamb of God, I come.

7 Just as I am, of that free love
The breadth, length, depth, and height to prove,
Here for a season, then above,
O Lamb of God, I come.

Charlotte Elliott (1789–1871)

654
8 8 6. D

'God be merciful to me a sinner' Luke 18 v 13

1 Lord God Almighty, hear me now!
As I the chief of sinners bow
Before Thee, gracious God!
Forgive, forgive my guilt, my sin,
Redeem my soul, O make me clean
In Jesus' precious blood!

2 Merciful Lord in whom I trust,
Quickened by Thee, O Holy Ghost,
Confirm Thy pardoning Word!
Grant, grant assurance Holy Dove,
And fill my longing heart with love
For Christ, my blessèd Lord!

3 Eternal Lord, Immortal King,
With faltering lips, my praise I bring
To Thee, great majesty!
Now, now Thy mighty self enshrine
My heart, it is no longer mine;
Redeemed am I by Thee!

4 Father, O Father, on that Day,
When all decreed must pass away
Before Thy Son's dread gaze.
Raise, raise Thy child to be with Thee,
Father, Son, Spirit – Holy Three!
And see Him as He is.

© Copyright Control   *Howell Green (b.1942)*

655   87.87.337

*'Wilt thou not revive us again: that thy
people may rejoice in thee?'* Psalm 85 v 6

1 Lord, I hear of showers of blessing
Thou art scattering, full and free,
Showers the thirsty land refreshing;
Let some drops now fall on me.
Even me.

2 Pass me not, O gracious Father,
Sinful though my heart may be!
Thou might'st leave me, but the
rather
Let Thy mercy light on me.
Even me.

3 Pass me not, O tender Saviour!
Let me love and cling to Thee;
I am longing for Thy favour,
When Thou comest, call for me.
Even me.

4 Pass me not, O mighty Spirit!
Thou canst make the blind to see;
Witness of the Saviour's merit!
Speak the word of power to me.
Even me.

5 Love of God so pure and changeless,
Blood of Christ so rich and free,
Grace of God so strong and
boundless,
Magnify them all in me!
Even me.

Elizabeth Codner (1824–1919)

656   77.77.77

*'Draw nigh to God, and he will draw
nigh to you'* James 4 v 8

1 Lord, we lie before Thy feet;
Look on all our deep distress;
Thy rich mercy we may meet;
Clothe us with Thy righteousness;
Stretch forth Thine almighty hand,
Hold us up, and we shall stand.

2 O that closer we could cleave
To Thy bleeding, dying breast!
Give us firmly to believe,
And to enter into rest.
Lord, increase, increase our faith;
Make us faithful unto death.

3 Let us trust Thee evermore;
Every moment on Thee call
For new life, new will, new power;
Let us trust Thee, Lord, for all.
May we nothing know beside
Jesus, and Him crucified!

Joseph Hart (1712–68)

657   D.S.M.

'For one is your Master, even Christ'
Matthew 23 v 8

1 Make me a captive, Lord,
And then I shall be free;
Force me to render up my sword,
And I shall conqueror be.
I sink in life's alarms
When by myself I stand,
Imprison me within Thine arms,
And strong shall be my hand.

2 My heart is weak and poor
Until it master find;
It has no spring of action sure,
It varies with the wind:
It cannot freely move
Till Thou hast wrought its chain;
Enslave it with Thy matchless love,
And deathless it shall reign.

3 My will is not my own
Till Thou hast made it Thine;
If it would reach the monarch's
  throne
It must its crown resign:
It only stands unbent,
Amid the clashing strife,
When on Thy bosom it has leant,
And found in Thee its life.

George Matheson (1842–1906)

658   664.666.4

'Be not afraid, only believe' Mark 5 v 36

1 My faith looks up to Thee,
Thou Lamb of Calvary,
Saviour divine!
Now hear me while I pray;
Take all my guilt away;
O let me from this day
Be wholly Thine!

2 May Thy rich grace impart
Strength to my fainting heart,
My zeal inspire;
As Thou hast died for me,
O may my love to Thee
Pure, warm and changeless be,
A living fire.

3 While life's dark maze I tread,
And griefs around me spread,
Be Thou my guide;
Bid darkness turn to day,
Wipe sorrow's tears away,
Nor let me ever stray
From Thee aside.

4 When ends life's transient dream,
When death's cold, sullen stream
Shall o'er me roll,
Blest Saviour, then, in love,
Fear and distrust remove;
O bear me safe above,
A ransomed soul.

Ray Palmer (1808–87)

659   88.88.88

'He ... set my feet upon a rock'
Psalm 40 v 2

1 My hope is built in nothing less
Than Jesus' blood and righteous-
  ness;
I dare not trust the sweetest frame,
But wholly lean on Jesus' name.

On Christ, the solid Rock, I stand;
All other ground is sinking sand.

2 When darkness veils His lovely face,
I rest on His unchanging grace;
In every high and stormy gale,
My anchor holds within the veil.

3 His oath, His cov'nant, and His
  blood,
Support me in the whelming flood;
When all around my soul gives way,
He then is all my hope and stay.

4 When He shall come with trumpet
  sound,
O may I then in Him be found!
Clothed in His righteousness alone,
Faultless to stand before the throne.

Edward Mote (1797–1874)

660   C.M.

'Cast thy burden upon the LORD'
Psalm 55 v 22

1 My load of sin I now cast down
Before such pain divine.
Mountains of guilt Thy cross
  transforms
To glorious songs sublime.

2 Where'er I look, to east or south
To earth's far distant rim.
Through ages past or yet to come
There's none like unto Him.

3 His hands, so pure were stretched
  out wide
A crown of thorns He wore,
That vilest sinners might become
As linen white and pure.

4 Ascended now to heaven on high
To plead there for the weak.
Soon to His bosom He will clasp
My soul in succour sweet.

5 With Him above, I then shall be
When all the world's ablaze,
And on His lovely countenance
With growing joy, I'll gaze.

William Williams (1801–76)
© The Translator   Tr. Graham Stuart Harrison (b.1935)

661   8 10. 10 4

'For there is none other name under
heaven given among men, whereby we
must be saved' Acts 4 v 12

1 None other lamb, none other name,
None other hope in heaven or earth
or sea,
None other hiding-place from guilt
and shame,
None beside Thee.

2 My faith burns low, my hope burns
low,
Only my heart's desire cries out in
me,
By the deep thunder of its want and
woe,
Cries out to Thee.

3 Lord, Thou art life, though I be
dead;
Love's fire Thou art, however cold I
be:
Nor heaven have I, nor place to lay
my head,
Nor home, but Thee.

Christina Georgina Rossetti (1830–94)

662   8 7. 8 7. D

'Looking for the mercy of our Lord Jesus'
Jude v 21

1 O have mercy, gracious Saviour;
Look upon this heart of sin
Which has nothing more to offer
Than the stubborn pride within.
On the wall the dreadful writing,
Words of judgement and despair;
In the balances found wanting –
Jesus, Saviour, hear my prayer!

2 O give light and understanding,
Spirit of the living God;
In thy grace thy truth revealing,
Open thou thy precious Word.
Tell of virtues, grace and kindness
That from Calvary's hill do spring;
Speak of mercy and forgiveness
That my soul may ever sing.

3 Dip the pen, O Lord of glory,
In the blood of Jesus shed;
Write upon our hearts the story
Of atonement fully made.
Once inscribed upon the tablet
Of our hearts, let none erase;
There unmoved let it be fixèd,
Read for all eternal days.

William Vernon Higham (b. 1926)
© The Translator   Tr. Edmund Tudor Owen (b. 1935)

663   7 6. 7 6. D

'And they shall scourge him, and put him
to death' Luke 18 v 33

1 O teach me what it meaneth,
That cross uplifted high,
With one, the Man of Sorrows,
Condemned to bleed and die!
O teach me what it cost Thee
To make a sinner whole;
And teach me, Saviour, teach me
The value of a soul!

2 O teach me what it meaneth,
That sacred crimson tide,
The blood and water flowing
From Thine own wounded side.
Teach me that if none other
Had sinned, but I alone,
Yet still Thy blood, Lord Jesus,
Thine only, must atone.

3 O teach me what it meaneth,
Thy love beyond compare,
The love that reacheth deeper
Than depths of self-despair!
Yes, teach me, till there gloweth
In this cold heart of mine
Some feeble, pale reflection
Of that pure love of Thine.

4 O teach me what it meaneth,
For I am full of sin,
And grace alone can reach me,
And love alone can win.
O teach me, for I need Thee,
I have no hope beside –
The chief of all the sinners
For whom the Saviour died!

5 O Infinite Redeemer!
I bring no other plea;
Because Thou dost invite me
I cast myself on Thee.
Because Thou dost accept me
I love and I adore;
Because Thy love constraineth,
I'll praise Thee evermore!

Lucy Ann Bennett (1850–1927)

664   C.M.

'The sacrifices of God are a broken spirit'
Psalm 51 v 17

1 O tell me, Lord, what pleaseth Thee:
Is there an offering meet?
For in my heart I long to see
Thy smile of grace so sweet.

2 Search as I may in all my way
And all my work and toil,
I cannot find a worthy day
That sin has failed to soil.

3 This heart of mine with depths
profound
Yields disappointment keen,
And every effort I have found
Has leaned to self and sin.

4 Then I beheld the purest One,
With heart of love and peace,
Who shed His blood, a victory won,
And floods of joy release.

5 My heart is broken at the sight
Of such humility;
I stand amazed and bathe in light
Of this new dignity.

6 Now I can see my life is vain,
Contrition breaks my heart;
For now I know and feel the pain
That sin and shame impart.

7 Yet in some stange and wondrous
way
This breaking pleaseth Thee;
For Thou wilt not despise or slay
A holy sorrow's plea.

8 I feel Thy smile upon my face,
And I rejoice to know
The blessèd bliss of Thine embrace
In lifting one so low.

© The Author   William Vernon Higham (b.1926)

665   L.M.

*'And seeing the multitudes ... he opened
his mouth, and taught them'*
Matthew 5 vv 1,2

1 O Thou, whom once they flocked to
hear,
Thy words to hear, Thy power to
feel;
Suffer the sinners to draw near,
And graciously receive us still.

2 They that be whole, Thyself hast
said,
No need of a physician have;
But I am sick, and want Thine aid,
And want Thine utmost power to
save.

3 Thy power, and truth, and love
    divine,
  The same from age to age endure;
  A word, a gracious word of Thine,
  The most inveterate plague can cure.

4 Helpless howe'er my spirit lies,
  And long hath languished at the pool,
  A word of Thine shall make me rise,
  And speak me in a moment whole.

5 Make this the acceptable hour;
  Come, O my soul's physician Thou!
  Display Thy sanctifying power,
  And show me Thy salvation now.

Charles Wesley (1707–88)

666   7 6. 7 6. D

*'I am not worthy of the least of all the
mercies, and of all the truth, which thou
hast shewed unto thy servant'
Genesis 32 v 10*

1 Oh Lord, my soul approaches,
  Yet at a distance stand.
  By name I am a sinner,
  With nothing in my hand.
  My plea is for Thy mercy,
  Oh hear my sad complaint.
  Oh mercy grant Thou to me,
  Or into death I faint.

2 I know I am a sinner,
  Oh Lord what else am I?
  So poor, and so unworthy,
  Oh do not pass me by.
  I now confess my failure,
  From birth unto my grave,
  My plaintiff cry is 'Failure.'
  No peace for this poor slave.

3 I heard the name of Jesus,
  As One, who mercy shows.
  To those in degradation,
  His love to them bestows.
  Receive me, Oh receive me,
  Receive my soul in grace,
  Forgiving all transgressions
  No more my sin to face.

Thomas Williams (1761–1844)

667   Irregular

*'Delivered ... from the power of darkness'
Colossians 1 v 13*

1 Out of my bondage, sorrow and
    night,
  Jesus, I come; Jesus, I come;
  Into Thy freedom, gladness and
    light,
  Jesus, I come to Thee.
  Out of my sickness into Thy health,
  Out of my want and into Thy wealth,
  Out of my sin and into Thyself,
  Jesus, I come to Thee.

2 Out of my shameful failure and loss,
  Jesus, I come; Jesus, I come;
  Into the glorious gain of Thy cross,
  Jesus, I come to Thee.
  Out of earth's sorrows into Thy
    balm,
  Out of life's storm and into Thy
    calm,
  Out of distress to jubilant psalm,
  Jesus, I come to Thee.

3 Out of unrest and arrogant pride,
  Jesus, I come; Jesus, I come;
  Into Thy blessèd will to abide,
  Jesus, I come to Thee.
  Out of myself to dwell in Thy love,
  Out of despair into raptures above,
  Upward for aye on wings like a dove,
  Jesus, I come to Thee.

4 Out of the fear and dread of the
    tomb,
  Jesus, I come; Jesus, I come;
  Into the joy and light of Thy home,
  Jesus, I come to Thee.
  Out of the depths of ruin untold,
  Into the peace of Thy sheltering fold,
  Ever Thy glorious face to behold,
  Jesus, I come to Thee.

William True Sleeper (1819–1904)

668   8 7. 8 7. 8 8 7

Based on Psalm 130

1 Out of the depths I cry to Thee;
  Lord, hear me, I implore Thee;
  If Thou shouldst mark iniquity,
  Who, Lord, shall stand before Thee?
  O may Thine ear attend my cry!
  Lord, bid me to Thyself draw nigh,
  While now I call upon Thee.

2 'Tis Thee, O Lord, my soul doth
  seek,
  Upon Thy Word relying;
  Thou art a God who aids the meek,
  Their every need supplying.
  Lord, may I Thy forgiveness know,
  That I to Thee due fear may show,
  And humbly walk before Thee.

3 More doth my soul, Lord, for Thee
  wait
  Than those that long for morning,
  Who through the darkest hours of
  night
  Are watching for the dawning.
  From every sin, Lord, set me free;
  Make my whole life bring praise to
  Thee,
  For Thou alone art worthy.

4 Hope thou, my soul, then, in the
  Lord,
  Whose plentiful redemption
  And mercy shall to thee afford
  The promise of salvation.
  They hope in vain who think they
  can
  Escape from sin by strength of man:
  God only can deliver.

© The Author   *Graham Stuart Harrison (b.1935)*

669   8 5. 8 5 (with refrain)

'Lord, help me' Matthew 15 v 25

1 Pass me not, O gentle Saviour
  Hear my humble cry;
  While on others Thou art calling,
  Do not pass me by.

  Saviour! Saviour!
  Hear my humble cry,
  And while others Thou art calling,
  Do not pass me by.

2 Let me at a throne of mercy
  Find a sweet relief;
  Kneeling there in deep contrition,
  Help my unbelief.

3 Trusting only in Thy merit,
  Would I seek Thy face;
  Heal my wounded, broken spirit,
  Save me by Thy grace.

4 Thou the spring of all my comfort,
  More than life to me,
  Whom have I on earth beside Thee?
  Whom in heaven but Thee?

Frances Jane Crosby (1820–1915)

670   L.M.

Based on Psalm 51

1 Show pity, Lord; O Lord, forgive;
  Let a repenting rebel live:
  Are not Thy mercies large and free?
  May not a sinner trust in Thee?

2 A broken heart, my God, my King,
  Is all the sacrifice I bring;
  The God of grace will ne'er despise
  A broken heart for sacrifice.

3 My soul lies humbled in the dust,
  And owns Thy dreadful sentence
  just;
  Look down, O Lord, with pitying
  eye,
  And save the soul condemned to die.

4 Then will I teach the world Thy
  ways;
  Sinners shall learn Thy sovereign
  grace;
  I'll lead them to my Saviour's blood,
  And they shall praise a pardoning
  God.

5 O may Thy love inspire my tongue!
  Salvation shall be then my song;
  And all my powers shall join to bless
  The Lord my strength and
  righteousness.

Isaac Watts (1647–1748)

671   7 7.7 7

'God be merciful to me a sinner'
Luke 18 v 13

1 Sinful, sighing to be blest;
  Bound, and longing to be free;
  Weary, waiting for my rest:
  God be merciful to me!

2 Goodness I have none to plead;
  Sinfulness in all I see;
  I can only bring my need:
  God be merciful to me!

3 Broken heart and downcast eyes
  Dare not lift themselves to Thee;
  Yet Thou canst interpret sighs:
  God be merciful to me!

4 From this sinful heart of mine
  To Thy bosom I would flee;
  I am not my own, but Thine:
  God be merciful to me!

5 There is One beside the throne,
  And my only hope and plea
  Are in Him, and Him alone:
  God be merciful to me!

6 He my cause will undertake,
  My Interpreter will be;
  He's my all, and for His sake,
  God be merciful to me!

John Samuel Bewley Monsell (1811–75)

672   L.M.

'Let him deny himself, and take up his
cross, and follow me' Matthew 16 v 24

1 'Take up thy cross,' the Saviour said,
  'If thou wouldst My disciple be;
  Deny thyself, the world forsake,
  And humbly follow after Me.'

2 Take up thy cross; let not its weight
  Fill thy weak soul with vain alarm;
  His strength shall bear thy spirit up,
  And brace thy heart, and nerve thine
  arm.

3 Take up thy cross, nor heed the
  shame,
  Nor let thy foolish pride rebel;
  The Lord for thee the cross endured
  To save thy soul from death and hell.

4 Take up thy cross, then, in His
  strength,
  And calmly every danger brave;
  'Twill guide thee to a better home,
  And lead to victory o'er the grave.

5 Take up thy cross, and follow Christ,
  Nor think till death to lay it down;
  For only he who bears the cross
  May hope to wear the glorious
  crown.

Charles William Everest (1814–77)

673   8 7.8 7. D

'Christ Jesus came into the world to save
sinners; of whom I am chief'
1 Timothy 1 v 15

1 Though I am the chief of sinners,
  Burdened with a sense of sin,
  I behold a refuge open
  Wide enough to take me in:
  God, in Christ, has made provision
  Full and free and unto all,
  For salvation is now offered
  To the victims of the fall.

2 In the wounded hand of Jesus,
Who redeemed me on the tree,
I can see the golden sceptre
Graciously held out to me:
At His feet I'll fall confessing –
'I have sinned, O Lord, 'gainst Thee,
Cleanse me in the precious fountain
Opened on Mount Calvary.'

Ann Griffiths (1776–1805)
Tr. A. Olwyn Jones

674   S.M.

'Lord, help me' Matthew 15 v 25

1 To Christ for help I fly,
The Friend of sinners lost,
A refuge sweet and sure and nigh,
And there is all my trust.

2 No help in self I find,
And yet have sought it well;
The native treasure of my mind
Is sin and death and hell.

3 Lord, grant me free access
Unto Thy piercèd side,
For there I seek my dwelling-place,
And there my guilt would hide.

4 In every time of need
My helpless soul defend,
And save me from all evil deed,
And save me to the end.

5 And when the hour is near
That flesh and heart will fail,
Do Thou in all Thy grace appear,
And bid my faith prevail.

John Berridge (1716–93)

675   C.M.

'The love of Christ, which passeth
knowledge' Ephesians 3 v 19

1 To heart and soul how sweet Thou
    art,
O great High Priest of God!
My heart brought nigh to God's own
    heart
By Thy most precious blood.

2 No more my countless sins shall rise
To fill me with dismay;
That precious blood before His eyes
Hath put them all away.

3 My soul draws near with trust secure,
With boldness glad and free;
What matters it that I am poor,
For I am rich in Thee.

4 Forgotten every stain and spot,
Their memory past and gone,
For me, O God, Thou seest not,
Thou lookest on Thy Son.

5 Is all a dream? Thou canst not lie;
Thy Spirit and Thy blood
Proclaim to sinners such as I
The boundless love of God.

6 They tell Thy love, so deep, so free,
They tell the Father's heart;
Not what I am, or I must be,
They tell me what Thou art.

7 Come, weary sinners, great and
    small,
The open door stands wide,
The blessèd heart that welcomes all,
The Lamb of God, who died.

Gerhard Tersteegen (1697–1769)
Tr. Emma Frances Bevan (1827–1909)

676   10 10. 10 10

'Restore unto me the joy of thy salvation'
Psalm 51 v 12

1 Weary of earth, and laden with my
    sin,
I look at Heaven and long to enter in;
But there no evil thing may find a
    home,
And yet I hear a voice that bids me
    come.

2 So vile I am, how dare I hope to
    stand
In the pure glory of that holy land,
Before the whiteness of that throne
    appear?
Yet there are hands stretched out to
    draw me near.

3 The while I fain would tread the
heavenly way,
Evil is ever with me day by day;
Yet on mine ears the gracious tidings
fall:
'Repent, believe; thou shalt be
loosed from all.'

4 It is the voice of Jesus that I hear,
His are the hands stretched out to
draw me near,
And His the blood that can for all
atone,
And set me faultless there before the
throne.

5 O great Absolver, grant my soul may
wear
The lowliest garb of penitence and
prayer,
That in the Father's courts my
glorious dress
May be the garment of Thy
righteousness!

6 Yea, Thou wilt answer for me,
righteous Lord:
Thine all the merit, mine the great
reward;
Thine the sharp thorns, and mine
the golden crown;
Mine the life won, and Thine the life
laid down.

7 Naught can I bring, dear Lord, for all
I owe;
Yet let my full heart what it can
bestow:
Like ointment sweet, let my devotion
prove,
Forgiven greatly, how greatly I love.

Samuel John Stone (1839–1900)

677   8 8 6 . 8 8 6

*'He shall come to be glorified in his
saints' 2 Thessalonians 1 v 10*

1 When Thou, my righteous Judge,
shalt come
To fetch Thy ransomed people
home,
Shall I among them stand?
Shall such a worthless worm as I,
Who sometimes am afraid to die,
Be found at Thy right hand?

2 I love to meet among them now,
Before Thy gracious feet to bow,
Though vilest of them all;
But can I bear the piercing thought,
What if my name should be left out,
When Thou for them shalt call?

3 Provide, provide it by Thy grace;
Be Thou, dear Lord, my Hiding-
place
In this, the gospel day!
Thy pardoning voice, O let me hear,
To still my unbelieving fear,
Nor let me fall, I pray!

4 Let me among Thy saints be found,
Whene'er the archangel's trump
shall sound,
To see Thy smiling face:
Then loudest of the crowd I'll sing,
While heaven's resounding
mansions ring
With shouts of sovereign grace.

Lady Huntingdon's Hymn Book 1774

678

87.87.87

*'Thus hath the Lord dealt with me in the
days wherein he looked on me'*
Luke 1 v 25

1 Who is this that looked upon me
Dead in sins and woeful plight?
Who is this so great in mercy
Sent His Son to bring us light?
See the radiance, see the glory
Of the heart of God on high.

2 Why regard the world so sinful
So opposed to God's great love?
Why such scheme devised so careful
Set to gain all those who rove?
Only Jesus, only mercy
Can explain the plan above.

3 See the wounds on Christ inflicted.
See man's hatred in full span.
See the wage by law demanded
Paid in full for fallen man.
Such a wonder, such a mystery.
Full adoption is His plan.

4 O this vast and great creation
Nestles in the Godhead's palm.
Yet He sends His sweet salvation,
Now for sorrow sweet embalm.
Sight now fails me, faith now holds
me.
Troubled souls in mercy's calm.

© The Author   *William Vernon Higham (b.1926)*

679

L.M.

'God be merciful to me a sinner'
Luke 18 v 13

1 With broken heart and contrite sigh,
A trembling sinner, Lord, I cry;
Thy pardoning grace is rich and free,
O God, be merciful to me!

2 I smite upon my troubled breast,
With deep and conscious guilt
oppressed;
Christ and His cross my only plea:
O God, be merciful to me!

3 Far off I stand with tearful eyes,
Nor dare uplift them to the skies;
But Thou dost all my anguish see;
O God, be merciful to me!

4 Nor alms, nor deeds that I have
done,
Can for a single sin atone:
To Calvary alone I flee;
O God, be merciful to me!

5 And when, redeemed from sin and
hell,
With all the ransomed throng I
dwell,
My raptured song shall ever be:
God has been merciful to me!

Cornelius Elven (1797–1873)

THE CHRISTIAN LIFE

680
88.88.D

'Being confident of this very thing'
Philippians 1 v 6

1 A debtor to mercy alone,
   Of covenant mercy I sing;
   Nor fear, with Thy righteousness on,
   My person and offering to bring;
   The terrors of law and of God
   With me can have nothing to do;
   My Saviour's obedience and blood
   Hide all my transgressions from
      view.

2 The work which His goodness
      began,
   The arm of His strength will
      complete;
   His promise is Yea and Amen,
   And never was forfeited yet.
   Things future, nor things that are
      now,
   Not all things below nor above,
   Can make Him His purpose forgo,
   Or sever my soul from His love.

3 My name from the palms of His
      hands
   Eternity will not erase;
   Impressed on His heart it remains,
   In marks of indelible grace;
   Yes, I to the end shall endure,
   As sure as the earnest is given;
   More happy, but not more secure,
   The glorified spirits in heaven.

Augustus Montague Toplady (1740–78)

681
C.M.

'Thou wilt keep him in perfect peace,
whose mind is stayed on thee'
Isaiah 26 v 3

1 A mind at perfect peace with God;
   O what a word is this!
   A sinner reconciled through blood,
   This, this indeed is peace!

2 By nature and by practice far –
   How very far from God!
   Yet now by grace brought near to
      Him,
   Through faith in Jesus' blood.

3 So near, so very near to God,
   I cannot nearer be;
   For in the Person of His Son
   I am as near as He.

4 So dear, so very dear to God,
   More dear I cannot be;
   The love wherewith He loves the
      Son –
   Such is His love to me!

5 Why should I ever anxious be,
   Since such a God is mine?
   He watches o'er me night and day,
   And tells me Mine is Thine.

Catesby Paget

682
88.88.D

'O God of my salvation' Psalm 27 v 9

1 A sovereign Protector I have,
Unseen, yet for ever at hand,
Unchangeably faithful to save,
Almighty to rule and command.
He smiles, and my comforts abound;
His grace as the dew shall descend;
And walls of salvation surround
The soul He delights to defend.

2 Inspirer and Hearer of prayer,
Thou Shepherd and Guardian of
    Thine,
My all to Thy covenant care
I sleeping and waking resign.
If Thou art my Shield and my Sun,
The night is no darkness to me;
And fast as my moments roll on,
They bring me but nearer to Thee.

3 Kind Author and Ground of my
    hope,
Thee, Thee, for my God I avow;
My glad Ebenezer set up,
And own Thou hast helped me till
    now.
I muse on the years that are past,
Wherein my defence Thou hast
    proved;
Nor wilt Thou relinquish at last
A sinner so signally loved!

Augustus Montague Toplady (1740–78)

683
6 6. 6 6. 4 4. 4 4

'The Lord is not slack concerning his
promise, as some men count slackness'
2 Peter 3 v 9

1 Away, distrustful care!
I have Thy promise Lord:
To banish all despair
I have Thy pledge and Word;
And therefore I
Shall see Thy face
And then Thy grace
I'll magnify.

2 Though sin would make me doubt,
And fill my soul with fears,
Though God seem to shut out
My daily cries and tears:
Yet I shall rest
Upon the Word
Of Thee, my God,
That I am blest!

3 With Thy triumphant flock
I soon shall numbered be:
Built on the eternal Rock,
His glory I shall see:
The heavens so high,
With praise shall ring,
And all shall sing
In harmony.

4 The sun is but a spark
From the eternal Light!
Its brightest beams are dark
To Thy most glorious sight!
There the great choir
With one accord
Shall praise the Lord
For evermore!

Richard Baxter (1615–91)

684
S.M.

'Beloved, now are we the sons of God,
and it doth not yet appear what we
shall be' 1 John 3 v 2

1 Behold, what wondrous grace
The Father hath bestowed
On sinners of a mortal race,
To call them sons of God.

2 'Tis no surprising thing
That we should be unknown;
The Jewish world knew not their
    King,
God's everlasting Son.

3 Nor doth it yet appear
How great we must be made;
But when we see our Saviour here,
We shall be like our Head.

4 A hope so much divine
May trials well endure,
May purge our souls from sense and
sin,
As Christ the Lord is pure.

5 If in our Father's love
We share a filial part,
Send down Thy Spirit like a dove
To rest upon each heart.

6 We would no longer lie
Like slaves beneath Thy throne;
Our faith shall 'Abba, Father' cry,
And Thou the kindred own.

Isaac Watts (1674–1748)

685   Irregular

'Heirs of God, and joint-heirs with Christ'
Romans 8 v 17

1 Blessed assurance, Jesus is mine:
O what a foretaste of glory divine!
Heir of salvation, purchase of God,
Born of His Spirit, washed in His
blood.

*This is my story, this is my song,
Praising my Saviour all the day long.*

2 Perfect submission, perfect delight,
Visions of rapture burst on my sight;
Angels descending bring from above
Echoes of mercy, whispers of love.

3 Perfect submission, all is at rest,
I in my Saviour am happy and blest;
Watching and waiting, looking
above,
Filled with His goodness, lost in His
love.

Frances Jane Crosby (1820–1915)

686   C.M.

'An inheritance incorruptible, and
undefiled' 1 Peter 1 v 4

1 Blest be the everlasting God,
The Father of our Lord!
Be His abounding mercy praised,
His majesty adored!

2 When from the dead He raised His
Son,
And called Him to the sky,
He gave our souls a lively hope
That they should never die.

3 To an inheritance divine
He taught our hearts to rise;
'Tis uncorrupted, undefiled,
Unfading in the skies.

4 Saints by the power of God are kept,
Till the salvation come;
We walk by faith as strangers here,
Till Christ shall call us home.

Isaac Watts (1674–1748)

687   D.L.M.

'The Comforter, which is the Holy Ghost'
John 14 v 26

1 Come, Holy Ghost, my heart assure,
Dispel my fears, that I no more
May doubt that mercy now is mine,
Nor question promises divine;
Impress the seal, Thine image leave,
Confirm in power that grace I have,
That I may run the heavenly race
With joy, beholding Jesus' face.

2 Come, blessèd Comforter divine,
Relieve this doubting heart of mine;
Banish the clouds of unbelief,
O liberate my soul from grief,
Illumine me with heavenly light,
Scatter the thoughts of darkest
night!
With anxious sighs I look above,
Longing to know my Saviour's love.

3 Come, promise of the Father's love,
Abide within me, gentle Dove;
My soul assured, I then shall rest
On my Redeemer's tender breast
Until I come to heaven at last,
With all my sins and troubles past;
Truly to know that grace was sure,
Happy to know, and doubt no more!

© The Author   *Alan Charles Clifford (b.1941)*

688   6 6. 6 6 (with refrain)

'I will rejoice in thy salvation'
Psalm 9 v 14

1 Dear Saviour, Thou art mine,
  How sweet the thought to me!
  Let me repeat Thy name,
  And lift my heart to Thee.

  Mine! mine! mine! I know Thou art mine;
  Saviour, dear Saviour, I know Thou art
  mine.

2 Thou art the sinner's Friend,
  So I Thy friendship claim,
  A sinner saved by grace,
  When Thy sweet message came.

3 My hardened heart was touched;
  Thy pardoning voice I heard;
  And joy and peace came in,
  While listening to Thy Word.

4 So let me sing Thy praise,
  So let me call Thee mine;
  I cannot doubt Thy Word,
  I know that I am Thine.

                                Anna Hudson

689   C.M.

'The peace of God, which passeth all
understanding' Philippians 4 v 7

1 Father, whate'er of earthly bliss
  Thy sovereign will denies,
  Accepted at Thy throne of grace
  Let this petition rise:

2 Give me a calm, a thankful heart,
  From every murmur free;
  The blessings of Thy grace impart,
  And let me live to Thee.

3 Let the sweet hope that Thou art
    mine
  My path through life attend,
  Thy presence through my journey
    shine,
  And crown my journey's end.

                          Anne Steele (1717–78)

690   7 7. 7 7. D.

'I pray for them, I pray not for the world,
but for them which thou hast given me'
John 17 v 9

1 God eternal, can it be,
  From beyond the clouds of time,
  Thou hast chosen even me,
  Named me in Thy courts sublime?
  Timeless grace, immortal love
  Now in Christ has filled my soul,
  With this knowledge from above,
  That He took sin's heavy toll.

2 Though I search, I cannot bring
  Any merit that will gain;
  Tarnished, tainted, everything
  Sin has touched, my spirit slain.
  Was it, Lord, to such as I,
  Deep in sin's depravity,
  That Thy mercy called to fly
  Out of darkness unto Thee?

3 Chosen by Thy grace alone,
  Hidden reasons to Thee known;
  All I know, Thou didst atone,
  Claimed and took me as Thine own.
  Chosen Saviour to redeem,
  Costly mission to perform,
  Work peculiar, yet supreme,
  As He took our human form.

4 Thine I am, Thy prayer reveals,
  For the Father brought me nigh;
  Such security appeals
  That Thy truth will sanctify.
  Even me, how can it be
  That these lips should sing Thy
    praise?
  Sweet Redeemer, now I see
  What it costs to grant this grace.

© The Author   *William Vernon Higham (b.1926)*

691   L.M.

'Thou art my hiding place' Psalm 32 v 7

1 Hail, sovereign love, that first began
  The scheme to rescue fallen man!
  Hail, matchless, free, eternal grace,
  That gave my soul a hiding-place!

2 Against the God who rules the sky
I fought with hand uplifted high;
Despised the mention of His grace,
Too proud to seek a hiding-place.

3 But thus the eternal counsel ran:
'Almighty love, arrest that man!'
I felt the arrows of distress,
And found I had no hiding-place.

4 Indignant Justice stood in view;
To Sinai's fiery mount I flew;
But Justice cried, with frowning face,
'This mountain is no hiding-place!'

5 Ere long a heavenly voice I heard,
And Mercy's angel-form appeared;
She led me on, with placid pace,
To Jesus, as my Hiding-place.

6 Should storms of seven-fold thunder
roll,
And shake the globe from pole to
pole,
No flaming bolt could daunt my
face,
For Jesus is my Hiding-place.

7 On Him almighty vengeance fell,
That must have sunk a world to hell;
He bore it for a chosen race,
And thus became their Hiding-place.

8 A few more rolling suns, at most,
Will land me on fair Canaan's coast,
Where I shall sing the song of grace,
And see my glorious Hiding-place.

Jehoida Brewer (1751–1817)

692　　　　11 11. 11 11

*'For he hath said, I will never leave thee,
nor forsake thee' Hebrews 13 v 5*

1 How firm a foundation, ye saints of
the Lord,
Is laid for your faith in His excellent
Word!
What more can He say than to you
He has said –
All, who unto Jesus for refuge have
fled?

2 In every condition – in sickness, in
health,
In poverty's vale, or abounding in
wealth;
At home or abroad, on the land, on
the sea,
As days may demand, shall thy
strength ever be.

3 Fear not, I am with thee, O be not
dismayed!
I, I am thy God, and will still give
thee aid:
I'll strengthen thee, help thee, and
cause thee to stand,
Upheld by My righteous, omnipotent
hand.

4 When through the deep waters I
cause thee to go,
The rivers of woe shall not thee
overflow;
For I will be with thee, thy troubles
to bless,
And sanctify to thee thy deepest
distress.

5 When through fiery trials thy
pathway shall lie,
My grace all-sufficient shall be thy
supply;
The flame shall not hurt thee: I only
design
Thy dross to consume, and thy gold
to refine.

6 The soul that on Jesus has leaned for
repose
I will not, I will not desert to its foes;
That soul, though all hell should
endeavour to shake,
I'll never, no never, no never forsake!

'K' in Rippon's Selection 1787

693

88.88

'O the depth of the riches both of the
wisdom and knowledge of God'
Romans 11 v 33

1 How good is the God we adore,
Our faithful, unchangeable Friend!
His love is as great as His power,
And knows neither measure nor
end!

2 'Tis Jesus, the First and the Last,
Whose Spirit shall guide us safe
home;
We'll praise Him for all that is past,
And trust Him for all that's to come.

Joseph Hart (1712–68)

694

S.M.

'For we have not an high priest which
cannot be touched with the feeling of our
infirmities' Hebrews 4 v 15

1 How gracious, kind and good,
My great High Priest, art Thou!
As Aaron in the holiest stood,
So Christ in heaven now.

2 When conscience would despair,
By reason of my sin,
Thy blood can banish all its care,
And peace restore within.

3 It gives the anxious mind
A confidence in Thee;
Though nothing in ourselves we
find,
But insufficiency.

4 Whene'er my footsteps slide,
And when my spirit fails,
I flee to Thy dear bleeding side,
And humble faith prevails.

5 Then feels my deepest smart
The soul-reviving power,
And gently rests my troubled heart
Beneath the crimson shower.

Gerhard Tersteegen (1697–1769)
Tr. Leifchild's Original Hymns 1842

695

L.M.

'A strong consolation' Hebrews 6 v 18

1 How oft have sin and Satan strove
To rend my soul from Thee, my
God?
But everlasting is Thy love,
And Jesus seals it with His blood.

2 The oath and promise of the Lord
Join to confirm the wondrous grace;
Eternal power performs the word,
And fills all heaven with endless
praise.

3 Amidst temptations sharp and long,
My soul to this dear refuge flies:
Hope is my anchor, firm and strong,
While tempests blow and billows
rise.

4 The gospel bears my spirit up;
A faithful and unchanging God
Lays the foundation of my hope
In oaths, and promises, and blood.

Isaac Watts (1674–1748)

696

88.88.D

'The unsearchable riches of Christ'
Ephesians 3 v 8

1 How shall I my Saviour set forth?
How shall I His beauties declare?
Oh, how shall I speak of His worth!
Or what His chief dignities are?
His angels can never express,
Nor saints who sit nearest His
throne,
How rich are His treasures of grace;
No, this is a myst'ry unknown.

2 In Him all the fulness of God
For ever transcendently shines;
The Father's Anointed, He stood,
To finish His gracious designs:
Though once He was nailed to the
cross,
Vile rebels like me to set free,
His glory sustainèd no loss,
Eternal His kingdom shall be.

3 His wisdom, His love, and His
     power
  Seemed then with each other to vie,
  When sinners He stooped to restore,
  Poor sinners appointed to die.
  He came on the earth to reside,
  And dwelt in a cottage of clay;
  For sinners He suffered and died,
  To wash their pollutions away.

4 Ye sanctified sinners, adore
  This Saviour, so rich to redeem;
  No creature can ever explore
  The treasures of goodness in Him.
  He riches has ever in store,
  And treasures that never can waste;
  Here's pardon, here's grace; yea, and
     more,
  Here's glory eternal at last.

                       James Maxwell (1720–1800)

697   S.M.

*'Not unto us, O LORD … but unto thy
name give glory' Psalm 115 v 1*

1 I bless the Christ of God,
  I rest on love divine,
  And with unfaltering lip and heart
  I call this Saviour mine.

2 His cross dispels each doubt;
  I bury in His tomb
  Each thought of unbelief and fear,
  Each lingering shade of gloom.

3 I praise the God of grace,
  I trust His truth and might;
  He calls me His, I call Him mine,
  My God, my joy, my light.

4 In Him is only good,
  In me is only ill;
  My ill but draws His goodness forth,
  And me He loveth still.

5 'Tis He who saveth me,
  And freely pardon gives;
  I love because He loveth me,
  I live because He lives.

6 My life with Him is hid,
  My death has passed away,
  My clouds have melted into light,
  My midnight into day.

                       Horatius Bonar (1808–89)

698   C.M. (with refrain)

*'For I know whom I have believed'
2 Timothy 1 v 12*

1 I know not why God's wondrous
     grace
  To me has been made known,
  Nor why – unworthy as I am –
  He claimed me for His own.

  *But I know whom I have believèd,
  And am persuaded that He is able
  To keep that which I've committed
  Unto Him against that day.*

2 I know not how this saving faith
  To me He did impart,
  Or how believing in His Word
  Wrought peace within my heart.

3 I know not how the Spirit moves,
  Convincing men of sin,
  Revealing Jesus through the Word,
  Creating faith in Him.

4 I know not what of good or ill
  May be reserved for me–
  Of weary ways or golden days
  Before His face I see.

5 I know not when my Lord may
     come;
  I know not how, nor where;
  If I shall pass the vale of death,
  Or meet Him in the air.

                       Daniel Webster Whittle (1840–1901)

699
64.64

'Thy face, LORD, will I seek'
Psalm 27 v 8

1 I wait on Thee, O Lord,
Come to me here.
As I obey Thy Word,
Remove my fear.
For I have sought Thy face,
And long for Thee.
Oh let me know Thy grace,
Draw near to me!

2 Draw near to my poor soul,
Dear Lord, I pray.
And grant that I might know,
Thy peace today.
Oh let me trust in Thee.
My gracious God,
Pour out Thy grace on me,
O Son of God.

3 Shower my soul with peace,
O Holy Dove,
Let all my doubting cease,
Reveal Christ's love.
O may I feel Thy touch,
Deep in my heart,
Great God who lovest much,
O ne'er depart.

4 Send from Thy sovereign throne,
Joy, peace and rest.
That Christ might be alone,
My righteousness.
Let me now rest in Thee,
My gracious Lord,
Thou God of majesty,
Eternal Word.

© The Author   Robert Dickie (b.1950)

700
87.87.887

'LORD, thou hast been our dwelling place
in all generations' Psalm 90 v 1

1 Lord, Thou hast been our dwelling
place
In every generation;
Thy people still have known Thy
grace,
And blessed Thy consolation;
Through every age Thou heard'st our
cry;
Through every age we found Thee
nigh,
Our strength and our salvation.

2 Our cleaving sins we oft have wept,
And oft Thy patience proved;
But still Thy faith we fast have kept,
Thy name we still have loved:
And Thou hast kept and loved us
well,
Hast granted us in Thee to dwell,
Unshaken, unremovèd.

3 Lord, nothing from Thine arms of
love
Shall Thine own people sever:
Our helper never will remove,
Our God will fail us never.
Thy people, Lord, have dwelt in
Thee;
Our dwelling place Thou still wilt be
For ever and for ever.

Thomas Hornblower Gill (1819–1906)

701
S.M.

'Whether we live therefore, or die, we are
the Lord's' Romans 14 v 8

1 My Saviour, I am Thine,
By everlasting bands;
My name, my heart, I would resign,
My soul is in Thy hands.

2 To Thee I still would cleave,
With ever-growing zeal;
Let millions tempt me Christ to
leave,
They never shall prevail.

3 His Spirit shall unite
My soul to Him, my Head;
Shall form me to His image bright,
And teach His path to tread.

4 Death may my soul divide
From this abode of clay;
But love shall keep me near His side
Through all the gloomy way.

5 Since Christ and we are one,
What should remain to fear?
If He in heaven hath fixed His
    throne,
He'll fix His members there.

Philip Doddridge (1702–51)

702   8 8. 8 8. 8 8

*'Who have fled for refuge to lay hold
upon the hope set before us'
Hebrews 6 v 18*

1 Now I have found the ground
    wherein
Sure my soul's anchor may remain –
The wounds of Jesus, for my sin
Before the world's foundation slain;
Whose mercy shall unshaken stay,
When heaven and earth are fled away.

2 Father, Thine everlasting grace
Our scanty thought surpasses far,
Thy heart still melts with tenderness,
Thine arms of love still open are
Returning sinners to receive,
That mercy they may taste and live.

3 O Love, Thou bottomless abyss,
My sins are swallowed up in Thee!
Covered is my unrighteousness,
Nor spot of guilt remains on me.
While Jesus' blood, through earth
    and skies,
Mercy, free, boundless mercy cries!

4 With faith I plunge me in this sea,
Here is my hope, my joy, my rest;
Hither, when hell assails, I flee,
I look into my Saviour's breast:
Away, sad doubt and anxious fear!
Mercy is all that's written there.

5 Though waves and storms go o'er
    my head,
Though strength, and health, and
    friends be gone,
Though joys be withered all and
    dead,
Though every comfort be with-
    drawn,
On this my steadfast soul relies –
Father, Thy mercy never dies!

6 Fixed on this ground will I remain,
Though my heart fail and flesh
    decay:
This anchor shall my soul sustain,
When earth's foundations melt
    away:
Mercy's full power I then shall
    prove,
Loved with an everlasting love.

*Johann Andreas Rothe (1688–1758)
Tr. John Wesley (1703–91)*

703   7 7. 7 7

*'We also joy in God through our Lord
Jesus Christ' Romans 5 v 11*

1 O the power of love divine!
Who its heights and depths can
    tell –
Tell Jehovah's grand design
To redeem our souls from hell?

2 Mystery of redemption this;
All my sins on Christ were laid;
My offence was reckoned His;
He the grand atonement made.

3 Fully I am justified;
Free from sin and more than free:
Guiltless, since for me He died;
Righteous, since He lives for me.

4 Jesus, now to Thee I bow;
Let Thy praise my tongue employ;
Saved unto the utmost now,
Who can speak my heartfelt joy?

John Bradford (1750–1805)

704
S.M.

'Your life is hid with Christ in God'
Colossians 3 v 3

1 Our life is hid with Christ,
   With Christ in God above;
   Upward our hearts would go to Him,
   Whom, seeing not, we love.

2 He liveth and we live;
   His life for us prevails;
   His fullness fills our emptiness,
   His strength for us avails.

3 Life worketh in us now,
   And shall for evermore;
   Death shall be swallowed up of life,
   The grave its trust restore.

4 When He who is our life
   In glory shall appear,
   We too shall be revealed with Him,
   And His bright raiment wear.

5 In Him we then shall be
   Transformed and glorified,
   For we shall see Him as He is,
   And in His light abide.

Horatius Bonar (1808–89)

705
87. 87. D

'Speak the word only, and my servant
shall be healed' Matthew 8 v 8

1 Speak, I pray Thee, gentle Jesus!
   O how passing sweet Thy words,
   Breathing o'er my troubled spirit
   Peace which never earth affords.
   All the world's distracting voices,
   All the enticing tones of ill,
   At Thy accents mild, melodious,
   Are subdued, and all is still.

2 Tell me Thou art mine, O Saviour,
   Grant me an assurance clear;
   Banish all my dark misgivings,
   Still my doubting, calm my fear.
   O, my soul within me yearneth
   Now to hear Thy voice divine;
   So shall grief be gone for ever,
   And despair no more be mine.

William Williams (1717–91)
Tr. Richard Morris Lewis (1849–1918)

706
C.M.

Based on Romans 8 vv 34-39

1 The Saviour died, but rose again
   Triumphant from the grave;
   And pleads our cause at God's right
      hand,
   Omnipotent to save.

2 Who then can e'er divide us more
   From Jesus and His love?
   Or break the sacred chain that binds
   The earth to heaven above?

3 Let troubles rise and terrors frown,
   And days of darkness fall;
   Through Him all dangers we'll defy,
   And more than conquer all.

4 Nor death, nor life, nor earth, nor
      hell,
   Nor time's destroying sway,
   Can e'er efface us from His heart,
   Or make His love decay.

Scottish Paraphrases 1781

707

8 4. 8 4. 8 8. 8 4

'I know that it shall be well with them that fear God' Ecclesiastes 8 v 12

1 Through the love of God our Saviour
All will be well;
Free and changeless is His favour,
All, all is well:
Precious is the blood that healed us;
Perfect is the grace that sealed us;
Strong the hand stretched forth to
   shield us;
All must be well.

2 Though we pass through tribulation,
All will be well;
Christ hath purchased full salvation,
All, all is well:
Happy still in God confiding,
Fruitful, if in Christ abiding,
Holy, through the Spirit's guiding;
All must be well.

3 We expect a bright tomorrow;
All will be well;
Faith can sing through days of
   sorrow,
All, all is well:
On our Father's love relying,
Jesus every need supplying,
Then in living or in dying
All must be well.

Mary Peters (1813–56)

708

L.M.

'Because I live, ye shall live also'
John 14 v 19

1 When sins and fears prevailing rise,
And fainting hope almost expires,
Jesus, to Thee I lift my eyes,
To Thee I breathe my soul's desires.

2 Art Thou not mine, my living Lord?
And can my hope, my comfort die,
Fixed on Thy everlasting Word,
That Word which built the earth and
   sky?

3 If my immortal Saviour lives,
Then my immortal life is sure;
His Word a firm foundation gives:
Here let me build, and rest secure.

4 Here let my faith unshaken dwell;
Immovable Thy promise stands;
Not all the powers of earth or hell
Can e'er dissolve the sacred bands.

5 Here, O my soul, thy trust repose;
If Jesus is for ever mine,
Not death itself, that last of foes,
Shall break a union so divine!

Anne Steele (1717–78)

709

8 7. 8 7. D

'They that trust in the LORD shall be as
Mount Zion, which cannot be removed'
Psalm 42 v 1

1 Who trusts in God, a strong abode
In heaven and earth possesses;
Who looks in love to Christ above,
No fear his heart oppresses.
In Thee alone, dear Lord, we own
Sweet hope and consolation,
Our shield from foes, our balm from
   woes,
Our great and sure salvation.

2 Though Satan's wrath beset our
   path,
And worldly scorn assail us,
While Thou art near we will not fear,
Thy strength shall never fail us.
Thy rod and staff shall keep us safe,
And guide our steps forever;
Nor shades of death, nor hell
   beneath,
Our souls from Thee shall sever.

3 In all the strife of mortal life
Our feet shall stand securely;
Temptation's hour shall lose its
    power,
For Thou shalt guard us surely.
O God, renew, with heavenly dew,
Our body, soul and spirit,
Until we stand at Thy right hand,
Through Jesus' saving merit.

v 1 Joachim Magdeburg (b.c.1525)
vv 2 & 3 Anonymous 1597
Tr. Benjamin Hall Kennedy (1804–89) Altd

710   8 8 8

'Now thanks be unto God, which always
causeth us to triumph in Christ'
2 Corinthians 2 v 14

1 Why should I fear the darkest hour,
Or tremble at the tempter's power?
Jesus vouchsafes to be my tower.

2 Though hot the fight, why quit the
    field?
Why must I either fly or yield,
Since Jesus is my mighty shield?

3 When creature comforts fade and
    die,
Worldlings may weep, but why
    should I?
Jesus still lives and still is nigh.

4 I know not what may soon betide,
Or how my wants shall be supplied;
But Jesus knows, and will provide.

5 Though sin would fill me with
    distress,
The throne of grace I dare address,
For Jesus is my righteousness.

6 Though faint my prayers and cold
    my love,
My steadfast hope shall not remove,
While Jesus intercedes above.

7 Against me earth and hell combine;
But on my side is power divine;
Jesus is all, and He is mine!

John Newton (1725–1807)

711   S.M.

'Why weepest thou?' John 20 v 13

1 Why should I sorrow more?
I trust a Saviour slain,
And safe beneath His sheltering
    cross
Unmoved I shall remain.

2 Let Satan and the world
Now rage or now allure;
The promises in Christ are made
Immutable and sure.

3 The oath infallible
Is now my spirit's trust;
I know that He who spake the word
Is faithful, true and just.

4 He'll bring me on my way
Unto my journey's end;
He'll be my Father and my God,
My Saviour and my Friend.

5 So all my doubts and fears
Shall wholly flee away,
And every mournful night of tears
Be turned to joyous day.

6 All that remains for me
Is but to love and sing,
And wait until the angels come
To bear me to the King.

William Williams (1717–91)
and Charles Haddon Spurgeon (1834–92)

712   C.M.

'But we preach Christ crucified'
1 Corinthians 1 v 23

1 With glorious clouds encompassed
    round,
Whom angels dimly see,
Will the Unsearchable be found,
Or God appear to me?

2 Will He forsake His throne above,
Himself to men impart?
Answer, Thou Man of grief and love,
And speak it to my heart!

3 In manifested love explain
   Thy wonderful design;
   What meant the suffering Son of man,
   The streaming blood divine?

4 Didst Thou not in our flesh appear,
   And live and die below,
   That I may now perceive Thee near,
   And my Redeemer know?

5 Come, then, and to my soul reveal
   The heights and depths of grace,
   The wounds which all my sorrows
     heal,
   That dear disfigured face.

6 Before my eyes of faith confessed
   Stand forth a slaughtered Lamb:
   And clasp me to Thy blood-stained
     breast,
   And tell me all Thy name.

7 Jehovah in Thy Person show,
   Jehovah crucified!
   And then the pardoning God I know,
   And feel the blood applied.

8 I view the Lamb in His own light,
   Whom angels dimly see,
   And gaze, transported at the sight,
   To all eternity.

Charles Wesley (1707–88)

713   6 6. 6 6. 8 8

'Walk worthy of the Lord'
Colossians 1 v 10

1 Ye souls redeemed with blood
   And called by grace divine
   Walk worthy of your God
   And let your conduct shine;
   Keep Christ, your living Head in
     view
   In all you say, in all you do.

2 Has Jesus made you free?
   Then you are free indeed;
   Ye sons of liberty,
   Ye chosen royal seed,
   Walk worthy of your Lord and view
   Your glorious Head in all you do.

3 Increase our faith and love,
   And make us watch and pray;
   O fix our souls above,
   Nor let us ever stray;
   Dear Lord, do Thou our strength
     renew
   And lead us on with Christ in view.

William Gadsby (1773–1844)

714   S.M.

'Blessed are the pure in heart: for they
shall see God' Matthew 5 v 8

1 Blest are the pure in heart,
   For they shall see our God;
   The secret of the Lord is theirs,
   Their soul is Christ's abode.

2 The Lord, who left the heavens
   Our life and peace to bring,
   To dwell in lowliness with men,
   Their pattern and their King –

3 Still to the lowly soul
   He doth Himself impart,
   And for His dwelling and His throne
   Chooseth the pure in heart.

4 Lord, we Thy presence seek;
   May ours this blessing be;
   Give us a pure and lowly heart,
   A temple meet for Thee.

John Keble (1792–1866) and others

715   886. D

'Even so, come, Lord Jesus'
Revelation 22 v 20

1 Dear Jesus, come, my soul doth
     groan
   For nought but for Thyself alone,
   Thou art the pearl of price;
   For Thee, I'd part with all below,
   And every hardship undergo,
   Beneath the vaulted skies.

2 Thy presence can, without delay,
  Drive all my numerous cares away,
  As chaff before the wind;
  Compose my thoughts to adore and
        love
  Thee, as an object far above,
  To Thee alone inclined.

3 Release me from my heavy chain,
  Guilt, sin and shame, which still
        remain
  To bind me hand and foot;
  O, glorious Conqueror, enter in,
  Cast out my foes, destroy my sin,
  Both branch and spreading root.

4 Give me that knowledge pure,
        divine,
  To know and feel that Thou art
        mine,
  And Thee my portion call;
  That doubts and fears may flee away,
  And faith unfeignèd win the day,
  And triumph over all.

William Williams (1717–91)

716   D.C.M.

*'That I may know him, and the power of
his resurrection, and the fellowship of his
sufferings' Philippians 3 v 10*

1 Deep in my heart there is a sigh,
  A longing, Lord, for Thee;
  To know the depths that in Thee lie,
  The grace of Calvary.
  O grant that I might understand
  Thy glorious mystery,
  More of Thyself, and by Thy hand
  Obedience stir in me.

2 Thy living power I long to prove
  In resurrection might,
  With overcoming grace to move
  Each sin that dims this light.
  O grant that I may find the source
  Of hidden strength and stay,
  Whch flows from Thee, and on its
        course
  O draw my soul each day.

3 There is a fellowship of pain
  Deep in Thy heart of love,
  Of suffering sweet, eternal gain,
  The tears of heaven above.
  O grant me, Lord, to feel this joy,
  These tremors of Thy grace;
  Engraved by Thee, none can destroy
  The riches I embrace.

4 Then lead me in this wondrous way
  To die to self and sin;
  And take me, Lord, when Thou dost
        slay,
  And drive Thy grace within.
  O grant me now an image sweet
  Impressed upon my heart;
  With joy I lie beneath Thy feet,
  To weep and not depart.

© The Author   William Vernon Higham (b.1926)

717   7 6 7 6. D

*'For without me ye can do nothing'
John 15 v 5*

1 I could not do without Thee,
  O Saviour of the lost,
  Whose precious blood redeemed me
  At such tremendous cost;
  Thy righteousness, Thy pardon,
  Thy precious blood must be
  My only hope and comfort,
  My glory and my plea.

2 I could not do without Thee,
  I cannot stand alone,
  I have no strength or goodness,
  No wisdom of my own;
  But Thou, belovèd Saviour,
  Art all in all to me,
  And weakness will be power
  If leaning hard on Thee.

3 I could not do without Thee;
  No other friend can read
  The spirit's strange deep longings,
  Interpreting its need.
  No human heart could enter
  Each dim recess of mine,
  And soothe, and hush, and calm it,
  O blessèd Lord, but Thine.

4 I could not do without Thee;
For years are fleeting fast,
And soon in solemn loneness
The river must be passed:
But Thou wilt never leave me;
And though the waves roll high,
I know Thou wilt be near me
And whisper: 'It is I.'

Frances Ridley Havergal (1836–79)

718   6 4. 6 4. 10 10

'My beloved is mine, and I am his'
Song of Solomon 2 v 16

1 I lift my heart to Thee,
Saviour divine;
For Thou art all to me,
And I am Thine.
Is there on earth a closer bond than
this,
That my Beloved's mine and I am
His?

2 Thine am I by all ties;
But chiefly Thine,
That through Thy sacrifice
Thou, Lord, art mine.
By Thine own cords of love, so
sweetly wound
Around me, I to Thee am closely
bound.

3 To Thee, Thou dying Lamb,
I all things owe;
All that I have and am,
And all I know.
All that I have is now no longer
mine,
And I am not my own; Lord, I am
Thine.

4 How can I, Lord, withhold
Life's brightest hour
From Thee, or gathered gold,
Or any power?
Why should I keep one precious
thing from Thee,
When Thou hast given Thine own
dear self for me?

5 I pray Thee, Saviour, keep
Me in Thy love,
Until death's holy sleep
Shall me remove
To that fair realm where, sin and
sorrow o'er,
Thou and Thine own are one for
evermore.

Charles Edward Mudie (1818–90)

719   L.M.

'My soul thirsteth for God, for the living
God' *Psalm 42 v 2*

1 I thirst, Thou wounded Lamb of
God,
To wash me in Thy cleansing blood;
To dwell within Thy wounds; then
pain
Is sweet, and life or death is gain.

2 Take my poor heart, and let it be
For ever closed to all but Thee;
Seal Thou my breast, and let me
wear
That pledge of love for ever there.

3 How blest are they who still abide
Close sheltered in Thy bleeding side;
Who life and strength from thence
derive,
And by Thee move, and in Thee live!

4 What are our works but sin and
death,
Till Thou Thy quickening Spirit
breathe?
Thou giv'st the power Thy grace to
move:
O wondrous grace! O boundless
love!

5 How can it be, Thou heavenly King,
That Thou shouldst us to glory
bring;
Make slaves the partners of Thy
throne,
Decked with a never-fading crown?

6 Hence our hearts melt, our eyes o'er
   flow;
   Our words are lost; nor will we
   know,
   Nor will we think of aught beside,
   My Lord, my Love, is crucified!

7 Ah, Lord, enlarge our scanty
   thought,
   To know the wonders Thou hast
   wrought;
   Unloose our stammering tongues, to
   tell
   Thy love immense, unsearchable.

8 First-born of many brethren Thou!
   To Thee, lo! all our souls we bow;
   To Thee our hearts and hands we
   give:
   Thine may we die, Thine may we
   live!

vv 1, 2, & 7 Nicolaus Ludwig Von Zinzendorf (1700–60)
vv 3-6 Johann Nitschmann (1712–83)
v 8 Anna Nitschmann (1715–60)
Tr. John Wesley (1703–91)

720   8 7. 8 7. D

*'Having loved his own … he loved them
unto the end' John 13 v 1*

1 I've found a Friend, O such a Friend!
   He loved me ere I knew Him;
   He drew me with the cords of love,
   And thus He bound me to Him;
   And round my heart still closely
   twine
   Those ties which nought can sever;
   For I am His, and He is mine,
   For ever and for ever.

2 I've found a Friend, O such a Friend!
   He bled, He died to save me;
   And not alone the gift of life,
   But His own self He gave me.
   Nought that I have mine own I'll
   call,
   I'll hold it for the Giver;
   My heart, my strength, my life, my
   all
   Are His, and His for ever.

3 I've found a Friend, O such a Friend!
   All power to Him is given,
   To guard me on my onward course,
   And bring me safe to heaven.
   The eternal glories gleam afar,
   To nerve my faint endeavour;
   So now to watch! to work! to war!
   And then – to rest for ever.

4 I've found a Friend, O such a Friend,
   So kind, and true, and tender!
   So wise a Counsellor and Guide,
   So mighty a Defender!
   From Him who loves me now so
   well
   What power my soul can sever?
   Shall life or death, or earth or hell?
   No! I am His for ever.

James Grindlay Small (1817–88)

721   C.M.

*'A name which is above every name'
Philippians 2 v 9*

1 Jesus! exalted far on high,
   To whom a name is given,
   A name surpassing every name
   That's known in earth or heaven:

2 Before whose throne shall every
   knee
   Bow down with one accord,
   Before whose throne shall every
   tongue
   Confess that Thou art Lord.

3 Jesus! who in the form of God
   Didst equal honour claim,
   Yet, to redeem our guilty souls,
   Didst stoop to death and shame:

4 O may that mind in us be formed
   Which shone so bright in Thee!
   May we be humble, lowly, meek,
   From pride and envy free.

5 May we to others stoop, and learn
   To emulate Thy love:
   So shall we bear Thine image here,
   And share thy throne above.

Thomas Cotterill (1779–1823)

722

8 7. 8 5. D (with refrain)

'Rest in the LORD' Psalm 37 v 7

1 Jesus, I am resting, resting
In the joy of what Thou art;
I am finding out the greatness
Of Thy loving heart.
Thou hast bid me gaze upon Thee,
And Thy beauty fills my soul,
For by Thy transforming power
Thou hast made me whole.

Jesus, I am resting, resting
In the joy of what Thou art;
I am finding out the greatness
Of Thy loving heart.

2 O how great Thy lovingkindness,
Vaster, broader than the sea!
O how marvellous Thy goodness,
Lavished all on me!
Yes, I rest in Thee, Belovèd,
Know what wealth of grace is Thine,
Know Thy certainty of promise,
And have made it mine.

3 Simply trusting Thee, Lord Jesus,
I behold Thee as Thou art,
And Thy love, so pure, so
changeless,
Satisfies my heart;
Satisfies its deepest longings,
Meets, supplies its every need,
Compasseth me round with
blessings;
Thine is love indeed!

4 Ever lift Thy face upon me,
As I work and wait for Thee;
Resting 'neath Thy smile, Lord
Jesus,
Earth's dark shadows flee.
Brightness of my Father's glory,
Sunshine of my Father's face,
Keep my ever trusting, resting;
Fill me with Thy grace.

Jean Sophia Pigott (1845–82)

723

8 7. 8 7. 4 7

'For it pleased the Father that in him
should all fullness dwell'
Colossians 1 v 19

1 Jesus, Jesus, all-sufficient,
Beyond telling is Thy worth;
In Thy name lie greater treasures
Than the richest found on earth.
Such abundance
Is my portion with my God.

2 In Thy gracious face there's beauty
Far surpassing every thing
Found in all the earth's great
wonders
Mortal eye hath ever seen.
Rose of Sharon,
Thou Thyself art heaven's delight.

William Williams (1717–91)
© The Translator *Tr. Robert Maynard (Bobi) Jones (b.1929)*

724

8 8. 8 8. 8 8

'For the love of Christ constraineth us'
2 Corinthians 5 v 14

1 Jesus, Thy boundless love to me
No thought can reach, no tongue
declare;
O knit my thankful heart to Thee,
And reign without a rival there!
Thine wholly, Thine alone, I am,
Be Thou alone my constant flame.

2 O grant that nothing in my soul
May dwell, but Thy pure love alone;
O may Thy love possess me whole,
My joy, my treasure, and my crown!
Strange flames far from my heart
remove;
My every act, word, thought, be love.

3 O Love, how cheering is Thy ray!
All pain before Thy presence flies,
Care, anguish, sorrow, melt away,
Where'er Thy healing beams arise:
O Jesus, nothing may I see,
Nothing desire, or seek, but Thee!

4 Unwearied may I this pursue,
Dauntless to the high prize aspire;
Hourly within my soul renew
This holy flame, this heavenly fire;
And day and night be all my care
To guard the sacred treasure there.

5 In suffering, be Thy love my peace;
In weakness, be Thy love my power;
And, when the storms of life shall
cease,
Jesus, in that tremendous hour,
In death, as life, be Thou my Guide,
And save me, who for me hast died.

Paul Gerhardt (1607–76)
Tr. John Wesley (1703–92)

725   C.M.

'That they all may be one' John 17 v 21

1 Lord Jesus are we one with Thee?
O height, O depth of love!
With Thee we died upon the tree,
In Thee we live above.

2 Such was Thy grace, that for our
sake
Thou didst from heaven come down,
Thou didst of flesh and blood par-
take,
In all our sorrows one.

3 Our sins, our guilt, in love divine,
Confessed and borne by Thee:
The gall, the curse, the wrath were
Thine,
To set Thy members free.

4 Ascended now in glory bright,
Still one with us Thou art;
Nor life, nor death, nor depth, nor
height,
Thy saints and Thee can part.

5 O teach us, Lord, to know and own
This wondrous mystery,
That Thou with us art truly one,
And we are one with Thee!

6 Soon, soon shall come that glorious
day,
When, seated on thy throne,
Thou shalt to wondering worlds dis-
play
That Thou with us art one.

James George Deck (1802–84)

726   87.87.D

'The love of Christ, which passeth
knowledge' Ephesians 3 v 19

1 Love divine, all loves excelling,
Joy of heaven, to earth come down,
Fix in us Thy humble dwelling,
All Thy faithful mercies crown.
Jesus, Thou art all compassion,
Pure, unbounded love Thou art;
Visit us with Thy salvation,
Enter every trembling heart.

2 Breathe, O breathe Thy loving Spirit
Into every troubled breast;
Let us all in Thee inherit,
Let us find Thy promised rest.
Take away the love of sinning,
Alpha and Omega be;
End of faith, as its beginning,
Set our hearts at liberty

3 Come, almighty to deliver,
Let us all Thy grace receive;
Suddenly return and never,
Never more Thy temples leave:
Thee we would be always blessing,
Serve Thee as Thy hosts above,
Pray, and praise Thee, without
ceasing,
Glory in Thy perfect love.

4 Finish then Thy new creation,
Pure and spotless may we be;
Let us see our whole salvation
Perfectly restored in Thee;
Changed from glory into glory,
Till in heaven we take our place,
Till we cast our crowns before Thee,
Lost in wonder, love and praise.

Charles Wesley (1707–88)

727

87.85

'Let this mind be in you, which was also in Christ Jesus' Philippians 2 v 5

1 May the mind of Christ my Saviour
Live in me from day to day,
By His love and power controlling
All I do and say.

2 May the Word of God dwell richly
In my heart from hour to hour,
So that all may see I triumph
Only through His power.

3 May the peace of God my Father
Rule my life in everything,
That I may be calm to comfort
Sick and sorrowing.

4 May the love of Jesus fill me
As the waters fill the sea;
Him exalting, self abasing,
This is victory.

5 May I run the race before me,
Strong and brave to face the foe,
Looking only unto Jesus
As I onward go.

6 May His beauty rest upon me
As I seek the lost to win,
And may they forget the channel,
Seeing only Him.

Katie Barclay Wilkinson (1859–1928)

728

C.M.

'A far more exceeding and eternal weight of glory' 2 Corinthians 4 v 17

1 My thoughts surmount these lower
skies,
And look within the veil;
There springs of endless pleasure
rise,
The waters never fail.

2 There I behold, with sweet delight,
The blessèd Three in One;
And strong affections fix my sight
On God's incarnate Son.

3 His promise stands for ever firm,
His grace shall ne'er depart;
He binds my name upon His arm,
And seals it on His heart.

4 Light are the pains that nature
brings;
How short our sorrows are,
When with eternal future things
The present we compare!

5 I would not be a stranger still
To that celestial place,
Where I for ever hope to dwell,
Near my Redeemer's face.

Isaac Watts (1674–1748)

729

9 10. 9 10

'Draw me, we will run after thee' Song of Solomon 1 v 4

1 Nearer, still nearer, close to Thy
heart,
Draw me, my Saviour, so precious
Thou art;
Fold me, O fold me close to Thy
breast,
Shelter me safe in that 'Haven of
Rest'.

2 Nearer, still nearer, nothing I bring,
Nought as an offering to Jesus my
King;
Only my sinful, now contrite heart;
Grant me the cleansing Thy blood
doth impart.

3 Nearer, still nearer, Lord to be Thine,
Sin, with its follies, I gladly resign,
All of its pleasures, pomp and its
pride;
Give me but Jesus, my Lord crucified.

4 Nearer, still nearer, while life shall
last,
Till all its struggles and trials are
past;
Then though eternity, ever I'll be
Nearer, my Saviour, still nearer to
Thee.

Leila Naylor Morris (1862–1929)

730 C.M.

'Until Christ be formed in you'
Galatians 4 v 19

1 O Jesus Christ, grow Thou in me,
  And all things else recede:
  My heart be daily nearer Thee,
  From sin be daily freed.

2 Each day let Thy supporting might
  My weakness still embrace;
  My darkness vanish in Thy light,
  Thy life my death efface.

3 In Thy bright beams which on me
    fall,
  Fade every evil thought;
  That I am nothing, Thou art all,
  I would be daily taught.

4 More of Thy glory let me see,
  Thou Holy, Wise, and True!
  I would Thy living image be,
  In joy and sorrow too.

5 Fill me with gladness from above,
  Hold me by strength divine!
  Lord, let the glow of Thy great love
  Through my whole being shine.

6 Make this poor self grow less and
    less.
  Be Thou my life and aim;
  O make me daily, through Thy grace,
  More meet to bear Thy name!

Johann Caspar Lavater (1741–1801)
Tr. Elizabeth Lee Smith (1817–98)

731 7 6. 7 6. D

'There is a friend that sticketh closer than
a brother' Proverbs 18 v 24

1 O Jesus, Friend unfailing,
  How dear art Thou to me!
  Are cares or fears assailing?
  I find my strength in Thee,
  Why should my feet grow weary
  Of this my pilgrim way?
  Rough though the path and dreary,
  It ends in perfect day.

2 What fills my soul with gladness?
  'Tis Thine abounding grace:
  Where can I look in sadness
  But, Jesus, on Thy face?
  My all is Thy providing,
  Thy love can ne'er grow cold:
  In Thee, my refuge, hiding,
  No good wilt Thou withhold.

3 Why should I droop in sorrow?
  Thou'rt ever by my side:
  Why trembling dread the morrow?
  What ill can e'er betide?
  If I my cross have taken
  'Tis but to follow Thee;
  If scorned, despised, forsaken,
  Nought severs Thee from me.

4 For every tribulation,
  For every sore distress,
  In Christ I've full salvation,
  Sure help and quiet rest.
  No fear of foes prevailing,
  I triumph, Lord, in Thee:
  O Jesus, Friend unfailing,
  How dear art Thou to me!

Samuel Christian Gottfried Kuster (1762–1838)
Tr. Hannah Kilham Burlingham (1842–1901)

732 8 8 6. D

'The love of God is shed abroad in our
hearts' Romans 5 v 5

1 O love divine, how sweet Thou art!
  When shall I find my willing heart
  All taken up by Thee?
  I thirst, I faint, I die to prove
  The greatness of redeeming love,
  The love of Christ to me.

2 Stronger His love than death or hell;
  Its riches are unsearchable;
  The first-born sons of light
  Desire in vain its depths to see;
  They cannot reach the mystery,
  The length, and breadth, and height.

3 God only knows the love of God;
O that it now were shed abroad
In this poor stony heart!
For love I sigh, for love I pine;
This only portion, Lord, be mine,
Be mine this better part!

4 O that I could for ever sit
With Mary at the Master's feet!
Be this my happy choice:
My only care, delight, and bliss,
My joy, my heaven on earth, be this –
To hear the Bridegroom's voice!

Charles Wesley (1707–88)

733   7 6. 7 6. 8 6. 8 6

'Rejoice evermore' 1 Thessalonians 5 v 16

1 Rejoice; 'tis not in sorrow
To dim that fount of joy;
No darkening tomorrow
Its brightness can destroy.
For in the Christian's heart is found
One spot of sacred ground –
The storm may rage in fury loud
Thy peace it can't confound.

2 Rejoice; when thou art feeling
The keenest earthly smart,
For then the Lord is sealing
His name upon thy heart.
For even through the weary day
God's cloud protects thy way,
And in the starless midnight hour
Still shines His perfect ray.

3 Rejoice; though thou art waging
A ceaseless war within,
With evil spirits raging,
A heart that's prone to sin.
For with Thy fiercest enemy
Christ's fought, and won the day,
His strength and love surround thee
still,
Rejoice – in victory.

John Charles Ryle (1816–1900)

734   8 7. 8 7

'And the Lord turned, and looked upon Peter' Luke 22 v 61

1 Saviour, look on Thy belovèd;
Triumph over all my foes;
Turn to happy joy my mourning;
Turn to gladness all my woes.

2 Live or die, or work or suffer,
Let my weary soul abide
In all changes whatsoever
Sure and steadfast by Thy side.

3 Nothing will preserve my goings
But salvation full and free;
Nothing will my feet dishearten
But my absence, Lord, from Thee.

4 Nothing can delay my progress,
Nothing can disturb my rest,
If I shall, where'er I wander,
Lean my spirit on Thy breast.

William Williams (1717–91)

735   D.C.M.

'Show me thy glory 'Exodus 33 v 18

1 Show me Thy face! – one transient
gleam
Of loveliness divine,
And I shall never think or dream
Of other love save Thine;
All lesser light will darken quite,
All lower glories wane;
The beautiful of earth will scarce
Seem beautiful again.

2 Show me Thy face! – my faith and
love
Shall henceforth fixèd be,
And nothing here have power to
move
My soul's serenity;
My life shall seem a trance, a dream,
And all I feel and see,
Illusive, visionary – Thou
The one reality!

3 Show me Thy face! – I shall forget
  The weary days of yore;
  The fretting ghosts of vain regret
  Shall haunt my soul no more;
  All doubts and fears for future years
  In quiet rest subside,
  And nought but blest content and
      calm
  Within my breast abide.

4 Show my Thy face! – the heaviest
      cross
  Will then seem light to bear;
  There will be gain in every loss,
  And peace with every care;
  With such light feet the years will
      fleet,
  Life seem as brief as blest,
  Till I have laid my burden down,
  And entered into rest.

Stockwell Gems

736   C.M.

'For to me to live is Christ, and to die is
gain' Philippians 1 v 21

1 There's none but Jesus, lovely Lord,
  My satisfaction found.
  My comfort all in sweet concord,
  Now from His death abound.

2 There's nought that captivates my
      heart,
  Or calms life's troubled maze,
  But constant gazing is my part,
  On God's redemptive grace.

3 I see a place in His rich wound,
  For guilty ones to hide.
  A place where nought but peace is
      found,
  My all in Him confide

4 The payment paid on lonely hill,
  My sure foundation is.
  I'll follow Jesus Christ until
  In heaven I'm ever His.

vv 1-3 William Edwards (1773–1853)
v 4 William Jones (1764–1822)

737   C.M.

'Thou art a priest for ever after the order
of Melchizedek' Psalm 110 v 4

1 Thou dear Redeemer, dying Lamb,
  We love to hear of Thee;
  No music's like Thy charming name,
  Nor half so sweet can be.

2 O, let us ever hear Thy voice,
  In mercy to us speak!
  And in our Priest we will rejoice,
  Thou great Melchizedek.

3 Our Jesus shall be still our theme
  While in this world we stay:
  We'll sing our Jesus' lovely name,
  When all things else decay.

4 When we appear in yonder cloud,
  With all Thy favoured throng,
  Then will we sing more sweet, more
      loud,
  And Christ shall be our song.

John Cennick (1718–55)

738   88.88.88

'The author of eternal salvation unto all
them that obey him' Hebrews 5 v 9

1 Thou hidden source of calm repose,
  Thou all-sufficient love divine,
  My help and refuge from my foes,
  Secure I am, if Thou art mine:
  And lo! From sin, and grief, and
      shame,
  I hide me, Jesus, in Thy name.

2 Thy mighty name salvation is,
  And keeps my happy soul above;
  Comfort it brings, and power, and
      peace,
  And joy, and everlasting love:
  To me, with Thy dear name, are
      given
  Pardon, and holiness, and heaven.

3 Jesus, my All in all Thou art,
My rest in toil, my ease in pain,
The medicine of my broken heart,
In war my peace, in loss my gain,
My smile beneath the tyrant's frown,
In shame my glory and my crown:

4 In want my plentiful supply,
In weakness my almighty power,
In bonds my perfect liberty,
My light in Satan's darkest hour,
My help and stay whene'er I call,
My life in death, my heaven, my all.

Charles Wesley (1707–88)

739   L.M.

'Lord, to whom shall we go? thou hast
the words of eternal life' John 6 v 68

1 Thou only sovereign of my heart,
My refuge, my almighty friend –
And can my soul from Thee depart,
On whom alone my hopes depend?

2 Whither, ah! whither shall I go,
A wretched wanderer from my Lord?
Can this dark world of sin and woe,
One glimpse of happiness afford?

3 Eternal life Thy words impart,
On these my fainting spirit lives;
Here sweeter comforts cheer my
heart
Than all the round of nature gives.

4 Let earth's alluring joys combine,
While Thou art near, in vain they
call;
One smile, one blissful smile of
Thine,
My dearest Lord, outweighs them
all.

5 Thy name my inmost powers adore,
Thou art my life, my joy, my care:
Depart from Thee – 'tis death, 'tis
more,
'Tis endless ruin, deep despair.

6 Low at Thy feet my soul would lie,
Here safety dwells, and peace divine;
Still let me live beneath Thine eye,
For life, eternal life, is Thine.

Anne Steele (1716–1778)

740   8 8. 8 8. D

'He shall feed his flock like a shepherd'
Isaiah 40 v 11

1 Thou Shepherd of Israel, and mine,
The joy and desire of my heart,
For closer communion I pine,
I long to reside where Thou art:
The pasture I languish to find
Where all, who their Shepherd obey,
Are fed, on Thy bosom reclined,
And screened from the heat of the
day.

2 Ah! show me that happiest place,
The place of Thy people's abode,
Where saints in an ecstasy gaze,
And hang on a crucified God;
Thy love for a sinner declare,
Thy passion and death on the tree;
My spirit to Calvary bear,
To suffer and triumph with Thee.

3 'Tis there, with the lambs of Thy flock,
There only, I covet to rest,
To lie at the foot of the rock,
Or rise to be hid in Thy breast;
'Tis there I would always abide,
And never a moment depart,
Concealed in the cleft of Thy side,
Eternally held in Thy heart.

Charles Wesley (1707–88)

741   8 7. 8 7. 7 7

'Thou shalt call his name JESUS: for he
shall save his people' Matthew 1 v 21

1 Those whose name is callèd Jesus,
Risen Lord of life and power,
O it is so sweet to trust Thee
Every day and every hour!
Of Thy wondrous grace I sing,
Saviour, Counsellor and King.

2 Thou canst keep my feet from
   falling,
   Even my poor wayward feet –
   Thou who dost present me faultless,
   In Thy righteousness complete;
   Jesus, Lord, in knowing Thee,
   O what strength and victory!

3 All the sin in me, my Saviour,
   Thou canst conquer and subdue;
   With Thy sanctifying power
   Permeate my spirit through;
   Let Thy government increase
   Risen, crownèd, Prince of Peace.

4 Thou canst keep me upward
   looking,
   Ever upward in Thy face;
   Thou canst make me stand,
   upholden
   By the greatness of Thy grace;
   Every promise of Thy Word
   Now I claim from Thee, dear Lord.

5 O what joy to trust Thee, Jesus,
   Mighty Victor o'er the grave,
   And to learn amid earth's shadows
   Thine unceasing power to save!
   Only those who prove Thee know
   What the grace Thou dost bestow.

6 Make my life a bright outshining
   Of thy life, that all may see
   Thine own resurrection power
   Mightily put forth in me;
   Ever let my heart become
   Yet more consciously Thy home.

   Jean Sophia Pigott (1845–82)

742   L.M.

'The LORD is my portion, saith my soul'
Lamentations 3 v 24

1 Though all the world my choice
   deride,
   Yet Jesus shall my portion be;
   For I am pleased with none beside;
   The fairest of the fair is He.

2 Sweet is the vision of Thy face,
   And kindness o'er Thy lips is shed;
   Lovely art Thou and full of grace,
   And glory beams around Thy head.

3 E'en whilst I hated, Thou didst love,
   And o'er Thy rebel creature yearn;
   For me Thou pleadest still above –
   And shall I not such love return?

4 Thy sufferings I embrace with Thee,
   Thy poverty and shameful cross;
   The pleasures of the world I flee,
   And deem its treasures worthless
   dross.

5 Be daily dearer to my heart,
   And ever let me feel Thee near;
   Then willingly with all I'd part,
   Nor count it worthy of a tear.

6 O keep my heart and love with Thee
   Until my mortal work is done;
   And then in heaven Thy face I'll see,
   To be with Thee for ever one!

   Gerhard Tersteegen (1697–1769)
   Tr. Samuel Jackson 1832

743   8 7. 8 7

'My beloved is ... the chiefest among ten
thousand' Song of Solomon 5 v 10

1 Who can cheer the heart like Jesus,
   By His presence all divine?
   True and tender, pure and precious,
   O how blest to call Him mine!

   All that thrills my soul is Jesus;
   He is more than life to me;
   And the fairest of ten thousand
   In my blessèd Lord I see.

2 Love of Christ so freely given,
   Grace of God beyond degree,
   Mercy higher than the heaven,
   Deeper than the deepest sea!

3 What a wonderful redemption!
   Never can a mortal know
   How my sin, though red like
   crimson,
   Can be whiter than the snow.

4 Every need His hand supplying,
Every good in Him I see;
On His strength divine relying,
He is all in all to me.

5 By the crystal-flowing river
With the ransomed I will sing,
And for ever and for ever
Praise and glorify the King.

© *Thoro Harris*

744   C.M.

Based on Psalm 42

1 As pants the hart for cooling
       streams,
When heated in the chase,
So longs my soul, O God, for Thee,
And Thy refreshing grace!

2 For Thee, my God, the living God,
My thirsty soul doth pine;
O when shall I behold Thy face,
Thou majesty divine!

3 God of my strength, how long
       shall I,
Like one forgotten, mourn?
Forlorn, forsaken, and exposed
To my oppressor's scorn.

4 Why restless, why cast down, my
       soul?
Hope still, and thou shalt sing
The praise of Him who is thy God,
Thy health's eternal spring.

Nahum Tate (1652–1715)
and Nicholas Brady (1659–1726)

745   L.M.

*'Blessed are they that mourn: for they
shall be comforted' Matthew 5 v 4*

1 Blest are the humble souls that see
Their emptiness and poverty;
Treasures of grace to them are given,
And crowns of joy laid up in heaven.

2 Blest are the men of broken heart,
Who mourn for sin with inward
       smart;
The blood of Christ divinely flows,
A healing balm for all their woes.

3 Blest are the meek, who stand afar
From rage and passion, noise and
       war;
God will secure their happy state,
And plead their cause against the
       great.

4 Blest are the souls that thirst for
       grace,
Hunger and long for righteousness;
They shall be well supplied and fed,
With living streams and living bread.

5 Blest are the men whose hearts do
       move
And melt with sympathy and love;
From Christ the Lord shall they
       obtain
Like sympathy and love again.

6 Blest are the pure, whose hearts are
       clean
From the defiling powers of sin;
With endless pleasure they shall see
A God of spotless purity.

7 Blest are the men of peaceful life,
Who quench the coals of growing
       strife;
They shall be called the heirs of
       bliss,
The sons of God, the God of peace.

8 Blest are the sufferers who partake
Of pain and shame for Jesus' sake;
Their souls shall triumph in the
       Lord,
Glory and joy are their reward.

Isaac Watts (1674–1748)

746
87.87

Based on Psalm 1

1 Blest is he who loves God's precepts,
Who from sin restrains his feet,
He who will not stand with sinners,
He who shuns the scorners' seat.

2 Blest is he who makes the statutes
Of the Lord his chief delight,
In the law of God rejoicing,
Meditating day and night.

3 He is like a tree well planted
By the flowing river's side,
Ever green of leaf and fruitful;
Thus shall all his works abide.

4 Like the driven chaff the wicked
Shall be swept from off the land;
With the just they shall not gather,
Nor shall in the judgement stand.

5 Well the Lord will guard the
righteous,
For their way to Him is known;
But the way of evildoers
Shall by Him be overthrown.

Psalter Hymnal 1959

747
S.M.

*'He breathed on them, and saith unto
them, Receive ye the Holy Ghost'*
John 20 v 22

1 Breathe on me, Breath of God;
Fill me with life anew,
That I may love what Thou dost love,
And do what Thou wouldst do.

2 Breathe on me, Breath of God,
Until my heart is pure,
Until with Thee I will one will,
To do and to endure.

3 Breathe on me, Breath of God,
Till I am wholly Thine,
Until this earthly part of me
Glows with Thy fire divine.

4 Breathe on me, Breath of God;
So shall I never die,
But live with Thee the perfect life
Of Thine eternity.

Edwin Hatch (1835–89)

748
C.M.

'Love the Lord thy God with all thy heart'
Matthew 22 v 37

1 Enthrone thy God within thy heart,
Thy being's inmost shrine:
He doth to thee the power impart
To live the life divine.

2 Seek truth in Him with Christ-like
mind;
With faith His will discern;
Walk in life's way with Him, and
find
Thy heart within thee burn.

3 With love that overflows thy soul
Love Him who first loved thee;
Is not His love thy life, thy goal,
Thy soul's eternity?

4 Serve Him in His sufficing strength:
Heart, mind and soul employ;
And He shall crown thy days at
length
With everlasting joy.

© Copyright Control   *William Jospeh Penn (1875–1956)*

749
C.M.

*'But unto you that fear my name shall
the Sun of righteousness arise'*
Malachi 4 v 2

1 Eternal Sun of righteousness,
Display Thy beams divine,
And cause the glories of Thy face
Upon my heart to shine.

2 Light in Thy light O may I see,
Thy grace and mercy prove,
Revived and cheered and blessed by
Thee,
The God of pardoning love.

3 Lift up Thy countenance serene,
  And let Thy happy child
  Behold, without a cloud between,
  The Godhead reconciled.

4 That all-comprising peace bestow
  On me, through grace forgiven;
  The joys of holiness below,
  And then the joys of heaven.

                              Charles Wesley (1707–88)

750   C.M.

*'He staggered not at the promise of God
through unbelief" Romans 4 v 20*

1 Father of Jesus Christ, my Lord,
  My Saviour, and my Head,
  I trust in Thee, whose powerful word
  Hath raised Him from the dead.

2 Eternal life to lost mankind
  Thou hast in Jesus given;
  And all who seek, in Him shall find
  The happiness of heaven.

3 Faith in Thy power Thou seest I
    have,
  For Thou this faith hast wrought;
  Dead souls Thou callest from their
    grave,
  And speakest worlds from nought.

4 In hope, against all human hope,
  Self-desperate, I believe;
  Thy quickening Word shall raise me
    up,
  Thou shalt Thy Spirit give.

5 Faith, mighty faith, the promise
    sees,
  And looks to that alone;
  Laughs at impossibilities,
  And cries: It shall be done!

                              Charles Wesley (1707–88)

751   10 7.10 7 (with refrain)

*'I love my master … I will not go out
free' Exodus 21 v 5*

1 I am Thine, O Lord; I have heard Thy
    voice,
  And it told Thy love to me;
  But I long to rise in the arms of
    faith,
  And be closer drawn to Thee.

  *Draw me nearer, nearer, blessèd Lord,
  To the cross where Thou hast died:
  Draw me nearer, nearer, nearer, blessèd
    Lord,
  To Thy precious, bleeding side.*

2 Consecrate me now to Thy service,
    Lord,
  By the power of grace divine;
  Let my soul look up with a steadfast
    hope,
  And my will be lost in Thine.

3 O the pure delight of a single hour
  That before Thy throne I spend,
  When I kneel in prayer, and with
    Thee, my God,
  I commune as friend with friend.

4 There are depths of love that I can
    not know
  Till I cross the narrow sea;
  There are heights of joy that I may
    not reach
  Till I rest in peace with Thee.

                        Frances Jane Crosby (1820–1915)

752

88.88.88

*'God hath not given us the spirit of fear;
but of power, and of love, and of a sound
mind'* 2 Timothy 1 v 7

1 I want the Spirit of power within,
Of love, and of a healthful mind:
Of power, to conquer in bred sin;
Of love, to Thee and all mankind;
Of health, that pain and death
  defies,
Most vigorous when the body dies.

2 When shall I hear the inward voice
Which only faithful souls can hear?
Pardon, and peace, and heavenly joys
Attend the promised Comforter:
O come! and righteousness divine,
And Christ, and all with Christ, are
  mine.

3 O that the Comforter would come!
Nor visit as a transient guest,
But fix in me His constant home,
And take possession of my breast,
And fix in me His loved abode,
The temple of indwelling God.

4 Come, Holy Ghost, my heart inspire!
Attest that I am born again;
Come, and baptize me now with fire,
Nor let Thy former gifts be vain:
I cannot rest in sins forgiven;
Where is the earnest of my heaven?

5 Where the indubitable seal
That ascertains the kingdom mine?
The powerful stamp I long to feel,
The signature of love divine:
O shed it in my heart abroad,
Fulness of love, of heaven, of God!

Charles Wesley (1707–88)

753

87.87.D

'Come, take up the cross, and follow me'
Mark 10 v 21

1 Jesus, I my cross have taken,
All to leave, and follow Thee;
Destitute, despised, forsaken,
Thou from hence my all shalt be:
Perish every fond ambition,
All I've sought, and hoped, and
  known;
Yet how rich is my condition!
God and heaven are still mine own.

2 Let the world despise and leave me,
They have left my Saviour too;
Human hearts and looks deceive me;
Thou art not, like man, untrue:
And, while Thou shalt smile upon me,
God of wisdom, love, and might,
Foes may have, and friends may
  shun me;
Show Thy face, and all is bright.

3 Man may trouble and distress me,
'Twill but drive me to Thy breast;
Life with trials hard may press me,
Heaven will bring me sweeter rest.
O 'tis not in grief to harm me,
While Thy love is left to me!
O 'twere not in joy to charm me,
Were that joy unmixed with Thee!

4 Take, my soul, thy full salvation;
Rise o'er sin, and fear, and care:
Joy to find in every station
Something still to do or bear.
Think what Spirit dwells within thee,
What a Father's smile is thine,
What a Saviour died to win thee:
Child of heaven, shouldst thou
  repine?

5 Haste then on from grace to glory,
Armed by faith, and winged by
prayer;
Heaven's eternal day's before thee;
God's own hand shall guide thee
there.
Soon shall close thine earthly
mission,
Swift shall pass thy pilgrim days,
Hope soon change to glad fruition,
Faith to sight and prayer to praise.

Henry Francis Lyte (1793–1847)

754   8 8 8. 4

'The hour of prayer' Acts 3 v 1

1 My God, is any hour so sweet,
From blush of morn to evening star,
As that which calls me to Thy feet,
The hour of prayer?

2 Then is my strength by Thee
renewed;
Then are my sins by Thee forgiven;
Then dost Thou cheer my solitude
With hope of heaven.

3 No words can tell what blest relief
There for my every want I find;
What strength for warfare, balm for
grief,
What peace of mind!

4 Hushed is each doubt, gone every
fear;
My spirit seems in heaven to stay;
And e'en the penitential tear
Is wiped away.

5 Lord, till I reach yon blissful shore,
No privilege so dear shall be,
As thus my inmost soul to pour
In prayer to Thee.

Charlotte Elliott (1789–1871)

755   6 4. 6 4. 6 6 4

'Surely the LORD is in this place'
Genesis 28 v 16

1 Nearer, my God to Thee,
Nearer to Thee!
E'en though it be a cross
That raiseth me,
Still all my song shall be,
Nearer, my God, to Thee
Nearer to Thee!

2 Though, like the wanderer,
The sun gone down,
Darkness be over me,
My rest a stone,
Yet in my dreams I'd be
Nearer, my God, to Thee,
Nearer to Thee!

3 There let the way appear
Steps unto heaven:
All that Thou send'st to me
In mercy given;
Angels to beckon me
Nearer, my God, to Thee,
Nearer to Thee.

4 Then, with my waking thoughts
Bright with Thy praise,
Out of my stony griefs
Bethel I'll raise;
So by my woes to be
Nearer, my God, to Thee,
Nearer to Thee!

5 Or if on joyful wing
Cleaving the sky,
Sun, moon, and stars forgot,
Upward I fly,
Still all my song shall be,
Nearer, my God, to Thee,
Nearer to Thee!

6 Christ alone beareth me
Where Thou dost shine;
Joint-heir He maketh me
Of the divine!
In Christ my soul shall be
Nearest, my God, to Thee,
Nearest to Thee.

Sarah Fuller Adams (1805–48)
v 6 Arthur Tozer Russell (1806–74)

756 C.M.

Based on Psalm 63

1 O God, Thou art my God alone,
Early, to Thee my soul shall cry,
A pilgrim in a land unknown,
A thirsty land whose springs are dry.

2 Yet through this rough and thorny
maze
I follow hard on Thee, my God;
Thine hand unseen upholds my
ways;
I safely tread where Thou hast trod.

3 Thee, in the watches of the night,
When I remember on my bed,
Thy presence makes the darkness
light;
Thy guardian wings around my
head.

4 Better than life itself Thy love,
Dearer than all beside to me;
For whom have I in heaven above,
Or what on earth, compared with
Thee?

5 Praise, with my heart, my mind, my
voice,
For all Thy mercy I will give;
My soul shall still in God rejoice;
My tongue shall bless Thee while I
live.

James Montgomery (1771–1854)

757 C.M.

'Delight thyself also in the LORD'
Psalm 37 v 4

1 O Lord, I would delight in Thee,
And on Thy care depend;
To Thee in every trouble flee,
My best, my only Friend.

2 When all created streams are dried,
Thy fulness is the same;
May I with this be satisfied,
And glory in Thy name!

3 No good in creatures can be found,
But may be found in Thee;
I must have all things, and abound,
While God is God to me.

4 O that I had a stronger faith,
To look within the veil,
To rest on what my Saviour saith,
Whose word can never fail!

5 He that has made my heaven secure
Will here all good provide;
While Christ is rich, can I be poor?
What can I want beside?

6 O Lord, I cast my care on Thee,
I triumph and adore;
Henceforth my great concern shall
be
To love and please Thee more.

John Ryland (1753–1825)

758 C.M.

'And you hath he quickened, who were
dead in trespasses and sins'
Ephesians 2 v 1

1 O Lord, Thy touch hath stirred my
soul
And caused my heart to love;
My quickened mind hath been made
whole
To seek those things above.

2 There is a path of thought so true
That brings me to Thy throne,
And there my heart may mercy sue
And claim Thy grace my own.

3 Eye hath not seen, nor ear hath
heard
Those things that Thou hast there:
For every promise of Thy Word
Awaits my soul to dare.

4 O why should I let sorrow reign,
When such a God is mine,
Who gives to me and gives again,
And tells me, 'Mine is thine'?

5 The riches He hath stored for me
No measurement can tell;
For in the love of Calvary
All with my God is well.

6 Thy Holy Spirit now hath taught
My being to adore;
The blessings Jesus Christ hath
wrought
Shall cause my soul to soar.

© The Author   William Vernon Higham (b.1926)

759   68.88

Based on Psalm 24 vv 1-6

1 O Lord, who shall ascend
That holy hill to seek Thy face?
Where is the man who dares to
stand
And worship in Thy holy place?

2 The man whose hands are clean,
With lowly heart, and lips kept pure,
Who knows the cleansing of Christ's
blood,
Has access there that will endure.

3 To such the Lord shall give
The blessing of His righteousness:
He calls His saints to seek His face
And throng His courts that He may
bless.

© The Author   Eluned Harrison (b.1934)

760   76.76.77.76

'Led by the Spirit of God' Romans 8 v 14

1 Open, Lord, my inward ear,
And bid my heart rejoice;
Bid my quiet spirit hear
Thy comfortable voice;
Never in the whirlwind found,
Or where the earthquakes rock the
place,
Still and silent is the sound,
The whisper of Thy grace.

2 From the world of sin, and noise,
And hurry I withdraw;
For the small and inward voice
I wait with humble awe;
Silent am I now and still,
Dare not in Thy presence move;
To my waiting soul reveal
The secret of Thy love.

3 Thou didst undertake for me,
For me to death wast sold;
Wisdom in a mystery
Of bleeding love unfold;
Teach the lesson of Thy cross,
Let me die with Thee to reign;
All things let me count but loss,
So I may Thee regain.

4 Show me, as my soul can bear,
The depth of inbred sin;
All the unbelief declare,
The pride that lurks within;
Take me, whom Thyself hast
bought,
Bring into captivity
Every high aspiring thought
That would not stoop to Thee.

5 Lord, my time is in Thy hand,
My soul to Thee convert;
Thou canst make me understand,
Though I am slow of heart;
Thine in whom I live and move,
Thine the work, the praise is Thine;
Thou art wisdom, power, and love,
And all Thou art is mine.

Charles Wesley (1707–88)

761 76.76.77.76

'Seek those things which are above'
Colossians 3 v 1

1 Rise, my soul, and stretch thy wings,
Thy better portion trace:
Rise from transitory things
Toward heaven, thy native place.
Sun and moon and stars decay,
Time shall soon this earth remove;
Rise, my soul, and haste away
To seats prepared above.

2 Rivers to the ocean run,
Nor stay in all their course;
Fire, ascending, seeks the sun;
Both speed them to their source:
So a soul that's born of God
Pants to view His glorious face,
Upward tends to His abode,
To rest in His embrace.

3 Cease, ye pilgrims, cease to mourn;
Press onward to the prize;
Soon our Saviour will return
Triumphant in the skies:
Yet a season, and ye know
Happy entrance will be given,
All our sorrows left below,
And earth exchanged for heaven.

Robert Seagrove (1693–1750)

762 C.M.

'And the LORD talked with Moses'
Exodus 33 v 9

1 Talk with us, Lord, Thyself reveal,
While here on earth we rove;
Speak to our hearts, and let us feel
The kindling of Thy love.

2 With Thee conversing, we forget
All time and toil and care;
Labour is rest, and pain is sweet,
If Thou, my God, art there.

3 Here then, my God, vouchsafe to stay,
And bid my heart rejoice;
My bounding heart shall own Thy sway,
And echo to Thy voice.

4 Thou callest me to seek Thy face,
'Tis all I wish to seek;
To attend the whispers of Thy grace,
And hear Thee inly speak.

5 Let this my every hour employ
Till I Thy glory see,
Enter into my Master's joy,
And find my heaven in Thee.

Charles Wesley (1707–88)

763 8 8 6. D

'I will not leave you comfortless: I will come to you' John 14 v 18

1 Thou great mysterious God unknown,
Whose love hath gently led me on,
E'en from my infant days,
Mine inmost soul expose to view,
Thy justifying grace.

2 If I have only know Thy fear,
And followed with a heart sincere
Thy drawings from above,
Now, now the further grace bestow,
And let my sprinkled conscience know
Thy sweet forgiving love.

3 Short of Thy love I would not stop,
A stranger to the gospel hope,
The sense of sin forgiven;
I would not, Lord, my soul deceive,
Without the inward witness live,
That foretaste now of heaven.

4 If now the witness were in me,
Would He not testify of Thee
In Jesus reconciled?
And should I not in faith draw nigh,
And boldly Abba, Father! cry,
And know myself Thy child?

5 Whate'er obstructs Thy pardoning
    love,
Or sin or righteousness, remove,
Thy glory to display;
Mine heart of unbelief convince,
And now absolve me from my sins,
And take them all away.

6 Father, in me reveal Thy Son,
And to my inmost soul make known
How merciful Thou art:
The secret of Thy love reveal,
And by Thine hallowing Spirit dwell
For ever in my heart.

Charles Wesley (1707–88)

764   8 8. 8 8. 8 8

'I will love thee, O LORD, my strength'
Psalm 18 v 1

1 Thou hidden love of God, whose
    height,
Whose depth unfathomed, no man
    knows,
I see from far Thy beauteous light,
And inly sigh for Thy repose;
My heart is pained, nor can it be
At rest, till it finds rest in Thee.

2 Is there a thing beneath the sun
That strives with Thee my heart to
    share?
Ah! Tear it thence, and reign alone,
And govern every motion there;
Then shall my heart from earth be
    free,
When it has found its all in Thee.

3 O hide this self from me, that I
No more, but Christ in me, may live!
My vile affections crucify,
Nor let one darling lust survive!
In all things nothing may I see,
Nothing desire or seek, but Thee.

4 Each moment draw from earth away
My heart, that lowly waits Thy call;
Speak to my inmost soul and say,
'I am thy Saviour God, thy All!'
To feel Thy power, to hear Thy voice,
To taste Thy love, be all my choice.

Gerhard Tersteegen (1697–1769)
Tr. John Wesley (1703–91)

765   L.M.

'Peace through the blood of his cross'
Colossians 1 v 20

1 Beneath Thy cross I lay me down,
And mourn to see Thy thorny crown;
Love drops in blood from every vein,
Love is the spring of all Thy pain.

2 Here, Jesus, I shall ever stay,
And spend my longing hours away,
Think on Thy bleeding wounds and
    pain,
And contemplate Thy woes again.

3 The rage of Satan and of sin,
Of foes without and fears within,
Shall ne'er my conquering soul
    remove,
Or from Thy cross, or from Thy love.

4 Secured from harm beneath Thy
    shade,
Here death and hell shall ne'er
    invade;
Nor Sinai, with its thundering noise,
Shall e'er disturb my happier joys.

5 O unmolested, happy rest,
Where inward fears are all
    suppressed!
Here I shall love and live secure,
And patiently my cross endure.

William Williams (1717–91)

766   S.M. (with refrain)

*'The redeemed of the LORD shall return,
and come with singing unto Zion'
Isaiah 51 v 11*

1 Come, we that love the Lord,
And let our joys be known;
Join in a song with sweet accord,
And thus surround the throne.

*We're marching to Zion,
Beautiful, beautiful Zion;
We're marching upward to Zion,
The beautiful City of God.*

2 The sorrows of the mind
Be banished from the place;
Religion never was designed
To make our pleasures less.

3 Let those refuse to sing
That never knew our God;
But children of the heavenly King
May speak their joys abroad.

4 The God who rules on high,
And thunders if He please,
Who rides upon the stormy sky
And manages the seas –

5 This awesome God is ours,
Our Father and our love;
He will send down His heavenly
    powers
To carry us above.

6 The men of grace have found
Glory begun below;
Celestial fruit on earthly ground
From faith and hope may grow.

7 The hill of Zion yields
A thousand sacred sweets,
Before we reach the heavenly fields,
Or walk the golden streets.

8 Then let our songs abound,
And every tear be dry;
We're marching through
    Immanuel's ground
To fairer worlds on high.

          Isaac Watts (1674–1748)
*[Omit verses 4–6 when using the refrain
We're marching to Zion]*

767   7 7.7 7

*'Happy is he that hath the God of Jacob
for his help' Psalm 146 v 5*

1 Happiness, thou lovely name,
Where's thy seat, O tell me, where?
Learning, pleasure, wealth, and
    fame,
All cry out, 'It is not here.'

2 Not the wisdom of the wise
Can inform me where it lies;
Not the grandeur of the great
Can the bliss I seek create.

3 Object of my first desire,
Jesus, crucified for me;
All to happiness aspire,
Only to be found in thee.

4 Thee to praise and Thee to know,
Constitute our bliss below;
Thee to see and Thee to love,
Constitute our bliss above.

5 Lord, it is not life to live,
If Thy presence Thou deny;
Lord, if Thou Thy presence give,
'Tis no longer death to die.

6 Source and Giver of repose,
Singly from thy smile it flows;
Happiness complete is Thine;
Mine it is, if Thou art mine.

    Augustus Montague Toplady (1740–78)

768   L.M.

*'Happy is the man that findeth wisdom'
Proverbs 3 v 13*

1 Happy the man that finds the grace,
The blessing of God's chosen race,
The wisdom coming from above,
The faith that sweetly works by love!

2 Happy beyond description he
Who knows: The Saviour died for
    me!
The gift unspeakable obtains,
And heavenly understanding gains.

3 Wisdom divine! who tells the price
Of wisdom's costly merchandise?
Wisdom to silver we prefer,
And gold is dross compared to her.

4 Her hands are filled with length of
days,
True riches, and immortal praise,
Riches of Christ, on all bestowed,
And honour that descends from
God.

5 To purest joys she all invites,
Chaste, holy, spiritual delights;
Her ways are ways of pleasantness,
And all her flowery paths are peace.

6 Happy the man who wisdom gains,
Thrice happy who his guest retains!
He owns, and shall for ever own:
Wisdom, and Christ, and heaven are
one.

Charles Wesley (1707–88)

769 6 6 9. D

*'Blessed is he whose transgression is
forgiven, whose sin is covered'*
Psalm 32 v 1

1 How happy are they
Who the Saviour obey,
And have laid up their treasure
above.
Tongue cannot express
The sweet comfort and peace
Of a soul in its earliest love.

2 That comfort was mine,
When the favour divine
I first found in the blood of the
Lamb;
When my heart it believed,
What a joy it received,
What a heaven in Jesus' great name!

3 Jesus all the day long
Was my joy and my song;
O that all His salvation may see!
He hath loved me, I cried,
He hath suffered, and died,
To redeem such a rebel as me.

4 O the rapturous height
Of the holy delight
Which I felt in the life-giving blood!
Of my Saviour possessed
I was perfectly blessed
As if filled with the fulness of God.

Charles Wesley (1707–88)

770 D.C.M.

*'Blessed is he whose transgression is
forgiven, whose sin is covered'*
Psalm 32 v 1

1 How happy every child of grace,
Who knows his sins forgiven!
This earth, he cries, is not my place,
I seek my place in heaven!
A country far from mortal sight;
Yet, O by faith I see
The land of rest, the saints' delight,
The heaven prepared for me.

2 A stranger in the world below,
I calmly sojourn here;
Nor can its happiness or woe
Provoke my hope or fear:
Its evils in a moment end,
Its joys as soon are past;
But O the bliss to which I tend
Eternally shall last.

3 To that Jerusalem above
With singing I repair;
While in the flesh, my hope and love,
My heart and soul, are there:
There my exalted Saviour stands,
My merciful High-priest,
And still extends His wounded hands
To take me to His breast.

4 O what a blessèd hope is ours,
While here on earth we stay,
We more than taste the heavenly
powers,
Anticipate that day:
We feel the resurrection near,
Our life in Christ concealed,
And with His glorious presence here
Our earthen vessels filled.

Charles Wesley (1707–88)

771

L.M.

'For all things are yours'
1 Corinthians 3 v 21

1 How vast the treasure we
    possess!
  How rich Thy bounty, King of grace!
  This world is ours, and worlds to
    come;
  Earth is our lodge, and heaven our
    home.

2 All things are ours, the gift of God,
  The purchase of a Saviour's blood;
  While the good Spirit shows us how
  To use, and to improve them too.

3 If peace and plenty crown my days,
  They help me, Lord, to speak Thy
    praise;
  If bread of sorrows be my food,
  Those sorrows work my lasting
    good.

4 I would not change my blest estate
  For all the world calls good or great;
  And while my faith can keep her
    hold,
  I envy not the sinner's gold.

5 Father, I wait Thy daily will;
  Thou shalt divide my portion still:
  Grant me on earth what seems Thee
    best,
  Till death and heaven reveal the rest.

Isaac Watts (1674–1748)

772

8 8. 8 8. 8 8. 8

'There is a friend that sticketh closer than
a brother' Proverbs 18 v 24

1 I have a Friend whose faithful love
  Is more than all the world to me,
  'Tis higher than the heights above,
  And deeper than the soundless sea;
  So old, so new, so strong, so true;
  Before the earth received its frame,
  He loved me – Blessèd be His name!

2 He held the highest place above,
  Adored by all the sons of flame,
  Yet, such His self-denying love,
  He laid aside His crown and came
  To seek the lost, and, at the cost
  Of heavenly rank and earthly fame,
  He sought me – Blessèd be His
    name!

3 It was a lonely path He trod,
  From every human soul apart,
  Known only to Himself and God
  Was all the grief that filled His heart:
  Yet from the track He turned not
    back
  Till where I lay in want and shame
  He found me – Blessèd be His name!

4 Then dawned at last that day of dread
  When, desolate but undismayed,
  With wearied frame and thorn-
    crowned head
  He, now forsaken and betrayed,
  Went up for me to Calvary,
  And dying there in grief and shame
  He saved me – Blessèd be His name!

5 Long as I live my song shall tell
  The wonders of His matchless love:
  And when at last I rise to dwell
  In the bright home prepared above,
  My joy shall be His face to see,
  And bowing then with loud acclaim,
  I'll praise Him – Blessèd be His
    name!

C. A. Tydeman

773

S.M.

'Therefore being justified by faith, we
have peace with God' Romans 5 v 1

1 I hear the words of love,
  I gaze upon the blood,
  I see the mighty sacrifice,
  And I have peace with God.

2 'Tis everlasting peace,
  Sure as Jehovah's name;
  'Tis stable as His steadfast throne,
  For evermore the same.

3 The clouds may come and go,
  And storms may sweep my sky –
  This blood-sealed friendship
      changes not:
  The cross is ever nigh.

4 My love is oft-times low,
  My joy still ebbs and flows;
  But peace with Him remains the
      same –
  No change Jehovah knows.

5 I change, He changes not,
  The Christ can never die;
  His love, not mine, the resting-place,
  His truth, not mine, the tie.

Horatius Bonar (1808–89)

774   D.C.M.

'Behold, the half was not told me' 1
Kings 10 v 7

1 I heard about the Son of man,
  His beauty failed to see;
  And wandered far, and vainly ran,
  Believing I was free.
  And then Thy kind restraining grace
  Upon my soul took hold.
  I stood amazed, and saw Thy face –
  The half had not been told!

2 Thy mercy led me through the vale;
  My heart, with sorrow laid,
  With trembling trust and visage pale,
  Beheld the price He paid.
  Such majesty and dignity!
  Though piercing crown was worn;
  This blood and sacrifice to me
  Brought peace and I was born.

3 O blessèd Jesus, lovely name,
  A rose amongst the thorns!
  I cannot see why men defame,
  And this my heart now mourns.
  O gracious Lord, hear now my
      praise,
  I on Thy bosom lean;
  Immortal source, eternal grace,
  Thy beauty I have seen.

© The Author   William Vernon Higham (b.1926)

775   L.M.

'I count all things but loss for the
excellency of the knowledge of Christ Jesus
my Lord' Philippians 3 v 8

1 I once believed my life a gain,
  And thought that I would grace
      attain:
  The Spirit showed me all the dross,
  And now I see it all but loss.

2 Then I beheld the Saviour's face,
  And looked upon a life of grace:
  When I compared my feeble chart,
  Shame and remorse then filled my
      heart.

3 O to be found in Christ alone,
  For on the cross He did atone:
  He took my sin and nailed it there,
  And gave a gown of grace to wear.

4 Now I dismiss my foolish pride,
  Covered in Christ in whom I hide:
  All this by faith that will not fail,
  Granted by God, I will prevail.

5 O wondrous joy the Lord to know,
  I will delight Thy name to show:
  Yet, I desire to know Thee more,
  I hunger for Thy boundless store.

6 Thy risen power I long to prove,
  Fully enabled in each move:
  Through fellowship of suffering
      sweet,
  I worship Thee and ever greet.

7 Confirm me now in image strange;
  Death worketh life, what great
      exchange!
  Yet I believe in Thine increase;
  Lord, evermore may I decrease.

8 Lord, all my life to do Thy will,
  This by Thy grace I will fulfill:
  Then Thou wilt change my body vile,
  Fashioned in Christ – I wait awhile.

© The Author   William Vernon Higham (b.1926)

776 11.11.11.11.

'Jehovah Tsidkenu' means 'The LORD our righteousness' Jeremiah 33 v 16

1 I once was a stranger to grace and to
    God;
  I knew not my danger, and felt not
    my load;
  Though friends spoke in rapture of
    Christ on the tree,
  Jehovah Tsidkenu was nothing to
    me.

2 Like tears from the daughters of
    Zion that roll,
  I wept when the waters went over
    His soul!
  Yet thought not that my sins had
    nailed to the tree
  Jehovah Tsidkenu – 'twas nothing to
    me.

3 When free grace awoke me, by light
    from on high,
  Then legal fears shook me, I
    trembled to die;
  No refuge, no safety in self could I
    see;
  Jehovah Tsidkenu my Saviour must
    be.

4 My terrors all vanished before the
    sweet name;
  My guilty fears banished, with
    boldness I came
  To drink at the fountain, life-giving
    and free:
  Jehovah Tsidkenu was all things to
    me.

5 E'en treading the valley, the shadow
    of death,
  This watchword shall rally my
    faltering breath;
  For, when from life's fever my God
    sets me free,
  Jehovah Tsidkenu my death-song
    shall be.

Robert Murray M'Cheyne (1813–43)

777 7 6.7 6. D

*'If God be for us, who can be against us?'
Romans 8 v 31*

1 If God Himself be for me,
  I may a host defy;
  For when I pray, before me
  My foes confounded fly.
  This I believe – yea, rather,
  Of this I make my boast –
  That God is my dear Father,
  The Friend who loves me most.

2 And that, whate'er betide me,
  My Saviour is at hand,
  Through stormy seas to guide me,
  And bring me safe to land.
  I build on this foundation,
  That Jesus and His blood
  Alone are my salvation,
  The true, eternal good.

3 His Holy Spirit dwelleth
  Within my willing heart,
  Tames it, when it rebelleth,
  And soothes the keenest smart;
  And when my soul is lying
  Weak, trembling and oppressed,
  He pleads with groans and sighing
  That cannot be expressed.

4 To mine His Spirit speaketh
  Sweet words of soothing power,
  How God, for him that seeketh
  For rest, hath rest in store:
  There God Himself prepareth
  My heritage and lot,
  And though my body weareth,
  My heaven shall fail me not.

*Paul Gerhardt (1607–76)
Tr. Richard Massie (1800–87)*

778   665.665.786

*'Unto you therefore which believe he is
precious' 1 Peter 2 v 7*

1 Jesus, priceless treasure,
Source of purest pleasure,
Truest Friend to me;
Ah! how long I've panted,
And my heart hath fainted,
Thirsting, Lord, for Thee!
Thine I am, O spotless Lamb,
I will suffer nought to hide Thee,
Nought I ask beside Thee.

2 In Thine arm I rest me;
Foes who would molest me
Cannot reach me here;
Though the earth be shaking,
Every heart be quaking,
Jesus calms my fear;
Sin and hell in conflict fell
With their bitter storms assail me:
Jesus will not fail me.

3 Hence, all fears and sadness!
For the Lord of gladness,
Jesus, enters in;
Those who love the Father,
Though the storms may gather,
Still have peace within;
Yea, whate'er I here must bear,
Still in Thee lies purest pleasure,
Jesus, priceless treasure!

Johann Franck (1618–77)
Tr. Catherine Winkworth (1827–78)

779   65.65.D

*'Thou wilt keep him in perfect peace,
whose mind is stayed on thee'
Isaiah 26 v 3*

1 Like a river glorious
Is God's perfect peace,
Over all victorious
In its bright increase;
Perfect, yet it floweth
Fuller every day;
Perfect, yet it groweth
Deeper all the way.

Stayed upon Jehovah
Hearts are fully blessed,
Finding, as He promised,
Perfect peace and rest.

2 Hidden in the hollow
Of His blessed hand,
Never foe can follow,
Never traitor stand;
We may trust Him fully
All for us to do;
They who trust Him wholly
Find Him wholly true.

Frances Ridley Havergal (1836–79)

780   77.77.D

*'I am my beloved's, and my beloved is
mine' Song of Solomon 6 v 3*

1 Loved with everlasting love,
Led by grace that love to know,
Spirit, breathing from above,
Thou hast taught me it is so.
O this full and perfect peace!
O this transport all divine!
In a love which cannot cease,
I am His and He is mine.

2 Heaven above is softer blue,
Earth around is sweeter green;
Something lives in every hue
Christless eyes have never seen:
Birds with gladder songs o'erflow,
Flowers with deeper beauties shine,
Since I know, as now I know,
I am His and He is mine.

3 His for ever, only His;
Who the Lord and me shall part?
Ah, with what a rest of bliss
Christ can fill the loving heart!
Heaven and earth may fade and flee,
First-born light in gloom decline,
But while God and I shall be,
I am His and He is mine.

George Wade Robinson (1838–77)

781 5 5 11. D

'Whether we live therefore, or die, we are the Lord's' Romans 14 v 8

1 My God, I am Thine;
What a comfort divine,
What a blessing to know that my
Jesus is mine!
In the heavenly Lamb
Thrice happy I am,
And my heart it doth dance at the
sound of his name.

2 True pleasures abound
In the rapturous sound;
And whoever hath found it hath
paradise found.
My Jesus to know
And feel His blood flow,
'Tis life everlasting, 'tis heaven
below.

3 Yet onward I haste
To the heavenly feast:
That, that is the fullness; but this is
the taste!
And this I shall prove,
Till with joy I remove,
To the heaven of heavens in Jesus'
great love.

Charles Wesley (1707–88)

782 C.M.

'We also joy in God through our Lord Jesus Christ' Romans 5 v 11

1 My God, the spring of all my joys,
The life of my delights,
The glory of my brightest days,
And comfort of my nights.

2 In darkest shades, if He appear,
My dawning is begun;
He is my soul's bright morning star,
And He my rising sun.

3 The opening heavens around me shine
With beams of sacred bliss,
While Jesus shows His heart is mine,
And whispers I am His.

4 My soul would leave this heavy clay
At that transporting word,
Run up with joy the shining way
To see and praise my Lord.

5 Long as I live, I'll bless Thy name,
My King, my God of love;
My work and joy shall be the same
In the bright world above.

Isaac Watts (1674–1748)

783 6 6. 6 6

'My soul thirsteth for thee' Psalm 63 v 1

1 My spirit longs for Thee
Within my troubled breast,
Though I unworthy be
Of so divine a guest.

2 Of so divine a guest
Unworthy though I be,
Yet has my heart no rest
Unless it come from Thee.

3 Unless it come from Thee,
In vain I look around;
In all that I can see
No rest is to be found.

4 No rest is to be found
But in Thy blessed love;
O let my wish be crowned,
And send it from above!

John Byrom (1692–1763)

784 10 10. 10 10

'Hereby we know that he abideth in us, by the Spirit which he hath given us' 1 John 3 v 24

1 Not what I am, O Lord, but what
Thou art!
That, that alone, can be my soul's
true rest;
Thy love, not mine, bids fear and
doubt depart,
And stills the tempest of my tossing
breast.

2 Thy name is Love! I hear it from the
cross;
Thy name is Love! I read it in the
tomb;
All meaner love is perishable dross,
But this shall light me through
time's thickest gloom.

3 Girt with the love of God on every
side,
Breathing that love as heaven's own
healing air,
I work or wait, still following my
Guide,
Braving each foe escaping every
snare.

4 'Tis what I know of Thee, my Lord
and God,
That fills my soul with peace, my
lips with song;
Thou art my health, my joy, my staff
and rod;
Leaning on Thee, in weakness I am
strong.

5 More of Thyself, O show me hour by
hour,
More of Thy glory, O my God and
Lord;
More of Thyself, in all Thy grace and
power;
More of Thy love and truth,
incarnate Word!

Horatius Bonar (1808–89)

785   10 10. 11 11

*'I will praise the LORD with my whole
heart' Psalm 111 v 1*

1 O what shall I do my Saviour to
praise?
So faithful and true, so plenteous in
grace,
So strong to deliver, so good to
redeem
The weakest believer that hangs
upon Him.

2 How happy the man whose heart is
set free,
The people that can be joyful in
Thee;
Their joy is to walk in the light of
Thy face,
And still they are talking of Jesus's
grace.

3 Their daily delight shall be in Thy
name;
They shall as their right Thy righteousness claim;
Thy righteousness wearing, and
cleansed by Thy blood,
Bold shall they appear in the
presence of God.

4 For Jesus, my Lord, is now my
defence;
I trust in His word, none plucks me
from thence;
Since I have found favour, He all
things will do;
My King and my Saviour shall make
me anew.

Charles Wesley (1707–88)

786   10 10

*'Thou wilt keep him in perfect peace,
whose mind is stayed on thee'
Isaiah 26 v 3*

1 Peace, perfect peace, in this dark
world of sin?
The blood of Jesus whispers peace
within.

2 Peace, perfect peace, by thronging
duties pressed?
To do the will of Jesus, this is rest.

3 Peace, perfect peace, with sorrows
surging round?
On Jesus' bosom nought but calm is
found.

4 Peace, perfect peace, with loved ones
far away?
In Jesus' keeping we are safe, and
they.

5 Peace, perfect peace, our future all
  unknown?
  Jesus we know, and He is on the
  throne?

6 Peace, perfect peace, death
  shadowing us and ours?
  Jesus has vanquished death and all
  its powers.

7 It is enough: earth's struggles soon
  shall cease,
  And Jesus call us to heaven's perfect
  peace.

Edward Henry Bickersteth (1825–1906)

787   7 7.7 7

'Thou wilt keep him in perfect peace,
whose mind is stayed on thee'
Isaiah 26 v 3

1 Prince of Peace, control my will;
  Bid this struggling heart be still:
  Bid my fears and doubtings cease:
  Hush my spirit into peace.

2 Thou hast bought me with Thy
    blood,
  Opened wide the gate to God:
  Peace I ask, but peace must be,
  Lord, in being one with Thee.

3 May Thy will, not mine, be done;
  May Thy will and mine be one;
  Chase these doubtings from my
    heart;
  Now Thy perfect peace impart.

4 Saviour, at Thy feet I fall;
  Thou my life, my God, my all!
  Let Thy happy servant be
  One for evermore with Thee!

Charles Wesley (1707–88)

788   9 8. 9 8 (with refrain)

'Let the redeemed of the LORD say so'
Psalm 107 v 2

1 Redeemed how I love to proclaim it,
  Redeemed by the blood of the Lamb;
  Redeemed through His infinite
    mercy,
  His child and forever I am.

  Redeemed, redeemed,
  Redeemed by the blood of the Lamb,
  Redeemed, redeemed,
  His child and forever I am.

2 Redeemed and so happy in Jesus,
  No language my rapture can tell;
  I know that the light of His presence
  With me doth continually dwell.

3 I think of my blessèd Redeemer,
  I think of Him all the day long;
  I sing, for I cannot be silent,
  His love is the theme of my song.

4 I know I shall see in His beauty,
  The King in whose law I delight;
  Who lovingly guardeth my footsteps,
  And giveth me songs in the night.

5 I know there's a crown that is waiting
  In yonder bright mansion for me;
  And soon with the spirits made
    perfect,
  At home with the Lord I shall be.

Frances Jane Crosby (1823–1915)

789   8 7. 8 7

Based on Psalm 23

1 The King of love my Shepherd is,
  Whose goodness faileth never;
  I nothing lack, if I am His,
  And He is mine for ever.

2 Where streams of living waters flow,
  My ransomed soul He leadeth,
  And, where the verdant pastures
    grow,
  With food celestial feedeth.

3 Perverse and foolish oft I strayed,
But yet in love He sought me,
And on His shoulder gently laid,
And home, rejoicing, brought me.

4 In death's dark vale I fear no ill,
With Thee, dear Lord, beside me;
Thy rod and staff my comfort still,
Thy cross before to guide me.

5 And so through all the length of
days,
Thy goodness faileth never:
Good Shepherd, may I sing Thy
praise
Within Thy house for ever!

Henry Williams Baker (1821–77)

790   C.M.

*'There is a friend that sticketh closer than
a brother' Proverbs 18 v 24*

1 There is a Friend whose matchless
love
Surpasses all beside,
'Tis Jesus Christ, the mighty God,
Who for His people died.

2 Yes, Jesus is a Friend indeed,
Whose love is always true!
And, sinners, if you feel your need,
He'll be a Friend to you.

3 If there's a praying heart within,
Though words be very few –
If but a tear, you need not fear,
He'll be a Friend to you.

4 And if you once shall taste His love,
That kindness He'll renew;
In every season you shall prove
He'll be a Friend to you.

5 And when the last great foe shall
stand
Before your trembling view,
Then at that scene He'll step
between,
And prove a Friend to you.

6 He'll guide your footsteps to the last,
To Canaan's happy shore,
Where you shall join the hosts
above,
To praise and to adore.

R. Sears

791   C.M.

*'The peace of God, which passeth all
understanding' Philippians 4 v 7*

1 We bless Thee for Thy peace, O God,
Deep as the unfathomed sea,
Which falls like sunshine on the
road
Of those who trust in Thee.

2 We ask not, Father, for repose
Which comes from outward rest,
If we may have through all life's woes
Thy peace within our breast.

3 That peace which suffers and is
strong,
Trusts where it cannot see,
Deems not the trial-way too long,
But leaves the end with Thee.

4 That peace which flows serene and
deep,
A river in the soul,
Whose banks a living verdure keep,
God's sunshine o'er the whole.

5 Father, give to our hearts this peace,
Whate'er the outward be,
Till all life's discipline shall cease,
And we go home to Thee.

Christian Melodies 1858

792   C.M.

*'The kings of the earth set themselves'
Psalm 2 v 2*

1 Which of the monarchs of the earth
Can boast a guard like ours,
Encircled from our second birth
With all the heavenly powers?

2 Myriads of bright, cherubic bands,
Sent by the King of kings,
Rejoice to bear us in their hands,
And shade us with their wings.

3 Angels, where'er we go, attend
Our steps, whate'er betide;
With watchful care their charge
defend,
And evil turn aside.

4 Our lives those holy angels keep
From every hostile power;
And, unconcerned, we sweetly sleep,
As Adam in his bower.

5 And when our spirits we resign,
On outstretched wings they bear,
And lodge us in the arms divine,
And leave us ever there.

Charles Wesley (1707–1788)

793   5 4. 5 4 D

'Sorrow and sighing shall flee away'
Isaiah 35 v 10

1 Light after darkness, gain after loss,
Strength after weakness, crown after
cross;
Sweet after bitter, hope after fears
Home after wandering, praise after
tears.

2 Sheaves after sowing, sun after rain,
Sight after mystery, peace after pain;
Joy after sorrow, calm after blast,
Rest after weariness; sweet rest at
last.

3 Near after distant, gleam after
gloom,
Love after loneliness, life after tomb;
After life's trial and loss, all
suffering gone
After life's rugged way, heaven is
won.

4 Praise to the Lord of light, Jesus our
King,
Gone now is sin's dark night, His
mercies sing,
He's gained the victory, all works for
good,
Pardon and peace at last; saved by
His blood.

Frances Ridley Havergal (1836–79)

794   C.M.

'All my springs are in thee'
Psalm 87 v 7

1 Now, dearest Lord, to praise Thy
name,
Let all our powers agree;
Worthy art Thou of endless fame;
Our springs are all in Thee.

2 Here in Thy love will we rejoice,
All sovereign, rich, and free;
Singing, we hope with heart and
voice,
Our springs are all in Thee.

3 To whom, dear Jesus, O to whom
Shall needy sinners flee,
But to Thyself, who bidst us come?
Our springs are all in Thee.

4 Some tempted, weak, and trembling
saint
Before Thee now may be;
Let not his hopes or wishes faint;
His springs are all in Thee.

5 The poor supply, the wounded heal,
Let sinners such as we,
Salvation's blessings taste and feel;
Our springs are all in Thee.

6 When we arrive at Zion's hill,
And all Thy glory see,
Our joyful songs shall echo still,
Our springs are all in Thee.

Samuel Medley (1738–99)

795
76. 76. D

'Unto the upright there ariseth light in
the darkness' Psalm 112 v 4

1 Sometimes a light surprises
The Christian while he sings;
It is the Lord who rises
With healing in His wings:
When comforts are declining,
He grants the soul again
A season of clear shining,
To cheer it after rain.

2 In holy contemplation,
We sweetly then pursue
The theme of God's salvation,
And find it ever new.
Set free from present sorrow,
We cheerfully can say,
'E'en let the unknown morrow
Bring with it what it may –

3 'It can bring with it nothing
But He will bear us through;
Who gives the lilies clothing
Will clothe His people too:
Beneath the spreading heavens
No creature but is fed;
And He who feeds the ravens
Will give His children bread.

4 'Though vine nor fig-tree neither
Their wonted fruit should bear
Though all the field should wither,
Nor flocks nor herds be there,
Yet God the same abiding,
His praise shall tune my voice;
For while in Him confiding,
I cannot but rejoice.'

William Cowper (1731–1800)

796
D.C.M.

'For without me ye can do nothing'
John 15 v 5

1 The Galilean fishers toil
All night and nothing take;
But Jesus comes – a wondrous spoil
Is lifted from the lake.
Lord, when our labours are in vain,
And vain the help of men,
When fruitless is our care and pain,
Come, blessèd Jesus, then!

2 The night is dark, the surges fill
The bark, the wild winds roar;
But Jesus comes; and all is still –
The ship is at the shore.
O Lord, when storms around us howl,
And all is dark and drear,
In all the tempests of the soul,
O blessèd Jesus, hear!

3 A frail one, thrice denying Thee,
Saw mercy in Thine eyes;
The penitent upon the tree
Was borne to Paradise.
In hours of sin, and deep distress,
O show us, Lord, Thy face;
In penitential loneliness,
O give us, Jesus, grace!

4 The faithful few retire in fear,
To their closed upper room;
But, suddenly, with joyful cheer
They see their Master come.
Lord, come to us, unloose our
    bands,
And bid our terrors cease;
Lift over us Thy blessèd hands,
Speak, holy Jesus, peace!

Christopher Wordsworth (1807–85)

797
C.M.

Based on Psalm 126

1 The Lord can clear the darkest skies,
Can give us day for night;
Make drops of sacred sorrow rise
To rivers of delight.

2 Let those that sow in sadness wait
Till the fair harvest come!
They shall confess their sheaves are
   great,
And shout the blessings home.

3 The seed, though buried long in dust,
Shall not deceive their hope:
The precious grain can ne'er be lost,
For grace ensures the crop.

Isaac Watts (1674–1748)

798   7 6 . 7 6 D

'I will put thee in a cleft of the rock'
Exodus 33 v 22

1 Thy grace, my God, is mighty,
Sufficient for my need;
And from Thy wondrous bounty
My soul will ever feed.
Thy matchless precious presence,
So full of truth and grace,
Shall be my only preference:
I'll ever seek Thy face.

2 Thy face, O my Redeemer,
With countenance so fair,
Delights my heart with wonder:
None can with Thee compare.
From wounds of merit costly
Flow pardon, peace and joy,
O blessèd, blessèd Calv'ry!
My God I will enjoy.

3 And yet, O Lord of mercy,
Withhold Thy hand at times,
For when Thou dost embrace me
My feeble frame declines.
The anguish of Thy glory
My trembling soul can't bear:
I sink in human frailty,
Without Thy covering care.

4 O fortify me, Saviour,
With strength that comes from Thee;
Endue my soul, Redeemer,
With sweet serenity.
I long to know such fulness,
But grant me grace to stand,
A vessel with new firmness
Controlled by Thy great hand.

© The Author   *William Vernon Higham (b.1926)*

799   D.C.M.

'Thy right hand shall hold me'
Psalm 139 v 10

1 'Twixt gleams of joy and clouds of
   doubt
Our feelings come and go;
Our best estate is tossed about
In ceaseless ebb and flow:
No mood of feeling, form of thought,
Is constant for a day;
But Thou, O Lord, Thou changest
   not;
The same Thou art alway.

2 I grasp Thy strength, make it mine
   own,
My heart with peace is blest:
I lose my hold, and then comes
   down
Darkness, and cold unrest.
Let me no more my comfort draw
From my frail hold of Thee;
In this alone rejoice with awe –
Thy mighty grasp of me.

3 Out of that weak, unquiet drift
That comes but to depart,
To that pure heaven my spirit lift
Where Thou unchanging art;
Lay hold of me with Thy strong grasp,
Let Thy almighty arm
In its embrace my weakness clasp,
And I shall fear no harm.

4 Thy purpose of eternal good
Let me but surely know;
On this I'll lean – let changing mood
And feeling come or go –
Glad when Thy sunshine fills my
   soul
Not 'lorn when clouds o'ercast,
Since Thou within Thy sure control
Of love dost hold me fast.

John Campbell Sharp

800 11 11. 11 11 (with refrain)

'Forget not all his benefits' Psalm 103 v 2

1 When upon life's billows you are
  tempest toss'd,
  When you are discouraged, thinking
  all is lost,
  Count your many blessings, name
  them one by one,
  And it will surprise you what the
  Lord hath done.

  *Count your blessings, name them one by
  one,
  Count your blessings, see what God hath
  done;
  Count your blessings, name them one by
  one,
  And it will surprise you what the Lord
  hath done.*

2 Are you ever burden'd with a load of
  care?
  Does the cross seem heavy you are
  called to bear?
  Count your many blessings, ev'ry
  doubt will fly,
  And you will be singing as the days
  go by.

3 When you look at others with their
  lands and gold,
  Think that Christ has promised you
  His wealth untold,
  Count your many blessings, money
  cannot buy
  Your reward in heaven, nor your
  home on high.

4 So amid the conflict, whether great
  or small,
  Do not be discouraged, God is over
  all,
  Count your many blessings, angels
  will attend,
  Help and comfort give you to your
  journey's end.

  Johnson Oatman Jr (1856–1922)

801 C.M.

*'How unsearchable are his judgements,
and his ways passed finding out!'
Romans 11 v 33*

1 Who fathoms the eternal thought?
  Who talks of scheme and plan?
  The Lord is God! He needeth not
  The poor device of man.

2 Here in the maddening maze of
  things,
  When tossed by storm and flood,
  To one fixed ground my spirit clings;
  I know that God is good!

3 I long for household voices gone,
  For vanished smiles I long;
  But God hath led my dear ones on,
  And He can do no wrong.

4 I know not what the future hath
  Of marvel or surprise,
  Assured alone that life and death
  His mercy underlies.

5 And if my heart and flesh are weak
  To bear an untried pain,
  The bruisèd reed He will not break,
  But strengthen and sustain.

6 No offering of my own I have,
  But Christ who died for me;
  Who came His sinless life to give
  From sin to set me free.

7 And so beside the silent sea
  I wait the muffled roar;
  No harm from Him can come to me
  On ocean or on shore.

8 I know not where the islands lift
  Their fronded palms in air;
  I only know I cannot drift
  Beyond His love and care.

  John Greenleaf Whittier (1807–92)

802 5 5. 5 5. 6 5. 6 5

'I will trust, and not be afraid'
Isaiah 12 v 2

1 Begone, unbelief;
My Saviour is near,
And for my relief
Will surely appear:
By prayer let me wrestle,
And He will perform;
With Christ in the vessel,
I smile at the storm.

2 Though dark be my way,
Since He is my guide,
'Tis mine to obey,
'Tis His to provide;
Though cisterns be broken,
And creatures all fail,
The word He has spoken
Shall surely prevail.

3 His love in time past
Forbids me to think
He'll leave me at last
In trouble to sink;
Each sweet Ebenezer
I have in review
Confirms His good pleasure
To help me quite through.

4 Determined to save,
He watched o'er my path,
When, Satan's blind slave,
I sported with death;
And can He have taught me
To trust in His name,
And thus far have brought me
To put me to shame?

5 Why should I complain
Of want or distress,
Temptation or pain?
He told me no less;
The heirs of salvation,
I know from His Word,
Through much tribulation
Must follow their Lord.

6 Since all that I meet
Shall work for my good,
The bitter is sweet,
The medicine is food;
Though painful at present,
'Twill cease before long;
And then, O how pleasant
The conqueror's song!

John Newton (1725–1807)

803 11 9. 11 9

'We are troubled on every side, yet not
distressed' 2 Corinthians 4 v 8

1 How strange is the course that a
Christian must steer!
How perplexed is the path he must
tread!
The hope of his happiness rises
from fear,
And his life he receives from the
dead.

2 His fairest pretensions must wholly
be waived,
And his best resolutions be crossed;
Nor can he expect to be perfectly
saved,
Till he finds himself utterly lost.

3 When all this is done, and his heart
is assured
Of the total remission of sins,
When his pardon is signed and his
peace is procured,
From that moment his conflict
begins.

Joseph Hart (1712–68)

804 L.M.

'That he might humble thee'
Deuteronomy 8 v 16

1 I asked the Lord that I might grow
In faith, and love, and every grace,
Might more of His salvation know,
And seek more earnestly His face.

2 'Twas He who taught me thus to
   pray,
And He, I trust, has answered
   prayer;
But it has been in such a way
As almost drove me to despair.

3 I hoped that in some favoured hour
At once He'd answer my request;
And, by His love's constraining
   power,
Subdue my sins, and give me rest.

4 Instead of this, He made me feel
The hidden evils of my heart,
And let the angry powers of hell
Assault my soul in every part.

5 Yea, more, with His own hand He
   seemed
Intent to aggravate my woe,
Crossed all the fair designs I
   schemed,
Blasted my gourds, and laid me low.

6 'Lord, why is this?' I trembling cried,
'Wilt Thou pursue Thy worm to
   death?'
'Tis in this way,' the Lord replied,
'I answer prayer for grace and faith.

7 'These inward trials I employ,
From self and pride to set thee free,
And break thy schemes of earthly
   joy,
That thou mayest seek thy all in Me.'

John Newton (1725–1807)

805   6 5. 6 5. D

*'I have prayed for thee, that thy faith fail
not' Luke 22 v 32*

1 In the hour of trial,
Jesus, pray for me,
Lest by base denial
I depart from Thee;
When Thou seest me waver,
With a look recall,
Nor, for fear or favour,
Suffer me to fall.

2 With its witching pleasures
Would this vain world charm,
Or its sordid treasures
Spread to work me harm –
Bring to my remembrance
Sad Gethsemane,
Or, in darker semblance,
Cross-crowned Calvary.

3 If with sore affliction
Thou in love chastise,
Pour Thy benediction
On the sacrifice;
Then, upon Thine altar
Freely offered up,
Though the flesh may falter,
Faith shall drink the cup.

4 When in dust and ashes
To the grave I sink,
While heaven's glory flashes
O'er the shelving brink,
On Thy truth relying
Through that mortal strife,
Lord, receive me, dying,
To eternal life.

James Montgomery (1771–1854)

806   S.M.

*'Look thou upon me, and be merciful
unto me' Psalm 119 v 132*

1 Lord Jesus, think on me,
And purge away my sin;
From earthborn passions set me free,
And make me pure within.

2 Lord Jesus, think on me,
With care and woe opprest;
Let me Thy loving servant be,
And taste Thy promised rest.

3 Lord Jesus, think on me,
Amid the battle's strife;
In all my pain and misery
Be Thou my health and life.

4 Lord Jesus, think on me,
Nor let me go astray;
Through darkness and perplexity
Point Thou the heavenly way.

5 Lord Jesus, think on me,
  When flows the tempest high;
  When on doth rush the enemy,
  O Saviour, be Thou nigh.

6 Lord Jesus, think on me,
  That, when the flood is past,
  I may the eternal brightness see,
  And share Thy joy at last.

Synesius of Cyrene (375–430)
Tr. Allen William Chatfield (1808–96)

807
7 6. 7 6. D

'These are they which follow the Lamb
withersoever he goeth' Revelation 14 v 4

1 O Jesus, I have promised
  To serve Thee to the end;
  Be Thou for ever near me,
  My Master and my Friend:
  I shall not fear the battle
  If Thou art by my side,
  Nor wander from the pathway
  If Thou wilt be my Guide.

2 O let me feel Thee near me:
  The world is ever near;
  I see the sights that dazzle,
  The tempting sounds I hear;
  My foes are ever near me,
  Around me and within;
  But, Jesus, draw Thou nearer,
  And shield my soul from sin.

3 O let me hear Thee speaking
  In accents clear and still,
  Above the storms of passion,
  The murmurs of self-will;
  O speak to reassure me,
  To hasten or control;
  O speak, and make me listen,
  Thou Guardian of my soul.

4 O Jesus, Thou hast promised,
  To all who follow Thee,
  That where Thou art in glory
  There shall Thy servant be;
  And, Jesus, I have promised
  To serve Thee to the end:
  O give me grace to follow,
  My Master and my Friend.

5 O let me see Thy footmarks,
  And in them plant mine own:
  My hope to follow duly
  Is in Thy strength alone.
  O guide me, call me, draw me,
  Uphold me to the end;
  And then in heaven receive me,
  My Saviour and my Friend.

John Ernest Bode (1816–74)

808
7 6. 7 6

'Your life is hid with Christ in God'
Colossians 3 v 3

1 O Lamb of God, still keep me
  Close to Thy piercèd side:
  'Tis only there in safety
  And peace I can abide.

2 What foes and snares surround me,
  What lusts and fears within!
  The grace that sought and found me
  Alone can keep me clean.

3 'Tis only in Thee hiding
  I feel myself secure;
  Only in Thee abiding,
  The conflict can endure.

4 Thine arm the victory gaineth
  O'er every hateful foe;
  Thy love my heart sustaineth
  In all its cares and woe.

5 Soon shall my eyes behold Thee
  With rapture face to face;
  One half hath not been told me
  Of all Thy power and grace.

6 Thy beauty, Lord, and glory,
  The wonders of Thy love,
  Shall be the endless story
  Of all Thy saints above.

James George Deck (1802–84)

809
11 11. 11 11

'Lead me to the rock that is higher than I'
Psalm 61 v 2

1 O safe to the Rock that is higher
than I
My soul in its conflicts and sorrows
would fly;
So sinful, so weary, Thine, Thine
would I be;
Thou blest Rock of Ages, I'm hiding
in Thee!

Hiding in Thee! hiding in Thee!
Thou blest Rock of Ages, I'm hiding in
Thee!

2 In the calm of the noontide, in
sorrow's lone hour,
In times when temptation casts o'er
me its power,
In the tempests of life, on its wide
heaving sea,
Thou blest Rock of Ages, I'm hiding
in Thee!

3 How oft in the conflict, when
pressed by the foe,
I have fled to my refuge and
breathed out my woe!
How often, when trials like
sea-billows roll,
Have I hidden in Thee, O Thou Rock
of my soul!

William Orcutt Cushing (1823–1903)

810
8 8 8. 6

'Seeing he ever liveth to make intercession
for them' Hebrews 7 v 25

1 O Thou, the contrite sinner's Friend,
Who, loving, lovest to the end,
On this alone my hopes depend,
That Thou wilt plead for me.

2 When, weary in the Christian race,
Far off appears my resting-place,
And, fainting, I mistrust Thy grace,
Then, Saviour, plead for me.

3 When I have erred, and gone astray
Afar from Thine and wisdom's way,
And see no glimmering, guiding ray,
Still, Saviour, plead for me.

4 When Satan, by my sins made bold,
Strives from Thy cross to loose my
hold,
Then with Thy pitying arms enfold,
And plead, O plead for me!

5 And when my dying hour draws near,
Darkened with anguish, guilt, and
fear,
Then to my fainting sight appear,
Pleading in heaven for me.

6 When the full light of heavenly day
Reveals my sins in dread array,
Say, 'I have washed them all away,
I plead, yea, plead for thee.'

Charlotte Elliot (1789–1871)

811
S.M.

'I am oppressed; undertake for me'
Isaiah 38 v 14

1 Oppressed with sin and woe,
A burdened heart I bear;
Opposed by many a mighty foe,
Yet will I not despair.

2 With this polluted heart,
I dare to come to Thee –
Holy and mighty as Thou art –
For Thou wilt pardon me.

3 I feel that I am weak,
And prone to every sin;
But Thou who giv'st to those who seek,
Wilt give me strength within.

4 I need not fear my foes;
I need not yield to care;
I need not sink beneath my woes,
For Thou wilt answer prayer.

5 In my Redeemer's name
I give myself to Thee;
And, all unworthy as I am,
My God will welcome me.

Anne Bronte (1820–49)

812 C.M.

'Search me, O God, and know my heart'
Psalm 139 v 23

1 Search me, O God! my actions try,
And let my life appear
As seen by Thine all-searching eye –
To mine my ways make clear.

2 Search all my senses, know my
heart,
Who only canst make known;
And let the deep, the hidden part
To me be fully shown.

3 Throw light into the darkened cells,
Where passion reigns within;
Quicken my conscience till it feels
The loathsomeness of sin.

4 Search, till Thy fiery glance has cast
Its holy light through all,
And I by grace am brought at last
Before Thy face to fall.

5 Thus prostrate I shall learn of Thee,
What now I feebly prove,
That God alone in Christ can be
Unutterable love!

Francis Bottome (1823–94)

813 86.84

'Make me to know my transgression and
my sin' Job 13 v 23

1 Show me myself, O holy Lord;
Help me to look within;
I will not turn me from the sight
Of all my sin.

2 Just as it is in Thy pure eyes
Would I behold my heart;
Bring every hidden spot to light,
Nor shrink the smart.

3 Not mine, the purity of heart
That shall at last see God;
Not mine, the following in the steps
The Saviour trod.

4 Not mine, the life I thought to live
When first I took His name:
Mine but the right to weep and
grieve
Over my shame.

5 Yet, Lord, I thank Thee for the sight
Thou hast vouchsafed to me;
And, humbled to the dust, I shrink
Closer to Thee.

6 And if Thy love will not disown
So frail a heart as mine,
Chasten and cleanse it as Thou wilt,
But keep it Thine!

Plymouth Hymnal 1893

814 S.M.

'The song of Moses ... and the song of the
Lamb' Revelation 15 v 3

1 Awake, and sing the song
Of Moses and the Lamb;
Wake every heart and every tongue
To praise the Saviour's name.

2 Sing of His dying love;
Sing of His rising power;
Sing how He intercedes above
For those whose sins He bore.

3 Ye pilgrims, on the road
To Zion's city, sing;
Rejoice ye in the Lamb of God,
In Christ, the eternal King.

4 Soon shall we hear Him say,
'Ye blessed children, come!'
Soon will He call us hence away,
And take His wanderers home.

5 There shall each raptured tongue
His endless praise proclaim,
And sing in sweeter notes the song
Of Moses and the Lamb.

William Hammond (1718–83)

815   L.M.

'I will mention the lovingkindnesses of the LORD' Isaiah 63 v 7

1 Awake, my soul, in joyful lays,
   And sing thy great Redeemer's
      praise;
   He justly claims a song from thee:
   His lovingkindness, O how free!

2 He saw me ruined in the Fall,
   Yet loved me, notwithstanding all;
   He saved me from my lost estate:
   His lovingkindness, O how great!

3 Though numerous hosts of mighty
      foes,
   Though earth and hell my way
      oppose,
   He safely leads my soul along:
   His lovingkindness, O how strong!

4 When trouble, like a gloomy cloud,
   Has gathered thick and thundered
      loud,
   He near my soul has always stood:
   His lovingkindness, O how good!

5 Often I feel my sinful heart
   Prone from my Saviour to depart;
   But though I have Him oft forgot,
   His lovingkindness changes not.

6 Soon shall I pass the gloomy vale,
   Soon all my mortal powers must fail;
   O may my last expiring breath
   His lovingkindness sing in death!

7 Then let me mount and soar away
   To the bright world of endless day,
   And sing with rapture and surprise
   His lovingkindness in the skies.

Samuel Medley (1738–99)

816   6 4. 6 4

'That ye love one another' John 13 v 34

1 Belovèd, let us love:
   Love is of God;
   In God alone hath love
   Its true abode.

2 Belovèd, let us love:
   For they who love,
   They only, are His sons,
   Born from above.

3 Belovèd, let us love:
   For love is rest,
   And he who loveth not
   Abides unblest.

4 Belovèd, let us love:
   In love is light,
   And he who loveth not,
   Dwelleth in night.

5 Belovèd, let us love:
   For only thus
   Shall we behold that God
   Who loveth us.

Horatius Bonar (1808–89)

817   6 6. 6 6. 8 8

'To him be glory' Revelation 1 v 6

1 Come, every thankful heart,
   That loves the Saviour's name,
   Your noblest powers exert
   To celebrate His fame!
   Tell all above and all below
   The debt of love to Him you owe.

2 He left His starry crown,
   He laid His robes aside,
   On wings of love came down,
   And wept, and bled, and died.
   What He endured no tongue can tell,
   To save our souls from death and
      hell.

3 From the dark grave He rose,
   The mansion of the dead,
   And thence His mighty foes
   In glorious triumph led:
   Up through the sky the Conqueror
      rode,
   And reigns on high the Saviour God.

4 From thence He'll quickly come,
His chariot will not stay,
And bear our spirits home
To realms of endless day:
Then shall we see His lovely face,
And ever dwell in His embrace.

5 Jesus, we ne'er can pay
The debt we owe Thy love;
Yet tell us how we may
Our gratitude approve:
Our hearts, our all, to Thee we give,
The gift, though small, do Thou
receive.

Samuel Stennett (c.1727–95)

818   8 7. 8 7. D

'Hitherto hath the LORD helped us'
1 Samuel 7 v 12

1 Come, Thou Fount of every blessing,
Tune my heart to sing Thy grace;
Streams of mercy, never ceasing,
Call for songs of loudest praise.
Teach me some melodious measure,
Sung by flaming worlds above;
O the vast, the boundless treasure
Of my Lord's unchanging love!

2 Here I raise my Ebenezer,
Hither by Thy help I'm come,
And I hope by Thy good pleasure
Safely to arrive at home.
Jesus sought me when a stranger,
Wandering from the fold of God;
He, to rescue me from danger,
Interposed His precious blood.

3 O to grace how great a debtor
Daily I'm constrained to be!
Let that grace, Lord, like a fetter,
Bind my wandering heart to Thee.
Prone to wander, Lord, I feel it,
Prone to leave the God I love;
Take my heart, O take and seal it,
Seal it from Thy courts above!

Robert Robinson (1735–90)

819   C.M.

'What shall I render unto the LORD for
all his benefits toward me?'
Psalm 116 v 12

1 For mercies countless as the sands,
Which daily I receive
From Jesus, my Redeemer's hands,
My soul, what canst thou give?

2 Alas! From such a heart as mine
What can I bring Him forth?
My best is stained and dyed with sin,
My all is nothing worth.

3 Yet this acknowledgment I'll make,
For all He has bestowed:
Salvation's sacred cup I'll take,
And call upon my God.

John Newton (1725–1807)

820   L.M.

'I will sing praise to my God while I have
my being' Psalm 104 v 33

1 God of my life, through all my days
My grateful powers shall sound Thy
praise;
My song shall wake with opening
light,
And cheer the dark and silent night.

2 When anxious cares would break my
rest,
And griefs would tear my throbbing
breast,
Thy tuneful praises, raised on high,
Shall check the murmur and the
sigh.

3 When death o'er nature shall prevail,
And all the powers of language fail,
Joy through my swimming eyes shall
break,
And mean the thanks I cannot
speak.

4 But O when that last conflict's o'er,
And I am chained to earth no more,
With what glad accents shall I rise
To join the music of the skies!

5 Soon shall I learn the exalted strains
Which echo through the heavenly
plains;
And emulate, with joy unknown,
The glowing seraphs round the
throne.

6 The cheerful tribute will I give
Long as a deathless soul shall live;
A word so sweet, a theme so high,
Demands and crowns eternity.

Philip Doddridge (1702–51)

821   7 7. 7 7

'Thou knowest that I love thee'
John 21 v 16

1 Hark, my soul! it is the Lord;
'Tis thy Saviour, hear His word;
Jesus speaks, and speaks to thee:
'Say, poor sinner, lov'st thou Me?

2 'I delivered thee when bound,
And, when bleeding, healed thy
wound;
Sought thee wandering, set thee
right,
Turned thy darkness into light.

3 'Can a woman's tender care
Cease towards the child she bare?
Yes, she may forgetful be,
Yet will I remember thee.

4 'Mine is an unchanging love,
Higher than the heights above,
Deeper than the depths beneath,
Free and faithful, strong as death.

5 'Thou shalt see My glory soon,
When the work of grace is done;
Partner of My throne shalt be:
Say, poor sinner, lov'st thou Me?'

6 Lord, it is my chief complaint
That my love is weak and faint;
Yet I love Thee, and adore;
O for grace to love Thee more!

William Cowper (1731–1800)

822   8 7. 8 7. D

'Unto you therefore which believe he is
precious' 1 Peter 2 v 7

1 I have not seen Thy face, O Lord,
Yet with my heart I love Thee;
For Thou hast plucked each tender
cord
With pleasing touch of mercy.
O Saviour, Lord, my King and
Friend,
I worship Thee with gladness;
And by Thy grace I will defend
The name that brought me
kindness.

2 I have not known Thee here on
earth,
Yet with my soul I trust Thee;
For Thou hast stirred my thought to
birth
Of God and heaven and glory.
O precious Saviour, hear my praise
With songs of joy and wonder;
For Thou hast taught my lips to raise
A theme of words so tender.

3 Now I have seen Thy glorious face,
With eyes of faith unveiling
The splendour of the theme of grace,
All to my mind revealing.
Such bliss and happiness is mine
To know the God of glory;
For who could call the Lord divine
But for Thy grace and mercy?

© The Author   William Vernon Higham (b.1926)

823

87.87.D

'The Son of God, who loved me, and gave himself for me' Galatians 2 v 20

1 I will sing the wondrous story
Of the Christ who died for me;
How He left His home in glory
For the cross on Calvary.
I was lost: but Jesus found me,
Found the sheep that went astray;
Threw His loving arms around me,
Drew me back into His way.

2 I was bruised; but Jesus healed me –
Faint was I from many a fall;
Sight was gone, and fears possessed
me:
But He freed me from them all.
Days of darkness still come o'er me;
Sorrow's paths I often tread;
But the Saviour still is with me,
By His hand I'm safely led.

3 He will keep me till the river
Rolls its waters at my feet:
Then He'll bear me safely over,
Where the loved ones I shall meet.
Yes, I'll sing the wondrous story
Of the Christ who died for me;
Sing it with the saints in glory,
Gathered by the crystal sea.

© Copyright Control   Francis Harold Rowley (1854–1952)

824

8 8. 8 6 (with refrain)

'He brought me up' Psalm 40 v 2

1 In loving-kindness Jesus came,
My soul in mercy to reclaim,
And from the depths of sin and
shame
Through grace He lifted me.

From sinking sand He lifted me;
With tender hand He lifted me;
From shades of night to plains of light,
O praise His name, He lifted me!

2 He called me long before I heard,
Before my sinful heart was stirred;
But when I took Him at His word,
Forgiven He lifted me.

3 His brow was pierced with many a
thorn,
His hands by cruel nails were torn,
When from my guilt and grief,
forlorn,
In love He lifted me.

4 Now on a higher plane I dwell,
And with my soul I know 'tis well;
Yet how or why, I cannot tell,
He should have lifted me.

Charles Homer Gabriel (1856–1932)

825

Irregular

'The precious blood of Christ'
1 Peter 1 v 19

1 In tenderness He sought me,
Weary and sick with sin,
And on His shoulders brought me
Back to His fold again;
While angels in His presence sang,
Until the courts of heaven rang.

O the love that sought me!
O the blood that bought me!
O the grace that brought me to the fold,
Wondrous grace that brought me to the
fold!

2 He washed the bleeding sin-wounds,
And poured in oil and wine;
He whispered to assure me
'I've found thee, thou art Mine';
I never heard a sweeter voice,
It made my aching heart rejoice.

3 He pointed to the nail-prints –
For me His blood was shed;
A mocking crown so thorny
Was placed upon His head:
I wondered what He saw in me
To suffer such deep agony.

4 I'm sitting in His presence,
The sunshine of His face,
While with adoring wonder
His blessings I retrace.
It seems as if eternal days
Are far too short to sound His
praise.

5 So, while the hours are passing,
All now is perfect rest;
I'm waiting for the morning,
The brightest and the best,
When He will call us to His side
To be with Him, His spotless bride.

W. Spencer Walton (1850–1906)

826   66.66.88

*'How precious also are thy thoughts unto
me, O God!' Psalm 139 v 17*

1 Indulgent God, how kind
Are all Thy ways to me,
Whose dark benighted mind
Was enmity with Thee;
Yet now, subdued by sovereign grace,
My spirit longs for Thy embrace!

2 How precious are Thy thoughts
Which o'er my bosom roll!
They swell beyond my faults
And captivate my soul;
How great their sum, how high they
rise,
Can ne'er be known beneath the
skies.

3 Preserved in Jesus when
My feet made haste to hell;
And there should I have gone
But Thou dost all things well;
Thy love was great, Thy mercy free,
Which from the pit delivered me.

4 A monument of grace,
A sinner saved by blood,
The streams of love I trace
Up to the fountain, God;
And in His wondrous mercy see
Eternal thoughts of love to me.

John Kent (1766–1843)

827   88.88.88

'Lovest thou me?' John 21 v 15

1 Jesus, my Lord, my God, my All,
Hear me, blest Saviour, when I call;
Hear me, and from Thy dwelling-
place
Pour down the riches of Thy grace:

*Jesus, my Lord, I Thee adore;
O make me love Thee more and more.*

2 Jesus, too late I Thee have sought;
How can I love Thee as I ought?
And how extol Thy matchless fame,
The glorious beauty of Thy name?

3 Jesus, what didst Thou find in me,
That Thou hast dealt so lovingly?
How great the joy that Thou hast
brought,
So far exceeding hope or thought!

4 Jesus, of Thee shall be my song;
To Thee my heart and soul belong;
All that I have or am is Thine,
And Thou, blest Saviour, Thou art
mine.

Henry Collins (1827–1919)

828   87.87.77

*'Him that ... washed us from our sins in
his own blood' Revelation 1 v 5*

1 Let us love, and sing, and wonder,
Let us praise the Saviour's name!
He has hushed the Law's loud
thunder,
He has quenched Mount Sinai's
flame;
He has washed us with His blood,
He has bought us nigh to God.

2 Let us love the Lord who bought us,
Pitied us when enemies,
Called us by His grace and taught
us,
Gave us ears, and gave us eyes:
He has washed us with His blood,
He presents our souls to God.

3 Let us sing, though fierce
  temptations
  Threaten hard to bear us down!
  For the Lord, our strong Salvation,
  Holds in view the conqueror's crown:
  He who washed us with His blood
  Soon will bring us home to God.

4 Let us wonder; grace and justice
  Join, and point to mercy's store;
  When through grace in Christ our
    trust is,
  Justice smiles, and asks no more.
  He who washed us with His blood
  Has secured our way to God.

5 Let us praise and join the chorus
  Of the saints enthroned on high;
  Here they trusted Him before us,
  Now their praises fill the sky:
  'Thou hast washed us with His
    blood;
  Thou art worthy, Lamb of God.'

John Newton (1725–1807)

829   8 8 6. D

'I am the light of the world' John 8 v 12

1 Light of the world, Thy beams I
    bless;
  On Thee, bright Sun of
    Righteousness,
  My faith hath fixed its eye;
  Guided by Thee, through all I go,
  Nor fear the ruin spread below,
  For Thou art always nigh.

2 Not all the powers of hell can fright
  A soul that walks with Christ in light;
  He walks, and cannot fall:
  Clearly he sees, and wins his way,
  Shining unto the perfect day,
  And more than conquers all.

3 I rest in Thine almighty power;
  The name of Jesus is a tower,
  That hides my life above:
  Thou canst, Thou wilt my Helper be;
  My confidence is all in Thee,
  The faithful God of love.

4 Wherefore, in never-ceasing prayer,
  My soul to Thy continual care
  I faithfully commend;
  Assured that Thou through life shall
    save,
  And show Thyself beyond the grave
  My everlasting Friend.

Charles Wesley (1707–88)

830   8 7. 8 7. D

*'For thou lovest me before the foundation
of the world' John 17 v 24*

1 Loved with love which knows no
    measure
  Save the Father's love to Thee,
  Blessèd Lord, our hearts would
    treasure
  All the Father's thoughts of Thee.
  All His joy, His rest, His pleasure –
  All His deepest heart's delight –
  Lord, Thy heart alone can measure
  What Thou art in His pure sight.

2 How He set His love upon Thee –
  Called Thee His belovèd Son;
  Yet for us He did not spare Thee,
  By Thy death our life was won.
  Blood-bought people, saved and
    spotless,
  Here we come to show Thy grace;
  Soon, presented by Thee faultless,
  We shall see Thee face to face.

3 O! the joy, the wondrous singing,
  When we see Thee as Thou art;
  Thy blest name, Lord Jesus, bringing
  Sweetest music to God's heart,
  Notes of gladness, songs unceasing,
  Hymns of everlasting praise;
  Psalms of glory, joy increasing,
  Through God's endless day of days.

C. A. Wellesley

831 C.M.

'Thou are fairer than the children of men'
Psalm 45 v 2

1 Majestic sweetness sits enthroned
Upon the Saviour's brow;
His head with radiant glories
   crowned,
His lips with grace o'erflow.

2 He saw me plunged in deep distress,
He flew to my relief;
For me He bore the shameful cross,
And carried all my grief.

3 To Him I owe my life and breath,
And all the joys I have;
He makes me triumph over death,
He saves me from the grave.

4 To heaven, the place of His abode,
He brings my weary feet;
Shows me the glories of my God,
And makes my joys complete.

5 Since from His bounty I receive
Such proofs of love divine,
Had I a thousand hearts to give,
Lord, they should all be Thine!

Samuel Stennett (c.1727–95)

832 11 11. 11 11

'I will love thee, O LORD, my strength'
Psalm 18 v 1

1 My Jesus, I love Thee, I know Thou
   art mine;
For thee all the pleasures of sin I
   resign;
My gracious Redeemer, my Saviour
   art Thou,
If ever I loved Thee, my Jesus, 'tis now.

2 I love Thee because Thou hast first
   lovèd me,
And purchased my pardon on
   Calvary's tree;
I love Thee for wearing the thorns on
   Thy brow,
If ever I loved Thee, my Jesus, 'tis now.

3 I will love Thee in life, I will love
   Thee in death,
And praise Thee as long as Thou
   lendest me breath;
And say, when the death-dew lies
   cold on my brow,
If ever I loved Thee, my Jesus, 'tis now.

4 In mansions of glory and endless
   delight,
I'll ever adore Thee in heaven so
   bright;
I'll sing with the glittering crown on
   my brow,
If ever I loved Thee, my Jesus, 'tis now.

William Ralph Featherston (1842–70)

833 S.M.

'I will ... ascribe righteousness to my
Maker' Job 36 v 3

1 My Maker, and my King,
To Thee my all I owe;
Thy sovereign bounty is the spring
From whence my blessings flow.

2 Thou ever good, and kind,
A thousand reasons move,
A thousand obligations bind,
My heart to grateful love.

3 The creature of Thy hand,
On Thee alone I live:
My God, Thy benefits demand
More praise than life can give.

4 Oh! what can I impart,
When all is Thine before?
Thy love demands a thankful heart;
The gift, alas, how poor!

5 Shall I withhold Thy due?
And shall my passions rove?
Lord, form this wretched heart anew,
And fill it with Thy love.

6 O let Thy grace inspire
My soul with strength divine;
Let all my powers to Thee aspire,
And all my days be Thine.

Anne Steele (1717–78)

834

11 10. 11 10

'O LORD my God, thou art very great'
Psalm 104 v 1

1 O Lord my God, I stand and gaze in
  wonder
  On the vast heavens Thy wisdom
  hath ordained;
  Sun, moon and stars continue at Thy
  pleasure,
  From nothing called and by Thy
  power sustained.

  O mighty God, my heart cries out to Thee,
  How great Thou art! how great Thou art!
  Thy praise shall sound throughout
  eternity,
  How great Thou art! how great Thou art!

2 Sometimes I hear the heavens rent
  by thunder,
  Or see dread lightening leap across
  the sky,
  Then in the cloud I see the promised
  rainbow
  Stilling my fears with mercy from on
  high.

3 This earth once heard the sound of
  angels singing –
  This earth that wept the day that
  Adam fell –
  For Jesus came from purest heights
  of glory,
  An Infant weak, to break the powers
  of hell.

4 Nailed to a tree, the great Creator
  suffered
  When that dread weight of foulest
  sin He bare.
  Lo! Satan flees! the Lord of glory
  triumphs!
  Nothing can with this mighty love
  compare.

© The Author   Eluned Harrison (b.1934)
          Based on Carl Gustaf Boberg (1856–1940)

835

8 8 8. 4

'The living God, who giveth us richly all
things to enjoy' 1Timothy 6 v 17

1 O Lord of heaven, and earth, and
    sea,
  To Thee all praise and glory be;
  How shall we show our love to Thee,
  Who givest all?

2 The golden sunshine, vernal air,
  Sweet flowers and fruits, Thy love
    declare;
  Where harvests ripen, Thou art
    there,
  Who givest all.

3 For peaceful homes and healthful
    days,
  For all the blessings earth displays,
  We owe Thee thankfulness and
    praise,
  Who givest all.

4 Thou didst not spare Thine only
    Son,
  But gav'st Him for a world undone,
  And freely with that blessèd One
  Thou givest all.

5 Thou giv'st the Spirit's blessèd
    dower,
  Spirit of life, and love, and power,
  And dost His sevenfold graces
    shower
  Upon us all.

6 For souls redeemed, for sins
    forgiven,
  For means of grace and hopes of
    heaven,
  Father, what can to Thee be given,
  Who givest all?

7 To Thee, from whom we all derive
  Our life, our gifts, our power to give!
  O may we ever with Thee live,
  Who givest all!

          Christopher Wordsworth (1807–85)

836

66.66.88

'Whosoever believeth in Him should not perish' John 3 v 16

1 The gospel of Thy grace
My stubborn heart has won;
For God so loved the world,
He gave His only Son,
That 'Whosoever will believe,
Shall everlasting life receive!'

2 The serpent lifted up
Could life and healing give,
So Jesus on the cross
Bids me to look and live;
That 'Whosoever will believe,
Shall everlasting life receive!'

3 The soul that sins shall die:
My awful doom I heard;
I was for ever lost,
But for Thy gracious word,
That 'Whosoever will believe,
Shall everlasting life receive!'

4 Not to condemn the world
The Man of sorrows came;
But that the world might have
Salvation through His name;
For 'Whosoever will believe,
Shall everlasting life receive!'

5 Lord, help my unbelief!
Give me the peace of faith,
To rest with childlike trust
On what Thy gospel saith,
That 'Whosoever will believe,
Shall everlasting life receive!'

Arthur Tappan Pierson (1837–1911)
James McGranahan (1840–1907)

837

D.C.M.

'For he hath clothed me with the garments of salvation, he hath covered me with the robe of righteousness' Isaiah 61 v 10

1 The robe of righteousness I wear
Was bought, dear Lord, by Thee,
Thy suffering broken body hung,
In shame on Calvary's tree.
By hands of sinners such as I
Thy precious blood was shed,
That men might know Thy pow'r
o'er sin,
Thou quickener of the dead.

2 I did not willingly take part
In this thine agony.
I was not there, I did not raise
An angry fist t'wards Thee;
But sin has joined my guilty hands
With those who nailed Thee there,
An enemy of Christ my God,
In all their guilt I share.

3 Thy 'It is finished' was a cry
Of victory, not defeat,
All Satan's accusations now
Thy cleansing blood doth meet,
He can no longer claim dominion
O'er my life and soul,
For, by Thy grace and mercy, Thou
Hast made this sinner whole.

4 How can I tell the beauty of
A life that's clean, forgiv'n?
It's glories I'll not fully know
Until I reach Thy heaven.
What bliss to know my precious
Lord,
Within Thy sight to dwell,
Washed clean and saved from
death – its sting,
The grave and powers of hell.

5 How can I pay Thee what I owe?
A debt too great to count.
But Thou dost not require of me
One fraction of the amount.
'Tis grace alone enables me
To stand before Thy throne.
This robe of righteousness is mine
By grace and grace alone.

© The Author   *Hilary Sykes (b.1960)*

838   8 8. 8 8. 8 8

'I will love thee, O LORD, my strength'
Psalm 18 v 1

1 Thee will I love, my strength, my
    tower,
Thee will I love, my joy, my crown,
Thee will I love with all my power,
In all Thy works, and Thee alone;
Thee will I love, till the pure fire
Fill my whole soul with chaste
    desire.

2 In darkness willingly I strayed,
I sought Thee, yet from Thee I roved,
Far wide my wandering thoughts
    were spread,
Thy creatures more than Thee I
    loved;
And now if more at length I see,
'Tis through Thy light, and comes
    from Thee.

3 I thank Thee, uncreated Sun,
That Thy bright beams on me have
    shined;
I thank Thee, who hast overthrown
My foes, and healed my wounded
    mind;
I thank Thee, whose enlivening voice
Bids my freed heart in Thee rejoice.

4 Uphold me in the doubtful race,
Nor suffer me again to stray;
Strengthen my feet with steady pace
Still to press forward in Thy way;
My soul and flesh, O Lord of might,
Transfigure with Thy heavenly light.

5 Thee will I love, my joy, my crown,
Thee will I love, my Lord, my God;
Thee will I love, beneath Thy frown
Or smile, Thy sceptre or Thy rod;
What thought my flesh and heart
    decay?
Thee shall I love in endless day!

Johann Scheffler (1624–77)
Tr. John Wesley (1703–91)

839   C.M.

*'What shall I render unto the LORD for
all his benefits toward me?'*
Psalm 116 v 12

1 What shall I render to my God
For all His mercy's store?
I'll take the gifts He hath bestowed,
And humbly ask for more.

2 The sacred cup of saving grace
I will with thanks receive,
And all His promises embrace,
And to His glory live.

3 My vows I will to His great name
Before His people pay,
And all I have, and all I am,
Upon His altar lay.

4 Thy hands created me, Thy hands
From sin have set me free;
The mercy that hath loosed my
    bands
Hath bound me fast to Thee.

5 The God of all-redeeming grace
My God I will proclaim;
Offer the sacrifice of praise,
And call upon His name.

6 Praise Him, ye saints, the God of
    love,
Who hath my sins forgiven;
Till, gathered to the church above,
We sing the songs of heaven.

Charles Wesley (1707–88)

840
S.M.

Based on Psalm 137

1 Your harps, ye trembling saints,
Down from the willows take;
Loud to the praise of love divine
Bid every string awake.

2 Though in a foreign land,
We are not far from home;
And nearer to our house above
We every moment come.

3 His grace will to the end
Stronger and brighter shine;
Nor present things, nor things to
come,
Shall quench the grace divine.

4 When we in darkness walk,
Nor feel the heavenly flame,
Then is the time to trust our God,
And rest upon His name.

5 Soon shall our doubts and fears
Subside at His control;
His lovingkindness shall break
through
The midnight of the soul.

6 Blest is the man, O God,
That stays himself on Thee,
Who wait for Thy salvation, Lord,
Shall Thy salvation see.

Augustus Montague Toplady (1740–78)

841
L.M.

*'Being then made free from sin, ye became
the servants of righteousness'*
Romans 6 v 18

1 And dost Thou say, 'Ask what thou
wilt?'
Lord, I would seize the golden hour;
I pray to be released from guilt,
And freed from sin and Satan's power.

2 More of Thy presence, Lord, impart,
More of Thine image let me bear;
Erect Thy throne within my heart,
And reign without a rival there.

3 Give me to read my pardon sealed,
And from Thy joy to draw my
strength,
To have Thy boundless love revealed,
Its height, and depth, its breadth,
and length.

4 Grant these requests, I ask no more,
But to Thy care the rest resign;
Living or dying, rich or poor,
All shall be well if Thou art mine.

John Newton (1725–1807)

842
L.M.

'Teach me thy way, O LORD'
Psalm 27 v 11

1 Be with me, Lord, where'er I go;
Teach me what Thou wouldst have
me do;
Suggest whate'er I think or say;
Direct me in the narrow way.

2 Work in me, lest I harbour pride,
Lest I in my own strength confide;
Show me my weakness, let me see
I have my power, my all, from Thee.

3 Assist and teach me how to pray;
Incline my nature to obey;
What Thou abhorrest let me flee,
And only love what pleases Thee.

John Cennick (1718–55)

843
S.M.

*'Because strait is the gate, and narrow is
the way, which leadeth unto life'*
Matthew 7 v 14

1 Believe not those who say
The upward path is smooth,
Lest thou shouldst stumble in the
way
And faint before the truth.

2 It is the only road
Unto the realms of joy;
But he who seeks that blest abode
Must all his powers employ.

3 Arm, arm thee for the fight!
Cast useless loads away;
Watch through the darkest hours of
night;
Toil through the hottest day.

4 To labour and to love,
To pardon and endure,
To lift thy heart to God above,
And keep thy conscience pure –

5 Be this thy constant aim,
Thy hope, thy chief delight;
What matter who should whisper
blame
Or who should scorn or slight,

6 If but thy God approve,
And if, within thy breast,
Thou feel the comfort of His love,
The earnest of His rest.

Anne Bronte (1820–49)

844   7 7.7 7

'For with thee is the fountain of life'
Psalm 36 v 9

1 Christ, of all my hopes the ground,
Christ, the spring of all my joy,
Still in Thee may I be found,
Still for Thee my powers employ.

2 Let Thy love my heart inflame,
Keep Thy fear before my sight,
Be Thy praise my highest aim,
Be Thy smile my chief delight.

3 Fountain of overflowing grace,
Freely from Thy fullness give;
Till I close my earthly race,
May I prove it 'Christ to live'.

4 Firmly trusting in Thy blood,
Nothing shall my heart confound;
Safely I shall pass the flood,
Safely reach Immanuel's ground.

5 Thus, O thus, an entrance give
To the land of cloudless sky;
Having known it 'Christ to live',
Let me know it 'gain to die'.

Ralph Wardlaw (1779–1853)

845   8 8 8. D

'They were all filled with the Holy Ghost'
Acts 4 v 31

1 Come, Holy Ghost, all-quickening
fire,
Come, and my hallowed heart
inspire,
Sprinkled with the atoning blood;
Now to my soul Thyself reveal,
Thy mighty working let me feel,
And know that I am born of God.

2 Humble, and teachable, and mild,
O may I, as a little child,
My lowly Master's steps pursue!
Be anger to my soul unknown,
Hate, envy, jealousy, be gone;
In love create Thou all things new.

3 Let earth no more my heart divide,
With Christ may I be crucified,
To Thee with my whole soul aspire;
Dead to the world and all its toys,
Its idle pomp, and fading joys,
Be Thou alone my one desire!

4 My will be swallowed up in Thee;
Light in Thy light still may I see,
Beholding Thee with open face;
Called the full power of faith to
prove,
Let all my hallowed heart be love,
And all my ransomed life be praise.

Charles Wesley (1707–88)

846   L.M.

'The love of God is shed abroad in our
hearts by the Holy Ghost' Romans 5 v 5

1 Come, Saviour, Jesus, from above!
Assist me with Thy heavenly grace;
Empty my heart of earthly love,
And for Thyself prepare the place.

2 O let Thy sacred presence fill,
And set my longing spirit free,
Which pants to have no other will,
But day and night to feast on Thee.

3 While in this region here below,
No other good will I pursue;
I'll bid this world of noise and show,
With all its glittering snares, adieu!

4 That path with humble speed I'll
    seek,
In which my Saviour's footsteps
    shine;
Nor will I hear, nor will I speak,
Of any other love but Thine.

5 Henceforth may no profane delight
Divide this consecrated soul;
Possess it Thou, who hast the right,
As Lord and Master of the whole.

6 Wealth, honour, pleasure, and what
    else
This short-enduring world can give,
Tempt as ye will, my soul repels,
To Christ alone resolved to live.

7 Thee can I love, and Thee alone,
With pure delight and inward bliss:
To know Thou tak'st me for Thine
    own,
O what a happiness is this!

8 Nothing on earth do I desire,
But Thy pure love within my breast;
This, only this, will I require,
And freely give up all the rest.

Antoinette Bourignon (1616–80)
Tr. John Wesley (1703–91)

847   C.M.

'He is altogether lovely'
Song of Solomon 5 v 16

1 Compared with Christ, in all beside
No comeliness I see;
The one thing needful, dearest Lord,
Is to be one with Thee.

2 The sense of Thy expiring love
Into my soul convey;
Thyself bestow; for Thee alone,
My All in all, I pray.

3 Less than Thyself will not suffice
My comfort to restore;
More than Thyself I cannot crave;
And Thou canst give no more.

4 Loved of my God, for Him again
With love intense I burn;
Chosen of Thee ere time began,
I choose Thee in return.

5 Whate'er consists not with Thy love,
O teach me to resign;
I'm rich to all the intents of bliss,
If Thou, O God, art mine!

Augustus Montague Toplady (1740–78)

848   C.M.

*'Grow in grace, and in the knowledge of
our Lord and Saviour Jesus Christ'*
2 Peter 3 v 18

1 Father of peace, and God of love,
We own Thy power to save,
That power by which our Shepherd
    rose
Victorious o'er the grave.

2 Him from the dead Thou brought'st
    again,
When, by His sacred blood,
Confirmed and sealed for evermore
The eternal covenant stood.

3 O may Thy Spirit seal our souls,
And mould them to Thy will,
That our weak hearts no more may
    stray,
But keep Thy precepts still;

4 That to perfection's sacred height
We nearer still may rise,
And all we think, and all we do,
Be pleasing in Thine eyes.

Philip Doddridge (1702–51)

849 7 7.7 7

'Whom have I in heaven but Thee?'
Psalm 73 v 25

1 Jesus, all-atoning Lamb,
Thine, and only Thine, I am:
Take my body, spirit, soul;
Only Thou possess the whole.

2 Thou my one thing needful be;
Let me ever cleave to Thee;
Let me choose the better part;
Let me give Thee all my heart.

3 Fairer than the sons of men,
Do not let me turn again,
Leave the fountain-head of bliss,
Stoop to creature-happiness.

4 Whom have I on earth below?
Thee, and only Thee, I know;
Whom have I in heaven but Thee?
Thou art all in all to me.

5 All my treasure is above,
All my riches is Thy love:
Whom the worth of love can tell?
Infinite, unsearchable.

Charles Wesley (1707–88)

850 7 6. 7 6 (with refrain)

'The cross of our Lord Jesus Christ'
Galatians 6 v 14

1 Jesus, keep me near the cross:
There a precious fountain,
Free to all, a healing stream,
Flows from Calvary's mountain.

In the cross, in the cross,
Be my glory ever,
Till my raptured soul shall find
Rest beyond the river.

2 Near the cross, a trembling soul,
Love and mercy found me;
There the bright and morning Star
Shed its beams around me.

3 Near the cross! O Lamb of God,
Bring its scenes before me;
Help me walk from day to day
With its shadow o'er me.

4 Near the cross I'll watch and wait,
Hoping, trusting ever,
Till I reach the golden strand,
Just beyond the river.

Frances Jane Crosby (1820–1915)

851 D.S.M.

'I can do all things through Christ which
strengtheneth me' Philippians 4 v 13

1 Jesus, my strength, my hope,
On Thee I cast my care,
With humble confidence look up,
And know Thou hear'st my prayer.
Give me on Thee to wait,
Till I can all things do,
On Thee, almighty to create,
Almighty to renew.

2 I want a godly fear,
A quick-discerning eye
That looks to Thee when sin is near,
And sees the tempter fly;
A spirit still prepared,
And armed with jealous care,
For ever standing on its guard
And watching unto prayer.

3 I want a true regard,
A single, steady aim,
Unmoved by threatening or reward,
To Thee and Thy great name;
A jealous, just concern
For Thine immortal praise;
A pure desire that all may learn
And glorify Thy grace.

4 I rest upon Thy Word;
The promise is for me;
My succour and salvation, Lord,
Shall surely come from Thee:
But let me still abide,
Nor from my hope remove,
Till Thou my patient spirit guide
Into Thy perfect love.

Charles Wesley (1707–88)

852 C.M.

'The love of God is shed abroad in our
hearts by the Holy Ghost' Romans 5 v 5

1 Jesus, Thine all-victorious love
  Sheds in my soul abroad;
  Then shall my feet no longer rove,
  Rooted and fixed in God.

2 O that in me the sacred fire
  Might now begin to glow,
  Burn up the dross of base desire
  And make the mountains flow!

3 O that it now from heaven might
    fall,
  And all my sins consume!
  Come, Holy Ghost, for Thee I call;
  Spirit of burning, come!

4 Refining fire, go through my heart,
  Illuminate my soul;
  Scatter Thy life through every part,
  And sanctify the whole.

5 My steadfast soul, from falling free,
  Shall then no longer move,
  While Christ is all the world to me,
  And all my heart is love.

Charles Wesley (1707–88)

853 C.M.

'Blest are the pure in heart: for they shall
see God' Matthew 5 v 8

1 O for a heart to praise my God,
  A heart from sin set free;
  A heart that always feels Thy blood
  So freely shed for me.

2 A heart resigned, submissive, meek,
  My great Redeemer's throne,
  Where only Christ is heard to speak,
  Where Jesus reigns alone.

3 A humble, lowly, contrite heart,
  Believing, true, and clean.
  Which neither life nor death can part
  From Him that dwells within.

4 A heart in every thought renewed
  And full of love divine,
  Perfect and right and pure and good:
  A copy, Lord, of Thine.

5 Thy nature, gracious Lord, impart;
  Come quickly from above;
  Write Thy new name upon my heart,
  Thy new best name of love.

Charles Wesley (1707–88)

854 C.M.

'Teach me thy way, O LORD'
Psalm 27 v 11

1 O that the Lord would guide my
    ways
  To keep His statutes still!
  O that my God would grant me grace
  To know and do His will!

2 O send Thy Spirit down to write
  Thy law upon my heart;
  Nor let my tongue indulge deceit,
  Nor act the liar's part.

3 From vanity, Lord, turn my eyes;
  Let no corrupt design,
  Nor covetous desires arise
  Within this soul of mine.

4 Order my footsteps by Thy Word,
  And make my heart sincere;
  Let sin have no dominion, Lord,
  But keep my conscience clear.

5 Make me to walk in Thy commands;
  'Tis a delightful road;
  Nor let my head, or heart, or hands,
  Offend against my God.

Isaac Watts (1674–1748)

855 8 8 8. 3

'Seek ye first the kingdom of God, and his
righteousness' Matthew 6 v 34

1 Seek ye first, not earthly pleasure,
  Fading joy and failing treasure;
  But the love that knows no measure
  Seek ye first.

2 Seek ye first God's peace and
blessing –
Ye have all if this possessing;
Come, your need and sin confessing:
Seek Him first.

3 Seek Him first; then, when forgiven,
Pardoned, made an heir of heaven,
Let your life to Him be given:
Seek this first.

4 Seek this first: be pure and holy,
Like the Master, meek and lowly,
Yielded to His service wholly:
Seek this first.

5 Seek this first, His promise trying –
It is sure, all need supplying;
Heavenly things – on Him relying –
Seek ye first.

Georgianna Mary Taylor (1848–1915)

856 L.M.

*'Adorn the doctrine of God our Saviour in
all things' Titus 2 v 10*

1 So let our lips and lives express
The holy gospel we profess;
So let our works and virtues shine,
To prove the doctrine all divine.

2 Thus shall we best proclaim abroad
The honours of our Saviour God,
When His salvation reigns within,
And grace subdues the power of sin.

3 Our flesh and sense must be denied,
Passion and envy, lust and pride,
While justice, temperance, truth and
love,
Our inward godliness approve.

4 Religion bears our spirits up,
While we expect that blessèd hope,
The bright appearance of the Lord:
And faith stands leaning on His
Word.

Isaac Watts (1674–1748)

857 11 11.11 11

*'Sanctify yourselves therefore, and be ye
holy: for I am the Lord your God'
Leviticus 20 v 7*

1 Take time to be holy, speak oft with
thy Lord;
Abide in Him always, and feed on
His Word
Make friends of God's children, help
those who are weak;
Forgetting in nothing His blessing
to seek.

2 Take time to be holy, the world
rushes on;
Spend much time in secret with
Jesus alone.
By looking to Jesus like Him thou
shalt be;
Thy friends, in thy conduct, His
likeness shall see.

3 Take time to be holy, let Him be thy
guide:
And run not before Him whatever
betide:
In joy or in sorrow still follow thy
Lord,
And, looking to Jesus, still trust in
His Word.

4 Take time to be holy, be calm in thy
soul;
Each thought and each temper
beneath His control.
Thus led by His Spirit and filled with
His love,
Thou soon shalt be fitted for service
above.

William Dunn Longstaff (1822–94)

858
C.M.

'Walk in the light, as he is in the light'
1 John 1 v 7

1 Walk in the light, and thou shalt
    own
Thy darkness passed away,
Because that light hath on thee
    shone
In which is perfect day.

2 Walk in the light, and thou shalt find
Thy heart made truly His
Who dwells in cloudless light
    enshrined,
In Whom no darkness is.

3 Walk in the light, and sin abhorred
Shall ne'er defile again;
The blood of Jesus Christ, thy Lord,
Shall cleanse from every stain.

4 Walk in the light, so shalt thou know
That fellowship of love
His Spirit only can bestow,
Who reigns in light above.

5 Walk in the light, and e'en the tomb
No fearful shade shall wear;
Glory shall chase away its gloom,
For Christ has conquered there.

6 Walk in the light; pursue thy way
Till faith be turned to sight;
For in the land of endless day
God is Himself the Light.

Bernard Barton (1784–1849) Altd

859
C.M.

*'Thou therefore endure hardness, as a
good soldier of Jesus Christ'*
2 Timothy 2 v 3

1 Are we the soldiers of the cross,
The followers of the Lamb?
And shall we fear to own His cause,
Or blush to speak His name?

2 No! We must fight if we would
    reign:
Increase our courage, Lord;
We'll bear the toil, endure the pain,
Supported by Thy Word.

3 Thy saints in all this glorious war
Shall conquer, though they're slain;
They see the triumph from afar,
And shall with Jesus reign.

4 When that illustrious day shall rise,
And all Thine armies shine
In robes of victory through the skies,
The glory shall be Thine.

Isaac Watts (1674–1748)

860
77.73

'Watch and pray' Mark 13 v 33

1 Christian, seek not yet repose;
Cast thy dreams of ease away;
Thou art in the midst of foes:
Watch and pray.

2 Principalities and powers,
Mustering their unseen array,
Wait for thy unguarded hours:
Watch and pray.

3 Gird thy heavenly armour on;
Wear it ever, night and day;
Ambushed lies the evil one:
Watch and pray.

4 Hear the victors who o'ercame;
Still they mark each warrior's way;
All with one sweet voice exclaim,
'Watch and pray.'

5 Hear, above all, hear thy Lord,
Him thou lovest to obey;
Hide within thy heart His word:
'Watch and pray.'

6 Watch, as if on that alone
Hung the issue of the day;
Pray, that help may be sent down:
Watch and pray.

Charlotte Elliott (1789–1871)

861

L.M.

'Fight the good fight of faith'
1 Timothy 6 v 12

1 Fight the good fight with all thy
    might;
    Christ is thy strength, and Christ thy
    right;
    Lay hold on life, and it shall be
    Thy joy and crown eternally.

2 Run the straight race through God's
    good grace,
    Lift up thine eyes and seek His face;
    Life with its path before thee lies,
    Christ is the way, and Christ the
    prize.

3 Cast care aside, lean on thy Guide;
    His boundless mercy will provide;
    Trust, and thy trusting soul shall
    prove
    Christ is its life and Christ its love.

4 Faint not nor fear, His arms are
    near;
    He changeth not, and thou art dear;
    Only believe, and thou shalt see
    That Christ is All in all to thee.

John Samuel Bewley Monsell (1811–75)

862

7 6.7 6

Based on Psalm 27

1 God is my strong salvation:
    What foe have I to fear?
    In darkness and temptation
    My light, my help is near.

2 Though hosts encamp around me,
    Firm to the fight I stand;
    What terror can confound me,
    With God at my right hand?

3 Place on the Lord reliance;
    My soul, with courage wait;
    His truth be thine affiance,
    When faint and desolate.

4 His might thine heart shall
    strengthen,
    His love thy joy increase;
    Mercy thy days shall lengthen;
    The Lord will give thee peace.

James Montgomery (1771–1854)

863

11 11. 11 11

'O thou afflicted, tossed with tempest'
Isaiah 54 v 11

1 O Zion, afflicted with wave upon
    wave,
    Whom no man can comfort, whom
    no man can save;
    With darkness surrounded, by
    terrors dismayed,
    In toiling and rowing Thy strength is
    decayed.

2 Loud roaring, the billows now nigh
    overwhelm;
    But skilful's the Pilot who sits at the
    helm;
    His wisdom conducts thee, His
    power thee defends,
    In safety and quiet thy warfare He
    ends.

3 'O fearful, O faithless!' In mercy He
    cries;
    'My promise, My truth, are they light
    in thine eyes?
    Still, still I am with thee; My promise
    shall stand;
    Through tempest and tossing, I'll
    bring thee to land.'

4 'Forget thee I will not, I cannot; Thy
    name
    Engraved on My heart does forever
    remain;
    The palms of My hands while I look
    on I see
    The wounds I receivèd when
    suffering for thee.'

5 'I feel at My heart all thy sighs and
  thy groans,
  For thou art most near me, my flesh
  and my bones;
  In all thy distresses thy Head feels
  the pain;
  Yet all are most needful; not one is in
  vain.'

6 'Then trust Me, and fear not; thy life
  is secure;
  My wisdom is perfect, supreme is
  My power;
  In love I correct thee, thy soul to
  refine,
  To make thee at length, in My
  likeness to shine.'

James Grant (d.1785)

864

10 10. 11 11

'*Yea, the Almighty shall be thy defence*'
Job 22 v 25

1 Omnipotent Lord, my Saviour and
  King,
  Thy succour afford, Thy righteous-
  ness bring;
  Thy promises bind Thee compassion
  to have;
  Now, now let me find Thee almighty
  to save.

2 Rejoicing in hope, and patient in
  grief,
  To Thee I look up for certain relief;
  I fear no denial, no danger I fear,
  Nor start from the trial, while Jesus
  is near.

3 Yet God is above men, devils, and
  sin,
  My Jesus's love the battle shall win,
  So terribly glorious His coming shall
  be,
  His love all-victorious shall conquer
  for me.

4 He all shall break through; His truth
  and His grace
  Shall bring me into the plentiful place,
  Through much tribulation, through
  water and fire,
  Through floods of temptation and
  flames of desire.

5 On Jesus, my power, till then I rely,
  All evil before His presence shall fly;
  When I have my Saviour, my sin
  shall depart,
  And Jesus for ever shall reign in my
  heart.

Charles Wesley (1707–88)

865

6 5. 6 5. D (with refrain)

'*I will build my church; and the gates of
hell shall not prevail against it*'
Matthew 16 v18

1 Onward! Christian soldiers,
  Marching as to war,
  Looking unto Jesus,
  Who is gone before:
  Christ, the royal Master,
  Leads against the foe;
  Forward into battle,
  See, His banners go!

  *Onward! Christian soldiers,
  Marching as to war,
  Looking unto Jesus,
  Who is gone before.*

2 At the name of Jesus,
  Satan's host doth flee;
  On then, Christian soldiers,
  On to victory!
  Hell's foundations quiver
  At the shout of praise:
  Brothers, lift your voices;
  Loud your anthem raise.

3 Like a mighty army
  Moves the church of God;
  Brothers, we are treading
  Where the saints have trod:
  We are not divided,
  All one body we,
  One in hope and doctrine,
  One in charity.

4 Crowns and thrones may perish,
Kingdoms rise and wane;
But the church of Jesus
Constant will remain:
Gates of hell can never
'Gainst that church prevail;
We have Christ's own promise,
And that cannot fail.

5 Onward, then, ye people!
Join our happy throng;
Blend with ours your voices
In the triumph-song:
'Glory, praise, and honour,
Unto Christ the King!'
This through countless ages
Men and angels sing.

Sabine Baring-Gould (1834–1924)

866 L.M.

'I can do all things through Christ which strengtheneth me' Philippians 4 v 13

1 Shall I, for fear of feeble man,
The Spirit's course in me restrain?
Or, undismayed, in deed and word
Be a true witness for my Lord?

2 Saviour of men, Thy searching eye
Doth all my inmost thoughts descry;
Doth aught on earth my wishes
raise,
Or the world's pleasures or its
praise?

3 The love of Christ doth me constrain
To seek the wandering souls of men;
With cries, entreaties, tears, to save,
To snatch them from the gaping
grave.

4 My life, my blood, I here present,
If for Thy truth they may be spent:
Fulfil Thy sovereign counsel, Lord;
Thy will be done, Thy name adored.

5 Give me Thy strength, O God of
power;
Then, let winds blow or thunders
roar,
Thy faithful witness will I be:
'Tis fixed; I can do all through Thee!

Johann Joseph Winckler (1670–1722)
Tr. John Wesley (1703–91)

867 D.S.M.

'Put on the whole armour of God'
Ephesians 6 v 11

1 Soldiers of Christ, arise,
And put your armour on;
Strong in the strength which God
supplies,
Through His eternal Son;
Strong in the Lord of hosts,
And in His mighty power;
Who in the strength of Jesus trusts
Is more than conqueror.

2 Stand, then in His great might,
With all His strength endued;
And take, to arm you for the fight,
The panoply of God.
To keep your armour bright
Attend with constant care,
Still serving in your Captain's sight,
And watching unto prayer.

3 From strength to strength go on;
Wrestle and fight and pray;
Tread all the powers of darkness
down,
And win the well-fought day;
That, having all things done,
And all your conflicts past,
Ye may o'ercome through Christ
alone,
And stand complete at last.

Charles Wesley (1707–88)

868
7 6. 7 6. D

*'Watch ye, stand fast in the faith, quit
you like men, be strong'*
1 Corinthians 16 v 13

1 Stand up, stand up for Jesus,
Ye soldiers of the cross!
Lift high His royal banner,
It must not suffer loss.
From victory unto victory
His army shall He lead,
Till every foe is vanquished,
And Christ is Lord indeed.

2 Stand up, stand up for Jesus!
The trumpet-call obey;
Forth to the mighty conflict
In this His glorious day!
Ye that are men, now serve Him
Against unnumbered foes;
Let courage rise with danger,
And strength to strength oppose.

3 Stand up, stand up for Jesus!
Stand in His strength alone;
The arm of flesh will fail you;
Ye dare not trust your own.
Put on the gospel armour,
Each piece put on with prayer;
Where duty calls, or danger,
Be never wanting there.

4 Stand up, stand up for Jesus!
The strife will not be long;
This day the noise of battle,
The next the victor's song.
To him that overcometh
A crown of life shall be;
He with the King of glory
Shall reign eternally.

George Duffield (1818–88)

869
11 10. 11 10. 11 10

*'For we rest on thee, and in thy name we
go'* 2 Chronicles 14 v 11

1 We rest on Thee, our Shield and our
Defender!
We go not forth alone against the
foe;
Strong in Thy strength, safe in Thy
keeping tender,
We rest on Thee, and in Thy name
we go.

2 Yes, in Thy name, O Captain of
salvation!
In Thy dear name, all other names
above;
Jesus our Righteousness, our sure
Foundation,
Our Prince of glory and our King of
love.

3 We go in faith, our own great
weakness feeling,
And needing more each day Thy
grace to know;
Yet from our hearts a song of
triumph pealing:
We rest on Thee, and in Thy name
we go.

4 We rest on Thee, our Shield and our
Defender!
Thine is the battle; Thine shall be
the praise
When passing through the gates of
pearly splendour,
Victors, we rest with Thee, through
endless days.

Edith Adeline Gilling Cherry (1872–97)

870

6 5. 6 5. Ter

'Who is on the LORD'S side?'
Exodus 32 v 26

1 Who is on the Lord's side?
Who will serve the King?
Who will be His helpers
Other lives to bring?
Who will leave the world's side?
Who will face the foe?
Who is on the Lord's side?
Who for Him will go?
By Thy call of mercy,
By Thy grace divine,
We are on the Lord's side;
Saviour, we are Thine.

2 Jesus, Thou hast bought us,
Not with gold or gem,
But with Thine own life-blood,
For Thy diadem.
With Thy blessing filling
Each who comes to Thee,
Thou hast made us willing,
Thou hast made us free.
By Thy grand redemption,
By Thy grace divine,
We are on the Lord's side;
Saviour, we are Thine.

3 Fierce may be the conflict,
Strong may be the foe;
But the King's own army
None can overthrow;
Round His standard ranging,
Victory is secure,
For His truth unchanging
Makes the triumph sure.
Joyfully enlisting,
By Thy grace divine,
We are on the Lord's side;
Saviour, we are Thine.

4 Chosen to be soldiers,
In an alien land,
Chosen, called, and faithful,
For our Captain's band,
In the service royal,
Let us not grow cold;
Let us be right loyal,
Noble, true and bold.
Master, Thou wilt keep us,
By Thy grace divine,
Always on the Lord's side,
Saviour, always Thine.

Frances Ridley Havergal (1836–79)

871

D.C.M.

Based on Psalm 27

1 Whom shall I fear on earth below
With such a God on high?
My light to guide, my strength to
save –
Thou, Lord, art ever nigh.
Let wicked men, my enemies,
Rise in malicious pride,
In this will I be confident:
Safe in my Lord I hide.

2 One thing desired I of the Lord,
One thing alone I've sought:
That long as life shall last on earth
I may to Thee be brought.
Within Thy house my days I'd spend,
Thy beauty to behold,
Enquire of Thee, and sing that praise
Whose end can ne'er be told.

3 He'll hide me in His secret place
When trouble rages sore;
Upon the rock of steadfast love
My feet are set secure.
He lifts my head in triumph high
Mine enemies above;
And so with joy my praise shall rise
To God, the King of love.

4 Hear, gracious Lord this voice that
    cries;
Have mercy, is my plea:
Let not thine anger hide Thy face
Far, far away from me.
Thou only hast my helper been;
Forsake me not, I sigh;
Lift up Thy lovely face, and shine
Its beauty from on high.

5 Unless I had believed to see
His goodness while below,
What else in this sad land of sin
But faintness would I know?
Wait on the Lord, with courage wait,
And thy weak heart shall find
The mighty strength of God within
Thy heart and soul and mind.

© The Author   Graham Stuart Harrison (b.1935)

872   C.M.

*'These are they which follow the Lamb
whithersoever he goeth' Revelation 14 v 4*

1 A pilgrim in a desert land,
I wander far and wide,
Expecting I may some time come
Close to my Father's side.

2 Ahead of me I think I hear
Sounds of a heavenly choir,
A conquering host already gone
Through tempest, flood and fire.

3 Come, Holy Spirit, fire by night,
Pillar of cloud by day;
Lead, for I dare not take a step
Unless Thou show the way.

4 So prone am I when on my own
To stray from side to side,
I need, each step to Paradise,
My God to be my guide.

5 I have a yearning for that land,
Where the unnumbered throng
Extol the death on Calvary
In heaven's unending song.

William Williams (1717–91)
© The Translator Tr. Robert (Bobi) Maynard Jones (b.1929)

873   C.M.

'Strangers and pilgrims' Hebrews 11 v 13

1 A pilgrim through this lonely world,
The blessèd Saviour passed;
A mourner all His life was He,
A dying Lamb at last.

2 That tender heart, that felt for all,
For us its life-blood gave;
It found on earth no resting-place,
Save only in the grave.

3 Such was our Lord – and shall we
    fear
The cross, with all its scorn?
Or love a faithless, evil world,
That wreathed His brow with thorn?

4 No! Facing all its frowns or smiles,
Like Him, obedient still,
We homeward press, through storm
    or calm,
To Zion's blessèd hill.

5 In tents we dwell amid the waste,
Nor turn aside to roam
In folly's path, nor seek our rest
Where Jesus had no home.

6 Dead to the world with Him who
    died
To win our hearts, our love,
We, risen with our risen Head,
In spirit dwell above.

Edward Denny (1796–1889)

874   8 7. 8 7. D

*'Thou shalt remember all the way which
the LORD thy God led thee'
Deuteronomy 8 v 2*

1 All the way my Saviour leads me:
What have I to ask beside?
Can I doubt His tender mercy,
Who through life has been my
    guide?
Heavenly peace, divinest comfort,
Here by faith in Him to dwell!
For I know whate'er befall me,
Jesus doeth all things well.

2 All the way my Saviour leads me:
Cheers each winding path I tread,
Gives me grace for every trial,
Feeds me with the living bread.
Though my weary steps may falter,
And my soul athirst may be,
Gushing from the rock before me,
Lo! a spring of joy I see.

3 All the way my Saviour leads me;
O the fullness of His love!
Perfect rest to me is promised
In my Father's house above.
When my spirit, clothed, immortal,
Wings its flight to realms of day,
This my song through endless ages –
Jesus led me all the way.

Frances Jane Crosby (1820–1915)

875 10 10. 10 10

*'Thou hast been a shelter for me, and a
strong tower from the enemy'*
Psalm 61 v 3

1 Be Thou my vision, O Lord of my
  heart;
Nought be all else to me, save that
  Thou art;
Thou my best thought, by day or by
  night,
Waking or sleeping, Thy presence
  my light.

2 Be Thou my wisdom, be thou my
  true Word;
I ever with Thee, and Thou with me,
  Lord;
Thou my great Father, and I Thy true
  son;
Thou in me dwelling, and I with
  Thee one.

3 Be Thou my battle-shield, my sword
  for the fight;
Be Thou my armour, and be Thou
  my might;
Thou my soul's shelter, and Thou
  my high tower;
Raise Thou me heavenward, O
  Power of my power.

4 Riches I heed not, nor man's empty
  praise;
Thou mine inheritance, now and
  always;
Thou and Thou only, the first in my
  heart,
High King of heaven, my treasure
  Thou art.

5 High King of heaven, after victory
  won,
May I reach heaven's joy, O bright
  heaven's Sun!
Heart of my own heart, whatever
  befall,
Still be my vision, O Ruler of all.

Irish c.8th Century
Tr. Mary Elizabeth Byrne (1880–1931)
Versified by Eleanor Henrietta Hull (1860–1935)

876 8 8. 8 8. 8 8

'A leader and commander to the people'
Isaiah 55 v 4

1 Captain of Israel's host, and Guide
Of all who seek the land above,
Beneath Thy shadow we abide,
The cloud of Thy protecting love;
Our strength, Thy grace; our rule,
  Thy Word;
Our end, the glory of the Lord.

2 By Thine unerring Spirit led,
We shall not in the desert stray;
We shall not full direction need,
Nor miss our providential way;
As far from danger as from fear,
While love, almighty love, is near.

3 Raised by the breath of love divine,
We urge our way with strength
  renewed;
The church of the first-born to join,
We travel to the mount of God,
With joy upon our heads arise,
And meet our Captain in the skies.

Charles Wesley (1707–88)

877
77.77

'The ransomed of the LORD shall return,
and come to Zion with songs'
Isaiah 35 v 10

1 Children of the heavenly King,
As ye journey, sweetly sing;
Sing your Saviour's worthy praise,
Glorious in His works and ways.

2 We are travelling home to God
In the way the fathers trod;
They are happy now, and we
Soon their happiness shall see.

3 Shout, ye little flock and blest!
You on Jesus' throne shall rest;
There your seat is now prepared,
There your kingdom and reward.

4 Lift your eyes, ye sons of light;
Zion's city is in sight;
There our endless home shall be,
There our Lord we soon shall see.

5 Fear not brethren; joyful stand
On the borders of your land;
Jesus Christ, your Father's Son,
Bids you undismayed go on.

6 Lord, obediently we go,
Gladly leaving all below:
Only Thou our Leader be,
And we still will follow Thee.

John Cennick (1718–55)

878
87.87.47

'Thou shalt guide me with thy counsel'
Psalm 73 v 24

1 Guide me, O Thou great Jehovah,
Pilgrim through this barren land;
I am weak, but Thou art mighty,
Hold me with Thy powerful hand;
Bread of heaven,
Feed me till I want no more.

2 Open Thou the crystal fountain
Whence the healing stream doth
flow;
Let the fiery, cloudy pillar
Lead me all my journey through;
Strong Deliverer,
Be Thou still my strength and shield.

3 When I tread the verge of Jordan,
Bid my anxious fears subside;
Death of death, and hell's
destruction,
Land me safe on Canaan's side;
Songs of praises
I will ever give to Thee.

William Williams (1717–91)
Tr. Peter Williams (1721–96)

879
L.M.

'To me to live is Christ' Philippians 1 v 21

1 How blest is life if lived for Thee,
My loving Saviour and my Lord:
No pleasures that the world can give
Such perfect gladness can afford.

2 To know I am Thy ransomed child,
Bought by Thine own most precious
blood,
And from Thy loving hand to take
With grateful heart each gift of
good;

3 All day to walk beneath Thy smile,
Watching Thine eye to guide me
still,
To rest at night beneath Thy care,
Guarded by Thee from every ill;

4 To feel that though I journey on
By stony paths and rugged ways,
Thy blessèd feet have gone before,
And strength is given for weary days.

5 Such love shall ever make me glad,
Strong in Thy strength to work or
rest,
Until I see Thee face to face,
And in Thy light am fully blest.

Prust's Supplementary Hymn Book 1869

880 76.76.D

'Fear not, little flock' Luke 12 v 32

1 In heavenly love abiding,
No change my heart shall fear;
And safe is such confiding,
For nothing changes here:
The storm may roar without me,
My heart may low be laid;
But God is round about me,
And can I be dismayed?

2 Wherever He may guide me,
No want shall turn me back;
My Shepherd is beside me,
And nothing can I lack:
His wisdom ever waketh,
His sight is never dim;
He knows the way He taketh,
And I will walk with Him.

3 Green pastures are before me,
Which yet I have not seen;
Bright skies will soon be o'er me,
Where the dark clouds have been:
My hope I cannot measure,
My path to life is free;
My Saviour has my treasure,
And He will walk with me.

Anna Laetitia Waring (1823–1910)

881 55.88.55

'His way is perfect' Psalm 18 v 30

1 Jesus, still lead on,
Till our rest be won;
And, although the way be cheerless,
We will follow, calm and fearless;
Guide us by Thy hand
To our fatherland.

2 If the way be drear,
If the foe be near,
Let not faithless fears o'ertake us,
Let not faith and hope forsake us;
For, through many a foe,
To our home we go.

3 When we seek relief
From a long-felt grief,
When oppressed by new temptations,
Lord, increase and perfect patience;
Show us that bright shore
Where we weep no more.

4 When sweet earth and skies
Fade before our eyes;
When through death we look to
heaven,
And our sins are all forgiven,
From Thy bright abode,
Call us home to God.

5 Jesus, still lead on,
Till our rest be won;
Heavenly Leader, still direct us,
Still support, console, protect us,
Till we safely stand in our
fatherland.

Nicolaus Ludwig von Zinzendorf (1700–60)
Tr. Jane Laurie Borthwick (1813–97)

882 87.87.87

'He led them forth by the right way'
Psalm 107 v 7

1 Lead us, Heavenly Father, lead us
O'er the world's tempestuous sea;
Guard us, guide us, keep us, feed us,
For we have no help but Thee;
Yet possessing every blessing
If our God our Father be.

2 Saviour, breathe forgiveness o'er us;
All our weakness Thou dost know;
Thou didst tread this earth before
us,
Thou didst feel its keenest woe;
Lone and dreary, faint and weary,
Through the desert Thou didst go.

3 Spirit of our God, descending,
Fill our hearts with heavenly joy,
Love with every passion blending,
Pleasure that can never cloy;
Thus provided, pardoned, guided,
Nothing can our peace destroy.

James Edmenston (1791–1867)

883

88.88.88

'He led them forth by the right way'
Psalm 107 v 7

1 Leader of faithful souls, and Guide
Of all that travel to the sky,
Come and with us, ev'n us, abide,
Who would on Thee alone rely,
On Thee alone our spirits stay,
While held in life's uneven way.

2 Strangers and pilgrims here below,
This earth, we know, is not our
place;
But hasten through the vale of woe,
And, restless to behold Thy face,
Swift to our heavenly country move,
Our everlasting home above.

3 We've no abiding city here,
But seek a city out of sight;
Thither our steady course we steer,
Aspiring to the plains of light,
Jerusalem, the saints' abode,
Whose founder is the living God.

4 Through Thee, who all our saints
hast borne,
Freely and graciously forgiven,
With songs to Zion we return,
Contending for our native heaven;
That palace of our glorious King,
We find it nearer while we sing.

5 Raised by the breath of love divine,
We urge our way with strength
renewed;
The church of the first-born to join,
We travel to the mount of God,
With joy upon our heads arise,
And meet our Captain in the skies.

Charles Wesley (1707–88)

884

C.M.

Based on Genesis 28 vv 20-21

1 O God of Bethel! by whose hand
Thy people still are fed;
Who through this weary pilgrimage
Hast all our fathers led:

2 Our vows, our prayers, we now
present
Before Thy throne of grace:
God of our fathers, be the God
Of their succeeding race.

3 Through each perplexing path of life
Our wandering footsteps guide;
Give us each day our daily bread,
And raiment fit provide.

4 O spread Thy covering wings around,
Till all our wanderings cease,
And at our Father's loved abode
Our souls arrive in peace.

5 Such blessings from Thy gracious
hand
Our humble prayers implore;
And Thou shalt be our chosen God,
And portion evermore.

Philip Doddridge (1702–51)

885

76.76

*'Behold, we have forsaken all, and
followed thee; what shall we have
therefore?' Matthew 19 v 27*

1 O happy band of pilgrims,
If onward ye will tread,
With Jesus as your Fellow,
To Jesus as your Head!

2 O happy if ye labour
As Jesus did for men;
O happy if ye hunger
As Jesus hungered then!

3 The cross that Jesus carried,
He carried as your due;
The crown that Jesus weareth,
He weareth it for you.

4 The faith by which ye see Him,
The hope in which ye yearn,
The love that through all troubles
To Him alone will turn,

5 The trials that beset you,
The sorrows ye endure,
The manifold temptations
That death alone can cure:

6 What are they but His jewels
Of right celestial worth?
What are they but the ladder
Set up to heaven on earth?

7 O happy band of pilgrims,
Look upward to the skies,
Where such a light affliction
Shall win you such a prize.

John Mason Neale (1818–66)
Based on Joseph the Hymnographer 9th Century

886 L.M.

'The house of my pilgrimage'
Psalm 119 v 54

1 O, mighty Lord, give Thou Thy hand
To succour one in barren land,
That he may in his up-ward quest
Through conflicts find eternal rest.

2 All graces that the church can know,
In heav'n above or earth below,
I claim them all as my due right,
If I possess Thy nature's might.

3 I'll cling to Thee while I have breath,
I'll praise the virtues of Thy death,
I'll bear the cross, I'll breast the tide,
If Thou Thyself in me abide.

David Charles (1762–1834)
Tr. Robert Davies (1769–1835)

887 77.77.D

Based on Psalm 84

1 Pleasant are Thy courts above,
In the land of light and love;
Pleasant are Thy courts below,
In this land of sin and woe.

2 O! my spirit longs and faints
For the converse of Thy saints,
For the brightness of Thy face,
For Thy fullness, God of grace!

3 Happy birds that sing and fly
Round Thine altars, O Most High!
Happier souls that find a rest
In a heavenly Father's breast!

4 Like the wandering dove that found
No repose on earth around
They can to their ark repair,
And enjoy it ever there.

5 Happy souls! their praises flow
Even in this vale of woe;
Waters in the desert rise,
Manna feeds them from the skies.

6 On they go from strength to
strength,
Till they reach Thy throne at length,
At Thy feet adoring fall,
Who hast led them safe through all.

7 Lord, be mine this prize to win;
Guide me through a world of sin;
Keep me by Thy saving grace;
Give me at Thy side a place.

8 Sun and shield alike Thou art;
Guide and guard my erring heart;
Grace and glory flow from Thee;
Shower, O shower them, Lord on
me!

Henry Francis Lyte (1793–1847)

888 88.88.88

'The breadth, and length, and depth and
height' Ephesians 3 v 18

1 Stupendous height of heavenly love,
Of pitying tenderness divine!
It brought the Saviour from above,
It caused the springing day to shine;
The Sun of Righteousness to appear,
And gild our gloomy hemisphere.

2 God did in Christ Himself reveal,
To chase our darkness by His light,
Our sin and ignorance dispel,
Direct our wandering feet aright,
And bring our souls, with pardon
blest,
To realms of everlasting rest.

3 Come then, O Lord, Thy light
      impart,
   The faith that bids our terrors cease;
   Into Thy love direct our heart,
   Into Thy way of perfect peace;
   And cheer the souls of death afraid,
   And guide them through the
      dreadful shade.

4 Answer Thy mercy's whole design,
   My God incarnated for me;
   My spirit make Thy radiant shrine,
   My light and full salvation be;
   And through the shades of death
      unknown
   Conduct me to Thy dazzling throne.

Charles Wesley (1707–88)

889   7 7.7 7

'We are thine' Isaiah 63 v 19

1 Thine forever! God of love,
   Hear us from Thy throne above;
   Thine forever may we be,
   Here and in eternity.

2 Thine forever! Lord of life,
   Shield us through our earthly strife;
   Thou, the Life, the Truth, the Way,
   Guide us to the realms of day.

3 Thine forever! O how blest
   They who find in Thee their rest!
   Saviour, Guardian, heavenly Friend,
   O defend us to the end!

4 Thine forever! Saviour, keep
   These Thy frail and trembling sheep,
   Safe alone beneath Thy care,
   Let us all Thy goodness share.

5 Thine forever! Thou our Guide,
   All our wants by Thee supplied,
   All our sins by Thee forgiven,
   Lead us, Lord, from earth to heaven.

Mary Fawler Maude (1819–1913)

890   8 7.8 7

*'And the LORD went before them by day
in a pillar of cloud … and by night in a
pillar of fire' Exodus 13 v 21*

1 Through the night of doubt and
      sorrow,
   Onward goes the pilgrim band,
   Singing songs of expectation,
   Marching to the promised land.

2 Clear before us through the
      darkness
   Gleams and burns the guiding light;
   Brother clasps the hand of brother,
   Stepping fearless through the night.

3 One the light of God's own
      presence,
   O'er His ransomed people shed,
   Chasing far the gloom and terror,
   Brightening all the path we tread;

4 One the object of our journey,
   One the faith which never tires,
   One the earnest looking forward,
   One the hope our God inspires;

5 One the strain that lips of thousands
   Lift as from the heart of one;
   One the conflict, one the peril,
   One the march in God begun;

6 One the gladness of rejoicing
   On the far eternal shore,
   Where the one almighty Father
   Reigns in love for evermore.

7 Onward therefore, pilgrim brothers,
   Onward with the cross our aid!
   Bear its shame, and fight its battle,
   Till we rest beneath its shade.

8 Soon shall come the great awaking,
   Soon the rending of the tomb;
   Then the scattering of all shadows,
   And the end of toil and gloom.

Bernhardt Severin Ingemann (1789–1862)
Tr. Sabine Baring-Gould (1834–1924)

891
66.66

'Not as I will, but as thou wilt'
Matthew 26 v 39

1 Thy way, not mine, O Lord,
However dark it be!
Lead me by Thine own hand,
Choose out the path for me.

2 Smooth let it be, or rough,
It will be still the best;
Winding, or straight, it leads
Right onward to Thy rest.

3 I dare not choose my lot;
I would not if I might;
Choose Thou for me, my God,
So shall I walk aright.

4 The kingdom that I seek
Is Thine, so let the way
That leads to it be Thine,
Else I must surely stray.

5 Take Thou my cup, and it
With joy or sorrow fill,
As best to Thee may seem;
Choose Thou my good and ill.

6 Choose Thou for me my friends,
My sickness or my health;
Choose Thou my cares for me,
My poverty or wealth.

7 Not mine, not mine the choice,
In things or great or small;
Be Thou my Guide, my Strength,
My Wisdom, and my All.

Horatius Bonar (1808–89)

892
10 4. 10 4. 10 10

Based on Psalm 121

1 Unto the hills around do I lift up
My longing eyes
O whence for me shall my salvation
come,
From whence arise?
From God, the Lord, doth come my
certain aid,
From God, the Lord, Who heaven
and earth hath made.

2 He will not suffer that thy foot be
moved:
Safe shalt thou be.
No careless slumber shall His
eyelids close,
Who keepeth thee.
Behold our God, the Lord, He
slumbereth ne'er,
Who keepeth Israel in His holy care.

3 Jehovah is Himself thy Keeper true,
Thy changeless shade;
Jehovah thy defence on thy right
hand
Himself hath made.
And thee no sun by day shall ever
smite,
No moon shall harm thee in the
silent night.

4 From every evil shall He keep thy
soul,
From every sin;
Jehovah shall preserve thy going out,
Thy coming in.
Above thee watching, He, whom we
adore
Shall keep thee henceforth, yea,
forevermore.

John Douglas Sutherland Campbell (1845–1914)

893
77.77

'Until the day break, and the shadows
flee away' Song of Solomon 2 v 17

1 When we cannot see our way,
Let us trust and still obey;
He who bids us forward go
Cannot fail the way to show.

2 Though the sea be deep and wide,
Though a passage seem denied,
Fearless let us still proceed,
Since the Lord vouchsafes to lead.

3 Though it be the gloom of night,
Though we see no ray of light,
Since the Lord Himself is there,
'Tis not meet that we should fear.

4 Night with Him is never night;
   Where He is, there all is light;
   When He calls us, why delay?
   They are happy who obey.

5 Be it ours, then, while we're here,
   Him to follow without fear;
   Where He calls us, there to go,
   What He bids us, that to do.

Thomas Kelly (1769–1855)

894   6 5. 6 5. 6 6. 6 5

*'Speak unto the children of Israel, that
they go forward' Exodus 14 v 15*

1 Who would true valour see,
   Let him come hither;
   One here will constant be,
   Come wind, come weather;
   There's no discouragement
   Shall make him once relent
   His first avowed intent
   To be a pilgrim.

2 Whoso beset him round
   With dismal stories,
   Do but themselves confound;
   His strength the more is.
   No lion can him fright;
   He'll with a giant fight,
   But he will have a right
   To be a pilgrim.

3 Hobgoblin nor foul fiend
   Can daunt his spirit;
   He knows he at the end
   Shall life inherit.
   Then fancies fly away;
   He'll fear not what men say;
   He'll labour night and day
   To be a pilgrim.

John Bunyan (1628–88)

895   C.M.

*'Thou art my trust from my youth'
Psalm 71 v 5*

1 Almighty Father of mankind,
   On Thee my hopes remain;
   And when the day of trouble comes,
   I shall not trust in vain.

2 In early days Thou wast my Guide,
   And of my youth the Friend:
   And as my days began with Thee,
   With Thee my days shall end.

3 I know the power in whom I trust,
   The arm on which I lean;
   He will my Saviour ever be,
   Who has my Saviour been.

4 My God, who causedst me to hope,
   When life began to beat,
   And when a stranger in the world,
   Didst guide my wandering feet;

5 Thou wilt not cast me off when age
   And evil days descend!
   Thou wilt not leave me in despair,
   To mourn my latter end.

6 Therefore in life I'll trust to Thee,
   In death I will adore,
   And after death I'll sing Thy praise,
   When time shall be no more.

Michael Bruce (1746–67)

896   10 10. 10 10. 10 10

*'Be still, and know that I am God'
Psalm 46 v 10*

1 Be still, my soul: the Lord is on thy
   side;
   Bear patiently the cross of grief or
   pain;
   Leave to thy God to order and
   provide;
   In every change He faithful will
   remain.
   Be still, my soul: thy best, thy
   heavenly Friend
   Through thorny ways leads to a
   joyful end.

2 Be still, my soul: thy God doth
   undertake
To guide the future as He has the
   past.
Thy hope, thy confidence, let
   nothing shake;
All now mysterious shall be bright at
   last.
Be still, my soul: the waves and
   winds still know
His voice who ruled them while He
   dwelt below.

3 Be still, my soul: the hour is
   hastening on
When we shall be for ever with the
   Lord,
When disappointment, grief and
   fear are gone,
Sorrow forgot, love's purest joys
   restored.
Be still, my soul: when change and
   tears are past,
All safe and blessèd we shall meet at
   last.

Katharina von Schlegel (b.1697)
Tr. Jane Laurie Borthwick (1813–97)

897   D.S.M.

'In all thy ways acknowledge him, and
he shall direct thy paths' Proverbs 3 v 6

1 Give to the winds thy fears;
Hope, and be undismayed:
God hears thy sighs, and counts thy
   tears;
God shall lift up thy head.
Through waves, and clouds, and
   storms
He gently clears thy way;
Wait thou His time, so shall this
   night
Soon end in joyous day.

2 Leave to His sovereign sway
To choose and to command;
So shalt thou wondering own his
   way,
How wise, how strong His hand.
Far, far above thy thought
His counsel shall appear,
When fully He the work hath
   wrought
That caused thy needless fear.

3 Thou seeset our weakness, Lord;
Our hearts are known to Thee:
O lift Thou up the sinking hand,
Confirm the feeble knee!
Let us in life, in death,
Thy steadfast truth declare,
And publish with our latest breath
Thy love and guardian care.

Paul Gerhardt (1607–76)
Tr. John Wesley (1703–91)

898   8 4. 8 8 4

'He knoweth the way that I take'
Job 23 v 10

1 God holds the key of all unknown,
And I am glad:
If other hands should hold the key,
Or if He trusted it to me,
I might be sad.

2 What if tomorrow's cares were here
Without its rest?
I'd rather He unlocked the day,
And, as the hours swing open, say,
'My will is best.'

3 The very dimness of my sight
Makes me secure;
For, groping in my misty way,
I feel His hand; I hear Him say,
'My help is sure.'

4 I cannot read His future plans;
But this I know:
I have the smiling of His face,
And all the refuge of His grace,
While here below.

5 Enough: this covers all my wants;
And so I rest!
For what I cannot, He can see,
And in His care I saved shall be,
For ever blest.

Joseph Parker (1830–1902)

899   5 4. 5 4. D

*'As the clay is in the potters hand, so are
ye in mine hand' Jeremiah 18 v 6*

1 Have Thine own way, Lord,
Have Thine own way;
Thou art the Potter,
I am the clay.
Mould me and make me
After Thy will,
While I am waiting
Yielded and still.

2 Have Thine own way, Lord,
Have Thine own way;
Search me and try me,
Master, today.
Whiter than snow, Lord,
Wash me just now,
As in Thy presence
Humbly I bow.

3 Have Thine own way, Lord,
Have Thine own way;
Wounded and weary,
Help me, I pray.
Power, all power,
Surely is Thine;
Touch me and heal me,
Saviour divine.

4 Have Thine own way, Lord,
Have Thine own way;
Hold o'er my being
Absolute sway.
Fill with Thy Spirit
Till all shall see
Christ only, always,
Living in me.

Adelaide Addison Pollard (1862–1934)

900   L.M.

*'If any man serve me, let him follow me'
John 12 v 26*

1 How shall I follow Him I serve?
How shall I copy Him I love,
Nor from those blessèd footsteps
swerve
Which lead me to His seat above?

2 Privations, sorrows, bitter scorn,
The life of toil, the mean abode,
The faithless kiss, the crown of
thorn –
Are these the consecrated road?

3 'Twas thus He suffered, though a
Son,
Foreknowing, choosing, feeling all,
Until the perfect work was done,
And drank the bitter cup of gall.

4 Lord, should my path through
suffering lie,
Forbid it I should e'er repine;
Still let me turn to Calvary,
Nor heed my griefs, remembering
Thine.

5 To faint, to grieve, to die for me
Thou camest, not Thyself to please;
And, dear as earthly comforts be,
Shall I not love Thee more than
these?

6 Yes, I would count them all but loss,
That I may follow after Thee;
Flesh shrinks and trembles at the
cross,
But Thou canst give the victory.

Josiah Conder (1789–1855)

901

888.7

'Christ Jesus came into the world to save sinners' 1 Timothy 1 v 15

1 I am not skilled to understand
What God hath willed, what God
    hath planned;
I only know at His right hand
Stands One who is my Saviour.

2 I take Him at His word and deed:
'Christ died for sinners', this I read;
And in my heart I find a need
Of Him to be my Saviour.

3 That He should leave His place on
    high,
And come for sinful man to die,
You count it strange? – so once did I,
Before I knew my Saviour.

4 And O that He fulfilled may see
The travail of His soul in me,
And with His work contented be,
As I with my dear Saviour!

5 Yea, living, dying, let me bring
My strength, my solace, from this
    spring,
That He who lives to be my King
Once died to be my Saviour.

Dorothy Greenwell (1821–82)

902

C.M.

'It is the LORD: let him do what seemeth him good' 1 Samuel 3 v 18

1 It is the Lord, my covenant God,
Whose claims are all divine,
Who has an undisputed right
To govern me and mine.

2 It is the Lord! Should I distrust
Or contradict His will,
Who cannot do but what is just
And must be righteous still?

3 It is the Lord who gives me all,
My wealth, my friends, my ease,
And of His bounties may recall
Whatever part He please.

4 It is the Lord who can sustain
Beneath the heaviest load,
From whom assistance I obtain
To tread the thorny road.

5 It is the Lord, whose matchless skill
Can from afflictions raise
Matter eternity to fill
With ever-growing praise.

6 It is the Lord, my covenant God,
Thrice blessèd be His name!
Whose gracious promise, sealed
    with blood,
Must ever be the same.

Thomas Greene 1780

903

L.M.

'But one thing is needful' Luke 10 v 42

1 Jesus, engrave it on my heart,
That Thou the one thing needful art;
I could from all things parted be,
But never, never, Lord, from Thee.

2 Needful art Thou to make me live;
Needful art Thou all grace to give;
Needful to guide me, lest I stray;
Needful to help me every day.

3 Needful is Thy most precious blood;
Needful is Thy correcting rod;
Needful is Thy indulgent care;
Needful Thy all-prevailing prayer.

4 Needful Thy presence, dearest Lord,
True peace and comfort to afford;
Needful Thy promise to impart
Fresh life and vigour to my heart.

5 Needful art Thou, my soul can say,
Through all life's dark and thorny
    way;
In death Thou wilt most needful be,
When I yield up my soul to Thee.

6 Needful art Thou, to raise my dust
In shining glory with the just;
Needful when I in heaven appear,
To crown and to present me there.

Samuel Medley (1738–99)

904
L.M.

'There is a friend that sticketh closer than a brother' Proverbs 18 v 24

1 Jesus, our best-belovèd Friend,
Draw out our souls in pure desire;
Jesus, in love to us descend,
Baptize us with Thy Spirit's fire.

2 On Thy redeeming name we call,
Poor and unworthy though we be;
Pardon and sanctify us all;
Let each Thy full salvation see.

3 Our souls and bodies we resign
To fear and follow Thy commands;
O take our hearts, our hearts are
Thine,
Accept the service of our hands.

4 Firm, faithful, watching unto prayer,
May we Thy blessèed will obey,
Toil in Thy vineyard here, and bear
The heat and burden of the day.

5 Yet, Lord, for us a resting-place
In heaven at Thy right hand prepare;
And till we see Thee face to face
Be all our conversation there.

James Montgomery (1771–1854)

905
88.88.88

'Commit thy way unto the LORD; trust also in him; and he shall bring it to pass' Psalm 37 v 5

1 Leave God to order all thy ways,
And hope in Him whate'er betide;
Thou'lt find Him in the evil days
Thy all-sufficient strength and
Guide:
Who trusts in God's unchanging
love
Builds on the Rock that nought can
move.

2 Only thy restless heart keep still,
And wait in cheerful hope, content
To take whate'er His gracious will,
His all-discerning love, hath sent;
Nor doubt our inmost wants are
known
To Him who choose us for His own.

3 Sing, pray, and swerve not from His
ways,
But do thine own part faithfully;
Trust His rich promises of grace,
So shall they be fulfilled in thee:
God never yet forsook at need
The souls that trusted Him indeed.

Georg Christian Neumark (1621–81)
Tr. Catherine Winkworth (1827–78)

906
87.87.D

'Peace I leave with you, my peace I give unto you' John 14 v 27

1 Let my rest in Thee be peaceful
'Neath the palm trees of Thy love;
Let me rest with pilgrims faithful
On their path to heaven above.
There relate Thy faithful mercies
In the wilderness we face,
Then forget our great distresses
As we praise Thy powerful grace.

2 O how sweet a company travelling
With their gaze fixed on their home;
Not a tongue in malice piercing,
Not a heart with guile may roam.
See the dew on souls descending,
Hear their confidence in Him,
Listen to their heartfelt longing
As they love to speak of heaven.

3 Hold me, Lord, in all my travelling,
There is little left at best;
On my soul Thy sunshine warming,
Bidding me at last to rest.
Let the breeze of heaven so gently
Touch me, keep me, from all ill,
Yet my feet now standing firmly
On the heights of Zion's hill.

Ambrose Williams
© The Translator   *Tr. William Vernon Higham (b.1926)*

907 C.M.

'For to me to live is Christ, and to die is gain' Philippians 1 v 21

1 Lord, it belongs not to my care
Whether I die or live;
To love and serve Thee is my share,
And this Thy grace must give.

2 If life be long, I will be glad
That I may long obey;
If short, yet why should I be sad
To soar to endless day?

3 Christ leads me through no darker
rooms
Than He went through before;
And he that to God's kingdom
comes
Must enter by this door.

4 Come, Lord, when grace has made
me meet
Thy blessèd face to see;
For if Thy work on earth be sweet,
What will Thy glory be?

5 Then I shall end my sad complaints
And weary, sinful days;
And join with the triumphant saints
Who sing Jehovah's praise.

6 My knowledge of that life is small,
The eye of faith is dim;
But 'tis enough that Christ knows
all,
And I shall be with Him.

Richard Baxter (1615– 91)

908 88.84

'O my Father ... not as I will, but as thou wilt' Matthew 26 v 39

1 My God, my Father, while I stray
Far from my home on life's rough
way,
Oh teach me from my heart to say –
Thy will be done!

2 If Thou shouldst call me to resign
What I most prize – it ne'er was
mine –
I only yield Thee what was Thine:
Thy will be done!

3 Should pining sickness waste away
My life, in premature decay –
My Father, still I strive to say,
Thy will be done!

4 If but my fainting heart be blest
With Thy sweet Spirit for its guest,
My God, to Thee I leave the rest;
Thy will be done!

5 Renew my will from day to day;
Blend it with Thine, and take away
All that now makes it hard to say,
Thy will be done!

6 Then, when on earth I breathe no
more,
The prayer, oft mixed with tears
I'll sing upon a happier shore –
Thy will be done!

Charlotte Elliott (1789–1871)

909 D.C.M.

'God is the strength of my heart, and my portion for ever' Psalm 73 v 26

1 My heart is resting, O my God,
I will give thanks and sing;
My heart is at the secret source
Of every precious thing:
Now the frail vessel Thou hast made
No hand but Thine shall fill;
The waters of the earth have failed,
And I am thirsty still.

2 I thirst for springs of heavenly life,
And here all day they rise;
I seek the treasure of Thy love,
And close at hand it lies;
And a new song is in my mouth
To long-loved music set:
Glory to Thee for all the grace
I have not tasted yet!

3 Glory to Thee for strength withheld,
For want and weakness known,
The fear that sends me to Thy breast
For what is most my own.
I have a heritage of joy
That yet I must not see;
The hand that bled to make it mine
Is keeping it for me.

4 My heart is resting, O my God,
My heart is in Thy care;
I hear the voice of joy and health
Resounding everywhere.
'Thou art my portion,' saith my soul,
Ten thousand voices say;
The music of their glad Amen
Will never die away.

Anna Laetitia Waring (1823–1910)

910   S.M.

'Father, into thy hands I commend my spirit' Luke 23 v 46

1 My spirit on Thy care,
Blest Saviour, I recline;
Thou wilt not leave me to despair,
For Thou art love divine.

2 In Thee I place my trust,
On Thee I calmly rest;
I know Thee good, I know Thee just,
And count Thy choice the best.

3 Whate'er events betide,
Thy will they all perform;
Safe in Thy breast my head I hide,
Nor fear the coming storm.

4 Let good or ill befall,
It must be good for me;
Secure of having Thee in all,
Of having all in Thee.

Henry Francis Lyte (1793–1847)

911   S.M.

'My times are in thy hand'
Psalm 31 v 15

1 My times are in Thy hand:
My God, I wish them there;
My life, my friends, my soul I leave
Entirely to Thy care.

2 My times are in Thy hand,
Whatever they may be,
Pleasing or painful, dark or bright,
As best may seem to Thee.

3 My times are in Thy hand:
Why should I doubt or fear?
A Father's hand will never cause
His child a needless tear.

4 My times are in Thy hand,
Jesus, the Crucified;
Those hands my cruel sins had
pierced
Are now my guard and guide.

5 My times are in Thy hand:
I'll always trust in Thee;
And, after death, at Thy right hand
I shall for ever be.

William Freeman Lloyd (1791–1853)

912   88.886

'How shall I give thee up?' Hosea 11 v 8

1 O Love, that wilt not let me go,
I rest my weary soul in Thee;
I give Thee back the life I owe,
That in Thine ocean depths its flow
May richer, fuller be.

2 O Light, that followest all my way,
I yield my flickering torch to Thee;
My heart restores its borrowed ray,
That in Thy sunshine's blaze its day
May brighter, fairer be.

3 O Joy, that seekest me through pain,
I cannot close my heart to Thee;
I trace the rainbow through the rain,
And feel the promise is not vain
That morn shall tearless be.

4 O Cross, that liftest up my head,
I dare not ask to fly from thee;
I lay in dust life's glory dead,
And from the ground there blos-
soms red
Life that shall endless be.

George Matheson (1842–1906)

913   6 4. 6 4. 6 6. 6 4

*'Teach me thy way, and lead me in a
plain path' Psalm 27 v 11*

1 Teach me Thy way, O Lord,
Teach me Thy way;
Thy gracious aid afford,
Teach me Thy way;
Help me to walk aright,
More by faith, less by sight;
Lead me with heavenly light:
Teach me Thy way.

2 When doubts and fears arise,
Teach me Thy way;
When storms o'respread the skies,
Teach me Thy way;
Shine through the cold and rain,
Through sorrow, toil, and pain;
Make Thou my pathway plain:
Teach me Thy way.

3 Long as my life shall last,
Teach me Thy way;
Where'er my lot be cast,
Teach me Thy way;
Until the race is run,
Until the journey's done,
Until the crown is won,
Teach me Thy way.

Benjamin Mansell Ramsey (1849–1923)

914   L.M.

*'I am thine, save me; for I have sought
thy precepts' Psalm 119 v 94*

1 Thee, dearest Lord, my soul adores,
I would be Thine, and only Thine;
To Thee, my heart and all its powers,
With full consent, I would resign.

2 But ah! This weak inconstant mind,
How frail, how apt from Thee to
stray;
Trifles, as empty as the wind,
Can tempt my roving thoughts away.

3 Sure I am Thine, or why this load
When earthly vanities beguile?
Why do I mourn my absent God,
And languish for Thy cheering
smile?

4 If Thou return, how sweet the joy,
Though mix'd with penitential
smart!
Then I despise each tempting toy,
And long to give Thee all my heart.

5 Come, Lord, Thy saving power dis
play,
Resistless power of love divine!
And drive Thy hated foes away,
And make me Thine, and only
Thine.

Anne Steele (1716–78)

915   8 7. 8 7. 8 8 8

*'As for God, his way is perfect'
Psalm 18 v 30*

1 Whate'er my God ordains is right:
Holy His will abideth;
I will be still whate'er He doth,
And follow where He guideth:
He is my God;
Though dark my road,
He holds me that I shall not fall:
Wherefore to Him I leave it all.

2 Whate'er my God ordains is right:
He never will deceive me;
He leads me by the proper path;
I know He will not leave me.
I take, content,
What He hath sent;
His hand can turn my griefs away,
And patiently I wait His day.

3 Whate'er my God ordains is right:
   Though now this cup, in drinking,
   May bitter seem to my faint heart,
   I take it, all unshrinking:
   Tears pass away;
   With dawn of day;
   Sweet comfort yet shall fill my heart,
   And pain and sorrow shall depart.

4 Whate'er my God ordains is right:
   Here shall my stand be taken;
   Though sorrow, need, or death be
        mine,
   Yet I am not forsaken.
   My Father's care
   Is round me there;
   He holds me that I shall not fall:
   And so to Him I leave it all.

Samuel Rodigast (1649–1708)
Tr. Catherine Winkworth (1827–78)

916 C.M.

'Be careful for nothing' Philippians 4 v 6

1 When I survey life's varied scene
   Amid the darkest hours,
   Sweet rays of comfort shine between,
   And thorns are mixed with flowers.

2 Lord, teach me to adore the hand
   From whence my comforts flow,
   And let me in this desert land
   A glimpse of Canaan know.

3 And O, whate'er of earthly bliss
   Thy sovereign hand denies,
   Accepted at Thy throne of grace
   Let this petition rise:

4 Give me a calm, a thankful heart,
   From every murmur free;
   The blessings of Thy grace impart,
   And let me live to Thee,

5 Let the sweet hope that Thou art
        mine
   My path of life attend,
   Thy presence through my journey
        shine,
   And crown my journey's end.

Anne Steele (1717–78)

917 Irregular

'Is it well with thee?' ... 'It is well'
2 Kings 4 v 26

1 When peace, like a river, attendeth
        my way,
   When sorrows like sea billows, roll,
   Whatever my lot, Thou has taught
        me to say,
   It is well, it is well with my soul.

   It is well with my soul;
   It is well, it is well with my soul.

2 Though Satan should buffet, though
        trials should come,
   Let this blest assurance control,
   That Christ has regarded my
        helpless estate,
   And hath shed His own blood for my
        soul.

3 My sin – oh, the bliss of this
        glorious thought!
   My sin, not in part, but the whole,
   Is nailed to His cross, and I bear it
        no more:
   Praise the Lord, praise the Lord, O
        my soul!

4 For me, be it Christ, be it Christ
        hence to live:
   If Jordan above me shall roll,
   No pang shall be mine, for in death
        as in life
   Thou wilt whisper Thy peace to my
        soul.

5 But, Lord, 'tis for Thee, for Thy
        coming we wait,
   The sky, not the grave, is our goal;
   Oh trump of the angel! Oh voice of
        the Lord!
   Blessèd hope! blessèd rest of my
        soul!

Horatio Gates Spafford (1828–88)

918

6 6 9. D (with refrain)

'Walk as children of light'
Ephesians 5 v 8

1 When we walk with the Lord,
In the light of His Word,
What a glory He sheds on our way!
While we do His good will,
He abides with us still,
And with all who will trust and obey!

Trust and obey!
For there's no other way
To be happy in Jesus,
But to trust and obey.

2 Not a shadow can rise,
Not a cloud in the skies,
But His smile quickly drives it away;
Not a doubt nor a fear,
Not a sigh nor a tear,
Can abide while we trust and obey!

3 Not a burden we bear,
Not a sorrow we share,
But our toil He doth richly repay:
Not a grief nor a loss,
Not a frown nor a cross,
But is blest if we trust and obey.

4 But we never can prove
The delights of His love
Until all on the altar we lay;
For the favour He shows,
For the joy He bestows,
Are for them who will trust and
obey.

5 Then in fellowship sweet
We will sit at His feet.
Or we'll walk by His side in the way;
What He says we will do,
Where He sends we will go –
Never fear, only trust and obey!

John Henry Sammis (1846–1919)

919

C.M.

'Gird up the loins of your mind'
1 Peter 1 v 13

1 Awake, my soul, stretch every nerve,
And press with vigour on;
A heavenly race demands thy zeal,
And an immortal crown.

2 A cloud of witnesses around
Hold thee in full survey:
Forget the steps already trod,
And onward urge thy way.

3 'Tis God's all-animating voice
That calls thee from on high
'Tis His own hand presents the prize
To thine aspiring eye.

4 Blest Saviour, introduced by Thee,
Have I my race begun;
And, crowned with victory, at Thy
feet
I'll lay my honours down.

Philip Doddridge (1702–51)

920

7 6. 7 6. D

'I must preach the kingdom of God to
other cities also' Luke 4 v 43

1 Facing a task unfinished,
That drives us to our knees,
A need that, undiminished,
Rebukes our slothful ease,
We, who rejoice to know Thee,
Renew before Thy throne
The solemn pledge we owe Thee
To go and make Thee known.

2 Where other lords beside Thee
Hold their unhindered sway,
Where forces that defied Thee
Defy Thee still today,
With none to heed their crying
For life, and love, and light,
Unnumbered souls are dying,
And pass into the night.

3 We bear the torch that flaming
 Fell from the hands of those
 Who gave their lives proclaiming
 That Jesus died and rose.
 Ours is the same commission,
 The same glad message ours,
 Fired by the same ambition,
 To Thee we yield our powers.

4 O Father who sustained them,
 O Spirit who inspired,
 Saviour, whose love constrained
  them
 To toil with zeal untired,
 From cowardice defend us,
 From lethargy awake!
 Forth on Thine errands send us
 To labour for Thy sake.

© OMF International (UK)   *Frank Houghton (1894–1972)*

921   L.M.

'Be ye steadfast, unmoveable'
1 Corinthians 15 v 58

1 Father, though storm on storm
  appear,
 Let not our faith forgo her hold;
 Deliver us from craven fear,
 And make us steadfast, firm and
  bold.

2 Out of our weakness make us
  strong;
 Arm us as in the ancient days;
 Loose in Thy cause each stammering
  tongue,
 And perfect, e'en in us, Thy praise.

3 Come, holy, holy, holy Lord;
 O Father, Son and Spirit, come;
 Be mindful of Thy changeless Word,
 And make the faithful soul Thy
  home.

4 If we can witness, Lord, for Thee,
 Let us despise our fleeting breath;
 Give us the opening heaven to see,
 And make us faithful unto death.

Charles Wesley (1707–88)

922   C.M.

'This people … shall show forth my
praise' Isaiah 43 v 21

1 Fill Thou my life, O Lord my God,
 In every part with praise,
 That my whole being may proclaim
 Thy being and Thy ways.

2 Not for the lip of praise alone,
 Nor e'en the praising heart,
 I ask, but for the life made up
 Of praise in every part:

3 Praise in the common things of life,
 Its goings out and in;
 Praise in each duty and each deed,
 However small and mean.

4 Fill every part of me with praise;
 Let all my being speak
 Of Thee and of Thy love, O Lord,
 Poor though I be and weak.

5 So shalt Thou, Lord, from me, e'en
  me,
 Receive the glory due;
 And so shall I begin on earth
 The song for ever new.

6 So shall no part of day or night
 From sacredness be free;
 But all my life, in every step
 Be fellowship with Thee.

Horatius Bonar (1808–89)

923   L.M.

'I have set the LORD always before me'
Psalm 16 v 8

1 Forth in Thy name, O Lord I go,
 My daily labour to pursue,
 Thee, only Thee, resolved to know
 In all I think, or speak, or do.

2 The task Thy wisdom hath assigned
 O let me cheerfully fulfil,
 In all my works Thy presence find,
 And prove Thy good and perfect will.

3 Thee may I set at my right hand,
Whose eyes my inmost substance
see,
And labour on at Thy command,
And offer all my works to Thee.

4 Give me to bear Thy easy yoke,
And every moment watch and pray,
And still to things eternal look,
And hasten to Thy glorious day;

5 For Thee delightfully employ
Whate'er Thy bounteous grace hath
given,
And run my course with even joy,
And closely walk with Thee to heaven.

Charles Wesley (1707–88)

924 L.M.

'They ... first gave their own selves to the Lord' 2 Corinthians 8 v 5

1 Go, labour on; spend, and be spent,
Thy joy to do the Father's will;
It is the way the Master went;
Should not the servant tread it still?

2 Go, labour on; 'tis not for nought;
Thy earthly loss is heavenly gain;
Men heed thee, love thee, praise thee
not;
The Master praises: what are men?

3 Go, labour on; your hands are weak,
Yours knees are faint, your soul cast
down;
Yet falter not; the prize you seek
Is near – a kingdom and a crown!

4 Go, labour on, while it is day;
The world's dark night is hastening
on;
Speed, speed thy work, cast sloth
away;
It is not thus that souls are won.

5 Toil on, faint not, keep watch, and
pray;
Be wise the erring soul to sin;
Go forth into the world's highway,
Compel the wanderer to come in.

6 Toil on, and in thy toil rejoice;
For toil comes rest, for exile home;
Soon shalt thou hear the
Bridegroom's voice,
The midnight cry, 'Behold, I come!'

Horatius Bonar (1808–89)

925 C.M.

'I am not ashamed' 2 Timothy 1 v 12

1 I'm not ashamed to own my Lord,
Or to defend His cause;
Maintain the honour of His Word,
The glory of His cross.

2 Jesus, my God! I know His name,
His name is all my trust;
Nor will He put my soul to shame,
Nor let my hope be lost.

3 Firm as His throne His promise
stands,
And He can well secure
What I've committed to His hands
Till the decisive hour.

4 Then will He own my worthless
name
Before His Father's face;
And, in the new Jerusalem,
Appoint my soul a place.

Isaac Watts (1674–1748)

926 L.M.

'Ashamed of me' Mark 8 v 38

1 Jesus, and shall it ever be
A mortal man ashamed of Thee,
Ashamed of Thee, whom angels
praise,
Whose glories shine through
endless days?

2 Ashamed of Jesus, of my God,
Who purchased me with His own
blood!
Of Him who, to retrieve my loss,
Despised the shame, endured the
cross!

3 Ashamed of Jesus, that dear Friend,
On whom my hopes of heaven
depend!
No, when I blush, be this my shame,
That I no more revere His name.

4 Ashamed of Jesus! yes, I may
When I've no guilt to wash away,
No tear to wipe, no good to crave,
No fears to quell, no soul to save.

5 Ashamed of Jesus, of my Lord,
By all heaven's glorious hosts
adored!
No, I will make my boast of Thee,
In time and in eternity!

6 Till then, nor is my boasting vain,
Till then I boast a Saviour slain!
And O may this my glory be
That Christ is not ashamed of me!

Joseph Grigg (c.1720–68)
and Benjamin Francis (1734–99)

927   87.87

'How often would I have gathered thy
children together?' Matthew 23 v 37

1 Jesus calls us! O'er the tumult
Of our life's wild restless sea,
Day by day His sweet voice
soundeth,
Saying, 'Christian, follow Me':

2 As of old apostles heard it
By the Galilean lake,
Turned from home and toil and
kindred,
Leaving all for His dear sake.

3 Jesus calls us from the worship
Of the vain world's golden store,
From each idol that would keep us,
Saying, 'Christian, love Me more!'

4 In our joys and in our sorrows,
Days of toil and hours of ease,
Still He calls, in cares and pleasures,
That we love Him more than these.

5 Jesus calls us! By Thy mercies,
Saviour, make us hear Thy call,
Give our hearts to Thy obedience,
Serve and love Thee best of all.

Cecil Frances Alexander (1818–95)

928   L.M.

'Speak, LORD: for thy servant heareth'
1 Samuel 3 v 9

1 Lord, speak to me, that I may speak
In living echoes of Thy tone;
As Thou hast sought, so let me seek
Thy erring children lost and lone.

2 O lead me, Lord, that I may lead
The wandering and the wavering
feet;
O feed me, Lord, that I may feed
Thy hungering ones with manna
sweet.

3 O strengthen me, that, while I stand
Firm on the rock, and strong in Thee,
I may stretch out a loving hand
To wrestlers with the troubled sea.

4 O teach me, Lord, that I may teach
The precious things Thou dost
impart;
And wing my words, that they may
reach
The hidden depths of many a heart.

5 O give Thine own sweet rest to me,
That I may speak with soothing power
A word in season, as from Thee,
To weary ones in needful hour.

6 O fill me with Thy fullness, Lord,
Until my very heart o'erflow
In kindling thought and glowing
word,
Thy love to tell, Thy praise to show.

7 O use me, Lord, use even me,
Just as Thou wilt, and when, and
where;
Until Thy blessèd face I see,
Thy rest, Thy joy, Thy glory share.

Frances Ridley Havergal (1836–79)

929

87.87.77

'*Speak LORD: for thy servant heareth*'
1 Samuel 3 v 9

1 Master, speak! Thy servant heareth,
   Waiting for Thy gracious word,
   Longing for Thy voice that cheereth,
   Master, let it now be heard.
   I am listening, Lord, for Thee;
   What hast Thou to say to me?

2 Speak to me by name, O Master,
   Let me know it is to me;
   Speak, that I may follow faster,
   With a step more firm and free,
   Where the Shepherd leads the flock
   In the shadow of the Rock.

3 Master, speak! though least and
      lowest,
   Let me not unheard depart;
   Master, speak! for O Thou knowest
   All the yearning of my heart;
   Knowest all its truest need;
   Speak, and make me blest indeed.

4 Master, speak! and make me ready,
   When Thy voice is truly heard,
   With obedience glad and steady
   Still to follow every word.
   I am listening, Lord, for Thee;
   Master, speak! O speak to me!

Frances Ridley Havergal (1836–79)

930

L.M.

'*For none of us liveth unto himself, and
no man dieth unto himself*'
Romans 14 v 7

1 My gracious Lord, I own Thy right
   To every service I can pay;
   And call it my supreme delight
   To hear Thy dictates and obey.

2 What is my being but for Thee,
   Its sure support, its noblest end;
   Thy ever-smiling face to see,
   And serve the cause of such a
      Friend?

3 I would not breathe for worldly joy,
   Or to increase my worldly good;
   Nor future days or powers employ
   To spread a sounding name abroad.

4 'Tis to my Saviour I would live,
   To Him who for my ransom died:
   Nor could untainted Eden give
   Such bliss as blossoms at His side.

5 His work my hoary age shall bless,
   When youthful vigour is no more;
   And my last hour of life confess
   His love hath animating power.

Philip Doddridge (1702–51)

931

L.M.

'*Ye shall bring your offering*'
Leviticus 1 v 2

1 O Lord, what offerings can we bring
   In gratitude for saving love?
   Each gift comes down from Thee,
      our King,
   Father of lights, in heaven above.

2 Thou givest strength to garner
      wealth;
   Then all we have is Thine, not ours;
   Skills, money, intellect or health,
   Stewards of all within our powers.

3 Thy glorious Son, took flesh, and
      shed
   The outward marks of heavenly
      fame;
   Had not a place to lay His head,
   Made poor, to make us rich again.

4 That He should poverty embrace,
   And live the perfect life as man,
   Then die to save our guilty race;
   Amazing love – Thy generous plan.

5 And shall we then, Thy cause
      impede
   By wasting all that Thou hast given
   On useless luxuries and greed?
   No, may we lay it up in heaven.

6 Gladly to spend and to be spent;
  Surrender all for Christ our Lord;
  At any cost our firm intent
  To spread Thy glorious gospel word.

© The Author   Stephen J. Ford (b.1949)

932   L.M.

*'He shall baptize you with the Holy
Ghost and with fire' Luke 3 v 16*

1 O Thou who camest from above
  The pure celestial fire to impart,
  Kindle a flame of sacred love
  On the mean altar of my heart!

2 There let it for Thy glory burn
  With inextinguishable blaze,
  And trembling to its source return
  In humble prayer and fervent praise.

3 Jesus, confirm my heart's desire
  To work and speak and think for
      Thee;
  Still let me guard the holy fire,
  And still stir up Thy gift in me.

4 Ready for all Thy perfect will,
  My acts of faith and love repeat,
  Till death Thine endless mercies seal,
  And make the sacrifice complete.

                    Charles Wesley (1707–88)

933   6 4. 6 4. 6 6. 6 4

*'And who then is willing to consecrate his
service this day unto the Lord?*
1 Chronicles 29 v 5

1 Saviour, Thy dying love
  Thou gavest me;
  Nor should I aught withhold,
  My Lord, from Thee;
  In love my soul would bow,
  My heart fulfil its vow,
  Some offering bring Thee now,
  Something for Thee.

2 At the blest mercy-seat
  Pleading for me,
  My feeble faith looks up,
  Jesus, to Thee;

Help me the cross to bear,
Thy wondrous love declare,
Some song to raise, or prayer –
Something for Thee.

3 Give me a faithful heart,
  Likeness to Thee,
  That each departing day
  Henceforth may see
  Some work of love begun,
  Some deed of kindness done,
  Some wanderer sought and won –
  Something for Thee.

4 All that I am and have,
  Thy gifts so free,
  In joy, in grief, through life,
  O Lord, for Thee!
  And when Thy face I see,
  My ransomed soul shall be,
  Through all eternity,
  Something for Thee.

            Sylvanus Dryden Phelps (1816–95)

934   S.M.

*'In the morning sow thy seed, and in the
evening withhold not thy hand'*
Ecclesiastes 11 v 6

1 Sow in the morn thy seed,
  At eve hold not thine hand;
  To doubt and fear give thou no heed;
  Broadcast it o'er the land.

2 Thou know'st not which may thrive,
  The late or early sown;
  Grace keeps the chosen germ alive,
  When and wherever strown.

3 And duly shall appear
  In verdure, beauty, strength,
  The tender blade, the stalk, the ear,
  And the full corn at length.

4 Thou canst not toil in vain;
  Cold, heat, and moist, and dry
  Shall foster and mature the grain
  For garners in the sky.

5 Thence, when the glorious end,
The day of God, is come,
The angel-reapers shall descend
And heaven cry, 'Harvest-home!'

James Montgomery (1771–1854)

935 77.77

'Ye are not your own ... ye are bought
with a price' 1 Corinthians 6 vv 19-20

1 Take my life, and let it be
Consecrated, Lord, to Thee;
Take my moments and my days,
Let them flow in ceaseless praise.

2 Take my hands, and let them move
At the impulse of Thy love;
Take my feet, and let them be
Swift and beautiful for Thee.

3 Take my voice, and let me sing
Always, only for my King;
Take my lips, and let them be
Filled with messages from Thee.

4 Take my silver and my gold,
Not a mite would I withhold;
Take my intellect, and use
Every power as Thou shalt choose.

5 Take my will, and make it Thine;
It shall be no longer mine:
Take my heart, it is Thine own;
It shall be Thy royal throne.

6 Take my love; my Lord, I pour
At thy feet its treasure-store:
Take myself, and I will be
Ever, only, all for Thee!

Frances Ridley Havergal (1836–79)

936 66.66.66

'I lay down my life for the sheep'
John 10 v 15

1 Thy life was given for me,
Thy blood, O Lord, was shed,
That I might ransomed be,
And quickened from the dead:
Thy life was given for me;
What have I given for Thee?

2 Long years were spent for me
In weariness and woe,
That through eternity
Thy glory I might know:
Long years were spent for me;
Have I spent one for Thee?

3 Thou, Lord, hast borne for me
More than my tongue can tell
Of bitterest agony,
To rescue me from hell:
Thou suffer'dst all for me;
What have I borne for Thee?

4 And Thou hast brought to me
Down from Thy home above
Salvation full and free,
Thy pardon and Thy love:
Great gifts Thou broughtest me;
What have I brought to Thee?

5 O let my life be given,
My years for Thee be spent,
World-fetters all be riven,
And joy with suffering blent:
Thou gav'st Thyself for me;
I give myself to Thee.

Frances Ridley Havergal (1836–79)

937 S.M.

'Blessed are those servants, whom the
lord, when he cometh shall find
watching' Luke 12 v 37

1 Ye servants of the Lord,
Each in his office wait,
Observant of His heavenly Word,
And watchful at His gate.

2 Let all your lamps be bright,
And trim the golden flame;
Gird up your loins as in His sight,
For holy is His name.

3 Watch! 'tis your Lord's command,
And while we speak He's near;
Mark the first signal of His hand,
And ready all appear.

4 O happy servant he,
In such a posture found!
He shall his Lord with rapture see,
And be with honour crowned.

5 Christ shall the banquet spread
   With His own royal hand,
   And raise that faithful servant's head
   Amid the angelic band.

Philip Doddridge (1702–51)

938   8 8. 8 8. 8 8

'And Jacob was left alone; and there
wrestled a man with him until the
breaking of the day' Genesis 32 v 24

Short Version

1 Come, O Thou Traveller unknown,
   Whom still I hold, but cannot see!
   My company before is gone,
   And I am left alone with Thee;
   With Thee all night I mean to stay,
   And wrestle till the break of day.

2 I need not tell Thee who I am,
   My misery and sin declare;
   Thyself hast called me by my name;
   Look on Thy hands, and read it there:
   But who, I ask Thee, who art Thou?
   Tell me Thy name, and tell me now.

3 In vain Thou strugglest to get free;
   I never will unloose my hold!
   Art Thou the Man that died for me?
   The secret of Thy love unfold:
   Wrestling, I will not let Thee go,
   Till I Thy name, Thy nature know.

4 Yield to me now; for I am weak,
   But confident in self-despair;
   Speak to my heart, in blessings
        speak,
   Be conquered by my instant prayer;
   Speak, or Thou never hence shalt
        move,
   And tell me if Thy name is Love.

5 'Tis Love! 'tis Love! Thou diedst for
        me!
   I hear Thy whisper in my heart;
   The morning breaks, the shadows
        flee,
   Pure, universal love Thou art;
   To me, to all, Thy mercies move:
   Thy nature and Thy name is Love.

6 I know Thee, Saviour, who Thou art,
   Jesus, the feeble sinner's Friend;
   Nor wilt Thou with the night depart,
   But stay and love me to the end;
   Thy mercies never shall remove:
   Thy nature and Thy name is Love.

Full Version

1 Come, O Thou Traveller unknown,
   Whom still I hold, but cannot see!
   My company before is gone,
   And I am left alone with Thee;
   With Thee all night I mean to stay,
   And wrestle till the break of day.

2 I need not tell Thee who I am,
   My misery and sin declare;
   Thyself hast called me by my name;
   Look on Thy hands, and read it there:
   But who, I ask Thee, who art Thou?
   Tell me Thy name, and tell me now.

3 In vain Thou strugglest to get free;
   I never will unloose my hold!
   Art Thou the Man that died for me?
   The secret of Thy love unfold:
   Wrestling, I will not let Thee go,
   Till I Thy name, Thy nature know.

4 Wilt Thou not yet to me reveal
   Thy new, unutterable name?
   Tell me, I still beseech Thee, tell;
   To know it now resolved I am:
   Wrestling, I will not let Thee go,
   Till I Thy name, Thy nature know.

5 What though my shrinking flesh
        complain,
   And murmur to contend so long?
   I rise superior to my pain,
   When I am weak, then I am strong;
   And when my all of strength shall fail,
   I shall with the God-Man prevail.

6 Yield to me now; for I am weak,
   But confident in self-despair;
   Speak to my heart, in blessings speak,
   Be conquered by my instant prayer;
   Speak, or Thou never hence shalt
        move,
   And tell me if Thy name is Love.

7 'Tis Love! 'tis Love! Thou diedst for
   me!
I hear Thy whisper in my heart;
The morning breaks, the shadows
   flee,
Pure, universal love Thou art;
To me, to all, Thy mercies move:
Thy nature and Thy name is Love.

8 My prayer hath power with God; the
   grace
Unspeakable I now receive;
Through faith I see Thee face to face,
I see Thee face to face, and live!
In vain I have not wept and strove:
Thy nature and Thy name is Love.

9 I know Thee, Saviour, who Thou art,
Jesus, the feeble sinner's Friend;
Nor wilt Thou with the night depart,
But stay and love me to the end;
Thy mercies never shall remove:
Thy nature and Thy name is Love.

10 The Sun of righteousness on me
Hath risen with healing in His
   wings;
Withered my nature's strength, from
   Thee
My soul its life and succour brings;
My help is all laid up above:
Thy nature and Thy name is Love.

11 Contented now upon my thigh
I halt, till life's short journey end;
All helplessness, all weakness, I
On Thee alone for strength depend;
Nor have I power from Thee to
   move:
Thy nature and Thy name is Love.

12 Lame as I am, I take the prey,
Hell, earth, and sin with ease
   o'ercome;
I leap for joy, pursue my way,
And as a bounding hart fly home,
Through all eternity to prove
Thy nature and Thy name is Love.

Charles Wesley (1707–88)

939   7 7.7 7

'God be merciful to me a sinner'
Luke 18 v 13

1 Depth of mercy! can there be
Mercy still reserved for me?
Can my God His wrath forbear?
Me, the chief of sinners, spare?

2 I have long withstood His grace,
Long provoked Him to His face,
Would not hearken to His calls,
Grieved Him by a thousand falls.

3 Whence to me this waste of love?
Ask my Advocate above!
See the cause in Jesu's face,
Now before the throne of grace.

4 There for me the Saviour stands;
Shows His wounds and spreads His
   hands.
God is love; I know, I feel;
Jesus lives, and loves me still.

5 Jesus, answer from above:
Is not all Thy nature love?
Wilt Thou not the wrong forget?
Suffer me to kiss Thy feet?

6 If I rightly read Thy heart,
If Thou all compassion art,
Bow Thine ear, in mercy bow;
Pardon and accept me now.

Charles Wesley (1707–88)

940   8 7.8 7.8 8 7

Based on Psalm 130

1 From deep distress I cry to Thee,
Lord, hear me, I implore Thee;
Bend down Thy gracious ear to me,
Regard my prayer before thee;
If Thou rememberest each misdeed,
If each should have its rightful
   meed,
Who may abide Thy presence?

2 Our pardon is Thy gift; Thy love
And grace alone avail us;
Our works could ne'er our guilt
  remove,
The strictest life would fail us;
That none may boast himself of
  aught,
But own in fear Thy grace hath
  wrought
What in him seemeth righteous.

3 And thus my hope is in the Lord
And not in mine own merit;
I rest upon His faithful Word
To them of contrite spirit;
That He is merciful and just –
Here is my comfort and my trust;
His help I wait with patience.

4 Though great our sins and sore our
  woes,
His grace much more aboundeth;
His helping love no limit knows,
Our utmost need it soundeth;
Our kind and faithful Shepherd he,
Who shall at last set Israel free
From all their sin and sorrow.

Martin Luther (1483–1546)
Tr. Catherine Winkworth (1827–78)

941   C.M.

*'I will heal their backsliding, I will love
them freely' Hosea 14 v 4*

1 How oft, alas, this wretched heart
Has wandered from the Lord!
How oft my roving thoughts depart,
Forgetful of His Word!

2 Yet sovereign mercy calls, Return:
Dear Lord, and may I come?
My vile ingratitude I mourn;
O take the wanderer home.

3 And canst Thou, wilt Thou yet
  forgive,
And bid my crimes remove?
And shall a pardon'd rebel live
To speak Thy wondrous love?

4 Almighty grace, Thy healing power
How glorious, how divine!
That can to life and bliss restore
So vile a heart as mine.

5 Thy pardoning love, so free, so
  sweet,
Dear Saviour, I adore;
O keep me at Thy sacred feet,
And let me rove no more.

Anne Steele (1716–88)

942   7 6. 7 6. 7 7. 7 6

*'O turn unto me, and have mercy upon
me' Psalm 86 v 16*

1 Jesus, Friend of sinners, hear
A feeble creature pray;
From my debt of sin set clear,
For I have nought to pay.
Speak, O speak my kind release,
My backsliding soul restore;
Love me freely, seal my peace,
And let me rove no more.

2 Though my sins as mountains rise,
And swell and reach to heaven,
Mercy is above the skies
And I shall stand forgiven.
Mighty is my guilt's increase,
Greater is Thy mercy's store;
Love me freely, seal my peace,
And let me rove no more.

3 From the oppressive weight of sin
My struggling spirit free;
Blood and righteousness divine
Can rescue even me.
Holy Spirit, shed Thy grace,
Let me feel the softening shower;
Love me freely, seal my peace,
And let me rove no more.

Charles Wesley (1707–88)

943   7 6. 7 6. D

'Walk before me, and be thou perfect'
Genesis 17 v 1

1 O for a closer walk with God,
   A calm and heavenly frame,
   A light to shine upon the road
   That leads me to the Lamb!

2 Where is the blessedness I knew
   When first I saw the Lord?
   Where is the soul-refreshing view
   Of Jesus and His Word?

3 What peaceful hours I once enjoyed!
   How sweet their memory still!
   But they have left an aching void
   The world can never fill.

4 Return, O holy Dove! return,
   Sweet messenger of rest!
   I hate the sins that made Thee
      mourn,
   And drove Thee from my breast.

5 The dearest idol I have known,
   Whate'er that idol be,
   Help me to tear it from Thy throne,
   And worship only Thee.

6 So shall my walk be close with God,
   Calm and serene my frame;
   So purer light shall mark the road
   That leads me to the Lamb.

William Cowper (1731–1800)

944   7 6. 7 6. D

'I will heal their backsliding, I will love
them freely' Hosea 14 v 4

1 O Jesus, full of truth and grace,
   More full of grace than I of sin,
   Yet once again I seek Thy face;
   Open Thine arms, and take me in,
   And freely my backslidings heal,
   And love the faithless sinner still.

2 Thou knowest the way to bring me
      back,
   My fallen spirit to restore:
   O for Thy truth and mercy's sake,
   Forgive, and bid me sin no more;
   The ruins of my soul repair,
   And make my heart a house of
      prayer.

3 The stone to flesh again convert,
   The veil of sin again remove;
   Sprinkle Thy blood upon my heart,
   And melt it by Thy dying love;
   This rebel heart by love subdue,
   And make it soft, and make it new.

4 Ah! give me, Lord, the tender heart
   That trembles at the approach of sin;
   A godly fear of sin impart,
   Implant, and root it deep within,
   That I may dread Thy gracious
      power,
   And never dare to offend Thee more.

Charles Wesley (1707–88)

945   L.M.

'Return ... and I will heal your
backslidings' Jeremiah 3 v 22

1 Return, O wanderer, return,
   And seek an injured Father's face;
   Those warm desires that in thee burn
   Were kindled by reclaiming grace.

2 Return, O wanderer, return,
   And seek a Father's melting heart;
   Whose pitying eyes thy grief discern,
   Whose hand can heal thy inward
      smart.

3 Return, O wanderer, return;
   He heard thy deep repentant sigh;
   He saw thy softened spirit mourn
   When no intruding ear was nigh.

4 Return, O wanderer, return;
   Thy Saviour bids thy spirit live;
   Go to His bleeding feet, and learn
   How freely Jesus can forgive.

William Bengo Collyer (1782–1854)

946

87.87.D

'Saw ye him whom my soul loveth?'
Song of Solomon 3 v 3

1 What is this, the cloud that darkens,
  Cloud which hides the Lord above?
  What this covering shade that
      thickens,
  Keeps me from the One I love?
  Speak, my Jesus, tell what ails me,
  May I view again Thy face;
  Smile upon me, do not leave me
  In distress, O Lord of grace.

2 Is it mist from off Thy mountain
  Makes my heart so cold and drear?
  Is it that my Lord is teaching
  By declining to draw near?
  Speak, my Jesus, what the lesson?
  What the message I should heed?
  Grant Thine aid and heaven open;
  Shed Thy light upon my need.

3 Is it from the nether regions
  That thick vapours fill the air?
  Work of Satan and his legions
  Who would drive me to despair?
  Speak, my Jesus, of Thy power,
  Of Thy saving, mighty arm.
  To the depths Thy mercy lower
  And deliver me from harm.

William Vernon Higham (b.1926)
© The Translator Tr. Edmund Tudor Owen (b.1935)

947

L.M.

'Let us run with patience the race that is
set before us' Hebrews 12 v 1

1 Awake, our souls! away, our fears!
  Let every trembling thought be gone!
  Awake, and run the heavenly race,
  And put a cheerful courage on.

2 True, 'tis a strait and thorny road,
  And mortal spirits tire and faint;
  But they forget the mighty God
  Who feeds the strength of every
      saint.

3 Thee, mighty God, whose matchless
      power
  Is ever new, and ever young,
  And firm endures, while endless
      years
  Their everlasting circles run.

4 From Thee, the ever-flowing spring,
  Our souls shall drink a fresh supply;
  While such as trust their native
      strength
  Shall melt away, and droop, and die.

5 Swift as the eagle cuts the air,
  We'll mount aloft to Thine abode;
  On wings of love our souls shall fly,
  Nor tire along the heavenly road.

Isaac Watts (1674–1748)

948

L.M.

'Hope thou in God' Psalm 42 v 5

1 Be still, my heart! These anxious
      cares
  To thee are burdens, thorns and
      snares,
  They cast dishonour on the Lord
  And contradict His gracious Word.

2 Brought safely by His hand thus far,
  Why wilt thou now give place to
      fear?
  How canst thou want if He provide?
  Or lose thy way with such a guide?

3 When first, before His mercy seat,
  Thou didst to Him thy all commit,
  He gave thee warrant from that hour
  To trust His wisdom, love and
      power.

4 Did ever trouble yet befall
  And He refuse to hear thy call?
  And has He not His promise passed,
  That thou shalt overcome at last?

5 He who has helped me hitherto
  Will help me all my journey through,
  And give me daily cause to raise
  New Ebenezers to His praise.

6 Though rough and thorny be the
   road,
  It leads thee home apace to God;
  Then count thy present trials small,
  For heaven will make amends for all.

John Newton (1725–1807)

949 S.M.

*'Wait on the LORD: be of good courage,
and he shall strengthen thine heart'
Psalm 27 v 14*

1 Blest is the man, O God,
  That stays himself on Thee;
  Who waits for Thy salvation, Lord,
  Shall Thy salvation see.

2 When we in darkness walk,
  Nor feel the heavenly flame,
  Then is the time to trust our God,
  And rest upon His name.

3 Soon shall our doubts and fears
  Subside at His control;
  His lovingkindness shall break
    through
  The midnight of the soul.

4 His grace will to the end
  Stronger and brighter shine;
  Nor present things, nor things to
    come,
  Shall quench the life divine.

Augustus Montague Toplady (1740–78)

950 77.77

*'Cast thy burden on the LORD, and he
shall sustain thee' Psalm 55 v 22*

1 Cast thy burden on the Lord;
  Only lean upon His Word;
  Thou wilt soon have cause to bless
  His eternal faithfulness.

2 He sustains thee by His hand;
  He enables thee to stand;
  Those whom Jesus once hath loved
  From His grace are ne'er removed.

3 Human counsels come to nought;
  That will stand which God hath
    wrought;
  His compassion, love and power
  Are the same for evermore.

4 Heaven and earth may pass away,
  God's free grace shall not decay;
  He hath promised to fulfil
  All the pleasure of His will.

5 Jesus, Guardian of Thy flock,
  Be Thyself our constant Rock;
  Make us, by Thy powerful hand,
  Strong as Zion's mountain stand.

Rowland Hill's Psalms and Hymns 1783

951 65.65.66.65

*'My flesh longeth for thee in a dry and
thirsty land' Psalm 63 v 2*

1 Far off I see the goal;
  O Saviour, guide me;
  I feel my strength is small;
  Be Thou beside me:
  With vision ever clear,
  With love that conquers fear,
  And grace to persevere,
  O Lord, provide me.

2 Whene'er Thy way seems strange,
  Go Thou before me;
  And lest my heart should change,
  O Lord, watch o'er me;
  But should my faith prove frail,
  And I through blindness fail,
  O let Thy grace prevail,
  And still restore me.

3 Should earthly pleasures wane,
  And joy forsake me,
  If lonely hours of pain
  At length o'ertake me,
  My hand in Thine hold fast
  Till sorrow be o'erpast,
  And gentle death at last
  For heaven awake me.

4 There with the ransomed throng
Who praise for ever
The love that made them strong
To serve for ever,
I too would see Thy face,
Thy finished work retrace,
And magnify Thy grace,
Redeemed for ever.

© Copyright Control   *Robert Rowland Roberts (1865–1945)*

952   12 11. 12 11 (with refrain)

'*Much more the grace of God*'
Romans 5 v 15

1 He giveth more grace when the
burdens grow greater,
He sendeth more strength when the
labours increase;
To added affliction He addeth His
mercy,
To multiplied trials, His multiplied
peace.

*His love has no limit, His grace has no
measure,*
*His power has no boundary known unto
men;*
For out of His infinite riches in Jesus
He giveth, and giveth, and giveth again!

2 When we have exhausted our store
of endurance,
When our strength has failed ere the
day is half done,
When we reach the end of our
hoarded resources,
Our Father's full giving is only
begun.

Annie Johnson Flint

953   8 8. 8 8. 8 8

'*Let us lift up our heart with our hands
unto God in the heavens*'
Lamentations 3 v 41

1 Jesus, to Thee our hearts we lift –
May all our hearts with love
o'erflow –
With thanks for Thy continued gift,
That still Thy precious name we
know,
Retain our sense of sin forgiven,
And wait for all our inward heaven.

2 What mighty troubles hast Thou
shown
Thy feeble, tempted followers here!
We have through fire and water
gone,
But saw Thee on the floods appear,
But felt Thee present in the flame,
And shouted our Deliverer's name.

3 All are not lost or wandered back;
All have not left Thy church and
Thee;
There are who suffer for Thy sake,
Enjoy Thy glorious infamy,
Esteem the scandal of Thy cross,
And only seek divine applause.

4 Thou who hast kept us to this hour,
O keep us faithful to the end:
When, robed with majesty and
power,
Our Jesus shall from heaven
descend,
His friends and witnesses to own,
And seat us on His glorious throne.

Charles Wesley (1707–88)

954   8 8 8. 6

'*Lord, save us: we perish*'
Matthew 8 v 25

1 Lo! The storms of life are breaking,
Faithless fears our hearts are
shaking;
For our succour undertaking,
Lord and Saviour, help us.

2 Lo! the world, from Thee rebelling,
Round Thy church in pride is
swelling;
With Thy Word their madness
quelling,
Lord and Saviour, help us.

3 On Thine own command relying,
We our onward task are plying,
Unto Thee for safety sighing,
Lord and Saviour, help us.

4 Steadfast we, in faith abiding,
In Thy secret presence hiding,
In Thy love and grace confiding;
Lord and Saviour, help us.

5 By Thy birth, Thy cross, Thy
passion,
By Thy tears of deep compassion,
By Thy mighty intercession,
Lord and Saviour, help us.

Henry Alford (1810–71)

955 C.M.

'Have faith in God' *Mark 11 v 22*

1 O for a faith that will not shrink,
Though pressed by many a foe;
That will not tremble on the brink
Of poverty or woe;

2 That will not murmur or complain
Beneath the chastening rod;
But in the hour of grief or pain
Can lean upon its God;

3 A faith that shines more bright and
clear
When tempests rage without;
That when in danger knows no fear,
In darkness feels no doubt;

4 A faith that keeps the narrow way
Till life's last spark is fled,
And with a pure and heavenly ray
Lights up the dying bed.

5 Lord, give me such a faith as this,
And then, whate'er may come,
I taste e'en now the hallowed bliss
Of an eternal home.

William Hiley Bathurst (1796–1877)

956 L.M.

'In thee is my trust' *Psalm 141 v 8*

1 O Thou to whose all-searching sight
The darkness shineth as the light,
Search, prove my heart; it pants for
Thee;
O burst these bonds, and set it free!

2 Wash out its stains, refine its dross,
Nail my affections to the cross;
Hallow each thought; let all within
Be clean, as Thou, my Lord, art
clean.

3 When rising floods my soul
o'erflow,
When sinks my heart in waves of woe,
Jesus, Thy timely aid impart,
And raise my head, and cheer my
heart.

4 Saviour, where'er Thy steps I see,
Dauntless, untired, I follow Thee;
O let Thy hand support me still,
And lead me to Thy holy hill.

Nicolaus Ludwig von Zinzendorf (1700–60)
Tr. John Wesley (1703–91)

957 11 10. 11 10

'The peace of God, which passeth all
understanding' *Philippians 4 v 7*

1 Oh! For that peace, beyond all
understanding
Peace, heavenly peace, bought by
eternal pain,
That my frail soul, beneath life's
cruel pounding
At rest at Jesu's cross may still
remain.

2 Oh! Give the peace, that in the
stormiest fight
Can never tire and still is amply
blest,
So that my soul in midst of blackest
night
Can rest on God, my heavenly
Father's breast.

3 Grant me the peace that leads to
 sweet endeavour
In heavenly work, in disappointment's hour,
Without a fear, but resting in the
 favour
Of God's great love, despite the
 storm's great power.

4 Oh! For the peace, that like that river
 flowing
Through heaven's city and the trees
 of life.
Peace after war, to heavenward
 pilgrims going
Beyond the vale, to joy and end of
 strife.

Howell Elvis Lewis (1860–1953)
© Copyright Control *Tr. D. Martyn Lloyd-Jones (1899–1981)*

958   C.M.

'You life is hid with Christ in God'
Colossians 3 v 3

1 Rejoice, believer, in the Lord,
 Who makes your cause His own!
The hope that's built upon His Word
 Can ne'er be overthrown.

2 Though many foes beset your road,
 And feeble is your arm,
Your life is hid with Christ in God,
 Beyond the reach of harm.

3 Weak as you are, you shall not faint,
 Or fainting, shall not die;
Jesus, the strength of every saint,
 Will aid you from on high.

4 Though unperceived by mortal
 sense,
Faith sees Him always near,
A guide, a glory, a defence;
 Then what have you to fear?

5 As surely as He overcame
 And triumphed once for you,
So surely you that love His name
 Shall triumph in Him too.

John Newton (1725–1807)

959   10 10. 11 11

'Jehovah-jireh' Genesis 22 v 14

1 Though troubles assail and dangers
 afright,
Though friends should all fail and
 foes all unite,
Yet one thing secures us, whatever
 betide,
The Scripture assures us the Lord
 will provide.

2 When Satan appears to stop up our
 path,
And fills us with fears, we triumph
 by faith;
He cannot take from us, though oft
 he has tried,
This heart cheering promise, the
 Lord will provide.

3 His call we obey like Abram of old,
 Not knowing our way, but faith
 makes us bold;
For though we are strangers we have
 a good guide,
And trust, in all dangers, the Lord
 will provide.

4 No strength of our own or goodness
 we claim;
Yet, since we have known the
 Saviour's great name,
In this our strong tower for safety we
 hide,
The Lord is our power, the Lord will
 provide.

John Newton (1725–1807)

960   C.M.

'His compassions fail not'
Lamentations 3 v 22

1 We praise and bless Thee, gracious
 Lord,
Our Saviour kind and true,
For all the old things passed away,
For all Thou hast made new.

2 The old security is gone,
In which so long we lay;
The sleep of death Thou hast
dispelled,
The darkness rolled away.

3 New hopes, new purposes, desires
And joys, Thy grace has given;
Old ties are broken from the earth,
New ties attach to heaven.

4 But yet how much must be
destroyed,
How much renewed must be,
Ere we can fully stand complete
In likeness, Lord, to Thee.

5 Thou, only Thou, must carry on
The work Thou hast begun;
Of Thine own strength Thou must
impart,
In Thine own ways to run.

6 So shall we faultless stand at last
Before Thy Father's throne,
The blessedness for ever ours,
The glory all Thine own.

Carl Johann Philipp Spitta (1801–59)
Tr. Jane Laurie Borthwick (1813–97)

961 L.M.

Based on Romans 8 vv 33-39

1 Who shall the Lord's elect condemn?
'Tis God that justifies their souls,
And mercy, like a mighty stream
O'er all their sins divinely rolls.

2 Who shall adjudge the saints to hell?
'Tis Christ that suffered in their
stead;
And their salvation to fulfil,
Behold Him rising from the dead.

3 He lives, He lives, and sits above,
For ever interceding there;
Who shall divide us from His love?
Or what should tempt us to despair?

4 Shall persecution or distress,
Famine, or sword, or nakedness?
He that hath loved us bears us
through,
And makes us more than conquerors
too.

5 Faith hath an overcoming power,
It triumphs in the dying hour:
Christ is our life, our hope, our joy,
Nor can our foes that hope destroy.

6 Not all that men on earth can do,
Nor powers on high, nor powers
below,
Shall cause His mercy to remove,
Or wean our hearts from Christ our
love.

Isaac Watts (1674–1748)

962 L.M.

*'I press toward the mark for the prize of
the high calling of God in Christ Jesus'*
Philippians 3 v 14

1 Why is my faith so weak and faint?
When God has promised every saint
That comes to Him in Jesus' name,
Fires to subdue and floods to tame.

2 Oh gracious Spirit, give to me
The eye of faith that I may see,
When Satan thrusts me to the
ground
The heavenly hosts encamped
around.

3 And though I tread a weary road
And though I feel the tempter's
goad,
May Jesus Christ my refuge be
And I, by faith, blest Zion see.

4 Encouraged thus, Lord, may I rise
And press toward the heavenly prize;
Serve Thee until I hear at last
Come, faithful child, thy toils are
past.

5 Now hasten on that longed for day,
When sinful flesh is stripped away,
My feeble faith is turned to sight
And Christ appears in glories bright.

Andrew Boorman (1967–2007)

963   11 8. 11 8

'The righteous also shall hold on his way'
Job 17 v 9

1 Ye pilgrims of Zion and chosen of
   God
  Whose spirits are filled with dismay,
  Since ye have eternal redemption
    through blood,
  Ye cannot but hold on your way.

2 As Jesus in covenant love did engage
  A fullness of grace to display,
  The powers of darkness in malice
    may rage,
  The righteous shall hold on his way.

3 This truth, like its Author, eternal
   shall stand,
  Though all things in nature decay;
  Upheld by Jehovah's omnipotent
   hand,
  The righteous shall hold on his way.

4 They may in the storms of
   temptation be tossed,
  Their sorrows may swell as the sea,
  But none of the ransomed shall ever
   be lost,
  The righteous shall hold on his way.

5 Surrounded with sorrows,
   temptations and cares,
  This truth with delight we survey,
  And sing, as we pass through this
   valley of tears,
  The righteous shall hold on his way.

Henry Fowler (1779–1838)

964   10 10. 10 10

'Abide with us: for it is toward evening'
Luke 24 v 29

1 Abide with me: fast falls the
   eventide;
  The darkness deepens; Lord, with
   me abide!
  When other helpers fail, and
   comforts flee,
  Help of the helpless, O abide with
   me.

2 Swift to its close ebbs out life's little
   day;
  Earth's joys grow dim, its glories
   pass away;
  Change and decay in all around I
   see:
  O Thou who changest not, abide
   with me.

3 I need Thy presence every passing
   hour;
  What but Thy grace can foil the
   tempter's power?
  Who like Thyself my guide and stay
   can be?
  Through cloud and sunshine, Lord,
   abide with me.

4 I fear no foe, with Thee at hand to
   bless;
  Ills have no weight, and tears no
   bitterness:
  Where is death's sting? Where,
   grave, thy victory?
  I triumph still, if Thou abide with
   me.

5 Hold Thou Thy cross before my
   closing eyes;
  Shine through the gloom, and point
   me to the skies;
  Heaven's morning breaks, and
   earth's vain shadows flee:
  In life, in death, O Lord, abide with
   me.

Henry Francis Lyte (1793–1847)

965
D.S.M.

'And so shall we ever be with the Lord'
1 Thessalonians 4 v 17

1 'For ever with the Lord!'
Amen, so let it be!
Life from the dead is in that word,
'Tis immortality.
Here in the body pent,
Absent from Him I roam,
Yet nightly pitch my moving tent
A day's march nearer home.

2 My Father's house on high,
Home of my soul, how near
At times to faith's foreseeing eye
Thy golden gates appear!
Ah! Then my spirit faints
To reach the land I love,
The bright inheritance of saints,
Jerusalem above.

3 'For ever with the Lord!'
Father, if 'tis Thy will,
The promise of that faithful word
E'en here to me fulfil.
Be Thou at my right hand,
Then can I never fail;
Uphold Thou me, and I shall stand;
Fight, and I must prevail.

4 So when my latest breath
Shall rend the veil in twain,
By death I shall escape from death,
And life eternal gain.
That resurrection word,
That shout of victory:
Once more, 'For ever with the Lord!'
Amen, so let it be!

James Montgomery (1771–1854)

966
98.98.D

'The city of the living God, the heavenly Jerusalem' Hebrews 12 v 22

1 From heavenly Jerusalem's towers,
The path through the desert they
trace;
And every affliction they suffered
Redounds to the glory of grace;
Their look they cast back on the
tempests,
On fears, on grim death and the
grave,
Rejoicing that now they're in safety,
Through Him that is mighty to save.

2 And we, from the wilds of the
desert,
Shall flee to the land of the blest;
Life's tears shall be changed to
rejoicing,
Its labours and toil into rest.
There we shall find refuge eternal,
From sin, from affliction, from pain,
And in the sweet love of the Saviour,
A joy without end shall attain.

David Charles (1762–1834)
Tr. Lewis Edwards (1809–87)

967
C.M.

'These were redeemed from among men'
Revelation 14 v 4

1 Give me the wings of faith to rise
Within the veil, and see
The saints above, how great their
joys,
How bright their glories be.

2 Once they were mourning here
below,
With sighings and with tears;
They wrestled hard, as we do now,
With sins and doubts and fears.

3 I ask them whence their victory
came;
They, with united breath,
Ascribe their conquest to the Lamb,
Their triumph to His death.

4 They marked the footsteps that He
   trod,
  His zeal inspired their breast,
  And, following their incarnate God,
  Possess the promised rest.

5 Our glorious Leader claims our praise
  For His own pattern given;
  While the long cloud of witnesses
  Show the same path to heaven.

Isaac Watts (1674–1748)

968   C.M.

Based on Revelation 7 vv 13-17

1 How bright these glorious spirits
   shine!
  Whence all their white array?
  How came they to the blissful seats
  Of everlasting day?

2 Lo! these are they from sufferings
   great
  Who came to realms of light;
  And in the blood of Christ have
   washed
  Those robes that shine so bright.

3 Now with triumphal palms they
   stand
  Before the throne on high,
  And serve the God they love amidst
  The glories of the sky.

4 His presence fills each heart with
   joy,
  Tunes every voice to sing;
  By day, by night, the sacred courts
  With glad hosannas ring.

5 Hunger and thirst are felt no more,
  Nor sun with scorching ray;
  God is their Sun, whose cheering
   beams
  Diffuse eternal day.

6 The Lamb, who dwells amidst the
   throne,
  Shall o'er them still preside,
  Feed them with nourishment divine,
  And all their footsteps guide.

7 In pastures green He'll lead His
   flock,
  Where living streams appear;
  And God the Lord from every eye
  Shall wipe off every tear.

8 To Him who sits upon the throne,
  The God whom we adore,
  And to the Lamb that once was slain,
  Be glory evermore!

Isaac Watts (1674–1748)

969   9 8. 9 8. D

'I will never leave thee, nor forsake thee'
Hebrews 13 v 5

1 I saw a new vision of Jesus,
  A view I'd not seen here before,
  Beholding in glory so wondrous
  With beauty I had to adore.
  I stood on the shores of my
   weakness,
  And gazed at the brink of such fear;
  'Twas then that I saw Him in
   newness,
  Regarding Him fair and so dear.

2 My Saviour will never forsake me,
  Unveiling His merciful face,
  His presence and promise almighty,
  Redeeming His loved ones by grace.
  In shades of the valley's dark terror,
  Where hell and its horror hold sway,
  My Jesus will reach out in power,
  And save me by His only way.

3 For yonder a light shines eternal,
  Which spreads through the valley of
   gloom;
  Lord Jesus, resplendent and regal,
  Drives fear far away from the tomb.
  Our God is the end of the journey,
  His pleasant and glorious domain;
  For there are the children of mercy,
  Who praise Him for Calvary's pain.

© The Author   *William Vernon Higham (b.1926)*

970

S.M.

'For to me ... to die is gain'
Philippians 1 v 21

1 It is not death to die,
To leave this weary road,
And, 'midst the brotherhood on
high,
To be at home with God.

2 It is not death to close
The eye long dimmed by tears,
And wake in glorious repose
To spend eternal years.

3 It is not death to bear
The wrench that sets us free
From dungeon chain, to breathe the
air
Of boundless liberty.

4 It is not death to fling
Aside this sinful dust,
And rise on strong, exulting wing
To live among the just.

5 Jesus, Thou Prince of life!
Thy chosen cannot die;
Like Thee, they conquer in the strife,
To reign with Thee on high.

Henri Abraham Cesar Malan (1787–1864)
Tr. George Washington Bethune (1805–62)

971

7 6. 7 6. D

*'That great city, the holy Jerusalem,
descending out of heaven from God'*
Revelation 21 v 10

1 Jerusalem the golden,
With milk and honey blessed,
Beneath thy contemplation
Sink heart and voice oppressed:
I know not, O I know not
What joys await us there,
What radiancy of glory,
What bliss beyond compare.

2 They stand, those halls of Zion,
All jubilant with song,
And bright with many an angel,
And all the martyr throng;
The Prince is ever in them;
The daylight is serene;
The pastures of the blessèd
Are decked in glorious sheen.

3 There is the throne of David;
And there, from care released,
The shout of them that triumph,
The song of them that feast;
And they, who with their Leader
Have conquered in the fight,
For ever and for ever
Are clad in robes of white.

4 O sweet and blessèd country,
The home of God's elect!
O sweet and blessèd country
That eager hearts expect!
Jesus, in mercy bring us
To that dear land of rest,
Who art, with God the Father
And Spirit, ever blessed!

Bernard of Cluny 12th Century
Tr. John Mason Neale (1818–66)

972

L.M.

*'And God shall wipe away all tears from
their eyes' Revelation 7 v 17*

1 Lo, round the throne, a glorious
band,
The saints in countless myriads
stand,
Of every tongue redeemed to God,
Arrayed in garments washed in
blood.

2 Through tribulation great they came;
They bore the cross, despised the
shame;
From all their labours now they rest,
In God's eternal glory blest.

3 They see their Saviour face to face,
  And sing the triumphs of his grace;
  Him day and night they ceaseless
    praise,
  To Him the loud thanksgiving raise:

4 'Worthy the Lamb, for sinners slain,
  Through endless years to live and
    reign!
  Thou hast redeemed us by Thy
    blood,
  And made us kings and priests to
    God.'

5 O may we tread the sacred road
  That saints and holy martyrs trod;
  Wage to the end the glorious strife,
  And win, like them, a crown of life.

Based on Rowland Hill (1744–1833)

973   11 11. 11 11

'There the weary be at rest' Job 3 v 17

1 My rest is in heaven, my rest is not
  here,
  Then why should I tremble when
    trials are near?
  Be calm anxious spirit, the worst
    that can come
  But shortens the journey, and
    hastens me home.

2 It is not for me to be seeking my
    bliss,
  Or building my hopes in a region
    like this;
  I look for a city that hands have not
    piled,
  I look for a country by sin undefiled.

3 Afflictions may press me, they
    cannot destroy;
  One glimpse of His love turns them
    all into joy;
  Let doubt, then, and danger my
    progress oppose,
  They only make heaven more sweet
    at the close.

4 Come joy or come sorrow, whate'er
    may befall,
  An hour with my God will make up
    for them all.
  The road may be rough, but it will
    not be long;
  I'll walk it by faith, while rejoicing in
    song.

Henry Francis Lyte (1793–1847)

974   8 7. 8 7. D

'For I have received of the Lord that which
also I delivered unto you'
1 Corinthians 11 v 23

1 Oh, what love! So vast and mighty,
  Irresistible the grace,
  Heaven's own seal upon the
    covenant,
  That no power can e'er efface;
  This alone is my sure anchor,
  While I cross the stormy deep,
  God's decree shall stand for ever,
  All in Christ He'll safely keep.

2 In the deep and surging waters,
  When the billows o'er me roll,
  None but Jesus, my Redeemer,
  Can uphold my trembling soul;
  While I cross the swelling Jordan,
  I shall sing above its roar,
  For He'll press me to His bosom,
  As He bears me safely o'er.

Ann Griffiths (1776–1805)
Tr. A. Olwyn Jones

975   7 6. 7 6. 7 6. 7 5

'Thy land, O Immanuel' Isaiah 8 v 8

1 The sands of time are sinking;
  The dawn of heaven breaks;
  The summer morn I've sighed for,
  The fair, sweet morn, awakes:
  Dark, dark hath been the midnight,
  But day-spring is at hand,
  And glory, glory dwelleth
  In Immanuel's land.

2 O Christ, He is the fountain,
The deep, sweet well of love;
The streams on earth I've tasted,
More deep I'll drink above;
There, to an ocean fullness,
His mercy doth expand,
And glory, glory dwelleth
In Immanuel's land.

3 The King there, in His beauty,
Without a veil is seen;
It were a well-spent journey,
Though seven deaths lay between;
The Lamb with His fair army
Doth on Mount Zion stand,
And glory, glory dwelleth
In Immanuel's land.

4 I've wrestled on towards heaven,
'Gainst storm and wind and tide;
Now, like a weary traveller
That leans upon his guide,
Amid the shades of evening,
While sinks life's lingering sand,
I hail the glory dawning
From Immanuel's land.

5 With mercy and with judgement
My web of time He wove,
And aye the dews of sorrow
Were lustred with His love:
I'll bless the hand that guided,
I'll bless the heart that planned,
When throned where glory dwelleth
In Immanuel's land.

6 The bride eyes not her garment,
But her dear bridegroom's face;
I will not gaze at glory,
But on my King of grace;
Not at the crown He giveth,
But on His piercèd hand:
The Lamb is all the glory
Of Immanuel's land.

Anne Ross Cousin (1824–1906)

976 C.M.

'They shall behold the land that is very far off' Isaiah 33 v 17

1 There is a land of pure delight,
Where saints immortal reign;
Infinite day excludes the night,
And pleasures banish pain.

2 There everlasting spring abides,
And never-withering flowers;
Death, like a narrow sea, divides
This heavenly land from ours.

3 Sweet fields, beyond the swelling
flood,
Stand dressed in living green;
So to the Jews old Canaan stood,
While Jordan rolled between.

4 But timorous mortals start and
shrink
To cross this narrow sea;
And linger, shivering on the brink,
And fear to launch away.

5 O could we make our doubts
remove,
Those gloomy thoughts that rise,
And see the Canaan that we love
With unclouded eyes!

6 Could we but climb where Moses
stood,
And view the landscape o'er,
Not Jordan's stream, nor death's
cold flood,
Should fright us from the shore.

Isaac Watts (1674–1748)

977 C.M.

'It is appointed unto man once to die' Hebrews 9 v 27

1 There is an hour when I must part
With all I hold most dear;
And life with its best hopes will then
As nothingness appear.

2 There is an hour when I must sink
  Beneath the stroke of death,
  And yield to Him, who gave it first,
  My struggling, vital breath.

3 There is an hour when I must stand
  Before the judgement-seat,
  And all my sins, and all my foes,
  In awful vision meet.

4 There is an hour when I must look
  On one eternity;
  And nameless woe, or blissful life,
  My endless portion be.

5 O Saviour, then, in all my need,
  Be near, be near to me;
  And let my soul by steadfast faith
  Find life and heaven in Thee.

Andrew Reed (1787–1862)

978   88.88.88

*'A partaker of the glory that shall be
revealed' 1 Peter 5 v 1*

1 What will it be to dwell above,
  And with the Lord of glory reign,
  Since the sweet earnest of His love
  So brightens all this dreary plain?
  No heart can think, no tongue
    explain
  What joy 'twill be with Christ to
    reign.

2 When sin no more obstructs our
    sight,
  When sorrow pains the heart no
    more,
  When we shall see the Prince of
    light,
  And all His works of grace explore,
  What heights and depths of love
    divine
  Will there through endless ages
    shine!

3 Our God has fixed the happy day
  When the last tear shall dim our
    eyes,
  When He will wipe all tears away,
  And fill our hearts with glad
    surprise,
  To hear His voice, to see His face,
  And know the riches of His grace.

4 This is the joy we seek to know,
  For this with patience we would
    wait,
  Till called from earth and all below,
  We rise, our gracious Lord to meet;
  To wave our palm, our crown to
    wear,
  And praise the love that brought us
    there.

Joseph Swain (1761–96)

979   77.77.77

*'Then shall I know even as also I am
known' I Corinthians 13 v 12*

1 When this passing world is done,
  When has sunk yon radiant sun,
  When we stand with Christ on high,
  Looking o'er life's history,
  Then, Lord, shall I fully know,
  Not till then, how much I owe.

2 When I stand before the throne,
  Dressed in beauty not my own,
  When I see Thee as Thou art,
  Love Thee with unsinning heart,
  Then Lord, shall I fully know,
  Not till then, how much I owe.

3 When the praise of heaven I hear,
  Loud as thunders to the ear,
  Loud as many waters' noise,
  Sweet as harp's melodious voice,
  Then, Lord, shall I fully know,
  Not till then, how much I owe.

4 Chosen not for good in me,
Wakened up from wrath to flee,
Hidden in the Saviour's side,
By the Spirit sanctified,
Teach me, Lord, on earth to show,
By my love, how much I owe.

Robert Murray M'Cheyne (1813–43)

980   64.64.66.64

'Who is this that cometh from Edom?'
Isaiah 63 v 1

1 Who is this fearful foe
With presence chill –
His gaze and word of woe,
Unbending will?
He comes to high and low,
With unrelenting flow;
The fear of all below,
This death so still.

2 Yet men forget their end,
From God they flee:
They on themselves depend,
With pride their plea.
Yet all their life is vain,
And foolish all their claim;
And though they death disdain,
They are not free.

3 Who is this Warrior true
Who now appears?
A mighty form who slew
Our dreadful fears!
Begotten from above,
With grace of heaven's Dove,
He is the Lord of love:
Their debt He clears.

4 Now sin and death have failed
In all their scheme;
And Satan's work destroyed:
God's strength is seen.
The price of sin is paid,
A path of heaven is laid,
With life that cannot fade:
O glorious theme!

© The Author   *William Vernon Higham (b.1926)*

THE
CHURCH OF CHRIST

981

C.M.

Based on 1 John 3 vv 1-4

1 Behold the amazing gift of love
The Father hath bestowed
On us, the sinful sons of men,
To call us sons of God.

2 Concealed as yet this honour lies,
By this dark world unknown,
A world that knew not when He
came,
Ev'n God's eternal Son.

3 High is the rank we now possess,
But higher we shall rise;
Though what we shall hereafter be
Is hid from mortal eyes:

4 Our souls, we know, when He
appears,
Shall bear His image bright;
For all His glory, full disclosed,
Shall open to our sight.

5 A hope so great, and so divine,
May trials well endure;
And purge the soul from sense and
sin,
As Christ Himself is pure.

Scottish Paraphrases 1781

982

L.M.

*'Let my beloved come into his garden,
and eat his pleasant fruits'*
Song of Solomon 4 v 16

1 Christ has a garden walled around,
A paradise of fruitful ground,
Chosen by love and fenced by grace
From out the world's wide
wilderness.

2 Like trees of spice His servants
stand,
There planted by His mighty hand;
By Eden's gracious streams, that
flow
To feed their beauty where they
grow.

3 Awake, O wind of heaven, and bear
Their sweetest perfume through the
air:
Stir up, O south, the boughs that
bloom,
Till the belovèd Master come.

4 That He may come, and linger yet
Among the trees that He has set;
That He may evermore be seen
To walk amid the springing green.

Isaac Watts (1674–1748) Altd

983
66.66.44.44

'Jesus Christ himself being the chief corner stone' Ephesians 2 v 20

1 Christ is our corner stone,
On Him alone we build;
With His true saints alone
The courts of heaven are filled;
On His great love
Our hopes we place
Of present grace
And joys above.

2 O then with hymns of praise
These hallowed courts shall ring;
Our voices we will raise
The Three in One to sing;
And thus proclaim
In joyful song,
Both loud and long,
That glorious name.

3 Here, gracious God, do Thou
For evermore draw nigh;
Accept each faithful vow,
And mark each suppliant sigh;
In copious shower
On all who pray
Each holy day
Thy blessings pour.

4 Here may we gain from heaven
The grace which we implore;
And may that grace, once given,
Be with us evermore,
Until that day
When all the blest
To endless rest
Are called away.

Latin 6th or 7th Century
Tr. John Chandler (1806–76)

984
65.65.D

'I have set my affection to the house of my God' 1 Chronicles 29 v 3

1 Christ is the foundation
Of the house we raise;
Be its walls salvation,
And its gateways praise;
May its threshold lowly
To the Lord be dear;
May the hearts be holy
That shall worship here.

2 Here the vow be sealed
By Thy Spirit, Lord;
Here the sick be healed,
And the lost restored;
Here the broken-hearted
Thy forgiveness prove;
Here the friends long parted
Be restored to love.

3 Here may every token
Of Thy presence be;
Here may chains be broken,
Prisoners here set free;
Here may light illumine
Every soul of Thine,
Lifting up the human
Into the divine.

4 Here may God the Father,
Christ the Saviour – Son,
With the Holy Spirit,
Be adored as One;
Till the whole creation
At Thy footstool fall,
And in adoration
Own Thee Lord of all.

John Samuel Bewley Monsell (1811–75)

985

8 7.8 7. D

'Glorious things are spoken of thee, O city of God' Psalm 87 v 3

1 Glorious things of thee are spoken,
   Zion, city of our God!
   He, whose word cannot be broken,
   Formed thee for His own abode.
   On the Rock of Ages founded,
   What can shake thy sure repose?
   With salvation's walls surrounded,
   Thou may'st smile at all thy foes.

2 See! the streams of living waters,
   Springing from eternal love,
   Well supply thy sons and daughters,
   And all fear of want remove:
   Who can faint while such a river
   Ever flows their thirst to assuage –
   Grace which, like the Lord the Giver,
   Never fails from age to age?

3 Round each habitation hovering,
   See! the cloud and fire appear,
   For a glory and a covering,
   Showing that the Lord is near:
   Blest inhabitants of Zion,
   Washed in the Redeemer's blood –
   Jesus, whom their souls rely on,
   Makes them kings and priests to
      God.

4 Saviour, if of Zion's city
   I through grace a member am,
   Let the world deride or pity,
   I will glory in Thy name:
   Fading is the worldling's pleasure,
   All his boasted pomp and show;
   Solid joys and lasting treasure
   None but Zion's children know.

John Newton (1725–1807)

986

C.M.

'Fellowcitizens with the saints' Ephesians 2 v 19

1 Happy the souls to Jesus joined,
   And saved by grace alone;
   Walking in all His ways, they find
   Their heaven on earth begun.

2 The church triumphant in Thy love,
   Their mighty joys we know;
   They sing the Lamb in hymns above,
   And we in hymns below.

3 Thee in Thy glorious realm they
      praise,
   And bow before Thy throne;
   We in the kingdom of Thy grace:
   The kingdoms are but one.

4 The holy to the holiest leads,
   From thence our spirits rise;
   And he that in Thy statutes treads
   Shall meet Thee in the skies.

Charles Wesley (1707–88)

987

C.M.

Based on Isaiah 26 vv 1-7

1 How glorious Zion's courts appear,
   The city of our God!
   His throne He hath established here,
   Here fixed His loved abode.

2 Its walls, defended by His grace,
   No power shall e'er o'erthrow,
   Salvation is its bulwark sure
   Against the assaulting foe.

3 Lift up the everlasting gates,
   The doors wide open fling;
   Enter, ye nations, who obey
   The statutes of our King.

4 Here shall ye taste unmingled joys,
   And dwell in perfect peace,
   Ye, who have known Jehovah's
      name,
   And trusted in His grace.

5 Trust in the Lord, for ever trust,
And banish all your fears;
Strength in the Lord Jehovah dwells,
Eternal as His years.

Scottish Paraphrases 1781

988 C.M.

Based on Psalm 84

1 How lovely are Thy dwellings fair!
O Lord of hosts, how dear
The pleasant tabernacles are,
Where Thou dost dwell so near!

2 My soul doth long and almost die
Thy courts, O Lord, to see;
My heart and flesh aloud do cry,
O living God, for Thee.

3 Happy who in Thy house reside,
Where Thee they ever praise!
Happy whose strength in Thee doth
'bide,
And in their hearts Thy ways!

4 They journey on from strength to
strength
With joy and gladsome cheer,
Till all before our God at length
In Zion do appear.

5 For God, the Lord, both sun and
shield,
Gives grace and glory bright;
No good from them shall be
withheld
Whose ways are just and right.

6 Lord God of hosts, that reign'st on
high,
That man is truly blest
Who only on Thee doth rely,
And in Thee only rest.

John Milton (1608–74)

989 668.D

Based on Psalm 122

1 How pleased and blest was I
To hear the people cry,
'Come, let us seek our God today!'
Yes, with a cheerful zeal
We haste to Zion's hill,
And there our vows and honours
pay.

2 Zion, thrice happy place,
Adorned with wondrous grace,
And walls of strength embrace thee
round;
In thee our tribes appear,
To pray, and praise, and hear
The sacred gospel's joyful sound.

3 There David's greater Son
Has fixed His royal throne,
He sits for grace and judgment
there;
He bids the saint be glad,
He makes the sinner sad,
And humble souls rejoice with fear.

4 May peace attend thy gate,
And joy within thee wait,
To bless the soul of every guest!
The man that seeks thy peace,
And wishes thine increase,
A thousand blessings on him rest!

5 My tongue repeats her vows,
Peace to this sacred house!
For there my friends and kindred
dwell;
And, since my glorious God
Makes thee His blest abode,
My soul shall ever love thee well!

Isaac Watts (1674–1748)

990 S.M.

'For where two or three are gathered together in my name, there am I in the midst of them' Matthew 18 v 20

1 Jesus, we look to Thee,
Thy promised presence claim;
Thou in the midst of us shalt be,
Assembled in Thy name.

2 Thy name salvation is,
Which here we come to prove;
Thy name is life, and health, and peace,
And everlasting love.

3 We meet, the grace to take
Which Thou hast freely given;
We meet on earth for Thy dear sake,
That we may meet in heaven.

4 Present we know Thou art,
But O Thyself reveal!
Now, Lord, let every bounding heart
The mighty comfort feel.

5 O may Thy quickening voice
The death of sin remove;
And bid our inmost souls rejoice
In hope of perfect love!

Charles Wesley (1707–88)

991 6 6. 6 6. 4 4. 4 4

Based on Psalm 84

1 Lord of the worlds above,
How pleasant and how fair
The dwellings of Thy love,
Thine earthly temples, are!
To Thine abode
My heart aspires,
With warm desires
To see my God.

2 O happy souls that pray
Where God delights to hear!
O happy men that pay
Their constant service there!
They praise Thee still,
And happy they
Who love the way
To Zion's hill!

3 They go from strength to strength,
Through this dark vale of tears
Till each arrive at length,
Till each in heaven appears:
O glorious seat!
Thou, God our King,
Shalt thither bring
Our willing feet!

4 To spend one sacred day
Where God and saints abide,
Affords diviner joy
Than thousand days beside;
Where God resorts,
I love it more
To keep the door
Than shine in courts.

5 God is our sun and shield,
Our light and our defence;
With gifts His hands are filled,
We draw our blessings thence:
He shall bestow
On Jacob's race
Peculiar grace
And glory too.

6 The Lord His people loves;
His hand no good withholds
From those His heart approves,
From holy, humble souls:
Thrice happy he,
O God of hosts,
Whose spirit trusts
Alone in Thee!

Isaac Watts (1674–1748)

992 C.M.

Based on Psalm 122

1 O 'twas a joyful sound to hear
Our tribes devoutly say,
'Up, Israel, to the temple haste,
And keep your festal day.'

2 At Salem's courts we must appear,
With our assembled powers,
In strong and beauteous order ranged,
Like her united towers.

3 O pray we then for Salem's peace,
  For they shall prosperous be,
  Thou holy city of our God,
  Who bear true love to thee.

4 May peace within thy sacred walls
  A constant guest be found,
  With plenty and prosperity
  Thy palaces be crowned.

5 For my dear brethren's sake, and
    friends
  No less than brethren dear,
  I'll pray, 'May peace in Salem's
    towers
  A constant guest appear.'

6 But most of all I'll seek thy good,
  And ever wish thee well,
  For Zion and the temple's sake,
  Where God vouchsafes to dwell.

Nahum Tate (1652–1715)
and Nicholas Brady (1659–1726)

993   7 6. 7 6. D

'For other foundation can no man lay
than that is laid, which is Jesus Christ'
1 Corinthians 3 v 11

1 The church's one foundation
  Is Jesus Christ her Lord;
  She is His new creation
  By water and the Word;
  From heaven He came and sought
    her
  To be His holy bride;
  With His own blood He bought her,
  And for her life He died.

2 Elect from every nation,
  Yet one o'er all the earth;
  Her charter of salvation –
  One Lord, one faith, one birth;
  One holy name she blesses,
  Partakes one holy food;
  And to one hope she presses,
  With every grace endued.

3 Though with a scornful wonder
  Men see her sore oppressed,
  By schisms rent asunder,
  By heresies distressed,
  Yet saints their watch are keeping,
  Their cry goes up, 'How long?'
  And soon the night of weeping
  Shall be the morn of song.

4 'Mid toil and tribulation,
  And tumult of her war,
  She waits the consummation
  Of peace for evermore;
  Till with the vision glorious
  Her longing eyes are blest,
  And the great church victorious
  Shall be the church at rest.

5 Yet she on earth hath union
  With God the Three in One,
  And mystic sweet communion
  With those whose rest is won.
  O happy ones and holy!
  Lord, give us grace that we,
  Like them, the meek and lowly,
  On high may dwell with Thee!

Samuel John Stone (1839–1900)

994   6 6. 6 6

'LORD, I have loved the habitation of thy
house, and the place where thine honour
dwelleth' Psalm 26 v 8

1 We love the place, O God,
  Wherein Thine honour dwells;
  The joy of Thine abode
  All earthly joy excels.

2 It is the house of prayer
  Wherein Thy servants meet;
  And Thou, O Lord, art there,
  Thy chosen flock to greet.

3 We love the Word of life,
  The Word that tells of peace,
  Of comfort in the strife,
  And joys that never cease.

4 We love to sing below
Of mercies freely given;
But, O, we long to know
The triumph song of Heaven!

5 Lord Jesus, give us grace,
On earth to love Thee more,
In Heaven to see Thy face,
And with Thy saints adore.

William Bullock (1798–1874)
and Henry Williams Baker (1821–77)

995 C.M.

'Wherefore comfort yourselves together,
and edify one another'
1 Thessalonians 5 v 11

1 All praise to our redeeming Lord,
Who joins us by His grace,
And bids us, each to each restored,
Together seek His face.

2 He bids us build each other up;
And, gathered into one,
To our high calling's glorious hope
We hand in hand go on.

3 The gift which He on one bestows,
We all delight to prove;
The grace through every vessel
flows,
In purest streams of love.

4 Even now we think and speak the
same,
And cordially agree;
Concentred all, through Jesu's
name,
In perfect harmony.

5 We all partake the joy of one,
The common peace we feel,
A peace to sensual minds unknown,
A joy unspeakable.

6 And if our fellowship below
In Jesus be so sweet,
What heights of rapture shall we
know
When round His throne we meet.

Charles Wesley (1707–88)

996 S.M.

'Who redeemeth thy life from destruction'
Psalm 103 v 4

1 And are we yet alive,
And see each other's face?
Glory and praise to Jesus give
For His redeeming grace!

2 Preserved by power divine
To full salvation here,
Again in Jesu's praise we join,
And in His sight appear.

3 What troubles have we seen,
What conflicts have we passed,
Fightings without, and fears within,
Since we assembled last!

4 But out of all the Lord
Hath brought us by His love;
And still He doth His help afford,
And hides our life above.

5 Then let us make our boast
Of His redeeming power,
Which saves us to the uttermost,
Till we can sin no more:

6 Let us take up the cross,
Till we the crown obtain;
And gladly reckon all things loss,
So we may Jesus gain.

Charles Wesley (1707–78)

997 C.M.

'Behold, how good and how pleasant it is
for brethren to dwell together in unity!'
Psalm 133 v 1

1 Behold, how blessed is the place
Where brethren meet in love;
For they have known the Spirit's
grace,
As gentle as a dove.

2 Precious the brow that feels the
balm
Of healing incense sweet;
The savour of eternal calm
Its glorious God now greet.

3 Silent the dew on Zion's hills,
Eternal stillness lies;
The promise of a God who wills
His bountiful supplies.

4 Command the blessing there, O
Lord
Of everlasting life;
Compel Thy people by Thy Word
To cease from sinful strife.

5 Come quickly to Thy people, now,
And hear our humble cry;
Grant us Thy blessing as we bow
In contrite unity.

6 Sweet is the balm and fresh the dew
Of Thy redeeming grace;
Thy presence, real to us, yet few;
We see Thy beauteous face.

7 Now let Thy blessing leap abroad
Reviving sons of light;
Many shall praise their new-found
Lord,
The God of their delight.

© The Author   William Vernon Higham (b.1926)

998   S.M.

'Let brotherly love continue'
Hebrews 13 v 1

1 Blest be the tie that binds
Our hearts in Christian love;
The fellowship of kindred minds
Is like to that above.

2 Before our Father's throne
We pour our ardent prayers;
Our fears, our hopes, our aims are
one,
Our comforts and our cares.

3 We share our mutual woes,
Our mutual burdens bear;
And often for each other flows
The sympathizing tear.

4 When for a while we part,
This thought will soothe our pain,
That we shall still be joined in heart,
And hope to meet again.

5 This glorious hope revives
Our courage by the way,
While each in expectation lives,
And longs to see the day.

6 From sorrow, toil, and pain,
And sin we shall be free;
And perfect love and friendship
reign
Through all eternity.

John Fawcett (1739–1817)

999   7 7.7 7

'The grace of our Lord Jesus Christ be
with you' 1 Corinthians 16 v 23

1 For a season called to part,
Let us now ourselves commend
To the gracious eye and heart
Of our ever-present Friend.

2 Jesus, hear our humble prayer,
Tender Shepherd of Thy sheep!
Let Thy mercy and Thy care
All our souls in safety keep!

3 In Thy strength may we be strong,
Sweeten every cross and pain;
Give us, if we live, ere long
Here to meet in peace again.

John Newton (1725–1807)

1000   8 7.8 7. D

'Behold, how good and how pleasant it is
for brethren to dwell together in unity!'
Psalm 133 v 1

1 Gaze upon the hills of Zion,
Rising in their strong array,
There the dew of gentle Hermon,
Springs with purity each day.
Sweet the incense of Thy freshness,
Sweet the presence of our King;
Glorious is Thy ready kindness,
This Thy saints will ever sing.

2 Blessed sight to see each brother,
Pleasant is their happy part;
One in Thee and in each other;
Blessed unity of heart.
Like the kindness of God's favour
Shed in fragrance on their gown;
Blessed garment of Thy splendour;
Sweet the incense of Thy dawn.

3 There the blessing God commanded;
There in hearts united, strong;
There the person of the Godhead;
Blessed Saviour be their song.
Hail! all hail our blest Redeemer!
Hail, Thy coming now to stay;
Praise and glory be for ever,
Let Thy sceptre gently sway.

© The Author   *William Vernon Higham (b.1926)*

1001   7 7 7 . 5

Based on 1 Corinthians 13

1 Gracious Spirit, Holy Ghost,
Taught by Thee, we covet most,
Of Thy gifts at Pentecost,
Holy, heavenly love.

2 Faith that mountains could remove,
Tongues of earth or heaven above,
Knowledge, all things, empty prove
Without heavenly love.

3 Though I as a martyr bleed,
Give my goods the poor to feed,
All in vain if love I need;
Therefore give me love.

4 Love is kind, and suffers long,
Love is meek, and thinks no wrong,
Love than death itself more strong;
Therefore give us love.

5 Prophecy will fade away,
Melting in the light of day;
Love will ever with us stay;
Therefore give us love.

6 Faith, and hope, and love we see,
Joining hand in hand, agree;
But the greatest of the three,
And the best, is love.

Christopher Wordsworth (1807–85)

1002   C.M.

*'Thou shalt surely help him to lift them
up again' Deuteronomy 22 v 4*

1 Help us to help each other, Lord,
Each other's cross to bear,
Let each his friendly aid afford
And feel his brother's care.

2 Help us to build each other up,
Our little stock improve;
Increase our faith, confirm our hope
And perfect us in love.

3 Up into Thee, our living Head,
Let us in all things grow,
Till Thou hast made us free indeed,
And spotless here below.

4 Touched by the loadstone of Thy love,
Let all our hearts agree;
And ever toward each other move,
And ever move toward Thee.

5 To Thee, inseparably joined,
Let all our spirits cleave;
O may we all the loving mind
That was in Thee, receive.

6 Still let us own our common Lord,
And bear Thine easy yoke,
A bond of love, a threefold cord
Which never can be broke.

Charles Wesley (1707–88)

1003   6 6 . 6 6 . 8 8

Based on Psalm 133

1 How beautiful the sight
Of brethren who agree
In friendship to unite,
And bonds of charity!
'Tis like the precious ointment shed
O'er all his robes from Aaron's head.

2 'Tis like the dews that fill
The cups of Hermon's flowers;
Or Zion's fruitful hill,
Bright with the drops of showers,
When mingling odours breathe
   around,
And glory rests on all the ground.

3 For there the Lord commands
Blessings, a boundless store,
From His unsparing hands,
Yea, life for evermore:
Thrice happy they who meet above
To spend eternity in love!

James Montgomery (1771–1854)

1004 S.M.

'Pray for the peace of Jerusalem: they shall prosper that love thee'
Psalm 122 v 6

1 I love Thy kingdom, Lord,
The house of Thine abode,
The church our blest Redeemer
saved
With His own precious blood.

2 I love Thy church, O God:
Her walls before Thee stand,
Dear as the apple of Thine eye,
And graven on Thy hand.

3 For her my tears shall fall,
For her my prayers ascend,
To her my cares and toils be given,
Till toils and cares shall end.

4 Beyond my highest joy
I prize her heavenly ways,
Her sweet communion, solemn
vows,
Her hymns of love and praise.

5 Jesus, Thou Friend divine,
Our Saviour and our King,
Thy hand from every snare and foe
Shall great deliverance bring.

6 Sure as Thy truth shall last,
To Zion shall be given
The brightest glories earth can yield,
And brighter bliss of heaven.

Timothy Dwight (1752–1817)

1005 87.87.47

'Serve the LORD with fear' Psalm 2 v 11

1 In Thy name, O Lord, assembling,
We, Thy people, now draw near;
Teach us to rejoice with trembling;
Speak, and let Thy servants hear;
Hear with meekness,
Hear Thy Word with godly fear.

2 Grant us, Lord, some gracious token
Of Thy love before we part;
Crown Thy Word which will be
spoken,
Life and peace to each impart,
And all blessings
Which will sanctify the heart.

3 While our days on earth are
lengthened,
May we give them, Lord, to Thee;
Cheered by hope, and daily
strengthened,
May we run, nor weary be,
Till Thy glory
Without cloud in heaven we see.

4 There, in worship purer, sweeter,
Thee Thy people shall adore,
Tasting of enjoyment greater
Far than thought conceived before:
Full enjoyment,
Full, unmixed and evermore.

Thomas Kelly (1769–1855)

1006 77.77

'Likeminded one toward another'
Romans 15 v 5

1 Jesus, Lord, we look to Thee,
Let us in Thy name agree;
Show Thyself the Prince of Peace;
Bid all strife for ever cease.

2 By Thy reconciling love
Every stumbling-block remove;
Each to each unite, endear,
Come, and spread Thy banner here.

3 Make us of one heart and mind,
Courteous, pitiful, and kind,
Lowly, meek, in thought and word,
Altogether like our Lord.

4 Let us for each other care,
Each the other's burden bear,
To Thy church the pattern give,
Show how true believers live.

5 Free from anger and from pride.
Let us thus in God abide;
All the depths of love express,
All the heights of holiness.

6 Let us then with joy remove
To the family above;
On the wings of angels fly,
Show how true believers die.

Charles Wesley (1707–88)

1007   77.77

*'For where two or three are gathered toge-
ther in my name, there am I in the midst
of them' Matthew 18 v 20*

1 Jesus, we Thy promise claim,
We are gathered in Thy name,
In the midst do Thou appear,
Manifest Thy presence here.

2 Sanctify us, Lord, and bless,
Breathe Thy Spirit, give Thy peace;
Come and dwell within each heart,
Light, and life, and joy impart.

3 Plant in us Thy humble mind;
Patient, pitiful and kind,
Meek and lowly let us be,
Full of goodness, full of Thee.

4 Make us all in Thee complete,
Make us all for glory meet,
Meet to appear before Thy sight,
Partners with the saints in light.

5 Call, O call us each by name
To the marriage of the Lamb;
Let us lean upon Thy breast,
Love be there our endless feast.

Charles Wesley (1707–88)

1008   77.77.D

*'Be of the same mind in the Lord'
Philippians 4 v 2*

1 Lord from whom all blessings flow,
Perfecting the church below,
Steadfast may we cleave to Thee,
Love, the mystic union be;
Join our faithful spirits, join
Each to each, and all to Thine;
Lead us through the paths of peace
On to perfect holiness.

2 Move and actuate and guide;
Diverse gifts to each divide;
Placed according to Thy will,
Let us all our work fulfil;
Never from our office move;
Needful to each other prove;
Use the grace on each bestowed,
Tempered by the art of God.

3 Sweetly may we all agree,
Touched with softest sympathy;
There is neither bond nor free,
Great nor servile, Lord, in Thee:
Love, like death, hath all destroyed,
Rendered all distinctions void;
Names and sects and parties fall,
Thou, O Christ, art All in all.

Charles Wesley (1707–88)

1009   C.M.

Taken from Psalms 116, 122 and 133

1 Pray that Jerusalem may have
Peace and felicity:
Let them that love thee and thy peace
Have still prosperity.

2 Behold how good a thing it is,
And how becoming well,
Together such as brethren are,
In unity to dwell.

3 Therefore I wish that peace may still
Within thy walls remain;
And ever may thy palaces
Prosperity retain.

4 Now for my friends' and brethren's
  sake,
Peace be in thee, I'll say;
And for the house of God our Lord
I'll seek thy good alway.

5 Within the courts of God's own
  house,
Within the midst of thee,
O City of Jerusalem,
Praise to the Lord give ye.

Scottish Psalter 1650

1010   6 6. 6 6. 8 8

*'The wise, and their works, are in the
hand of God' Ecclesiastes 9 v 1*

1 Thou God of truth and love,
  We seek Thy perfect way,
Ready Thy choice to approve,
  Thy providence to obey:
Enter into Thy wise design,
And sweetly lose our will in Thine.

2 Surely Thou dost unite
  Our kindred spirits here,
That all hereafter might
  Before Thy throne appear;
Meet at the marriage of the Lamb,
And all Thy glorious love proclaim.

3 Then let us ever bear
  The blessèd end in view,
And join, with mutual care,
  To fight our passage through;
And kindly help each other on,
Till all receive the starry crown.

4 O may Thy Spirit seal
  Our souls unto that day,
With all Thy fullness fill,
  And then transport away –
Away to our eternal rest,
Away to our Redeemer's breast!

Charles Wesley (1707–88)

1011   8 7. 8 7. 8 8 7

*'My father's God, and I will exalt Him'
Exodus 15 v 2*

1 We come unto our fathers' God,
  Their Rock is our salvation;
Th'eternal arms, their dear abode,
  We make our habitation;
We bring Thee, Lord, the praise they
  brought,
We seek Thee as Thy saints have
  sought
In every generation.

2 The fire divine their steps that led
  Still goeth bright before us;
The heavenly shield around them
  spread
Is still high holden o'er us;
The grace those sinners that subdued,
The strength those weaklings that
  renewed,
Doth vanquish, doth restore us.

3 The cleaving sins that brought them
  low
Are still our souls oppressing.
The tears that from their eyes did
  flow
Fall fast, our shame confessing;
As with Thee, Lord, prevailed their cry,
So our strong prayer ascends on high
And bringeth down Thy blessing,

4 Their joy unto their Lord we bring;
  Their song to us descendeth;
The Spirit who in them did sing
  To us His music lendeth;
His song in them, in us, is one;
We raise it high, we send it on –
The song that never endeth.

5 Ye saints to come, take up the strain,
  The same sweet theme endeavour;
Unbroken be the golden chain,
  Keep on the song forever!
Safe in the same dear dwelling place,
Rich with the same eternal grace,
Bless the same boundless Giver!

Thomas Hornblower Gill (1819–1906)

1012   8 7. 8 7. 6 6. 6 6 7

'God is our refuge and strength, a very present help in trouble' Psalm 46 v 1

1 A safe stronghold our God is still,
A trusty shield and weapon;
He'll help us clear from all the ill
That hath us now o'ertaken.
The ancient prince of hell
Hath risen with purpose fell;
Strong mail of craft and power
He weareth in this hour;
On earth is not his fellow.

2 With force of arms we nothing can,
Full soon were we down-ridden;
But for us fights the proper Man,
Whom God Himself hath bidden.
Ask ye, Who is this same?
Christ Jesus is His name,
The Lord Sabaoth's Son;
He, and no other one,
Shall conquer in the battle.

3 And were this world all devils o'er,
And watching to devour us,
We lay it not to heart so sore;
Not they can overpower us.
And let the prince of ill
Look grim as e'er he will,
He harms us not a whit:
For why? His doom is writ;
A word shall quickly slay him.

4 God's Word, for all their craft and
force,
One moment will not linger,
But, spite of hell, shall have its
course;
'Tis written by His finger.
And though they take our life,
Goods, honour, children, wife,
Yet is their profit small:
These things shall vanish all;
The city of God remaineth.

Martin Luther (1483–1546)
Tr. Thomas Carlyle (1795–1881)

1013   D.C.M.

'Of whom the whole family in heaven and earth is named' Ephesians 3 v 15

1 Come, let us join our friends above
That have obtained the prize,
And on the eagle wings of love
To joys celestial rise:
Let saints below in concert sing
With those to glory gone;
For all the servants of our King
In earth and heaven are one.

2 One family we dwell in Him,
One church, above, beneath,
Though now divided by the stream,
The narrow stream of death:
One army of the living God,
To His command we bow;
Part of His host have crossed the flood,
And part are crossing now.

3 Our spirits too shall quickly join
With theirs in glory crowned,
And shout to see our Captain's sign,
To hear His trumpet sound.
O that we now might grasp our Guide!
O that the word were given!
Come, Lord of hosts, the waves divide,
And land us all in heaven.

Charles Wesley (1707-88)

1014   10 10. 10 4

'Compassed about with so great a cloud of witnesses' Hebrews 12 v 1

1 For all the saints who from their
labours rest,
Who Thee by faith before the world
confessed,
Thy name, O Jesus, be for ever blest.
Hallelujah!

2 Thou wast their Rock, their Fortress,
and their might;
Thou, Lord, their Captain in the
well-fought fight;
Thou in the darkness drear, their
one true Light.
Hallelujah!

3 O may Thy soldiers, faithful, true
   and bold,
Fight as the saints who nobly fought
   of old,
And win, with them, the victor's
   crown of gold.
Hallelujah!

4 O blest communion, fellowship
   divine!
We feebly struggle, they in glory
   shine;
Yet all are one in Thee, for all are
   Thine.
Hallelujah!

5 And when the strife is fierce, the
   warfare long,
Steals on the ear the distant triumph
   song,
And hearts are strong again, and
   arms are strong.
Hallelujah!

6 The golden evening brightens in the
   west;
Soon, soon to faithful warriors
   cometh rest,
Sweet is the calm of Paradise the
   blest.
Hallelujah!

7 But lo! There breaks a yet more
   glorious day;
The saints triumphant rise in bright
   array;
The King of Glory passes on His
   way.
Hallelujah!

8 From earth's wide bounds, from
   ocean's farthest coast,
Through gates of pearl streams in
   the countless host,
Singing to Father, Son and Holy
   Ghost.
Hallelujah!

William Walsham How (1823–97)

1015   6 5. 6 5. Ter

*'Speak unto the children of Israel, that
they go forward' Exodus 14 v 15*

1 'Forward!' be our watchword,
   Steps and voices joined;
Seek the things before us,
   Not a look behind;
Burns the fiery pillar
   At our army's head;
Who shall dream of shrinking,
   By our Captain led?
Forward through the desert,
   Through the toil and fight:
Jordan flows before us,
   Zion beams with light.

2 Forward, flock of Jesus,
   Salt of all the earth,
Till each yearning purpose
   Springs to glorious birth.
Sick, they ask for healing,
   Blind, they grope for day;
Pour upon the nations
   Wisdom's loving ray.
Forward, out of error,
   Leave behind the night;
Forward through the darkness,
   Forward into light.

3 Glories upon glories
   Has our God prepared,
By the souls that love Him
   One day to be shared;
Eye has not beheld them,
   Ear has never heard,
Nor of these has uttered
   Thought or speech a word.
Forward, marching forward,
   Clad in armour bright,
Till the veil be lifted,
   Till our faith be sight.

Henry Alford (1810-71)

1016   7 7. 4 4. 7. D

'Christ is the head of the church'
Ephesians 5 v 23

1 Head of Thy church triumphant,
  We joyfully adore Thee;
  Till Thou appear
  Thy members here
  Shall sing like those in glory.
  We lift our hearts and voices
  With blest anticipation,
  And cry aloud,
  And give to God
  The praise of our salvation.

2 While in affliction's furnace,
  And passing through the fire,
  Thy love we praise,
  Which knows our days
  And ever brings us nigher.
  We clap our hands exulting
  In Thine almighty favour;
  The love divine
  Which made us Thine
  Shall keep us Thine for ever.

3 By faith we see the glory
  To which Thou shalt restore us;
  The cross despise
  For that high prize
  Which Thou hast set before us.
  And if Thou count us worthy,
  We each, as dying Stephen,
  Shall see Thee stand
  At God's right hand,
  To take us up to heaven.

Charles Wesley (1707–88)

1017   8 8. 8 8. D

'Glory to God in the highest' Luke 2 v 14

1 All glory to God in the sky,
  And peace upon earth be restored!
  O Jesus, exalted on high,
  Appear our omnipotent Lord!
  Who, meanly in Bethlehem born,
  Didst stoop to redeem a lost race,
  Once more to Thy creatures return,
  And reign in Thy kingdom of grace.

2 When Thou in our flesh didst
    appear,
  All nature acknowledged Thy birth;
  Arose the acceptable year,
  And heaven was opened on earth:
  Receiving its Lord from above,
  The world was united to bless
  The Giver of concord and love,
  The Prince and the Author of peace.

3 O wouldst Thou again be made
    known!
  Again in Thy Spirit descend,
  And set up in each of Thine own
  A kingdom that never shall end.
  Thou only art able to bless,
  And make the glad nations obey,
  And bid the dire enmity cease,
  And bow the whole world to Thy
    sway.

4 Come then to Thy servants again,
  Who long Thy appearing to know,
  Thy quiet and peaceable reign
  In mercy establish below;
  All sorrow before Thee shall fly,
  And anger and hatred be o'er,
  And envy and malice shall die,
  And discord afflict us no more.

Charles Wesley (1707–88)

1018   C.M.

'He shall glorify me' John 16 v 14

1 Come, Holy Spirit, heavenly Dove,
  With all Thy quickening powers;
  Kindle a flame of sacred love
  In these cold hearts of ours.

2 In vain we tune our formal songs,
  In vain we strive to rise;
  Hosannas languish on our tongues,
  And our devotion dies.

3 And shall we then for ever live
  At this poor dying rate?
  Our love so faint, so cold to Thee,
  And Thine to us so great?

4 Come, Holy Spirit, heavenly Dove,
With all Thy quickening powers;
Come, shed abroad the Saviour's
love,
And that shall kindle ours.

Isaac Watts (1674–1748)

1019 C.M.

Based on Hosea 6 vv 1-4

1 Come, let us to the Lord our God
With contrite hearts return;
Our God is gracious, nor will leave
The desolate to mourn.

2 His voice commands the tempest
forth,
And stills the stormy wave;
And though His arm be strong to
smite,
'Tis also strong to save.

3 Long hath the night of sorrow
reigned;
The dawn shall bring us light;
God shall appear, and we shall rise
With gladness in His sight.

4 Our hearts, if God we seek to know,
Shall know Him and rejoice;
His coming like the morn shall be,
Like morning songs His voice.

5 As dew upon the tender herb,
Diffusing fragrance round;
As showers that usher in the spring,
And cheer the thirsty ground:

6 So shall His presence bless our
souls,
And shed a joyful light;
That hallowed morn shall chase
away
The sorrows of the night.

Scottish Paraphrases 1781

1020 64.64.66.64

*'Draw nigh to God, and he will draw
nigh to you' James 4 v 8*

1 Here from the world we turn,
Jesus to seek;
Here may His loving voice
Tenderly speak.
Jesus, our dearest Friend,
While at Thy feet we bend,
O let Thy smile descend!
'Tis Thee we seek.

2 Come, Holy Comforter,
Presence divine,
Now in our longing hearts
Graciously shine;
O for Thy mighty power!
O for a blessèd shower,
Filling this hallowed hour
With joy divine!

3 Saviour, Thy work revive,
Here may we see
Those who are dead in sin
Quickened by Thee.
Come to our hearts' delight,
Make every burden light,
Cheer Thou our waiting sight;
We long for Thee.

Frances Jane Crosby (1820–1915)

1021 77.77

'The life was the light of men' John 1 v 4

1 Light of life, seraphic fire,
Love divine, Thyself impart;
Every fainting soul inspire,
Shine in every drooping heart.

2 Every mournful sinner cheer,
Scatter all our guilty gloom,
Son of God, appear, appear!
To Thy human temples come.

3 Come in this accepted hour;
Bring Thy heavenly kingdom in;
Fill us with Thy glorious power,
Rooting out the seeds of sin.

4 Nothing more can we require,
We will ask for nothing less;
Be Thou all our hearts' desire,
All our joy, and all our peace.

Charles Wesley (1707–88)

1022 C.M.

'Arise, O LORD, into thy rest; thou, and the ark of thy strength' Psalm 132 v 8

1 Light up this house with glory, Lord:
Enter and claim Thine own;
Receive the homage of our souls,
Erect Thy temple-throne.

2 We rear no altar – Thou hast died;
We deck no priestly shrine:
What need have we of creature-aid?
The power to save is Thine.

3 We ask no bright shekinah-cloud
To glorify the place;
Give, Lord, the substance of that
sign –
A plentitude of grace.

4 No rushing mighty wind we ask,
No tongues of flame desire;
Grant us the Spirit's quickening
light,
His purifying fire.

5 Light up this house with glory, Lord –
The glory of that love
Which forms and saves a church
below,
And makes a heaven above.

John Harris (1802–56)

1023 98.98

'O LORD, revive thy work in the midst of the years' Habakkuk 3 v 2

1 O Breath of life, come sweeping
through us,
Revive Thy church with life and
power,
O Breath of life, come, cleanse,
renew us,
And fit Thy church to meet this hour.

2 O Wind of God, come, bend us,
break us,
Till humbly we confess our need;
Then in Thy tenderness remake us,
Revive, restore; for this we plead.

3 O Breath of love, come, breathe
within us,
Renewing thought and will and
heart:
Come, Love of Christ, afresh to win
us,
Revive Thy church in every part.

4 Revive us Lord! Is zeal abating
While harvest fields are vast and
white?
Revive us Lord, the world is waiting,
Equip Thy church to spread the
light.

© SIM - UK / N. Europe   *Elizabeth Ann Head (1850–1936)*

1024 S.M.

'For he must reign' 1 Corinthians 15 v 25

1 O Lord our God, arise!
The cause of truth maintain,
And wide o'er all the peopled world
Extend her blessèd reign.

2 Thou Prince of life, arise!
Nor let Thy glory cease;
Far spread the conquests of Thy
grace,
And bless the earth with peace.

3 O Holy Ghost, arise!
Expand Thy quickening wing,
And o'er a dark and ruined world
Let light and order spring.

4 All on the earth, arise!
To God the Saviour sing;
From shore to shore, from earth to
heaven,
Let echoing anthems ring.

Ralph Wardlaw (1779–1853)

1025 L.M.

'Give ear, O Shepherd of Israel, thou that leadest Joseph like a flock' Psalm 80 v 1

1 O Shepherd of the church, give ear,
Lord above highest angels – hear;
Thou who didst lead Thy chosen
sheep
Safe through the desert and the
deep.

2 Lord, Thou hast planted with Thy
hands
A lovely vine in heathen lands;
How did those spreading branches
shoot
And bless the nations with their
fruit!

3 But now its beauty is defaced,
And foes have laid her fences waste;
Return, O God! How long? Return!
Nor let Thy failing vineyard mourn.

4 Lord, when this vine in Canaan
grew,
Thou gavest strength and glory too;
Kept it through years from
numerous foes
Until the Branch of promise rose.

5 Fair Branch, ordained of old to shoot
From David's stock, from Jacob's
root,
Our Saviour came to Israel's land,
Down from His throne at Thy right
hand.

6 O for His sake attend our cry,
Shine on our churches lest they die,
Turn us to Thee, revive, restore,
We shall be saved and blessed once
more.

Isaac Watts (1674–1748)

1026 C.M.

'Make thy face to shine upon thy servant' Psalm 31 v 16

1 Our God! Our God! Thou shinest
here;
Thine own this latter day:
To us Thy radiant steps appear;
We watch Thy glorious way.

2 Not only olden ages felt
The presence of the Lord;
Not only with the fathers dwelt
Thy Spirit and Thy Word.

3 Doth not the Spirit still descend
And bring the heavenly fire?
Doth not He still Thy church extend,
And waiting souls inspire?

4 Come, Holy Ghost, in us arise;
Be this Thy mighty hour,
And make Thy willing people wise
To know Thy day of power.

5 Bear us aloft, more glad, more strong
On Thy celestial wing;
And grant us grace to look and long
For our returning King.

6 He draweth near, He standeth by,
He fills our eyes, our ears;
Come, King of grace, Thy people cry,
And bring the glorious years.

Thomas Hornblower Gill (1819–1906)

1027 L.M.

'He that descended is the same also that ascended up far above all heavens' Ephesians 4 v 10

1 Our Jesus is gone up on high,
For us the blessing to receive;
It now comes streaming from the sky,
The Spirit comes, and sinners live.

2 Lord, we believe to us and ours
The apostolic promise given;
We wait the Pentecostal powers,
The Holy Ghost sent down from
heaven.

3 Ah! Leave us not to mourn below,
Or long for Thy return to pine;
Now, Lord, the Comforter bestow,
And fix in us the Guest divine.

4 Assembled here with one accord,
Calmly we wait the promised grace,
The purchase of our dying Lord:
Come, Holy Ghost, and fill the
place.

5 If every one that asks may find,
If still Thou dost on sinners fall,
Come as a mighty rushing wind;
Great grace be now upon us all.

Charles Wesley (1707–88)

1028   8 7. 8 7. D

*'Oh that thou wouldest rend the heavens,
that thou wouldest come down'*
Isaiah 64 v 1

1 Rend the heavens Thou Prince of
glory,
Melt the mountains with Thy grace;
Pour Thy presence, show Thy mercy
And the radiance of Thy face.
We believe that Thou art able
In Thy greatness and Thy love;
Make the nations fear and tremble,
As Thou comest from above.

2 Rend our hearts in sorrow sighing,
Stir our souls to seek for Thee;
Turn Thy wrath and meet our crying;
Help us from our sin to flee.
There is none that seeketh rightly,
Yet, O Father, we are Thine!
Come, O come, revive us quickly –
Make our hearts to Thee incline.

3 Thou dost meet the heart that seeks
Thee,
Righteousness His robe and joy;
Thou delightest in Thy mercy
When our souls Thy grace employ.
Since the world began its journey
Eye and ear have never seen,
All the wonders of the glory
God provides, beyond our dream.

4 Lord the sight of our condition,
Degradation is our way;
Filthy garments our destruction,
Sin would hold its evil sway.
Like a faded leaf we wither,
Causèd by the wind to fly:
Brief our life and we can never
Stay the hand that bids us die.

5 Cause us now to call upon Thee,
Call upon the Name of names;
Stir our hearts to gaze at Calvary,
There behold reviving flames.
Holy gates of Zion City,
Now let Israel see Thy face,
For the God of might and glory
Dwells within Thy holy place.

© The Author   *William Vernon Higham (b.1926)*

1029   S.M.

'O LORD, revive thy work'
Habakkuk 3 v 2

1 Revive Thy work, O Lord,
Thy mighty arm make bare;
Speak with the voice that wakes the
dead,
And make Thy people hear!

2 Revive Thy work, O Lord,
While here to Thee we bow;
Descend, O gracious Lord, descend:
O come and bless us now!

3 Revive, Thy work, O Lord,
Disturb the sleep of death;
Quicken the smouldering embers
now
By Thine almighty breath!

4 Revive Thy work, O Lord,
Create soul-thirst for Thee;
And hungering for the Bread of Life,
O may our spirits be!

5 Revive Thy work, O Lord,
Exalt Thy precious name;
And, by the Holy Ghost, our love
For Thee and Thine inflame!

6 Revive Thy work, O Lord,
And give refreshing showers;
The glory shall be all Thine own,
The blessing, Lord, be ours!

Albert Midlane (1825–1909)

1030   8 7. 8 7 (with refrain)

'There shall be showers of blessing'
Ezekiel 34 v 26

1 There shall be showers of blessing:
This is the promise of love!
There shall be seasons refreshing
Sent from the Saviour above.

Showers of blessing,
Showers of blessing we need;
Mercy-drops round us are falling
But for the showers we plead.

2 There shall be showers of blessing
Precious reviving again;
Over the hills and the valleys,
Sound of abundance of rain.

3 There shall be showers of blessing:
Send them upon us, O Lord!
Grant to us now a refreshing:
Come and now honour Thy word.

4 There shall be showers of blessing:
O that today they might fall,
Now as to God we're confessing,
Now as on Jesus we call!

Daniel Webster Whittle (1840–1901)

1031   L.M.

'O LORD, revive thy work'
Habakkuk 3 v 2

1 Thou glorious Sovereign of the skies,
And wilt Thou bow Thy gracious ear?
While feeble mortals raise their cries,
Wilt Thou, the great Jehovah, hear?

2 How shall Thy servants give Thee rest,
Till Zion's mouldering walls Thou
raise?
Till Thine own power shall stand
confessed,
And make Jerusalem a praise?

3 Triumphant here let Jesus reign,
And on His vineyard sweetly smile;
While all the virtues of His train
Adorn our church, adorn our isle.

4 On all our souls let grace descend,
Like heavenly dew in copious
showers,
That we may call our God our Friend,
That we may hail salvation ours.

5 Then shall each age and rank agree
United shouts of joy to raise;
And Zion, made a praise by Thee,
To Thee shall render back the praise.

Philip Doddridge (1702–51)

1032   L.M.

Based on Psalm 48

1 Triumphant Zion, lift thy head
From dust and ashes and the dead;
Thou, humbled long, awake at
length,
And gird thee with thy Saviour's
strength.

2 Put all thy beauteous garments on,
And let thine excellence be known;
Decked in the robe of righteousness,
The world thy glories shall confess.

3 No more shall foes unclean invade,
And fill thy hallowed walls with
dread;
No more shall hell's insulting host
Their victory and thy sorrows boast.

4 God from on high has heard thy
prayer;
His hand thy ruins shall repair;
Reared and adorned by love divine
Thy towers and battlements shall
shine.

5 Grace shall dispose my heart and
voice
To share and echo back her joys;
Nor will thy watchful Monarch cease
To guard thee in eternal peace.

Philip Doddridge (1702–51)

1033 C.M.

'Pour out your heart before him'
Psalm 62 v 8

1 Approach, my soul, the mercy-seat,
Where Jesus answers prayer;
There humbly fall before His feet,
For none can perish there.

2 Thy promise is my only plea;
With this I venture nigh;
Thou calledst burdened souls to
Thee,
And such, O Lord, am I!

3 Bowed down beneath a load of sin,
By Satan sorely pressed,
By war without, and fears within,
I come to Thee for rest.

4 Be Thou my shield and hiding-place,
That, sheltered near Thy side,
I may my fierce accuser face,
And tell him Thou hast died.

5 O wondrous love! To bleed and die,
To bear the cross and shame,
That guilty sinners such as I,
Might plead Thy gracious name!

John Newton (1725–1807)

1034 S.M.

'Let us therefore come boldly unto the
throne of grace' Hebrews 4 v 16

1 Behold the throne of grace,
The promise calls us near;
There Jesus shows a smiling face,
And waits to answer prayer.

2 That rich atoning blood,
Which sprinkled round we see,
Provides for those who come to God
An all-prevailing plea.

3 Beyond our utmost wants
His love and power can bless;
To praying souls He always grants
More than they can express.

4 Thine image, Lord, bestow,
Thy presence and Thy love;
We ask to serve Thee here below,
And reign with Thee above.

5 Abiding in Thy faith,
Our will conformed to Thine,
Let us victorious be in death,
And then in glory shine.

John Newton (1725–1807)

1035 78.78.88

'Watch and pray' Matthew 26 v 41

1 Blessed Jesus, at Thy word
We are gathered all to hear Thee;
Let our minds and wills be stirred
Now to seek and love and fear Thee;
By Thy teachings true and holy
Drawn from earth to love Thee
solely.

2 All our knowledge, sense and sight,
Lie in deepest darkness shrouded,
Till Thy Spirit breaks our night
With the beams of truth unclouded;
Thou alone to God canst win us,
Thou must work all good within us.

3 Glorious Lord, Thyself impart,
Light of light, from God proceeding,
Open Thou each mind and heart,
Help us by Thy Spirit's pleading.
Hear the cry Thy church now raises;
Lord, accept our prayers and praises.

Tobias Clausnitzer (1619–84)
Tr. Catherine Winkworth (1827–78)

1036 77.77

'Ask, and it shall be given you' Luke 11 v 9

1 Come, my soul, thy suit prepare,
Jesus loves to answer prayer;
He Himself has bid thee pray,
Therefore will not say thee nay.

2 Thou art coming to a King,
Large petitions with thee bring;
For His grace and power are such,
None can ever ask too much.

3 With my burden I begin:
  Lord, remove this load of sin;
  Let Thy blood, for sinners spilt,
  Set my conscience free from guilt.

4 Lord, I come to Thee for rest;
  Take possession of my breast;
  There Thy blood-bought right
       maintain,
  And without a rival reign.

5 While I am a pilgrim here,
  Let Thy love my spirit cheer;
  As my Guide, my Guard, my Friend,
  Lead me to my journey's end.

6 Show me what I have to do;
  Every hour my strength renew;
  Let me live a life of faith;
  Let me die Thy people's death.

John Newton (1725–1807)

1037   L.M.

'For I will appear in the cloud upon the
mercy seat' *Leviticus 16 v 2*

1 From every stormy wind that blows,
  From every swelling tide of woes,
  There is a calm, a safe retreat:
  'Tis found beneath the mercy seat.

2 There is a place where Jesus sheds
  The oil of gladness on our heads,
  A place than all beside more sweet;
  It is the blood-stained mercy seat.

3 There is a spot where spirits blend,
  Where friend holds fellowship with
       friend;
  Though sundered far, by faith we
       meet
  Around one common mercy seat.

4 There, there, on eagle wing we soar,
  And time and sense seem all no
       more,
  And heaven comes down our souls
       to greet,
  And glory crowns the mercy seat.

5 O let my hands forget their skill,
  My tongue be silent, cold, and still,
  This bounding heart forget to beat,
  If I forget the mercy seat!

Hugh Stowell (1799–1865)

1038   7 7 7. 5

'Like as a father pitieth his children, so
the Lord pitieth them that fear him'
Psalm 103 v 13

1 God of pity, God of grace,
  When we humbly seek Thy face,
  Bend from heaven, Thy dwelling-
       place;
  Hear, forgive, and save.

2 When we in Thy temple meet,
  Spread our wants before Thy feet,
  Pleading at Thy mercy seat,
  Look from heaven and save.

3 When Thy love our hearts shall fill,
  And we long to do Thy will,
  Turning to Thy holy hill,
  Lord, accept and save.

4 Should we wander from Thy fold,
  And our love to Thee grow cold,
  With a pitying eye behold;
  Lord, forgive and save.

5 Should the hand of sorrow press,
  Earthly care and want distress,
  May our souls Thy peace possess;
  Jesus, hear and save.

6 And whate'er our cry may be,
  When we lift our hearts to Thee,
  From our burden set us free;
  Hear, forgive, and save.

Eliza Frances Morris (1821–74)

1039   C.M.

'Lord teach us to pray' *Luke 11 v 1*

1 Great Shepherd of Thy people, hear;
  Thy presence now display;
  As Thou hast given a place for prayer,
  So give us hearts to pray.

2 Show us some tokens of Thy love,
Our fainting hopes to raise;
And pour Thy blessing from above,
That we may render praise.

3 Within these walls let holy peace,
And love and concord dwell;
Here give the troubled conscience
ease,
The wounded spirit heal.

4 May we in faith receive Thy Word,
In faith present our prayers,
And in the presence of our Lord
Unburden all our cares.

5 The hearing ear, the seeing eye,
The contrite heart bestow:
And shine upon us from on high,
That we in grace may grow.

John Newton (1725–1807)

1040   L.M.

'Lo, I am with you alway'
Matthew 28 v 20

1 Head of the church and Lord of all,
Hear from Thy throne our suppliant
call:
We come the promised grace to
seek,
Of which aforetime Thou didst
speak.

2 'Lo, I am with you' – that sweet
word,
Lord Jesus, meekly be it heard,
And stamped with all-inspiring
power
On our weak souls this favoured
hour.

3 Without Thy presence, King of
saints,
Our purpose fails, our spirit faints;
Thou must our wavering faith renew,
Ere we can yield Thee service true.

4 Thy consecrating might we ask –
Or vain the toil, unblest the task;
And impotent of fruit will be
Love's holiest effort wrought for
Thee.

5 'Lo, I am with you' – even so,
Thy joy our strength, we fearless go:
And praise shall crown the
suppliant's call,
Head of the church, and Lord of all!

Joseph Tritton (1819–87)

1041   6 5. 6 5

'Jesus himself stood in the midst of them'
Luke 24 v 36

1 Jesus! stand among us
In Thy risen power,
Let this time of worship
Be a hallowed hour.

2 Breathe Thy Holy Spirit
Into every heart,
Bid the fears and sorrows
From each soul depart.

3 Thus with quickened footsteps,
We'll pursue our way,
Watching for the dawning
Of eternal day.

William Pennefather (1816–73)

1042   8 8. 8 8. 8 8

'The Spirit also helpeth our infirmities'
Romans 8 v 26

1 Jesus, Thou sovereign Lord of all,
The same through one eternal day,
Attend Thy feeblest followers' call,
And O instruct us how to pray!
Pour out Thy supplicating grace,
And stir us up to seek Thy face.

2 We cannot think a gracious thought,
We cannot feel a good desire,
Till Thou, who call'dst a world from
nought,
The power into our hearts inspire;
And then we in Thy Spirit groan,
And then we give Thee back Thine
own.

3 Jesus, regard the joint complaint
Of all Thy tempted followers here,
And now supply the common want,
And send us down the Comforter;
The Spirit of ceaseless prayer impart,
And fix Thy Agent in our heart.

4 To help our soul's infirmity,
To heal Thy sin-sick people's care,
To urge our God-commanding plea,
And make our hearts a house of
prayer,
The promised Intercessor give,
And let us now Thyself receive.

5 Come in Thy pleading Spirit down
To us who for Thy coming stay;
Of all Thy gifts we ask but one,
We ask the constant power to pray:
Indulge us, Lord, in this request;
Thou canst not then deny the rest.

Charles Wesley (1707–88)

1043   L.M.

*'I dwell ... with him also that is of a
contrite and humble spirit'
Isaiah 57 v 15*

1 Jesus, where'er Thy people meet,
There they behold Thy mercy seat;
Where'er they seek Thee Thou art
found,
And every place is hallowed ground.

2 For Thou, within no walls confined,
Inhabitest the humble mind;
Such ever bring Thee where they
come,
And going, take Thee to their home.

3 Dear Shepherd of Thy chosen few,
Thy former mercies here renew;
Here to our waiting hearts proclaim
The sweetness of Thy saving name.

4 Here may we prove the power of
prayer,
To strengthen faith and sweeten
care,
To teach our faint desires to rise,
And bring all heaven before our
eyes.

5 Lord, we are few, but Thou art near,
Nor short Thine arm, nor deaf Thine
ear;
O rend the heavens, come quickly
down,
And make a thousand hearts Thine
own!

William Cowper (1731–1800)

1044   L.M.

*'There am I in the midst of them'
Matthew 18 v 20*

1 Lord Jesus Christ, we seek Thy face;
Within the veil we bow the knee;
O let Thy glory fill the place,
And bless us while we wait on Thee.

2 We thank Thee for the precious blood
That purged our sins and brought us
nigh,
And cleansed and sanctified to God,
Thy holy name to magnify.

3 Shut in with Thee, far, far above
The restless world that wars below,
We seek to learn and prove Thy love,
Thy wisdom and Thy grace to know.

4 The brow that once with thorns was
bound,
Thy hands, Thy side, we fain would
see;
Draw near, Lord Jesus, glory-
crowned,
And bless us while we wait on Thee.

Alexander Stewart (1843–1923)

1045
C.M.

'Lord, teach us to pray' Luke 11 v 1

1 Lord, teach us how to pray aright,
With reverence and with fear;
Though dust and ashes in Thy sight,
We may, we must draw near.

2 We perish if we cease from prayer;
O grant us power to pray!
And when to meet Thee we prepare,
O meet us by the way.

3 Burdened with guilt, convinced of
sin,
In weakness, want and woe,
Fightings without, and fears within;
Lord, whither shall we go?

4 God of all grace, we come to Thee
With broken, contrite hearts;
Give what Thine eye delights to see,
Truth in the inward parts.

5 Give deep humility; the sense
Of godly sorrow give;
A strong, desiring confidence
To hear Thy voice and live.

6 Faith is the only sacrifice
That can for sin atone;
To cast our hopes, to fix our eyes,
On Christ, on Christ alone.

7 Patience to watch and wait and
weep,
Though mercy long delay;
Courage, our fainting souls to keep,
And trust Thee though Thou slay.

8 Give these, and then Thy will be
done;
Thus strengthened with Thy might,
We by Thy Spirit and Thy Son
Shall pray, and pray aright.

James Montgomery (1771–1854)

1046
7 7.7 7

'I will not let thee go, except thou bless
me' Genesis 3 2 v 2 6

1 Lord, we come before Thee now;
At Thy feet we humbly bow:
O do not our suit distain!
Shall we seek Thee, Lord, in vain?

2 Lord, on Thee our souls depend:
In compassion now descend;
Fill our hearts with Thy rich grace;
Tune our lips to sing Thy praise.

3 In Thine own appointed way,
Now we seek Thee; here we stay;
Lord, from hence we would not go,
Till a blessing Thou bestow.

4 Send some message from Thy Word,
That may joy and peace afford;
Let Thy Spirit now impart
Full salvation to each heart.

5 Comfort those who weep and
mourn;
Let the time of joy return;
Those that are cast down lift up;
Make them strong in faith and hope.

6 Grant that those who seek may find
Thee a God supremely kind;
Heal the sick, the captive free;
Let us all rejoice in Thee.

William Hammond (1718–83)

1047
C.M.

'A broken and contrite heart'
Psalm 5 1 v 1 7

1 Lord, when we bend before Thy
throne,
And our confessions pour,
Teach us to feel the sins we own,
And hate what we deplore.

2 Our broken spirits pitying see,
True penitence impart;
Then let a kindling glance from Thee
Beam hope upon the heart.

3 When we disclose our wants in prayer,
May we our wills resign;
That not a thought may enter there
Which is not wholly Thine.

4 May faith each weak petition fill,
And waft it to the skies,
And teach our hearts 'tis goodness still
That grants it or denies.

Joseph Dacre Carlyle (1758–1804)

1048   S.M.

*'Our fellowship is with the Father, and
with his Son Jesus Christ' 1 John 1 v 3*

1 Our heavenly Father calls,
And Christ invites us near;
With both, our friendship shall be
   sweet,
And our communion dear.

2 God pities all our griefs;
He pardons every day;
Almighty to protect our souls,
And wise to guide our way.

3 How large His bounties are!
What various stores of good,
Diffused with our Redeemer's hand,
And purchased with His blood!

4 Jesus, our living Head,
We bless Thy faithful care;
Our Advocate before the throne,
And our Forerunner there.

5 Here fix, my roving heart!
Here wait, my warmest love!
Till the communion be complete
In nobler scenes above.

Philip Doddridge (1702–51)

1049   S.M.

Based on Matthew 6 vv 9-13

1 Our heavenly Father, hear
The prayer we offer now;
Thy name be hallowed far and near,
To Thee all nations bow.

2 Thy kingdom come! Thy will
On earth be done in love,
As saints and seraphim fulfil
Thy perfect law above.

3 Our daily bread supply,
While by Thy Word we live;
The guilt of our iniquity
Forgive, as we forgive.

4 From dark temptation's power,
From Satan's wiles defend;
Deliver in the evil hour,
And guide us to the end.

5 Thine, then, for ever be
Glory and power divine;
The sceptre, throne and majesty
Of heaven and earth are Thine.

James Montgomery (1771–1854)

1050   D.S.M.

*'Men ought always to pray, and not to
faint' Luke 18 v 1*

1 Pray, without ceasing pray,
Your Captain gives the word;
His summons cheerfully obey,
And call upon the Lord:
To God your every want
In instant prayer display;
Pray always; pray, and never faint;
Pray, without ceasing pray!

2 In fellowship, alone,
To God with faith draw near,
Approach His courts, besiege His
   throne
With all the powers of prayer:
Go to His temple, go,
Nor from His altar move;
Let every house His worship know,
And every heart His love.

3 Pour out your souls to God,
And bow them with your knees,
And spread your hearts and hands
    abroad,
And pray for Zion's peace;
Your guides and brethren bear
For ever on your mind;
Extend the arms of mighty prayer,
In grasping all mankind.

4 From strength to strength go on,
Wrestle, and fight, and pray,
Tread all the powers of darkness
    down,
And win the well-fought day;
Still let the Spirit cry
In all His soldiers: 'Come!'
Till Christ the Lord descend from
    high,
And take the conquerors home.

Charles Wesley (1707–88)

1051   D.C.M.

*'Praying always with all prayer and
supplication in the Spirit'*
Ephesians 6 v 18

1 Prayer is the soul's sincere desire,
Uttered or unexpressed,
The motion of a hidden fire
That trembles in the breast.
Prayer is the burden of a sigh,
The falling of a tear,
The upward glancing of an eye
When none but God is near.

2 Prayer is the simplest form of speech
That infant lips can try;
Prayer, the sublimest strains that
    reach
The Majesty on high.
Prayer is the Christian's vital breath,
The Christian's native air,
His watchword at the gate of death;
He enters heaven with prayer.

3 Prayer is the contrite sinner's voice,
Returning from his ways;
While angels in their songs rejoice
And cry, 'Behold, he prays!'
O Thou by whom we come to God,
The Life, the Truth, the Way!
The path of prayer Thyself hast trod;
Lord, teach us how to pray!

James Montgomery (1771–1854)

1052   C.M.

*'I will not let thee go, except thou bless
me' Genesis 32 v 26*

1 Shepherd divine, our wants relieve
In this our evil day,
To all Thy tempted followers give
The power to watch and pray.

2 Long as our fiery trials last,
Long as the cross we bear,
O let our souls on Thee be cast
In never-ceasing prayer!

3 The Spirit of interceding grace
Give us in faith to claim;
To wrestle till we see Thy face,
And know Thy hidden name.

4 Till Thou Thy perfect love impart,
Till Thou Thyself bestow,
Be this the cry of every heart:
I will not let Thee go –

5 I will not let Thee go, unless
Thou tell Thy name to me,
With all Thy great salvation bless,
And make me all like Thee.

6 Then let me on the mountain-top
Behold Thy open face,
Where faith in sight is swallowed
    up,
And prayer in endless praise.

Charles Wesley (1707–88)

1053

87.87.D

'His ears are open unto their prayers'
1 Peter 3 v 12

1 What a Friend we have in Jesus,
All our sins and griefs to bear!
What a privilege to carry
Everything to God in prayer!
O what peace we often forfeit,
O what needless pain we bear,
All because we do not carry
Everything to God in prayer!

2 Have we trials and temptations?
Is there trouble anywhere?
We should never be discouraged:
Take it to the Lord in prayer.
Can we find a friend so faithful,
Who will all our sorrows share?
Jesus knows our every weakness:
Take it to the Lord in prayer.

3 Are we weak and heavy-laden,
Cumbered with a load of care?
Precious Saviour, still our refuge:
Take it to the Lord in prayer.
Do your friends despise, forsake
thee?
Take it to the Lord in prayer;
In His arms He'll take and shield
thee;
Thou wilt find a solace there.

Joseph Medlicott Scriven (1819–86)

1054

L.M.

'He will answer thee' Isaiah 30 v 19

1 What various hindrances we meet
In coming to the mercy seat;
Yet who that knows the worth of
prayer,
But wishes to be often there.

2 Prayer makes the darkened cloud
withdraw,
Prayer climbs the ladder Jacob saw;
Gives exercise to faith and love,
Brings every blessing from above.

3 Restraining prayer, we cease to fight;
Prayer makes the Christian's armour
bright;
And Satan trembles, when he sees
The weakest saint upon his knees.

4 While Moses stood with arms spread
wide,
Success was found on Israel's side;
But when through weariness they
failed,
That moment Amalek prevailed.

5 Have you no words? Ah, think again,
Words flow apace when you complain;
And fill your fellow creature's ear
With the sad tale of all your care.

6 Were half the breath thus vainly
spent,
To heaven in supplication sent;
Your cheerful song would oftener be,
'Hear what the Lord has done for
me.'

William Cowper (1731–1800)

1055

C.M.

'Lord, teach us to pray' Luke 11 v 1

1 When cold our hearts, and far from
Thee
Our wandering spirits stray,
And thoughts and lips move heavily,
Lord, teach us how to pray.

2 Too vile to venture near Thy throne,
Too poor to turn away,
Depending on Thy help alone,
Lord, teach us how to pray.

3 We know not how to seek Thy face
Unless Thou lead the way;
We have no words, unless Thy grace,
Lord, teach us how to pray.

4 Here every thought and fond desire
We on Thine altar lay;
And when our souls have caught Thy
fire,
Lord, teach us how to pray.

John Samuel Bewley Monsell (1811–75)

1056

7 6. 7 6. D

*'Buried with him in baptism, wherein
also ye are risen with him'*
Colossians 2 v 12

1 Around Thy grave, Lord Jesus,
Thine empty grave, we stand,
With hearts all full of gladness,
To keep Thy blest command;
By faith our souls rejoicing
To trace Thy path of love,
Through death's dark angry billows,
Up to the throne above.

2 Lord Jesus, we remember
The travail of Thy soul,
When in Thy love's deep pity
The waves did o'er Thee roll:
Baptized in death's cold waters,
For us Thy blood was shed;
For us the Lord of glory
Was numbered with the dead.

3 O Lord, Thou now art risen,
Thy travail all is o'er,
For sin Thou once hast suffered,
Thou liv'st to die no more!
Sin, death and hell are vanquished
By Thee, Thy church's Head:
And lo! we share Thy triumphs,
Thou First-born from the dead.

4 Into Thy death baptized,
We own with Thee we died;
With Thee, our Life, are risen,
And in Thee glorified;
From sin, the world and Satan,
We're ransomed by Thy blood,
And now would walk as strangers
Alive with Thee to God.

James George Deck (1802–84)

1057

L.M.

*'Baptising them in the name of the
Father, and of the Son, and of the Holy
Ghost' Matthew 28 v 19*

1 Come, Holy Spirit, Dove divine,
On these baptismal waters shine,
And teach our hearts in highest
strain
To praise the Lamb for sinners slain.

2 We love Thy name, we love Thy laws,
And joyfully embrace Thy cause,
We love Thy cross, the shame, the
pain,
O Lamb of God, for sinners slain.

3 And as we rise with Thee to live,
O let the Holy Spirit give
The sealing unction from above,
The breath of life, the fire of love.

Adoniram Judson (1788–1850)

1058

C.M.

*'Buried with him in baptism, wherein
also ye are risen with him'*
Colossians 2 v 12

1 Come, ye who bow to sovereign
grace,
Record Immanuel's love;
Join in a song of noble praise
To Him who reigns above.

2 Once in the gloomy grave He lay,
But, by His rising power,
He bore the gates of death away:
Hail, mighty Conqueror!

3 Buried with Him beneath this flood,
We glory in His death:
We own our great incarnate God,
And rise with Him by faith.

4 As saints of old confessed His name
In Jordan's flowing tide,
So we adore the stricken Lamb,
Renouncing all beside.

5 No trust in water do we place,
  'Tis but an outward sign;
  The great reality is grace,
  The fountain, blood divine.

vv 1-2, 4-5 Maria De Fleury (d.c.1794)
v 3 Charles Haddon Spurgeon (1834–92)

1059 L.M.

'And I, if I be lifted up from the earth,
will draw all men unto me' John 12 v 32

1 Glory to God, whose Spirit draws
  Fresh soldiers to the Saviour's cause,
  Who thus, baptized into His name,
  His goodness and their faith
    proclaim.

2 For these now added to the host,
  Who in their Lord and Saviour boast,
  And consecrate to Him their days,
  Accept, O God, our grateful praise.

3 Thus may Thy mighty Spirit draw
  All here to love and keep His law;
  Themselves His subjects to declare,
  And place themselves beneath His
    care.

4 Lead them at once their Lord to own,
  To glory in His cross alone;
  And then, baptized, His truth to
    teach,
  His love to share, His heaven to
    reach.

Baptist Wriothesley Noel (1799–1873)

1060 8 7. 8 7. 4 7

'If any man will come after me, let him
deny himself, and take up his cross, and
follow me' Matthew 16 v 24

1 Hast Thou said, exalted Jesus,
  'Take thy cross and follow Me?'
  Shall the word with terror seize us?
  Shall we from the burden flee?
  Lord, I'll take it,
  And, rejoicing, follow Thee.

2 Sweet the sign that thus reminds me,
  Saviour, of Thy love for me;
  Sweeter still the love that binds me
  In its deathless bond to Thee:
  O what pleasure,
  Buried with my Lord to be!

3 Then, baptized in love and glory,
  Lamb of God, Thy praise I'll sing;
  Loudly with the immortal story
  All the harps of heaven shall ring:
  Saints and angels
  Sound it loud from every string.

John Eustace Giles (1805–75)

1061 C.M.

'For thou, O God, hast heard my vows'
Psalm 61 v 5

1 Witness, ye men and angels now,
  Before the Lord we speak;
  To Him we make our solemn vow,
  A vow we dare not break;

2 That, long as life itself shall last,
  Ourselves to Christ we yield;
  Nor from His cause will we depart,
  Or ever quit the field.

3 We trust not in our native strength,
  But on His grace rely,
  That, with returning wants, the Lord
  Will all our need supply.

4 O guide our doubtful feet aright,
  And keep us in Thy ways;
  And while we turn our vows to
    prayers,
  Turn Thou our prayers to praise.

Benjamin Beddome (1717–95)

1062 S.M.

'Peace I leave with you, my peace I give
unto you' John 14 v 27

1 A parting hymn we sing
  Around Thy table, Lord;
  Again our grateful tribute bring,
  Our solemn vows record.

2 Here we have seen Thy face,
And felt Thy presence near;
So may the savour of Thy grace
In word and life appear.

3 In self-forgetting love
Be our communion shown,
Until we join the church above,
And know as we are known.

Aaron Robarts Wolfe (1821–1902)

1063   C.M.

'This do in remembrance of me'
Luke 22 v 19

1 According to Thy gracious Word,
In meek humility,
This will I do, my dying Lord,
I will remember Thee.

2 Thy body, broken for my sake,
My bread from heaven shall be;
Thy testamental cup I take,
And thus remember Thee.

3 Gethsemane can I forget?
Or there Thy conflict see,
Thine agony and bloody sweat,
And not remember Thee?

4 When to the cross I turn my eyes,
And rest on Calvary,
O Lamb of God, my Sacrifice!
I must remember Thee:

5 Remember Thee, and all Thy pains,
And all Thy love to me:
Yes, while a breath, a pulse remains,
Will I remember Thee.

6 And when these failing lips grow
dumb,
And mind and memory flee,
When Thou shalt in Thy kingdom
come,
Jesus, remember me.

James Montgomery (1771–1854)

1064   L.M.

'Then ... came Jesus and stood in the
midst' John 20 v 19

1 Amidst us our Belovèd stands,
And bidst us view His piercèd hands;
Points to His wounded feet and side,
Blest emblems of the Crucified.

2 What food luxurious loads the
board,
When at His table sits the Lord!
The wine how rich, the bread how
sweet,
When Jesus deigns the guests to meet!

3 If now, with eyes defiled and dim,
We see the signs but see not Him,
O may His love the scales displace,
And bid us see Him face to face!

4 Our former transports we recount,
When with Him in the holy mount,
These cause our souls to thirst anew
His marred but lovely face to view.

5 Thou glorious Bridegroom of our
hearts,
Thy present smile a heaven imparts;
O lift the veil, if veil there be,
Let every saint Thy beauties see!

Charles Haddon Spurgeon (1834–92)

1065   66.66.88

'The Lord's table' 1 Corinthians 10 v 21

1 Author of life divine,
Who hast a table spread,
Furnished with mystic wine
And everlasting bread,
Preserve the life Thyself hast given,
And feed and train us up for heaven.

2 Our needy souls sustain
With fresh supplies of love,
Till all Thy life we gain
And all Thy fullness prove,
And, strengthened by Thy perfect
grace,
Behold without a veil Thy face.

Charles Wesley (1707–88)

1066 C.M.

'And now abideth faith, hope, charity,
these three' 1 Corinthians 13 v 13

1 Be known to us in breaking bread,
But do not then depart;
Saviour, abide with us, and spread
Thy table in our heart.

2 There sup with us in love divine;
Thy body and Thy blood,
That living bread, that heavenly wine,
Be our immortal food.

3 We would not live by bread alone,
But by Thy Word of grace,
In strength of which we travel on
To our abiding place.

vv 1 & 2 James Montgomery (1771–1854)
v 3 Anonymous

1067 77.77.77

'For my flesh is meat indeed, and my
blood is drink indeed' John 6 v 55

1 Bread of heaven! on Thee I feed,
For Thy flesh is meat indeed:
Ever may my soul be fed
With the true and living bread;
Day by day with strength supplied
Through the life of Him who died.

2 Vine of heaven! Thy blood supplies
This blest cup of sacrifice:
'Tis Thy wounds my healing give;
To Thy cross I look and live:
Thou my Life, O let me be
Rooted, grafted, built on Thee!

Josiah Conder (1789–1855)

1068 88.84

'Ye do show the Lord's death till he come'
1 Corinthians 11 v 26

1 By Christ redeemed, in Christ
restored,
We keep the memory adored,
And show the death of our dear Lord
Until He come.

2 His body broken in our stead
Is seen in this memorial bread,
And so our feeble love is fed
Until He come.

3 The drops of His dread agony,
His life-blood shed for us, we see;
The wine shall tell the mystery
Until He come.

4 And thus that dark betrayal-night
With the last advent we unite,
By one blest chain of loving rite,
Until He come:

5 Until the trump of God be heard,
Until the ancient graves be stirred,
And with the great commanding
word
The Lord shall come.

6 O blessèd hope! With this elate,
Let not our hearts be desolate,
But, strong in faith, in patience wait
Until He come.

George Rawson (1807–89)

1069 S.M.

'Until that day' Matthew 26 v 29

1 Dear Lord, before we part
From Thy sweet earthly feast,
Give us the earnest in our heart
Of Thine eternal rest.

2 Lift up our drooping eyes
To the great banquet there;
And ever for the crowning prize
Our waiting souls prepare.

3 So each a glorious seat
Shall in Thy kingdom claim;
And there, in heavenly triumph, eat
The supper of the Lamb.

Psalms and Hymns 1858

1070

77.76

'Thanks be unto God for his unspeakable gift' 2 Corinthians 9 v 15

1 For the bread and for the wine,
For the pledge that seals Him mine,
For the words of love divine,
We give Thee thanks, O Lord.

2 For the words that turn our eye
To the cross of Calvary,
Bidding us in faith draw nigh,
We give Thee thanks, O Lord.

3 For the words that tell of home,
Pointing us beyond the tomb,
'Do ye this, until I come!'
We give Thee thanks, O Lord.

4 Till He come we take the bread,
Type of Him on whom we feed,
Him who liveth and was dead!
We give Thee thanks, O Lord.

5 Till He come we take the cup;
As we at His table sup,
Eye and heart are lifted up!
We give Thee thanks, O Lord.

6 For that coming, here foreshown,
For that day to man unknown,
For the glory and the throne,
We give Thee thanks, O Lord.

Horatius Bonar (1808–89)

1071

10 10. 10 10

'Called unto the fellowship of his Son' 1 Corinthians 1 v 9

Part One

1 Here, O my Lord, I see Thee face to
face;
Here would I touch and handle
things unseen,
Here grasp with firmer hand the
eternal grace,
And all my weariness upon Thee
lean.

2 Here would I feed upon the bread of
God,
Here drink with Thee the royal wine
of heaven;
Here would I lay aside each earthly
load,
Here taste afresh the calm of sin
forgiven.

3 Mine is the sin, but Thine the
righteousness;
Mine is the guilt, but Thine the
cleansing blood!
Here is my robe, my refuge and my
peace –
Thy blood, Thy righteousness, O
Lord my God.

4 This is the hour of banquet and of
song;
This is the heavenly table spread for
me;
Here let me feast, and, feasting, still
prolong
The brief, bright hour of fellowship
with Thee.

Part Two

5 Too soon we rise; the symbols
disappear;
The feast, though not the love, is
past and gone;
The bread and wine remove, but
Thou art here,
Nearer than ever, still my Shield and
Sun.

6 I have no help but Thine; nor do I
need
Another arm save Thine to lean
upon;
It is enough, my Lord, enough
indeed;
My strength is in Thy might, Thy
might alone.

7 Feast after feast thus comes and
   passes by,
   Yet, passing, points to the glad feast
   above,
   Giving sweet foretaste of the festal
   joy,
   The Lamb's great bridal feast of bliss
   and love.

Horatius Bonar (1808–89)

1072 C.M.

*'Then came Jesus, the doors being shut,
and stood in the midst' John 20 v 26*

1 How sweet and awesome is the place
   With Christ within the doors,
   While everlasting love displays
   The choicest of her stores.

2 Here, all the mercy of our God
   With soft compassion rolls;
   Here peace and pardon, bought with
   blood,
   Is food for dying souls.

3 While all our hearts and all our
   songs
   Join to admire the feast,
   Each of us cry, with thankful
   tongues,
   Lord, why was I a guest?

4 Why was I made to hear Thy voice,
   And enter while there's room?
   When thousands make a wretched
   choice,
   And rather starve than come.

5 'Twas the same love that spread the
   feast,
   That sweetly forced us in;
   Else we had still refused to taste
   And perished in our sin.

Isaac Watts (1674–1748)

1073 66.66

'My soul thirsteth for thee' Psalm 63 v 1

1 I hunger and I thirst;
   Jesus, my manna be;
   Ye living waters, burst
   Out of the rock for me.

2 Thou bruised and broken Bread,
   My life-long wants supply;
   As living souls are fed,
   O feed me, or I die.

3 Thou true life-giving Vine,
   Let me Thy sweetness prove;
   Renew my life with Thine,
   Refresh my soul with love,

4 Rough paths my feet have trod,
   Since first their course began;
   Feed me, Thou Bread of God;
   Help me, Thou Son of Man.

5 For still the desert lies
   My thirsting soul before;
   O living waters, rise
   Within me evermore.

John Samuel Bewley Monsell (1811–75)

1074 C.M.

*'His great love wherewith he loved us'
Ephesians 2 v 4*

1 In memory of the Saviour's love,
   We keep the sacred feast,
   Where every humble contrite heart
   Is made a welcome guest.

2 By faith we take the bread of life,
   With which our souls are fed;
   And drink the token of His blood
   That was for sinners shed.

3 Under His banner thus we sing
   The wonders of His love,
   And thus anticipate by faith
   The heavenly feast above.

Thomas Cotterill (1779–1823) Altd

1075　　S.M.

*'For as the body is one, and hath many
members … so also is Christ'*
1 Corinthians 12 v 12

1 Jesus invites His saints
To meet around His board;
Here pardoned rebels sit and hold
Communion with their Lord.

2 This holy bread and wine
Maintain our fainting breath,
By union with our living Lord,
And interest in His death.

3 Our heavenly Father calls
Christ and His members one;
We the young children of His love,
And He the first-born Son.

4 We are but several parts
Of the same broken bread;
One body hath its several limbs,
But Jesus is the Head.

5 Let all our powers be joined
His glorious name to raise;
Pleasure and love fill every mind,
And every voice be praise.

Isaac Watts (1674–1748)

1076　　S.M.

*'He brought me to the banqueting house,
and his banner over me was love'*
Song of Solomon 2 v 4

1 Jesus, we thus obey
Thy last and kindest word;
Here in Thine own appointed way
We come to meet our Lord.

2 Our hearts we open wide,
To make the Saviour room;
And lo! the Lamb, the Crucified,
The sinner's Friend is come.

3 Thus we remember Thee,
And take this bread and wine
As Thine own dying legacy,
And our redemption's sign.

4 With high and heavenly bliss
Thou dost our spirits cheer;
Thy house of banqueting is this,
And Thou hast brought us here.

5 Thy presence makes the feast;
Now let our spirits feel
The glory not to be expressed,
The joy unspeakable.

6 Now let our souls be fed
With manna from above,
And over us Thy banner spread
Of everlasting love.

Charles Wesley (1707–88)

1077　　L.M.

'We would see Jesus' John 12 v 21

1 Lord in this blest and hallowed hour
Reveal Thy presence and Thy power;
Show to my faith Thy hands and side,
My Lord and God, the Crucified!

2 Fain would I find a calm retreat
From vain distractions near Thy feet;
And, borne above all earthly care,
Be joyful in Thy house of prayer.

3 Or let me through the opening skies
Catch one bright glimpse of Paradise,
And realize, with raptured awe,
The vision dying Stephen saw.

4 But, if unworthy of such joy,
Still shall Thy love my heart employ;
For, of Thy favoured children's fare,
'Twere bliss the very crumbs to share.

5 Yet never can my soul be fed
With less than Thee, the living Bread;
Thyself unto my soul impart,
And with Thy presence fill my heart.

Josiah Conder (1789–1855)

1078

77.77.77

*'For as often as ye eat this bread, and
drink this cup, ye do show the Lord's
death till he come'* 1 Corinthians 11 v 26

1 Meeting in the Saviour's name,
Breaking bread by His command,
To the world we thus proclaim
On what ground we hope to stand,
When the Lord shall come with
    clouds,
Joined by heaven's exulting crowds.

2 From the cross our hope we draw,
'Tis the sinner's blest resource;
Jesus magnified the law;
Jesus bore its awful curse:
What a joyful truth is this!
O how full of hope it is!

3 Jesus died and then arose;
Yes, He rose, He lives, He reigns!
Jesus vanquished all His foes,
Jesus led them all in chains:
His the triumph and the crown,
His the glory and renown.

4 Sing we then of Him who died,
Sing of Him who rose again;
By His blood we're justified,
And with Him we hope to reign:
Yes, we wait to see our Lord,
And to share His bright reward.

Thomas Kelly (1769–1855)

1079

L.M.

'That ye may eat and drink at my table'
Luke 22 v 30

1 My God, and is Thy table spread?
And does Thy cup with love
    o'erflow?
Thither be all Thy children led,
And let them all its sweetness know.

2 Why are these emblems still in vain
Before unwilling hearts displayed?
Was not for you the Victim slain?
Are you forbid the children's bread?

3 O let Thy table honoured be,
And furnished well with joyful
    guests;
And may each soul salvation see,
That here its sacred pledges tastes.

4 Revive Thy dying churches, Lord,
And bid our drooping graces live;
And more, that energy afford
A Saviour's grace alone can give.

Philip Doddridge (1702–51)

1080

10 10. 10 10

*'I will come in to him, and will sup with
him, and he with me'* Revelation 3 v 20

1 Not worthy, Lord, to gather up the
    crumbs
With trembling hand that from Thy
    table fall,
A weary heavy-laden sinner comes
To plead Thy promise and obey Thy
    call.

2 I am not worthy to be thought Thy
    child,
Nor sit the last and lowest at Thy
    board;
Too long a wanderer, and too oft
    beguiled,
I only ask one reconciling word.

3 One word from Thee, my Lord, one
    smile, one look,
And I could face the cold, rough
    world again;
And with that treasure in my heart
    could brook
The wrath of devils and the scorn of
    men.

4 I hear Thy voice: Thou bidd'st me
    come and rest;
I come, I kneel, I clasp Thy piercèd
    feet;
Thou bidd'st me take my place, a
    welcome guest,
Among Thy saints, and of Thy
    banquet eat.

5 My praise can only breathe itself in
   prayer,
   My prayer can only lose itself in
   Thee;
   Dwell Thou for ever in my heart, and
   there,
   Lord, let me sup with Thee: sup
   Thou with me.

Edward Henry Bickersteth (1825–1906)

1081   8 8. 8 6

*'Yea, I have loved thee with an
everlasting love' Jeremiah 31 v 3*

1 O Saviour, I have nought to plead,
  In earth beneath, or heaven above,
  But just my own exceeding need,
  And Thy exceeding love.

2 The need will soon be past and gone,
  Exceeding great, but quickly o'er;
  Thy love unbought is all Thine own,
  And lasts for evermore.

Jane Crewdson (1809–63)

1082   C.M.

'I am that bread of life' John 6 v 48

1 O Thou who this mysterious bread
  Didst in Emmaus break,
  Return herewith our souls to feed
  And to Thy followers speak.

2 Unseal the volume of Thy grace,
  Apply the gospel word,
  Open our eyes to see Thy face,
  Our hearts to know the Lord.

3 Of Thee we commune still, and
   mourn
   Till Thou the veil remove,
   Talk with us, and our hearts shall
   burn
   With flames of fervent love.

4 Enkindle now the heavenly zeal,
  And make Thy mercy known,
  And give our pardoning souls to feel
  That God and love are one.

Charles Wesley (1707–88)

1083   7 6. 7 6. D

*'The Lord Jesus the same night in which
he was betrayed took bread'
1 Corinthians 11 v 23*

1 On that same night, Lord Jesus,
  In which Thou wast betrayed,
  When without cause man's hatred
  Against Thee was displayed,
  We hear Thy gracious accents:
  This do; remember Me;
  With joyful hearts responding
  We would remember Thee.

2 We think of all the darkness
  Which round Thy spirit pressed,
  Of all those waves and billows
  Which rolled across Thy breast;
  'Tis there Thy grace unbounded
  And perfect love we see;
  With joy and yet with sorrow
  We do remember Thee.

3 We know Thee now as risen,
  The First-born from the dead;
  We see Thee now ascended,
  The Church's glorious Head:
  In Thee by grace accepted,
  With heart and mind set free,
  We think of all Thy sorrow,
  And thus remember Thee.

4 Till Thou shalt come in glory
  And call us hence away,
  To share with Thee the brightness
  Of that unclouded day,
  We show Thy death, Lord Jesus,
  And here would seek to be
  More to that death conformed
  Whilst we remember Thee.

George West Fraser (1840–96)

1084

77.76

'This is my body which is given for you:
this do in remembrance of me'
Luke 22 v 19

1 Saviour, we remember Thee!
Thy deep woe and agony,
All Thy suffering on the tree:
Saviour, we adore Thee.

2 Calvary! O Calvary!
Mercy's vast unfathomed sea,
Love, eternal love to me:
Saviour, we adore Thee.

3 Darkness hung around Thy head,
When for sin Thy blood was shed,
Victim in the sinner's stead:
Saviour, we adore Thee.

4 Jesus, Lord, Thou now art risen!
Thou hast all our sins forgiven;
Haste we to our home in heaven:
Saviour, we adore Thee.

5 Soon with joyful, glad surprise
We shall hear Thy word: 'Arise!'
Mounting upward to the skies:
Glory, glory, glory!

6 Saviour, we Thy love adore;
We will praise Thee more and more;
Spread Thy name from shore to
    shore,
Saviour, we adore Thee.

Samuel Trevor Francis (1834–1925)

1085

87.87.47

'The angel of the LORD that stood
amongst the myrtle trees'
Zechariah 1 v 11

1 See among the myrtles standing
One so worthy of my love,
Though but dimly I perceive Him
Far all earthly things above;
Hail that morning
When I'll see Him as He is!

2 Rose of Sharon, so men name Him,
White and ruddy, form so fair,
Far excelling all ten thousand
Of the world's delights so rare:
Friend of sinners,
He's their Pilot o'er the sea.

3 What have I to do henceforward
With base idols of the earth?
When compared with my great Jesus
All, I vouch, are nothing worth:
O to linger
All my lifetime in His love.

Ann Griffiths (1776–1805)
© The Translator   *Tr. Graham Stuart Harrison (b.1935)*

1086

S.M.

'Until that day when I drink it new with
you in my Father's kingdom'
Matthew 26 v 29

1 Sweet feast of love divine!
'Tis grace that makes us free
To feed upon this bread and wine,
In memory, Lord, of Thee.

2 Here every welcome guest
Waits, Lord, from Thee to learn
The secrets of Thy Father's breast,
And all Thy grace discern.

3 Here conscience ends its strife,
And faith delights to prove
The sweetness of the Bread of life,
The fullness of Thy love.

4 The blood that flowed for sin;
In symbol here we see,
And feel the blessèd pledge within
That we are loved of Thee.

5 O if this glimpse of love
Is so divinely sweet,
What will it be, O Lord, above,
They gladdening smile to meet?

6 To see Thee face to face,
Thy perfect likeness wear,
And all Thy ways of wondrous grace
Through endless years declare!

Edward Denny (1796–1889)

1087

87.87

'Her sins, which are many, are forgiven;
for she loved much' Luke 7 v 47

1 Sweet the moments, rich in blessing,
Which before the cross I spend,
Life and health, and peace
    possessing
From the sinner's dying Friend!

2 Here I rest, in wonder viewing
All my sins on Jesus laid,
And a full redemption flowing
From the sacrifice He made.

3 Here I find my hope of heaven,
While upon the Lamb I gaze;
Loving much, and much forgiven,
Let my heart o'erflow in praise.

4 Love and grief my heart dividing,
With my tears His feet I'll bathe,
Constant still in faith abiding,
Life deriving from His death.

5 Lord, in ceaseless contemplation
Fix my thankful heart on Thee!
Till I taste Thy full salvation,
And Thine unveiled glory see.

William Walter Shirley (1725–86) and others
Based on James Allen (1734–1804)

1088

77.77.77.

'Till he come' 1 Corinthians 11 v 26

1 Till He come! O let the words
Linger on the trembling chords!
Let the little while between
In their golden light be seen;
Let us think how heaven and home
Lie beyond that till He come!

2 When the weary ones we love
Enter on their rest above,
Seems the earth so poor and vast,
All our life-joy overcast:
Hush! be every murmur dumb,
It is only till He come!

3 Clouds and conflicts round us press;
Would we have one sorrow less?
All the sharpness of the cross,
All that tells the world is loss,
Death and darkness and the tomb,
Only whisper, till He come!

4 See, the feast of love is spread,
Drink the wine and break the bread;
Sweet memorials, till the Lord
Call us round His heavenly board;
Some from earth, from glory some,
Severed only till He come!

Edward Henry Bickersteth (1825–1906)

1089

C.M.

'For the transgression of my people was
he stricken' Isaiah 53 v 8

1 To Calvary, Lord, in spirit now
Our weary souls repair,
To dwell upon Thy dying love,
And taste its sweetness there.

2 Sweet resting-place of every heart
That feels the plague of sin,
Yet knows that deep mysterious joy,
The peace of God within.

3 There through Thine hour of deepest
    woe,
Thy suffering spirit passed;
Grace there its wondrous victory
    gained,
And love endured its last.

4 Dear suffering Lamb! Thy bleeding
    wounds,
With cords of love divine,
Have drawn our willing hearts to
    Thee,
And linked our life with Thine.

5 Our longing eyes would fain behold
That bright and blessèd brow,
Once wrung with bitterest anguish,
    wear
Its crown of glory now.

6 Why linger then? Come, Saviour,
  come,
Responsive to our call;
Come, claim Thy ancient power and
  reign,
The Heir and Lord of all.

Edward Denny (1796–1889)

1090   7 7. 7 7

*'And when they were come to the place,
which is called Calvary, there they
crucified him' Luke 23 v 33*

1 When on Calvary I rest,
God in flesh made manifest,
Shines in my Redeemer's face,
Full of beauty, truth, and grace.

2 Here I would for ever stay,
Weep and gaze my soul away;
Thou art heaven on earth to me,
Lovely, mournful, Calvary.

James Montgomery (1771–1854)

1091   8 7. 8 7. D

*'While the king sitteth at his table'
Song of Solomon 1 v 12*

1 While in sweet communion feeding
On this earthly bread and wine,
Saviour, may we see Thee bleeding
On the cross to make us Thine!
Now our eyes we would be closing
To this fleeting world below,
And, upon Thyself reposing,
More of grace and mercy know.

2 Though unseen, be ever near us,
With the still small voice of love,
Whispering words of peace to cheer
  us,
Every doubt and fear remove;
Bring before us all the story
Of Thy life, and death of woe,
And, with hopes of endless glory,
Wean our hearts from all below.

Edward Denny (1796–1889)

1092   8 8. 8 8. 8 8

*'I am thine, save me; for I have sought
thy precepts' Psalm 119 v 94*

1 Behold the servant of the Lord!
I wait Thy guiding eye to feel,
To hear and keep Thy every word,
To prove and do Thy perfect will,
Joyful from my own works to cease,
Glad to fulfil all righteousness.

2 Me, if Thy grace vouchsafe to use,
Meanest of all Thy creatures me,
The deed, the time, the manner
  choose,
Let all my fruit be found in Thee;
Let all my works in Thee be
  wrought,
By Thee to full perfection brought.

3 My every weak though good design,
O'errule, or change, as seems Thee
  meet;
Jesus, let all my work be Thine!
Thy work, O Lord, is all complete,
And pleasing in Thy Father's sight;
Thou only hast done all things right.

4 Here then to Thee Thy own I leave;
Mould as thou wilt Thy passive clay;
But let me all Thy stamp receive,
But let me all Thy words obey,
Serve with a single heart and eye,
And to Thy glory live and die.

Charles Wesley (1707–88)

1093   L.M.

*'Strive together with me in your prayers
to God for me' Romans 15 v 30*

1 Father of mercies, bow Thine ear,
Attentive to our earnest prayer;
We plead for those who plead for
  Thee;
Successful pleaders may they be!

2 How great their work, how vast their
charge!
Do Thou their anxious souls enlarge:
Their best acquirements are our
gain;
We share the blessings they obtain.

3 Clothe, then, with energy divine,
Their words, and let those words be
Thine;
To them Thy sacred truth reveal,
Suppress their fear, inflame their
zeal.

4 Teach them to sow the precious
seed,
Teach them Thy chosen flock to
feed;
Teach them immortal souls to gain,
Souls that will well reward their
pain.

5 Let thronging multitudes around
Hear from their lips the joyful
sound,
In humble strains Thy grace
implore,
And feel Thy new-creating power.

Benjamin Beddome (1717–95)

1094   88.88.88

'And now abideth faith, hope, charity,
these three; but the greatest of these is
charity' 1 Corinthians 13 v 13

1 Give me the faith which can remove
And sink the mountain to a plain;
Give me the child-like praying love,
Which longs to build Thy house again;
Thy love, let it my heart o'erpower,
And all my simple soul devour.

2 I want an even strong desire,
I want a calmly fervent zeal,
To save poor souls out of the fire,
To snatch them from the verge of
hell,
And turn them to a pardoning God,
And quench the brands in Jesu's
blood.

3 I would the precious time redeem,
And longer live for this alone,
To spend, and to be spent, for them
Who have not yet my Saviour known;
Fully on these my mission prove,
And only breathe to breathe Thy
love.

4 My talents, gifts, and graces, Lord,
Into Thy blessèd hand receive;
And let me live to preach Thy Word,
And let me to Thy glory live;
My every sacred moment spend
In publishing the sinners' Friend.

5 Enlarge, inflame, and fill my heart
With boundless charity divine!
So shall I all my strength exert,
And love them with a zeal like Thine;
And lead them to Thy open side,
The sheep for whom their Shepherd
died.

Charles Wesley (1707–88)

1095   S.M.

'How beautiful are the feet of them that
preach the gospel of peace'
Romans 10 v 15

1 How beauteous are their feet
Who stand on Zion's hill,
Who bring salvation on their
tongues
And words of peace reveal!

2 How charming is their voice,
How sweet the tidings are!
Zion, behold thy Saviour King,
He reigns and triumphs here.

3 How happy are our ears,
That hear this joyful sound,
Which kings and prophets waited
for,
And sought but never found!

4 How blessèd are our eyes,
That see this heavenly light!
Prophets and kings desired it long,
But died without the sight.

5 The watchmen join their voice,
And tuneful notes employ:
Jerusalem breaks forth in song,
And deserts learn the joy.

6 The Lord makes bare His arm
Through all the earth abroad;
Let every nation now behold
Their Saviour and their God.

Isaac Watts (1674–1748)

1096   8 8 6. D

'Prayer was made without ceasing of the church unto God for him' Acts 12 v 5

1 Lord of the church, we humbly pray
For those who guide us in Thy way,
And speak Thy holy Word;
With love divine their hearts inspire,
And touch their lips with hallowed fire,
And needful grace afford.

2 Help them to preach the truth of God
Redemption through the Saviour's blood;
Nor let Thy Spirit cease
On all the church His gifts to shower –
To them, a messenger of power,
To us, of life and peace.

3 So may they live to Thee alone;
Then hear the welcome word, 'Well done!'
And take their crown above;
Enter into their Master's joy,
And all eternity employ
In praise and bliss and love!

Edward Osler (1798–1863)

1097   L.M.

'Let thy priests be clothed with righteousness' Psalm 132 v 9

1 Pour out Thy Spirit from on high,
Lord, Thine ordainèd servants bless;
Graces and gifts to each supply,
And clothe them with Thy righteousness.

2 Within Thy temples when they stand,
To teach the truth, as taught by Thee,
Saviour, like stars in Thy right hand
The angels of the churches be!

3 Wisdom and zeal and faith impart,
Firmness with meekness, from above,
To bear Thy people on their heart,
And love the souls whom Thou dost love;

4 To watch and pray, and never faint,
By day and night strict guard to keep,
To warn the sinner, cheer the saint,
Nourish Thy lambs and feed Thy sheep;

5 Then, when their work is finished here,
And they in hope their charge resign,
When the Chief Shepherd shall appear,
May they, O God, in glory shine!

James Montgomery (1771–1854)

1098   6 6. 6 6. D

'The LORD make his face shine upon thee' Numbers 6 v 25

1 Shine Thou upon us, Lord,
True Light of men, to-day;
And through the written word
Thy very self display;
That so, from hearts which burn
With gazing on Thy face,
Thy people here may learn
The wonders of Thy grace.

2 Breathe Thou upon us, Lord,
Thy Spirit's living flame,
That so with one accord
Our lips may tell Thy name;
Give Thou the hearing ear,
Fix Thou the wandering thought,
That those we teach may hear
The great things Thou hast wrought.

3 Speak Thou for us, O Lord,
In all we say of Thee;
According to Thy word
Let all our teaching be;
That so Thy lambs may know
Their own true Shepherd's voice,
Where'er He leads them go,
And in His love rejoice.

4 Live Thou within us, Lord;
Thy mind and will be ours;
Be Thou beloved, adored,
And served, with all our powers;
That so our lives may teach
Thy children what Thou art,
And plead, by more than speech,
For Thee with every heart.

John Ellerton (1826–93)

1099   8 8 6. D

'For without me ye can do nothing'
John 15 v 5

1 The means of grace are in my hand,
The blessing is at God's command,
Who must the work fulfil;
And though I read, and watch and
pray,
Yet here the Lord directs my way,
And worketh all things still.

2 I cannot speak a proper word,
Nor think aright, but from the Lord
Preparing heart and tongue;
In nature I can see no good,
But all my good proceeds from God,
And does to grace belong.

3 I see it now, and do confess
My utter need of Jesus' grace,
And of His Spirit's light;
I beg His kind and daily care;
O Lord, my heart and tongue
prepare
To think and speak aright.

4 Prepare my heart to love Thee well,
And love Thy truth which doth excel,
And love Thy children dear;
Instruct me how to live by faith,
And feel the virtue of Thy death,
And find Thy presence near,

5 Prepare my tongue to pray and
praise,
To speak of providential ways,
And heavenly truth unfold;
To strengthen well a feeble soul,
Correct the wanton, rouse the dull,
And silence sinners bold.

John Berridge (1716–93)

1100   L.M.

'Receive him therefore in the Lord with all
gladness; and hold such in reputation'
Philippians 2 v 29

1 We bid thee welcome in the name
Of Jesus our exalted Head;
Come as a servant: so He came;
And we receive thee in His stead.

2 Come as a shepherd: guard and keep
This fold from hell and earth and
sin;
Nourish the lambs, and feed the
sheep,
The wounded heal, the lost bring in.

3 Come as a watchman: take thy stand
Upon thy tower amidst the sky;
And when the sword comes on the
land,
Call us to fight, or warn to fly.

4 Come as an angel, hence to guide
A band of pilgrims on their way;
That, safely walking at thy side,
We fail not, faint not, turn nor stray.

5 Come as a teacher, sent from God,
Charged His whole counsel to
declare:
Lift o'er our ranks the prophet's rod,
While we uphold thy hands with
prayer.

James Montgomery (1771–1854)

THE GREAT COMMISSION

1101   87.87.D

*'Go ye into all the world, and preach the
gospel to every creature' Mark 16 v 15*

1 'For My sake and the gospel's, go
And tell redemption's story;'
His heralds answer, 'Be it so,
And Thine, Lord, all the glory!'
They preach His life, His birth, His
   cross,
The love of His atonement,
For whom they count the world but
   loss,
His rising, His enthronement.

2 Hark, hark, the trump of jubilee
Proclaims to every nation,
From pole to pole, by land and sea,
Glad tidings of salvation.
As nearer draws the day of doom,
While still the battle rages,
The heavenly Day-spring through
   the gloom
Breaks on the night of ages.

3 Still on and on the anthems spread
Of hallelujah voices,
In concert with the holy dead
The warrior church rejoices;
Their snow-white robes are washed
   in blood,
Their golden harps are ringing;
Earth and the paradise of God
One triumph-song are singing.

4 He comes, whose advent-trumpet
   drowns
The last of time's evangels,
Immanuel crowned with many
   crowns,
The Lord of saints and angels:
O Life, Light, Love, the great I AM,
Triune, who changest never,
The throne of God and of the Lamb
Is Thine, and Thine for ever!

Edward Henry Bickersteth (1825–1906)

1102   L.M.

*'Go ye therefore, and teach all nations'
Matthew 28 v 19*

1 Go quickly, for the fading hours
With haste are sinking in the west;
Exert with zeal thy ransomed powers,
Nor think it yet the time for rest.

2 Go quickly, for the sons of time
Are journeying to a hopeless grave,
And tell to earth's remotest clime
Of Him who came to seek and save.

3 Go quickly to the realms of sin;
Invite as many as you find;
And welcome all to enter in –
The poor, the maimed, the halt, the
   blind.

4 Go quickly with the living Word
Sent to the nations from above,
Till every heart on earth has heard
The tidings of redeeming love.

     William Wileman (1848–1944)

1103 L.M.

'O LORD God of Abraham, Isaac and Israel, our fathers' 1 Chronicles 29 v 18

1 Great God of Abraham! Hear our
  prayer;
  Let Abraham's seed Thy mercy
  share:
  O may they now at length return
  And look on Him they pierced, and
  mourn!

2 Remember Jacob's flock of old;
  Bring home the wanderers to Thy
  fold;
  Remember too Thy promised word,
  'Israel at last shall seek the Lord.'

3 Though outcasts still, estranged
  from Thee,
  Cut off from their own olive tree,
  Why should they longer such
  remain?
  For Thou canst graft them in again.

4 Lord, put Thy law within their
  hearts,
  And write it in their inward parts;
  The veil of darkness rend in two,
  Which hides Messiah from their
  view.

5 O haste the day, foretold so long,
  When Jew and Greek, a glorious
  throng,
  One house shall seek, one prayer
  shall pour,
  And one Redeemer shall adore!

Thomas Cotterill (1779–1823)

1104 6 6. 6 6. 4 4. 4 4

'But unto you that fear my name shall the Sun of righteousness arise with healing in his wings' Malachi 4 v 2

1 In doubt and dread dismay,
  Midst superstition's gloom,
  The godless grope their way,
  And joyless reach the tomb:
  No holy light,
  No healing ray
  Of gospel day
  Has blessed their sight.

2 Rise, Sun of Righteousness,
  And on Thy gracious wing,
  Be pleased to heal and bless,
  And Thy salvation bring.
  Let darkened minds
  Thy brightness see;
  O set them free
  From sin that blinds.

3 With searching beams explore
  The dark strongholds of sin;
  And on sin's prisoners pour
  Transforming light within:
  Bright Morning-Star,
  Unveil Thy face,
  And shed Thy grace
  Both near and far.

4 Lord Jesus, Light of life!
  Arouse the world from sleep;
  Send love in place of strife,
  And joy to those who weep:
  Great King of kings,
  Thy Spirit give,
  That souls may live
  Beneath Thy wings!

William Henry Havergal (1793–1870) Altd

1105 C.M.

'The armies which were in heaven followed him' Revelation 19 v 14

1 Lift up your heads, ye gates of brass,
  Ye bars of iron, yield,
  And let the King of glory pass;
  The cross is in the field.

2 Ye armies of the living God,
His dedicated host,
Where hallowed footsteps never trod
Take your appointed post.

3 Follow the cross; the ark of peace
Accompany your path;
To slaves and rebels bring release
From bondage and from wrath.

4 Though few and small and weak
your bands,
Strong in your Captain's strength,
Go to the conquest of all lands;
All must be His at length.

5 Then fear not, faint not, halt not
now;
Quit you like men, be strong;
To Christ shall all the nations bow,
And sing the triumph-song:

6 Uplifted are the gates of brass,
The bars of iron yield;
Behold the King of glory pass;
The cross hath won the field.

James Montgomery (1771–1854) Altd

1106   L.M.

'To give light to them that sit in darkness' Luke 1 v 79

1 O Christ, our true and only Light,
Illumine those who sit in night;
Let those afar now hear Thy voice,
And in Thy fold with us rejoice.

2 And all who else have strayed from
Thee,
O gently seek! Thy healing be
To every wounded conscience given,
And let them also share Thy heaven.

3 O make the deaf to hear Thy Word,
And teach the dumb to speak, dear
Lord,
Who dare not yet the faith avow,
Though secretly they hold it now.

4 Shine on the darkened and the cold,
Recall the wanderers from Thy fold;
Those now unite who walk apart,
Confirm the weak and doubting
heart.

5 So they with us may evermore
Such grace with wondering thanks
adore,
And endless praise to Thee be given
By all Thy church in earth and
heaven.

Johann Heermann (1585–1647)
Tr. Catherine Winkworth (1827–78)

1107   L.M.

'Unto the uttermost part of the earth'
Acts 1 v 8

1 Send forth the gospel! Let it run
Southward and northward, east and
west;
Tell all the earth Christ died and lives
Who giveth pardon, life, and rest.

2 Send forth Thy gospel, gracious
Lord!
Thine was the blood for sinners
shed;
Thy voice still pleads in human
hearts;
To Thee Thine other sheep be led.

3 Send forth Thy gospel, holy Lord!
Kindle in us love's sacred flame;
Love giving all and grudging naught
For Jesus' sake, in Jesus' name.

4 Send forth the gospel! Tell it out!
Go, brothers, at the Master's call;
Prepare His way, who comes to reign
The King of kings and Lord of all.

Henry E. Fox (1841–1926)

1108

87.87.47

'Go ye therefore, and teach all nations ...
and, lo, I am with you alway'
Matthew 28 vv 19, 20

1 Speed Thy servants, Saviour, speed
    them;
  Thou art Lord of winds and waves:
  They were bound, but Thou hast
    freed them;
  Now they go to free the slaves.
  Be Thou with them:
  'Tis Thine arm alone that saves.

2 Friends, and home, and all
    forsaking,
  Lord, they go at Thy command;
  As their stay Thy promise taking,
  While they traverse sea and land:
  O be with them!
  Lead them safely by the hand.

3 When they think of home, now
    dearer
  Than it ever seemed before,
  Bring the promised glory nearer,
  Let them see that peaceful shore,
  Where Thy people
  Rest from toil and weep no more.

4 Where no fruit appears to cheer
    them,
  And they seem to toil in vain,
  Then in mercy, Lord, draw near
    them,
  Then their sinking hopes sustain;
  Thus supported,
  Let their zeal revive again.

5 In the midst of opposition,
  Let them trust, O Lord, in Thee;
  When success attends their mission,
  Let Thy servants humbler be;
  Never leave them,
  Till Thy face in heaven they see:

6 There to reap in joy for ever
  Fruit that grows from seed here
    sown,
  There to be with Him who never
  Ceases to preserve His own,
  And with gladness
  Give the praise to Him alone.

Thomas Kelly (1769–1855)

1109

73.73.77.73

'All the ends of the earth shall see the
salvation of our God' Isaiah 52 v 10

1 We have heard the joyful sound:
  Jesus saves!
  Spread the tidings all around:
  Jesus saves!
  Bear the news to every land,
  Climb the steeps and cross the
    waves;
  Onward! 'tis our Lord's command:
  Jesus saves!

2 Sing above the battle strife:
  Jesus saves!
  By His death and endless life,
  Jesus saves!
  Shout it brightly through the gloom,
  When the heart for mercy craves;
  Sing in triumph o'er the tomb:
  Jesus saves!

3 Give the winds a mighty voice:
  Jesus saves!
  Let the nations now rejoice:
  Jesus saves!
  Shout salvation full and free;
  Highest hills and deepest caves;
  This our song of victory:
  Jesus saves!

Priscilla Jane Owens (1829–1907)

1110 87.87.D

'Behold, I lay in Sion a chief corner stone'
1 Peter 2 v 6

1 Ye that know the Lord is gracious,
  Ye for whom a Cornerstone
  Stands, of God elect and precious,
  Laid that ye may build thereon,
  See that on that sure foundation
  Ye a living temple raise,
  Towers that may tell forth salvation,
  Walls that may re-echo praise.

2 Living stones, by God appointed
  Each to his allotted place,
  Kings and priests, by God anointed,
  Shall ye not declare his grace?
  Ye, a royal generation,
  Tell the tidings of your birth,
  Tidings of a new creation
  To an old and weary earth.

3 Tell the praise of Him who called
    you
  Out of darkness into light,
  Broke the fetters that enthralled you,
  Gave you freedom, peace and sight:
  Tell the tale of sins forgiven,
  Strength renewed and hope
    restored,
  Till the earth, in tune with heaven,
  Praise and magnify the Lord!

© Copyright Control *Cyril Argentine Alington (1872–1955)*

1111 L.M.

'Awake, awake, put on strength, O arm
of the LORD' Isaiah 51 v 9

1 Arm of the Lord, awake, awake!
  Thy power unconquerable take;
  Thy strength put on, assert Thy
    might,
  And triumph in the dreadful fight.

2 Why dost Thou tarry, mighty Lord?
  Why slumbers in its sheath Thy
    sword?
  O rouse Thee, for Thine honour's
    sake;
  Arm of the Lord, awake, awake!

3 Behold, what numbers still
    withstand
  Thy sovereign rule and just command,
  Reject Thy grace, Thy threats despise,
  And hurl defiance at the skies.

4 Haste then, but come not to destroy;
  Mercy is Thine, Thy crown, Thy joy:
  Their hatred quell, their pride
    remove,
  But melt with grace, subdue with
    love.

5 Why dost Thou from the conquest
    stay?
  Why do Thy chariot wheels delay?
  Lift up Thyself, hell's kingdom
    shake;
  Arm of the Lord, awake, awake!

Henry March (1791–1869)

1112 C.M.

Based on Isaiah 2 vv 2-6

1 Behold, the mountain of the Lord
  In latter days shall rise
  On mountain tops above the hills,
  And draw the wondering eyes.

2 To this the joyful nations round,
  All tribes and tongues shall flow;
  Up to the hill of God, they'll say,
  And to His house we'll go.

3 The beam that shines from Zion's
    hill
  Shall lighten every land;
  The King who reigns in Salem's
    towers
  Shall all the world command.

4 Among the nations He shall judge;
  His judgements truth shall guide;
  His sceptre shall protect the just,
  And quell the sinner's pride.

5 No strife shall rage, nor hostile feuds
  Disturb those peaceful years;
  To ploughshares men shall beat
    their swords,
  To pruning-hooks their spears.

6 Come then, O come from every land,
  To worship at His shrine;
  And, walking in the light of God,
  With holy beauties shine.

Michael Bruce (1746–67)

1113   77.77

'Thy kingdom come' Matthew 6 v 10

1 Father, let Thy kingdom come,
  Let it come with living power!
  Speak at length the final word,
  Usher in the triumph hour.

2 As it came in days of old,
  In the deepest hearts of men,
  When Thy martyrs died for Thee,
  Let it come, O God, again!

3 Tyrant thrones and idol shrines,
  Let them from their place be hurled:
  Enter on Thy better reign,
  Wear the crown of Thine own world.

4 O what long, sad years have gone,
  Since Thy church was taught this
      prayer!
  O what eyes have watched and wept
  For the dawning everywhere!

5 Break, triumphant day of God!
  Break at last, our hearts to cheer;
  Throbbing souls and holy songs
  Wait to hail Thy dawning here.

6 Empires, temples, sceptres, thrones –
  May they all for God be won;
  And, in every human heart,
  Father, let Thy kingdom come!

John Page Hopps (1834–1911)

1114   77.77.77

Based on Psalm 67

1 God of mercy! God of grace!
  Show the brightness of Thy face;
  Shine upon us, Saviour, shine;
  Fill Thy church with light divine;
  And Thy saving health extend
  Unto earth's remotest end.

2 Let the people praise Thee, Lord;
  Be by all that live adored:
  Let the nations shout and sing
  Glory to their Saviour King;
  At Thy feet their tribute pay,
  And Thy holy will obey.

3 Let the people praise Thee, Lord;
  Earth shall then her fruits afford;
  God to man His blessings give;
  Man to God devoted live:
  All below, and all above,
  One in joy and light and love.

Henry Francis Lyte (1793–1847)

1115   76.76.D

Based on Psalm 72

1 Hail to the Lord's Anointed,
  Great David's greater Son!
  Hail, in the time appointed,
  His reign on earth begun!
  He comes to break oppression,
  To set the captive free,
  To take away transgression,
  And rule in equity.

2 He shall come down like showers
  Upon the fruitful earth,
  And love, joy, hope, like flowers,
  Spring in His path to birth:
  Before Him on the mountains
  Shall peace, the herald, go;
  And righteousness, in fountains,
  From hill to valley flow.

3 Kings shall fall down before Him,
  And gold and incense bring;
  All nations shall adore Him,
  His praise all people sing;
  To Him shall prayer unceasing
  And daily vows ascend;
  His kingdom still increasing,
  A kingdom without end.

4 He comes with succour speedy
To those who suffer wrong;
To help the poor and needy,
And bid the weak be strong;
To give them songs for sighing,
Their darkness turn to light,
Whose souls, condemned and dying,
Were precious in His sight.

5 O'er every foe victorious,
He on His throne shall rest;
From age to age more glorious,
All-blessing and all-blest:
The tide of time shall never
His covenant remove;
His name shall stand for ever,
His changeless name of Love.

James Montgomery (1771–1854)

1116 Irregular

'This is indeed the Christ, the Saviour of the world' John 4 v 42

1 I cannot tell why He, whom angels
worship,
Should set His love upon the sons of
men,
Or why, as Shepherd, He should
seek the wanderers,
To bring them back, they know not
how or when.
But this I know, that He was born of
Mary,
When Bethlehem's manger was His
only home,
And that He lived at Nazareth and
laboured,
And so the Saviour, Saviour of the
world, is come.

2 I cannot tell how silently He suffered,
As with His peace He graced this
place of tears,
Or how His heart upon the cross was
broken,
The crown of pain to three and thirty
years.
But this I know, He heals the
broken-hearted,
And stays our sin, and calms our
lurking fear,
And lifts the burden from the heavy
laden,
For yet the Saviour, Saviour of the
world, is here.

3 I cannot tell how He will win the
nations,
How He will claim His earthly
heritage,
How satisfy the needs and aspirations
Of East and West, of sinner and of
sage.
But this I know, all flesh shall see
His glory,
And He shall reap the harvest He has
sown,
And some glad day His sun shall
shine in splendour
When He the Saviour, Saviour of the
world, is known.

4 I cannot tell how all the lands shall
worship,
When, at His bidding, every storm is
stilled,
Or who can say how great the
jubilation
When all the hearts of men with love
are filled.
But this I know, the skies will thrill
with rapture,
And myriad, myriad human voices
sing,
And earth to heaven, and heaven to
earth will answer:
At last the Saviour, Saviour of the
world, is King!

William Young Fullerton (1857–1932)

1117

87.87.47

Based on Psalm 45 vv 1-6

1 Let us sing the King Messiah,
King of righteousness and peace;
Hail Him, all His happy subjects,
Never let His praises cease:
Ever hail Him;
Never let His praises cease.

2 How transcendent are Thy glories,
Fairer than the sons of men,
While Thy blessèd meditation
Brings us back to God again:
Blest Redeemer,
How we triumph in Thy reign!

3 Gird Thy sword on, mighty Hero!
Make the Word of truth Thy car;
Prosper in Thy course majestic;
All success attend Thy war!
Gracious Victor,
Let mankind before Thee bow!

4 Majesty combined with meekness,
Righteousness and peace unite
To ensure Thy blessèd conquests;
On, great Prince, assert Thy right:
Ride triumphant
All around the conquered globe.

5 Blest are all that touch Thy sceptre;
Blest are all that own Thy reign,
Freed from sin, that worst of tyrants,
Rescued from its galling chain:
Saints and angels,
All who know Thee bless Thy reign.

John Ryland (1753–1825)

1118

C.M.

'There shall come a Star out of Jacob'
Numbers 24 v 17

1 Light of the lonely pilgrim's heart,
Star of the coming day!
Arise, and with Thy morning beams
Chase all our griefs away.

2 Come, blessèd Lord, bid every shore
And answering island sing
The praises of Thy royal name,
And own Thee as their King.

3 Bid the whole earth, responsive now
To the bright world above,
Break forth in rapturous strains of
joy
In memory of Thy love.

4 Jesus, Thy fair creation groans,
The air, the earth, the sea,
In unison with all our hearts,
And calls aloud for Thee.

5 Thine was the cross, with all its
fruits
Of grace and peace divine;
Be Thine the crown of glory now,
The palm of victory Thine.

Edward Denny (1796–1889)

1119

87.87.D

'And what I say unto you I say unto all,
Watch' Mark 13 v 37

1 Lord, her watch Thy church is
keeping;
When shall earth Thy rule obey?
When shall end the night of
weeping?
When shall break the promised day?
See the whitening harvest languish,
Waiting still the labourers' toil;
Was it vain, Thy Son's deep anguish?
Shall the strong retain the spoil?

2 Tidings, sent to every creature,
Millions yet have never heard;
Can they hear without a preacher?
Lord Almighty, give the Word:
Give the Word; in every nation
Let the gospel trumpet sound,
Witnessing a world's salvation
To the earth's remotest bound.

3 Then the end: Thy church
   completed,
All Thy chosen gathered in,
With their King in glory seated,
Satan bound, and banished sin;
Gone for ever parting, weeping,
Hunger, sorrow, death, and pain:
Lo! her watch Thy church is keeping;
Come, Lord Jesus, come to reign!

Henry Downton (1818–85)

1120   7 6. 7 6. D

*'I say unto you, Lift up your eyes, and
look on the fields; for they are white
already to harvest' John 4 v 35*

1 Lord of the living harvest
That whitens o'er the plain,
Where angels soon shall gather
Their sheaves of golden grain;
Accept these hands to labour,
These hearts to trust and love,
And deign with them to hasten
Thy kingdom from above.

2 As labourers in Thy vineyard,
Still faithful may we be,
Content to bear with burden
Of weary days for Thee;
We ask no other wages,
When Thou shalt call us home,
But to have shared the travail
That makes Thy kingdom come.

3 Come down, Thou Holy Spirit,
And fill our souls with light,
Clothe us in spotless raiment,
In vesture clean and white;
Within Thy sacred temple
Be with us, where we stand,
And sanctify Thy people
In this and every land.

4 Be with us, God the Father!
Be with us, God the Son!
Be with us, God the Spirit!
O blessèd Three in One!
Make us a royal priesthood,
Thee rightly to adore,
And fill us with Thy fullness,
Both now and evermore.

John Samuel Bewley Monsell (1811–75)

1121   8 8. 8 8. 8 8

Based on Psalm 45 vv 1-4

1 My heart is full of Christ, and longs
Its glorious matter to declare!
Of him I make my loftier songs,
I cannot from His praise forbear;
My ready tongue makes haste to sing
The glories of my heavenly King.

2 Fairer than all the earth-born race,
Perfect in comeliness Thou art;
Replenished are Thy lips with grace,
And full of love Thy tender heart:
God ever blest! we bow the knee,
And own all fullness dwells in Thee.

3 Gird on Thy thigh the Spirit's sword,
And take to Thee Thy power divine;
Stir up Thy strength, Almighty Lord,
All power and majesty are Thine:
Assert Thy worship and renown;
O all-redeeming God, come down!

4 Come, and maintain Thy righteous
   cause,
And let Thy glorious toil succeed;
O spread the victory of Thy cross,
Ride on, and prosper in Thy deed!
Through earth triumphantly ride on,
And reign in every heart alone.

Charles Wesley (1707–88)

1122

88.88.88

'To redeem them that were under the law'
Galatians 4 v 5

1 O come, O come, Immanuel,
And ransom captive Israel,
That mourns in lonely exile here
Until the Son of God appear.

Rejoice! rejoice! Immanuel
Shall come to thee, O Israel!

2 O come, O come, Thou Lord of
might,
Who to Thy tribes on Sinai's height,
In ancient times didst give the law
In cloud and majesty and awe.

3 O come, Thou Rod of Jesse, free
Thine own from Satan's tyranny;
From depths of hell Thy people save,
And give them victory o'er the grave.

4 O come, Thou Day-spring, come and
cheer
Our spirits by Thine advent here;
Disperse the gloomy clouds of night,
And death's dark shadows put to
flight.

5 O come, Thou Key of David, come,
And open wide our heavenly home;
Make safe the way that leads on
high,
And close the path to misery.

Latin 12th Century
Tr. John Mason Neale (1818–66) Altd

1123

87.87.47

'The people which sat in darkness saw
great light' Matthew 4 v 16

1 O'er the gloomy hills of darkness
Look, my soul; be still, and gaze;
All the promises do travail
With a glorious day of grace:
Blessèd jubilee!
Let thy glorious morning dawn.

2 Kingdoms wide that sit in darkness,
Grant them, Lord, Thy glorious
light;
And from eastern coast to western
May the morning chase the night;
And redemption,
Freely purchased, win the day.

3 May the glorious day approaching
End their night of sin and shame,
And the everlasting gospel
Spread abroad Thy holy name
O'er the borders
Of the great Immanuel's land!

4 Fly abroad, thou mighty gospel,
Win and conquer, never cease;
May thy lasting wide dominion
Multiply and still increase!
Sway Thy sceptre,
Saviour, all the world around.

William Williams (1717–91)

1124

87.87. D

'The Lamb shall overcome them: for he is
Lord of lords, and King of kings'
Revelation 17 v 14

1 Onward march, all-conquering
Jesus,
Gird Thee on Thy mighty sword;
Sinful earth can ne'er oppose Thee;
Hell itself quails at Thy Word.
Thy great name is so exalted,
Every foe shrinks back in fear;
Terror creeps through all creation,
When it knows that Thou art near.

2 Free my soul from sin's foul
bondage;
Hasten now the glorious dawn;
Break proud Babel's gates in sunder;
Let the massive bolts be drawn.
Forth, like ocean's heaving surges,
Bring in myriad ransomed slaves,
Host on host, with shouts of
triumph,
Endless, countless as the waves.

3 E'en today I hear sweet music,
Praises of a blood-freed throng;
Full deliverance, glorious freedom,
Are their themes for endless song;
Whiter than the snow their raiment,
Victor palms they wave on high,
As they pass, with fullest glory,
Into life's felicity.

4 How my raptured soul rejoices
That the jubilee is near;
Every word will be accomplished
Spoken by our Saviour here.
North and South, in countless
    myriads,
From earth's darkest ends they
    come,
With the dance and gladsome music,
Into heaven's eternal home.

William Williams (1717–91)
Tr. William Howells (1855–1932)

1125   77.77.D

'I am come to send fire on the earth'
Luke 12 v 49

1 See how great the flame aspires,
Kindled by a spark of grace!
Jesu's love the nations fires,
Sets the kingdoms on a blaze;
Fire to bring on earth He came;
Kindled in some hearts it is:
O that all might catch the flame,
All partake the glorious bliss!

2 When He first the work begun,
Small and feeble was His day:
Now the word doth swiftly run,
Now it wins its widening way;
More and more it spreads and
    grows,
Ever mighty to prevail;
Sin's strongholds it now o'erthrows,
Shakes the trembling gates of hell.

3 Sons of God, your Saviour praise;
He the door hath opened wide,
He hath given the word of grace,
Jesu's word is glorified;
Jesus, mighty to redeem,
He alone the work hath wrought;
Worthy is the work of Him,
Him who spake a world from
    nought.

4 Saw ye not the cloud arise,
Little as a human hand?
Now it spreads along the skies,
Hangs o'er all the thirsty land;
Lo! the promise of a shower
Drops already from above;
But the Lord will shortly pour
All the Spirit of His love.

Charles Wesley (1707–88)

SPECIAL OCCASIONS

1126
L.M.

'For God is my defence, and the God of my mercy' Psalm 59 v 17

1 Another year has now begun
With silent pace its course to run;
Our hearts and voices let us raise
To God in prayer and songs of
praise.

2 Father, Thy bounteous love we bless,
For gifts and mercies numberless;
For life and health, for grace and
peace,
For hope of joys that never cease.

3 O Son of God, in faith and fear
Teach us to walk as strangers here,
With hearts in heaven, that we may
come
To where Thou art, our Father's
home.

4 Grant us, O Comforter, Thy grace,
And speed us on our earthly race,
In body, spirit, and in soul,
Right onward to the heavenly goal.

5 Thou, Lord, who makest all things
new,
O give us hearts both pure and true;
That we, as jewels, ever Thine,
In new Jerusalem may shine.

6 Blest Three in One, to Thee we pray;
Defend and guide us on our way;
That we at last with joy may see
The new year of eternity!

Christopher Wordsworth (1807–85)

1127
5 5. 5 11

'I press toward the mark for the prize of the high calling of God in Christ Jesus' Philippians 3 v 14

1 Come, let us anew
Our journey pursue,
Roll round with the year,
And never stand still till the Master
appear.

2 His adorable will
Let us gladly fulfil,
And our talents improve,
By the patience of hope and the
labour of love.

3 Our life is a dream;
Our time as a stream
Glides swiftly away,
And the fugitive moment refuses to
stay.

4 O that each in the day
Of His coming may say:
I have fought my way through,
I have finished the work Thou didst
give me to do!

5 O that each from his Lord
May receive the glad word:
Well and faithfully done;
Enter into My joy, and sit down on
My throne!

Charles Wesley (1707–88)

1128
7 5. 7 5. D

'My times are in thy hand'
Psalm 31 v 15

1 Father, let me dedicate
All this year to Thee,
In whatever earthly state
Thou wilt have me be.
Not from sorrow, pain, or care
Freedom dare I claim;
This alone shall be my prayer:
Glorify Thy name.

2 Can a child presume to choose
Where or how to live?
Can a father's love refuse
All the best to give?
More Thou givest every day
Than the best can claim
Nor withholdest aught that may
Glorify Thy name.

3 If in mercy Thou wilt spare
Joys that yet are mine;
If on life, serene and fair,
Brighter rays may shine,
Let my glad heart while it sings
Thee in all proclaim
And, whate'er the future brings,
Glorify Thy name.

4 If Thou callest to the cross
And its shadow come,
Turning all my gain to loss,
Shrouding heart and home,
Let me think how Thy dear Son
To His glory came
And in deepest woe pray on:
'Glorify Thy name.'

Lawrence Tuttiett (1825–97)

1129
L.M.

'Having therefore obtained help of God, I
continue unto this day' Acts 26 v 32

1 Great God, we sing that guiding
hand,
By which supported still we stand;
The opening year Thy mercy shows,
Let mercy crown it till its close.

2 By day, by night, at home, abroad,
Still are we guarded by our God,
By His incessant bounty fed,
By His unerring counsel led.

3 With grateful hearts the past we
own;
The future, all to us unknown,
We to Thy guardian care commit,
And peaceful leave before Thy feet.

4 In scenes exalted or depressed,
Be Thou our joy and Thou our rest;
Thy goodness all our hopes shall
raise,
Adored through all our changing
days.

5 When death shall interrupt these
songs,
And seal in silence mortal tongues,
Our Helper, God, in whom we trust,
Shall keep our souls and guard our
dust.

Philip Doddridge (1702–51)

1130
L.M.

'My help cometh from the LORD'
Psalm 121 v 2

1 My Helper, God! I bless His name,
Whose love for ever is the same;
The tokens of whose gracious care
Open, and crown, and close the year.

2 I midst ten thousand dangers stand,
Supported by His guardian hand,
And see, when I review my ways,
Ten thousand monuments of praise.

3 Thus far His arm hath led me on,
Thus far I make His mercy known;
And while I tread this desert land,
New mercies shall new songs
demand.

4 My grateful soul, on Jordan's shore,
Shall raise one sacred pillar more;
Then bear in His bright courts above
Inscriptions of immortal love.

Philip Doddridge (1702–51)

1131   C.M.

'Let us come before his presence with thanksgiving' Psalm 95 v 2

1 Sing to the great Jehovah's praise;
   All praise to Him belongs;
   Who kindly lengthens out our days
   Demands our choicest songs.

2 His providence hath brought us
       through
   Another various year;
   We all with vows and anthems new
   Before our God appear.

3 Father, Thy mercies past we own;
   Thy still continued care;
   To Thee presenting, through Thy
       Son,
   Whate'er we have or are.

4 Our lips and lives shall gladly show
   The wonders of Thy love,
   While on in Jesu's steps we go
   To see Thy face above.

5 Our residue of days or hours
   Thine, wholly Thine, shall be;
   And all our consecrated powers
   A sacrifice to Thee:

6 Till Jesus in the clouds appear
   To saints on earth forgiven
   And bring the grand sabbatic year,
   The jubilee of heaven.

Charles Wesley (1707–88)

1132   7 7. 7 7. D

Based on Matthew 13 vv 36-43

1 Come, ye thankful people, come,
   Raise the song of harvest-home:
   All is safely gathered in
   Ere the winter storms begin;
   God our Maker doth provide
   For our wants to be supplied:
   Come to God's own temple, come,
   Raise the song of harvest-home.

2 All the world is God's own field,
   Fruit unto His praise to yield;
   Wheat and tares together sown,
   Unto joy or sorrow grown;
   First the blade, and then the ear,
   Then the full corn shall appear:
   Lord of harvest, grant that we
   Wholesome grain and pure may be.

3 For the Lord our God shall come,
   And shall take His harvest home;
   From His field shall in that day
   All offences purge away;
   Give His angels charge at last
   In the fire the tares to cast,
   But the fruitful ears to store
   In His garner evermore.

4 Even so, Lord, quickly come
   To Thy final harvest-home:
   Gather Thou Thy people in,
   Free from sorrow, free from sin;
   There, for ever purified,
   In Thy presence to abide:
   Come, with all Thine angels come,
   Raise the glorious harvest-home.

Henry Alford (1810–71)

1133   8 7. 8 7. D (with refrain)

'Thou crownest the year with thy goodness' Psalm 65 v 11

1 Now the year is crowned with
       blessing
   As we gather in the grain;
   And, our grateful thanks expressing,
   Loud we raise a joyous strain.
   Bygone days of toil and sadness
   Cannot now our peace destroy;
   For the hills are clothed with
       gladness,
   And the valleys shout for joy.

   To the Lord their first-fruits bringing
   All His thankful people come,
   To the Father praises singing
   For the joy of harvest-home.

2 In the spring the smiling meadows
Donned their robes of living green,
As the sunshine chased the shadows
Swiftly o'er the changing scene;
In the summer-time the story
Of a riper hope was told;
Then the rich autumnal glory
Decked the fields in cloth of gold.

3 Shall not we, whose hearts are
swelling
With the thought of former days,
Sing a joyous song foretelling
Future gladness, fuller praise?
For the cloud the bow retaineth
With its covenant of peace,
That, as long as earth remaineth,
Harvest-time shall never cease.

Ellen Thorneycroft Felkin (1860–1929)

1134 8 7. 8 7. D (with refrain)

'He … filleth thee with the finest of the wheat' Psalm 147 v 14

1 To Thee, O Lord, our hearts we raise
In hymns of adoration,
To Thee bring sacrifice of praise
With shouts of exultation;
Bright robes of gold the fields adorn,
The hills with joy are ringing,
The valleys stand so thick with corn
That even they are singing.

2 And now, on this our festal day,
Thy bounteous hand confessing,
Before Thee thankfully we lay
The first-fruits of Thy blessing.
By Thee the souls of men are fed
With gifts of grace supernal;
Thou who dost give us earthly bread,
Give us the bread eternal.

3 We bear the burden of the day,
And often toil seems dreary;
But labour ends with sunset ray,
And rest comes for the weary:
May we, the angel-reaping o'er,
Stand at the last accepted,
Christ's golden sheaves for evermore
To garners bright elected.

4 O blessèd is that land of God
Where saints abide for ever,
Where golden fields spread far and
broad,
Where flows the crystal river.
The strains of all its holy throng
With ours today are blending;
Thrice blessèd is that harvest song
Which never hath an ending.

William Chatterton Dix (1837–98)

1135 7 6. 7 6. (with refrain)

*'Every good gift … is from above'
James 1 v 17*

1 We plough the fields, and scatter
The good seed on the land,
But it is fed and watered
By God's almighty hand;
He sends the snow in winter,
The warmth to swell the grain,
The breezes and the sunshine,
And soft refreshing rain.

*All good gifts around us
Are sent from heaven above,
Then thank the Lord, O thank the Lord,
For all His love.*

2 He only is the Maker
Of all things near and far;
He paints the wayside flower;
He lights the evening star;
The winds and waves obey Him,
By Him the birds are fed;
Much more to us, His children,
He gives our daily bread.

3 We thank Thee, then, O Father,
For all things bright and good,
The seed-time and the harvest,
Our life, our health, our food;
No gifts have we to offer,
For all Thy love imparts,
But that which Thou desirest,
Our humble, thankful hearts.

*Matthias Claudius (1740–1815)
Tr. Jane Montgomery Campbell (1817–78)*

1136   L.M.

'The LORD is good to all' Psalm 145 v 9

1 Yes, God is good; in earth and sky,
From ocean depths and spreading
    wood,
Ten thousand voices seem to cry –
God made us all, and God is good.

2 The sun that keeps his trackless way,
And downward pours his golden
    flood,
Night's sparkling host, all seem to
    say,
In accents clear, that God is good.

3 The merry birds prolong the strain,
Their song with every spring
    renewed;
And balmy air, and falling rain,
Each softly whisper – God is good.

4 I hear it in the rushing breeze;
The hills that have for ages stood,
The echoing sky and roaring seas,
All swell the chorus – God is good.

5 Yes, God is good, all nature says,
By God's own hand with speech
    endued;
And man, in louder notes of praise,
Should sing for joy that God is good.

6 For all Thy gifts we bless Thee, Lord;
But most for Thy redeeming blood,
Thy pardoning grace, Thy quicken-
    ing word,
These prompt our songs that God is
    good.

John Hampden Gurney (1802–62)

1137   C.M.

'Have mercy upon us' Psalm 123 v 2

1 Almighty God, before Thy throne
Thy mourning people bend;
'Tis on Thy pardoning grace alone
Our prostrate hopes depend.

2 Dire judgements from Thy heavy hand
Thy dreadful power display;
Yet mercy spares our guilty land,
And still we live to pray.

3 O turn us, turn us, mighty Lord,
By Thy subduing grace;
So shall our hearts obey Thy Word,
And we shall see Thy face.

4 When evil smites, when foes invade,
We shall not sink or fear,
Secure of all-sufficient aid
When God, our God, is near!

Anne Steele (1717–78)

1138   88.88.88

'Even the winds and the sea obey him!'
Matthew 8 v 27

1 Eternal Father, strong to save,
Whose arm hath bound the restless
    wave,
Who bidd'st the mighty ocean deep
Its own appointed limits keep:
O hear us when we cry to Thee
For those in peril on the sea!

2 O Christ, whose voice the waters heard,
And hushed their raging at Thy word,
Who walkedst on the foaming deep,
And calm amid the storm didst
    sleep;
O hear us when we cry to Thee
For those in peril on the sea!

3 O Holy Spirit, who didst brood
Upon the waters dark and rude,
And bid their angry tumult cease,
And give, for wild confusion, peace:
O hear us when we cry to Thee
For those in peril on the sea!

4 O Trinity of love and power,
Our brethren shield in danger's hour;
From rock and tempest, fire and foe,
Protect them wheresoe'er they go:
Thus evermore shall rise to Thee
Glad hymns of praise from land and
    sea.

William Whiting (1825–78)

1139

11 10. 11 10

'A time of peace' Ecclesiastes 3 v 8

1 God the All-terrible! King who
ordainest
Great winds Thy clarions, the light-
nings Thy sword:
Show forth Thy pity on high where
Thou reignest;
Give to us peace in our time, O Lord!

2 God the All-merciful! earth hath
forsaken
Meekness and mercy, and slighted
Thy word;
Bid not Thy wrath in its terrors
awaken;
Give to us peace in our time, O Lord!

3 God the All-righteous One! man
hath defied Thee;
Yet to eternity standeth Thy Word;
Falsehood and wrong shall not tarry
beside Thee;
Give to us peace in our time, O Lord!

4 God the All-wise! by the fire of Thy
chastening,
Earth shall to freedom and truth be
restored;
Through the thick darkness Thy
kingdom is hastening;
Thou wilt give peace in our time, O
Lord!

5 So shall Thy children, with thankful
devotion,
Praise Him who saved them from
peril and sword,
Singing in chorus from ocean to
ocean:
Peace to the nations and praise to
the Lord.

vv 1,2,3,5 Henry Fothergill Chorley (1808–72)
v 4 John Ellerton (1826–93)

1140

L.M.

'King of Salem, which is, King of peace'
Hebrews 7 v 2

1 O God of love, O King of peace,
Make wars throughout the world to
cease;
The wrath of sinful men restrain;
Give peace, O God, give peace again.

2 Remember, Lord, Thy works of old,
The wonders that our fathers told;
Remember not our sin's dark stain;
Give peace, O God, give peace again.

3 Whom shall we trust but Thee, O
Lord:
Where rest but on Thy faithful
Word?
None ever called on Thee in vain;
Give peace, O God, give peace again.

4 Where saints and angels dwell
above,
All hearts are knit in holy love;
O bind us in that heavenly chain;
Give peace, O God, give peace again.

Henry Williams Baker (1821–1877)

1141

7 7. 7 7

'As obedient children' 1 Peter 1 v 14

1 God of mercy, hear our prayer
For the children Thou hast given;
Let them all Thy blessings share,
Grace on earth, and bliss in heaven.

2 In the morning of their days
May their hearts be drawn to Thee;
Let them learn to lisp Thy praise
In their earliest infancy.

3 Cleanse their souls from every stain,
Through the Saviour's precious
blood;
Let them all be born again,
And be reconciled to God.

4 For this mercy, Lord, we cry;
  Bend Thine ever-gracious ear;
  While on Thee our souls rely,
  Hear our prayer, in mercy hear!

Thomas Hastings (1784–1872)

1142   C.M.

'To show piety at home' 1 Timothy 5 v 4

1 Happy the home when God is there,
  And love fills every breast;
  When one their wish, and one their
      prayer,
  And one their heavenly rest.

2 Happy the home where Jesus' name
  Is sweet to every ear;
  Where children early lisp His fame,
  And parents hold Him dear.

3 Happy the home where prayer is
      heard,
  And praise is wont to rise;
  Where parents love the sacred Word
  That makes us truly wise.

4 Lord, let us in our homes agree,
  This blessèd peace to gain;
  Unite our hearts in love to Thee,
  And love to all will reign.

Henry Ware (1794–1843)

1143   7 6. 7 6. D

*'Except the LORD build the house, they
labour in vain that build it'*
Psalm 127 v 1

1 O Father, all-creating,
  Whose wisdom, love, and power
  First bound two lives together
  In Eden's primal hour,
  Today to these Thy children
  Thine earliest gifts renew:
  A home by Thee made happy,
  A love by Thee kept true.

2 O Saviour, Guest most bounteous
  Of old in Galilee,
  Vouchsafe today Thy presence
  With those who call on Thee;
  Their store of earthly gladness
  Transform to heavenly wine,
  And teach them in the tasting
  To know the gift is Thine.

3 O Spirit of the Father,
  Breathe on them from above,
  So mighty in Thy pureness,
  So tender in Thy love;
  That, guarded by Thy presence,
  From sin and strife kept free.
  Their lives may own Thy guidance,
  Their hearts be ruled by Thee.

4 Except Thou build it, Father,
  The house is built in vain;
  Except Thou, Saviour, bless it,
  The joy will turn to pain:
  But nought can break the union
  Of hearts in Thee made one;
  And love Thy Spirit hallows
  Is endless love begun.

John Ellerton (1826–93)

1144   11 10. 11 10. 11 10

*'Thy wife shall be as a fruitful vine …
thy children like olive plants'*
Psalm 127 v 5

1 O give us homes built firm upon the
      Saviour,
  Where Christ is Head and
      Counsellor and Guide;
  Where every child is taught His love
      and favour
  And gives its heart to Christ the
      Crucified;
  How sweet to know that though its
      footsteps waver
  The faithful Lord is walking by its
      side!

2 O give us homes with godly fathers,
  mothers,
  Who always place their hope and
  trust in Him;
  Whose tender patience turmoil never
  bothers,
  Whose calm and courage trouble
  cannot dim;
  A home where each finds joy in
  serving others,
  And love still shines though days be
  dark and grim.

3 O give us homes where Christ is
  Lord and Master,
  The Bible read, the precious hymns
  still sung;
  Where prayer comes first in peace or
  in disaster,
  And praise is natural speech to every
  tongue;
  Where mountains move before a
  faith that's vaster,
  And Christ sufficient is for old and
  young.

4 O Lord, our God, our homes are
  Thine for ever!
  We trust to Thee their problems, toil
  and care;
  Their bonds of love no enemy can
  sever
  If Thou art always Lord and Master
  there;
  Be Thou the centre of our least
  endeavour,
  Be Thou our guest, our hearts and
  homes to share.

Barbara B. Hart (b.1916)

1145   88.88.88

'I will make him an help meet for him'
Genesis 2 v 18

1 O God who didst from Adam's side
  Fashion an help meet for his bride,
  Flesh of his flesh, bone of his bone,
  That both might feel and love as
  one!
  Make these Thy servants one in
  heart;
  Whom Thou hast joined let no man
  part.

2 Lord of the church, whose bleeding
  side
  Gave life to Thy redeemèd bride;
  Whose grace through every member
  spread
  Joins the whole body to its Head:
  O let Thy love their model be,
  As they together live to Thee.

3 O Thou who once, a Guest divine,
  Didst turn the water into wine!
  Thy presence, not unsought, afford;
  Fill Thou their cup, and bless them,
  Lord;
  And while each heart Thy Word
  obeys,
  May all their joy be turned to praise.

4 Spirit of grace and holiness,
  Who does these bodies now possess,
  As living temples, which to stain
  Were God's own dwelling to
  profane,
  May these Thy servants, honouring
  Thee,
  Be kept in love and purity.

Josiah Conder (1789–1855) Altd

1146

11 10. 11 10

'And they shall be one flesh'
Genesis 2 v 24

1 O happy home where Thou art loved
  the dearest,
  Thou loving Friend, and Saviour of
  our race,
  And where among the guests there
  never cometh
  One who can hold such high and
  honoured place!

2 O happy home where two in heart
  united
  In holy faith and blessèd hope are
  one,
  Whom death a little while alone
  divideth,
  And cannot end the union here
  begun!

3 O happy home whose little ones are
  given
  Early to Thee, in humble faith and
  prayer,
  To Thee, their Friend, who from the
  heights of heaven
  Guides them, and guards with more
  than mother's care!

4 O happy home where each one
  serves Thee, lowly,
  Whatever his appointed work may
  be,
  Till every common task seems great
  and holy,
  When it is done, O Lord, as unto
  Thee!

5 O happy home where Thou art not
  forgotten
  When joy is overflowing, full and
  free;
  O happy home where every wounded
  spirit
  Is brought, Physician, Comforter, to
  Thee.

6 Until at last, when earth's day's
  work is ended,
  All meet Thee in the blessèd home
  above,
  From whence Thou camest, where
  Thou hast ascended,
  Thy everlasting home of peace and
  love!

Carl Johann Philipp Spitta (1801–59)
Tr. Sarah Laurie Findlater (1823–1907)

1147

C.M.

'Suffer little children, and forbid them
not, to come unto me' Matthew 19 v 14

1 O Lord, behold us at Thy feet,
  A needy, sinful band;
  As suppliants round Thy mercy-seat
  We come at Thy command.

2 'Tis for our children we would plead,
  The offspring Thou hast given;
  Where shall we go in time of need
  But to the God of heaven?

3 We ask not for them wealth or fame,
  Amid the worldly strife;
  But, in the all-prevailing name,
  We ask eternal life.

4 We crave the Spirit's quickening
  grace,
  To make them pure in heart,
  That they may stand before Thy face,
  And see Thee as Thou art.

Thomas Hastings (1784–1872)

1148

11 10. 11 10

'As Christ also loved the church'
Ephesians 5 v 25

1 O perfect Love, all human thought
  transcending,
  Lowly we kneel in prayer before Thy
  throne,
  That theirs may be the love which
  knows no ending
  Whom Thou for evermore dost join
  in one.

2 O perfect Life, be Thou their full
assurance
Of tender charity and steadfast faith,
Of patient hope, and quiet brave
endurance,
With childlike trust that fears not
pain nor death

3 Grant them the joy which brightens
earthly sorrow;
Grant them the peace which calms
all earthly strife;
And to life's day the glorious
unknown morrow
That dawns upon eternal love and
life.

Dorothy Frances Gurney (1858–1932)

1149 C.M.

'For the promise is unto you, and to your
children' Acts 2 v 39

1 Our children, Lord, in faith and
prayer
We now present to Thee;
Let them Thy covenant mercies
share,
And Thy salvation see.

2 Such helpless babes Thou didst
embrace,
While dwelling here below;
To us and ours, O God of grace,
The same compassion show.

3 In early days their hearts secure
From worldly snares, we pray;
And may they to the end endure
In every righteous way.

4 Before them let their parents live
In godly faith and fear,
Then, Lord, to heaven their souls
receive,
And bring their children there.

Thomas Haweis (1733–1820) Altd

1150 87.87.D

'The peace of God, which passeth all
understanding' Philippians 4 v 7

1 Peace be to this habitation;
Peace to all that dwell therein;
Peace, the earnest of salvation,
Peace, the fruit of pardoned sin;
Peace that speaks the heavenly Giver,
Peace to worldly minds unknown;
Peace divine that lasts for ever;
Peace that comes from God alone.

2 Jesus, Prince of Peace, be near us,
Fix in all our hearts thy home;
With Thy gracious presence cheer
us,
Let they sacred kingdom come.
Raise to heaven our expectation;
Give our ransomed souls to prove
Glorious and complete salvation
In the realms of bliss above.

Charles Wesley (1707–88)

1151 C.M.

'And he took them up in his arms, put his
hands upon them, and blessed them'
Matthew 10 v 16

1 See Israel's gentle Shepherd stand
With all-engaging charms;
Hark how He calls the tender lambs,
And folds them in His arms!

2 Permit them to approach, He cries,
Nor scorn their humble name;
For 'twas to bless such souls as
these
The Lord of angels came.

3 We bring them, Lord, in thankful
hands,
And yield them up to Thee;
Joyful that we ourselves are Thine,
Thine let our children be.

Philip Doddridge (1702–51)

1152   76.76

'And God blessed them' Genesis 1 v 28

1 The voice that breathed o'er Eden,
That earliest wedding-day,
The primal marriage blessing,
It hath not passed away.

2 Be present, heavenly Father,
To give away this bride,
As Eve Thou gav'st to Adam
Out of his own pierced side.

3 Be present, gracious Saviour,
To join their loving hands,
As Thou didst bind two natures
In Thine eternal bands.

4 Be present, Holy Spirit,
To bless them as they kneel,
As Thou for Christ the Bridegroom
The heavenly spouse dost seal.

5 O spread Thy pure wings o'er them!
Let no ill power find place,
When onward through life's journey
The hallowed path they trace,

6 To cast their crowns before Thee,
In perfect sacrifice,
Till to the home of gladness
With Christ's own bride they rise.

John Keble (1792–1866)

1153   C.M.

'And they shall be one flesh'
Genesis 2 v 24

1 Thou who at Cana didst appear,
To bless a marriage feast,
Vouchsafe Thy gracious presence here;
Be Thou with us as Guest.

2 Upon the bridal pair look down,
Who now have plighted hands;
Their union with Thy favour crown,
And bless their nuptial bands.

3 With gifts of grace their hearts endow,
Of all rich dowries best;
Their substance bless, and peace
   bestow
To sweeten all the rest.

4 In purest love their souls unite,
That they, with Christian care,
May make domestic burdens light,
By taking mutual share.

5 Through life their every step attend
With tokens of Thy love;
And, having reached their journey's
   end,
Complete their bliss above.

John Berridge (1716–93)

1154   C.M.

'So God created man in his own image'
Genesis 1 v 27

1 We worship Thee, the King of grace,
With heart and soul and voice;
O grant that mercy's smiling face
May cause us to rejoice

2 Along life's path we have been led
By Thee, our Lord and Friend;
And we have tasted of the bread
Of life, which Thou dost send.

3 We come to Thee for blessing now
Upon this wedding-day;
We ask Thee, Lord, Thy grace bestow
And may Thy presence stay.

4 We come our promises to make,
Present our vows to Thee;
Our humble prayer, O gently take,
That we may faithful be.

5 Upon our hearts O grant Thy peace,
Thy guidance in our lives;
That we may walk the way of grace,
And be in all things wise.

6 Upon our home Thy blessing give,
A haven from the storm,
A place of comfort, where we live
In harmony and calm.

7 We look to Thee, our sovereign God,
For unction and for grace;
And when our journey we have trod,
We'll see Thy blessed face.

© The Author   *William Vernom Higham (b.1926)*

HYMNS FOR CHILDREN

1155

76.76

'And God saw every thing that he had made, and, behold, it was very good'
Genesis 1 v 31

All things bright and beautiful,
All creatures great and small,
All things wise and wonderful,
The Lord God made them all.

1 Each little flower that opens,
Each little bird that sings,
He made their glowing colours,
He made their tiny wings:

2 The purple-headed mountain,
The river running by,
The sunset, and the morning
That brightens up the sky:

3 The cold wind in the winter,
The pleasant summer sun,
The ripe fruits in the garden,
He made them every one:

4 He gave us eyes to see them,
And lips that we might tell
How great is God Almighty,
Who has made all things well:

Cecil Frances Alexander (1818–95)

1156

11 11. 11 11

'And laid him in a manger' Luke 2 v 7

1 Away in a manger, no crib for a bed,
The little Lord Jesus laid down His sweet head.
The stars in the bright sky looked down where He lay,
The little Lord Jesus asleep on the hay.

2 The cattle are lowing, the Baby awakes
But little Lord Jesus no crying He makes.
I love Thee, Lord Jesus! look down from the sky,
And stay by my side until morning is nigh.

3 Be near me, Lord Jesus; I ask Thee to stay
Close by me for ever, and love me, I pray.
Bless all the dear children in Thy tender care,
And fit us for heaven, to live with Thee there.

Anonymous

1157

7 7. 7 7

'And the children crying in the temple,
and saying, Hosanna to the son of
David' Matthew 21 v 15

1 Children of Jerusalem
   Sang the praise of Jesus' name:
   Children, too, of modern days,
   Join to sing the Saviour's praise.

   Hark, hark, hark! while infant voices
     sing,
   Hark, hark, hark! while infant voices
     sing,
   Loud hosannas, loud hosannas,
   Loud hosannas to our King.

2 We are taught to love the Lord,
   We are taught to read His Word,
   We are taught the way to heaven:
   Praise for all to God be given.

3 Parents, teachers, old and young,
   All unite to swell the song;
   Higher and yet higher rise,
   Till hosannas reach the skies.

                          John Henley (1800–42)

1158

7 7. 7 7. 7 7

'Every good gift and every perfect gift is
from above' James 1 v 17

1 For the beauty of the earth,
   For the beauty of the skies,
   For the love which from our birth
   Over and around us lies:
   Gracious God, to Thee we raise
   This our sacrifice of praise.

2 For the beauty of each hour
   Of the day and of the night,
   Hill and vale, and tree and flower,
   Sun and moon and stars of light:
   Gracious God, to Thee we raise
   This our sacrifice of praise.

3 For the joy of human love,
   Brother, sister, parent, child,
   Friends on earth and friends above,
   For all gentle thoughts and mild:
   Gracious God, to Thee we raise
   This our sacrifice of praise.

4 For each perfect gift of Thine
   To our race so freely given,
   Graces human and divine,
   Flowers and buds of earth and heaven:
   Gracious God, to Thee we raise
   This our sacrifice of praise.

             Folliott Stanford Pierpoint (1835–1917)

1159

5 6. 6 4

'There shall no evil befall thee'
Psalm 91 v 10

1 God, who made the earth,
   The air, the sky, the sea,
   Who gave the light its birth,
   Careth for me.

2 God, who made the grass,
   The flower, the fruit, the tree,
   The day and night to pass,
   Careth for me.

3 God, who made the sun,
   The moon, the stars, is He
   Who, when life's clouds come on,
   Careth for me.

4 God, who sent His Son
   To die on Calvary,
   He, if I lean on Him,
   Will care for me.

5 When in heaven's bright land
   I all His loved ones see,
   I'll sing with that blest band,
   'God cared for me.'

                    Sarah Betts Rhodes (1829–1904)

1160

66.66.88

'Speak, LORD; for thy servant heareth'
1 Samuel 3 v 9

1 Hushed was the evening hymn,
The temple courts were dark;
The lamp was burning dim
Before the sacred ark;
When suddenly a voice divine
Rang through the silence of the
    shrine.

2 The priest of Israel, slept,
The old man meek and mild;
Watch in the temple kept,
The little Levite child;
And what from Eli's sense was sealed
The Lord to Hannah's son revealed.

3 O give me Samuel's ear,
The open ear, O Lord!
Alive and quick to hear
Each whisper of Thy Word;
Like him to answer at Thy call,
And to obey Thee first of all.

4 O give me Samuel's heart!
A lowly heart, that waits
Where in Thy house Thou art,
Or watches at Thy gates;
By day and night a heart that still
Moves at the breathing of Thy will.

5 O give me Samuel's mind!
A sweet unmurmuring faith,
Obedient and resigned
To Thee in life and death;
That I may read with childlike eyes
Truths that are hidden from the wise.

James Drummond Burns (1823–64)

1161

S.M.

'Draw near with a true heart'
Hebrews 10 v 22

1 I often say my prayers,
But do I ever pray?
And do the wishes of my heart
Go with the words I say?

2 I may as well kneel down
And worship gods of stone,
As offer to the living God
A prayer of words alone.

3 For words without the heart
The Lord will never hear;
Nor will He to those lips attend
Whose prayers are not sincere.

4 Lord, teach me what I need,
And teach me how to pray;
Nor let me ask Thee for Thy grace,
Not meaning what I say.

John Burton (1803–77)

1162

L.M.

'We love him, because he first loved us'
1 John 4 v 19

1 It is a thing most wonderful,
Almost too wonderful to be,
That God's own Son should come
    from heaven,
And die to save a child like me.

2 And yet I know that it is true;
He came to this poor world below,
And wept and toiled and mourned
    and died,
Only because He loved us so.

3 I cannot tell how He could love
A child so weak and full of sin;
His love must be most wonderful,
If He could die my love to win.

4 I sometimes think about the cross,
And shut my eyes, and try to see
The cruel nails, and crown of thorns,
And Jesus crucified for me.

5 But even could I see Him die,
I could but see a little part
Of that great love which, like a fire,
Is always burning in His heart.

6 It is most wonderful to know
His love for me so free and sure;
But 'tis more wonderful to see
My love for Him so faint and poor.

7 And yet I want to love Thee, Lord;
O light the flame within my heart,
And I will love Thee more and more,
Until I see Thee as Thou art.

William Walsham How (1823–97)

1163   C.M.

'*Lord, teach us to pray*' Luke 11 v 1

1 Lord, teach a little child to pray,
Thy grace to me impart;
And grant Thy Holy Spirit may
Renew my youthful heart.

2 A sinful creature I was born,
And from my birth have strayed;
I must be wretched and forlorn
Without Thy mercy's aid.

3 But Christ can all my sins forgive,
And wash away their stain;
Can fit my soul with Him to live,
And in His kingdom reign.

4 To Him let little children come,
For He has said they may;
His bosom then shall be their home,
Their tears He'll wipe away.

5 For all who early seek His face
Shall surely taste His love;
Jesus shall guide them by His grace
To dwell with Him above.

John Ryland (1753–1825)

1164   7 7.7 7

'*The sheep follow him: for they know his voice*' John 10 v 4

1 Loving Shepherd of Thy sheep,
Keep me now, in safety keep;
Nothing can Thy power withstand,
None can pluck me from Thy hand.

2 Loving Saviour, Thou didst give
Thine own life that I might live,
And the hands outstretched to bless
Bear the cruel nails' impress.

3 I would praise Thee every day,
Gladly all Thy will obey,
Like Thy blessed ones above
Happy in Thy precious love.

4 Loving Shepherd, ever near,
Teach me now Thy voice to hear;
Suffer not my steps to stray
From the strait and narrow way.

5 Where Thou leadest I would go,
Walking in Thy steps below,
Till before my Father's throne
I shall know as I am known.

Jane Eliza Leeson (1809–81)

1165   L.M. (with refrain)

'*Then shall we know, if we follow on to know the LORD*' Hosea 6 v 3

1 More about Jesus would I know,
More of His grace to others show,
More of His saving fullness see,
More of His love – who died for me.

More, more about Jesus,
More, more about Jesus;
More of His saving fulness see,
More of His love who died for me.

2 More about Jesus let me learn,
More of His holy will discern;
Spirit of God, my Teacher be,
Showing the things of Christ to me.

3 More about Jesus, in His Word,
Holding communion with my Lord;
Hearing His voice in every line,
Making each faithful saying mine.

4 More about Jesus, on His throne,
Riches in glory all His own;
More of His kingdom's sure
increase;
More of His coming, Prince of
Peace!

Eliza Edmunds Hewitt (1851–1920)

1166 S.M.

'Thy word is true' Psalm 119 v 160

1 The Bible is God's Book,
Though human was the pen:
The seeing eye discerns how well
His Spirit guided men.

2 How kind of God to write
A Book to be my guide;
When other books have turned to
dust,
The Scriptures shall abide.

3 Such simple words are here
A child may understand;
While earthly wisdom fails to read
Its truth profoundly grand.

4 What noble songs are here!
What lovely stories too!
Its promises shall be fulfilled,
Its prophecies come true.

5 Its choir of voices join
To make a Saviour known,
Till all the praise and glory crown
The Lamb upon the throne.

6 Thou who didst write the Book,
Come with Thy light divine,
Shine in my heart and on the page,
And make its treasures mine.

C. C. White

1167 6 6. 5 5. 6

'There shall in no wise enter into it anything that defileth' Revelation 21 v 27

1 There is a city bright;
Closed are its gates to sin;
Naught that defileth,
Naught that defileth,
Can ever enter in.

2 Saviour, I come to Thee!
O Lamb of God, I pray,
Cleanse me and save me,
Cleanse me and save me,
Wash all my sins away.

3 Lord, make me, from this hour,
Thy loving child to be,
Kept by Thy power,
Kept by Thy power,
From all that grieveth Thee:

4 Till in the snowy dress
Of Thy redeemed I stand,
Faultless and stainless,
Faultless and stainless,
Safe in that happy land!

Mary Ann Sanderson Deck (1813–1903)

1168 C.M.

'The Son of God, who loved me, and gave
himself for me' Galatians 2 v 20

1 There is a green hill far away,
Outside a city wall,
Where the dear Lord was crucified,
Who died to save us all.

2 We may not know, we cannot tell,
What pains He had to bear;
But we believe it was for us
He hung and suffered there.

3 He died that we might be forgiven,
He died to make us good,
That we might go at last to heaven,
Saved by His precious blood.

4 There was no other good enough
To pay the price of sin;
He only could unlock the gate
Of heaven and let us in.

5 O dearly, dearly has He loved,
And we must love Him, too,
And trust in His redeeming blood,
And try His works to do.

Cecil Frances Alexander (1818–95)

1169   6 5. 6 5. D (with refrain)

*'And whatsoever ye do ... do all in the
name of the Lord Jesus' Colossians 3 v 17*

1 There's a work for Jesus
Ready at your hand,
'Tis a task the Master
Just for you has planned.
Haste to do His bidding,
Yield Him service true;
There's a work for Jesus,
None but you can do.

*Work for Jesus, day by day,
Serve Him ever, falter never, Christ obey.
Yield Him service, loyal, true:
There's a work for Jesus none but you can
do.*

2 There's a work for Jesus,
Humble though it be,
'Tis the very service
He would ask of Thee.
Go where fields are whitened,
And the labourers few;
There's a work for Jesus,
None but you can do.

3 There's a work for Jesus,
Precious souls to bring,
Tell them of His mercies,
Tell them of your King.
Faint not, grow not weary,
He will strength renew;
There's a work for Jesus,
None but you can do.

Elsie Yale (c.1912)

1170   11 11. 11 12 (with refrain)

*'But the Lord is faithful, who shall
stablish you, and keep you from evil'
2 Thessalonians 3 v 3*

1 Yield not to temptation, for yielding
is sin;
Each victory will help you some
other to win;
Fight manfully onward; dark
passions subdue;
Look ever to Jesus, He'll carry you
through.

*Ask the Saviour to help you,
Comfort, strengthen and keep you;
He is willing to aid you,
He will carry you through.*

2 Shun evil companions, bad language
disdain,
God's Name hold in reverence, nor
take it in vain;
Be thoughtful and earnest, kind-
hearted and true;
Look ever to Jesus, He'll carry you
through.

3 To him that o'ercometh, God giveth
a crown;
Through faith we shall conquer,
though often cast down;
He who is our Saviour our strength
will renew;
Look ever to Jesus, He will carry you
through.

Horatio Richmond Palmer (1834–1907)

CLOSE OF WORSHIP

1171 L.M.

'And now the eventide was come'
Mark 11 v 11

1 At even, ere the sun was set,
The sick, O Lord, around Thee lay;
O in what diverse pains they met!
O with what joy they went away!

2 Once more 'tis eventide, and we
Oppressed with various ills draw
near;
What if Thy form we cannot see?
We know and feel that Thou art
here.

3 O Saviour Christ, our woes dispel;
For some are sick, and some are sad,
And some have never loved Thee well,
And some have lost the love they
had.

4 And some have found the world is
vain,
Yet from the world they break not
free;
And some have friends who give
them pain,
Yet have not sought a friend in Thee.

5 And none, O Lord, have perfect rest,
For none are wholly free from sin;
And they who fain would serve Thee
best
Are conscious most of wrong within.

6 O Saviour Christ, Thou too art man;
Thou hast been troubled, tempted,
tried;
Thy kind but searching glance can
scan
The very wounds that shame would
hide.

7 Thy touch has still its ancient power;
No word from Thee can fruitless fall;
Hear in this solemn evening hour,
And in Thy mercy heal us all.

Henry Twells (1823–1900)

1172 L.M.

'That Christ may dwell in your hearts by
faith' Ephesians 3 v 17

1 Come, dearest Lord, descend and
dwell,
By faith and love, in every breast;
Then shall we know, and taste, and
feel
The joys that cannot be expressed.

2 Come, fill our hearts with inward
strength,
Make our enlarged souls possess,
And learn the height and breadth
and length
Of Thine immeasurable grace.

3 Now to the God whose power can do
More than our thoughts or wishes
know,
Be everlasting honours done
By all the church, through Christ His
Son.

Isaac Watts (1674–1748)

1173
8. 3 3. 6

'For so he giveth his beloved sleep'
Psalm 127 v 2

1 Ere I sleep, for every favour
This day showed
By my God,
I will bless my Saviour.

2 O my Lord, what shall I render
To Thy name,
Still the same,
Merciful and tender?

3 Thou hast ordered all my goings
In Thy way,
Heard me pray,
Sanctified my doings.

4 Leave me not, but ever love me;
Let Thy peace
Be my bliss,
Till Thou hence remove me.

5 Visit me with Thy salvation,
Let Thy care
Now be near
Round my habitation.

6 Thou my rock, my guard, my tower,
Safely keep
While I sleep,
Me, with all Thy power.

7 So, whene'er in death I slumber,
Let me rise
With the wise,
Counted in their number.

John Cennick (1718–55)

1174
8 8 7. D

'Deliver us from evil' Luke 11 v 4

1 Father, in high heaven dwelling,
May our evening song be telling
Of Thy mercy large and free:
Through the day Thy love hath fed us,
Through the day Thy care hath led
us,
With divinest charity.

2 This day's sins, O pardon, Saviour!
Evil thoughts, perverse behaviour,
Envy, pride and vanity;
From the world, the flesh, deliver,
Save us now, and save us ever,
O Thou Lamb of Calvary!

3 From enticements of the devil,
From the might of spirits evil,
Be our shield and panoply:
Let Thy power this night defend us,
And a heavenly peace attend us,
And angelic company.

4 Whilst the night dews are distilling,
Holy Ghost, each heart be filling
With Thine own serenity;
Softly let the eyes be closing,
Loving souls on Thee reposing,
Ever-blessed Trinity!

George Rawson (1807–89)

1175
L.M.

'And under his wings shalt thou trust'
Psalm 91 v 4

1 Glory to Thee, my God, this night,
For all the blessings of the light:
Keep me, O keep me, King of kings,
Beneath Thine own almighty wings.

2 Forgive me, Lord, for Thy dear Son,
The ill that I this day have done;
That with the world, myself, and
Thee,
I, ere I sleep, at peace may be.

3 Teach me to live, that I may dread
The grave as little as my bed;
Teach me to die, that so I may
Rise glorious at the judgment day.

4 O may my soul on Thee repose,
And may sweet sleep mine eyelids
close,
Sleep that may me more vigorous
make
To serve my God when I awake.

5 If in the night I sleepless lie,
  My soul with heavenly thoughts
    supply;
  Let no ill dreams disturb my rest,
  No powers of darkness me molest.

6 Praise God, from whom all blessings
    flow;
  Praise Him, all creatures here below;
  Praise Him above, ye heavenly host;
  Praise Father, Son, and Holy Ghost.

Thomas Ken (1637–1710)

1176   Irregular

'Lead me, O LORD, in thy righteousness'
Psalm 5 v 8

1 Lead me, Lord, lead me in Thy
    righteousness;
  Make Thy way plain before my face.
  Lead me, Lord, lead me in Thy
    righteousness;
  Make Thy way plain before my face.

2 For it is Thou, Lord, Thou, Lord,
    only,
  That makest me dwell in saftey.
  For it is Thou, Lord, Thou, Lord,
    only,
  That makest me dwell in safety.

Anonymous

1177   87.87.47

'And went unto their tents joyful and
glad of heart' 1 Kings 8 v 66

1 Lord, dismiss us with Thy blessing;
  Fill our hearts with joy and peace;
  Let us each Thy love possessing,
  Triumph in redeeming grace.
  O refresh us,
  Traveling through this wilderness.

2 Thanks we give and adoration
  For Thy gospel's joyful sound;
  May the fruits of Thy salvation
  In our hearts and lives abound.
  Ever faithful,
  To the truth may we be found.

3 So that whene'er the signal's given
  Us from earth to call away,
  Borne on angels' wings to heaven,
  Glad Thy summons to obey,
  May we ever,
  Reign with Thee in endless day!

John Fawcett (1739–1817)

1178   87.87

Based on 2 Corinthians 13 v 14

1 May the grace of Christ our Saviour,
  And the Father's boundless love,
  With the Holy Spirit's favour,
  Rest upon us from above.

2 Thus may we abide in union
  With each other and the Lord,
  And possess, in sweet communion,
  Joys which earth cannot afford.

John Newton (1725–1807)

1179   77.77

Based on Hebrews 13 vv 20, 21

1 Now may He, who from the dead
  Brought the Shepherd of the sheep,
  Jesus Christ, our King and Head,
  All our souls in safety keep.

2 May He teach us to fulfil
  What is pleasing in His sight,
  Perfect us in all His will,
  And preserve us day and night.

3 To that dear Redeemer's praise,
  Who the covenant sealed with blood,
  Let our hearts and voices raise
  Loud thanksgivings to our God.

John Newton (1725–1807)

1180

66.66

'Praise ye the LORD' Psalm 135 v 1

1 Once more before we part,
We bless the Saviour's Name;
Let every tongue and heart
Join to extol the Lamb.

2 Jesus, the sinner's Friend,
He whom our souls adore,
His praises have no end,
Praise Him for evermore.

3 Lord, in Thy grace we came,
Thy blessing still impart;
We met in Jesus' name,
And in His name we part.

4 If here we meet no more,
May we in realms above,
With all the saints adore
Redeeming grace and love.

Joseph Hart (1712–68)
and Robert Hawker (1753–1827)

1181

10 10. 10 10

'Peace I leave with you, my peace I give unto you' John 14 v 27

1 Saviour, again to Thy dear name we raise
With one accord our parting hymn of praise;
We stand to bless Thee ere our worship cease,
Then, lowly kneeling, wait Thy word of peace.

2 Grant us Thy peace upon our homeward way;
With Thee began, with Thee shall end the day;
Guard Thou the lips from sin, the hearts from shame,
That in this house have called upon Thy name.

3 Grant us Thy peace, Lord, through the coming night,
Turn Thou for us its darkness into light;
From harm and danger keep Thy children free,
For dark and light are both alike to Thee.

4 Grant us Thy peace throughout our earthly life,
Our balm in sorrow, and our stay in strife;
Then, when Thy voice shall bid our conflict cease,
Call us, O Lord, to Thine eternal peace.

John Ellerton (1826–93)

1182

L.M.

'Abide with us' Luke 24 v 29

1 Sun of my soul, Thou Saviour dear,
It is not night if Thou be near;
O may no earth-born cloud arise
To hide Thee from Thy servant's eyes.

2 When the soft dews of kindly sleep
My wearied eyelids gently steep,
Be my last thought, how sweet to rest
For ever on my Saviour's breast!

3 Abide with me from morn till eve,
For without Thee I cannot live;
Abide with me when night is nigh,
For without Thee I dare not die.

4 If some poor wandering child of Thine
Have spurned today the voice divine,
Now Lord, the gracious work begin;
Let him no more lie down in sin.

5 Watch by the sick; enrich the poor
With blessings from Thy boundless store;
Be every mourner's sleep tonight
Like infant's slumbers, pure and light.

6 Come near and bless us when we
  wake,
  Ere through the world our way we
  take;
  Till in the ocean of Thy love
  We lose ourselves in heaven above.

John Keble (1792–1866)

1183   8 7. 8 7 (iambic)

*'From the rising of the sun unto the going
down of the same the LORD's name is to
be praised' Psalm 113 v 3*

1 The day departs;
  Our souls and hearts
  Long for that better morrow,
  When Christ shall set His people
  free
  From every care and sorrow.

2 The sunshine bright
  Is lost in night;
  O Lord, Thyself unveiling,
  Shine on our souls with beams of
  love,
  All darkness there dispelling.

3 The land above,
  Of peace and love,
  No earthly beams need brighten;
  For all its borders Christ Himself
  Doth with His glory lighten.

4 May we be there,
  That joy to share,
  Glad hallelujahs singing;
  With all the ransomed evermore
  Our joyful praises bringing.

5 Lord Jesus, Thou
  Our refuge now,
  Forsake Thy servants never;
  Uphold and guide, that we may
  stand
  Before Thy throne for ever.

Johann Anastasius Freylinghausen (1670–1739)
Tr. Jane Laurie Borthwick (1813–97)

1184   9 8. 9 8

*'From the rising of the sun unto the going
down of the same the LORD's name is to
be praised' Psalm 113 v 3*

1 The day Thou gavest, Lord, is ended,
  The darkness falls at Thy behest;
  To Thee our morning hymns
  ascended,
  Thy praise shall sanctify our rest.

2 We thank Thee that Thy church
  unsleeping,
  While earth rolls onward into light,
  Through all the world her watch is
  keeping,
  And rests not now by day or night.

3 As o'er each continent and island
  The dawn leads on another day,
  The voice of prayer is never silent,
  Nor dies the strain of praise away.

4 The sun that bids us rest is waking
  Our brethren 'neath the western sky,
  And hour by hour fresh lips are
  making
  Thy wondrous doings heard on
  high.

5 So be it, Lord! Thy throne shall
  never,
  Like earth's proud empires, pass
  away,
  Thy kingdom stands, and grows for
  ever,
  Till all thy creatures own Thy sway.

John Ellerton (1826–93)

1185
87.87.77

'*To show forth thy lovingkindness in the morning, and thy faithfulness every night*' Psalm 92 v 2

1 Through the day Thy love hath
   spared us;
  Now we lay us down to rest;
  Through the silent watches guard us,
  Let no foe our peace molest:
  Jesus, Thou our Guardian be;
  Sweet it is to trust in Thee.

2 Pilgrims here on earth and strangers,
  Dwelling in the midst of foes,
  Us and ours preserve from dangers;
  In Thine arms may we repose!
  And, when life's sad day is past,
  Rest with Thee in heaven at last.

Thomas Kelly (1769–1855)

1186
5 5.5 5.6 5.6 5

'*Glory to God in the highest*' Luke 2 v 14

Give glory to God,
Ye children of men,
And publish abroad,
Again and again,
The Son's glorious merit,
The Father's free grace,
The gift of the Spirit,
To Adam's lost race.

Joseph Hart (1712–68)

1187
87.87

'*But God … hath quickened us together with Christ*' Ephesians 2 vv 4,5

1 Hallelujah! Hallelujah!
  Earth and heaven, in sweet accord,
  Join to tell Jehovah's praises,
  Tell the glory of the Lord.

2 Hallelujah! Hallelujah!
  Magnify Jehovah's name,
  Praise the living God, your Maker;
  All that breathe, His praise proclaim.

Psalter Hymnal 1959

1188
87.87.87

'*Thy kingdom come. Thy will be done in earth, as it is in heaven*' Matthew 6 v 10

Now to Him who loved us, gave us
Every pledge that love could give,
Freely shed His blood to save us,
Gave His life that we might live,
Be the kingdom and dominion
And the glory evermore.

Samuel Miller Waring (1792–1827)

1189
L.M.

'*Praise waiteth for thee, O God, in Sion*' Psalm 65 v 1

Praise God, from whom all blessings
   flow;
Praise Him, all creatures here below;
Praise Him above, ye heavenly host;
Praise Father, Son and Holy Ghost!

Thomas Ken (1637–1710)

1190
87.87

'*God blessed for ever. Amen*' Romans 9 v 5

1 Praise the God of all creation,
  Praise the Father's boundless love;
  Praise the Lamb, our expiration,
  Priest and King enthroned above.

2 Praise the Fountain of salvation,
  Him by whom our spirits live;
  Undivided adoration
  To the one Jehovah give.

Josiah Conder (1789–1855)

1191
L.M.

'*Whatsoever ye do, do all to the glory of God*' 1 Corinthians 10 v 31

To God the Father, God the Son,
And God the Spirit, Three in One,
Be honour, praise and glory given,
By all on earth, and all in heaven.

Isaac Watts (1674–1748)

INDEX

AUTHORS, TRANSLATORS AND SOURCES OF WORDS

INDEX

SUBJECTS IN THE PSALMS

68:32–35; 72:1–7, 8–16,17–19; 89:14–17, 18–23, 24–29; 93:1–5; 99:1–5; 104:1–5; 110:1–4; 118:19–25; 138:1–5,6–8; 145:1–7, 8–16, 17–21; 146:5–10

Resurrection 16:5–11; 18:7–18; 20:5–9; 21:1–7; 30:1–5; 40:1–5; 61:6–8; 116:1–8

Second Coming 7:6–11; 24:7–10; 25:20–22; 50:1–6; 96:8–13; 98:5–9; 130:1–8; 145(2):17–21

Sufferings 11:1–7; 12:1–8; 22:1–6, 7–12, 13–21; 27:1 6; 31:1–8, 9–14, 15–18; 35:1–10; 38:8–16; 42:1–5; 54:1–7; 69:1–4, 12–21; 109:23–31; 118:10–18

Teaching 40:9–10; 78:1–4; 119

Temptation 17:1–4, 5–9; 91:13–16

Church 45:9 17; 48:1–9, 10–14; 50:1–2; 60:1–5; 63:1–8; 65:1–5; 66:13–20; 84:1–7, 8–12; 100:1–5; 101:1–8; 122:1–9; 132:7–18; 137:1–9; 144:11–15; 147:12–20; 149:1–5

Blessing 36:5–10; 48:10–14; 67:1–7; 68:7–11, 24–31; 87:1–7; 89:15–18; 92:11–15; 144:11–15

Dedication 24:7–10; 118:19–25, 28–29; 122:1–9

Fellowship 122:1–9; 133:1–3; 137:1–6

God's House 5:1–7; 15:1–5; 23:1–6; 26:8–12; 27:1–6; 36:5–10; 42:1–5; 43:3–5; 46:1–7; 48:1–2, 10–14; 65:1–4; 84:1–7, 8–12; 102(2):13–22; 116:13–19; 122:1–9; 132:7–9, 13–16

Growth 72:8–15, 16–19; 80:8–11; 87:1–7; 147:1–8, 12–20

Reformation 51:15–19; 68:1–6; 69:30–36; 72:16–19; 101:1–8

Revival 28:7–9; 51:15–19; 67(2):1–7; 68:7–11, 24–26; 69:30–36; 72:16–19; 74:1–3, 7–12, 18–23; 77:5–13; 79:8–13; 80:1–7, 14–19; 85:6–13; 90:13–17; 92:10–15; 94:14–19; 102:13–16, 17–22; 108:1–6; 115:12–18; 119:25–32, 81–88, 121–128, 153–160; 126:1–6; 127:1–5; 132:13–18; 143(2):6–12; 147:1–7

Unity 42:1–5; 122:1–9; 133:1–3

Worship 5:1–7; 15:1–5; 22:22–26; 24:1–6; 26:1–7, 8–12; 27:1–6; 43:3–5; 48:10–14; 50:1–6; 51:15–18; 63:1–8; 65:1–4; 66:1–4, 13–20; 67(2):1–7; 68:24–26; 84:1–5; 89:5–8, 14–18; 93:1–5; 95:1–6; 96:1–7, 8–13; 100:1–5; 108:1–6; 111:1–5; 116:13–19; 118:19–25, 26–29; 122:1–9; 132:1–10, 11–18; 134:1–2; 138:1–5; 149:1–4

Comfort

General 23:1–6; 25:15–22; 71:15–21; 86:12–17; 94:14–19

Bereavement 9:7–11; 13:1–6; 23:1–6; 25:15–22; 27:7–14; 31:19–24; 34:1–10, 18–22; 42:1–5; 46:1–5; 57:1–2; 61:1–5; 62:5–8; 71:20–24; 73:23–28; 90:14–17; 91:1–4; 94:14–19; 103:8–12, 13–18; 116:1–8; 121:1–8; 123:1–4; 147:1–5

Commandments, Divine 1:1–6; 19:7–14; 78:4b–7; 103:13–18; 111:8–10; 119:1–8, 9–16, 33–40, 89–94, 169–176

Communion 4:1–8; 5:1–7; 15; 17:5–9; 20:1–5; 22:1–5; 23:1–6; 24:1–6, 7–10; 25:1–7, 8–14, 15–22; 27:1–6, 7–14; 31:1–6; 37:1–7; 42:1–5; 43:3–5; 57:1–2;

61:1–5; 62:5–8; 63:1–8; 71:1–8; 73:23–28; 84:1–7, 8–12; 91:1–4; 123:1–4; 141:1–2; 143(2):6–12

Confession & Pardon 25:8–14, 15–22; 32:1–5; 51:1–6, 7–13, 14–19; 65:1–4; 78:32–39; 103:8–12; 130:1–8

Consecration 4:1–5; 16:6–11; 18:1–3; 24:1–6, 7–10; 25:1–7; 57:7–9; 62:5–8; 73:23–28; 86:1–4; 116:13–19; 131:1–3

Conviction of Sin 32:1–6; 38:1–9; 39:7–13; 40:11–17; 45:1–5; 51:1–6, 7–13, 14–19; 61:1–5; 85:1–5; 90:8–12; 116:1–8; 130:1–1–8; 141:1–5; 142:1–7; 143(2):1–5, 6–12; 147:1–3

Courage 3:1–8; 9:1–6; 11:1–7; 18:1–3, 28–36; 27:1–6, 7–14; 31:19–24; 34:1–10; 37:1–7, 34–40; 44:1–8; 52:1–9; 54:1–7; 56:1–4, 5–13; 60:1–5; 62:1–8; 68:1–6; 71:14–16; 76:7–12; 78:5–11; 91:1–4, 5–13; 112:5–10; 118:1–9, 10–14; 119:113–120; 124(2):1–8; 138:1–8

Covenant of Grace 89:1–7, 24–28, 29–34, 35–46, 47–52; 103:13–18; 105:1–10; 111:1–5

Creation 8:1–9; 19:1–6; 33:6–9; 95:1–6; 102:25–28; 103:19–22; 104:1–5, 31–34; 136(2):1–9; 146:5–10; 148(2):1–14

Death 16:6–11; 23:1–6; 37:34–40; 39:4–8, 9–13; 49:6–13, 14–20; 68:18–20; 73:12–22, 23–28; 90:1–12; 102:23–28; 103:13–18; 116:1–8, 9–19; 121:1–8

Declension & Recovery 13:1–6; 23:1–6; 43:3–5; 51:7–13; 80:1–7, 17–19; 81:8–16; 90:13–17; 107:10–16, 17–22; 116:1–8; 119:25–32, 33–44, 81–88, 105–112, 145–152, 153–160; 138:6–8; 143(2):6–12; 145:8–14

Decree, Eternal 2:7–12; 33:10–22; 105:1–6; 139:15–18; 148:1–6

Dependence upon God 17:5–9; 25:1–7; 27:1–4, 7–8, 13–14; 28:6–9; 31:1–6; 34:1–4; 40:1–5; 61:1–5, 8; 62:5–8; 73:1–2, 23–26; 84:8–12; 89:15–18; 91:1–4; 121:1–8; 130:1–8; 143(2):1, 6–8; 146:1–2, 5–10

Depression 30:1–5, 6–12; 31:9–16; 34:1–10, 17–22; 42:1–5, 6–11; 43:3–5; 51:7–13; 77:7–14; 112:4–10; 123:1–4; 130:1–8; 138:1–3; 142:1–7; 143(2):1–5, 6–7, 8–12

Desertion, Spiritual 13:1–6; 22:1–6, 6–11; 43:3–5; 44:17–26; 60:1–5; 71:9–13; 74:1–3; 77:7–14; 80:1–7; 88:1–9; 102:1–12; 130:1–8; 134:1–6; 142:1–7; 143(2):6–8

Dismission 28:6–9; 61:1–5, 8; 67(2):1–7; 72:17–19; 89:15–18; 103:19–22; 117:1–2; 121:1–8; 122:6–9; 146:5–10

Doxologies 68:19–20; 72:17–19; 103:19–22; 106:48; 117:1–2

Election, Sovereign 65:1–4; 105:1–6, 38–45; 135:1–5

Evangelism 20:1–5; 37:29–33; 40:1–5, 9–11; 51:7–13; 60:1–5; 66:16–20; 67(2):1–7; 68:7–11; 96:8–13; 98:1–4; 107:1–9, 17–22; 119:41–48, 129–136, 169–176; 126:1–6

Evening 4:1–8; 16:7–11; 22:1–5; 30:1–5; 42:6–11; 63:1–6; 74:16–23; 92:1–4; 104:19–23; 141:1–5

*Compiled by Malcolm H. Watts and published by
Emmanuel Church, Salisbury, 2008*

INDEX

SCRIPTURE PARAPHRASES
(INCLUDING HYMNS BASED ON PSALMS)

INDEX

BIBLICAL REFERENCES AND ALLUSIONS

INDEX

FIRST LINES OF
PSALMS AND HYMNS
(METRICAL PSALMS ARE SHOWN IN ITALICS)